# THE FRANKLIN REPORT™
## The Insider's Guide to Home Services

www.franklinreport.com

## New York City

❖ ❖ ❖

Allgood Press
New York

# AN ALLGOOD PRESS PUBLICATION

MANAGING EDITOR
Elizabeth Franklin

PROJECT MANAGER
Melissa Foster

MAIN CONTRIBUTERS
Emily Bodine, Liza Bulos, Jason Carpenter,
Kate Delimitros, Dan D'Lauro, Rebecca Fisher,
Barbara Glatt, Michelle Habash, Deborah Horn,
Angela Miata, Chase Palmer, Paige Sutherland

GRAPHICS/TECHNOLOGY DIRECTOR
Sarah Heffez

TECHNOLOGY TEAM
Michael Brennan, Christya Izett,
Charles "Skip" Schloss, Laura Wahl

SPECIAL THANKS TO
Leah Becker, Paula Crown,
Kathy Kaplan, Pete Mueller

Allgood Press
New York

# TABLE OF CONTENTS

# THE FRANKLIN REPORT™
## The Insider's Guide to Home Services

# INTRODUCTION

Welcome to the new second edition of *The Franklin Report™* (*New York City*), the regional edition of a national series of guides. The Franklin Report has created a comprehensive survey, based on client reviews, of the city's top home service providers. Some of these companies and individuals have been profiled in national magazines, and others are well-kept secrets or rising stars, but all reportedly excel in their fields.

In this guide, you will find factual information and opinions about service providers from architects and interior designers to electricians and pest control specialists. We invite you to use this guide and participate in our project. To submit reports on providers you have used, please visit our website at www.franklinreport.com or use the postcard or reference forms provided at the end of this book. We are committed to keeping all reviews absolutely anonymous.

Our mission is to simplify the task of choosing a home service provider by codifying the "word-of-mouth" approach. We do the homework for you with detailed fact checking, research and extensive interviews of both vendors and clients. We then give you and the community a chance to contribute to this ongoing dialogue. We hope you will join us.

The evaluations and reports on the service providers in *The Franklin Report* are based on factual information from the providers themselves, publicly available information, industry experts and thousands of in-depth customer interviews and surveys submitted through our website and by email, fax, telephone and in person. The Summary, Specific Comments and Ratings that make up each entry are based on these sources and do not reflect the opinion of The Franklin Report.

We have gone to great lengths to ensure that our information originates from verifiable and reliable sources, and conducted followup interviews when any questions arose. In addition, it is our policy to disregard any unsubstantiated information or surveys that differ markedly from the consensus view.

Each service category opens with a brief, informative introduction to the specific home service industry. These summaries provide facts and valuable insights on how to choose a service provider, including realistic expectations and cost considerations. Armed with this information, you'll be well prepared to speak to service providers listed in *The Franklin Report* and make your best choice. In addition, the following section, "What You Should Know About Hiring a Service Provider," covers general issues that apply to all the home service categories, from interior design to air conditioning.

Each listing contains the following components:

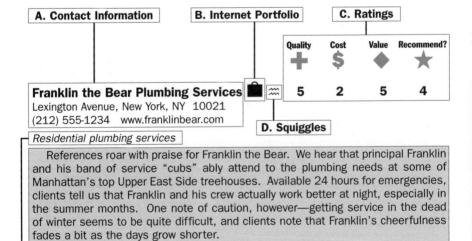

**A. Contact Information:** Vendors are listed alphabetically by the first word in the name of the company (Alexander Zed Designs comes before Elizabeth Anderson Designs). Some vendors provide multiple home services and are listed in more than one category.

**B. Internet Portfolio:** Visit The Franklin Report website at www.franklinreport.com to see a portfolio of online images of this company's work and a description of their philosophy.

**C. Ratings:** Providers are rated in four columns—Quality, Cost, Value and Recommend?—on a 5-point scale, with 5 as the highest rating. Keep in mind that because we only include the firms that received the most positive reviews, a 3 in Quality is still an excellent score: the ratings differentiate the top providers.

Note also that while a high rating is generally better, a higher Cost rating means that vendor is more expensive. Reading the introductory section of each home service category will help you understand the specific pricing structure in each profession. Value is determined by the relationship between Quality and Cost. Recommend? indicates whether the customer would use the provider again or recommend the firm to a friend.

**Quality**
5 – Highest Imaginable
4 – Outstanding
3 – High End
2 – Good
1 – Adequate

**Cost**
5 – Over the Top
4 – Very Expensive
3 – High End
2 – Moderate
1 – Inexpensive

**Value**
5 – Worth Every Penny
4 – Good Value
3 – Fair Deal
2 – Not Great
1 – Poor Value

**Recommend**?
5 – My First and Only Choice
4 – On My Short List, Would Recommend to a Friend
3 – Very Satisfied, Might Hire Again
2 – Have Reservations
1 – Not Pleased, Would Not Hire Again

 Open folders indicate that we did not feel we had enough information to issue a rating. If you have worked with any of the firms with open folders, please fill out reference reports on these providers on our website or on the forms provided in this book.

**D. Squiggles:** The graphic of two squiggly lines indicates a significant number of mixed reviews about a provider.

**E. Services and Specialties:** This describes the main services the company provides.

**F. Summary and Specific Comments:** *The Franklin Report* editors distilled information from all sources to write a summary profiling each service provider that reflects the consensus view. In select categories, where appropriate, we use several abbreviations to indicate certain special recognitions the firm has received:

KB 2000: featured in a Kips Bay Showhouse in that year
AD 100, 2000: listed in *Architectural Digest*'s top 100 in that year
HB Top Designers, 2000: listed in *House Beautiful*'s annual compendium
ID Hall of Fame: Interior Design's Hall of Fame Award

A number of schools are mentioned throughout this section, with the indicated abbreviations: Fashion Institute of Technology ("FIT"), New York School of Interior Design ("NYSID"), Parsons School of Design ("Parsons"), and Rhode Island School of Design ("RISD").

In Specific Comments, clients describe the process of working with the service provider—and the end results—in their own words.

# What You Should Know About Hiring a Service Provider

Hiring a service provider to work in your home is not a task to be undertaken lightly. In addition to issues of quality, cost and scheduling, keep in mind that these professionals and their team may become an integral, albeit temporary, part of your life. The following eight-step process will help you make the best choice.

## 1. Determine Your Needs

First, you need to think about the nature and scope of your project. The service firm that may be perfect for a full-scale renovation may be unresponsive and unnecessarily costly for repair or maintenance work. Are you looking for simple built-in bookcases or an integrated, elaborate library? Do you want an heirloom-quality sofa or a playroom sleeper? Next, weigh your priorities. Is it crucial that the project is done by the holidays? Or is it more important to get a particular style? Is budget a driving factor? Evaluating your requirements will make it easier to decide upon a vendor, because you will know where you can compromise and where you can't. Your requirements may evolve as you learn more about what is in the marketplace, but it's a good idea not to stray too far from your original intent.

## 2. Identify Possible Candidates

To find the best professional for the job, start by asking for recommendations from friends, colleagues, neighbors, your building superintendent or related service providers you trust. The Franklin Report will help you evaluate those candidates and identify others by offering insight into their competitive strengths and weaknesses.

## 3. Check Public Records

To make most efficient use of your time, first do quick background checks of the candidates to eliminate those with questionable records. For all categories you should check with the Better Business Bureau (212-533-6200 or www.bbb.org) to see if any complaints have been filed against the vendor. In addition, for each specific category, licenses may be required or professional associations may offer additional information (check The Franklin Report overviews for each category for specifics). If you are investigating The Franklin Report service providers, you will be informed of past client satisfaction in this book and on our regularly updated website, www.franklinreport.com.

## 4. Interview Service Providers

While it may not be necessary to conduct a face-to-face interview with a provider who is going to do a one- or two-day project, phone interviews are recommended before they show up. For larger projects, it is wise to meet with the potential providers to learn all you possibly can about process, expectations, quality and price and to judge your potential compatibility. Don't be shy. Personality and style "fit" are extremely important for longer-term projects that will involve design decisions or complicated ongoing dialogues, but are less critical when seeking a professional steam cleaner.

The following are general interview questions that will help you make the most of discussions with potential vendors. More specific questions that apply to each specific profession may be found in the category overviews.

✧ How long have you been in the business?
✧ What are your areas of expertise?
✧ Have you recently completed similar jobs? Can I speak with these clients for a reference?
✧ Who will be my primary day-to-day contact? What percentage of time will they spend on site?
✧ What sections of the job will be done by your employees and what sections will be subcontracted?
✧ Are you licensed, registered and insured? What about the subcontractors? (It is crucial to verify that all workers are covered by worker's compensation—otherwise, you may be liable for any worksite injuries.)
✧ How long will the project take? Any concerns or qualifications?
✧ Do you offer warranties? Do you provide written contracts? Will the contract have an arbitration clause?
✧ Are you a member of any national or local professional associations? (While not essential, this can show dedication to the profession.)
✧ How will we communicate? Will we have regular meetings?

Other things to consider:
✧ How long it took them to return your initial phone call.
✧ Whether or not the firm's principal attended the meeting.
✧ How receptive they were to your ideas.
✧ How thoughtful and flexible they were in pricing, budgeting and scheduling.
✧ Personality/fit and how interested they were in your project.

Licenses, registrations, insurance, bonding and permits are key parts of the equation, but are category dependent (again, check the overviews). Any suspicious activity on this front, like a contractor who asks you to get the permits yourself or can't seem to find his proof of insurance, is a red-flag event. Similarly, anyone who refuses to give you references, asks for all the money up front or who tells you what a great deal you can have if you sign today should be eliminated from your list.

## 5. SPEAK WITH PAST CLIENTS

In discussions with references provided by the potential candidates, be aware that these clients should be their greatest fans. For a more balanced view, review their Franklin Report write-up.

Suggested questions for client references:
✧ What was the scope of your project?
✧ Were you happy with both the process and quality of the result?
✧ How involved were you in the process?
✧ Were they responsive to your concerns?
✧ Were work crews timely and courteous, and did they leave the worksite clean?
✧ Did they stick to schedule and budget?
✧ Were they worth the cost?
✧ Were they communicative and professional about any issues or changes?
✧ Were they available for any necessary post-mortem followup?
✧ Would you use this firm again?

Once the contract is written, you may want an attorney to review and identify any potential issues. While most homeowners do not take this step, it could save you from costly and frustrating complications further down the road.

## 6. Ask About Cost

Each service category works differently in terms of pricing structure. Projects may be priced on a flat fee, estimated or actual time, a percentage over materials, a percent of the total job (if other contractors are involved) and a host of other variations. What appears difficult and costly to some providers may be routine for others. Many providers will be responsive to working with you on price (and it is always worth a try). However, under strong economic conditions, the service provider may only be pushed so far—they may actually be interviewing *you* during your call. For more specific details and recommendations, see the pricing discussions in each of The Franklin Report category overviews.

## 7. Evaluate the Bids and Make Your Choice

Narrow your list and ask for at least three bids for substantial jobs. Describe your project clearly and thoroughly, including any timing constraints. Once received, do your best to compare the bids on an "apples to apples" basis. Ask each provider to break down their bids so you can see whether some include more services or higher quality specifications (processes and materials) than others. Don't be afraid to keep asking questions until you fully understand the differences between the bids.

Cheaper is not always better, as a bid might be lower because the workers are less skilled or the materials are of lower quality. Compare samples where possible. If speed is important, you may be willing to pay more for the person who can start next week instead of six months from now and who checked out to be more reliable on timing.

## 8. Negotiate a Contract

Just as with pricing, you will need to understand what the acceptable business practices are within each industry and negotiate a contract, if appropriate. Most service professionals have standard contracts that they prefer.

SMALLER JOBS: For one-time-only situations that you will be supervising (rug cleaning, window washing, etc.) a full-blown contract approved by your lawyer hardly seems necessary. Just ask for a written estimate after you thoroughly discuss the job with the provider.

LARGER JOBS: For larger projects, like a general contracting job that will cost multiple thousands of dollars and will involve many people and lots of materials, a detailed contract is essential. Don't be afraid to ask about anything that is unclear to you. This is all part of the communication process, and you don't want to be working with a service provider who intimidates you into accepting anything that you don't understand.

The contract should clearly spell out, in plain English, the following:
 ✧ The scope of the project in specific, sequential stages.
 ✧ A detailed list of all required building materials, including quality specifications. Assume that they are just meeting minimum code standards unless otherwise specified.
 ✧ Timing expectations. Don't be too harsh here, since much may be contingent upon building conditions or supply deliveries. Some, but very few providers are open to a bonus/ penalty system in meeting specific timing deadlines.
 ✧ A payment schedule, which is usually triggered by completion of the stages above, offering incentives to move on to the next stage.
 ✧ Permit issues and responsibilities if applicable.
 ✧ A description of how any design changes ("change orders") will be processed and priced.
 ✧ The specific tasks and accountability of the service provider, noting exactly what they will and will not do.

Once the contract is written, you may want an attorney to review and identify any potential issues. While most homeowners do not take this step, it could save you from costly and frustrating complications further down the road.

### 9. Overseeing the Job

No matter how professional your team of service providers may be, they need your input and direction to satisfactorily complete the job. Be specific as to who will supervise on-site and who will be the overall project manager (responsible for the interaction between service providers and, ultimately, the dreaded punch lists). This task will fall to you unless you assign it away.

On larger projects, generally the architect (usually within their standard fee contract) or the interior designer (usually for an additional fee) will fulfill the project manager role. You should be available and encourage periodic meetings to ensure that there are no surprises in design, timing or budget. Whether or not you have a project manager, stay on top of the process (but do not get in the way), as this will be your home long after the dust settles and these professionals move on to the next project.

The *Franklin Report* website—a virtual companion to this reference book—is updated regularly with new vendor commentaries and other helpful material about home repairs, maintenance and renovations. With expert, accessible information guiding you through the process and dedicated professionals on the job, every stage of your home project will move smoothly toward completion. Knowledge is power, regardless of whether you're engaging a plumber for a contained upgrade or a general contractor for a complete renovation. *The Franklin Report* is your companion in this process, with current, insightful home service information.

# Hiring an Air Conditioning &
# Heating Service Provider

Known in the trades as Heating, Ventilation and Air Conditioning (HVAC), this home service industry keeps your climate controlled and family comfortable. It is also often responsible for custom sheet metal work, such as kitchen hoods and copper window dressing. An HVAC unit means central air, central heat, central convenience. To keep your home fit for human habitation throughout New York's stifling summers and icy winters, an HVAC system—expertly installed and maintained—will keep you smiling smugly at whatever Mother Nature throws your way.

## An HVAC Primer

All air conditioning (A/C) systems operate under the same principle: a fan sucks in your home's warm air across coils that contain a refrigerant (freon), and the cooled air is then blown into the room. Central A/C operates with two principle components: a condensing unit and evaporator coil. The condenser pressurizes the refrigerant to cool it. Heat is released in the process, so the condenser must be located outside of the home or with an opening to the outside. The cooled refrigerant is then pushed to the evaporator coil, where it cools and dehumidifies the warm air collected from your plenum (the dead space above the ceiling). Finally, this cool air is directed via ductwork back into the rooms. (And you thought an air conditioner just contained a fan and a block of dry ice!)

Heating is supplied in one of three ways: forced air, hydronic or steam. In the forced air system, air is heated by your furnace or a heat pump and a blower pushes air through the heat source, then into your home. While a furnace heats the air through burning natural gas, oil, wood or coal, a heat pump functions like an air conditioner with the refrigerant cycle reversed. Chill is captured by the condenser and warm air is produced with the evaporator coil. The air is further heated through electric heating coils at the blower. In the hydronic system, water is heated via gas or electricity in a boiler and distributed to radiators. The steam system works similarly to a boiler, with steam, rather than water, distributed directly to radiators.

## How Much Do You Need

Believe it or not, it's not the air that makes your room a delightful temperature. It's math. By understanding the following, your eyes will not glaze over when your mechanical man starts spouting acronyms such as BTU, EER and CFM. All of this has to do with the efficiency of your system. Heating is measured in BTUs (British Thermal Units). Cooling is measured in tons. The capacities of furnaces, boilers, heat pumps and air conditioners are determined by how many tons or BTUs they carry. The standard for an 800-square-foot area is 30,000 BTUs of heat and one ton of air conditioning. Obviously, the bigger the space, the more capacity you will need.

The EER, or Energy Efficiency Rating, measures the relationship between space and the energy needed to properly condition its climate. Equipment with higher EERs will properly condition more space with less capacity. The higher the EER, the higher the quality (and cost) of the equipment and the lower your energy bills. Ducts are a significant aspect of HVAC system efficiency. Obviously, you want to have as direct a path as possible between the heat/cool source and the space it's to condition. If the ductwork is too small—the distance from the source too far, or if there are too many bends and jogs, the airflow will suffer. Designers specify the amount of CFMs (the measurement of the airflow through your ductwork) necessary to properly condition a space. If this isn't met, the efficiency of your system is compromised because your equipment has to work harder than it should for a given space.

## ON COST AND CONTRACTS

As in any other trade, you'll be charged for labor, materials and a ten to twenty percent markup for overhead and profit, plus tax. Demand a flat fee for equipment and installation of new systems. Make sure the estimate specifies any other associated work—electrical, plumbing, plaster—that may be necessary for the installation if you expect someone to do it. All makes and models of equipment should be spelled out on the bid proposal. It's okay to sign off on the bid proposal to execute the work, but it should refer to drawings (best generated by an engineer as opposed to a sketch on the back of a napkin) and they should be attached. Clean-up, transportation, commencement and completion dates, payment schedule, change order procedure, licensing and insurance information should all be included in the contract, if not on the bid proposal. The technician should be responsible for the cost and time of obtaining permits. If your HVAC professional is fishing for a service agreement to cover the gaps in the warranty, see if you can get him to discount his price if you accept.

## ON SERVICE

There are a lot of variables in HVAC, so warranties count. One year for parts and labor is typical. You should get your mechanical contractor to do a check-up once a year. Many offer early-bird spring maintenance specials before the busy A/C season of summer, when pinning down a date with a technician takes more contacts than snagging front-row tickets to "The Producers." Service calls may include a travel or truck fee just to show up for the diagnostic, and hourly rates in the city run on average $85 an hour for a single technician, $125 for a team—reflected in a baseline rating of 3 in Cost in *The Franklin Report*.

Treat HVAC like a dentist—you wouldn't neglect to brush your teeth between check-ups, and you shouldn't neglect your filters between visits from the HVAC guy. Change them once a month in the summer—dirty filters will degrade the system's efficiency. It's easy to do—just get a lesson before the installer leaves. Also know where the gauges and valves are and how to read them. And try to maintain a good relationship with your mechanical man after the job. You don't want to have to pay someone else to become familiar with your custom-designed, intricate home system.

## WHAT SHOULD I LOOK FOR IN AN HVAC PROFESSIONAL?

Your HVAC service provider is essentially putting the lungs into your house, and you don't pick your surgeon based on a nudge and a wink. Talk to general contractors and ask who they recommend. Know that HVAC invariably involves plumbing and electrical work. You want to know whether the person you hire can handle the work necessary to make the system function, or if you'll have to bring in other trades to assist. If there is going to be work in and around your existing space, find out how clean and careful he is.

Choose the service provider and system best suited to your project. For renovations in tight spaces like apartments, where ceiling height is precious, high-pressure air conditioning systems that utilize small-diameter ducts permit retrofitting with little disruption to the surrounding structure. When renovating around steam, many HVAC professionals will recommend switching to hydronic. Your research into a good HVAC person will be more effective if you learn a few things about how these systems work. There's more to HVAC than thermostats. Learn the language so that when the installer asks if he can cut ducts in your apartment, you won't immediately report him to People for the Ethical Treatment of Animals.

## CREDENTIALS, PLEASE

HVAC is a complicated field. With all the inter-trade coordination, mechanical speak and math involved, your mechanical contractor should be backed up with the required licensing and insurance. This includes coverage for general liability, worker's comp and property damage. Manufacturers and distributors are a great source for recommending mechanical contractors, and often distinguish the best with awards. Nationally the EPA requires anyone working with refrigerant to be licensed, and New York City Department of Consumer Affairs requires these businesses be licensed for home improvement—essentially a business license. For more information check out the Air Conditioning Contractors of America website at www.acca.org.

### QUESTIONS YOUR HVAC CONTRACTOR WILL ASK

- ✧ Where is the interior unit going to go? Large utility room? A closet?
- ✧ Do you have permission to place a condenser outside? From the co-op? The city?
- ✧ Is there enough ceiling height to add ductwork?
- ✧ Where do you want the controls? How many zones?

| | Quality | Cost | Value | Recommend? |
|---|---|---|---|---|
| |  |  | |  |

## AIR CONDITIONING & HEATING

### Air Care
**3   3   4   3**

58-30 Maspeth Avenue, Maspeth, NY  11378
(718) 894 - 8313

*Window A/C unit repair, sales and installation*

Begun in 1953 as a TV repair service, today the only thing Air Care keeps on-air is cool air.  This small shop gets big work, both residential and commercial, repairing window air conditioning units, primarily in Manhattan.  Clients can either drop off their sputtering A/C units for service or arrange to have them picked up, fixed and returned home for an additional fee.  Air Care's specialties include emergency service, new unit sales and installation as well as winter storage.

### Airtronics Air Conditioning
**4.5   3   4.5   4.5**

63 West 38th Street, New York, NY  10018
(212) 302 - 2020

*Design/build for central and incremental air conditioning systems*

Airtronics specializes in service/repair and design/build for central air conditioning systems and incremental heating and cooling units for commercial and high-end residential clients.  References find the firm's staff of eight and outside support team (composed of two separate custom sheet metal shops) to be "thoroughly professional" and "inventive."  After thirty years in business, architects, manufacturers and homeowners often call Airtronics to set right the errors of less adept mechanical contractors.  We hear principal Mike Novack, whose father is also a veteran of the business, not only designs Airtronics's installations himself, but brings complex problems down to workable solutions.  He is known to "value engineer" overdone and unnecessarily expensive plans, creating greater efficiency at less cost without sacrificing quality.

We're told the company's work looks good, works well and stays within its engineering needs.  Clients say response time is quick, and the crews caring.  The firm even has a group to cut holes, patch and paint, so that the job is top quality throughout.  One-year parts and labor are included in warranties and preventative maintenance service contracts are also offered.  Pricing is fairly standard for the higher level of work.

*"Reliable, knowledgeable, accessible.  One of the best companies I have contracted."  "A very reliable and responsible company doing quality work.  They did what they said they would do, on time and for the cost quoted."*

### All Aire Conditioning Co. Inc.
**4   3.5   4   4**

41 East 29th Street, New York, NY  10016
(212) 683 - 9090

*High-end central air conditioning design, installation and service*

Discriminating building supers, high-end general contractors and savvy homeowners all turn to this family-run business, which has kept high-end residences climate-comfortable for a dozen years.  All Aire services existing central A/C systems in Park Avenue penthouses, performs brownstone retrofits and offers full design/build capabilities for new installation of the top manufacturers.  To maintain a premium level of quality, All Aire does all its own custom sheet metal and piping in house.  We're told one of the, top priorities for the firm is to create a safe, protected environment. The company is also familiar with ductless and split systems, can service such high pressure A/C systems as Space Pak or Unico, but will not work on window or thru-wall A/C units.

All Aire boasts CAD engineering services and employs fifteen service vehicles on the road. While we hear this firm is expensive, it provides a quality and value commensurate with the superior final product. To get a service technician to your door, a one-time charge is assessed that includes two hours of free labor. This charge is only competitive if the work is indeed expected to take such time. In the end, clients could not speak more highly of the firm or the family.

*"Solid. Full of integrity. Safe. It's a great, great company." "Truly unique. We've worked with them for years." "I could go on and on about how great they were."*

## AMHAC      4.5   3.5   5   5
365 White Plains Road, Eastchester, NY 10709
(914) 337 - 5555   www.amhac.com
*HVAC design, installation and service*

Specializing in challenging high-end retrofits, All Makes Heating and Air Conditioning (AMHAC) is a full-service HVAC contractor clients call "thoughtful" and "reliable." With over 40 years in the business, this well-equipped firm serves over 15,000 residential and commercial clients in Manhattan, the Bronx and Fairfield and Westchester counties. Clients are impressed by the company's "professional" and "polite" staff of 70, including design engineers, licensed electricians and field technicians, who we hear tackle the most complex installations and the most mundane maintenance items with equal dedication.

Still it's the intimidating projects—like multizone hot-water heating systems and radiant floor heating—that has the region's most discriminating general contractors turning to AMHAC. The firm is only one of two Carrier Distinguished Dealers in the area, also specializes in Alerton Systems and, as the name implies, can work with pretty much any and all makes.

AMHAC's 30,000-square-foot Eastchester facility hosts a showroom that has on display different types of heating and air conditioning units as well as zoning controls, lighting controls and more. AMHAC's deep resources, which include a fleet of service vehicles, enable it to offer 24-hour heating and 48-hour A/C response times. Response can be even quicker if you have an ongoing maintenance contract. The firm also offers Saturday office hours and a 24/7 phone service. Cost is often at the high end of the scale, but customers insist it's worth it.

*"A unique company. AMHAC cares." "They excel in customer service." "Would recommend with flying colors." "A job well done and worth paying more for." "Their proposal was the most professional and they actually follow up." "The only contractor who we felt was both honest and full service."*

## Amrus Mechanical Company Inc.     4   3   5   4.5
26-12 4th Street, Astoria, NY 11102
(718) 932 - 2444
*Central HVAC design, installation and service*

Those looking for central air solutions turn to Amrus for expert work and friendly service. Be it design and installation of new systems in loft build-outs, retrofitting brownstones with minimal disruption or service for an existing system, this company is said to deliver the quality its mostly high-end Manhattan projects demand. We're told the firm's in-house engineers are often asked to provide design services for architects. Amrus works in all makes and models, from ductless climate control systems to pool dehumidification systems.

Amrus offers a wide option of preventive maintenance programs, each tailored to meet a client's specific needs. These include regularly scheduled inspections that can run from two to twenty times a year. Customers also appreciate features such as emergency service and expert field supervision. Amrus typically sends two technicians, at a rate that is slightly more expensive than most, but it's worth it, according to clients.

*"They're so knowledgeable and professional. My HVAC system works very well."*

## Arista    4    4    4    4
38-26 10th Street, Long Island City, NY  11101
(718) 937 - 1400

*HVAC installation and service*

Prime-time professionals in New York residential construction recommend Arista. They note the company is incredibly knowledgeable about the complicated high-tech systems that are so prevalent in high-end residential work, as a result of skills drawn from the firm's commercial operations. Clients tell us the owner Stanley Berger, his son Scott and the rest of the staff are enjoyable to work with, but wish the same mechanic would be consistently sent to each job. We're also told Arista's post-construction maintenance program is the best in the city. However, some deem Arista's top-quality work, taken line-item by line-item with others, "too expensive."

*"The best in the city, hands down." "They are so dedicated to service." "As good and bad as anyone."*

## Blackstone HVAC    4.5    3.5    4.5    4
14 Chauncey Avenue, New Rochelle, NY  10801
(914) 235 - 0809

*High-end HVAC installation and service*

This small company, helmed by owner James Black, is a rock-solid choice for heating and cooling installation and service, references say. Established five years ago, the majority of Blackstone's work is in Manhattan and Westchester County. Black can take on most mechanical systems, including air balancing, but tends to stick with the high-end gear like geothermal systems. We're told Blackstone excels in systems design, conjuring up innovative and conscientious solutions. Clients say the work and site Blackstone personnel leave behind are immaculate, noting they make sure installations run quietly and have fail-safe measures. If something does go wrong, past clients are serviced on a 24-hour emergency basis. Blackstone isn't the lowest-cost company out there, but it's reflected in the extra effort put into each thing the company does. It's this reputation for excellence that can get Blackstone overbooked.

*"Fabulous at solving problems and making things fit." "Don't wait until summer to reach him!"*

| | Quality | Cost | Value | Recommend? |
|---|---|---|---|---|
| | + | $ | ◆ | ★ |

## Charles W. Beers Inc.      4    4    4    4
45-33 Davis Avenue, Long Island City, NY 11101
(718) 361 - 7322
*HVAC sales, installation and service*

This two-generation family-run business has gained a good reputation and impressive track record doing high-end, residential HVAC work throughout Manhattan. Clients say principal Charles Beers knows how to deal with co-ops, building codes and time restrictions, and is especially familiar with the standards of both quality and customer service demanded. We hear Beers helps architects and interior designers realize their designs without having to get overly technical, yet is creative enough in his custom work to hide the guts of any HVAC installation, making something potentially unsightly disappear into the architectural integrity of the home.

## Comfort Air      4    4    4    4.5
162 West Park Avenue, Long Beach, NY 11561
(516) 889 - 1540
*Central HVAC system design and installation, trade oriented*

Top-tier general contractors trust this "installation boutique" that specializes in new central air systems for gut renovations at high-end residences like a Fifth Avenue penthouse or Park Avenue townhouse. A small company, Comfort is oriented toward working directly under architects and builders, often in a design/ build capacity, although existing homeowner clients reap the rewards of this mindful and experienced company's preventative maintenance plan and service operations. Comfort also excels at control work, specifically those that integrate with other automated systems in the home.

Principal David Kliers, familiar with the ins and outs of the HVAC biz through his father, started Comfort Air in 1989. References say Kliers is "hands-on" and knows the job. He anticipates needs and potential issues are resolved in advance—much more so than others, industry sources report. The caliber of Comfort's work, executed as it is by professionals, is high and doesn't come cheap. Yet it is a tremendous value, we're told, considering Comfort's service costs for past clients.

*"Always willing to go the extra mile." "He's great." "As a GC, I can always get information from Kliers that I can't get from other mechanical subcontractors."*

## Cool Air Inc.      📁    📁    📁    📁
336 East 78th Street, New York, NY 10021
(212) 744 - 4224
*Window and thru-wall A/C unit repair, sales, installation and storage*

From the Hudson to East rivers, from Battery Park to 125th Street, Cool Air has kept Manhattan chilled for 60 years. This firm provides cleaning, service, sales and installation of window and thru-wall air conditioning units. We hear appointments are scheduled with the customer's time in mind, and the company always tries to be forthright about how long it will take to make a service call. Cool Air also offers winter storage and spring-cleaning specials. The diagnostic rate is reasonable.

## Ely Cooling Corp.      3    3    4    4
459 Columbus Avenue, Suite 118, New York, NY 10024
(212) 534 - 6610
*Central HVAC installation and service*

It's no surprise after 25 years of selling, installing and servicing central air conditioning systems for Manhattan residences, in addition to a broad array of

commercial work, Ely excels at cooling customers old, new and repeat. This company fields a staff of four, including founder Ely Franco who still lends hands-on expertise to projects. Ely and company are veterans of working in difficult or museum-type existing spaces in the most upscale of addresses, and according to references, are very respectful, tidy and efficient to their homes.

Full-time emergency service is available, and Ely carries a large stock of parts for more immediate service. All work is guaranteed in writing and quite reasonably priced. Fees for a diagnostic service call are deducted from the estimate of the work if the client goes with Ely. There is no estimation charge for installation of new equipment and Ely provides maintenance contracts.

## Figlia & Sons Inc.                    3.5      2.5      4.5      4
746 East 9th Street, New York, NY 10009
(212) 686 - 0094
*Incremental heating and cooling system sales, installation and service*

Family-owned and in business for over 40 years, this company sells, installs, cleans and repairs incremental heating and cooling systems and window A/C units for primarily residential customers. Clients, contractors and management companies call on Figlia for what we're told is prompt, professional service in Manhattan. Replacement units for Icecap, WeatherTwin, Zoneaire, Traine, Fredrich, Climatemaster, McQuay and many more makes are held in stock year round in a vast warehouse downtown, facilitating Figlia's quick response time. Figlia's staff can troubleshoot over the phone, make adjustments on site or take the units away for service, and always keeps things clean. Figlia does not, however, perform new window unit installations, nor does it service central systems with ductwork. According to references, this company's prices are very competitive.

*"Very quick. We use them for our hotel rooms where time is critical. They will pick up the unit, fix it and get it back within a matter of hours." "One of the few people in Manhattan who do what they say and charge reasonable prices."*

## Hamilton Air                          4.5      4        4        5
2 West 45th Street, New York, NY 10036
(212) 682 - 2710   www.hamiltonair.com
*Full-service HVAC sales, installation and maintenance*

Clients say this is as professional and reliable a heating and cooling company as there is in Manhattan. We hear Hamilton has the resources and know-how to pull off the most complex of installations others won't touch, taking on everything from ducted central systems to ductless split systems to through-the-wall and window units. Top contractors and management companies say Hamilton is most in its element working in high-end residences. Most residential clients say Hamilton is prompt, while a few feel they get lost in the shuffle.

Hamilton boasts an engineering department that oversees the design, application and installation of central A/C systems. Its service arm handles equipment repairs, warranty work and maintenance for over 6,000 Manhattanites. Both are backed by a factory in New Jersey that handles factory warranty work, service, cleaning and overhauling of equipment and manufacture of custom sheet metal. Hamilton's office staff will even assist with landmark applications. It's recommended to call as early as January for maintenance, before the summer crunch.

*"Highly professional and responsible." "Does great work. As a decorator I wouldn't let anyone else in my client's apartment." "I hear they are the best, but they never return my phone calls." "Worth it for the tough installations." "They give you alternatives for cost. Not just one way to do anything."*

| Quality | Cost | Value | Recommend? |

## Island Wide Mechanical Systems Inc.

4    3.5    4.5    4

105 Bridge Road, Hauppauge, NY 11788
(631) 851 - 9400

*HVAC sales, installation and service*

A legion of thankful homeowners, architects and contractors celebrated this design/build pro of custom mechanical systems' ten-year anniversary, along with Island Wide creators (and brothers) Anthony, Brian and Neil Concagh. We're told Island Wide can outfit the toughest spaces in Manhattan penthouses and introduce the most elaborate systems imaginable for Hampton homesteads. The firm forges all its custom sheet metal and grills, and is recognized for excellence by the top manufacturers with whom the company works. In addition to working in high pressure or ductless HVAC systems, Island Wide can also tackle radiant and hydronic heat, as well as boilers and dehumidifiers. The firm can even coordinate construction of custom cabinets to hide unsightly equipment.

We hear the first-generation Irish-American Concagh boys still personally supervise work of their fourteen employees, and treat every single service call with hard work, honesty and integrity. Clients say they are polite, respectful and meticulous about detail. From 24-hour service to design engineers on staff, this firm takes on jobs large and small for high-end clients. Island Wide uses state-of-the art tools to run its business, including a website where one can schedule service calls, computerized project management, estimating and technical support. Island Wide can price a job within 24 to 48 hours. All this service translates into a slightly more costly experience, but clients say they are 100 percent satisfied, and the work speaks for itself.

## Nu-Way Air Conditioning

4    3.5    4.5    4.5

5-45 47th Avenue, Long Island City, NY 11101
(718) 472 - 9890

*Custom HVAC design, installation and repair*

Clients praise the Nu-Way to custom HVAC design and installation as the only way. Sources tell us principal Thomas Queenan is a thoughtful, knowledgeable problem solver who is as familiar working in the city's most prestigious residences as working with the most high-end central air conditioning systems. Clients, contractors and building supervisors all admire Nu-Way's excellent customer service and top-quality work. Nu-Way's design acumen is also often employed by the city's finest architects. The company employs its own sheet metal mechanics and A/C technicians for custom installations. Headquartered only five minutes from midtown, Nu-Way's service usually comes in a flash, according to clients, but can get backlogged during the busy summer season. Work on through-the-wall or window units is limited to past customers, who highly recommend this pleasant, qualified firm.

*"A delight to work with." "Wonderful at problem solving in a helpful and timely manner." "Seemed great but were more expensive than the guy I chose instead. However, that guy took an extra month because he brought in the wrong machine. Oops!" "Always works through a problem until it is resolved, and always with a smile."*

## Power Cooling Inc.

3    2.5    4.5    4

43-43 Vernon Boulevard, Long Island City, NY 11101
(718) 784 - 1300

*HVAC installation and service*

Power Cooling Inc. has used its considerable muscle in all five boroughs of New York for over 35 years. References say the company, with its staff of 90, has evolved into a well-resourced, efficient and reliable establishment. The firm takes on both residential and commercial HVAC projects: installing, cleaning, repairing and selling a wide variety of air conditioning systems. Architects and contractors, as well as homeowners, turn to this HVAC specialist.

## Pro-Tech Heating & Plumbing Corp.

150-44 11th Avenue, Whitestone, NY 11357
(718) 767 - 9067 www.protech-plbg.com

*Plumbing and heating services*

    See Pro-Tech Heating & Plumbing Corp.'s full report under the heading Plumbers

## Stanley Ruth        3.5    3.5    4     4

287 Walton Avenue, Bronx, NY 10451
(718) 993 - 4000

*Window air conditioning unit repair, sales and installation*

    For many throughout the city where window or through-the-wall air conditioning units are concerned, whether it's new installation or service, repair on site or back at the company's shop, Stanley Ruth is the preferred choice. Most clients comment that the firm has, for the most part, responded to issues in a timely fashion, efficiently and without hesitation, it's staff is pleasant on the phone. Others question the company's reliability under such great demand. However, we hear that once you make Stanley Ruth's client list, service is never a problem. Just make sure to call way in advance (think January) for a spring maintenance appointment. We're told Stanley Ruth's pricing is reasonable and its service valued by some very prestigious co-op buildings in Manhattan.

    *"We have worked with several companies specializing in through-the-wall air conditioning over the years and find Stanley Ruth to be the best." "Came when they said and did a good job." "I saw the van and called eight times before they called back. But once they came they were fine."*

## Winds Mechanical       4    3.5    4.5    4

1883 Barnes Avenue, Bronx, NY 10462
(718) 824 - 6700 www.hometown.aol.com/windshvac

*HVAC design and installation*

    Winds Mechanical is a small family-run company with a big reputation for reliability and even bigger capabilities. From design and installation of custom top-of-the-line central A/C systems to setting window A/C units, to brand new construction to retrofitting existing buildings, this firm can handle the call, we hear. Its sister service firm, Winds Service (contact information below), covers all repair and maintenance contract work. While the majority of its work is in Manhattan, more significant projects take Winds up to Westchester County. The city's most established general contractors and the industry's leading manufacturers, such as SpacePak, trust Winds.

    Trade veterens of over 28 years, partners Charles and William Babish are reported to be dedicated to providing the maximum amount of comfort at a minimum amount of operation and maintenance costs. Clients concur, saying these trade winds blow in all the right directions.

## Winds Service         4     3    4.5    4

1883 Barnes Avenue, Bronx, NY 10462
(718) 828 - 8585

*HVAC repair and preventative maintenance*

    The service branch of Winds Mechanical (above) handles repairs and preventative maintenance. This includes things like fine adjustments, cleaning and lubrication of motors, fans, electrical contacts, checking refrigerant charges and cleaning filters, and is best done prior to the summer and winter seasons. The company offers service contracts that references say help save on fuel costs, high repair bills and provide longer lasting comfort systems. Equipped with two-way radio service trucks carrying the necessary parts to keep systems in operation, clients swear any problems are gone with the Winds.

# Hiring an Appraiser

Do you need to know the value of a necklace so you can sell it, or do you suspect that the IRS has overvalued and overbilled you? Or have you been watching the "Antiques Road Show" and suspect that the antique clock you just inherited could finance your child's college education? Appraisals are customized to meet the needs of a property owner, so examine your motives before seeking an appraisal. You may realize that you do not need a professional appraisal at all. For instance, if you're simply curious about the value of your grandparents' silverware or your aunt's antique hairpin, an informal estimate from a knowledgeable professional—also known as a verbal appraisal—will probably suffice. Such estimates are significantly cheaper and quicker to obtain than true appraisals. If, however, your property needs to be valued for a specific transactional purpose such as an insurance policy, taxation, a pre-nuptial agreement, sale, donation or equitable distribution, you probably need a signed and binding appraisal from a professional.

## What Kind of Appraiser Do I Need?

Once you have determined that you need a professional appraiser, assess the size, nature and scope of the property that needs appraising. If an entire estate needs to be evaluated for insurance, probate or taxation purposes, your best option is probably either a generalist or a large appraisal firm with various specialists who together have the expertise needed to evaluate the diverse contents of the estate. On the other hand, if you need an appraisal for a single item or homogenous collection of like items—such as a manuscript or set of manuscripts that you contemplate donating to a museum—a specialist would be ideal.

The purpose of the appraisal usually dictates the kind of appraisal you should seek. Property can be evaluated for its fair market value (FMV), replacement value, income value, etc. There's no such thing as intrinsic value, and sentimental value is in your eyes alone. Note that each kind of valuation will probably yield a different dollar figure and serve a different purpose. For instance, while replacement value might be most appropriate for an insurance policy, fair market value might be a more useful valuation if you want to sell an item. Discuss your requirements with the professional appraiser to ensure that he or she gets the right kind of valuation.

## Keeping It Official

Contrary to popular belief, professionals cannot produce appraisals upon a glance. While informal estimates may certainly be had in this fashion, as evidenced on the "Antiques Roadshow," accredited professionals may require extensive research to do a thorough, official job. They must produce a signed and binding report presenting the appraiser's objectivity, an account of the valuation process, the source of the data used and the methodology adopted and the limitations of the appraisal and the appraiser in relation to the item.

Valuations for legal transactions must be conducted by qualified, accredited appraisers who have no conflicting interest in the property, such as wanting to purchase it or to act as an agent for a potential sale. If appraisers seem to have an interest in the property they are appraising, the integrity of their appraisal may later be questioned and the property subsequently valued at a different rate. You then could become involved in lengthy negotiations and costly litigation in order to collect the money you expected. So if you're looking to have a painting evaluated for insurance purposes, having an auction house conduct the appraisal would not be appropriate. If an item is to be auctioned, however, the auction house usually appraises it. This is because any potential conflict of the appraiser's interest in the property is entirely transparent and can only work to the advantage of the property owner.

PRICING SYSTEMS: Appraisers usually charge either by the hour—sometimes stipulating to a minimum number of hours per project—or by the day, plus travel expenses. Daily rates average from $1,500 to $2,000. Typically, hourly rates range from $100 (a 1 on our Cost scale) to $500 (a 5+ on our Cost scale), depending on the reputation of the appraiser and the kind of valuation required. Informal estimates are considerably cheaper than formal appraisals and usually involve a flat rate. Auction houses often offer a discount on their appraisal rates if the property is to be consigned to them for sale.

## THE APPRAISING PROFESSION

Appraisers of personal property are accredited by the American Society of Appraisers (ASA). To receive accreditation, appraisers must pass rigorous written and oral exams totaling a minimum of eight hours and submit sample appraisal reports for review. They are subject to local credit and background investigations and are screened by an ethics committee. Each appraiser earns a professional designation in one or more specialized areas, such as jewelry, fine art, manuscripts or antique silver. Hiring an accredited appraiser ensures high standards of knowledge, professionalism and experience. Owners seeking professional appraisals should contact their local ASA chapter to perform a preliminary background check—they can also file grievances about appraisers with this organization. The ASA can be reached at (703) 478-2228 or www.appraisers.org.

### UNDERSTANDING APPRAISAL VALUE JARGON

- ✧ **Fair market value (FMV)**, also called fair value, is the price that an interested (but not desperate) party would be willing to pay for an item on the open market. The FMV method is generally used for appraising art, antiques and other valuables for the purpose of sale or equitable distribution.
- ✧ **Replacement value** is the estimated cost of replacing an item. It includes the premium over FMV that an individual might be willing to pay in order to obtain a lost or destroyed item. Replacement value is used most frequently for insurance purposes.
- ✧ **Income value** is the estimated value of income that an item will yield over time. Generally used with real estate, income value is also used to assess the value of items that are being loaned or rented, such as jewelry and works of art. Income value appraisals show up in New York divorce court, too. The income value of a professional degree earned during a marriage is assessed so that both parties may benefit equally from the income it will yield in the future.

## APPRAISERS – ART & ANTIQUES

### AirSea Packing Group Ltd.
40-45 22nd Street, Long Island City, NY 11101
(718) 937 - 6800   www.airseapacking.com
*Packing and shipping of delicate and valuable items*
See AirSea Packing Group Ltd.'s full report under the heading Movers

### Alex Rosenberg Fine Art                 4.5      4      4.5      5
3 East 69th Street, Suite 11B, New York, NY 10021
(212) 628 - 0606   www.alexrosenbergfineart.com
*Fine art appraisal services*

Veteran appraiser Alex Rosenberg receives high praise from clients for his integrity and judgement in matters of fine art appraisals. With over 30 years experience, clients rely on Rosenberg's expertise in estates and insurance valuation and as an expert trial witness and consultant. Clients admire his excellent judgement and note that while they may have used the services of other appraisers, none have lived up to Rosenberg's high standards.

A former president of the Appraisers Association of America (AAA), Rosenberg also offers his services to clients interested in buying or selling at auction as well as assisting with donations to museums. Both the AAA and American Society of Appraisers (ASA) list Rosenberg as a certified senior member.

*"Superb work." "Very knowledgeable and accurate with his appraisals." "Excellent research and great judgment."*

### Anita deCarlo Inc.
605 Madison Avenue, New York, NY 10022
(212) 759 - 1145
*Antique rug restoration, brokerage, cleaning and maintenance*
See Anita deCarlo Inc.'s full report under the heading Rugs – Cleaning, Installation & Repair

### Antiquorum                 4      3      4.5      4
609 Fifth Avenue, Suite 503, New York, NY 10017
(212) 750 - 1103   www.antiquorum.com
*Appraisal and auction-house services, specializing in timepieces and jewelry*

This impressive Swiss auctioneer has carved a niche for itself by promoting wristwatch and clock collecting internationally. With over a quarter-century of experience, we hear that Antiquorum is the place to go to have your antique timepiece evaluated. With a brief description and photo, the company will provide you with a prompt evaluation of your timepiece via email. As an innovative auctioneer, Antiquorum does not limit itself to timepieces, but is also known as one of the leading appraisers and auctioneers of rare gems and jewelry.

### Appraisal Resource Associates Inc.                 3      3      4      4
133 Pacific Street, Brooklyn, NY 11201
(718) 852 - 4961   www.appraisalresources.com
*Personal property appraisal services*

With over 20 years of experience, Appraisal Resource Associates is known as an established firm with highly qualified professionals available to appraise all personal property including antiques, decorative art, porcelain, silver and collectibles. The firm employs a staff gemologist as well as specialists for books and manuscripts, Oriental rugs and Native American art. Appraisers are available to travel to any destination to evaluate a clients personal property.

This full-service firm prides itself on maintaining a high level of professional standards for its appraisers, each with a minimum of five years experience. Appraisers are required to attend ongoing educational classes in their related field and members of the American Society of Appraisers (ASA) are required to recertify every five years. Clients report that the firm's knowledgeable appraisers contribute to the fine quality of its work.

## Appraisal Services Associates
232 Madison Avenue, Suite 605, New York, NY  10016
(212) 679 - 3400

*Litigation support and fine art appraisal services*

This independent appraisal company provides appraising services for 19th and 20th-century fine arts, antiques and decorative arts. Charles Rostoff, principal of the firm, is accredited by the American Society of Appraisers. Rostoff divides his time between appraising and teaching in the New York University Appraisal Studies program. Members of the firm also provide litigation support by appearing in court as expert witnesses.

## Beverlee N. Friedman
**3     2     4     3.5**
245 East 93rd Street, Suite 4K, New York, NY  10128
(212) 348 - 1335

*Personal property, antiques and decorative art appraisal services*

A member of the board of the Appraisers Association of America (AAA), sole proprietor Beverlee N. Friedman specializes in appraising personal property, antiques and decorative art. Friedman, a senior appraiser with the American Society of Appraisers (ASA), works with the residential and corporate communities alike, and will travel to meet a client's needs. References report fees are reasonable and praise Friedman for her attention to detail.

## Christie's
**5     3.5     4.5     5**
20 Rockefeller Plaza, New York, NY  10020
(212) 636 - 2000   www.christies.com

*Auction appraisal services*

An institution in both American and European auction communities, Christie's is considered a global leader in the art and antiques world. From the firm's first auction in 1766 in London by James Christie to its New York headquarters move in 1999 to Rockefeller Center, Christie's has a long and impressive record for auctioning the unique and beautiful.

Christie's primary line of business is auctions—its appraisal services are geared to that activity and represent the seller's interests. The large staff of Christie's covers a wide range of specialty areas, including American furniture and decorative art, American paintings, antiquities, books and manuscripts, Chinese ceramics and works of art, Chinese paintings, contemporary art, European ceramics and glass, European furniture and European works of art. Most clients give Christie's staffers high marks for their professional manner and knowledge, although some clients felt their appraiser lacked sufficient knowledge in all areas. Fees are charged per hour and are rebated if the client chooses to sell at auction through Christies within one year of the appraisal.

*"A great experience—very polite and professional." "Came within days for the appraisal—they were well-versed and very knowledgeable."*

## Consolidated Appraisal Co. Inc.     4.5   3   4.5   5
60 East 42nd Street, Suite 1464, New York, NY 10165
(212) 682 - 1650   www.consolidatedappraisal.com
*Residential, estate, industrial and commercial appraisal services*

In business for over 82 years, Consolidated Appraisal Company is a full-service independent appraisal company with both commercial and residential divisions. Consolidated's staff is trained to appraise general furnishings and fine-arts, including paintings, sculpture, graphics, ceramics and rugs. The firm also has specialists employed to appraise jewelry, rare books, coins, Oriental art and other ethnological art. This large firm claims the most appraisals of residential contents for insurance purposes than any other firm in the country. Clients use Consolidated to appraise the entire contents of their home or a collection of items—the company is not geared to appraise a single item. Fees are calculated hourly with a minimum charge.

We are told the company believes in educating the client about appraisals by dedicating some of its effort toward community education. Consolidated puts out a newsletter, *The Consolidated Appraisal Report*, which keeps the firm in touch with its client base and provides up-to-date information on the industry and the importance of appraisals for financial purposes.

*"We have used Consolidated for over thirty years—they have always been professional—we wouldn't use anyone else."*

## Cynthia S.H. Bowers     3   2   4   3
145 East 74th Street, New York, NY 10021
(212) 288 - 2860
*Estate and insurance appraisal services*

Cynthia Bowers' boutique firm specializes in appraisal services for fine and decorative antiques, fine art and silver for estate and insurance purposes. With over 20 years experience, this company's expertise is in valuing estates and providing appraisals for insurance prior to a residential move. Clients include corporations, law firms and financial institutions. Bowers' hourly fee is said to be very reasonable.

## Eli Wilner & Co.     4.5   5   3.5   4.5
1525 York Avenue, New York, NY 10028
(212) 744 - 6521   www.eliwilner.com
*Antique frame restoration and appraisal services*

Affectionately known in the industry as "Mr. Frame," Eli Wilner is considered the ultimate authority on antique American and European frames. Since 1983, Wilner and his professional staff have carved a niche for themselves as specialists in period framing. Wilner is a leading frame dealer, restorer, appraiser and collector's authority with an A-list clientele that includes the White House, the Metropolitan Museum of Art and Sotheby's. We're told that clients appreciate his sensitivity and discerning eye.

Appraisals are provided based on client photographs or in-house consultations. Each frame is personally appraised by Wilner himself. Both verbal and written appraisals are available, with verbal appraisals at a considerably lesser cost.

## Equitable Appraisal Co. Inc.

| | Quality | Cost | Value | Recommend? |
|---|---|---|---|---|
| | 4 | 2.5 | 5 | 4 |

19 East 75th Street, New York, NY  10021
(212) 535 - 3160

*Fine art appraisal services*

Equitable Appraisal Company is best known for its fine art appraisals. Clients include individual collectors, corporations, museums and insurance companies. Among its many notable projects, Equitable appraised the facades and the statue of Prometheus at Rockefeller Center.

## Gemini

188A East 65th Street, New York, NY  10021
(212) 779 - 9110

*Painting appraisal services*

Sole proprietor Elizabeth Clement is a member of the American Society of Appraisers (ASA), specializing in both old master and modern paintings. Clement, previously worked as an appraisal expert at an insurance company and has also taught at the NYU Appraisal Studies program.

## Hirschl & Adler Galleries

4    3.5    4.5    4

21 East 70th Street, New York, NY  10021
(212) 535 - 8810   www.hirschlandadler.com

*Fine art appraisal services*

Founded in 1952, Hirschl & Adler Galleries specializes in the areas of American and European paintings, watercolors, drawings and sculpture. Its professionals also cover American prints of all periods and 19th-century American decorative arts. The firm's contemporary arm, Hirschl & Adler Modern, shows a comprehensive array of American and European art from the postwar period. Though primarily an art gallery, Hirschl & Adler does offer appraisal services for fine art based on a minimum fee and per hour basis.

## Jason Rahm & Associates

4.5    3    4.5    5

310 East 70th Street, New York, NY  10021
(212) 772 - 0319   www.jasonrahm.com

*Fine art and estate appraisal services*

For over two decades, Jason Rahm and Associates has been providing independent appraisal services in the New York City area. The firm's areas of expertise include paintings, sculpture, silver, decorative art, furniture and porcelain. Clients include private collectors, insurance companies, attorneys, movers and estate planners. Rahm, an accredited senior member of the American Society of Appraisers (ASA), personally visits the client's home or office to photograph and examine each article to be appraised. Within a matter of weeks, an appraisal report, including color photographs, is personally presented to the client. The firm receives praise from clients for its experience and personal attention. Fees are based on a per-hour rate, with a minimum initial charge.

*"A gentleman." "We have enjoyed a long-term relationship with this firm—they provide excellent service."*

## Lauren Stanley

3    2.5    4.5    4

300 East 51st Street, New York, NY  10022
(212) 888 - 6732   www.laurenstanley.com

*Silver appraisal services*

| | Quality | Cost | Value | Recommend? |
|---|---------|------|-------|------------|
| | ✚ | $ | ◆ | ★ |

Lauren Stanley specializes in appraising museum-quality American silver. This boutique firm carries the largest inventory of 19th-century silver in the country, and its expertise renders it one of the best-known appraisers of silver items. The firm's distinguished client base includes museums and collectors from around the world. The firm provides appraisals at what we are told is a very reasonable hourly fee.

## Masterson Gurr Johns    5    4    5    5

122 East 55th Street, 2nd Floor, New York, NY  10022
(212) 486 - 7373   www.gurrjohns.com

*Fine and decorative art appraisal services*

This independent appraisal and art consulting firm has offices in both New York and London. For over 60 years, the New York headquarters has focused on providing appraisal services to the banking, legal and insurance industries. Masterson Gurr Johns is known for its expertise in the International fine arts market and offers art consultation services to collectors as well. Clients offer praise for the company's ability to provide appraisals for a wide variety of jobs—they will appraise a single item as well as large collections. Fees are billed at a fixed rate on an hourly basis.

The company prides itself on the high level of expertise it brings to each job. With a staff of three generalists and twenty specialists, experience is paramount to the firm's success. Each general appraiser has over ten years experience, and all are members or pending members of the American Association of Appraisers (AAA). Specialists have an average of 25 years of experience in their chosen fields.

*"One of the best." "They provide the highest level of expertise, and we would definitely refer their firm to future clients."*

## Michael Capo Appraisals    5    4.5    4.5    5

43 Greenwich Avenue, New York, NY  10014
(212) 242 - 7179

*Fine art and antiques consulting and appraisal services*

A third-generation antique dealer, Michael Capo buys and sells antiques and provides consultation services as a buying agent. He uses his extensive knowledge of more than 30 years of experience to appraise antique furniture, paintings, silver and decorative art. Capo has executed appraisals for the White House and the Brooklyn Museum, and has testified as an expert witness. Clients report the highest regard for his work—many have maintained a professional working relationship with him for decades. Several of the top auction houses have him on their "recommend" list. Capo has been known to travel for clients, and charges a per hour fee with a minimum, plus traveling expenses. Capo is an adjunct professor at New York University and at the New School for Social Research.

*"We always refer our clients to Mr. Capo." "His work is impeccable." "Worked with him for over 20 years—that's how much we respect him."*

| Quality | Cost | Value | Recommend? |
|---------|------|-------|------------|
| + | $ | ◆ | ★ |

## O'Toole-Ewald Art Associates Inc.

4.5    4    4.5    5

1133 Broadway, Suite 1107, New York, NY  10010
(212) 989 - 5151   www.otoole-ewald.com
*Expert witness and appraisal services*

Established in 1932, this national firm offers a wide range of independent professional appraisal services, including appraisals for estate taxes, insurance policies, corporate art collections and charitable donations.  Its professionals also perform damage, loss and fraud reporting and provide expert witness testimony for a wide variety of clientele including major law firms, the FBI and the Department of Justice.  The firm has a variety of specialists on staff who cover a wide range of fine and decorative art areas, including paintings, textiles and rugs, silver, glass, ceramics, books, photography and gems.  Principal Elin Lake Ewald is an accredited senior appraiser with the American Society of Appraisers (ASA), and the firm adheres to the Appraisal Foundation's Uniform Standards of Professional Appraisal Practice.

## Phillips Auctioneers

4.5    3    4.5    4

3 West 57th Street, New York, NY  10019
(212) 570 - 4830   www.phillips-auctions.com
*Fine and decorative art auction services*

For over two centuries, Phillips Fine Art Auctioneers has been a leading international auction house.  Founded in 1796, this firm has auctioned items for famous clients including Marie Antoinette, Beau Brummel and Queen Victoria. Today, with offices in more than fifteen countries around the world, Phillips caters to a more diverse, yet no less prestigious clientele.  The firm's appraisal specialists will provide private and corporate clients with formal written valuations on anything from a single item to full-house contents for insurance, probate, trusts and estates.  The company's expertise spans a wide range including jewelry, decorative objects, watches, rare coins, paintings and antique rugs, to name a few. Phillips' New York office conducts free walk-in appraisals and valuations, and each specialist department offers an informal on-line valuation service to give the customer an idea of the likely auction value of an item.

## Sotheby's

4    3.5    4.5    5

1334 York Avenue, New York, NY  10021
(212) 606 - 7000   www.sothebys.com
*Auction appraisal services*

One of the oldest fine auction houses in the world, Sotheby's has been at the forefront of the auction market for more than 250 years, since its beginnings in London with the sale of a manuscript by the firm's founder Samuel Becker.  Today, Sotheby's is an institution in the auction community with an international presence and 100 offices around the world.

In addition to its renowned auction capabilities, Sotheby's appraisal services has a staff of 200 specialists that represent over 70 collecting categories including jewelry, furniture and decorative arts, porcelain, silver, antique rugs, prints and paintings.  Appraisals are prepared to suit the clients needs—whether it be estate planning, insurance, charitable contributions or fair market value (FMV) for collection evaluation.  Appraisal fees are based on the volume and the nature of the property, as well as the time and the number of specialists involved in the appraisal.  If the appraised property is consigned to Sotheby's for sale within one year of the appraisal, a pro-rated portion of the fee is refunded.  For larger estates and collections, fees for written evaluations are negotiable and are generally very competitive.  Professionalism and expertise are the adjectives echoed by many satisfied clients.

*"Wonderful specialists—I learned so much from my appraisal experience."*

| | Quality + | Cost $ | Value ◆ | Recommend? ★ |
|---|---|---|---|---|

## Swann Galleries Inc.
**3 3 4 4**

104 East 25th Street, New York, NY 10010
(212) 254 - 4710  www.swanngalleries.com

*Auction appraisal services*

Established in 1941, Swann Galleries is known as the largest rare-book auctioneer in the world. This firm began as a specialist in rare books, maps, atlases and manuscripts. Today, Swann Galleries also markets the visual arts, which includes posters, photographs, prints and drawings. Appraisal services are usually rendered for large collections and only in connection with items to be auctioned by Swann Galleries.

## Tepper Galleries
**3.5 3.5 4 4**

110 East 25th Street, New York, NY 10010
(212) 677 - 5300  www.teppergalleries.com

*Auction appraisal services*

New York's oldest privately held auction house, Tepper Galleries, is known for its lively auctions of antique and reproduction furniture, jewelry, art, silver, carpets and decorative objects. This full-service firm offers weekly walk-in appraisals, and for items too large for transport, Tepper's staff will appraise them on-site by appointment. Verbal estimates are offered free of charge. Written appraisals, which contain a complete description of the item, including its provenance and fair market value, are charged a minimum fee plus an hourly rate.

## William Doyle Galleries Inc.
**4 3 4 4.5**

175 East 87th Street, New York, NY 10028
(212) 427 - 2730  www.doylenewyork.com

*Auction appraisal services*

Established in 1963, William Doyle Galleries is one of New York's best-known boutique auction galleries. Under the stewardship of Kathleen Doyle, this privately held company is known for its auctions of paintings, jewelry, furniture and haute couture clothing. Walk-in auction appraisals are available every Tuesday, but appointments are necessary for rug appraisals. Verbal appraisals are provided at no charge, while written appraisals prepared for insurance or estate planning are provided for a fee. Many of the firms appraisal specialists are regulars on the PBS series "Antiques Roadshow."

# Hiring an Architect

Creating a home will be one of the largest investments in your lifetime. An excellent architect may bring your dreams to life and furthermore, may avoid potential construction nightmares. He's your ally in ensuring that the construction process delivers exactly what you have envisioned and protects your investment. Famous architects have made history through their brilliant work as well as their eccentricities, such as Frank Lloyd Wright's demands to control every inch of design in the home, right down to the table settings, and Stanford White's headline-making personal life (and death). But don't get your heart set on achieving fame through an architect who brings celebrity to your address. The best matches are usually with talented, hard-working and experienced professionals who commit themselves to your project. The work of architects lives on indefinitely making their mark on people's lives and on the community itself.

The architect is your guide through the entire building process—from refining your vision and defining your needs to documenting them in plans and specifications; from suggesting contractors to counseling on budget; from monitoring progress and quality of construction to certifying payment to the contractor; and from answering questions to settling disputes. He is the point man working on behalf of your interests. The clarity and thoroughness of the drawings and the extensiveness of the involvement in the process are keystones to a successful job. If the architect misses a beam, the whole job could come crashing down—or more likely, you'll have to pay a little extra to get that beam retrofitted.

## Where Do I Start?

Choosing an architect isn't easy. Each professional has his or her own design philosophy, style and way of doing business. Talk to friends, realtors and contractors. You should interview three to five firms to get a sense of what you're looking for. Make sure to meet with the individual who will be designing the project, not just a principal selling you the firm. If you and the architect don't click, move on. The most important thing to look for is stylistic understanding and good chemistry. You're going to be working closely for a long time, bouncing ideas and problems off each other with a lot at stake. You want somebody with whom you'll enjoy the ride. Not surprisingly, architects consider the same thing when choosing which clients to take on.

Get a sense of the quality of the architect's past designs. Ask to see not only the portfolio, but the blueprints of those past jobs. The architect's clarity and thoroughness will be evident in the detailing and the notes. Not all blueprints are created equal, and the same goes for the people who draft them. Another important step is to get feedback from past clients. You want to know if a prospect was accessible and collaborative, if he was expedient in turning drawings around, responsive to questions and revisions and if he visited the site and met with the contractor regularly.

If an architect makes his living doing leading-edge homes and you have a historic brownstone, it's clear that this collaboration isn't going to work. Go with somebody who is well versed in the style you're looking for. Also keep in mind that the specific task to be designed is as important as the style. An architect who has never designed a rooftop addition in Manhattan is bound to be ignorant of certain details and codes that will inevitably become major factors in the job. This may also be the case if you are renovating an old townhouse in Gramercy Park and are subject to historic preservation restrictions. Your architect should relate to your personality and preferences, vision, logistical constraints and lifestyle.

## SPECIFIC CONSIDERATIONS

It's very important you have a realistic sense of constraints and possibilities regarding budget and code. It's the architect's job to define these things for you. Identify how familiar a candidate is with the local codes, and whether he is sensitive to cost. He needs to be able to help you navigate the permitting and inspection process and massage the budget by substituting materials and methods or modifying the design. Also, be vocal about any special stylistic interests and timing specifications you have from the outset. If using a particular contractor is important to you, or building an environmentally considerate and efficient home, speak up. Remember, certain architects only dabble their toes in certain ponds.

## ON COST AND CONTRACTS

If you think you've found a partner, it's time to start thinking about the fee. There are no set fees for architectural services. The scope of the job, the level of quality and detail, the pace and length of schedule and the amount of other clients the firm has already taken on all factor into how an architect calculates his service. An architect will typically charge an hourly rate or percentage of construction, but many do a combination of the two. For example, many architects may charge hourly through the schematics stage, and then charge a percentage of construction cost for the remainder of the project. Alternatively, there may be a fixed fee based on hourly, or an hourly rate not to exceed a certain percentage for construction. Regardless of the method of calculation, fees will typically range from 15 to 18 percent of the total cost of construction, which is considered standard for New York. Larger projects generally have smaller fee percentages, and for some of the more established and high profile firms, the percentage can also be elevated, partially based on status and reputation in the industry.

This fee, the responsibilities associated with it (revisions through permitting, frequency of on-site visits, payment certifications, punch list review) and the compensation procedure for any extra work should be spelled out in a contract. This can be an Architect's Letter of Agreement or a standard AIA contract as issued by The American Institute of Architects.

## LICENSES AND PERMITS

To earn his title, an architect must have a state license. He does not have to be a member of the AIA (Frank Lloyd Wright never joined). The typical qualifications for licensing are: 1) a degree from an accredited school of architecture, requiring three or more years of study, 2) three years of apprenticeship under the supervision of a licensed architect and 3) passage of a five-day exam. Exact requirements vary from state to state. Remember, if using a New York firm for say, your Greenwich summer home, verify they have an architect around to sign and seal (a signature and certifying stamp) the drawings in the state of the job. Cities require that drawings submitted for permit review be certified by a state-licensed architect.

It is also essential your architect be quite familiar with the local code requirements and regulations. Local codes vary widely, and a small misunderstanding can lead to a big inflation of budget and schedule after everyone's committed. In New York, as in most places, any alteration that does not fit the building code's definition of a minor repair requires an architect's application and certification of plans for approval and issuance of a building permit. The City Building Department also requires the architect to certify completion of the construction before anyone can occupy the space. If you live in a landmark building, you will also have to consider the approval of your plans by the Landmarks Commission. Your architect should be responsible for filing all the appropriate paperwork and addressing any code concerns during the permitting process.

## THE ARCHITECTURAL DESIGN PROCESS

Whether you're courting your architect or have already made the plunge, communication is critical. You're choosing someone to translate an epic fantasy only you have in your imagination. For an architect to develop an idea of what's in your head, you need to be able to convey in detail what it is you are looking for. Bring sketches, pictures, notes, clippings, Rorschach tests—anything that will tune him in to the same frequency. And take your turn to listen. Your architect will invariably come up with design ideas offering inventive solutions and innovative alternatives to your rough-hewn proposal. Also, you want an architect who can deliver options.

Once you've made your architect the designer of record, your first big discussion should begin to flesh out your nebulous dreams into cold hard details. The number of rooms, how and when you will use them and the flow of space are questions he will need answered in order to come up with a first round of schematic designs. Don't panic at their incompleteness. These rough sketches and drawings will be revised and refined as you review them until you are satisfied. The architect may produce a model to help you visualize the layout of your future residence.

## HOW LONG WILL IT TAKE TO DRAW UP A PLAN?

The easy answer: as long as you keep changing your mind. Even though you're the one spending the pretty penny and the design plan is for your home, you'll be astounded by the number of people who get to throw their two cents into your architectural plan. After you and your architect have come to terms, your drawings may pass through the hands of co-op boards; various historical, design or landmark review boards; planning and zoning, structural, mechanical, electrical, plumbing, fire life/safety and Americans with Disabilities Act (ADA) reviewers and your kids. You'll know how a writer feels when he tries to get his screenplay through the Hollywood system unscathed. When it comes to architectural plans, it's design by committee. Depending on the complexity of the job and profile of the location, expect the process to take from two to six months, or much longer if you make a hobby of it.

Once basic layout is approved, the architect can strike forward to prepare more detailed drawings to define the scale and scope of the project. The devil, never more true than in construction, is in the details. You must communicate absolutely everything your little heart desires. Finishes, brands, models, installation methods, notations on code, fixture selection, materials to be used—it all needs to be documented in plans and specs by the architect. At this point, the estimate for cost gets a whole lot clearer.

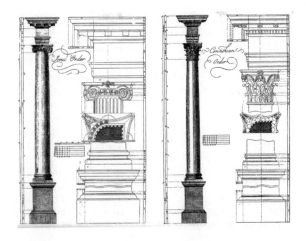

### The Architect Through the Process

It is only with thorough and clear documents that you should approach a contractor to bid. Your architect will manage (or assist you in) the process of hiring a contractor to coordinate construction. He should have a selective stable of reliable and friendly contractors with whom he has had good experiences and can recommend, or you may have your own ideas. As it is typical for several contractors to bid a job, he can help you sift through the proposals to make sure everything is included and you are comparing the same bang for the buck. Ultimately, however, the decision to hire the contractor is yours.

Throughout construction it is your architect's responsibility to make frequent appearances on site in order to monitor job progress, troubleshoot, answer questions and verify that all details and code requirements are being met per his plans and specs. It is becoming increasingly common for banks to require the architect of record to certify pay applications in order to release funding to the contractor. Again this requires the architect to visit the site to assess whether or not the work completed is commensurate with the request for payment. As construction draws to a close, he must lead the "punch list process" of those missing, incomplete, unpolished and mishandled loose ends. Working with an architect who is the perfect match for your personality, ideas and particular project will make this one of the most memorable adventures of your life. You may enjoy it so much that, like Thomas Jefferson, you'll immediately start to eye another project. "Architecture is my delight," wrote Jefferson, "and putting up and pulling down one of my favorite amusements."

### Drawing Is Just the Beginning. You Hire an Architect To:

- ✧ Interpret code.
- ✧ Estimate budget and schedule.
- ✧ Offer options for materials and methods.
- ✧ Recommend contractors and review bids.
- ✧ Document contractual obligations.
- ✧ Sign and seal plans for permitting.
- ✧ Review and certify pay applications.
- ✧ Monitor progress and quality.

---

## ARCHITECTS

### 1100 Architect PC

| | | | |
|---|---|---|---|
| 4 | 4 | 4 | 4.5 |

435 Hudson Street, New York, NY  10014
(212) 645 - 1011

*Modern institutional, residential and retail architecture*

Clients report this firm effectively projects a "modern contemporary expression" and praise partners David Piscukas and Juergen Riehm for their innovative choice and use of materials—ranging from resin to unique wood treatments and skin-like synthetics. Piscukas and Riehm are recognized for their distinctive and refined modernistic yet human approach, with a particular richness of texture, color and light. Clients say the firm's handsome interiors are inviting and elegant, often incorporating the undisguised use of wood and stone to counterbalance contemporary lines.   While restrained and disciplined, the firm's work is not considered minimalist. About half of 1100 Architect's 20 to 25 yearly projects are residential, which are evenly split between gut renovations and new construction.

Clients applaud the firm for acknowledging the fact that real people must live and work comfortably, and that the designs belong to the owners and not the architects.   1100 Architects generally takes on substantial projects and has recently worked a great deal on the Upper East Side and in TriBeCa.   The firm works largely in Manhattan, but also works in the Hamptons and Westchester and Fairfield counties.   Clients include noted retail establishments and institutions such as TSE Cashmere, J. Crew, Rene Lezard, Shiseido, the Robert Mapplethorpe Foundation and Little Red Schoolhouse. Celebrity clients include Jasper Johns, April Gornik, Liam Neeson, Willem Dafoe and Christy Turlington.

David Piscukas received a BA from Brown, studied at RISD and received an MA in architecture from the University of California. Juergen Riehm received a diploma in architecture from Fachhochschule Rheinland-Pfalz. The two worked together with Walter Chatham from 1983 to 1986 and then began their own venture.   Sources say they appreciate the firm's constant architectural exploration in every project, rendering each space unique and forward-thinking.   In addition to the partners' great success with architecture, they are also lauded for innovative interior design with coordinating cabinetry and accessories.   References recommend the firm highly for those seeking a modern aesthetic on a human scale. Many top interior designers are also fans of the firm, which generally charges a standard percentage of total construction costs, with smaller projects commanding a slightly higher percentage.

*"Their ability to innovate and create spaces of functional elegance is uncanny." "They find new and fresh ways to tell a story with openness highlighting enclosures of light." "My home is truly a work of art, original down to the last detail." "While ornament-free, they are leading a new wave of modernistic architecture that is disciplined, but has warmth and soul." "Despite their expertise and obvious talent, an overabundance of ego was never a problem."*

### Adams Soffes Wood

📁  📁  📁  📁

158 West 27th Street, Floor 11, New York, NY  10001
(212) 929 - 0083   www.aswdesign.com

*HB Top Designers, 2000.*

| | Quality | Cost | Value | Recommend? |
|---|---|---|---|---|
| | + | $ | ◆ | ★ |

## Ageloff & Associates 🛍

| | 4 | 3 | 5 | 5 |

57 East 11th Street, 8th Floor, New York, NY 10003
(212) 375 - 0678

*High-end residential interior architecture and design*

Clients say "Scott won't accept anything but the best," and tell us they won't accept anyone but Ageloff & Associates. As dean of the New York School of Interior Design, with both an undergraduate and an MA in architecture from Yale, Ageloff is extremely well versed, and some say brilliant, in combining design and architecture. He collaborates with clients to make their own style resonate with his strong knowledge of architecture and design. They tell us he has "a very good sense of relational elements, mixing old details of the structure with a modern livable look." We hear clients' favorite element about working with Ageloff is that he "often suggests wonderful things that I would have never thought of, touches that makes the place great, and that end up being my favorite parts of the home." Organization is another Ageloff strength, as is his kind and pleasant demeanor. Clients add his followup is "terrific" and "when he says one week, he means one week." Ageloff has worked in some of the most prominent buildings in Manhattan, and is also happy to undertake smaller spaces. Adept at bringing people with different points of view together to find a happy solution, he is often recommended by high-end contractors.

References also cite Ageloff's ability to work within a budget and to offer a wide range of product choices, though some wish he could "send up more flares" to alert them on price. He works on a reasonable hourly rate with a small markup over net on products. All clients say that his fees are absolutely worth the price and he saves them from potentially costly errors. His ability to do architectural work as well as interior design further controls costs. ASID.

*"I am really not into the whole designing, shopping thing, so for me to say it was painless is really saying something." "A very honest and correct gentleman." "He's not the type of person who says, 'this is my style and this is what you hired me for.' He listens to what you want." "I still call him years after our renovation to ask his opinion about subsequent purchases." "I am so sad that we will not have another project anytime soon because I so enjoy working with him." "My husband originally chose Scott, but I wanted to be cheap. I wanted to spend $150,000, but Scott was honest enough to say it could not be done for that. There were no surprises with Ageloff & Associates."*

## Alexander Gorlin

| | 5 | 4.5 | 5 | 5 |

137 Varick Street, 5th Floor, New York, NY 10013
(212) 229 - 1199   www.gorlinarchitect.com

*Contemporary high-end architecture*

Sources praise Alexander Gorlin for creating modern, sensual spaces that maximize the use of space and natural light. Described as highly intellectual and extremely talented, Gorlin has earned respect from the industry and clients alike since establishing this firm of nine in 1987. His portfolio is diverse and includes designs for household items, furniture, apartments, houses, office buildings, synagogues, museums and city parks. Gorlin, the sole proprietor of the firm, takes on 7 to 10 residential projects each year and 15 to 20 in total, many of which are large new home construction or gut renovations. Both industry insiders and clients alike laud Gorlin for his ability to work seamlessly within the surrounding environment of the spaces he creates. Recent jobs include the modern gut renovation of a 6,000-square-foot townhouse in Manhattan, two New York area synagogues and the reconstruction of Liberty Harbor North in New Jersey.

Gorlin holds degrees from Cooper Union and Yale and trained with I.M. Pei. Gorlin also taught at the Yale School of Architecture from 1980 to 1982 and has long been sought by clients in the media and fashion industries. About half of the firm's work has been residential, including Hamptons pool houses and gardens, Rocky Mountain retreats, TriBeCa lofts, Florida seaside homes and midtown apartments.

Clients say that Gorlin is committed to creating a work of art, though some caution that he can be a bit rigid in his thinking about style. Regardless, Gorlin draws praise for his "impeccable taste" and design sense. To that end, Rizzoli has published a monograph of his work featuring 28 projects. The firm charges a percentage of construction costs that is comparable or slightly higher to other high-end firms. Recently, Gorlin wrote and edited *The New American Townhouse.* AD 100, 2000.

*"He has a great sense of design, style and integrity." "I love the simplicity of the design—we didn't want complicated, contemporary design—we wanted straight and simple, which is what he gave us." "We never even talked to another architect, we picked him straight away." "The plans are very detailed. In fact, the contractor said they are the most complete and explicit plans he's ever seen." "He was very quick to pick up on exactly what we wanted and I love his tremendous artistic expertise."*

## Alison Spear, AIA 💼
131 East 70th Street, Suite 3E, New York, NY 10021
(212) 439 - 8506  www.alisonspear.com
*Iconoclastic, colorful and bold interior design and architecture*

See Allison Spear, AIA's full report under the heading Interior Designers & Decorators.

## Allen + Killcoyne Architects 💼    4    3    4.5    4.5
160 Fifth Avenue, Suite 608, New York, NY 10010
(212) 645 - 2222  www.allen-killcoyne.com
*Innovative residential and corporate architecture*

Approached often for the firm's skills in designing apartment and loft conversions, Allen + Killcoyne also take on new home construction. Insiders tell us the firm will not hesitate to assume smaller projects, provided they are interesting and challenging endeavors. These practitioners are always willing to extend themselves for loyal clients and unique projects. Approximately 30 percent of the firm's work is residential and 80 percent of all of its projects are in Manhattan. The firm will take on projects outside the metro area, venturing out to the Hamptons, Fairfield County, Martha's Vineyard and Aspen. Allen + Killcoyne is best known for its modern design as well as several functional and cost-effective Park Avenue gym projects. This firm, described by clients as young and hip, draws praise for fresh ideas and creative solutions.

Principals of the firm are David Allen and Stephen Killcoyne, both of whom earned degrees from Syracuse. The firm was established in 1986 and currently has a staff of twelve. Clients say the firm practices exemplary customer service and client relations, resulting in highly personalized custom spaces. The firm's recent jobs include the joining of two Manhattan apartments, offices for E! Entertainment Television and the design of several departments for FAO Schwartz: Dollhouse, Schweetz and the revamped Star Wars section (with extensive animation and lighting). Outside the city, projects have included several houses, a large yacht club renovation and a new chapel for the Audubon Society.

Current projects include a multi-million dollar, 3,500-square-foot apartment on Central Park West, a six-story loft conversion building in TriBeCa and consulting on a 9,000-square-foot home in Aspen. The firm generally charges a flat fee, based on the standard percentage of total construction costs. The firm will also take on interior design duties for some projects.

| | Quality | Cost | Value | Recommend? |
|---|---|---|---|---|
| | ✚ | $ | ◆ | ★ |

*"It's not every day you can find a firm that does high-quality work, yet has compassion for clients as well as the project." "The staff was willing to work closely with me and answer all of my sometimes annoying questions." "They were the only architecture firm of the three we talked with who did a mock-up for our board before we committed to build a gym. Due to their efforts, the board agreed to go ahead."*

## Anderson Architects                4    3.5    4.5    4.5
555 West 25th Street, 6th Floor, New York, NY  10013
(212) 620 - 0996

*Modern-edged commercial and residential architecture*

Ross Anderson is recognized for his forward-thinking modern design customized to fit the specific landscapes in which the spaces are found. About 30 percent of the firm's work is residential and approximately 30 percent of the firm's yearly workload takes place in Manhattan. Anderson generally takes on substantial new-home construction and renovation projects that can reach seven figures. Well known for his talent and creativity, Anderson has been widely published in prominent design and architectural magazines, and is admired by his contemporaries. Clients tell us Anderson is adept at taking local building styles and transforming them with a new perspective. One example is his own Vermont cabin, as featured in *The New York Times*, which evokes a covered bridge located down the road.

This firm of seventeen has existed under the current name for the past five years, but was known for eight years prior as Anderson Schwartz Architects. Principals of the firm are Ross Anderson, who holds degrees from Stanford and Harvard Graduate School and M.J. Sagan, who studied at Penn State.

The firm has worked on a number of downtown residential projects, particularly in TriBeCa. Recent commercial jobs include offices for bn.com and the late Tibor Kalman's firm, M&Co. Anderson has designed a one-million-square-foot office campus for Abercrombie and Fitch in Ohio and refurbished Manhattan's Friends Seminary. In addition, Anderson Architects takes on numerous commercial projects that include art galleries and high-end office space—including a 30,000-square-foot office for *Talk Magazine*. The firm charges a standard hourly rate or percentage of total construction costs that increases for smaller projects.

*"Most anybody can be trained to design a space, but what Ross did was understand our intentions, live our lifestyle and feel what we felt." "He understands the DNA of our company and translated that into a magnificent space." "It's great to deal with someone who's so smart, so talented and just a great guy." "He's very confident is his business, but we challenged him, he accepted—and he pulled it off superbly." "A very talented and prominent practitioner."*

## Atkin Kramer Architects            4    2.5    4.5    4.5
490 West End Avenue, New York, NY  10024
(212) 877 - 7994

*Versatile residential architecture*

Terry Atkin will not shy away from smaller projects, particularly if she makes a positive connection with the potential client. Best known for her detailed work on Manhattan's prewar buildings, Atkin has extensive experience with duplex renovations in some of the city's most exclusive neighborhoods. Clients say Atkin has a loyal appreciation for both the bones of these older edifices as well as clients' preferences for the spacious aspects and detail of the prewar building. Atkin is also a seasoned architect of new home design and clients say that although she can initially come across as "extremely confident," she soon warms up to the client. It is said that Atkin is adept at creating a vernacular feel to her work while maintaining a personalized approach to client relations, without leaning toward a specific style.

| | Quality | Cost | Value | Recommend? |
|---|---|---|---|---|
| | ✚ | $ | ◆ | ★ |

Atkin is a sole practitioner of this nineteen-year-old firm and holds architecture degrees from the Universities of Virginia and Pennsylvania. The vast majority of Atkin's work is residential and most projects take place in Manhattan. In addition to her work in New York City, Atkin also ventures into the Hamptons, Westchester and Fairfield County areas. Some recent projects include a new home on Long Island's North Fork—a 4,000-square-foot building that was featured in the pages of *This Old House Magazine*, and a 4,000-square-foot Park Avenue duplex.

Clients tell us Atkin's versatility is the hallmark of her style and has the ability to effectively manage construction, pay heed to budgetary constraints and actively incorporate clients' ideas into her work. The firm enjoys numerous return clients who recruit Atkin' services for multiple projects. Atkin has a reputation for charging a lower hourly rate without compromising quality.

*"I cannot say how glad I was that Terry was so effective in managing the construction process." "Terry was always available to take my calls or was quick to respond to my messages." "It's such a joy to have an architect so willing to dedicate the time and effort to the project as well as the client."*

## BKSK 🛍                                  4      4      4      5
28 West 25th Street, New York, NY 10010
(212) 807 - 9600  www.bksarch.com
*Modern residential and commercial architecture*

Often working on projects that have a historic component, BKSK has attracted clients whose projects include new home construction, historic preservations and multi-story apartment buildings. The firm generally takes on substantially sized projects that range up to $30 million. We hear the firm is not committed to a particular style and takes pride in its versatility, creating designs from modern to traditional. BKSK is adept at creating modern, livable designs and effectively merges its clients' tastes and needs into dictates of a project's setting. We have heard, however, that junior architects at the firm may take on more of the workload than clients expected.

Principals of the firm are Steven Burns, Harry Kendall, George Schieferdecker and Joan Krevlin. The firm had been in business since 1985 as BKS, but added another "K" when the firm combined forces with Krevlin in 1992. Of the firm's annual workload, about 70 percent is dedicated to residential projects. Roughly half of the company's projects occur in Manhattan, but BKSK also takes on projects in the Hamptons as well as the Westchester County area.

Some current projects include a fifteen-story loft-style apartment building in the historic district of TriBeCa, a new 15,000-square-foot visitor's center for the Queens Botanical Gardens, and a 25,000-square-foot townhouse development in the Bronx. BKSK charges an hourly fee to a maximum not to exceed a standard percentage of total construction costs.

*"The house is spectacular, the product is great." "Their followup was excellent and the firm really knew the coding issues well." "They get the highest rating in regards to articulating our ideas into the plan." "They have great integrity—doing everything they said they would do." "We think of them as friends—how often does that happen with an architect after a multimillion-dollar project?"*

## Bogdanow Partners                        4      4      4      4.5
215 Grand Street, 8th Floor, New York, NY 10012
(212) 966 - 0313  www.bogdanow.com
*Updated, classical commercial and residential architecture*

We are told Bogdanow Partners shies away from committing to a particular style, instead creating custom styles to suit the personalities of its clients—although we hear the firm has an affinity for the Arts and Crafts movement. In addition to being known for its restaurant and hospitality projects such as the Cub Room, Union Square Cafe and the 10,000-square-foot atrium of the TriBeCa Grand Hotel, Bogdanow also offers architectural design and functionality to residential clients. We are told the firm makes ample use of natural materials—including environmentally sound woods, natural-fiber textiles and metals to accentuate what clients say are warm and comfortable environments. The firm takes on projects of all types, although we hear it does more gut renovations of existing houses than new construction.

There are fourteen architects at this firm, which was established in 1978. Partners Larry Bogdanow and Warren Ashworth both graduated from Washington University, and Bogdanow also holds a degree from Pratt. Sources tell us each project is managed by a team of architects, with Bogdanow determining the overall design and Ashworth overseeing details, administration and creating custom lighting and furniture. Recently, Bogdanow Partners has also done many loft conversions and taken on multimillion-dollar projects, but remains flexible enough to accept smaller renovations.

About 30 percent of Bogdanow's projects are residential, and the vast majority of those take place in Manhattan. Recent projects include the restoration of an 1,800-square-foot 1920s cottage in the Hamptons and a multimillion-dollar SoHo loft renovation of 5,500 square feet. The firm charges a percentage of total construction costs that is slightly higher than the standard.

*"Their use of natural materials is a classy touch to their already excellent design." "Their work is genuine and honest, yet full of happy surprises." "Larry is like a tailor—if you order a tuxedo, he'll give you one. If you just want a sport jacket, that's exactly what you'll get." "They are personable, pleasant guys—and very successful despite a very competitive marketplace."*

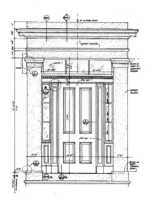

### Boris Baranovich Architects     4    4    4    5
153 Waverly Place, Suite 1200, New York, NY 10014
(212) 627 - 1150

*Traditional residential architecture*

Boris Baranovich is recognized by clients and peers mostly for his traditional, classical style of architectural design with an emphasis on French, English and American Shingle styles. The firm takes on six to eight new projects each year, with as many as twelve to fifteen projects in various stages of completion at any time. Baranovich is also known for being a "finisher"—always tying up loose ends. While some say his style can be a bit heavy, all appreciate his attention to detail and high-quality work. Clients also praise Boris Baranovich for his accommodating nature and ability to execute their wishes. They describe him as thoughtful, polite, honest and a strong communicator.

Baranovich holds a degree from Pratt and is the sole principal of this eighteen-person firm that has been in business since 1984. The firm mainly takes on large projects that start under $1 million and go up to the tens of millions. All of his work is residential, evenly split between gut rehabilitations and new single-family home construction. Many well-heeled families highly recommend him for projects in the metro area as well as the Hamptons. Contractors compliment his talent and organized approach.

Current projects include the gut renovation and addition to an 8,000-square-foot duplex Manhattan penthouse and the complete gut renovation of a massive traditional home in Connecticut—essentially doubling the size of the home with an addition. The firm charges an hourly rate that is translated into a standard percentage of total construction costs.

*"His extensive knowledge of traditional architecture is beyond what we expected." "He's good and he knows it, but Boris is worth every penny." "He is always ready to make a trip out to the site within minutes." "Delivers what he claims—and then some."*

### Brian O'Keefe Architects PC     4    3    5    5
410 West 53rd Street, Suite 122, New York, NY 10019
(212) 957 - 9790
*Traditional residential architecture*

With a solid reputation for creating fresh new designs for renovation projects, Brian O'Keefe is in demand by clients for incorporating tasteful traditional elements of design to residential spaces. He is also known for his design of substantial additions and apartment renovations in the city. O'Keefe works exclusively on residential projects, with about 20 percent taking place in Manhattan. In addition to his work in the city, O'Keefe has worked on projects in the Hamptons, Connecticut, Palm Beach and Miami. The firm generally takes on larger projects, whose total construction costs can range up to several million dollars.

This firm of five is currently expanding and has been in business for eight years, with O'Keefe as the sole principal. O'Keefe studied at Mississippi State University and trained under industry giant Peter Marino. Some current projects include a Park Avenue penthouse addition, which totals 2,500 square feet, a 10,000-square-foot guest house/barn/greenhouse/garden in Greenwich and a 10,000-square-foot, single-family six-story townhouse renovation on the Upper East Side.

O'Keefe has won applause from many clients for his creativity, talent and exceptional problem-solving skills. Clients say his style stays true to period details and materials, and we have heard his top-quality work is worth every penny. The firm charges an hourly rate or a standard percentage of total construction costs.

*"He really has become an outstanding architect in his own right." "A nice guy who has trained with the best." "He really took the time to listen to my ideas and make them fit into his vision."*

### Bromley/Caldari Architects     4    4    4    4.5
242 West 27th Street, New York, NY 10001
(212) 620 - 4250   www.bromleycaldari.com
*Residential and commercial architecture*

Adept at designing beach houses in the Hamptons, apartment renovations in Manhattan or free-standing new homes in the suburbs, sources tell us Bromley Caldari is a versatile firm. About 60 percent of its annual commissions are residential projects, the majority of which are in Manhattan. The duo is known for their enthusiasm for their work and commitment to personal service—as well as finding challenges and excitement in every project. A patio without furniture? A bathroom on a fire escape? We hear they can make it happen, although some say the firm tends to create overly-detailed and designed drawings. We understand the firm "makes new out of the old" by employing its distinctive modern style that features clean, classical original design with minimalist characteristics.

This firm currently employs ten, evenly split between architects and interior decorators and generally does the interior decorating for projects that it served as the architecture firm. The firm began in 1974 with Scott Bromley as the sole principal and evolved into a partnership with Jerry Caldari in 1991. Bromley holds a degree from Yale—Calderi from Clemson. The firm also does work in the Hamptons, Westchester and Fairfield counties, Brazil, Russia and more than 30 states in the United States.

Current projects include a small powder room on Fire Island made almost completely of beach glass, the gut renovation and combination of two Upper East Side townhouses and the renovation of the Greek Orthodox Church on 91st Street. The firm, which boasts many return clients, also designed the notorious Studio 54 in the 70s and some of today's trendiest Manhattan eateries. Bromley and Caldari also do a fair share of pro bono work for nonprofit organizations. The firm charges an hourly rate with a maximum not to exceed a higher-than-standard percentage of total construction costs. The firm has been published in prestigious periodicals in the United States and abroad. ID Hall of Fame.

*"Scott's strength is his spacial relations—he really knows how to create an inviting openness." "It was Scott who provided the complex chemistry to incorporate our ideas into the whole." "There's a tendency to draw too much." "The firm has an amazing take on the American beach house."*

## Buttrick White & Burtis                    4.5    4.5    5    4
475 Tenth Avenue, New York NY    10018
(212) 967 - 3333   www.bwb.com
*Institutional and restoration architecture*

Buttrick White & Burtis is one of a handful of architecture firms that are regularly called upon by the most established institutions of New York for refurbishments and enhancements. Respectful of history and tradition, the firm usually works within established contexts and vocabularies. It can also translate historically based works to a more modern vernacular. Recently working with the Spence School in its much-publicized renovation of the William Goadby Loew building, the firm has also worked for the Frick, the Trinity School, the Harvard Club, Columbia University (Casa Italiana) and the Chapin School, and has done buildings in Central Park for the Parks Department.

About one-third of the firm's work has been residential, including over 300 Manhattan apartments and regional homes over the years. The firm was established in 1978 by Harold Buttrick (now at Murphy, Burnham & Buttrick) and is led by Samuel G. White (Harvard College, master's in architecture from the University of Pennsylvania), grandson of Stanford White. Clients praise the integrity of the firm, saying the partners would never promise anything that was not absolutely deliverable and of perfect proportion.

*"I am famous in my town because of the beauty of the house Sam designed for me. It looks like it has been here 100 years and was so welcomed by the community." "They bring exuberance to every detail." "There is such quality and empathy between their design and the site." "The interiors the firm created were so gorgeous that I didn't even feel the need for paint or furniture." "I thought it was so incredible to be able to find anyone in New York with such extraordinary talent and such graceful character."*

## Campion A. Platt Architects     4    4    4    5
152 Madison Avenue Suite 900, New York, NY 10016
(212) 779 - 3835   www.campionplatt.com
*Eclectic, modern-edged residential architecture and interiors*

With a holistic approach and an appreciation for a wide variety of worldly architectural styles, Campion Platt is known for creating monochromatic spaces awash with contrasting textures provided by furniture, art and plants. Sources are quick to praise Platt's outgoing personality, thoroughness in providing weekly budget reports and close supervision of contractors. Stylistically, clients say Platt is a modernist who integrates his work into the existing environment—such as the renovation of an 1850s house in Sag Harbor which retains period themes and the influence of the sea, while incorporating modern twists.

Platt generally takes on about ten new projects each year, most of which are complete gut renovations that generally hover around the half million-dollar mark. He usually designs much of the interiors to complement his architectural work, including rugs, light fixtures, furniture and shelves. The firm, which was created in 1984 by its sole principal and namesake, currently employs six full-time in addition to several interior designers hired on a consultation basis. Platt holds degrees from the University of Michigan as well as Columbia School of Architecture. We are told he frequently travels to Europe and the Far East to purchase art and furniture for his clients—and to incorporate exotic influences into his practice. To that end, some clients say Platt can be rigid about his visions, but the end product is always superior—perhaps too superior for some clients' budgets.

Typical of his work is the recent 4,800-square-foot gut renovation of a modern, slightly eclectic duplex townhouse in Manhattan featuring a garden, new finishes and custom furniture. He also designed SoHo's MercBar—an amalgamation of Adirondack chic, Wild West ruggedness and New York hip. Platt frequently undertakes residential work uptown as well as in the Hamptons. Platt's architectural fees and product markups are in the standard range, with standard oversight fees. AD 100, 2000.

*"He has a good balance between creative design and functionality." "He's big into written responses." "He maybe chose higher-end products than we probably would have liked to." "I think he's extremely talented—with a good, creative eye." "He should work with high-end customers who appreciate the highest quality." "Immediately reacts and responds to my ideas." "He is a style-maker."*

## Centerbrook Architects & Planners LLC    5    3.5    5    5
67 Main Street, P.O. Box 955, Centerbrook, CT 06409
(860) 767 - 0175   www.centerbrook.com
*Residential, commercial and institutional architecture and planning*

This large, national firm has earned praise from clients, peers, the media and some of the world's finest educational institutions for designing a wide range of spaces—from those that house families to those that encompass schools of law, art collections and film festivals. With an approach that is distinctly American, sources tell us Centerbrook has extended itself to not only participate, but to excel in numerous architectural styles—from modern to traditional, based on the needs of the client.

Centerbrook was established in 1975 and is located in a renovated factory on the Falls River in Centerbrook, Connecticut. This firm of 70 architects takes on dozens of projects each year, of which about 15 percent are residential. Partners of the firm are William Grover, Jefferson Riley, Mark Simon, Chad Floyd and James C. Childress. James A Coan serves as the principal of the firm. Of its annual workload, only five percent takes place in Manhattan.

Clients express enthusiasm for the firm's meticulous attention to detail, noting that it has an uncanny ability to work out all the details while keeping clients' visions at the forefront. Others commend Centerbrook for the ability to deliver within estimated timetables and its overall design quality. Insiders say the firm's innovative work and stylistic versatility has won them many awards as well as many happy clients—with 75 percent of the firm's work coming from repeat clients. Residential projects include new construction, renovation and additions and range from $500,000 to $15 million.

Current projects include the Film Theater and Visions Center at the University of Nebraska, and the University of Colorado School of Law, among many others. This prominent firm has received national recognition for its work, including the American Institute of Architect's Firm Award. Centerbrook has also been featured in numerous articles and books. The firm charges a standard percentage of overall construction costs.

*"The architects designed a work of art that is also a wonderfully comfortable home to live in." "Working with them was one of the most exhilarating experiences."*

### Charles Warren Architect                4    4    4    5
1239 Broadway, Suite 1600, New York, NY 10001
(212) 689 - 0907

*Updated traditional residential architecture*

Charles Warren is hailed by clients for his extraordinary ability to create detailed drawings and transpose those ideas into livable, sensible design that is appropriate to the surrounding landscape and townscape. We are told Warren strives to meld the traditional elements of classic architecture with the most modern offerings of technology, creating distinctive commercial and residential buildings and interiors. Clients say they are drawn to Warren for his meticulous organization from start to finish in creating major additions to existing homes and substantial new custom single-family homes. He is also known for his skills at redesigning completely gutted apartments and townhouses in the city. Described as having a stringent vision of what a space should look like, we are told Warren retains a sense of humor throughout the course of the project.

Warren, the sole practitioner of this respected firm, earned his undergraduate degree from Skidmore College and his MA from Columbia. In addition to his work in Manhattan, which comprises approximately 80 percent of his yearly workload, Warren also takes on projects in the Hamptons, Westchester and Fairfield counties, Boston and Florida. The firm works with a well-heeled clientele and usually takes on larger comprehensive projects in which Warren has a hand in all elements of the project—from the landscaping to the interiors. While some clients say Warren's designs are pricey, they are quick to commend the overall quality of his work as "extremely high-end."

*"He has excellent judgement in terms of making design decisions and translating them into practical drawings." "Uses historically correct materials and design methodologies." "Opinionated without being dogmatic." "He is very detailed in his plans and his planning." "He was unusually attentive to construction." "Knowledgeable about history and a stickler for detail." "You've got to make sure your aesthetic is reasonably consistent with his before you hire him."*

41

| | Quality | Cost | Value | Recommend? |
|---|---|---|---|---|
| | **+** | **$** | **◆** | **★** |

## Cicognani Kalla Architects

| 4.5 | 4 | 5 | 4 |

16 East 53rd Street, 8th Floor, New York, NY 10022
(212) 308 - 4811

*Clean, handsome modern residential architecture*

An internationally renowned firm, Cicognani Kalla is a mid-size practice known for modern designs that feature clean lines, though sources say the firm's work is not strictly modernist. They tell us Cicognani Kalla will take on just about any style of project and prefers to take each one on its own merit, allowing the space to evolve in style with strong client input throughout the design phase. Working both in rural and urban settings, the firm is versatile in its range of abilities. From new single-family home construction in the country to gut renovations on Park Avenue and historic preservations across the country, sources tell us Cicognani Kalla will take on projects of all sizes—providing they prove to be an interesting challenge. Although those at the firm tend to be tight-lipped about their projects, clients tell us the end result of working with Cicognani Kalla is a space that is "rich, yet comfortable."

We hear the firm likes to have a hand in the creation of all aspects of a particular space—including the design of pools, garden and interiors. In addition to residential projects, the firm has designed art galleries, offices and restaurants. Described by references as enthusiastic and intelligent, Ann Kalla was educated at Carnegie Mellon and Columbia University. Awarded an AIA medal in 1980, Kalla held an assistant professorship at Columbia for three years and worked on several invitational international competition projects. In 1985 she and Pietro Cicognani founded this firm. Cicognani was also educated at Columbia, then spent several years after graduation on commercial and institutional projects around the globe.

*"They are both as much educators as they are architects." "Ann really gets into a project—and it's obvious she loves what she's doing." "They would be our first choice for our next project." "Such an elegant style, but it still feels like home."*

## Cooper, Robertson & Partners

| 5 | 4 | 5 | 5 |

311 West 43rd Street, 13th Floor, New York, NY 10036
(212) 247 - 1717

*Residential and institutional architecture and urban design*

With the belief that architecture, planning, landscape and urban design are critically interconnected, Cooper, Robertson & Partners has been involved with the planning and design of Battery Park City, the development of the MoMA Art Center, and campus master plans for Yale University, Trinity College, Duke University and Colgate University. While mainly involved in larger institutional projects and urban design, the firm has been featured in *Architectural Digest* for very high-end residential work. Following the firm's overall design philosophy, its individual residences reflect the social, cultural and political climate around them, and the belief that whatever the client's agenda for the house is, it will ultimately have to serve several subsequent owners.

Though interior design is not the firm's focus, partner Jaquelin Robertson has shown versatility by designing furniture and other pieces when he has been unable to locate exactly what he was looking for. Cooper Robertson & Partners has an impressive list of very satisfied high-profile clients. Their residential projects have been described as "works of art," and can be seen from Martha's Vineyard and the Hamptons to Casa de Campo and Europe. We hear this firm is extremely professional, and references comment on what an enjoyable experience it is to work with Robertson.

This firm is headed up by Alexander, Cooper, Jaquelin Robertson and David McGregor. Cooper, FAIA, founding partner, received his BA and MA in Architecture from Yale University. Robertson, FAIA, AICP, partner, received his BA from Oxford University, where he was a Rhodes Scholar. McGregor, Managing Director, received his BA from Harvard and PhD. from Columbia University. AD 100, 2000.

*"One of the best there is." "Mr. Robertson is the definition of a gentleman."*

| | Quality | Cost | Value | Recommend? |
|---|---|---|---|---|
| | + | $ | ◆ | ★ |

## Curtis + Ginsberg Architects LLP

| | 4 | 2.5 | 5 | 4.5 |

180 Varick Street, 5th Floor, New York, NY 10014
(212) 929 - 4417  www.cplusga.com

*Modern-focused residential and institutional architecture*

Sought out as one of the rare firms that is sympathetic to the client's needs, fears and overall input, Curtis + Ginsberg has earned a reputation among its clientele as "the kind of architects that most people want but can't find." Applauded by clients as easy going and grounded, Darby Curtis and Mark Ginsberg are said to work closely with clients to create spaces that closely follow their vision. The firm specializes in new multi-family home construction, but also does a fair amount of historical preservations in and out of the city. Additions, renovations to existing homes and combining of Manhattan apartments make up the remainder of Curtis and Ginsberg's body of work.

Sources tell us the firm leans toward a contemporary aesthetic, but is very adaptable. Clients say that the firm creates design solutions that are extremely pleasing to the eye, yet practical for modern living. Also described as flexible, practical, respectful of budget limitations and focused on time constraints, Curtis + Ginsberg is equally willing to do interiors or architecture. Generally taking on larger projects, we are told the firm will not hesitate to take on those of smaller scale. We are told the staff is extremely responsive to client input and takes the time to "walk" them through the entire process. It is this high level of customer service that clients say keeps them coming to the firm for repeat business.

This firm of nine has been in business for ten years with principals Curtis and Ginsberg personally overseeing each project. Curtis holds a degree from Columbia and Ginsberg from the University of Pennsylvania. The firm's projects are split equally each year between residential and commercial projects, with most taking place in Manhattan. Current projects include the combination of three apartments into one 2,400-square-foot living space in the city, and a 4,000-square-foot home renovation and addition in Westchester County. The firm charges an hourly fee not to exceed a standard percentage of total construction costs.

*"A rare case of high quality and integrity." "They came up with extremely creative solutions for our office renovations that met our rather tight budget constraints. Their team came up with very unique aspects for our office that were inexpensive." "I wouldn't think twice about hiring the firm again." "Her recommendations were great. Darby lead the team and was very responsive and patient with us."*

## Daniel Romualdez Architects

| | 4 | 4 | 4 | 4.5 |

119 West 23rd Street, Suite 909, New York, NY 10011
(212) 989 - 8429

*Edited, updated classical architecture*

References tell us that Daniel Romualdez is a charming, polished man who takes a calm and thoughtful approach to his work. Some clients have called the firm's work "beautiful" and "classical," while others have deemed it "chic, clean and serene." He is particularly adept at enhancing clients' art collections with appropriate settings.

Romualdez has a master's degree from Columbia School of Architecture. He worked for both Peter Marino and Robert Stern before starting his own firm in 1993. His firm has a staff of twelve and works mainly on high-end residential projects. Last year the firm added an interior design arm to offer clients a full range of services. HB Top Designers, 1999, 2000, 2001.

*"A modern look harkening to a classical past." "Amazing attention to detail." "From a dealers viewpoint, I think that he has an exquisite eye and taste."*

| | Quality + | Cost $ | Value ◆ | Recommend? ★ |
|---|---|---|---|---|

## Daniel Rowen Architects

4.5    4.5    4    4.5

448 West 37th Street, Studio 12B, New York, NY  10018
(212) 947 - 9109

*Edited, updated, classical architecture*

Internationally known for the simplicity, elegance and intelligence of the modern spaces he creates, Daniel Rowen is praised by his clients and contemporaries alike. His close-valued palette, sleek interiors and polished facades are very much in demand—predominantly by Manhattan's hip downtown crowd and innovative commercial clients. The vast majority of the firm's projects are gut renovations of large apartments, townhouses and offices in exclusive Manhattan locations. Rowen places strong emphasis on developing close relationships with each of his clients. Because of his relatively small practice and his lauded intellectual vision, he has the luxury of choosing his clientele and usually works only with those who share his creative point of view. Described as engaging and worldly by his clients, he is said to approach every project as though he is creating a unique and special work of art.

Rowen, the sole principal of this firm of seven, holds degrees from Brown and Yale. The firm has existed under its current name for six years, but Rowen has had his own practice since 1995, previously training under Charles Gwathmey. He has done all the commercial work for Martha Stewart over the last ten years, including her new 150,000-square-foot offices. In addition to Manhattan, Rowen has extended his services to London, Tokyo, San Francisco and the Hamptons. He is also the architect for the offices, showrooms and boutiques of Michael Kors. Recent residential work includes Ian Schrager's apartment—a collaboration with Philippe Starck, and participation in the Houses at Sagaponac, a residential development curated by Richard Meier.

Clients say Rowen is an extremely talented architect who also happens to be "the perfect lunch partner." The firm was awarded the 1998 Business Week/Architectural Record Design Award for work on a Lexington Avenue office. The firm works on a percentage of construction slightly higher than the standard rate.

*"Second to none in regards to accommodating the timelines, budgets and overall needs of clients." "He's as fun to have around as a friend as he is as an architect." "Extraordinary, but sometimes less practical" "There isn't a detail he doesn't miss. His work is just fantastic." "Dan's work is strong, chic, modern, cool and always elegant. We could not have realized these various projects without him."*

## David Bergman Architect 🎒

4    4    4    4.5

241 Eldridge Street, Suite 3R, New York, NY  10002
(212) 475 - 3106  www.cyberg.com

*Modern-edged residential and commercial architecture*

Praised as much for his trustworthy nature as his excellent skills as an architect, David Bergman has earned the respect of his loyal clientele. These clients tell us they refer Bergman to friends and family for projects that range from one-room renovations to sprawling single-family homes. We hear Bergman's style is fairly contemporary—"warm modern"—with distinct touches from the minds of his clients. Working in a close collaborative environment with Bergman, clients say the architect takes their ideas very seriously and point to Bergman's versatility in creating spaces ranging from traditional uptown townhouses to edgy downtown lofts. Bergman's designs are said to be flawless and his execution seamless— as in the case of a prewar building he recently renovated which, according to the client, showed no signs of an architect's remodeling whatsoever.

We are told Bergman is quick to solve problems that may arise throughout the course of a project and is a meticulous manager of any endeavor he undertakes. Most of Bergman's work takes place in Manhattan and is residential in nature. The firm also works in the Hamptons and Westchester and Fairfield counties. Recent projects include several loft renovations downtown and gut renovations of large apartments on the Upper West Side. Clients say they trust Bergman to the point of leaving large projects in his hands, unsupervised for long periods of time, with the confidence that he will deliver on time and on budget. Bergman's list of friends speaks volumes for his personality—many are former clients and colleagues.

Bergman received an MA from Princeton and currently teaches at Parsons. He has been lauded by clients and colleagues alike for his technical and aesthetic skills. He also designs his own line of "Fire & Water" lighting and furniture. The firm charges an hourly rate not to exceed a percentage of construction that can slightly exceed standard percentages on smaller projects.

*"A talented architect, but also just a good person." "He's almost too easy to work with." "His teaching skills clearly came through in my experience as I asked him many questions that probably drove him crazy." "Has a tremendous amount of patience."*

## David Gura Architects                    4        4        4        4.5

135 West 70th Street, Suite 2H, New York, NY 10023
(212) 874 - 5234  www.dgarch.com

*Forward thinking, high-tech, modern architecture*

Clients assure us that David Gura stands out among New York architects as a forward-thinking, technology-oriented man who takes into account modern living when creating his custom apartments and homes. A one-man operation, Gura takes on ten to fifteen projects each year, ranging from large townhouse renovations to small consulting or inspection jobs. When his workload swells, Gura works with a group of junior architects on a consultation basis. Stylistically, clients tell us Gura leans heavily toward modernism, featuring clean lines and incorporating the latest communications, computer and audio/visual technologies.

The vast majority of Gura's practice is residential and centered in Manhattan, and consists of high-end gut renovations of apartments and townhouses most recently on the Upper West Side. He will also take on the occasional project in the surrounding regional area. Sources tell us Gura generally works on large projects topping $1 million, but he will take on much smaller projects for repeat customers or if they present an interesting challenge.

Gura, a graduate of Kent State University created the firm more than 25 years ago and has worked with several celebrity clients including Robert Altman. Recent projects include the combination of three apartments into one totaling 2,200 square feet in Manhattan and the gut renovation of a 5,000-square-foot home in Briarcliff Manor with a bowling alley and pool. The firm charges an hourly or flat fee, translating into an approximate percentage of total construction costs that is slightly higher than standard rates.

*"His work is very functional, and he considers new technology so you don't get stuck with an outdated design." "He is knowledgeable, honest and sensitive to my needs and issues." "If there was a surprise, he was the first to tell me and we worked through it." "Projects like this get terse once in a while, but he shielded me from all that with the contractor—he's a great buffer."*

## David McMahon         4.5    4    4.5    5
341 East 62nd Street, Penthouse A, New York, NY 10021
(212) 755 - 2551

*Pedigreed, transitional residential architecture and interior design*

Clients say they approach David McMahon for his extensive experience and ability to communicate effectively with clients through a keen wit and pleasant demeanor. Without clear leanings, McMahon's style has a forward thinking approach, melding classic elements with modern ideas in a timeless, slightly eclectic design. Clients also tell us McMahon has an exemplary grasp on the traditional aesthetic—including a variety of period interiors such as Georgian and French. While bringing modern undertones to these traditional interiors, sources say McMahon creates refreshing spaces that exude a warm elegance. The firm also does interior design and has several interior designers on staff. McMahon is the primary client contact and is involved with all details of the interiors, including the purchasing of artwork (often in Paris).

McMahon studied at RISD and started this firm in 1997 after sixteen years as an architect with Parish-Hadley. Nearly all of McMahon's work is residential, and most of his projects are multi million-dollar apartment gut renovations that take place on the Upper East Side. Sources tell us, however, that McMahon will take on one-room renovations for repeat customers or that pose an intriguing architectural puzzle. In addition to his New York area clientele, McMahon has completed projects in Miami, Georgia, California, the Hamptons and Bermuda.

Some current projects include the design of a series of new Judith Leiber boutiques, an uptown penthouse renovation totaling 4,000 square feet and several Park Avenue office spaces. The firm charges an hourly rate or a standard percentage of construction costs that increases for smaller projects. For interiors, McMahon charges a low markup over net on design products, which is clearly shown on all bills. Some say McMahon could be slightly better organized regarding punch list items. McMahon's work has been featured in *House & Garden, House Beautiful, Architectural Digest* and *Elle Decor*.

*"He did such a nice job making our two floors flow together and he is brilliant with lighting." "I think hiring an architect can often be an exercise in futility, but I wholeheartedly recommend David." "He has become a mainstay on Park Avenue." "David is so helpful and an amazing resource—he deserves all the fame and fortune that is bound his way."*

## David Nahon Architects      3.5    2.5    4.5    4
340 West 89th Street, New York, NY 10024
(212) 580 - 0773

*Classical residential architecture with a modern focus*

With a talent for using soft colors with handsome lines in a modern aesthetic, David Nahon has earned accolades from clients for a combination of high quality and prices that won't break the bank. Clients appreciate the personalized service they receive from Nahon, which allows them to play an active role in the entire process—from design to construction. Nahon draws praise from clients for his ability to create plans and drawings quickly. Sources say a combination of excellent client relations and moderate pricing is a huge plus in working with the firm.

This firm has been in business for more than 30 years, and sole principal David Nahon holds two degrees from Columbia. All of Nahon's work is residential and takes place in the New York metro area. He takes on projects of all sizes—from one-room renovations to large brownstone gut rehabs. Sources tell us Nahon is well versed in many styles of design and will create spaces with the personal style and taste of his clients. Current projects include a 1,000-square-foot brownstone renovation on the Upper West Side and a 1,200-square-foot apartment combination on Central Park West. The firm charges an hourly rate or a lower percentage of total construction costs.

| | Quality | Cost | Value | Recommend? |
|---|---------|------|-------|------------|
| | + | $ | ◆ | ★ |

*"There is very little pressure in working with David—when I need to speak to him, he's always available." "It's so pleasantly different from what you'd think working with a high-end architect would be. Going to visit him is like going to a relative's house—it's so laid back." "The quality of the spaces he creates is great and I didn't have to dip into the kids' college funds."*

## David Netto Design LLC      4    3.5    4    4.5
270 Lafayette Street, New York, NY 10012
(212) 343 - 7415   www.davidnettodesign.com

*Fresh, young, classical residential architecture. HB Top Designers, 2001*

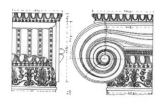

## Deamer + Phillips      4    3    4.5    5
149 Franklin Street, Suite 3 North, New York, NY 10013
(212) 925 - 4564

*Personalized, intelligent, modern architecture with traditional roots*

This husband-and-wife team is praised by clients for excellent design coupled with patience and honesty. We hear clients welcome the intensity of this small firm and the amount of effort and planning that goes into each project. With a cerebral approach in regards to materializing clients' visions, Deamer + Phillips style generally leans toward modernism, although the couple has completed numerous traditional projects. References describe the firm's work as modest but powerful in its use of contrasting materials and a heightened awareness of intricate detail. Because of the small nature of the firm, clients say the firm does not have the abundant resources of bigger firms.

This small firm of six is headed up by principals Peggy Deamer and Scott Phillips, and has been in business since 1987. Phillips holds a degree from the University of Washington and Deamer from Cooper Union. About 50 percent of the firm's work is residential, most of which is single-family home construction, with the remainder being additions or renovations. The firm's scope of projects ranges from smaller renovations to multi million-dollar new home construction.

Recent projects include a 1,200-square-foot addition to a Victorian home in Westchester County and the construction of a new 7,000-square-foot single-family home in Sherman, Connecticut. The firm charges an hourly fee not to exceed standard percentages of construction costs.

*"They are incredibly fair, patient and forthright." "I didn't lose a night's sleep because I felt like Scott and I were on the same wavelength." "I don't think I got a bargain, but I did get a jewel—it's just exquisite." "They just have an innate eye for good design, proportion and detail." "It's a small firm, so it's not fair to expect them to take on mammoth projects."*

## Deborah Berke Architect, PC      4.5    3.5    4.5    4.5
211 West 19th Street, 2nd Floor, New York, NY 10011
(212) 229 - 9211   www.dberke.com

*Residential, commercial and institutional architecture*

Deborah Berke, a Yale University associate professor of architecture, has gained an international following for her simple spaces designed in a distinctive, minimalist style. Berke and her "exceptional staff" have been described as very talented and totally professional, producing beautiful, elegant and functional designs. A co-editor of the 1997 book *Architecture of the Everyday*, Berke recognizes and emphasizes the allure of simple, serviceable materials in her designs. Clients who have retained Berke for residential work commend her as "an artist" and praise her work for its "ease of living."

The easy elegance of her work has earned her a number of distinguished jobs, including homes and stores in the planned community of Seaside, Florida, as well as CK Calvin Klein boutiques and the new Yale University School of Art.

*"On a scale of 1 to 5 for quality, I give her a 10!" "The ONLY problem with the project is that it is going to end soon."*

## Desai/Chia Studio

| | | | |
|---|---|---|---|
| 4 | 3.5 | 4.5 | 4.5 |

54 West 21st Street, New York , NY   10010
(212) 366 - 9630   www.desaichia.com

*High-end, tailored minimalist architecture*

Clients say they are drawn to this firm's simplistic, minimalist spaces and modern aesthetic. We are told the firm is adept at maximizing existing natural light and open space while incorporating innovative materials such as plastics, resin, concrete, metals and bamboo. Clients say they appreciate the clean flow of Desai/Chai spaces and the controlled manner in which the cutting-edge materials are presented. The firm takes on a variety of project types, but is probably best known for its elegant loft renovations. Desai/Chia also takes on apartment renovations, additions and smaller new construction projects. The firm generally takes on mid-sized renovations, but has also completed larger multi million-dollar projects.

This small firm of three was started in 1994. Principals of the firm are Arjun Desai, who holds degrees from M.I.T. and Bennington College and Katherine Chia, who has degrees from Amherst College and M.I.T. The firm takes on between ten to fifteen projects each year, the vast majority of which are in Manhattan and residential in nature.

Current projects include a 3,000-square-foot loft conversion with ample usage of glass, metal, acrylic and stainless steel and the gut renovation of a historic home, guest house and pool in Westchester County to give the 10,000-square-foot project a more modern appearance. The firm charges an hourly rate not to exceed the standard percentage of overall construction costs. HB Top Designers, 2000.

## DiDonno Associates Architects PC

| | | | |
|---|---|---|---|
| 3.5 | 3 | 4.5 | 4.5 |

694 10th Street, Brooklyn, NY  11215
(718) 788 - 2751

*Traditional residential architecture, preservation and interiors*

Clients generally approach DiDonno for its period restoration or the firm's adept skills of transforming lofts into contemporary living spaces as well as the preservation of existing rowhouses. This husband and wife-led team takes on about eight projects each year, which generally entail renovations or restoration endeavors. Clients tell us Guadalupe and Ron DiDonno believe design should evolve, instead of being imposed, indicating a high level of client involvement and contribution. We are also told the firm is very serious about getting the job done, yet maintain a pleasant working environment and are cordial to clients. We have heard the firm could improve their knowledge of specialty hardware and artistic interior suppliers. DiDonno has recently taken on some significant apartment combination projects, one in which a townhouse was converted from a five-family residence to a single-family dwelling.

In business since 1977, DiDonno Architects is a small firm of four with offices in Brooklyn. Both Guadalupe and Ron are principals of the firm and both attended Pratt. About 85 percent of the firm's work is residential in nature, and of that, more than half takes place in Manhattan. Recent projects include a 5,500-square-foot single-family home in Connecticut, a 4,000-square-foot loft in Brooklyn and a new home construction of a Hamptons summer home. The firm actively takes on projects in the Hamptons as well as the Westchester/Fairfield area and has done work as far away as Texas. DiDonno charges an hourly fee with the maximum reaching a lower percentage of total construction costs.

*"They are extremely thorough and conscientious." "They're not showy or flamboyant, just nose-to-the-grindstone people who get the job done." "They're lovely people who are quiet, reserved and certainly not pushy." "Well versed and organized, especially with handling the landmarks commission."*

## Dineen Nealy Architects LLP                    3      3      4      4
49 West 38th Street, Suite 12A, New York, NY 10018
(212) 396 - 2771

*Modern, romantic, innovative residential architecture and interior design*

Clients have hailed this firm's style as "romantic modern," incorporating mid-century feel into a high modern setting—what we are told is "progressive without being alienating." The firm does the interior decorating for most of its architectural projects, but will do interiors for projects the firm is not the architect on. Clients generally praise the firm's professionalism and commitment to the project once it is underway, but we hear the practices has been slow to start jobs, particularly those with smaller budgets. For the most part, we hear the staff is attentive at meetings, followup is excellent and the overall product is of high quality.

The firm is a mid-sized staff of eighteen—fourteen architects and four interior decorators. Principals Joan Dineen and Craig Nealy, both graduates of Cornell, started the firm three years ago. About half of the firm's work is done in Manhattan, although it also takes on projects in Westchester County, the Hamptons, South Florida, the Philippines, Asia and parts of Europe. Approximately 25 percent Dineen Nealy's annual projects are residential and cover a wide range or services—from gut renovations of multi million-dollar projects to the design of ashtrays. The firm generally takes on projects that fall somewhere in between and the bulk of their work starts with $250,000 construction projects.

Current projects include the combining of two duplex apartments into a 3,600-square-foot residence in a postwar building, and the gut renovation of a 3,600-square-foot jewel-box apartment in Manhattan. In addition to large residential renovations under way on Fifth Avenue and Central Park West, the firm has designed a lobby for the World Bank in Washington and the new Sotheby's restaurant in Manhattan. The firm charges a standard percentage of construction costs and standard markups over net for interiors, and handles each services with a separate contract. Dineen and Nealy's work has appeared on the cover of *House and Garden* (May 1999), as well as in *The New York Observer, House Beautiful* and *German Architectural Digest.*

*"I take Craig's opinion very seriously." "Very precise—I get minutes to meetings and I don't know many residential architects who draft meeting notes." "They are architects that show me function and form—they reproportioned the rooms masterfully." "They have strong opinions about certain things." "A junior architect wasn't up to snuff, so he was off the project and let go after two weeks." "The firm may have a lot of turnover."*

## Dwyer & Sae-Eng Inc.                    4      4      4      5
30 Gansevoort Street, New York, NY 10014
(212) 242 - 6767

*Traditional, preservationist residential architecture*

Aesthetically, Dwyer & Sae-Eng is best known for its traditional and historical preservation work. Insiders tell us this firm is extremely sensitive about retaining the strict historic integrity of its projects—to the point of being dubbed "fastidious preservationists." We hear principal Michael Dwyer has a strong command of historical reference and is adept at renovating prewar building interiors. We are told the firm is extremely confident in its historic preservation skills and may come across as rigid to the unsuspecting client. Sources also praise Dwyer's high intellect and charming nature. Insiders tell us this firm works extremely well and closely with some of the area's better-known interior decorators.

This firm currently employs a staff of six and was formed in 1995 by principals Michael Dwyer, a graduate of Penn and Unkun Sae-Eng, who was educated in Australia. Half of the firm's work takes place in Manhattan and takes on numerous projects in the Hamptons and Westchester counties. Around 65 percent of the firm's yearly workload is residential, ranging from high-end gut renovations to new home construction and alterations. The firm generally takes on mid-sized projects, but continues to take on smaller projects as well as large multi million-dollar endeavors.

Current projects include two multi million-dollar custom traditional homes in Greenwich, Connecticut—one totaling 13,000 square feet and the other 20,000 square feet. Dwyer & Sae-Eng charges an hourly rate or standard percentage of overall construction costs.

*"He understates rather than overstates." "He is an absolutely wonderful neo-classical designer." "Scrupulously honest." "I really appreciate their intellectual approach to the architectural challenge." "Unparalleled as a historic preservationist."*

## Edward Mills Architects PC     3.5     3     4.5     4
50 White Street, New York, NY  10013
(212) 334 - 9891  www.eimills.com

*High-modern residential and commercial architecture*

We hear Edward Mills can be a staunch perfectionist with strong opinions. Clients appreciate his dedication and speak of him warmly, calling him helpful and patient with a keen eye for fine detail. Sources tell us the firm's style can be considered high modern, but also well versed in classical restoration. They applaud his communications skills and his ability to guide clients through the entire design and construction process to keep surprises to a minimum. We are told Mills is an excellent arbiter, representing his clients well in dealing with contractors. We have heard that because of the desire to have a hand in all aspects of a project, he sometimes takes on too much responsibility instead of deferring to his staffers.

Leading this staff of ten is Mills, the sole principal and graduate of North Carolina State, and Harvard where he received an MA in architecture. He created the firm more than 22 years ago. The firm takes on about 20 projects each year of varying sizes, the majority of which are in Manhattan and the Hamptons. Roughly 20 percent of the firm's work is residential, and ranges from one-room renovations to complete gut rehabilitations of large townhouses.

Current projects include several Manhattan penthouse renovations—such as the 2,500-square-foot space at Sutton Place, and two 3,000-plus–square-foot projects on the Upper East Side. The firm generally charges an hourly fee not to exceed a standard percentage of overall construction costs.

*"He's a finisher—he really saved my hide." "He put me at ease because he's a straight-shooter." "He's brilliant. He also knows how to build economically if you need to." "Great at material selection and he also specializes in lighting." "I think he takes on too much and could delegate better."*

## ERG Architect     4.5     4.5     4     5
25 Lewis Street Suite 306, Greenwich, CT  06830
(203) 661 - 7472

*Highly customized, traditional, classical residential architecture*

For highly customized, classical design of major renovations, sprawling single-family homes and estates, clients say ERG is second to none. Clients extol the firm's disciplined and methodical approach to creating luxurious and elegant resi-

| | Quality | Cost | Value | Recommend? |
|---|---|---|---|---|
| | ✚ | $ | ◆ | ★ |

dential spaces. Based in Greenwich, Connecticut, insiders tell us ERG Architect is a small firm with big clients. Ron Geshue, sole proprietor of this three-person firm, has built up a clientele of those who live in the city, and household names who work in New York but live in exclusive neighborhoods outside the metro area. Insiders tell us it would be wise for potential clients to study this high-end firm's work before inquiring about services, particularly for projects with modest budgets.

Taking on about twelve large projects each year, whose construction costs often eclipse seven and eight figures, this firm was established in 1984 by Geshue who earned an MA in architecture from the University of Idaho. The vast majority of ERG's work is residential, although it has completed several high-profile commercial projects for the likes of Ford Models and various office spaces and art galleries. The firm generally focuses on major gut renovations and multi million dollar single-family new home construction, but will do smaller renovations or additions for repeat clients—which we hear make up nearly all of ERG's business.

Current projects include a 6,000-square-foot new single-family home in Lake Placid and a Beaux Arts style two-family mansion of 11,500 square feet on the Upper East Side. The firm is flexible in its fee structure and can charge an hourly rate, fixed price or a standard percentage of total construction costs. HB Top Designers, 2000.

*"Ron has a very good sense of balance and proportion and is able to effectively translate his ideas." "He's very well-regarded and has a very easy-going personality." "His greatest asset is that he has an unparalleled knowledge of the materials that make up these high-end types of projects." "I trust him to work on almost anything...we love our house and we're going to have him do a carriage house for us."*

## Eric J. Smith Architects PC

| | | | |
|---|---|---|---|
| 4.5 | 4 | 4 | 4.5 |

72 Spring Street 7th Floor, New York, NY 10012
(212) 334 - 3993

*Traditionally inspired residential architecture*

## Ethelind Coblin Architect PC ECAPC

| | | | |
|---|---|---|---|
| 3.5 | 3 | 4.5 | 4 |

505 Eighth Avenue, Suite 2202, New York, NY 10018
(212) 967 - 2490

*Commercial, government and residential architecture*

Known mostly for her traditional-style gut renovations in the city, Ethelind Coblin is said to take a highly collaborative approach with her clients. The firm is also known to take on projects of classical or modern design. Clients commend Coblin's soothing and charming personality, and say working with her firm is low-key and relaxed in a very professional way. We are told Coblin and her associates are willing take on every aspect of a project, from interior decorating down to the cabinet work and paint color selection. However, some say Coblin's back office could be increased.

This firm of six has been in business since 1989 with Coblin as the sole principal. She is a graduate of the University of Kentucky and Vanderbilt University where she earned an MA in architecture. Most of the firm's projects are fairly small in nature, reflective of Coblin's enjoyment of challenging small renovations. However, the firm's projects can range up to the half-million dollar mark. The firm typically takes on six to eight projects each year, in addition to consulting projects.

Nearly all of the firm's work is residential taking place in Manhattan, although Coblin will take on the occasional project in the Hamptons or the Westchester and Fairfield county areas. While most of the firm's work is in renovations, Coblin also works with co-op apartment buildings designing lobbies and other common areas and will also do small additions to existing structures. Current projects include a two-bedroom apartment gut renovation on the Upper East Side, a three bedroom gut rehab on the Upper West Side and several kitchen renovations. The firm charges a standard hourly fee.

*"She was very responsive to my concerns and made every effort to address them." "I found her very imaginative and creative in the brainstorming and design process." "She's very clear—communications were excellent." "Very professional and businesslike, but they could use a bigger back office."*

## Etienne Coffinier Design Ltd.

|  | 4 | 4 | 4.5 | 5 |
|---|---|---|---|---|

245 East 57th Street, New York, NY 10022
(212) 715 - 9699

*Residential architecture*

## Ferguson Shamamian & Rattner

|  | 5 | 4.5 | 4 | 5 |
|---|---|---|---|---|

270 Lafayette Street, Suite 300, New York, NY 10012
(212) 941 - 8088

*Classical, large-scale residential, institutional and commercial architecture*

This renowned firm is best known by clients (and peers alike) for its traditional styles of design, especially those borne of classical roots. Insiders tell us the firm is extremely efficient in its design process and pays close attention to providing personal service—with a principal involved in every project. Clients say the firm's designs are unique, detailed and highly customized within a traditional context. Ferguson Shamamian & Rattner has achieved iconic stature in architecture circles for its signature updated Hamptons Shingle Style. Regarding classicism as the purest form of design, we understand the firm's partners strongly prefer to work with clients who share their architectural philosophy. Clients say a combination of talent, quality and attention to detail makes this a much-sought-after firm, especially by those seeking the very best.

This large firm, created in 1988 by former employees of Parish-Hadley Associates, currently employs 65 in one office in New York City, although it takes on projects from coast to coast including the Hamptons, Nantucket, Martha's Vineyard, Georgia, South Carolina and Los Angeles. The partners of the firm are Mark Ferguson, who holds an MA from Princeton, Oscar Shamamian, who holds an MA from Columbia and Donald Rattner, who holds an MA from Princeton. The firm takes on somewhere between twelve and twenty projects each year. The firm dedicates nearly all of its services toward residential projects, about a quarter of which take place in Manhattan.

More than half the firm's current workload consists of single-family new home construction, the remainder being gut renovations, alterations and additions of apartments, townhouses and freestanding homes. Ferguson Shamamian & Rattner also offers master planning and design of resort communities Though the firm takes on many large Park and Fifth Avenue projects and celebrity clients (they recently finished Cindy Crawford's West Side apartment), it remains grounded and will accept a few projects with mid-level budgets for select clients. The firm charges an hourly rate which generally falls within the standard percentage of total construction costs.

*"They take great care with every detail. You can trust them to pick all the doorknobs and do it right." "Unbelievable team of professionals." "The Rolls-Royce of residential architects."*

| | Quality | Cost | Value | Recommend? |
|---|---|---|---|---|
| | + | $ | ◆ | ★ |

## FORM Architecture & Interiors

| | 4 | 4 | 4 | 4.5 |

1133 Broadway, New York, NY 10010
(212) 206 - 6430   www.formarch.com

*Full-service versatile, residential architecture*

Recently FORM Architecture has been on the receiving end of praise from clients and the media alike for its modern aesthetic. The firm is also known, however, for its ability to effectively execute projects of historic preservation and clients say the firm is adept at new home construction and large-scale renovations. Clients praise the firm for being sympathetic to their needs and answering questions with thoughtful, not rehearsed answers. We're also told the firm is quick with followups and approaches each project with enthusiasm.

Brent Leonard and Sean Webb are the principals of this eight-person firm that has been in business since 1999, although it has been around for much longer under different names. Leonard holds a degree from Parsons College and Webb holds an MA from the University of Texas. Approximately 90 percent of the firm's work is residential with about half taking place in Manhattan. In addition to working in the New York City area, FORM has also worked in the Hamptons, Westchester and Fairfield counties, Boston, Wyoming, California and Canada.

Current projects include a 10,000-square-foot modern residence in California, a SoHo spa in which the architects came up with new ways improving the flow and movement within the narrow space and a 3,000-square-foot loft in TriBeCa. The firm works on either an hourly rate or a standard percentage of total construction costs. The firm has been published in such publications as *Elle Decor, Interior Design* and *House Beautiful*. HB Top Designers, 2000.

*"Incredibly talented in all aspects of architecture and design." "Great customer relation abilities...he's always there when I need him." "Goes above and beyond the call of duty." "We saw their historic preservation work and looked no further."*

## Francois deMenil, Architect PC

| | 4 | 3.5 | 4.5 | 4.5 |

21 East 40th Street, Suite 2000, New York, NY 10016
(212) 779 - 3400

*Residential, commercial and retail architecture*

Known for selecting the appropriate materials based on their wide-ranging knowledge of the subject is what clients say sets Francois deMenil and his associates apart from the rest of New York's contemporary firms. From the most innovative synthetics to the humblest natural materials, Francois deMenil has been creating unique and elegant modern homes and apartments for the past ten years.

The firm generally takes on three to eight projects each year, most of which are larger projects with substantial budgets. Ranging from gut renovations of larger apartments and townhouses in Manhattan to new single-family home construction in the suburbs, sources say this firm of five is effective and efficient in the design process. Principal Francois deMenil, a graduate of Cooper Union plays an active role in every project the firm undertakes. We hear he is meticulously detail-oriented and a pleasure to work with professionally and to talk to personally. We are told deMenil takes on each project with class and creates designs that reflect his name and the client's vision with the highest integrity, caring as much about function as form.

Recent projects include a modern 8,700-square-foot home renovation in Manhattan and a 3,200-square-foot modern single family home in the Hamptons. We understand the firm is flexible in its methods of charging a fee, but the bottom line ends up being a standard to slightly lower percentage of total construction costs.

## Freyer Collaborative Architects

|   |   |   |   |
|---|---|---|---|
| 3.5 | 3.5 | 4 | 4.5 |

37 East 18th Street, 10th Floor, New York, NY
(212) 598 - 0900   freyerarchitects.com

*Modern residential and commercial architecture with historic sensitivity*

Best known for its gut renovations of existing homes and apartments, this firm's work is evenly split between residential and commercial architecture. Clients say Warren Freyer and his staff really listen to clients and actively incorporate their ideas into design. The firm usually accepts 20 to 30 new projects each year of varying sizes and scopes. In addition to taking on numerous apartment combinations, the firm also tackles loft renovations and rooftoop additions in the Manhattan, where most of its residential projects take place. Sources tell us the firm keeps detailed records and effectively manages contractors. We have heard the staff could be a bit more patient about the design process.

In business since 1991, Freyer Collaborative Architects is led by sole principal Warren Freyer, a graduate of the University of Illinois and Pratt. In addition to its Manhattan projects, the firm works on residences in the Hamptons as well commercial work across the country, including Telluride and Colorado. With a staff of nineteen, this firm has the resources to take on large mult million-dollar endeavors, but continues to take on small, challenging projects as well.

Recent projects include a large 4,200-square-foot loft renovation in a downtown industrial space, melding modern architecture to suit a fine collection of Far-Eastern antiques and a modern, yet historically detailed 1,800-square-foot rooftop renovation and addition including a large garden and a scaling wall inside for the rock-climbing owners. The firm also designed the Miramax Films offices downtown. Freyer often charges standard fixed fees based on a projection of total construction costs.

*"Their design sensibilities are really, really good." "I was looking for someone I felt comfortable with and someone I liked—and I found that in Warren Freyer." "Did a great job of being a buffer between me and the general contractor." "Whenever there was an issue, they were extremely responsive." "Everyone comes in here and loves the place—they always comment on it."*

## Gabellini Associates

|   |   |   |   |
|---|---|---|---|
| 4 | 4 | 4 | 4.5 |

665 Broadway, Suite 706, New York, NY  10012
(212) 388 - 1700   www.gabelliniassociates.com

*Modern, artistic high-end commercial and residential architecture*

Having designed the Giorgio Armani Center in Milan, the Nicole Farhi flagship store in New York and Jil Sander boutiques worldwide, Michael Gabellini is known for links to the fashion world, art galleries and museums. Highly respected and admired for its modern, minimalist style of design, this firm is lauded by clients for finding new ways interpret the modern aesthetic. Sources tell us the firm approaches each project with meticulous planning in order to create spacious, elegant designs that implement the importance of natural light through a simple means. New Yorkers (and tourists worldwide) have seen his work in the redesign of the Rockefeller Center Fifth Avenue facade. The firm also won an international competition for the redesign of the Piazza Isolo in Verona, Italy.

This firm, created in 1991, employs a staff of 31, led by principals Michael Gabellini, a graduate RISD, Daniel Garbowit, a graduate of Syracuse and Kimberly Sheppard, also a graduate of RISD. The firm takes on anywhere from 12 to 24 projects each year. Insiders describe Gabellini as an artist who works with architecture who initially enrolled at RISD to become a sculptor, but ended up studying architecture as well. We are told that Gabellini Associates focuses on large, high-end jobs, accepting few smaller projects. The firm has a small residential practice totaling roughly ten to twenty percent of its portfolio, mostly gut apartment renovations.

Recent projects include a twelve-story hotel in San Francisco totaling 80,000 square feet, and a 5,000-square-foot custom penthouse in the Cayman Islands. The firm works across the city, recently working in lower Manhattan, Midtown and the Upper East Side. The firm generally works on a fixed fee that usually ends up being on the higher end of the standard percentage of total construction costs based on a preconceived hypothetical estimation.

*"Exquisite minimalist work with an artist's touch."*

### GF55 Architects  3.5  3.5  4  5
19 West 21st Street, Suite 1201, New York, NY 10010
(212) 352 - 3099   www.gf55.com
*Residential, commercial and institutional architecture*

With numerous publications examining the exquisite restoration of mid-century modern American homes, it's no surprise that clients across the country trust their homes in the capable hands of GF55 Architects. Clients say they gravitate toward GF55 for the firm's well-respected neoclassical, traditional and modern designs with a specialty in high-end gut renovations of large city dwellings—brownstones, duplexes and triplexes. Clients praise the firm for its detailed drawings, swift execution and "New York quality without the New York attitude." We hear the firm's architects are consummate professionals who listen and respond to clients' needs while being inventive, suggesting refreshing new ideas.

This firm of eighteen has been in business since 1984 and is headed up by principals Leonard Fusco and David E. Gross. Fusco holds degrees from Columbia and Penn and Gross holds a degree from Penn. About one-third of GF55's annual workload is residential, with the remainder being a mix of commercial and institutional architecture. In addition to its architectural services GF55 will also decorate the interiors of projects they design. Approximately 40 percent of the firm's work takes place in Manhattan, although it does work in the rest of the regional area, Ohio and Florida.

Recent projects include a 2,500-square-foot gut rehab and addition in Rye, New York and a complete villa in Cleveland, Ohio that includes a 2,500-square-foot addition and total gut rehab of the existing structure. The firm is also known outside of the United States for its extensive design of commercial space across Central America. The firm charges a standard percentage of total construction costs. GF55 has been published in major magazines such as *Architectural Digest* (cover) and *House and Garden*. It has also been featured on HGTV and the recipient of AIA awards.

*"An excellent New York firm without New York snobbery."*

| | Quality | Cost | Value | Recommend? |
|---|---|---|---|---|

## Gleicher Design Group

| 4 | 3 | 4.5 | 4 |

330 West 38th Street, Suite 1101, New York, NY 10018
(212) 462 - 2789

*Renovation of apartments and brownstones*

A keen knowledge of zoning regulations and permitting issues coupled with the versatility to design both handsome modern and elegant traditional spaces is what clients say is the key to Paul Gleicher's success. We are told his honest, thoughtful and involved approach to design is just one of many reasons clients have returned for other projects. Clients tell us the firm excels in gut renovations of apartments and townhouses on the Upper East and Upper West Sides. Recently the firm has also accepted numerous projects combining two or more apartments into one and converting multi family townhouses back into single-family residences. Apart from his design sense, sources tell us Gleicher has a soothing personality and is able to take the stress out of any situation with his positive outlook.

This firm of six was created in 1989 by sole principal, Paul Gleicher, after spending time at Davis Brody & Associates and Haverson-Rockwell Architects. He holds degrees from SUNY Binghamton and Columbia architecture schools. Gleicher and his associates average about fifteen new projects each year, nearly all of which are residential spaces in the city. The firm also does interior decorating at the request of clients.

Gleicher has worked with numerous celebrity clients, most recently the renovation of Kevin Bacon's West Side apartment. Other recent projects include the combination of two traditional apartments into one totaling 6,200 square feet on the Upper West Side and the 2,800-square-foot modern apartment renovation in a prewar building also on the Upper West Side. The firm charges a standard percentage of overall construction costs.

*"I couldn't have been in better hands. Paul always had a great calm about him." "Totally flexible and accommodating." "We wanted a sharing experience and he gave us that—he was totally flexible and accommodating." "We needed it to come out beautifully, but quickly—and he delivered." "I am not given to change, so it took me a while to get used to it, but now if you try to change anything in that house, I'll break your hands. I just love it." "Terrific to work with. Paul Gleicher made the whole process as easy as it could be." "He is extremely honest. I felt totally in charge of the budget."*

## Goralnick & Buchanan Design

| 3.5 | 4 | 4 | 4.5 |

306 East 61st Street, 2nd Floor, New York, NY 10021
(212) 644 - 0334

*Residential architecture, interior design and furniture*

Specializing in gut renovations, Goralnick and Buchanan Design is approached by clients for the firm's ability to incorporate a contemporary take on traditional design. Clients applaud the firm's flexible approach and commend the staff of Goralnick and Buchanan for its skill in dramatizing the small spaces of New York apartments, working with color and furniture as well as architectural elements. The firm also offers interior design services, furniture and lighting product lines. Approximately 85 percent of the firm's annual commissions are residential, half of which takes place in Manhattan.

This firm of six was started in 1984 by principals Barry Goralnick, who holds a degree from Harvard Graduate School, and Michael Buchanan, who attended FIT. Sources tell us the firm generally takes on substantial projects, but will accept smaller ones providing the client connects with the philosophy of the firm and the project is challenging and interesting. The firm has taken on projects around the world, including the Hamptons, Westchester and Fairfield counties, Massachusetts, California, Maine and France.

| | Quality | Cost | Value | Recommend? |
|---|---|---|---|---|
| | ✚ | $ | ◆ | ★ |

Current projects include the design of an 8,500-square-foot home in Quogue and the interior decorating for a 20,000-square-foot home in Greenwich. The firm's work has been sought by a celebrity clientele and featured in many publications, including *Architectural Digest* and *Elle Decor*. The firm's proprietary designs appear in several high-end hotel and retail locations, including I. Magnin and the Trump casinos in Atlantic City. Goralnick and Buchanan generally charge a higher percentage of total construction cost, but occasionally will work on an hourly rate.

### Gustavson/Dundes Architecture Design

192 Lexington Avenue, New York, NY   10016
(212) 251 - 0212

*Residential, corporate and retail architecture and interiors*

### Gwathmey Siegel & Associates Architects   5    4    5    5

475 Tenth Avenue 3rd Floor, New York, NY   10018
(212) 947 - 1240   www.gwathmey-siegel.com

*Modern, dramatic institutional, commercial and residential architecture*

Praised by clients, acknowledged by the press and admired by industry professionals, the award-winning Gwathmey Siegel & Associates is one of country's most prestigious firms. Clients hail this firm for its intricate detail, completely original designs and passion for creating spaces of the highest quality and stylistic integrity. We are told the firm is even-handed in its selection of natural materials and clients say the firm leaves its indelible signature on every project without being repetitive—all while being sympathetic to the client's needs and tastes. Geometric and precise, and with great clarity of design, the firm's projects have won Charles Gwathmey and Robert Siegel a devoted following and more than 100 awards. The firm's projects put forth an unquestionable modernism, and this firm of 80 has been commended for displaying a sculptor's sensitivity to shape and light. Observers often describe the firm's work as luxurious and sleek. We are told these architects believe that complete architectural solutions should integrate the details of interior design.

Gwathmey, a Fulbright scholar, graduated in 1962 from Yale with a master's degree in architecture and became a Fellow of the AIA in 1981. Siegel is a graduate of Pratt and Harvard, became a Fellow in 1991 and remains active in the Pratt community. This partnership was founded in 1967 and both architects have taught at some of the country's most prestigious universities. The firm only accepts projects with broad budgets—each topping more than $5 million and any residential projects tend to be majestic single-family homes or large full-scale apartment renovations in New York and Los Angeles.

Current projects include the construction of a 20,000-square-foot sculptured and dynamic home in Bel-Air, the renovation of the 250,000-square-foot New York Public Library central circulation location on Fifth Avenue and the renovation or construction of the homes of numerous celebrities, including Jerry Seinfeld and Steven Spielberg. Other nonresidential projects have included the 1992 addition to the Solomon R. Guggenheim Museum, and buildings on the campuses of such universities as Harvard, Princeton and Cornell. The firm charges a higher percentage of total construction costs plus the fees for any necessary consultants or engineers. AD 100, 2000. ID Hall of Fame.

| | Quality | Cost | Value | Recommend? |
|---|---|---|---|---|
| | + | $ | ◆ | ★ |

*"We were able to get an architectural masterpiece without sacrificing practical living comfort." "It's been exhilarating, exciting and an education in the modern aesthetic." "The most amazing part about it was watching Charles's ideas come to fruition. I would do it all again." "The execution right down to the last detail was absolutely flawless." "It was a perfect collaboration of our ideas and enlightenment by them." "They were imaginative and creative—and it came out magnificently."*

## Helfand Myerberg Guggenheimer                4    3    5    5
428 Broadway, 2nd Floor, New York, NY 10013
(212) 925 - 2900  www.hmga.com
*Modern institutional, commercial and residential architecture*

Clients say this high-end firm displays a cerebral, intricate approach to architecture. While the firm's body of work reflects a definitive modern, minimal style, we are told the firm is also conversant in other vocabularies, especially traditional design. Helfand Myerberg Guggenheimer's work often references classical ideas, with a tangible element of experimentation. In addition to new and innovative design ideas, we are told the firm takes advantage of indigenous, industrial and recycled materials that lend new dimensions and economies to projects. Helfand Myerberg Guggenheimer will also do interior decorating at the request of the client. Clients say the firm's architects reflect its founders' charm and genuine talent for design, with the ability to assertively guide the client along the process without being too stern or soft. The architects also win fans for an ability to connect with clients and establish a personal rapport. Many clients applaud the firm for producing extraordinary design with ordinary spaces.

Industry insiders also stand behind HMG, including contractors who applaud the firm's ability to set forth reasonable timelines. This firm of 22 was formed 3 years ago and typically accepts 20 to 25 projects annually. Margaret Helfand, a Fellow of the AIA, was educated at the University of California at Berkeley and the Architectural Association of London. Henry Myerberg received an MA from Harvard University and has taught at Columbia. Peter Guggenheimer holds a degree from Pratt. All three partners had their own firms before joining to form this one.

Recent Manhattan projects include two large-scale renovations in the famous Dakota building, a modern loft-style penthouse and a Central Park West triplex. A number of high-end art dealers are included in their client list, as well as a variety of vacation homes and highly regarded institutional projects, such as Swarthmore College, Cornell University and the Museum of American Folk Art. The firm charges a standard percentage of total construction costs.

*"One of the most talented designers I know. They can really communicate with clients." "Their work is interesting, highly aesthetic." "Our space is beautiful, clever and very, very appropriate to our needs."*

## Henry Jessup                3.5    4.5    4    2
2067 Broadway, Suite 41, New York, NY 10023
(212) 580 - 8059
*Residential architecture and historic preservation*

We are told the firm generally prefers an eclectic style of design, but Henry Jessup is probably best known for his traditional and historically based renovations. Jessup's clients appreciate his professional demeanor, organizational skills and personable nature. Sources tell us that in order to maintain personal oversight of all projects and to offer high-level client relations, Jessup prefers to work alone. As a result, we are told he accepts only a few projects at any given time. The bulk of the architect's work is gut renovations and the new construction of single-family residences.

We hear this architect's services are always in high demand, and clients may wait up to a year to begin a project. Jessup prefers to work with a select group of contractors to ensure that their work is consistent with his standards. He is the

| Quality | Cost | Value | Recommend? |
| --- | --- | --- | --- |
| + | $ | ◆ | ★ |

sole principal of this firm he created 23 years ago and holds degrees from Brown and Columbia. Approximately 30 percent of Jessup's work is based in Manhattan, but he also works in Brooklyn, the Hamptons, Westchester and Fairfield counties and other parts of the regional area.

Recent projects include three single-family homes—a classic brick, an Italian Mediterranean and a Tudor-style—in Brooklyn ranging from 8,000 to 10,000 square feet. The firm also is currently building a 7,000-square-foot shingle-style home in Bedminister, New Jersey. The firm generally charges a lower percentage of overall construction costs, but will occasionally charge an hourly rate for repeat customers.

*"We really appreciated Henry's open attitude and lack of artistic ego, a quality rarely found among high-caliber designers in New York." "You can depend on Henry to deliver truly wonderful results."*

### Hottenroth & Joseph Architects        3.5    2.5    4    5
1181 Broadway, 5th Floor, New York, NY 10001
(212) 941 - 1900

*Traditional residential architecture specializing in renovations*

Sources tell us this firm has recently built a strong reputation for its exceptional treatment of traditional renovations and clients hail Hottenroth and Joseph as being meticulously respectful of the existing structure, going to great lengths to preserve the integrity of the design. In addition, the firm is also skilled at creating modern design and does so on occasion. Clients laud David Hottenroth and Jim Joseph for their tireless devotion to each project and a keen ability to solve problems on the fly. The firm offers both architectural and decorative services, creating a seamless product. We are told many happy clients in the city recommend the firm to friends and invite the architects to the Hamptons for projects there.

This firm of ten has been in business for eight years and is lead by principals David Hottenroth, a graduate of the University of Cincinnati and Jim Joseph, who also holds degrees from Cincinnati and Columbia. More than 80 percent of the firm's work is residential and includes numerous renovations and additions to existing homes, apartments and townhouses. The firm takes on projects with modest six-figure budgets and its staff can handle large, multi million-dollar residences.

More than half of the firm's work takes place within Manhattan, but Hottenroth & Joseph also takes on projects in the Hamptons, Westchester County, Montclair, Sun Valley and Palm Beach. Recent projects include the renovation of a West Village townhouse with an added penthouse and mezzanine totaling 4,000 square feet, and the gut renovation and addition of an elevator of a 6,000-square-foot townhouse on the Upper East Side. Their work has been featured on the pages of *Elle Decor* among other publications. The firm charges a standard percentage of overall construction costs.

*"They are gifted architects who combine the qualities of ingenuity, taste and professionalism." "Their distinct talents and characteristics complement each other, forming the ideal team to take on a wide variety of projects." "Has a true respect and admiration for the classics."*

### James Bodnar Architect        4    4    4    4.5
110 East 78th Street, New York, NY 10021
(212) 794 - 0744

*Highly detailed residential and commercial architecture*

Best known for his high-quality additions to existing homes and interior renovations of landmark historical buildings, James Bodnar has earned a reputation for staying true to style. Approximately half of his annual workload is residential, and his design style ranges from modern and contemporary to traditional. Bodnar is also known for his work in exterior preservation of historic buildings. We are told Bodnar spares no expense in search of aesthetic purity and refinement, to the delight of some and the concern of others.

Bodnar is the sole principal of this seven-person firm that he started in 1990. About half of his residential projects take place in Manhattan and the rest of his work extends from Santa Barbara to Nantucket, Westchester and Vermont. Bodnar studied at Catholic University, Yale and the American Academy in Rome. Clients praise Bodnar for extending himself to provide them with personalized up-to-date information about projects with a password protected area of his web site—where clients can review a complete archive of sketches and photographs. The firm takes on projects of all sizes, from small one-room renovations up to massive multi million-dollar homes.

Some notable recent projects include the renovation of a 12,000-square-foot landmark Midtown building for a not-for-profit company, an East Side townhouse of 17,000 square feet to become a private investment bank, and a 2,000-square-foot, seven-room addition to a suburban farmhouse. The firm charges an hourly fee up to a maximum (standard) percentage of total cost of construction.

*"Never pretentious, though he's a perfectionist." "A really decent human being, and a delight to work with." "A very good listener who tries to get everything just right for the client."*

### James D'Auria Associates, PC     4.5     4     4.5     4.5
20 West 36th Street, 12th Floor, New York, NY 10018
(212) 268 - 1142
*Versatile modern residential architecture*

With a broad understanding of multiple styles, clients say they gravitate toward James D'Auria for projects that range from cutting-edge modern design to traditional. Recently, the firm has received accolades from the press and clients for its modern, but not minimalist design. Clients say they appreciate D'Auria's keen ability to create environments that reflect clients' tastes. The firm's typical projects are gut renovations in Manhattan or new home construction in the suburbs. Ranging from small lofts to multi million-dollar homes, clients say D'Auria has a diversified practice. The firm offers interior design services, or projects that it acts as the architect for, and typically takes on both roles for many of its projects.

D'Auria, the sole principal of the firm, studied at the Art Institute and in Florence, Italy. The firm has been in business since 1974 and has grown to a staff of sixteen, with four interior designers and nine architects, and an administrative staff of three. D'Auria typically takes on 20 to 30 projects each year about 85 percent of which are in Manhattan. The firm will not shy away from smaller projects, and works in the Hamptons as well as the city.

Some recent projects include a large traditional apartment for Bryant Gumbel that was converted from three adjoining apartments. The firm also recently completed a 4,000-square-foot loft on Duane Street and a modern 4,000-square-foot home in Amagansett that was featured in a recent issue of *Elle Decor* magazine. The firm generally charges a higher percentage of total construction costs for its architectural services and standard hourly rates for its interior decorating services. The firm also offers store-planning services.

*"He was knowledgeable, open and honest about what could and could not be done." "Despite considerable expertise, he was always open to new ideas and willing to alter his plans and views." "On occasion, he pressed his view without being argumentative or condescending." "Ever aware that it's the client's project—not his, and that it's about the client's satisfaction—not his ego." "He not only completed the project on time and on budget, but he has become a dear friend."*

### John B. Murray Architect LLC

| | 4.5 | 4.5 | 4 | 4.5 |

36 West 25th Street, 9th Floor, New York, NY   10010
(212) 242 - 8600   www.jbmarch.com

*High-end traditional residential architecture*

This firm is considered by clients to be extremely traditionalist, with projects ranging from classical and formal to a relaxed vernacular. Principal John Murray, a founding partner of Ferguson, Murray & Shamamian before starting his own firm in 1998, generally embarks on large-scale gut renovations, although we hear the firm will take on smaller projects with an interesting twist or that pose an intriguing challenge. Clients praise Murray for his exceptional architectural sense and dedication to traditional design and form. Many say they approach him for his depth of experience and amiable personality. References report that Murray maintains a classic style with very traditional lines, matching the preferences of most of his clients. We have heard that Murray is extremely busy and not always easy to reach, although his followup is said to be very thorough.

While some say Murray's taste for the highest form of design occasionally leads him to suggest more changes than necessary, he is known to be receptive to clients' suggestions and sympathetic to their design and budgetary needs. Murray is a graduate of Carnegie Mellon. Slightly less than half of the firm's commissions are in Manhattan, with the rest spread across some of the surrounding area's most exclusive communities, serving a strong base of the New York area's carriage trade.

Current projects include a 16,000-square-foot renovation of a Georgian estate in Bedford Hills to double the scale of the house, and a 6,000-square-foot addition and renovation of a Greenwich Colonial Revival style home. Sources say that his fine work suits the highest-end tastes, he is considerably more affordable now that he is on his own. The firm generally charges a standard percentage of overall construction costs, but will occasionally work on an hourly rate.

*"He isn't a bargain, but he's a great value." "John loves to be involved and sometimes can get rather busy." "He watches and gives frequent budget reports." "His understanding and sensitivity to old buildings is his core strength." "He has dramatized the geometry of this historic building." "His followup is absolutely incredible." "A magnificent sense of classical design." "He upholds the very top standards of quality, at all times."*

### Kaehler/Moore Architects

| | 4 | 4 | 4 | 5 |

1 Fawcett Place, Greenwich, CT 06830
(203) 629 - 2212

*Residential architecture*

Clients return to this very versatile designer for beautifully detailed and beautifully executed construction. Kaehler/Moore's pragmatist style confidently integrates interiors and exteriors that are responsive to site conditions, social context and the client's interests. Clients rave about the firm's architectural interiors which integrates old furniture and fixtures into new construction with fabulous results. While schools and libraries count among this firm's institutional work, the tidal of its efforts flow mostly to residential new construction in the regional area. Much of the firm's residential renovation and addition work tends to be for past cus-

tomers, which has included build-outs of corporate space and second city homes. Thirty percent of Kaeler/Moore's work takes it across the country, to places like Colorado, California, Montana, and Maryland.

Principals Joeb Moore and Laura Kaehler are known to take time and pride in servicing clients. Moore tends to oversee the exteriors and partner Kaehler the interiors, but clients say both are attentive and available. The firm consists of thirteen architects and two assistants, and is considered to be very knowledgeable of environmental issues. Moore received his BA and first MA at Clemson, and holds a research degree at Yale. Laura holds a BA in Architecture from Rensselaer Polytechnic Institute. The firm offers its services for either a percentage of construction sliding on the upper end of the scale, especially for renovations, or at an hourly rate that is often the choice for clients with no cap of fees.

*"Listens to the client. Gives the client what they want." "Constantly working on the project. Constantly there." "Really tuned to the market. They get it." "Could not be more delightful people, with a critical eye for the highest quality."*

### Karen Jacobson Architects       4    3    5    5
103 Reade Street, New York, NY 10013
(212) 571 - 1116

*High-end residential architecture and design services*

Clients say they are drawn to Karen Jacobson's unique ability to address unforeseen issues, thorough drawings, high level client relations and overall outstanding end product. We are told Jacobson leans toward a modern-tinged classic aesthetic, but takes the client's stylistic cues. This Gwathmey-trained architect has a strong roster of famous clients who say they are devoted to her talent and unpretentious personality. Jacobson has a varied portfolio that includes new single-family home construction, major gut renovations and additions to existing homes, apartments, penthouses and townhouses. Jacobson is respected for her ability to work effectively with idiosyncratic spaces  such as carriage houses, apartment combinations, brownstone additions.

Half of the firm's work is in Manhattan—but it also takes on numerous projects in the Hamptons, Westchester and Fairfield counties. A fair amount of the firm's work is the design of new houses, primarily in upstate New York and Connecticut. Jacobson also does a considerable amount of work within the medical field, working on plastic surgeons' offices, in addition to offering interior design services. This small firm employs three and was created by Jacobson, a graduate of Princeton ten years ago. The projects the firm accepts tend to have substantial budgets that range from less than $1 million up to several million dollars.

Recent projects include the 6,000-square-foot gut renovation of a Hamptons summer home, the 2,000-square-foot addition to a Milbrook home and the new construction of a farmhouse on Shelter Island totaling 3,000 square feet. The firm charges an hourly rate not to exceed the standard to slightly lower percentage of overall construction costs.

*"I felt an immediate kinship with Karen. While she is very businesslike it is always in a completely nice way." "She steers you to the highest quality that is practical for your budget, but never pressures you." "I never would have made it through this process if I had not found Karen. She is a doer and a completer. She had a solution to every challenge." "She created a fabulous space from almost nothing."*

### Katherine Gormley, Architect    3.5   3.5   4    4
45 East End Avenue, New York, NY 10028
(212) 517 - 4121

*High-end residential architecture and interior design*

| | Quality | Cost | Value | Recommend? |
|---|---|---|---|---|
| | + | $ | ◆ | ★ |

## Kathryn McGraw Berry  3   3   4   4

143 West 20th Street, New York, NY 10011
(212) 807 - 1499

*Contemporary/transitional residential architecture*

Kathryn McGraw Berry creates high-end contemporary designs that have been described as "transitional modern with an eclectic twist." Working as a sole practitioner for over fifteen years, she has developed a strong following as a residential and commercial architect for clients on Park Avenue and downtown, working in brand-new buildings and on renovations. She also offers interior design services, and clients praise the clean lines and contemporary flair of her spaces.

An award-winning architect, Berry is selective about her work, taking on only a few jobs per year. Clients appreciate her delightful nature and natural grace. Berry was educated at the University of California at Berkeley and at the Cooper Union.

*"She's charming and very talented."*

## KSA Architects/Alfred Wen  3.5   3   4.5   4

45 West 34th Street, Suite 1209, New York, NY 10001
(212) 643 - 2655

*Highly detailed, personalized residential architecture*

Clients say Alfred Wen of KSA Architects is an excellent architect, careful listener and is senstive to his customers' vision. We are told this small firm pays close attention to detail—both in regards to the physical project and the notion of personalized client relations. KSA generally takes on traditional-style projects, with a strong inherent capability for the "exactly correct Park Avenue look," but remains flexible given the project. With a keen eye for proportion, clients say Wen's creative, collaborative approach is a valued asset of the firm.

Alfred Wen, a graduate of Princeton and Columbia, is the sole principal of this two-architect firm created in 1981. Approximately 60 percent of the firm's work is residential, the vast majority of which takes place in Manhattan—particularly on the Upper East Side. KSA also works in the Hamptons and Westchester and Fairfield counties. The firm's scope of projects range from small five-figure projects up to $1 million in terms of construction costs.

Current projects include a 3,000-square-foot gut renovation of a traditional apartment on the Upper East Side and the 2,000-square-foot combination of a traditional duplex on the Upper West Side. The firm has also worked on a number of restaurants and office interiors with developers. KSA charges a standard percentage of total construction costs.

*"A master of his craft, very talented." "I respected him very much." "Easy to work with—a gem." "He can easily emulate the old small base kitchens, because he has done it so many times." "That just-so look at way under the unexpected price."*

| | Quality | Cost | Value | Recommend? |
|---|---|---|---|---|
| | + | $ | ◆ | ★ |

## Lichten Craig Architects LLP
**4 3.5 4.5 5**

6 West 18th Street, New York, NY 10011
(212) 229 - 0200

*High-end residential architecture and interior design*

Classic style, impeccable standards and a personable approach are the qualities most often used to describe Lichten Craig Architects. Headed by Kevin Lichten and Joan Craig, the firm creates designs known for strong detail and handles projects ranging from traditional Park Avenue apartments to modern lofts. Many clients also use Craig for interior design. References describe the team as very willing and extremely able to accommodate clients' interests and style preferences. The firm receives high marks for strong project management skills, right through the very last punch list items.

While each of the principals had previously practiced separately for over a decade, they joined forces to create the current firm in 1995. Most clients are located in the NYC metro area, and other recent projects include residences in New Mexico, Brazil and New England. Lichten Craig's projects usually entail substantial renovations and new construction, but the firm is also willing to undertake smaller projects. References say that the principals are readily available and that the experienced support staff is excellent. Lichten holds a BA from Brown and an MA in architecture from Yale, and he practiced with both Edward Larrabee Barnes and Fox & Fowle. Craig holds a BA from Wesleyan and an MA in architecture from Princeton, and she practiced with Skidmore, Owings & Merrill as well as Buttrick, White & Burtis.

The firm charges standard architectural percentage rates or a fixed fee. Interior design is done on a standard hourly basis with net pricing, or on cost plus. Lichten Craig is highly recommended by clients for strong design vision that combines comfort, inventiveness and function.

*"Kevin was an absolute delight to work with—he knew exactly the 18th-century look I was after but added that magical sparkle of the here and now." "The coordination was terrific." "Joan listened to my ideas, then came up with creative solutions beyond my initial thoughts." "They stayed with me when the contractor said it was impossible to build a straight staircase between the three floors of my apartment. And they made it work just perfectly." "We have become great friends."*

## Louise Braverman, Architect
**4 4 4 5**

16 East 79th Street, Suite 43, New York, NY 10021
(212) 879 - 6155

*Artistic, yet functional residential architecture*

With impeccable followup practices and a style sources say is "forward thinking poetic modern," Louise Braverman has served the Manhattan area with high-end architectural design for the past decade. We are told Braverman works very closely with clients to interpret their abstract visions into the physical manifestation of the home, while taking into account an artistic merit and livability. We are told Braverman is cordial, down-to-earth and easily approachable. In addition to her satisfied clients, insiders tell us Braverman has earned the respect of her peers as well as contractors who say her attention to detail is of the highest standards.

Having received her MA in architecture from Yale University, Braverman established her own firm in 1991. She most commonly accepts gut renovations of apartments and townhouses in the city, but also takes on new home construction in the Hamptons and the Westchester and Fairfield counties, as well as a number of commercial and institutional endeavors.

Recent projects include the design of an eighteen-unit housing project, the conversion of two apartments into one penthouse and several renovations in landmark buildings. Her work has been widely published and received multiple awards—the New York Architectural League recognized her as an "Emerging Voice."

*"Her instincts to anticipate our needs and express our aesthetic were intuitive and totally on target." "I had such a positive experience working with Louise that if I didn't adore my location I'd love to totally renovate another apartment with her."*

| | Quality<br>+ | Cost<br>$ | Value<br>◆ | Recommend?<br>★ |
|---|---|---|---|---|

## Louis Mackall, Architect

|  | 4.5 | 3.5 | 5 | 5 |

135 Leetes Island Road, Guilford, CT 06437
(203) 458 - 8888 x88

*Collaborative, thoughtful architecture, millwork specialist*

Clients rave about Louis Mackall who is said to be brilliant, kind and keenly attuned to the clients needs. With fans from the Dakota in Manhattan to those in Connecticut, Westchester and Long Island, this "consistently creative" architect and Renaissance man is lauded for his willingness to both lead and be led down new design paths. Clients say he "constantly outdoes himself, making each rendition more exciting" and developing the maximum impact for reasonable dollars. A graduate of Yale and Yale Architecture School, Mackall has been practicing architecture since 1968, and also co-helms one of the region's best millwork outfits in Breakfast Woodworks.

Clients tell us they are impressed with Mackall's guidance during the project, saying that he turns around drawings and ideas swiftly, keeping the project on track. He is known to be gentle with clients and tough with subs in the same calm, measured manner that both respect. Clients tell us he "saves money on the spot," and that he is almost "too fair" when it comes to pricing, which he does typically on an hourly basis. We hear he takes on only a few jobs at a time and is completely dedicated to making each one a success.

*"I'm totally in love with Louis. So fair and so honest." "My friend had two ratty apartments. He combined them into a five million dollar spread." "He took into account our aesthetic and economic needs, and we decided together." "Half the price of everyone else because and that Murray does it right the first time." "Introduced me to every sub on the job, and they are all wonderful." "When our roof leaked, he was there within the hour and did not leave until the last nail was hammered in correctly." "If there is ever any questions, he pulls two computers out of his backpack and offers multiple solutions immediately." "True creative integrity." "He saved us."*

## May Architects

|  | 3 | 3 | 4 | 4 |

1449 Lexington Avenue, New York, NY 10128
(212) 534 - 2850   www.mayarchitects.com

*High-end, personalized architecture, sensitive to existing structures*

Manhattan apartment and loft owners look to Penny May and her small firm for large-scale gut renovations and rely on her ability to leave clues of existing architecture while incorporating modern hints. We understand May is adept at working on building of all kinds—prewar and postwar, modern and traditional. We hear May is highly involved in every project and puts clients at ease with her pleasant demeanor and ample personal attention.

This firm of four was created in 1991 by May, a graduate of Barnard College and the Columbia architecture school. Most of the firm's work is residential and is most often in Manhattan, with some in the regional areas.

## Mojo Stumer Associates

|  | 3.5 | 2 | 4 | 4.5 |

55 Bryant Avenue, Roslyn, NY 11576
(516) 625 - 3344

*Residential and corporate architecture, including interiors*

The architects at Mojo Stumer Associates work mainly on substantial jobs, including designing new high-end residences and renovating existing ones. While much of its work is on Long Island, this midsized firm also does projects throughout the New York area. Partners Thomas Mojo and Mark Stumer are cited for their interiors as well as their knowledgeable architectural work. References say that projects are well managed from start to finish, employing a range of contractors. The firm is particularly noted for giving sound advice on budget issues and for knowing the meaning of value.

In addition to residences, Mojo Stumer regularly works on corporate projects—we hear that these clients continue to come back for more, appreciative of the quality and consistency of Mojo Stumer's work. Other projects have included gyms and several country clubs. References say they enjoy working closely with these professionals.

*"They always go farther than necessary to help me."*

## MR Architecture & Decor    4    4    4    4.5
150 West 28 Street, Suite 1102, New York, NY   10001
(212) 989 - 9300
*High-end, minimalist modern architecture*

With a distinct Miës-inspired modern minimalist style, MR Architecture has designed numerous residential, commercial and retail spaces in Manhattan. Residential projects make up 30 percent of the firm's portfolio, and of those, the firm most commonly works on gut renovations of residences—nearly all of which are in the city. We are told the firm is rigorous in its design and planning of projects and mindful of budgetary constraints. Sources tell us the firm is so concerned about keeping to the parameters of initial budgets that it has been known to take the amount of overage off the final bill.

MR Architecture currently employs four and was created in 1995 by sole principal David Mann, a graduate of Pratt. Sources tell us Mann takes his work "beyond seriously" and is a very hands-on principal with heavy involvement in all projects, of which the firm takes on about fifteen each year. Recent projects include the minimalist modern renovation of an 11,000-square-foot downtown loft space and the 6,000-square-foot Takashimaya store located on Fifth Avenue. The firm charges a standard percentage of overall construction costs. HB Top Designers, 2000.

## Murphy Burnham & Buttrick Architects ■   4.5   3.5   5   4.5
1 West 37th Street, 9th Floor, New York, NY   10018
(212) 768 - 7676   www.mbbarch.com
*Residential and institutional architecture and interior design*

Clients of Murphy Burnham & Buttrick Architects applaud its strong expertise, established skill and very high-quality, detailed work that bridges the modern and traditional idioms. The firm does institutional, commercial and residential work, including projects for the Convent of the Sacred Heart, Riverside Park Volunteer House, a number of high-end LBO firms and various residences up and down Park and Fifth Avenues, as well as in Connecticut and Long Island. The three partners, Harry Buttrick, Mary Burnham and Jeffrey Murphy, each bring extensive knowledge gained from working on projects for some of New York's most treasured institutions. Most of the firm's work is done in New York and Connecticut, although it has also completed projects throughout the United States, Europe and Africa. The 20-person firm offers a complete range of architectural, planning and interior design services. Clients say that the team provides the personal attention and design focus of a small firm, with the services, technical expertise and production capabilities of a large firm.

Buttrick has worked as an architect in New York for 40 years; he previously founded Buttrick White & Burtis. He received his BA from Harvard College in 1953 and his Master of Architecture from Harvard University in 1959. Burnham (Buttrick's daughter) was principal of her own firm for six years after working at Richard Meier & Partners. She graduated from the University of Pennsylvania in 1983 and received her Master in Architecture from Yale University in 1987. Murphy practiced as principal of his own firm for seven years after being associated with I.M. Pei and Gwathmey Siegel & Associates. He received his BA in Architecture from the University of Virginia in 1982 and his Master of Architecture from Harvard University in 1986.

The firm charges standard architectural rates, structuring proposals to meet the needs of its clients. The majority of the firm's projects have substantial budgets that reach multi million-dollar proportions, but will also do smaller projects with modest budgets for repeat clients. Clients strongly recommend them as one of the only firms in New York to bring an "institutional memory" and distinct awareness of historically based traditions and "upscale nomenclature" to a project with classical proportions.

*"They understand what is correct." "Their attention to detail was so fine, there wasn't a single inch of the project that wasn't closely analyzed." "The work they put into the kitchen was amazing. It's so functional, yet beautiful. It feels like a suburban kitchen in the middle of the hustle and bustle of New York." "Jeff's follow up is very earnest, he's always calling to ask how we're doing. I really got to know him as a friend." "They renovated our historically based apartment, and it is as fresh and thoughtfully conceived as the original design was 80 years ago." "Harry's strength of character is reflected in his architectural work and in his client base."*

**Naiztat & Ham Architects**  4.5  3  5  5
45 Perry Street, New York, NY 10014
(212) 675 - 2932  www.naiztatandham.com
*Innovative, classic, residential and commercial architecture*

Clients find this experienced husband-and-wife team "truly a gem," while peers tell us they "keep getting better with each job as well." Not bad for a firm many already consider one of the most professional and talented architecture outfits in the city. Naiztat & Ham is equally comfortable designing in modernist or traditional styles, and creating interiors that are "at once innovative and classic." The two principals, Diane Naiztat and Alexander Ham, met while studying at Cornell. Their twelve-year-old firm commands a high volume of work, both residential and commercial, mostly within New York City. A gut renovation or sub renovation is the norm, running from $200,000 to $1 million. For new clients it needs to be a full project, but for old clients we're told the firm will do anything they can. It has undertaken work in Westchester County and Connecticut.

References describe the small shop as creative and reliable and its partners as very approachable and amazingly responsive, noting the team was "always on the spot during unexpected problems, devising solutions with care, compassion and efficiency." Clients add that Naiztat is "one of the most visionary designers they have had the opportunity to work with" and that she is thorough, meticulous and full of "great ideas with color and space." The firm is commended for its ability to listen to ideas while remaining honest to the integrity of the structure. Sources agree that "they know their business well and are fun and easy to work with" and say they will return for future projects. Naiztat & Ham charge a flat fee for a scope of work, hourly for anything above and beyond that established scope.

*"The professionalism and attention to detail that Diane Naiztat and Alexander Ham bring to each project is unsurpassed." "They take ownership of the project,*

67

| | Quality | Cost | Value | Recommend? |
|---|---|---|---|---|
| | + | $ | ◆ | ★ |

*deliver quality, customized service. We try to use them as much as we can." "They made a potentially stressful experience actually fun!" "I work with many well-known architects and have found Naiztat & Ham to be the most professional and talented around." "We feel fortunate to have found Naiztat & Ham Architects." "Having worked with dozens of architects they are the best I have seen and currently the only architects I will use on the 100 or so projects I will be doing."*

## Nasser Nakib Architect                 4     4     4     5

306 East 61st Street, 5th Floor, New York, NY 10021
(212) 759 – 1515

*Updated, traditional, residential architecture*

With work often described as "traditional with an edge," this architect comes highly recommended by both clients and decorators for his remarkable versatility and exceptional design. Catering mainly to a high-end residential clientele, Nasser Nakib is known to be sensitive to clients' needs and budgetary constraints. We hear he is extremely knowledgeable concerning every facet of a project and always presents insightful and inspired ideas for even the simplest of things. Nakib encourages the inclusion of interior designers in the early stages of a project in order to ensure a seamlessly integrated end result.

Nakib received his MA in architecture from Southern California Institute of Architecture. A significant portion of his work is in New York, with the rest reaching across the country and as far as Saudi Arabia. We're told this "absolutely beautiful work" comes at a cost, but all agree it's well worth it. HB 100, 2000.

*"A wonderful guy that is really making a name for himself." "He is always focused and still helpful even though our project was completed over two years ago."*

## Ogawa/Depardon Architects              4     5     3.5    5

137 Varick Street, New York, NY 10013
(212) 627 - 7390   www.oda-ny.com

*High-end, high-quality modern architecture and interior design*

The partnership of Gilles Depardon and Kathryn Ogawa is said to create clean modern architecture and interior design with "unlimited imagination and creativity" that stretches the expected borders. The firm concentrates much of its energy on apartments, townhouses and single-family houses across Manhattan and Brooklyn. It also does international and area second homes, and is respected for its commercial work. What differentiates Ogawa/Depardon, we're told, is the sensitivity to clients' needs. Described as attentive and talented, the principals are considered true advocates for their patrons. We hear they are extremely thorough at preparing drawings and dedicated to high-quality materials and construction— so don't expect them to cut any corners. Clients tell us Depardon and Ogawa's vision enables them to understand a space and design exactly what is required for it. They are also known as having "really good people" working for them. Fees consist of a combination cap percentage of construction cost that the accrued actual hourly is not to exceed.

*"Goes beyond what the architect is required to do. The firm's clients are extraordinarily lucky." "Modern, beautiful work. Gilles is exceptioanlly talented." "They are such a pleasure, and what wonderful insights, especially compared to the other architects I've used over the years." "Very attentive and talented. "My stone and glass 8,000-square-foot residence has gotten rave comments all around." "Won't compromise on quality, loyalty is to clients."*

## Opacic Architects                      4     2.5    5     4.5

24 North Astor, Irvington, NY 10533
(914) 591 - 4306

*Inventive, collaborative, residential architecture*

References are "completely blown away" by this architect's imaginative designs and incredibly detailed drawings. Opacic focuses on larger, extensive residential renovations, splitting its work between New York City and Westchester County. Clients tell us Opacic's specialty, besides the meticulous care the firm gives to all of the details of a design, is that each project is marked by direct and continuous involvement by the principal of the firm. They say he guides them through the design process from inception to completion, and while Rad Opacic "has definite ideas" he "always listens well." He is described as conscientious, considerate and enjoyable to work with. Schedules and budgets were easy to discuss with Opacic, we hear, with any changes along the way to the original plan "worked out well as to not delay the project." After such a "great experience" many have hired the firm since, and recommend Opacic to friends, who are also extremely pleased.

*"Wonderful work, wonderful people. Very fair, considerate, good listeners." "At the start of the project I gave each of the people at the firm Swatch watches to remind everyone that time was important. It must have worked because everything ran on schedule!" "Beautiful moldings, lovely woodwork, plans to die for—so detailed and well drawn." "Really, really, really nice. Overall, you are working with someone who is conscientious and extremely pleasant, so little things and slight delays do not matter." "Has great ideas. They do very detailed work and respond to my wishes."*

## Patrick Gerard Carmody                          4    3    5    4.5
523 Hudson Street, Suite 2FS, New York, NY 10014
(212) 691 - 0115

*Tasteful, elegant and traditional residential architecture*

Carmody's classical approach to architecture extends beyond style to execution. In his methodical management of details and patient attention to client preferences throughout many rounds of revisions, this young architect has come to produce "the best work by a sole practitioner I have ever seen," says one contractor. Carmody tends to work in a traditional vein with a light touch. Clients say he has particular gifts with space design and the relationship of functional elements. Before starting his own firm four years ago, Patrick Carmody studied architecture at Rice University and then worked at Saunders & Walsh. He now works mainly on high-end residential projects in New York City, many of them 3,000- to 4,000-square-foot gut renovations on Park and Fifth Avenues. Projects outside Manhattan have included a Shingle Style house in Westchester County and a clean, Art Deco-style home in Miami's South Beach.

Carmody is described as highly professional, efficient and a perfectionist by both clients and contractors. He is known to always have the best interest of the client at heart, who find him a "lovely man." They tell us he is "very good at managing the small and large details of the project which made me feel that nothing was getting lost between the cracks." Carmody's work is described as top-notch and well worth the comparatively modest fee based upon cost of construction.

*"A good listener. A lot of vision. Unbelievable attention to detail." "Our home is a grand but simple comfortable home with classical proportions and elegant details. We are always being told that it is the most beautiful home in the Houston area." "He is a pleasure to work with, making the architecture and design experience enjoyable and fun."*

## Peter L. Gluck & Partners                       4.5  3.5  5    4.5
19 Union Square West, 12th Floor, New York, NY 10003
(212) 255 - 1876

*Modern, integrated institutional, commercial and residential architecture*

Gluck creates the handsome and creative designs of a "practical modernist." A graduate of the Yale School of Architecture, Gluck spent a few years in Japan afterwards and the culture's influence on his work is apparent. Clean fluid lines

| | Quality | Cost | Value | Recommend? |
|---|---|---|---|---|
| | ✚ | $ | ◆ | ★ |

frame light and space. His firm, founded in 1972, is now twelve members strong. Gluck and his team take a holistic approach to architecture, handling all aspects of design, from interior decor to landscape planning. Clients and peers alike are extremely taken by his style and highly recommend his services, however suggest that potential clients familiarize themselves with his distinctive work before embarking upon a project. The Columbia University Business School is probably Gluck's most visible New York project, though he has also done a great deal of museum, gallery and residential work. AD 100, 2000.

*"His work is absolutely beautiful, but I think it takes a special kind of beholder."*

### Peter Marino & Associates          4.5     4.5     4     4.5
150 East 58th Street, 36th Floor, New York, NY 10022
(212) 752 - 5444

*Highest-end residential and retail architecture and interior design*

This "architect to the rich and famous" designs and decorates residential and retail spaces for some of the most prestigious names in New York, including Giorgio Armani, Barney's and Christian Dior. Peter Marino's comprehensive approach encompasses designing furniture, lamps and rugs for interiors, as well as offering collecting advice for residential clients. Reductive in style and taste, references call Marino's work "handsome" but not too provocatively modernist, harmonizing objects old and new. Top-of-the-line materials are an integral part of his design approach. He designed one recent apartment around and for a developing art collection—works by Willem de Kooning and Andy Warhol peacefully coexist with 18th-century chairs and coromandel screens.

With 80 architects and 25 interior designers, Marino's is one of the larger firms, with offices in New York, East Hampton, Philadelphia and London. Clients like the cutting-edge feel of the firm's design work, and though some believe Marino's reputation may outstrip his achievements by just a notch, the majority feel that the elegant classicism of his work is "as good as it gets." HB Top Designers, 1999, 2000. ID Hall of Fame.

*"Like eating out at a top restaurant—you pay a lot, but you get the highest quality." "Mercedes of the industry."*

### Peter Pennoyer Architects PC           4     4.5     5     2.5
1239 Broadway, New York, NY 10001
(212) 779 - 9765

*Residential and landmark architecture with historic references*

Peter Pennoyer is especially well-suited to execute challenging assignments involving historic structures. The firm approaches its work with an "imaginative historicism" inspired by classic Park Avenue style and distinct modern flourishes. The firm specializes in landmark work in New York City and beyond and does very high-end smaller jobs for clients. A number of commercial projects have also been undertaken recently, including the complete restoration of the residential Georgian Hotel, The Mark (which received the Friends of the Upper East Side Historic District Preservation Award). Current residential projects include several Upper East Side townhouses, a horse farm in Virginia, a home in Southampton, a lodge in the Adirondacks and a ski house in Utah.

Pennoyer received an MA in architecture from Columbia, and has worked with Robert Stern, the Smithsonian Institution and the New York City Landmarks Preservation Commission. For seventeen years he has directed his own firm, cultivating quite a following, who can't get enough of this "highly skilled and imaginative professional." We hear he is very selective about his jobs, taking great care and attention with each one. While Pennoyer decidedly keeps the reins on his firm's growth, references report he has a "serious office" populated with competent and talented staff. Pennoyer himself is known for a "responsible and cooperative" business attitude, however we're told his sensitivity to cost and budget can be tempered by his determination to deliver the highest possible quality for the client, be it through design or materials. Fees structure depends on the scope of the project.

*"Delightful to work with and open to our ideas and needs." "He is well known and well-liked by the carriage trade of New York." "The consummate professional." "His work is of the highest caliber." "He was delightful to work with and open to our ideas and needs."*

## Platt Byard Dovell Architects

19 Union Square West, 12th Floor, New York, NY 10003
(212) 691 - 2440

*Creative, high-end commercial, institutional and residential architecture*

Platt Byard Dovell is equally acclaimed for its inventive designs of new buildings in complex contemporary contexts and its significant volume of historical preservation work. Projects include residential, institutional, religious, retail and commercial commissions. Respected by both clients and fellow architects, the 30-person firm is led by Paul Byard, FAIA, Charles Platt, FAIA, and Ray Dovell. Projects range from Fifth Avenue penthouses to the Chanel building on 57th Street to the New 42nd Street Studios—a ten-story barn of rehearsal space with a facade that continuously transmutes into abstract fields of changing color. Landmark work includes comprehensive exterior renovation of the Foundation Building of Cooper Union, the complete renovation of the New Museum building in the SoHo Cast Iron Historic District and the restoration of Gould Memorial Library on the Bronx Community College campus—a spectacular space originally designed by Stanford White in 1900.

## Procter + Wang Architects

4 4 5 5

112 East 73rd Street, New York, NY 10021
(212) 288 - 5500   www.prowang.com

*Uptown, high-end residential architecture*

Situated in a townhouse on the Upper East Side, this capable husband-and-wife duo caters mostly to the Park and Fifth Avenue crowd. With a recognized emphasis on quality and a commitment to a high level of personalized service, clients say Diane Procter and Stephan Wang deliver originally conceived design, whether it is a penthouse addition to a Sutton Place building, the complete renovation of a carriage house or the addition of three floors to a townhouse. With a tendency to keep very tight control of each stage, Procter and Wang often contribute their skills to the interiors of their architectural assignments. Sources say both of these architects realize that the construction process can potentially be a very stressful experience for most homeowners, and clients are consistently impressed with the couple's willingness to listen and their collaborative approach. Professionals also commend this couple for its distinguished and professional demeanor, with one complimenting Procter as among the most charming architects he has ever worked with. These factors add up to ensure a smoothly run project, and explain why much of Procter and Wang's work is for repeat clients.

Procter and Wang began their practice in 1989, and have since opened an additional location on 55th Street. With most clients calling upon them for very significant renovations and additions, Procter + Wang charges a standard percentage of construction for most of their projects, depending on the scope of the project.

*"Clients love them, they keep things running smoothly." "Nice to deal with." "Traditional. Creative. They do different things." "Highest quality, does all Park Avenue." "They strike the perfect balance between maintaining standards and being accommodating."*

| | Quality + | Cost $ | Value ◆ | Recommend? ★ |
|---|---|---|---|---|

## R.M. Kliment & Frances Halsband
255 West 26th Street, 20th Floor, New York, NY 10001
(212) 243 - 7400   www.kliment-halsband.com

| | 4 | 4 | 4 | 4.5 |
|---|---|---|---|---|

*Versatile, residential, institutional, commercial and preservation architecture*

This highly respected and well-liked husband-and-wife team is known for the diversity of their projects and intelligence of their work. R.M. Kliment's & Frances Halsband's portfolio includes municipal buildings, museums, offices and a limited number of private residences in the Northeast, often new construction. We hear the product the firm delivers to its blue-chip clientele is "very carefully thought out and executed." Clients tell us the firm is mindful of the client's taste and circumstance in design, as well as considering the cultural and physical context of the home within the community. References describe the work as "spare with clean lines," "refreshing" and "engaging." The partners are probably best known for their contributions to academia—the firm has designed and renovated buildings for a number of universities, including Columbia, NYU and the University of Virginia, and both partners also taught architecture at a number of universities (Columbia, Yale, Harvard). R.M. Kliment & Frances Halsband was awarded the AIA's Architecture Firm Award in 1997 in recognition of its consistently excellent work and contributions to the profession.

Kliment and Halsband brought over 20 years of combined experience to the firm they created in 1972. Kliment received a graduate degree in architecture from Yale in 1959—Halsband earned hers from Columbia in 1968. From 1991 to 1994, she served as dean of the School of Architecture at the Pratt Institute in New York. Fees are based on a standard percentage of construction costs.

*"Sensitivity to their clients' needs is paramount." "Highly principled. Amazing execution." "This duo has thoughtfully executed a lot of award-winning work." "They did a fabulous job for me. On-time and on-budget."*

## Reed Rubey Architect
200 Park Avenue South, Suite 1515, New York, NY 10003
(212) 505 - 9982

| | 3.5 | 3 | 4.5 | 5 |
|---|---|---|---|---|

*Cerebral, meticulous residential architecture*

Reed Rubey has earned a reputation as a precise, intelligent and creative practitioner, with clients adding, "there cannot be a more sincere architect in New York." Clients are just as impressed with his honesty, integrity and warmth, making him a favorite of demanding clients throughout Manhattan. The majority of Rubey's work is Manhattan residences, with projects starting around $200,000—although he has performed work in Greenwich and the Hamptons. Rubey's design consists of conservative, elegant lines that are classically inspired, yet can just as well frame contemporary spaces. Ultimately, we hear each client's personality influences Rubey's style. He is known to always produce executable, well-thought-out design documents. Clients tell us Ruby's meticulous preparation ensures their projects are executed on budget and on time, however they warn prospective clients to be prepared to allow Rubey a bit of scheduling flexiblity in the planning stage.

Ruby studied at Stanford for his BA and received his MA at Harvard. Clients appreciate that Rubey's small practice—opened in 1984 and currently totaling two—affords the principal's direct focus. They tell us his great care extends beyond the plans to the handling of clients, who he follows up with long after a project has been completed. This firm typically bills by the hour.

*"He became part of our family." "Very efficient. Excellent drawing. Answers problems straight away." "Good with clients. Once a schedule is agreed upon, he will meet the time limits." "His clients are very happy. He is extremely careful, so careful he takes his time. Don't use him for something you want done in a hurry." "Reed came up with plans to my exact specifications. I loved them. Then he asked if I'd like to see what he would do with the space. When I saw his ideas, I pushed the others aside and we started the project immediately."*

| | Quality | Cost | Value | Recommend? |
|---|---|---|---|---|
| | **+** | **$** | **◆** | **★** |

## Richard Meier & Partners

| | | | |
|---|---|---|---|
| 5 | 4.5 | 5 | 5 |

475 Tenth Avenue, 6th Floor, New York, NY 10018
(212) 967 - 6060   www.richardmeier.com

*High-end, modern, forward-thinking institutional and residential architecture*

An architectural deity himself, it's fitting Richard Meier's clients include the Vatican. While museums, high-tech and medical facilities, commercial buildings and major civic commissions distinguish Meier's work, he still blesses residential clients with his renown talented. We hear the Cornell-educated Meier selects serious projects with serious, serious budgets. Recognized worldwide for his emphasis on light, geometric precision and extensive use of glass, Richard Meier's modern work exemplifies the architect's own definition of his profession—"architecture is the thoughtful making of space." His work shows the influence of Le Corbusier in the balance, mathematical rhythm and cubic forms it employs, but focuses on creating volumes of space within a building. Meier's predominantly white palette highlights vertical and horizontal elements and shifting grids, and porcelain panels often lend luminosity to otherwise monochromatic surfaces. A winner of the prestigious Pritzker Award in 1984, Meier's arguably most acclaimed work is the Getty Center in Los Angeles.

Recent projects of Richard Meier and Partners include courthouses opening in the fall of 2000 in Islip, New York, and Phoenix, Arizona. While the two works share some stylistic elements, each is uniquely suited to its environment, with the Phoenix building using natural airflow and water for cooling instead of air conditioning. AD 100, 2000. ID Hall of Fame.

*"As good as it gets." "The Itzhak Perlman of architecture." "The most serious architect working today."*

## Robert A.M. Stern

| | | | |
|---|---|---|---|
| 5 | 4.5 | 5 | 5 |

460 West 34th Street, 18th Floor, New York, NY  10001
(212) 967 - 5100

*High-end, intelligently-designed, institutional, commercial and residential architecture*

Robert Stern's influence in the architectural community is strong and deep. Stern is known as a passionate architect who views architecture as the embodiment of social values and culture. While about two-thirds of his projects are for large institutions, he made his name designing large homes. Stern will embark on a project only after he has familiarized himself with the local building traditions as well as the wishes and styles of the individual clients. He will usually combine styles and materials to suit each project. This includes sprawling, gabled Shingle Style houses on Long Island, a stately office tower in Boston, a Jeffersonian construct at the University of Virginia, a simple clapboard house in Massachusetts and an 85-foot version of Mickey's conical hat for Disney's new building in Burbank.

Stern's namesake firm employees 120 professionals, 30 of them registered architects. Remarkably, Stern reportedly is involved with the design of all projects, and reviews them at every stage. The firm usually does interior design work to complement the architecture, including the manufacture of custom furniture. Manhattan clients say that Stern tends to focus his design on one or more centers of the house, which always look phenomenal. Given his huge and loyal following, it is unsurprising that he is a bit less sensitive to the needs of the "mere mortal in need of good closet space," but still he is said to deliver something extraordinary every time.

Currently the dean of his alma mater, the Yale School of Architecture, he has written and edited over 20 books on design, taught thousands of students at Columbia and Yale and hosted a PBS series. As a practitioner, he was influenced early on by Le Corbusier, Frank Lloyd Wright and Robert Venturi. Through the years, however, he began incorporating classical elements (such as arches and moldings) into his clean, pared-down designs. Today, he describes himself as a modern traditionalist, and his works relate more closely to their historical prototypes. AD 100, 2000. ID Hall of Fame, 1993.

*When you sign on to the Stern program, you get a masterpiece." "The furnishings always looks fabulous, but sometimes form takes precedence over function." "Working with Bob is an experience I would not have traded for anything."*

## Robert Rich                                    3    3    4    4
160 Fifth Avenue, Suite 903, New York, NY  10010
(212) 645 - 4631

*Traditional, timeless residential architecture*

This self-described traditionalist strives for clear and well-defined architecture that clients admire as both unique and timeless.  The concept, we're told, is to create a canvass of space that is true to both the client and in tune with the site, and that exhibits fresh life with the brush strokes of cutting-edge ever-evolving decoration.  While not a declared speciality, many feel that his attention to detail is nicely tailored for renovation and period work. The firm chiefly has its hand in the remodeling of prewar apartments in Manhattan.   Projects range upwards of $250,000 and we hear Rich will travel for bigger jobs.   Current commissions include a renovation and major addition in North Carolina, new construction of a house, guest house and pool house in Rhode Island and for a past client an artist's studio in Egypt.  Rich will consider smaller projects that exhibit challenging design potential.

Rich holds a BA from Tulane and holds an MA in urban development. He established his practice 20 years ago and has remained small—only himself and an associate.  Customers mark this a positive, citing he personally spends a great deal of time and energy supervising each stage of construction.  They tell us in this managerial role, Rich ensures the entire team of contractors and subcontractors follows through with every phase of the project.  A high volume of repeat business speaks to the confidence that Rich, and his work, inspires in clients. We hear most projects are assessed at a set-fee for Rich's design efforts, while smaller ones are charged on an hourly basis.

*"Fastidious." "Extraordinarily nice to work with." "Oversees contractors very directly, so much so it probably drives them nuts."*

## Rodman Paul, Architect                          4    4    5    5
118 Chambers Street, 4th Floor, New York, NY   10007
(212) 587 - 1900

*Clean, traditional, residential, commercial and retail architecture*

This "extraordinary and unique" practice toplined by Rodman Paul and his partner Tarek Ashkar focuses on the architecture of big-ticket integrated residential projects, often in pairing with interior designers.  The principals' sister firm—Ashkar and Paul Associates—interior designs for projects helmed by other architects. It's this faculty for thorough integration that has clients talking. They tell us Rodman Paul's designs are clean and traditional, but are not rigidly beholden to one style. Instead, references report, his work displays a strong grasp of the interplay of lifestyle and design.

Rodman Paul's hands-on, hyper-responsive project management keeps clients worry free. They tell us he is an upstanding articulate guy whose depth of knowledge touches upon design, decorating and landscape architecture. One client said "he knew precisely what kinds of furniture finishes would stand the moisture in the air of the house on Long Island and directed us to think about styles that would work." Some caution that he can be intense in the pursuit of quality and top workmanship, but all agree he exhibits incredible dedication to his craft and his clients, who tell us he believes that "his work is his signature." It is this reason clients continue to approach Paul for autographs, from a townhouse in the city to second homes in the country.

While "he is careful with budgets," we hear, "he doesn't believe in cutting corners." The firm frequently charges a combination of percentage of construction and hourly rates.

*"Incredible dedication." "Clean, traditional, upper-end. Can handle Park Avenue." "Asked us about our lifestyle—right down to how many suits I had and how I hung them, so that the closet would be designed with the hangers at the right heights." "He is talented and his work is interesting, but not for everyone." "Takes himself very seriously." "They really care that all bits work—and are very deep into the detail and all aspects of the project."*

### Ronnette Riley Architect  3.5  3.5  4  4
350 Fifth Avenue, Suite 8001, New York, NY 10118
(212) 594 - 4015   www.ronnetteriley.com
*Warm, modern residential, commercial and retail architecture*

Ronnette Riley has been called "one of the most successful woman in architecture today." Riley is known for her inventive and hip retail, corporate and residential spaces around New York described as "modern with warm touches." Clients tell us she has become as much of a force in interior design as architecture, maintaining the widest possible view of today's business and architectural terrain. We hear Riley is very agile and adaptable, and her "can-do attitude" is a hit with clients. She received an MA in architecture from Harvard and was associated with Philip Johnson for eight years. Clients find her staff of eight "kind and understanding," and compliment the firm's quality and creativity.

Widely published and award-winning, the firm is located fittingly atop the Empire State Building. It has been at work on a variety of architecture and interior design projects including commercial spaces for New World Coffee, Yahoo! and Coca-Cola. A recent retail space for Emerald Planet in Silicon Alley makes creative use of a globe motif suggesting latitudes and longitudes, and earthy, natural colors, with frosted glass and stainless steel accents. A range of residential clients round out the client list for the firm, which has completed over 500 residential projects in Manhattan since its inception in 1987.

*"Very fun, very sociable, very talented, very driven, very busy." "Ronnette and her staff were responsive and helpful." "Ronnette Riley makes it her business to know new materials, new solutions." "All of the firm is easy to work with." "Never insist on their way."*

### Russell Riccardi Architect PC  4  3  5  5
16 East 65th Street, New York, NY 10021
(212) 439 - 9311
*High-end and sophisticated residential architecture*

Clients tell us this small firm buzzes with "lots of young energy." Principal Russell Riccardi delivers projects that encompass a complete range of high-end architectural, interior and landscape design, often in tandem with wife Erica Milar, a decorator. We hear his designs are said to be classic, sophisticated and highly detailed, drawn from a variety of styles. Clients applaud Riccardi's personal involvement in all stages of the project, from initial schematic design through construction. Riccardi is said to understand the importance of integrating technical requirements, budget and time into the process to ensure a winning project for all involved. City contractors who know better, see Riccardi nearing the upper stratosphere of the architectural community.

Riccardi was educated at Cornell University. Before forming his own firm, he worked with Skidmore, Owings & Merrill, Peter Marino, and Kohn, Pederson, Fox. Riccardi has completed projects in the New York metropolitan area, Boston, Southern California, France and Italy.

*"A wonderful experience and a truly beautiful result."*

## S. Russell Groves                                    4      3.5      4.5      4.5
210 11th Avenue, Suite 502, New York, NY 10001
(212) 966 - 6210   www.srussellgroves.com

*Open, practical residential and retail architecture and interior design*

The designs of S. Russell Groves are said to go beyond architecture to interiors, furniture, and to the lifestyles of his clients. Described as "minimal but practical" and "spare but elegant"—this architect's clean modern designs integrate tranquil open spaces warmed up by sensuous materials with distinctive silhouettes and a maze of hidden closets. In Groves' multifunctional universe walls don't just look beautiful, they work. Recent projects include the Giorgio Armani corporate showroom, the new Coach retail space on Madison Avenue, the Tea Box restaurant at Takashimaya and many residential lofts and apartments.

Insiders note that Groves is intense, yet "sweet" to clients, and fields "a great team." His residential clients tell us he provides great options concerning both aesthetics and budget. It is said "he's so in tune" with their needs and expectations that Groves' first suggestion often hits the mark. Some report that his attention to perfection can complicate the process, but all agree that the quality of his work is at the highest level. The firm charges a setfee on percentage of construction, and clients tell us "value is key with Russell." Groves comes highly recommended by admirers for his refined palette, commitment to excellence and clear vision. HB Top Designers, 1999, 2000.

*"A master of serene, clean, yet functional interiors." "Terrific appreciation of existing architecture but with a totally fresh and thoroughly modern eye." "Design that fits the times and stands the test of time." "So worth it. Russell never shortchanges you." "Russell listened to our entire family. Even our two-year old daughter." "Only question is some of the custom furniture may not be easy to maintain." "I liked the firm so much I wish I could become a partner."*

## Selldorf Architects                                   4       3       5      4.5
62 White Street, 5th Floor, New York, NY *10013*
(212) 219 - 9571

*Modern art-inspired residential architecture and interior design*

Recognized among artists for her skill at "designing for art," Annabelle Selldorf's modern-minimalist designs get maximum exposure in loft-like downtown galleries and living spaces. We're told Selldorf focuses on simplicity and function. Sleek and uncluttered spaces gain levity from the proportion, warmth and light she considers to be the core of each design. Clients comment on her careful use of white and muted colors, her respect for detail and the intelligence of her work.

Patrons find Selldorf's demeanor direct and unpretentious and her service "very professional," with the "best current sources available." We hear this inspired architect makes the completion of complex projects timely and efficient. Not heralded for the tightest drawings in the city, references report "she is quick to solve a problem."

Born in Germany to a family of architects, Selldorf has worked in Venice, Zurich and London as well as in New York. A recent project for chef Eberhard Muller of Lutece, a second home on the North Fork of Long Island, is notable for its supremely functional kitchen and simple yet beautiful living spaces. AD 100, 2000.

*"Many art gallery clients. She is a total modernist." "We highly recommend Selldorf Architects. They are very professional, creative and attentive." "High standards, very good work." "She is very lovely, very nice."*

### Shelton, Mindel & Associates           4.5          4.5          4          4.5
216 West 18th Street, PH, New York, NY 10011
(212) 243 - 3939

*Tailored, forward-thinking, residential, corporate and retail architecture and interior design*

Creators of "very handsome, cutting edge" design, Peter Shelton and Lee Mindel are known to "examine the polarity between modernism and traditional architecture" in their work. References laud the pair's ability to seamlessly integrate classical American icons of the past and a contemporary clarity to develop refined, controlled spaces that are minimal, yet rich in detail. They have achieved this with a wide range of residential and commercial undertakings, including the Manhattan headquarters of Polo/Ralph Lauren where a soaring lobby clothed in Black Watch tartan and a vast mahogany staircase meld into functional, neutral-colored conference rooms in the back. While not characterized by a signature style, after two decades in business, the firm is generally recognized as conservative modernists. It is intimately involved in the interior design of its spaces, often creating custom furniture and lighting schemes that are said to be "brushstrokes of the larger plan."

Clients report partners Shelton and Mindel are smart, likeable, forward-thinking architects who exhibit zero attitude. The firm is also highly respected throughout the building and design professions. While we hear the rigor with which the firm pursues the realization of its design vision sometimes leaves less regard for creature comforts, clients say they feel at home in Shelton & Mindel's highly original, deft architecture. Both began their studies at the University of Pennsylvania. Shelton graduated from Pratt in 1975 and then joined Edward Durell Stone and later Emery Roth & Sons. Mindel graduated from Harvard in 1976 and worked for Skidmore, Owings & Merill and then Rogers, Butler, Burgun.

The firm currently employs about fifteen people and has received many tributes, including fifteen AIA awards and a place in the Interior Design Hall of Fame. It charges a flat percentage of the overall construction to cover both their architecture and design fees. AD 100, 2000. HB Top Designers, 1999, 2000, 2001. ID Hall of Fame, 1996.

*"Lovely people. Chic." "I highly recommend them for their high standards, impeccable designs and strong professionalism." "While artfully amazing, you must do it their way." "Absolutely highest quality, and high cost." "They can also do traditional, but not the chintz thing."*

### Sidnam Petrone Gartner Architects          3.5          3          4.5          4.5
136 West 21st Street, 6th Floor, New York, NY 10011
(212) 366 - 5500   www.spgarchitects.com

*Clean modern residential and commercial architecture*

Sidnam Petrone Gartner is renowned for designing modernist interior spaces and free-standing buildings from materials that complement and resonate with the existing environment. To that end, the firm favors natural materials that are energy efficient, practical and environmentally sound. Caroline Sidnam founded the firm over 20 years ago and has since taken on two partners—William Petrone (1990) and Eric Gartner (1993). The practice now employs approximately fifteen architects who collectively draw inspiration from the rapport they develop with clients. The principals' and staff's pleasant demeanor and creativity wins them points for being "great to work with."

Residential projects make up only a third of the firm's "state-of-the-art" work, which include the renovation and construction of many co-op and condominium apartments, urban townhouses and second homes. We hear many of these private clients return to Sidman Petrone for projects concerning their commercial interests. This impressive client list includes AOL, Polo/Ralph Lauren, CK Calvin Klein and Time Warner, among others.

Sidnam did her undergraduate studies at Kenyon and Sarah Lawrence, and received her architecture degree from Carnegie Mellon University where she also taught. Gartner received both his BS, and MA in architecture from the University of Virginia.

*"Smart, precise and easy to talk to." "Everyone in the firm was so helpful through the entire project.*

## Siris/Coombs Architects

|  | 4 | 3.5 | 4.5 | 5 |

2112 Broadway, Suite 405, New York, NY 10014
(212) 580 - 2220

*Innovative, residential, commercial and institutional architecture, rooftop additions*

Clients "are thrilled with the artistry" of this firm's work which we hear combines "value with imagination—a rare commodity these days." Nationally known architects Jane Siris and Peter Coombs established their award-winning practice 20 years ago. Their vision is a "livable" modernism with an emphasis on clarity of plan organization, dynamic spatial forms, exploration into new materials and attentiveness to detail. Noted for a diversity of projects and striking designs, the company's resume includes commercial projects such as the original Green Street Cafe and a 20,000-square-foot SUNY Aerospace Training Facility at Republic Airport, as well as a series of private homes, townhouses, lofts and apartments in New York City and Connecticut. In addition, the design of rooftop residential additions has become a unique specialty for which the firm is widely recognized and respected. Siris/Coombs has cultivated a long list of distinguished and loyal clientele over the years.

Clients tell us the firm went beyond "my initially high expectations with their service." They found the design to be "especially imaginative" and "beautiful" yet "practical." In the planning process we hear the pair suggested a handful of design alternatives, yet quickly caught on to what clients wanted. References were equally impressed with Siris/Coombs' knowledge of "nuts and bolts" when dealing with contractors and city agencies. Jane Siris is described as "creative, highly professional and well organized." We're told both she and Peter have "topnotch" people skills, and display the conviction to do everything possible to make clients' homes "beautiful without bankrupting" them. A fee is typically a standard percentage of total construction cost.

*"Jane has no foibles. None. She has impeccable taste and is truly an intellectual. I loved working with her." "A clear design solution, clarity of detail and consistency of design." "I have finally become accustomed to the one word that typically accompanies the reactions of first-time visitors to my current loft—wow! Though they are not cheap, reactions like that made them worth every penny." "Jane and Peter designed for us an extraordinary beautiful apartment in a historic space within a historic district to accommodate not only the needs of our family but also our extensive collection of art nouveau furniture and paintings."*

## Spitzer & Associates, Architects

|  | 3.5 | 4.5 | 4.5 | 3 |

160 Fifth Avenue, Suite 611, New York, NY 10010
(212) 924 - 7454   www.4spitzer.org

*Detail-driven, residential architecture, planning and design*

This full-service architecture firm rolls out "fresh and practical" ideas in its design and execution. In light of the firm's reputation for "clear-cut planning with careful attention to detail," we hear it is as at it's best overseeing substantial renovation projects. These are mostly in Manhattan, but also can be found upstate, in Connecticut and the Hamptons and even Switzerland—from classic townhouses to some contemporary homes. President Hal Spitzer leads an "innovative, talented" staff of fifteen. Clients find Spitzer a "very knowledgeable and bright man who is capable of listening to clients' needs and desires," and conjuring them in 3-D. He is reputed to be "very flexible and responsive" without a strong ego getting in the way of cooperation and collaboration. Spitzer can commonly be found working with an affiliated company—Plan B—to work on the interiors of the firm's projects. His work is admired as both "stunning" and "beautiful."

Spitzer stays in close touch with clients about not only aesthetics, but cost too. Clients share Spitzer and Associates are "phenomenal budgeters," though the creative design "will provide temptations to go beyond." Many Spitzer clients fall to temptation, charged hourly rates and fee percentages based on cost of construction on par with other architects working in the top 5 percent of the residential market.

*"Attention to detail like no other." "Imaginative solutions given with diligent care." "Worked with twice. I was very pleased both times. Have recommended to many friends who have also been very happy with results." "The firm cares deeply about the quality of its work and the satisfaction of its clients." "They are always open to trying out clients' ideas, however crazy." "They really know what their ideas will cost."*

### Stephan Miller Seigel Architect     4    4    4    4
595 Madison Avenue, Suite 1300, New York, NY 10022
(212) 832 - 5400

*Traditionally inspired residential architecture.* HB Top Designers, 1999, 2000, 2001. KB 1999.

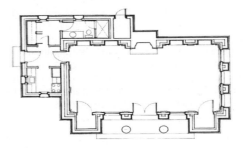

### Stephen Morgan 💼     4    2.5    5    4.5
16 East 96th Street, New York, NY 10128
(212) 996 - 0256

*Collaborative, eclectic, residential architecture*

Not only do "all the designers really like" Stephen Morgan, we hear he's a client's "dream architect." This small firm likes large renovations, predominately in uptown co-ops that baseline at $250,000 and go up from there. The firm's style is necessarily eclectic, fitted to the contextual aspects of each project. It's design of kitchens, baths and cabinetry stands out. In planning, detailing and oversight of projects clients say Morgan himself finds it important to demistify the process for them. They crow his promptness, honesty, and cordiality, combined with his technical skills and ability to coordinate with both contractor and owner make the design and construction process "a pleasant and rewarding experience, rather than a period of trial and tribulation." Morgan's elevated standards have been ratcheted up by years of working in demanding co-ops that force builders and designers to do the best of the things you cannot see.

Practicing independently over a decade, Morgan has vast experience in the industry, including associations with Peter Marino and the firm Buttrick, White & Burtis. Morgan was educated at Georgetown and Pratt. Clients consider the firm's fees reasonable and a good value.

*"Amazingly efficient, loyal and great to work with. An incredible combination." "Can not say better things. Top rate." "One of the nicest guys in the world, and reliable." "Superb skills—including strong conceptual abilities, excellent on-the-spot three-dimensional sketching, a careful attention to quality and details and a broad knowledge of accessories and suppliers." "Not only was Mr. Morgan professional and talented in his work, he was a true gentleman and a pleasure to work with."*

## Steven Harris Architects          4      4.5      3.5      3.5

50 Warren Street, New York, NY 10007

(212) 587 - 1108   www.stevenharrisarchitects.com

*Adaptive, residential architecture and townhouse renovations with intricate detail*

Clients describe Steven Harris as a "walking dictionary of architecture." We're told this Yale Professor is an intellectual and inventive problem-solver who can often see solutions where others cannot. Twenty-first century renovations are seamlessly integrated into pre-war buildings, a free-standing house on a cliff site in Mexico "springs to life from the site itself," and a 203-year old farmhouse is transformed into a playful variation on the theme of a rural compound. Recently completed projects include renovation of a number of NYC townhouses (a specialty), several large NYC apartments and loft renovations, the master plan for all buildings of an olive farm in Cape Town, South Africa, and offices for a small film production company in SoHo.

Sources say Harris combines wit and a down-to-earth demeanor with his sleek and sophisticated outlook. We hear the firm reviews all details, shielding the clients from the more arduous parts of the construction process. Most find the process is both educational and fun. Some advise looking carefully at Harris' plans before embarking on a project due to his decidedly strong and sometimes theoretical point of view. The result of his design approach they say can be at odds with the reality of construction, the community's wishes and ultimately the client's pocketbook. However, many past clients wouldn't consider anyone else for future projects, and say he can execute projects in a "timely, diligent and responsible" manner. In addition to architectural services, the firm offers interior design, a service we hear is encouraged in-house.

Harris earned a BFA from RISD and an MA in architecture from Princeton. He holds an associate professorship at Yale's architecture school and has also taught at Harvard. He is co-author with Deborah Berke of Architecture of the Everyday. Before starting his own firm in 1985 he worked with such architecture greats as Michael Grave and Charles Gwathmey. Harris either charges a slightly above-standard percentage of construction or a combination with an hourly fee. For his interior design services, he typically charges an hourly fee, passing discounts on to clients. While all fees depend on the scope of the project, we hear costs can add up quickly during the early design stages, and budgets can be an issue.

*"Incredibly talented and versatile." "It took him ten minutes to understand the space and see what could be done with it, and to explain it to me." "He is such a great teacher. He cannot help sharing his extraordinary depth and breadth of knowledge" "Must specifically like what he does." "They manage the whole project end-to-end with great follow-through and detail management." "There's no comparison with other firms that I've worked with."*

## Studio Morsa          ☞      ☞      ☞      ☞

247 Centre Street, New York, NY 10013

(212) 226 - 4324

*Residential architecture*

While Morsa's style has been described as avant-garde with an emphasis on natural light and linear simplicity, we're told the partners believe a client's preferences drive their designs. This small company undertakes jobs that include both interior

design and architectural renovation. The firm works worldwide, from Manhattan to Japan, South America and the Caribbean. A group of dedicated repeat customers keep coming back for more of the firm's attention to individual clients' needs.

## Toshiko Mori Architects

145 Hudson Street, 4th Floor, New York, NY 10013
(212) 274 - 8687

*Intellectual, modern residential architecture*

Clients say Toshiko Mori creates highly intelligent modernist interiors for a select clientele who describe her work as pure and unpretentious. An active voice in the academic and exhibition design community, we hear Mori reinterprets space with sensitivity and vision. References report these spaces are "calm and restful," if not a little austere. This small firm earns respect for both its residential and commercial work, mostly in Manhattan, though Mori has completed homes in Maine, Florida and Connecticut. We're told museums frequently call upon her expertise in curating and designing exhibitions. Mori is also a participant in and organizer of symposia and competition programs.

Mori herself is said to be intelligent, talented, sincere and lovely. In addition to being a Professor in practice at Harvard's Graduate School of Design, Mori is also an advisor to the Montreal Museum for Decorative Arts and the Greenwich Village Society for Historic Preservation. Before joining Harvard's team in 1995, she taught at Cooper Union and has been a visiting faculty member of Columbia and Yale. The firm's work has been widely published and has received awards internationally.

## Tsao & McKown Architects

|  | 4.5 | 3.5 | 4.5 | 4.5 |

20 Vandam Street, 10th Floor, New York, NY 10013
(212) 337 - 3800

*Forward-thinking, high-end commercial and residential architecture*

Unusual among young firms for the breadth of its practice, Calvin Tsao and Zack McKnown design with a "fresh take on the 20th Century." Since the establishment of their business partnership in 1985, Tsao and McKown have become known for "quirky, chic, elegant" modernist designs that enhance the subtleties of surface, texture and light. Their stylish designs are said to evolve from a very studied, earnest and arduous process of research and fact gathering about the subject and context of the project, seeking "to mirror the cosmology of the world." The firm's diverse project portfolio includes commercial buildings (many in Asia), hotel interiors, museum interiors and exhibitions, high-fashion boutiques, restaurants and of course, apartment and townhouse interiors. The firm's talents extend to the design of furniture and objects like sinks and bathtubs and dinnerware, candlesticks and picture frames.

Tsao & McKown's work can be seen in numerous downtown lofts, at JFK Airport's Virgin Atlantic Clubhouse, at Metrazur restaurant (on the East Balcony of Grand Central Station) and in guest rooms at the TriBeCa Grand Hotel. These projects spotlight the partnership's experience creating large-scale, technologically advanced corporate and commercial spaces while showing off its voracious attention to detail. Sources say the partners readily bring that same excellence to their residential work. HB Top Designers, 1999, 2000, 2001. ID Hall of Fame.

## Turino Kalberer Architects

|  | 4 | 3.5 | 4.5 | 5 |

462 Broadway, 3rd Floor, New York, NY 10013
(212) 219 - 3007

*Handsome, understated, traditional, residential architecture*

"If anyone could help you enjoy the process of home renovation, it would be Julie Kalberer," says an enthusiastic client. Sources suggest that homeowners looking for clean, traditional, understated elegance couldn't do better than to hire this architecture firm. The four-person firm is known for skilled execution and thoughtful attention to detail, and for creating cost-effective and budget-conscious designs. Half of the company's work is for Manhattan-based clients with midsized to large residences, with the other half consisting of residential work across the country.

Clients laud Kalberer for her lively, energetic and outgoing personality as well as her strong background in preservation. Both contractors and prominent local architects praise her flawless drawings and recognize her work as being of the highest caliber. Clients deem the firm to be very reasonably priced. Says one fan, "I felt that for the services provided, the firm didn't charge enough."

This widely published architect received her Master of Architecture from Columbia University. She then trained with Peter Pennoyer, considered one of the most distinguished architects in the city, before creating her own firm. Kalberer's work has been featured in *Architectural Digest, Design Times, Home Magazine* as well as others.

*"Julie was able to keep the spirit of the turn-of-century building in bringing my apartment up to the year 2001." "Simple. Amazing." I wish I could work with Julie more." "They know how to produce complete and accurate drawings." "Has a realistic budget and can stick to it. Keeps track of the job and how much it costs." "Great project management. Julie knows how to get things expedited."*

## Vail Associates Architects
4   3.5   5   5
53 West 72nd Street, New York, NY 10023
(212) 877 - 0094

*Thoughtful, attentive, high-end residential architecture*

Clients say this superb designer has clients calling him "our architect for life!" Thomas Vail caters his "creative, helpful and responsive" design services to a primarily uptown residential clientele. Projects are mostly gut renovations of apartments and townhouses, as well as new construction in Westchester County and out on the Cape. When not overwhelmed with clients wanting to con- script him for life, we hear Vail's small firm will to do small projects for anyone. Clients compliment the affable Thomas Vail for his thoughtful attention to detail and the amount of time he dedicates to addressing all their ideas and issues. He respects and encourages a client's taste, finding it critical to the realization of his design, which more often than not can be framed as traditional. While Vail's style changes with the customer climate, his service is said to be as solid as a ski mountain. Designers and contractors are as quick to recommend Vail Associates as clients.

Before going out on his own in 1990 Vail worked at Skidmore Owings & Merrill. The firm generally charges a percentage of construction which falls within stan- dard industry rates, depending on the scope of the project.

*"He made the project seamless and delighted the the client with the results." "Great creativity, smart work, terrific value, nice people and a pleasure to work with." "Tom is honest, direct and classically trained. He has become quite in demand and should consider hiring more administrative staff so he doesn't wear himself out. A great guy!" "Listens to the client, none of the usual architect 'if I didn't think of it, it must be bad' stuff."*

## Walter Chatham Architect
4   3   5   4
580 Broadway, Suite 1001, New York, NY 10012
(212) 925 - 2202

*Innovative, modern, residential architecture with wit*

Working very selectively in the design of "playful, inventive and colorful" modern interiors and homes, Walter Chatham is an established architectural force. Described as a charming and sophisticated man, Chatham prefers to collaborate with those who share his modernist approach and distinct philosophies, even if on a budget.  With spaces clients said to be "a model of simplicity," he has assembled an eclectic portfolio of work that is unified in its emphasis of natural light and color.  His work also includes the design of moldings and furniture.

With a strong New York City clientele, we hear Chatham's projects often take him outside the region as well.  Chatham's small, award-winning firm has been designing residences for nearly fifteen years, and has been involved with several "new towns" such as Seaside, Florida and the Aqua Allison Island community in Miami. This planned community, where Chatham is responsible for designing a condominium and loft complex, is a village of luxury island homes that combines modernism and traditional urbanism.  Ten notable designers and architects are collaborating on the project.

*"His clear perspective that life should be fun, makes it into his architecture." "Serious proponent of livable yet light-handed architecture."  "Very handsome modern houses."  "They treated our budget as gospel."*

### Weil Friedman Architects
3.5    2.5    5    5

30 East 92nd Street, New York, NY  10128
(212) 534 - 1240

*Updated, classical, residential architecture and interior design*

Barbara Friedman and Gretta Weil devote their practice entirely to residential design, creating a "classic, fresh look" that clients say is never overdone.  Patrons find the firm very practical about and responsive to "real-life" issues.  We hear Weil Friedman studies every aspect of living in a space from the perspective of the client, and integrates these discoveries in its architecture.  Clients appreciate the low-key style in which these architects use to guide them through the design process, while industry professionals acknowledge the excellence of the firm's drawings and project management.  Clients tell us all these attributes contribute to jobs running smoothly.  Furthermore, we hear the principals are "articulate" and share "a great sense of humor," making the process "fun."

After both gaining experience at Kohn, Petterson Fox, these two joined forces to engage mainly complete renovations of city residences and significant additions and renovations of client's second houses outside the city.  Projects in which these two talented women are currently working on include the combination of two apartments to create a duplex on the Upper East Side and a "significant" addition for a client in South Hampton.  Depending on the scope of a project, Weil Friedman typically charges a standard percentage of construction for its services, which often includes doing the interiors as well.

*"They have a great library at the office to help communicate thoughts and styles."  "Focus on having things simple and well-built.  Preserved the original lines of the saltbox in our Hamptons house while still achieving the objective." "Very efficient, the contractors have commented how they don't leave anything out of their plans."  "They manage projects well even from a distance and are very proactive about problem solving when things do crop up."*

### William Green & Associates
3    3    4    4

6 West 18th Street, 7th Floor, New York, NY  10011
(212) 924 - 2828   www.wgaarchitect.net

*Service-oriented, classically-rooted, residential and commercial architecture and interior design*

This boutique operation achieves what we hear is an elevated level of service as a result of principal William Green's full-tilt management style.  Green practices a classically-inspired brand of architecture that has translated nicely into contemporary design as well.  He helms a project team of four and projects are typically gut renovations, split between residential and commercial clients.  While Green has worked internationally, he now primarily takes on jobs in the city and Westchester County to maintain his one-to-one approach to clients. Green is known to control all aspects of a project, be it design of architecture, landscape, interiors or furniture, and we hear he pursues his vision through to the bitter end. Known as very dedicated, he often brings a serious artistic component to every project, such as sculpture on fireplaces. Green is also committed to ecological issues. He received his BFA from Tufts and his MA in architecture from University of Colorado. Before landing in New York in 1986, Green worked at SOM in Denver. The firm charges both hourly and as a percentage of construction, hinged on client and scope.

*"His approach is very hands-on." "A very gentle, yet highly focused architect."*

## William T. Georgis Architect                     4.5      4      5      5
275 Madison Avenue, Suite 2002, New York, NY 10016
(212) 557 - 6577

*Rich, modernist, residential architecture and interior design*

Architect and interior designer William T. Georgis is said to reinterpret modernism, combining clean lines with sumptuous materials. References report that Georgis takes pride in attending to every facet of his projects himself, often going so far as to design the furniture or hardware for a job. We hear he is creative, witty and refined, and that these qualities show clearly in his work. Edward Tuck joined Georgis as a principal in 1999, bringing with him extensive experience in residential, commercial and institutional design. The two lead six full time architects and an interior designer to create their "extremely high-end, extremely creative interiors."

Georgis' training includes a stint with architect/guru Robert Venturi and associate work with Robert A. M. Stern. His resume is distinguished by commercial renovation work of the public spaces at Lever House in New York City and the Envoy Club Hotel. Among recent residential projects are the renovation of a Manhattan townhouse and the design of a new home in the suburbs. Georgis was educated at Stanford and Princeton, and examples of his decorative work are included in the permanent collections at the Metropolitan Museum of Art and the Art Institute of Chicago. Before joining the firm, Tuck, a Princeton educated Architect, gained experience while working with Michael Graves, Robert A.M. Stern, Skidmore, Owings & Merrill. He spent two years running his own firm. KB 1996. AD 100, 2000.

*"Does extremely high-end work, he's very hands-on." "Fabulous designs and highly dependable." "Funny sensibility. Great guy." "Museum world. Gets a lot of art collectors."*

## workshop/apd, LLC 🛍                            3      3      5      5
115 West 29th Street, Suite 1105, New York, NY 10001
(212) 273 - 9712   www.workshopapd.com

*Adaptive residential architecture*

This rising star has gained a spot among the Manhattan design cosmos for its immense stylistic versatility and innovative design solutions. We understand the firm is equally capable at creating pared-down modern designs as it is more traditional interiors and residences, and while contemporary is the firm's preferred architectural trajectory, it all starts from the client's aesthetic interests. Projects span a wide scope, from very small to large and complex interiors, additions, free-standing or multi-use buildings. Some current projects include the renovation of a modern apartment on Central Park West, a large traditional/contemporary residence on Madison Avenue, a downtown loft renovation, as well as new construction and historic renovations on Nantucket, where the firm keeps a second office (PO Box 521, Nantucket, MA 02554 (508) 257-4018).

Clients tell us partners Andrew Kotchen and Matthew Berman are "charming and delightful." We're told the small firm's dedication and enthusiasm makes the process enjoyable for clients. Kotchen and Berman are acknowledged for maintaining the highest-quality standards and as sticklers for detail. All references are pleased with the principal's attentive and responsive personal service, remarking that they are full of exciting ideas.

Kotchen received his BA from Lehigh University and his MA in architecture from University of Michigan. He then established his own practice in Nantucket and relocated to New York City several years later. Berman also received his BA from Lehigh, and received his MA in architecture from Columbia. The firm has relatively low fees for its services, choosing to charge a flat fee or hourly charge based on the scope of the project not to exceed a lower percentage of construction. As a result, most clients "can't wait to work with" the firm again.

*"Completely dedicated to his clients and fulfilling their wishes." "Incredibly hard-working." "Simply an all-around, great guy. My dog loves him too!" "Truly talented and wonderful to work with." "We are starting another project with him and trust him completely." "I have recommended him to people who also hired him."*

**WYS Design Partnership Architects PC**    4    2.5    5    5
63 Greene Street, Suite 505, New York, NY 10012
(212) 431 - 1940

*Historically sensitive, residential, commercial and institutional architecture*

We hear this experienced firm produces some of the most "historically accurate work" in the city and the nation. Licensed in more than 25 states, the professionals at WYS Design Partnership are recognized for their considerable knowledge of architectural history and expertise in the areas of preservation, zoning and code compliance, particularly for landmark work in New York City. WYS Design Partnership is also considered one of the pioneering firms in loft conversions, particularly in SoHo. The firm typically tackles larger projects, from single apartment and co-op rehabs to loft space conversions of entire warehouse buildings for commercial developers. The firm also boasts wide-ranging experience in bar and restaurant design, as well as corporate interiors and institutional design. WYS will even attend to the interiors if asked. The aesthetic sensibility of this overachiever is dictated by the client.

Clients have found all of the partners and their employees "very honorable, reliable, dedicated and very comfortable to work with." They tell us the firm is "always going the extra mile for the project's sake," and delivers "good design and good supervision." The "mild-mannered" folks at WYS inspire confidence with careful attention to detail and to clients' needs, who report that the WYS education is a tremendous value.

*"Such beautiful work!" "They are serious and find ways to achieve the unusual at realistic prices with top contractors that finish work on time and do excellent quality work." "Knowledgeable about history of architecture." "Extremely committed. Very reasonably priced. Worth every penny."*

# Hiring an Audio/Video Design & Installation Service Provider

These days, one doesn't have to crave global domination to enjoy a room that can, at the push of a button, transform itself into a ground control headquarters that rivals any James Bond movie scene. Home theaters, multi-zone entertainment systems, home-automation and lighting controls, online capability—if you can dream it, they can hook it up. Just make sure you ask for the remote, or you may never be able to use what you paid for.

Audio/video (A/V) home service providers can seamlessly integrate almost anything—media walls, touch screen panels, speakers, structured cabling—into your existing components or into the architectural integrity of any room. If this isn't possible, they will build new cabinets to accommodate the equipment. Custom installation is the name of the game.

## What to Expect From an A/V Specialist

A/V providers can be contracted through general contractors, designers or directly by you. Whomever they bill, communication with the homeowner is essential. When courting your A/V guru, remember that they may specialize in only a few of the following areas: audio, video, telephone, Internet, security, lighting and climate control. A service provider who excels in home theater installation may not be as well versed in, or even deal with, security. You should also know whether the service provider can perform all the functions of integration. Determine your needs, get references, ask questions. Will the A/V specialist both design and engineer your project, or will he or she be coordinating with other trades?

Even when working through a designer, a good A/V contractor will want to meet with you one-on-one to assess your needs. Make the time. You don't want your system to outreach your ability or desire to operate it. Don't get swept up in your tech-happy A/V provider's enthusiasm for all the cool things available to you. Stand fast. Are you really looking for a movie palace complete with stadium seating, and does it really need to be tied into the landscape lighting and the air conditioner in the kitchen? Remember, the latest may not be the greatest if the newest innovation hasn't been around long enough to be tested. Some A/V contractors prefer a lag time of six months after the introduction of a product so that they can follow its performance before recommending it to their customers. If you're the first one in on a new gizmo, know that you may be the first one out of luck.

The means of customization and the materials used differ widely from shop to shop. Some contractors only work in certain brands. Others will install anything you want. Request that the bid proposal be itemized and a sketch attached if you want the finished product to perfectly match your dreams.

## Who Will Install My New System?

Although you'll first talk with either a principal or a representative of the A/V firm, traditionally a crew of field techs will be dispatched to perform the installation and service. Don't fret—this crew is likely to be as well informed and passionate about its business as any front man, so you should feel you're in good hands. It's invaluable to be able to speak to the same person from the beginning to the end of the project.

Miscommunication commonly surrounds the role of the electrician in an A/V installation. Some A/V providers want your electrician to pull the low voltage cable if he's already on site and already holds a permit, eliminating a coordination headache. Many prefer to do it themselves, knowing that some electricians treat delicate cables with the care of baggage handlers at JFK. Just check that someone's on it before the walls close up. Also, know that A/V contractors are not going to install or relocate the electrical receptacles that will power up your system and provide the jolt for the sub-woofers.

## PRICING AND SERVICE WARRANTIES

The cost of your A/V project will be a reflection of the design work involved, the degree of customization, the type and number of devices and pieces of equipment to be installed, the length of cable to be pulled and the anticipated man hours, plus overhead and profit. Many jobs require a deposit of up to 50 percent, with progress payments to be made when materials and equipment arrive on site, and again upon job completion. The warranty should appear on the bid proposal. A year of free service is standard.

## LICENSE CONSIDERATIONS

Because this is a new field, there is currently no licensing requirement for A/V services in New York City. Fortunately, this also means that no permit is required. Check your municipality, however, because where it's mandated, these service providers should be licensed and insured. If you're still confused, the Custom Electronic Design and Installation Association (CEDIA at www.cedia.org) is an excellent resource.

## THE HOTTEST NEW TRENDS

When it comes to home theater, blockbuster breakthroughs include Digital Video Disc (DVD) players, which offer much higher sound and visual quality than videos or laser discs. A movie on a DVD comes through at 500 lines of resolution, double the clarity of a 250-line videocassette. DVD players also offer lush Dolby Digital Surround Sound (DDSS). The quality of television output has advanced, too, with the advent of High Definition Television (HDTV) and Plasma TVs (those sleek, thin TVs, only four inches in depth that can be hung on the wall). Cutting-edge, multi-zone entertainment systems allow you to play CDs jukebox-style or listen to the radio or TV in any room of the house. For example, programming the system to air your favorite classical radio station through the bathroom speakers while you relax in the jacuzzi is simply a matter of pressing a touch screen.

Some A/V companies also provide a full line of home automation services, including wireless lighting controls that you can run from your phone (to turn the lights on if you'll be working late) or from a pad clipped onto your car visor. Home automation also applies to climate control, with wireless systems that let you turn on the heat, air conditioning or lawn sprinklers from any room in the house—or virtually anywhere, via telephone. Thanks to the latest user-friendly A/V programming systems, the days of not being able to program your VCR are over.

### HOW TO GET THE MOST OUT OF YOUR SYSTEM

- ✧ Sit down with the installer to discuss your wants and needs in detail.
- ✧ Don't rush for the newest technology.
- ✧ Only install gear you'll actually use.
- ✧ Don't fall asleep during the technician's instructions on how to program each device.

## Audio/Video Design & Installation

### Aaron's Media Inc.
3.5    2    5    4.5

107 Harper Terrace, Cedar Grove, NJ  07009
(973) 477 - 3544

*Audio/video and home theater installation and service*

Customers roundly praise Aaron's and its principal, Aaron Brown, as effective, attentive and up-to-date on the latest technology. We're told that this small, three-person company aims to please and will work closely with clients, architects and designers to build and install the system that best suits the customer's needs. References also note that they found Aaron's reliable and trustworthy—several have felt safe leaving their keys with Brown for installations. Aaron's works mainly on big jobs, such as whole home audio/video installation, but it will also do some smaller projects. The company works all over the regional region.

*"Service is his middle name." "No surprises." "Focuses on making sure the customer is happy." "Aaron made even my mother happy, which is not easy to do."*

### Ambiance Home Systems
3.5    3.5    4    4

1650 Route 9, Clifton Park, NY  12065
(518) 373 - 0770   www.ambiancehs.com

*Audio/video and home theater, lighting and multimedia installation and integration*

Many high-profile clients say they have been relying on Ambiance since its founding days in 1986. Ambiance has grown from a local company working with clients in upstate New York to ranking among the top 50 dealers nationwide, according to trade magazine *CE Pro*. Although the company's specialty is in high-end systems, it recently re-entered the mid-end residential market. Ambiance will work with clients or through their architect, contractor or designer to provide a range of technological solutions, including home theater, lighting control, home automation, data/communications and closed-circuit TV surveillance.

We're told every job is assigned to a project manager who is quick to answer questions and concerns. Clients also appreciate the on-call 24/7 availability service. Meticulous records are archived for future reference. The systems designed are described as fully integrated, highly customized and easy to use.

*"The technician spent a long time with me, making sure I understood how to use the system." "Very thorough instruction, and I felt comfortable using it from the start."*

### Audio by James Inc.
3.5    2.5    5    5

571 Knollwood Road, Ridgewood, NJ  07450
(201) 493 - 7282

*Audio/video installation and service*

Audio by James is a small audio and video installation firm specializing in the mid-fi to hi-fi range. The firm's clientele is both residential and commercial, with most clients in New York City and New Jersey. In order to maintain his personal stamp on the work, principal James Taylor has deliberately kept his business small, surrounding himself with no more than two or three employees. Clients appreciate the team's focus on the aesthetics of the installation, with particular attention directed to wire hiding and equipment placement.

In addition to home theater, multi-room and surround-sound installations, the firm also installs telephone systems, keypads and remote control relay and out-

| | Quality | Cost | Value | Recommend? |
|---|---|---|---|---|
| | + | $ | ◆ | ★ |

door speakers. Taylor's a perfectionist, and we hear the quality shows. In business since 1987, Audio by James has enjoyed its success through word-of-mouth from customers and peers. It's truly an insider's find.

*"He set up an amazing system for my home" "Very reliable—can call whenever we need him." "Gets the job done perfectly." "Definitely follows up." "Punctual and extremely neat."*

## Audio Command Systems                          4.5    4.5    4    4.5
694 Main Street, Westbury, NY 11590
(516) 997 - 5800   www.audiocommand.com
*Audio/video design, installation and integration and home automation*

Rated by CE Pro as the second-highest revenue-producing firm in the United States in 2000, Audio Command Systems (ACS) is recognized by clients and peers alike as one of the best in the business. We're told the ACS staff members are well versed in applying cutting-edge technologies to their field. Founded in 1976, ACS handles audio, video and home theater systems. In addition, the company coordinates the electronic management of automated lighting, home ventilation and air conditioning, security and other "smart house" system components.

Sources tell us ACS is in great demand and generally works on large, high-end projects. To serve clients, the firm has a staff of 75 technicians, with one project manager assigned to each client. One note of caution: we have heard that this firm is quick to respond to architects, contractors and clients with large installations but is somewhat less responsive to homeowners with small projects.

*"The best technology available, and extremely competent." "They know what to do and how to get it done." "Recommending these guys is the best favor I could do for any audiophile." "Always does a sound job for me."*

## Audio Den                                        4      4      4     4.5
2845 Middle Country Road, Lake Grove, NY 11755
(631) 585 - 5600   www.audioden.com
*Audio/video and home theater installation and service*

We hear that Audio Den has been delighting clients with its conceptual designs, installation and maintenance of high-end audio/video systems and custom home theaters since 1975. This firm works directly with homeowners in New York City, Long Island and the surrounding areas, and clients tell us that Audio Den delivers the correct products on time and provides service long after a job is complete. We are told the firm's technicians coordinate design schemes and project schedules with architects, builders and decorators. All in all, we hear this company is gifted at taking a homeowner's vision and bringing it to fruition.

*"Conscientious, careful and efficient." "Pleasant people designing outstanding systems."*

## Audio Interiors Inc.                             4.5    4.5    4      4
275 Marcus Boulevard, Hauppauge, NY 11788
(631) 434 - 4770
*Audio/video installation and integration*

Many clients offer high praise for Audio Interiors. Resources compliment this firm's work, calling it "high-end" and noting that its technicians have an outstanding knowledge base and provide quick and efficient service. The 22-person staff, we are told, is well trained, and although some customers say that listening to clients may not be its strong suit, all concede that the jobs are well designed and excellently installed. Most clients report high levels of satisfaction from Audio Interiors' work, while followup may be an issue with some. Trade magazine CE Pro recognizes Audio Interiors among the top 50 dealers nationwide.

*"Gets the job done with little hassle." "Spectacular, absolutely terrific." "Initial installation and response was great. Things got sticky from there."*

89

| | Quality | Cost | Value | Recommend? |
|---|---------|------|-------|------------|
| |  | $ | ◆ | ★ |

## Audio Systems Technologies (dba AST SOUND)

| Quality | Cost | Value | Recommend? |
|---------|------|-------|------------|
| 4 | 3.5 | 4.5 | 4 |

250 West Broadway, New York, NY 10013
(212) 226 - 7781   www.astaudio.com

*Audio/video and home theater and lighting installation*

This twelve-person firm has been equipping businesses and homes in the New York City area with up-to-date audio and video products and home theater and lighting systems since 1962. Audio Systems Technologies (AST) will design the equipment list, provide wire runs and do the final system hookup in-house or act as a subcontractor on site. AST also has a retail showroom for selection and sales, and provides maintenance for audio/video systems. While the company does not offer telephone installation as a stand-alone service, the firm will handle your home phones if integrated into the A/V system. Clients say AST's impressive work experience includes the recent sound system renovation at Chelsea Piers recreational complex, Global Financial Services, the Tunnel nightclub, American Stock Exchange and United States Military Academy at West Point.

## Audio Video Crafts

| Quality | Cost | Value | Recommend? |
|---------|------|-------|------------|
| 4.5 | 4 | 4.5 | 4 |

9-09 44th Avenue, Long Island City, NY 11101
(212) 996 - 8300

*Audio/video and home theater, intercom and lighting design, installation and integration*

Audio Video Craft's reputation for high-end, quality custom systems is backed by a client list with many high-profile celebrities. Rated by trade magazine CE Pro as one of the top 50 dealers nationwide, this mid-sized firm designs and installs custom home theaters, audio/video systems, lighting and intercoms. If the job is a big one (and we hear many of its projects are), the design, which is computer-aided, is free, as the firm charges retail for the components and installation services. References commend the company's expertise, but some smaller clients express concerns about customer service. Larger clients are very pleased with Audio Video Crafts' systems and service, and recommend the firm wholeheartedly.

*"They did a fantastic job designing my apartment-wide system, but it was tough to get them to come back to finish up." "Initial installation and response was great." "These guys are serious professionals. I respect their love of the business and desire to design to the highest quality standards."*

## Audio Video Systems Inc.

| Quality | Cost | Value | Recommend? |
|---------|------|-------|------------|
| 5 | 4 | 5 | 5 |

275 Hillside Avenue, Williston Park, NY 11596
(516) 739 - 1010   www.audiovideosystems.com

*Audio/video design, installation and integration and home automation*

In business for over 24 years, Audio Video Systems designs and installs high-end home entertainment and integration systems for a variety of residential and commercial customers. Acclaimed by manufacturers and industry publications alike, this 30-person firm delivers top-quality service to the greater New York area with its talented and accessible technicians and Greenwich, Connecticut showroom. Designers and contractors recommend the firm for its eye for detail and ability to coordinate, while clients are repeatedly impressed by follow-through and willingness to please after the job is finished. Audio Video Systems has established itself as one of the "best and brightest" in the industry, rated by CE Pro as the third-highest revenue-producing firm in the United States in 2000.

*"Went beyond the call of duty—exceeded all my expectations. Their technicians were courteous and professional, and their response time was quick and efficient." "Head and shoulders above the rest." "These are my guys. I wouldn't go with anyone else." "They make things idiot-proof." "Came back to teach my child about the system after he wasn't initially around to learn it." "They treated my project with the utmost respect and didn't make me feel like my job was too small for them. Customer service was great too—very friendly and informative."*

## Audio/Video Excellence, LLC     3    3    4    3.5

343 Manville Road, Pleasantville, NY 10570
(914) 747 - 1411
*Audio/video and home automation*

From the very simple to the most advanced custom home entertainment systems, Audio/Video Excellence delivers. For more than sixteen years, this firm has specialized in whole-house audio and video distribution, custom media rooms and home theater designs. Additionally, the company handles home automation by linking lighting, heating, ventilation, security and telephone systems to operate in total harmony. Sources are generally pleased using Audio/Video Excellence to refine their lifestyle by bringing 21st-century technology to their home.

## BJR Audio & Video Design     3    2.5    4.5    3.5

By appointment only, (718) 592 - 8930
*Audio/video design and installation*

BJR Audio and Video Design is a one-man operation that has been installing audio/video and home theater systems in the regional area since 1993. Principal Burt Rosen doesn't handle telephone, security, lighting or climate control systems. Sources tell us that his forte is setting up stereo systems in restaurants, nightclubs and bars, but we're told he does just as good of a job on residential projects. Clients say the cost for his high-end work is "more than fair."

*"Burt's great at spoon-feeding all the information from the owners manual in a way that's enjoyable."*

## Cerami & Associates, Inc.     4    4    4    5

317 Madison Avenue, Suite 220, New York, NY 10017
(212) 370 - 1776  www.ceramiassociates.com
*Audio/video system design, acoustical engineering and soundproofing*

An acoustical engineering firm, Cerami & Associates specializes in soundproofing and will consult on the sound implications of anything from audio/video systems to an apartment gym. Though the company does not actually sell or install systems, clients say Cerami makes excellent recommendations about the appropriate materials and design to meet clients' needs. Sources tell us the staff is extremely helpful and resourceful in tackling and solving complicated problems. Cerami is used by many high-end contractors and architects in the city.

*"The only game in town for high quality acoustical engineering." "They preserved my neighbor's sanity and our relationship due to the sound of my gym over their bedroom." "Great problem solvers."*

| | Quality  | Cost $ | Value ◆ | Recommend?  |
|---|---|---|---|---|

## Curt A. Barad Audio Video Inc.

| | 4 | 3.5 | 4.5 | 4.5 |

3585 Lawson Boulevard, Oceanside, NY  11572
(516) 763 - 4144

*Audio/video installation and service*

Clients praise Barad Audio for its strong technological audio/video expertise, excellent designs and quick custom work, as well as for offering a range of economic alternatives.  Recently, the company added lighting control to its list of services.  Barad's clients include many well-heeled uptown audiophiles and some celebrities. We hear the company is willing and able to assemble the ultimate system from scratch, customize a new system around your existing components or happily design a basic system.  The firm also wins points for thoroughness and follow-through on the whole, although there were a few timing hiccups mentioned in the fine-tuning stages.  Curt Barad is further lauded for honesty, straightforwardness and reasonable costs.

*"They are helpful, intelligent, focused guys with the best information, but they are not pushy or audio snobs.  They will do what is right for the client and the job."* *"As a high-end decorator, I love these guys.  They listen to the client and deliver the goods."*  *"They have common sense and understand priorities both in terms of timing and economics."*  *"You can trust them."*

## Electronic Environments

| | 3.5 | 3 | 4.5 | 4 |

247 West 37th Street, Suite 704, New York, NY  10018
(212) 997 - 1110

*Audio/video and telephone system installation and service*

We hear that accessibility, great ideas and an engaging personality are just a few of the things Kim Michels, principal of Electronic Environments, has to offer. The firm handles audio/video design and installation work, and its services come with an installation warranty that matches the duration of the warranty from the component manufacturer.  Electronic Environments also installs telephone systems and will consider projects of all sizes.  We are told that customer service and on-site training are also strengths of the company.

*"Terrific ideas, terrific service."*  *"Reliable and conscientious."*  *"A pleasure to work with, couldn't be happier with results."*  *"Articulate and classy."*

## Electronics Design Group, Inc.

| | 4.5 | 4 | 4.5 | 4 |

60 Ethel Road West, Suite 4, Piscataway, NJ  08854
(732) 650 - 9800  www.edgusa.com

*Audio/video and home theater, lighting and telephone/intercom systems design, installation and integration*

This New Jersey-based firm has been at work for fourteen years, providing state-of-the-art electronic technology for residents and corporations.  Recognized as one of the country's top 50 dealers by trade magazine *CE Pro*, Electronics Design Group specializes in the integration and installation of sophisticated home theater, multi-room audio, lighting, automation and telephone/intercom systems. Clients comment on the smooth interaction between Electronics Design Group and their architects, builders and interior designers, although the firm also works directly with homeowners.

*"An A+ rating from me."*  *"These guys proved to be the most efficient, reliable and overall best A/V company that I have had the pleasure of working with."*

## Harvey Electronics

| | 3 | 3 | 4 | 3.5 |

2 West 45th Street, New York, NY  10036
(212) 575 - 5000  www.harveyonline.com

*Audio/video and home theater installation and service*

| | Quality | Cost | Value | Recommend? |
|---|---|---|---|---|
| | + | $ | ◆ | ★ |

With six locations throughout New York, New Jersey and Connecticut and roots dating back to 1927, Harvey Electronics has become a household name. Customers tell us the staff at Harvey's has intimate industry know-how and deliver an excellent product. The company's specialty is installation and design of home theaters and audio systems, including consultation on design or collaboration with clients' architects or interior designers. Though clients note that working with Harvey involves paying retail, they report the company offers the added benefit of accepting trade-ins on old components. Customers report being pleased with the technicians' work.

*"A good dose of the new technologies here." "Offers tons of alternatives and the client service was much better than I expected."*

### HED (Home Entertainment Design)     3.5    2.5    4.5    4.5
43-22 12th Street, Long Island City, NY 11101
(718) 433 - 4434

*Audio/video and telephone installation and integration*

HED (Home Entertainment Design) provides services in the area of home theaters, audio/video systems, telephone systems, network wiring for computers and lighting controls. The firm does not address alarm systems. References have high praise for Alan Drespel's firm, which they say delivers courteous, attentive, professional service and great advice on systems and designs. One client was particularly impressed by the company's responsiveness to a pressing emergency, which involved driving out to the Hamptons on a moment's notice. Resources are uniformly pleased with the quality of work HED offers, and we hear top interior designers recommend HED to their clients.

*"Alan is fun to work with, and all the workers I met were courteous, respectful and knowledgeable." "First rate service." "Alan came up with a creative solution for dealing with my stereo equipment. At first I really had to be convinced, but now I realize it was exactly the right thing to do." "These guys are really impressive." "Alan was very responsive, even after he was paid."*

### Innerspace Electronics, Inc.     4     4     4     5
179 Summerfield Street, Scarsdale, NY 10583
(914) 725 - 4614

*Home management systems*

With thirteen years of experience in the business, the husband and wife team of Andrea and Barry Reiner has been designing and installing home theater, audio/video, lighting control, security, intercom systems and boardrooms for high-end clients locally and nationally. Clients praise the "sophisticated, yet simple to use" systems and references say Innerspace is the place to go for those interested in home management systems. Sources say the staff comes with a wealth of knowledge and the company receives high marks for remaining available to clients long after the project is finished. References are dedicated fans, a fact reflected in the excellent referrals and high recommendations received.

*"Responded right away when I messed things up." "I was going to give a bedroom to one of the workers, because he spent so much time at our house." "We're thinking of flying them to California to wire our home out there, because we can't find anyone else as good." "Committed to making things work."*

| | Quality  | Cost $ | Value ◆ | Recommend? ★ |
|---|---|---|---|---|

## Innovative Audio Video Showrooms

| 4 | 4 | 4 | 4 |

76 Montague Street, Brooklyn, NY 11201
(718) 596 - 0888   www.innovativeaudiovideo.com

*Custom multi-room and home theater systems*

Innovative boasts a large number of loyal clients, sources say, because the company really "knows its business." Since 1971, Innovative has been selling and installing complete audio/video systems, home theaters, lighting control and home automation. Clients tell us principal Elliot Fishkin and his team are flexible and attentive to individual needs. Innovative also handles telephones and security, but not as stand-alone systems. Clients especially report favorably about Innovative because of the "low-pressure, stress-free environment." Headquartered in Brooklyn and a showroom on the ground floor of the A&D Building in Manhattan, the firm works with designers, architects, builders and homeowners alike.

*"Designers of top of the line, stealth systems." "No pushy sales people." "Best products with the best service!"*

## Lyric Hi-Fi, Inc.

| 4 | 3.5 | 4.5 | 4.5 |

1221 Lexington Avenue, New York, NY 10028
(212) 535 - 5710   www.lyricusa.com

*Audio/video and home theater installation and service*

Since launching the business more than 40 years ago, Lyric remains on the cutting edge by identifying trends before they reach the market. As a pioneer of custom installation as well as the creator of some of the nation's first remote-controlled audio installations, owner Michael Kay earns respect and approval from references and peers alike. The firm's staff of 20 includes a full-time lighting specialist who also acts as design and architectural liaison. With store locations in Manhattan as well as in White Plains, Lyric is able to effectively cover a greater service region. The company's work can be seen and heard in homes around the country including the Bahamas, India, Brazil, the South of France and Italy.

Lyric is roundly applauded for its excellent followup, remaining available to clients long after the job is complete. Kay is a member of the Audio Engineering Society and became the first retailer inducted into the Academy for the Advancement of High End Audio's Hall of Fame.

*"Company is well trained and experienced." "The granddaddy of high-end audio/video stores." "Work was well thought out and included extra capacity wiring to allow for future capabilities." "Responded immediately whenever renovation contractor was ready for his work or had a question." "Was accommodating in respect to utilizing my old equipment to keep cost down."*

## Metro A.V.

| 3.5 | 3 | 4.5 | 4.5 |

128 Musgnug Avenue, Mineola, NY 11501
(516) 294 - 2949

*Audio/video and integration*

For twelve years, partners Tom Dolciotto and Chris Washburn have grown this small firm from the seeds of exemplary customer service, installing home theaters, audio systems, home integration and CCTV. We hear their attention and responsiveness have been welcomed from Westchester County and Greenwich to Manhattan and Long Island. Metro is known to work in concert with the client's architect and designer to get exactly what is needed both visually and technologically. Clients describe this firm as professional, honest, dependable and personable.

*"Well worth the money because they provide a value-added service that you can't get elsewhere." "Wiring up all the rooms of my penthouse was a challenge, but Tom Dolciotta and his staff did an excellent job."*

94

| | Quality | Cost | Value | Recommend? |
|---|---|---|---|---|
| | ✚ | $ | ◆ | ★ |

## Park Avenue Audio
**4  3.5  4.5  4.5**

425 Park Avenue South , New York, NY 10016
(212) 685 - 8101   www.parkavenueaudio.com

*Audio/video and integration*

For more than 25 years, Park Avenue Audio has been serving the needs of New York's most discerning clientele. Led by principal Denise Yetikyel, the firm receives high marks for satisfying the specific requirements of private home-owners, architects, builders and designers. This ten-person team offers audio and video distribution, custom home theaters and systems integration. Clients say they are happy to come back time and again to Park Avenue Audio for what they say are creative, elegant and upscale audio/video designs. References consistently commend this firm for its savvy expertise and efficient service.

*"Innovative designs." "Attentive to my needs as an audiophile." "Work done exactly as promised."*

## Performance Imaging
**4  4  4  4.5**

115 East Putnam Avenue, Greenwich, CT 06830
(203) 862 - 9600   www.performanceimaging.net

*Audio/video, integration and home theater installation*

Despite being in business for only five years, Performance Imaging has already established itself as an industry leader and is recognized by *CE Pro* to be among the top fifty dealers nationwide. Located in Greenwich, Connecticut, Performance Imaging receive enthusiastic applause from clients for their designs and installations of residential and commercial audio and video distribution, lighting, window automation and security—all fully integrated with a touch of a button (or a touch screen). Architects and designers praise Performance Imaging for creating systems that are invisible until activated. Homeowners agree and say their attention to detail and willingness to explain technical details is worth noting.

*"Accommodating, resourceful and sensitive to my budget concerns." "They were able to use my old equipment to keep costs down." "Dependable." "I am a lifelong audiophile, and I couldn't be happier or more impressed with the system they designed."*

## Scott Trusty
**4  2.5  5  5**

127 Joffre Avenue, Stamford, CT 06905
(203) 325 - 4881

*Audio/video, home theater installation and repair*

Clients trust Scott Trusty. Trusty's services include complete design, installation and repair of custom audio, video and home theater systems, with a particular interest in home automation and remote control. Trusty has been working in NYC and the surrounding areas for 33 years and has compiled a lengthy list of happy clients. One reference, himself a professional in a related field, tells us that Trusty knows everything about sound. We hear he is just as attentive on small jobs as he is on large projects and that he doesn't miss the details, down to working with the contractor on the appropriate type of plaster-board to be used for the ultimate acoustics or doing research on the perfect TV for a client's very specific space and budget needs. He'll work with clients directly or with architects or contractors, as appropriate. References concur that he's top notch.

*"Passionate about what he does, great with people and he delivers." "Absolutely fantastic." "Small projects done just as well as a large ones." "He's the only contractor my wife feels comfortable leaving alone in the house."*

| | Quality | Cost | Value | Recommend? |
|---|---|---|---|---|
| | + | $ | ◆ | ★ |

## Sony Style

| 3.5 | 3.5 | 4 | 4 |

550 Madison Avenue, New York, NY 10022
(212) 833 - 8800  www.sony.com

*Audio/video retail*

For those who choose Sony products for their audio/video needs, Sony Style is a great resource, located in a friendly atrium atmosphere. Sony Style has its own setup and installation department, and sources tell us the charge for these services is reasonable. Established in 1960, Sony stands behind its products and customers agree the systems provide a high level of luxury, are easy to use, are a good value and provide long-term reliability.

*"Sony has a great reputation for its products and I've found Sony Style to be equally as good for installation and friendly service." "You can't go wrong."*

## Sound by Singer

| 4.5 | 4 | 4.5 | 4.5 |

18 East 16th Street, New York, NY 10003
(212) 924 - 8600  www.soundbysinger.com

*Audio/video and home theater installation and service*

After 23 years, Sound by Singer has become an internationally recognized purveyor of the high-end audio and video experience. Based in Manhattan with a 15,000-square-foot audio/video demonstration showroom, this 20-person firm serves as consultant to many peers and has design and installation teams that serve clients around the world. For sole proprietor, Andrew Singer, high-end doesn't necessarily mean highly expensive—rather, he places emphasis on performance and execution. Sound by Singer can handle anything from home integration and control to home theaters and complex multi-room audio systems. Clients say Singer and his crew share a passion for providing the best entertainment system for the best price.

*"Sound by Singer is like staying at the Four Seasons—first-class service." "Great equipment at various price points." "Very accommodating to clients." "Andy isn't merely a vendor but a trusted advisor both to me and to countless others to whom I have wholeheartedly recommended." "Going to Sound by Singer has been my best shopping decision in years."*

## Sound City

| 3 | 2 | 4.5 | 4 |

58 West 45th Street, New York, NY 10036
(212) 575 - 0210  www.soundcityny.com

*Audio/video sales, service and installation*

Clients praise Sound City for its extensive retail showroom and excellent installation services. Since 1986, Sound City has been handling audio/video, home theater and security systems for residences and offices. Many longtime customers report that they can simply call and explain their needs, and Sound City's helpful staff finds the proper system, delivers it and installs it. We hear that the people at Sound City provide exemplary customer service and never "talk down" to customers. Sources tell us the staff at Sound City is very trustworthy and several references reported they felt comfortable turning over their house keys and letting Sound City take care of the entire project.

"Good responsiveness to initial start-up problems and trouble-free thereafter." "Service with a smile—yes-men. Whatever I asked or wanted—they did." "Very accommodating. . . loaned me a system to use for an impending party since my order was not yet delivered." "Delivery is quick. I received my order that same day."

## Sound Sight Technologies    3.5    3.5    4    3.5
124 West 30th Street, Suite 208, New York, NY  10001
(212) 760 - 0892   www.soundsightonline.com
*Audio/video integration, lighting design and climate control*

Led by principal, Robert Friedland, and established more than ten years ago, Sound Sight Technologies is dedicated not only to high-end audio/video, but also to full system integration. The firm offers design, installation and instruction services for such projects as brownstone renovations and corporate makeovers, without forgetting the smaller projects. While we hear that architects recommend them repeatedly to clients, there are, however, mixed reviews to their accessibility and responsiveness to the client.

"Excellent people—when our temporary satellite dish went down in a snowstorm, the president of the company climbed up onto the roof to clear off the snow at 9:00 pm." "They truly care that the client is satisfied." "Rob was hard to pin down at times—seemed like he might have been overextended—but when I finally got him to come out and do the work, I was pleased with it."

## Stereo Exchange    3    3    4    3.5
627 Broadway, New York, NY  10012
(212) 505 - 1111   www.stereoexchange.com
*Audio/video, home theater, integration and home automation*

Based in Manhattan, Stereo Exchange is a chief retailer and installation company that integrates high-end audio, video and automation systems into new construction and existing buildings for homes and businesses. Working closely with architects, designers, builders and homeowners, Stereo Exchange's 30-person staff understands the latest technologies and provides honest, knowledgeable information, without the techno-babble. Their reputation for what clients call "excellent systems" is the result of more than fifteen years spent integrating state-of-the-art equipment. Additionally, clients applaud this firm for its enthusiastic technical expertise and creative input.

## Ultimate Sound & Installation Inc.    4    3.5    4.5    4
36-16 29th Street, Long Island City, NY  11106
(718) 729 - 2111   www.ultimateinstallations.com
*Audio/video, home automation, lighting control and telephone systems*

Ultimate offers a wide variety of services to NYC-area clients (and, in fact, to some as far afield as Wyoming), including high-end telephone, audio, video, home theater, security and lighting control systems. One of the company's specialty areas is integrating multiple systems and providing remote access—so a client can execute such tasks as switching on the air conditioning from his or her car on the way home. Clients recommend Jack Borenstein and Ultimate to their friends because of the high level of service provided, especially in the area of followup. Sources say they appreciate and value the importance of conscientious followup for such complicated, high-end systems. Ultimate will work with clients directly, as well as with many of the top architects, designers and contractors in the city.

"Good work. Very professional, punctual and polite."

| | Quality | Cost | Value | Recommend? |
|---|---|---|---|---|

### Video Installations Plus

| | 4.5 | 3.5 | 5 | 5 |
|---|---|---|---|---|

45 East Hartsdale Avenue, Hartsdale, NY  10530
(914) 328 - 1771

*Audio/video design and installation*

Principal Alan Poltrack has been working in this field for eighteen years.  While working mostly in Manhattan, Video Installation Plus can integrate audio, video, satellite, telephone and lighting systems for clients from Westchester to Connecticut to Long Island—the company will even outfit your boat.  A small company that provides individual attention, Video Installations Plus earns glowing comments from customers about the thoughtfulness of the staff and the thoroughness of the service.  Female clients in particular lavish their praise on the firm's commitment to instruction and determination to clean up after themselves.

*"Very willing to explain and teach how to use the equipment." "They were absolutely wonderful in every way." "Work was completed on time and worth every cent." "Consistently does excellent work."*

### Woodbridge Stereo/Video

| | 3 | 3 | 4 | 3.5 |
|---|---|---|---|---|

751 Amboy Avenue, Woodbridge, NJ  07095
(732) 636 - 7777   www.woodbridgestereo.com

*Audio/video and home automation*

Established in 1971, Woodbridge Stereo/Video handles audio, video, home theaters, lighting control, security, telephone/intercom systems and home automation.  Although it is a sizeable operation, clients say that Woodbridge still gives personal and individual attention to each client.  Additionally, customers are impressed with the friendly crew and we hear they have an excellent maintenance and repair service.

# Hiring a Closet Designer

Are you embarrassed to take your guest's coat because you're not sure what's going to come crashing down as soon as you open the closet door? Are you tired of being late to dinner because you can't remember in which dark corner of your closet you last crammed your shoes? If you want to get maximum use out of minimum space, it's time to call a closet professional.

## Where Do I Start?

In a time when some homeowners view closet design just as important as kitchen and bath design, you have an endless choice of styles—from traditional to contemporary, casual to formal—and a large assortment of accessories.

There are many options to consider in designing custom closets. For example, for your bedroom closet you can choose to have more hanging space and fewer shelves, or vice versa, depending on your particular wardrobe. Hanging double rods (one above another) for short items such as jackets and shirts will maximize the hanging space. You can also incorporate drawers, shoe cubbies, sectioned jewelry drawers, and slide-out tie and belt racks, among numerous other "extras" such as fire-proof walls, a fold-out ironing board and steamer, a safe for valuables, cedar-lined walls and floors, a folding table, hydraulic lifts, valets, mirrored walls and doors, task lighting, a separate heating and air-conditioning system or designer hardware. Custom closets are just that—customized for your particular needs and space. Familiarize yourself with the options. If you can't visualize what you want or just need some ideas, start by visiting the closet companies. Many stores have showrooms that display their work. Some companies will come to your home to give a free consultation and estimate. Closet professionals can help you determine the exact configuration of shelving, hanging space and accessories to best organize your closets.

## Material Choices

Most closet professionals use similar materials. One of the most popular is pressed wood covered with either a wood veneer or melamine (also called laminate). Wood veneer is a thin layer of wood; melamine is a thin layer of vinyl. Some companies offer more than 30 colors to choose from. Pressed wood with a wood veneer gives the appearance of being solid wood. Melamine is durable and comes in numerous color choices, making it a favorite among customers.

Another popular material is vinyl-covered steel wire. It produces a clean and contemporary look. Because this surface is a wire grid and not solid, it allows good air circulation throughout the closet. However, the grids can leave an imprint on soft clothing, so a piece of cardboard or Plexiglas may be needed to cover shelves or the bottoms of baskets. Vinyl-covered steel wire sliding baskets allows you to see what is in the drawers without opening them, which can be a great benefit in the case of unreachable or hard-to-access spots. It is generally difficult to find closet companies that use solid wood because it is so expensive and can warp and change over time, however, it is very attractive, and generally used in the highest quality applications with a wood veneer.

In many cases your closet professional will be able to provide choices of materials that will match existing or more prominent millwork and cabinetry already in your home. This is a cost-efficient way to create a consistent look throughout the various rooms of your apartment.

## ON COST

The cost of custom closets depends on the size and scope of the specific job. There may be a retainer fee and/or a minimum installation fee. After the size of the job, which affects the amount of labor and materials involved, the most important influence on the price is the choice of material. Other details such as the condition of the existing walls will also influence the price. The more prep work a company has to do, the more expensive the job will be.

By far the most expensive material is solid wood. However, if it is important to you that your closet looks like a room in a mansion, with architectural details, inset panels and artistic moldings, you might consider talking to a millworker instead of a closet company.

Pressed wood is much more stable as well as less expensive. The cost of pressed wood with a veneer depends on what kind of wood veneer you choose. Cherry is more expensive than maple, for example. A wood veneer finish will be two to three times the price of melamine. Vinyl-covered steel wire is the cheapest closet system and the easiest to install.

A completely customized closet could be as much as $4,000, with an entire renovation of all closet and storage systems reaching beyond $500,000, but as mentioned above, there are many factors that affect this price, so be sure to discuss all options with your closet professional, and make sure all accessories and options are included in the final specifications and estimate of your project.

## WHAT SHOULD I EXPECT FROM A CLOSET DESIGNER?

Do not underestimate the professionalism needed for maximizing and organizing your home's storage spaces. Closet companies should be licensed, insured and bonded. You should also inquire about each company's warranty, which can range in duration anywhere from one year to a lifetime.

While some companies do everything themselves, from design to installation, others consult and design and then subcontract the actual installation to someone else. Ask exactly how much of the project is kept in house. You also want to find out how long the process takes. For example, if the company has to order your favorite brass doorknobs from Italy, it is going to take longer than using materials that are readily available. Consider your time constraints—are you willing to wait months for the perfect fittings? Also, note that a company might not be able to immediately install your closet due to demand, and it could take a few weeks to begin the job.

### BE A CLOSET MAVEN

- ❖ For the kids, install adjustable shelves that can accommodate a wardrobe that grows with them. If space allows, consider pullout bins for toys.
- ❖ Wire shelves (vinyl-covered or bare) and louvered doors offer better ventilation than pressed wood shelves. Towels or damp items will dry faster and the air will stay fresher. Consider using wire shelves for mudroom and bathroom closets, attics and basements.
- ❖ A cedar closet helps to protect off-season clothes from moths.
- ❖ Adding a drop-down ironing board in your walk-in closet allows you to quickly press out wrinkles.
- ❖ Install a light in your closet so you may see all of your items. You can even wire it so that the light goes on and off automatically when you open and close the door.
- ❖ Your choice of hangers not only effects the overall appearance of your closet, but can also effect the space used. Be sure to take this into consideration when planning the use of space.
- ❖ Decide whether you will rotate seasonal clothing before you design your closet.
- ❖ Remember that women need more long-garment hanging space than men.

# Closet Designers

## California Closet Company          3    3    4    4
1625 York Avenue, New York, NY 10028
(212) 517 - 7877  www.calclosets.com
*Closet consultation, design and installation*

One of the largest firms in the New York City, and the country, California Closet Company has been consulting, designing and installing home organizational units for nearly 20 years. Using modern computerized production methods, this company creates specific measurements according to the needs of the customer, mostly to match their standardized closet components. A variety of materials are available, ranging from wire to laminates (mostly used) to solid wood. California Closet will customize any closet, entertainment center, office or even laundry room at a reasonable cost. The diversity of the company's work can all be seen in its showroom located on the Upper East Side. Although clients say the size of the firm may seem overwhelming and unappealing at first, many were impressed with the company's professionalism and efficiency from beginning to the end, as long as you are not looking for something too elaborate.

*"Punctual and tidy." "Very knowledgeable and professional." "For your basic closet, they know just what to do. However, I would not recommend them for top millwork."*

## City Closet Company          ▱    ▱    ▱    ▱
200 Rector Place, New York, NY 10280
(212) 945 - 4010
*Closet consultation, design and installation*

## Closet Systems Group          2    3    3    3
810 Homboldt Street, Brooklyn, NY 11222
(212) 627 - 1717  www.closetsonline.com
*Closet consultation, design and installation*

This firm specializes in custom closets, combining modern machinery with skillfully trained craftsmen. Founded in 1980, The Closet Systems Group consists of 20 employees including both designers and installers. Each project is started and completed within the company, creating a truly customized closet system, yet insiders say Closet Systems is willing to work with the client's architect, interior designer or contractor as well. Clients say that its small size creates a sense of intimacy and high quality that is difficult to find among larger firms—although others had trouble contacting them when modifications were needed. Most tell us that Closet Systems Group is flexible about design schemes and is prompt at fixing problems when they arise.

## Closets by Design          4.5    3    5    5
1415 Blondell Avenue, Bronx, NY 10461
(718) 319 - 9255  www.closets-by-design.com
*Closet design and installation*

Closets By Design not only provides customized closets—it also builds home entertainment centers, offices, work areas and libraries. Although part of a bigger, national franchise, the local office receives high marks for its ability to provide both the personalized service of a small company and the resources of a larger one. Closets By Design's computerized three-dimensional drawings are useful in

| | Quality | Cost | Value | Recommend? |
|---|---|---|---|---|
| |  + | $ | ◆ | ★ |

designing a customized organizational system. Clients comment favorably on the firm's ability to create designs that are accessible to a wide range of budgets, with materials from laminate to solid wood. We've heard that owner Stuart Reisch is very personable and willing to accommodate his clients' needs and ideas.

*"One of the high points of our renovation process." "Did a fantastic job." "Delightful."*

### Closettec
**2    2    4    4**

17 Matinicock Avenue, Port Washington, NY  11050
(516) 883 - 6130   www.closettec.com
*Closet consultation, design and installation*

This family-owned and operated company offers a variety of pressed-wood closets, ranging from wood veneer to melamine.  A brand name, Closettec has twelve employees that provide free consultations as well as design and installation services.   Clients compliment the firm's flexibility and willingness to solve any problems, no matter how many times adjustments are necessary.  Although they do not offer solid woods, the company does offer practical solutions for closets at what references say is a very reasonable price.

### Creative Closets
**2.5    2.5    4    4**

364 Amsterdam Avenue, New York, NY  10024
(212) 496 - 2473
*Closet consultation, design and installation*

According to sources, Creative Closets was founded on the idea of good customer service at a reasonable price, and has been in business since 1984.  All nine employees are trained in both design and installation of open wire and solid melamine systems.  Creative Closets works on projects including the outfitting of every closet in a newly renovated Manhattan apartment to the installation of one or two smaller closet systems.

*"Work was done within the time frame and exactly at cost."*

### European Closet & Cabinet
**4    2    5    5**

214 49th Street, Brooklyn, NY  11220
(718) 567 - 7121   www.europeancloset.com
*Closet consultation, design and installation*

Established in 1982, this ten-person firm mainly uses laminate and high-density particle wood to create customized closet units and provides consulting, design and installation.  Clients say that European Closet & Cabinet offers modular closets, yet modifications can be made when needed.  This method of design provides customers with higher quality at more reasonable fees.

*"Even asked how the dry cleaners folded clothes." "No space wasted." "Very sophisticated." "Among the most professional people I've worked with."*

### George Wild Closets
**4    3    4.5    4.5**

1595 York Avenue, New York, NY  10028
(212) 737 - 4658
*Closet consultation, design and installation*

Trained in Germany, George Wild has been in business for over 30 years.  More of a craftsman than an organizer, sources say Wild makes all of his closets by hand, using laminate, wire and wood.  Projects range from single coat closets to entire dressing rooms.  Wild will gut the client's existing closet, plaster, paint and install the new setup in only a day.  Clients value George's practicality, great attention to detail and "old-world instincts.".  Also, many remark on his honesty and passion for his work.

*"An honest craftsman." "Friendly and knowledgeable." "He does not waste your time—after receiving a layout of the space by fax, he gets right to work."*

| | Quality | Cost | Value | Recommend? |
|---|---|---|---|---|
| | ✚ | $ | ◆ | ★ |

## Ken Dostis Custom Closet Interiors

| | 2.5 | 2 | 4 | 4 |

3134 51st Street, Woodside, NY 11377
(718) 932 - 4873

*Closet design and installation*

## Linda London Ltd.

| | 5 | 5 | 4 | 4.5 |

200 East 62nd Street, New York, NY 10021
(212) 751 - 5011

*Comprehensive home and office organization*

Sources tell us Linda London is more than a closet organizer—she can organize your entire home as well as your life. Known to many designers and people in the trade as the "closet lady to the stars," she has been working for more than thirteen years, with a staff of seven. London provides the design and then uses only select high-end craftsmen to create her intricate creations. Customers say they are amazed at her ability to maximize functionality without compromising style and tastefulness.

*"Overcame adversity." "Very funny." "Quality was great." "Great attention to detail and access to suppliers." "She is another world versus your typical high-volume closet company." "She understands the interests, needs and desires of the 'rich and famous' and designs to get it right the first time." "You get what you pay for—Linda is first rate."*

## Manhattan Cabinetry

227 East 59th Street, New York, NY 10022
(212) 750 - 9800   www.manhattancabinetry.com

*Custom cabinetry and furniture*

See Manhattan Cabinetry's full report under the heading Millwork & Cabinetry

## New York Closet Company

| | 3 | 2.5 | 4.5 | 4 |

1458 Third Avenue, New York, NY 10028
(212) 439 - 9500

*Closet consultation, design and installation*

Specializing in custom wire, laminate and veneer closets, New York Closet Company has been designing and installing closets for almost 20 years. Jan Riese, the owner, cost-conscientiously designs closet solutions. While "not the definition of organized," the firm gets the job done at a price well below that of the larger organizations. Since all closet companies use the same components, New York Closet has a cadre of loyal clients, both private and trade. Though clients say they would prefer a roomier showroom with more sample closets, they appreciate the wide variety of closet accessories available.

*"While it may not exactly be on schedule, the closets were installed sturdily and suit our needs, which were very functionally-oriented." "A one-woman show that works just fine." "While the firm could read a marketing manual, the end product makes sense."*

## Poliform USA

4.5    4    4.5    4.5

150 East 58th Street, 9th Floor, New York, NY 10155
(212) 421 - 1220   www.poliformusa.com

*Closet design and installation, kitchen and doors sales and installation*

Founded 50 years ago in Italy, Poliform commands a prominent position among clients and design professionals around the world.  This very high-end firm is called upon for kitchen design, closets, wall-to-wall storage solutions and wardrobe systems, most of which are described as sleek, contemporary and modern.  The firm offers complete renovations of kitchens (but not baths), providing design expertise and a wide selection of cabinetry, countertops, sophisticated closet components and Miele appliances.  Each piece is customized to suit the client's needs, and is offered in a variety of natural wood finishes and colors.  Specializing in Italian-based product lines of doors, closets and furniture, Poliform works with clients and their designers to create unique kitchens, closets and living spaces.

## The Closet Factory

3245 Hunterspoint Avenue, Long Island City, NY 11101
(718) 361 - 6310

*Closet design and installation*

## The Closet Lady Inc.

3.5    3    4.5    4.5

1 Lincoln Plaza, Suite 23P, New York, NY 10023
(212) 362 - 0428   www.closetlady.com

*Comprehensive home and office organization*

Labeling Doreen Tuman the Closet Lady is a modest way of describing this self-proclaimed perfectionist.  She not only designs closets—but organizes entire homes and offices as well.  We hear that her fourteen years of experience in the business is demonstrated in her specific designs and ability to understand the exact needs of clients.  All of her work is subcontracted, yet she only uses the finest of professionals and will work with architects, interior designers and contractors.  Although initial consultation and design fees may seem high, clients say the overall cost is very reasonable.  Her infectious enthusiasm and quality of service has won high praise among customers.

*"She organized my life, that's what I needed."  "She sees it through to the end."  "Can call her at any time."  "Her work is supreme."*

## Hiring a Computer Installation & Maintenance Service Provider

Maybe you'd like to connect the computer in your home office to the one in your teenager's room in order to share Internet access. You're worried, however, that if you do it yourself, your "network" will turn on the ceiling fans and trip the security system. Fortunately there are plenty of computer service providers who install networks and software, set up new computer systems and do other tasks that would take a lot of your precious time. Today's world requires a new approach to home computer needs, and computer technician professionals have up-to-the-minute knowledge. Though home networks aren't yet that common, they are fast becoming essential in a high-speed world of connectivity. Your computer setup needs to be as custom fit as a tailored suit for you to get the full benefit. While common sense dictates that you should leave the nitty-gritty details to a skilled technician, knowing what to expect will streamline the process.

### Do I Need a Computer Network?

What is a network, exactly? A cable modem? DSL? A wireless network? A firewall? And, most importantly, are any of these relevant to your needs or current system?

The most basic network is two computers hooked up to each other so that they can share files, Internet access and, perhaps, printers. If you have to save something to a disk, then put that disk into another computer to open a file in the second machine, you are not on a network. The size of networks is almost limitless and the largest corporations and government offices have a mind-boggling number of computers exchanging information. A common home network can consist of three computers: the home office computer, the kids' computer and maybe a laptop. In a network, computers are linked to an Ethernet hub, which is then linked to a printer and a modem. This usually requires running wire throughout the house, drilling and coordinating phone/cable jacks.

Why should you consider a home network? Quite simply, convenience. With a home network files can be transferred easily, printers and Internet access shared and the phone lines freed up for those important incoming calls from your mother-in-law. While this may seem like a sophisticated situation for a home, times are changing. More kids do their homework on the computer, more people work from home and everyone in the house wants to be on the Internet—at the same time. Home networks can save money because they avoid the added expense of multiple printers and Internet hookups. You'll need to buy a hub, the connection point for all elements of a network, which starts at about $50. Though most new computers already have network software installed, you may need to buy network cards, which cost from $15 to $50.

### High-Speed Internet Connections

Internet access through a conventional phone line severely limits your online speed and efficiency. Both a Digital Subscriber Line (DSL) and a cable modem are as much as 100 times faster than a standard analog (telephone) hook-up. A DSL line uses the same cabling as regular telephone lines, but it operates on a higher, idle frequency, allowing the user to be on the Internet and the phone at the same time. Also, DSL service is always connected, so the user never has to dial up and wait for a connection. Cable is a broadband connection, which means that lots of information can travel simultaneously (that's how all those cable channels can be available at the same time). A cable modem is also always "on," but it runs on TV cable lines. The speed is comparable to DSL with one difference: cable modems use a shared bandwidth. This means that speed depends on how many users are using that cable service: the more users, the more traffic, the slower the connection. Because DSL runs on single telephone lines, this isn't an issue. In both cases, find out whether the telephone lines and cable connections in your area are equipped with this service. There are various providers, and promotions offering free installation are common. Computer technician companies will install the DSL connection, but generally are not providers themselves. Monthly service for your connection will cost between $35 and $90. The monthly charge for superfast connections (usually for businesses) can be as high as $300.

Most broadband service packages and home network packages come with a firewall installed. This indispensable part of any Internet-ready computer protects the user from hackers and includes options such as a parental control feature, which allows parents to block inappropriate sites.

## THE WIRELESS ALTERNATIVE

Wireless networking is newly available and can be a practical choice in some cases. It saves having to drill holes through your walls and makes the layout of a home office or computer network more flexible. If the network needs to be expanded or rearranged, wireless networking makes the change easy and inexpensive. A wireless network consists of an Ethernet hub and PC cards inserted into the computers. These cards extend slightly from the machine with a small antenna from which information is sent and received. Wireless networks can operate as quickly as a standard network. The hub can cost anywhere from $300 to $900, and the PC cards are approximately $150. A computer technician can advise you whether or not a wireless system is best for your situation.

## BUYING A NEW COMPUTER: WHERE DO I START?

If your experience lies specifically with PCs (IBM compatible) or Macintoshes, you may want to stick with the type of computer already familiar to you. (Some technicians focus on one type or the other, which can narrow your search for a good techie, too). If there are children in the house, consider what computers their schools use. One computer technician suggests starting with an issue of *PC Magazine* or *Macworld* to see what's available and use it as a reference when you speak to a technician about models, memory sizes and accessories. This way you can get a clear idea of what appeals to you and have a more productive conversation with your computer consultant.

## ON COST

Computer technicians generally charge an hourly service fee, which can range from $65 to almost $200 per hour. In *The Franklin Report*, a baseline rating of 3 for Cost represents an hourly rate in the range of $100 to $115 per hour. However, please remember there are other factors that may affect the final cost. Before you hire a technician, ask whether the fee is calculated only in hourly increments. If you go 15 minutes into the next hour, are you charged for a full additional hour? In addition to the fee, you will be charged for whatever hardware or software you purchase. Discuss exactly what will be installed to avoid hidden costs. The key to any home service is the quality of the time spent, not the quantity. A good service provider will not squander the hours they are billing you for, but will arrive prepared to solve your problem as quickly as possible. Ask whether the technician charges for advice on the phone after he's made the house call. Often he will not charge for more time if you just need clarification on the service he recently provided. Once you're a customer, some technicians will even respond to a new question if it doesn't take too long, but others will want the clock to start running again. Find out your techie's policy and how flexible he is. Some consultants offer a package of a given number of hours of help, which can be a combination of an initial house call, followup help at home and time on the phone. This might be good for someone just starting out. It's comforting to know that someone is there to help when you panic.

## INSURANCE AND CONTRACTS

Most computer maintenance technicians carry some sort of business insurance which protects them from the repercussions of crashing your computer or network. This insurance is for everyone's benefit. Any service that handles office networks as well will carry this insurance. If you chose a smaller operation, ask them if and how they are covered. Computer service providers may have contracts with business accounts, but it is rare with home service. Ask your technician about the firm's policy.

## WHAT TO EXPECT FROM A TECHIE

Depending on the scope of the service, the principal of the company may perform the work personally or send out technicians. The key is finding someone who responds quickly and whose service is reliable. Also, since the computer industry moves at such a fast pace, it's infinitely helpful to work with someone who knows where it is going and shares that knowledge.

Steer clear of computer service professionals who act as if everyone should have been born with a computer gene. In truth, a lot of people just nod when they are told they need an updated USB port in order to handle the increased amount of EDI coming in over the DSL lines. You want someone who will listen to you, set up exactly what you need and ensure that you fully understand it. Try to quickly get a sense of whether the techie helping you only speaks in technobabble. Believe it or not, there are technicians out there who can make computers understandable to even you, and you should not have to put up with someone who does not patiently explain things in plain English.

Keep in mind that chimps in university labs can learn how to play computer games. If Cheeta can do it, so can you.

INTERNET JARGON
(AT LEAST YOU CAN SOUND LIKE YOU KNOW WHAT YOU'RE TALKING ABOUT.)

❖ **Bandwidth:** Measured in bits per second (bps), bandwidth is the amount of data that can be both sent and received through a connection.

❖ **Bozo Filter:** An email feature that allows the user to block messages from specific individuals. Can help reduce spam by creating a list of unwanted addresses affectionately named a "bozo list."

❖ **Cookie:** A message a Web server sends to your browser when certain Web pages are visited. The cookie is stored and a message is sent back every time the user requests that page. This allows the page to come up customized. For example, after you purchase something on Amazon.com, your user name will appear to welcome you every time you log on from the same computer.

❖ **Cyberspace:** The inter-connected non-physical space created by the Internet and the World Wide Web, where information is transferred and people communicate electronically through computer networks.

❖ **DSL (Digital Subscriber Line):** A method for sending data over regular phone lines. A DSL circuit is much faster than a regular phone connection. It uses the same wires already in place for regular phone service, but since it uses an unused frequency you can talk on the phone while connected to the Internet with only one line.

❖ **ISP (Internet Service Provider):** A company that provides access to the Internet, usually for a monthly fee. Most homes use an ISP to connect to the Internet.

❖ **LAN (Local Area Network):** A computer network limited to the immediate area, for example, a private residence. Ethernet is the most common type of connection used for LANs.

❖ **Modem:** A communication device that allows a computer to talk to other computers. Modems vary in speed from slower telephone modems to significantly faster DSL and cable modems.

❖ **Netiquette:** The accepted rules of conduct that define polite behavior in Cyberspace. If you breach the rules of netiquette, you can be sure your fellow users will let you know.

❖ **Network:** Any two or more computers connected together to share resources such as files, a printer or Internet access.

❖ **Newbie**: Term for someone who is new to computers or the Internet. It is not an insult but just a description. If you are reading this, you could be a Newbie.

❖ **Snail Mail:** Regular paper mail delivered by the US Postal Service. Why use the Postal Service when you can shoot a letter over in seconds via email?

❖ **Spam**: Junk mail over your email, which wastes your time and the network's bandwidth. Ways of combating spam include filters and private service providers like AOL.

❖ **T-1:** A wide bandwidth Internet connection that can carry data at 1.544 megabits per second. This is the fastest speed generally used to connect networks to the Internet.

❖ **URL (Uniform Resource Locator):** Represents the address used to locate a certain file, directory or page on the World Wide Web.

❖ **Web Browser:** Software such as Netscape Navigator or Internet Explorer that allows the user to access the World Wide Web by translating the language used to build web pages. Short term: "browser."

| Quality | Cost | Value | Recommend? |
|---------|------|-------|------------|
| **+** | **$** | **◆** | **★** |

## COMPUTER INSTALLATION & MAINTENANCE SERVICE PROVIDERS

### Amnet Solutions                                    3    3    4    4
229 East 53rd Street, New York, NY  10022
(212) 593 - 2425
*Computer networking and servicing*

For almost twelve years Amnet Solutions has provided individuals and small to mid-sized companies in Manhattan with networking, installation, consulting, training, maintenance and repair services for both PC and Macintosh systems. Additionally, the company specializes in data recovery and transfer. We hear the small, honest staff of three offers good service at a reasonable price.

*"Very reliable and trustworthy. We've used them for five years, and have found no reason to switch to another company." "You're in great hands with them." "No major complaints—a nice and responsive company."*

### AMTAC                                              3    3    4    4
50 West 23rd Street, 4th Floor, New York, NY  10010
(212) 675 - 3888
*Computer networking and training*

Although AMTAC may be known primarily for installing corporate intranet and Internet systems, we hear this high-end firm creates excellent home networks as well.  AMTAC works regularly with architects and interior designers, and clients recommend the company for its fast, efficient and comprehensive service.  They are commended for their training courses, as well as web design and website and domain hosting services.

### Brave New Consultants                              4.5   4.5   4    5
60 East 13th Street, New York, NY  10003
(212) 376 - 4000   www.brave.net
*Computer networking and servicing*

Brave New Consultants provides a wide variety of computer and web-related services targeted mainly at businesses, but sources tell us this upper-end firm will also install and repair residential networks if asked.  Clients are pleased with the service and the end results, but mention that commercial-minded prices may be a deterrent for some.  The company serves clients throughout Manhattan.

*"Did everything they promised and more." "It did cost more than we would have liked, but everything they did was excellent." "Techs were brilliant and the system they set up for me is solid as a rock."*

### CBI Connect                                        4.5   4    4.5   5
301 Elizabeth Street, New York, NY  10012
(212) 219 - 0278   www.cbi-connect.com
*Computer networking and servicing*

Dedicated to keeping clients in the New York City area well connected, CBI Connect offers local and wide-area networking solutions and Internet connectivity for both residential and business clients. Craig Bueker, who was profiled with his business in both *GQ*'s "Man of the Month" column and *New York Magazine*, comes

| Quality | Cost | Value | Recommend? |
|---|---|---|---|
| ✚ | $ | ◆ | ★ |

very highly recommended by those who appreciate his personal yet professional service. A host of high-powered clients in the arts call on Bueker for his talents—including Lou Reed and Ben Stiller—but sources tell us that hasn't altered the down-to-earth style he brings to his business.

Bueker and his staff of fourteen earn high ratings for their creative solutions to challenging problems and their courteous and efficient manner. Customer service and implementation are considered very reliable, and the company offers high-quality training as well. CBI has been handling both Macs and PCs for over six years, and recently Bueker has added managed firewall and security solutions to his company's repertoire, as well as broad-band service for residential and commercial use. Clients say the firm offers many billing options, including hourly fees, monthly retainer or project-based fees.

*"They met their guarantee of overall excellence." "They are able to conceive and execute solutions for difficult IT problems with ease." "He offers 200 percent and is quite personable as an instructor." "They are creative problem solvers and always on top of cutting-edge technologies." "CBI personnel are extremely efficient, courteous and always ready to help with any related computer problems. Phone calls are returned immediately, which I genuinely appreciate."*

### Clue Enterprises
101 Cassilis Avenue, Bronxville, NY  10708
(914) 961 - 2175

*Computer networking and servicing*

### Compushine
| | 3.5 | 3.5 | 4 | 5 |
30 East 60th Street, Suite 903, New York, NY  10022
(212) 371 - 1525  www.compushine.com

*Computer networking and servicing*

Clients enthusiastically recommend Compushine for its prompt and efficient service, as well as the range of services offered by its staff, including expertise in computer, telephone, satellite and audio/video systems. In business since 1995, Compushine employs a staff of 20, including certified technicians, and works with both residential and commercial customers in Manhattan and beyond.

Computer services offered by Compushine include installation, networking, troubleshooting and maintenance of systems, as well as consultation regarding hardware and software purchases and training. The company installs wireless networks—either apartment or full-building systems—and clients tell us the work is done skillfully. Telephone services offered include installation, wiring and maintenance for homeowners and businesses. Compushine handles Toshiba, Panasonic and Avaya systems.

*"You name it, they can do it." "Frank and speedy—very helpful. They spent almost 20 minutes on the phone with me, just answering my questions."*

### Computer ER
| | 3 | 2.5 | 4.5 | 5 |
605 Fifth Avenue, 3rd Floor, New York, NY  10017
(212) 317 - 9233

*Computer networking and servicing*

There's no computer trauma with this ER, a small company offering a variety of PC services for homes or small- to medium-sized businesses in the New York City area. Customers tell us this eight-year-old firm installs computer hardware—including home networks—and also provides on-site technical service (as well as phone help), consultation, training, sales and maintenance for PC systems. You can have the technicians make house calls for repair work, but we're told they offer a price break if you bring in your malfunctioning hardware. Computer ER is considered to be efficient and reasonably priced.

| Quality | Cost | Value | Recommend? |
|---|---|---|---|
| ✚ | $ | ◆ | ★ |

*"Good services, good prices and they always solve my problems quickly and efficiently." "We've worked with them for a couple of years—we've been very happy. He's like a member of the family to our small business. Very patient and gives us hands-on attention and support."*

## Computer Guru                    4     2     5     5
31 Union Square West, Suite 15E, New York, NY 10003
(212) 243 - 0532

*Computer training and troubleshooting*

The Computer Guru, A.K.A. David Silberman, is a dedicated technician who is available seven days a week, offering training and troubleshooting for both Macs and PCs. We hear he also provides installation, networking and consulting services to both businesses and individuals, and backs it up with phone support. Silberman does not sell hardware or software—nor does he do repairs—but he does offer consultation for clients looking for purchasing or repair advice. Most of his clientele are in Manhattan, although he will trek farther afield if traveling expenses are compensated. Clients report that David is generous with his time, and they are happy to recommend this fair and friendly company.

*"Top-notch in every regard—and a bargain." "I always recommend him to friends." "I consider it a plus that he calls to alert me that he'll be late." "He's an extremely honorable guy."*

## Computer Guys                    4     2.5     5     5
18 East 16th Street, 2nd Floor, New York, NY 10003
(212) 414 - 0321   www.computerguysny.com

*Computer networking, consulting, servicing, training and repair*

The guys (and gals) of Computer Guys are happy to assist in choosing the right system for your home or office (be it Mac or PC), install your new computer, set up your home or business network, repair your broken machine (they are Microsoft-certified), train you to use your software more effectively, help you get connected to the Internet and consult with you when things go wrong. About the only thing they won't do is sell you the hardware or software or offer you phone support. The six technicians work mainly in Manhattan and clients are consistently pleased with the results.

*"Very professional staff. I'm an extremely demanding and difficult client—they came up with some very simple but creative solutions which enhanced my business." "Computer Guys can fix anything in record time. I tried other computer services before I found them, but no one held a candle to them."*

| | Quality  | Cost $ | Value ◆ | Recommend? ★ |

## Computer Integrated Services
4  3.5  4.5  4

501 Fifth Avenue, Suite 602, New York, NY 10017
(212) 983 - 4936   www.computerintegrated.com

*Computer networking, consulting, servicing, training, repair and sales*

This company's computer-related services run the gamut from A to Z. CIS will install, upgrade, maintain, repair, consult, cable, train and network, and if you don't have a computer yet, they'll sell you the hardware and software to boot. Clients tell us CIS technicians are great at explaining things to the computer impaired—whether it's a Mac or PC—and have a broad range of experience in networking, web development, e-commerce and custom-integrated systems. Customers say they're nice, professional guys, who are eager to help you out. CIS also offers 24-hour service for those late night emergencies.

*"Quick to respond, which is important in my business." "We've been working with them for about three and a half years, and they've never left us in a bind." "We've had some serious viruses that have taken down our system numerous times, and they've always come to the rescue. They handle everything."*

## CPR Computer Services
3  2.5  4.5  4

28 West 39th Street, New York, NY 10018
(212) 768 - 9322

*Computer networking and troubleshooting*

CPR Computer Services has been breathing e-life into business for fifteen years. We hear the firm specializes in network systems installations for business clients, but occasionally accommodates individuals. According to sources, this company can solve most problems related to PC or Macintosh systems, including troubleshooting, maintenance and repair. CPR does not, however, sell products, nor do its technicians train their customers on software programs. CPR has eight technicians on staff, and we hear they are a capable and considerate group.

## Crocodile Computers
4  2  5  3.5

360 Amsterdam Avenue, New York, NY 10023
(212) 769 - 3400   www.crocs.com

*Computer repair and sales*

Crocodile Computers has taken a generous bite out of the PC repair business, offering reasonable prices—especially if you bring in your malfunctioning machine—as well as speedy service. Clients say don't expect to be coddled though. We hear service may be curt at times, but customers recognize this as part of the get it done ASAP attitude. Recommended by various publications including *New York Magazine* and *Smart Money Magazine*, Crocodile also sells software and new and used hardware. We hear that inventory turnover is high, so diligence is the key to finding what you're looking for.

Though sales and repair are Crocodile's bread and butter, sources tell us the company will also do some in-home network installation, for a three-hour minimum charge and a higher hourly rate.

## CTSI Consulting/Computer Tutor
3.5  3  4.5  4

118 West 79th Street, New York, NY 10024
(212) 787 - 6636

*Computer consulting and training*

Bruce Stark and CTSI Consulting/Computer Tutor has offered consulting and training services for all types of computers for nearly 20 years. While CTSI can help you research and purchase a system as well as provide training and limited support, it should be noted that the company does not provide support for computer networking, perform PC repairs or sell hardware or software. The firm has four technicians, and sources tell us the trustworthy staff is competent and reliable. The majority of CTSI's customers are in Manhattan, but we are told the staff will travel outside of the city—including Westchester County—for an added travel fee. Phone service is also available

*"Quick, responsible, honest, fair. Only good things to say about Bruce—he's our computer guy." "He's extremely trustworthy—I give him the keys to my house. I love this guy." "He's technically competent and personable to boot." "They're there when we need them."*

## Datavision                                3      3      4      5
445 Fifth Avenue, New York, NY  10016
(212) 689 - 1111   www.datavis.com
*Computer sales, consulting and installation*

Datavision, known mainly as a computer retailer selling both Macintosh and PC systems, also offers computer repair, configuration, networking, data retrieval, web design and consulting services. The company is an Authorized Service Center for all major manufacturers, and sources say that although the service is less personal than at a smaller firm, the range of expertise is great. We hear these professionals are at their best when in emergency mode, and with their rapid response time and expertise, it is said Datavision won't let you down.

*"Responsible, professional, competent, efficient and, most importantly, speedy."*

## Datum Computer Services Inc.              4     3.5    4.5     5
60 East 42nd Street, Suite 1310, New York, NY  10165
(212) 681 - 1212   www.datumcomputer.com
*Computer networking and consulting*

This small consulting firm has been around since 1992, helping New Yorkers with all their computer needs—from local and wide-area networking to Internet-access solutions from sales and installation to troubleshooting and repair of software and hardware. Clients laud Datum for its top-notch service and professional one-on-one instruction. The diagnostic services also receive high praise. One client notes how good the consultants are at identifying beforehand what you should contact the manufacturer about (to avoid costly service visits), and how pleasant it is that they don't try to sell you something new.

Datum works with both business and residential customers, and some clients are happily both. It does not, however, work with Macintosh systems. We hear the firm and its five technicians offer 24-hour service in emergency situations (although in general, two-day advance notice is preferred), and phone service is also available, billed at the normal hourly rate.

*"Never condescending in any way, even when I ask very basic questions." "Very knowledgeable, and really listens well." "Datum explains computers simply and easily for neophytes." "Extremely professional, and a joy to work with." "Can't say anything negative, only kudos."*

## De Castro Computer Services              3     1.5     5      4.5
228 Eighth Avenue, Suite 12, New York, NY  10011
(212) 206 - 8330   www.sdc.baweb.com
*Computer training and Web design*

We hear that Susan De Castro is particularly adept at Web design and graphics software support, two of the many services offered by this one-woman-show. Clients also tell us that De Castro is a patient and easygoing teacher, offering training, troubleshooting and Internet support for both the computer literate and the computer impaired, on both Macintosh and PC computers. De Castro Computer Services has been in business for eight years, offering on-site training in groups or one-on-one, for businesses as well as individuals. Whether it's providing computer support for a child trying to catch up with school work or parents trying to catch up with their child, she works well with all age groups, and clients appreciate her reasonable rates and down-to-earth service.

*"Susan is very patient with me and gladly answers all of my questions, no matter how rudimentary."*

## Domino Computing Inc.          4.5    4.5    4    5
325 West 38th Street, New York, NY  10018
(212) 594 - 2110   www.dominocomputing.com
*Computer networking, consulting and sales*

Domino Computing doesn't play games when it comes to computer support, we hear.  This full-service company works with all brands of computers and handles projects from the simple to the complex.  While Domino works mainly with small- to mid-sized businesses, it will also assist individuals in setting up home networks for personal or business use.  In addition to installation, diagnostic support, networking, consultation, security, server and Internet services, the company also sells both hardware and software.  A fairly new company—in business for less than a year—Domino has already won a loyal and satisfied following.

*"We wouldn't trade them for any other company."  "I have nothing but the highest regard for the work they do and the type of people they are."  "I had one tech experience before this which was very frustrating.  The other company was very hard to track down.  Domino's the opposite—they are very reliable, accessible and responsive."  "I couldn't be happier with them, and I wouldn't switch firms for anything."*

## Hank Unger          4    3.5    4.5    5
260 West 44th Street, Suite 501, New York, NY  10036
(212) 869 - 0070
*Computer consulting, troubleshooting and installation*

"Patient with the tech impaired" this "young, hip and professional" one-man enterprise tutors private clients and businesses all over New York City in the language of their computers while also offering purchasing, installation and networking services.  Clients say Unger offers clear, knowledgeable instruction and troubleshooting advice and "is realistic regarding time issues."  One client notes that she had worked with many other consultants before happening upon Unger, whom she found to be flexible, accessible and able to work with programs outside of the norm.  He is, we hear, very generous with his time.

*"Hank is honest and trustworthy, and a very hard worker."  "Terrific guy. On more than one occasion he's saved me from destroying my machine.  He even helped me lodge a complaint against a company that sold me a lemon, and they sent me a new computer."  "Marvelous personality—not arrogant at all."  "We are technologically impaired at our office, and even though we ask the most inane questions, he treats us cordially and with respect.  And, most importantly, he solves our problems for us."*

| | Quality + | Cost $ | Value ◆ | Recommend? ★ |
|---|---|---|---|---|

## Konanur Inc.

3     3     4     3

127 West 24th Street, New York, NY 10011
(212) 414 - 0700  www.konanurinc.com

*Computer consulting*

Dealing primarily with Macintosh computers, Konanur Inc. has been part of the Apple Solutions Network for over ten years. Konanur offers Website and database design in addition to the standard range of services for businesses and individuals including networking, systems integration and administration, tech support and training. Although the company does not sell hardware, Konanur's technicians are available to advise you on finding the right machine(s) for your needs. Clients praise the straightforward and friendly service.

## MacMechanix

4     3     4.5     4

50 Walker Street, 2nd Floor, New York, NY 10013
(212) 219 - 2080  www.macmechanix.com

*Computer consulting, installation, networking and repair*

John Greenleaf and his "band of merry techsters" are well regarded by the wide range of customers who call on them for help with their Macs. MacMechanix has been around for eleven years, installing, repairing, networking and consulting about Macintosh systems—as well as recovering lost data—for businesses and individuals in New York City. Greenleaf and his staff don't sell hardware or software, nor do they offer training. Clients cite the firm's response time as a plus, noting they usually get help the same day or the next. We also hear the firm gets particular praise from its graphics clients.

*"I've learned a lot from John—he is an extremely patient teacher, even when I ask very naive questions." "He's particularly good with graphics software, and is constantly updating his knowledge and skills." "I can't run my business without John."*

## MacTechnologies Consulting

3.5     3.5     4     4

545 Eighth Avenue, Suite 401, New York, NY 10018
(212) 201 - 1465  www.mactechnologies.com

*Computer consulting, networking and training*

As this company's name implies, MacTechnologies Consulting offers Macintosh consulting services, which it has done for eight years. In addition to consulting, Kem Tekinay and his staff provide custom programming, networking, troubleshooting, maintenance and on-site training including email, Internet and software support. MacTechnologies consults mainly in Manhattan (a one-hour minimum is required), although technicians will travel farther afield for a higher hourly rate and a two-hour minimum. Clients tell us that MacTechnologies does not sell Macs, but can comply with most other customer requests.

## NuLogic Inc.

4.5     4     4.5     4.5

360 East 88th Street, Suite 21C, New York, NY 10128
(212) 427 - 7408  www.nulinc.com

Whether building networks or firewalls, NuLogic gets New Yorkers's computer systems up and keeps them running. NuLogic specializes in Internet technologies and security, but also offers installation, upgrades, maintenance and consultation on all types of computers and platforms. Lars Larsen comes highly recommended by his clients, who concur that he is a master at his trade, and extremely responsible and pleasant to work with. Larsen doesn't sell hardware or software, but clients tell us he can help you sort out the good from the bad and recommend a system for you. Though NuLogic works with small, medium and large businesses, we hear that many individuals also call on the company for help with their home or home office needs. Larsen and his staff of consultants also do work in surrounding areas, including New Jersey, Westchester and Connecticut.

*"Lars has never ever let us down. He is always there, fixing our problems and keeping our business running smoothly." "Lars is reliable, dependable, brilliant— he can solve any problem, no matter how difficult." "Timely, responsive and, above all, a nice guy. I couldn't wish for a better computer guy." "Lars is exceptional at what he does, as well as extremely pleasant and very responsible. He is a valuable, irreplaceable part of my worklife."*

## RCS Computer Experience
3.5    3.5    4    4

575 Madison Avenue, New York, NY   10022
(212) 949 - 6935   www.rcseshop.com
*Computer sales and servicing*

Sales is the main attraction at RCS Computer Experience, although the company also offers service, installation and networking for both Macintoshes and PCs. We hear the sales staff is knowledgeable and friendly, and in spite of its size, the company offers personal service for both businesses and individuals in need of computer support and advice. In addition to the main retail store listed here, there are two additional retail locations in Manhattan—a store at 48th Street and Sixth Avenue and another at 47th Street and Fifth Avenue—as well as the website which sells nationally.

*"I called to get information on networking, and found the staff to be very helpful over the phone." "Sales is obviously number one here, but they were very clear and helpful."*

## Reality Works Consulting 🛍
4    3    4.5    5

19 Dixon Street, Tarrytown, NY  10591
(914) 366 - 7859
*Computer networking and high-speed connections*

Reality Works Consulting provides large corporate-level information technologies to small businesses and individuals in Manhattan and the regional area. The one-man-show featuring Chris Doherty, is particularly skilled at addressing connectivity solutions for high-speed Internet access. Additionally, Reality Works offers installation, troubleshooting, repair, networking and consultation services for both Macintosh and PC systems. References tell us that Doherty is patient and effective, and they appreciate his down-to-earth approach to explaining complicated problems in terms they can easily understand.

*"He has become a part of my life. We would be lost without Chris." "You could not find a nicer guy and he is always there in an emergency." "He works at it until he finds a solution."*

## RescueCom
🗁    🗁    🗁    🗁

(212) 406 - 0072
*Computer service and networking*

RescueCom technicians offer 911 service for Manhattan-area computer users whenever problems arise. The company is certified on Macs and PCs and is facile with both hardware and software. When called in for an emergency, the RescueCom squad strives to respond in one hour and charge accordingly— almost double their regular rate for scheduled calls. Technicians do much of their work at the customer's home or business, and are available up to as late as midnight. RescueCom can also assist with networking and Internet issues.

## Rivera Technics
3.5    4    4    4

127 West 24th Street, 5th Floor, New York, NY  10011
(212) 460 - 8862
*Computer installation and servicing*

This husband-and-wife team has been in business for twelve years, working exclusively on Macintosh computers for businesses and some long-standing residential clients in Manhattan. The couple offers consulting, tech support, networking and installation services. Clients tell us they are helpful, but not so attentive to new clients.

| | Quality + | Cost $ | Value ◆ | Recommend? ★ |
|---|---|---|---|---|

## SBA * Consulting Ltd.

| | 3.5 | 4 | 3.5 | 4 |
|---|---|---|---|---|

2711 Bellmore Avenue, Bellmore, NY 11710
(516) 221 - 3306   www.sbaconsulting.com

*Computer networking and servicing*

SBA * Consulting and its newer sister company, SBA.net.web, offer a range of computer services for the home or business user, including network design and installation, training, troubleshooting and Internet-related services such as e-commerce solutions and website design and hosting. We hear the majority of the company's residential work is done for home businesses in New York City, though some clients are as far afield as Paris and Texas. SBA * Consulting has been in business since 1985.

## Techknowledge/G

| | 3.5 | 3 | 4.5 | 5 |
|---|---|---|---|---|

130 East 18th Street, New York, NY 10003
(212) 254 - 8731   www.techknowledgeg.com

*Computer consulting, repair and troubleshooting*

Gail Heimberg of Techknowledge/G has been helping New Yorkers get a handle on their personal computers for almost twelve years. From advice on buying hardware and software to assistance with networking your family's jumble of computers to advice on optimizing your existing system, Heimberg can help. Her focus is on home systems and individuals—from novices to more technically adept users. She also works with small businesses, setting up networks and providing other consulting services.

Heimberg offers training and coaching on both Macs and PCs, and customers tell us she is a patient, competent and responsible teacher who keeps her clients' interests in mind at all times. Additional services include computer installation, troubleshooting, technical support and assistance with Internet access issues. We hear that area computer retailers often recommend Techknowledge/G.

*"When you are wandering through the wilderness, it is great to have someone show you the way." "Very reliable, never late, responsive. I think her rates are very fair."*

## Technology Management Resources

| | 4 | 3.5 | 4.5 | 5 |
|---|---|---|---|---|

(212) 243 - 3553

*Computer networking and servicing*

Though primarily dedicated to setting up computer systems for commercial customers, Technology Management Resources will also consult with residential clients on occasion. We hear TMR prefers to keep its client list low, as it is dedicated to customer-driven, high-quality work. TMR also offers ongoing tech support, maintenance, troubleshooting and crash rescues, and works with both PC and Macintosh systems. The dozen consultants at this firm operate on either a retainer or fee per hour, and although we hear that TMR is not inexpensive, we're told the technicians work honestly and very cost-consciously.

## Tekserve

| | 5 | 3 | 5 | 5 |
|---|---|---|---|---|

155 West 23rd Street, 4th Floor, New York, NY 10011
(212) 929 - 3645   www.tekserve.com

*Computer service, repair and upgrade*

Clients tell us that this is the place to go for repairs to your Macintosh or Macintosh clone and peripherals. Tekserve fixes hardware and software problems, upgrades systems and offers data recovery services (you pay only if they are successful). We're told its technicians operate on a first-come, first-serve basis, and clients report that they are very speedy, knowledgeable and accommodating. However, you will need to transport your machine to the Tekserve shop on your own (if you drive, they'll pay for up to three hours of parking at a nearby garage). The company also sells Macs and configures systems, but the company's real bread-and-butter—and strength, clients say—is in its service.

*"I can't say enough. They were unbelievably fast, reliable and competent."*

## Twin Peaks Geeks 　　　　　　　3.5　　3　　4.5　　5
47 Curtis Drive, Sound Beach, NY 11789
(631) 209 - 1320　www.twinpeaksgeeks.com
*Computer networking, consulting, installation, training and troubleshooting*

This pair of rock solid friends—Mike Avery and Sheryl Heller—works with small businesses and individuals in need of Macintosh solutions from installation and networking to upgrades, troubleshooting, training and equipment purchasing. The company is located in Long Island and works mainly with clients in the Hamptons, but has been found on their heels in Manhattan. We're told the two have been in business together for four years, initially in San Francisco and recently back East where they both grew up. They continue to work with loyal clients in California as well as in Florida, Boston and Arizona. Work is billed on an hourly basis, with a separate rate for tutoring services. The pair also offers phone support, and we hear they are readily available and responsive.

*"Mike is always very professional, informative, and extremely patient. He has never made me feel uncomfortable for not knowing simple computer tasks, and now that I've gained confidence in my skills, it's helped my productivity." "Supportive and creative. Superb personal skills. Consistent and available." "Mike and Sheryl are always there in a crisis, no matter the duration." "Always prompt and immediate in answering phone calls."*

## Wonderplay Inc. 　　　　　　　3　　3.5　　3.5　　3.5
235 West 76th Street, Suite 12E, New York, NY 10023
(212) 595 - 7894
*Computer training and installation*

Wonderplay's Stan Goldberg works with Macintosh systems, offering in-home installation, advice on system setup and purchases, support and training. Most clients appreciate this patient, focused, responsive Southern gentleman who is always accessible by beeper and will help you over the phone or by email. Occassionally, there are reported bumps with more complicated, unresolved systems issues, but mostly he is a good teacher who is organized, considerate and talented at explaining technology clearly and simply. Goldberg serves both individuals and small businesses, charging an hourly rate. Many friends pass on Goldberg's name to others.

*"With Stan Goldberg doing your computer work, you won't have any more worries." "He works well with busy executives, harried housewives and kids too." "If he buys equipment, he always looks for the best prices."*

# Hiring a Contractor or Builder

Understanding a big repair or renovation can be intimidating, especially the thought of selecting the top person in charge, the commander-in-chief—the contractor. That's why an excellent contractor is vital to any major household work. This professional, like a general, takes in the big picture as well as the details, is seasoned through experience, knows his troops and the system, gets the job done well and on time and wins your admiration in the process. Here's a field guide to enlisting a five-star contractor:

## Job Description

A traditional general contractor (GC) bids and builds from an architect's or designer's plans and specifications (the contract documents). The GC's duties are to interpret the drawings, execute the contracts, secure the permits, supervise the trades, manage the budget, make the schedule, deliver the quality and call it a day. There are design/build contracting firms that will draw up the contract documents, eliminating the need for an architect. Be aware, however, many firms which call themselves design/build really only offer conceptual assistance. They do not have practicing architects in-house, and must farm out design services to certified professionals. Some comment this one-stop shop approach more often than not results in uninspired design and cookie-cutter "McMansions," while others believe that nobody is more qualified to see a set of plans realized than its designer. This route is less costly than hiring an outside architect. However, an outside architect serves as a check and balance to the GC. Construction management offers an alternative to hiring the traditional GC. Clients themselves contract with individual trades and the construction manager handles all payments and project administration for a fee based on total job cost. Some clients laud this "open book" approach, while others say it lacks an incentive to save and can result in a less coordinated approach.

## What to Look for in a Contractor

Picking the right general contractor is all about communication. A homeowner needs to know as much about the GC's capabilities as the GC needs to know about a homeowner's expectations. With stakes this high—mortgages, reputations, living another day at your in-laws—it's time for everyone to feel completely secure in the leadership on the job and the direction of the project. You should feel comfortable stating your wishes to the contractor and have confidence in his ability to listen, explain, cooperate and delegate.

Before you approach a GC, make sure your contract documents are clear and thorough. If you choose to go design/build, look for a firm sympathetic and attuned to your sense of style, and make sure the company does indeed produce quality detailed drawings. Your candidate should be experienced in jobs of a similar type: restoration, renovation or new construction. Do you want a versatile GC or one that specializes? The GC should be well versed on the architectural features, building applications, specialty installations, customization and level of quality you expect. Consider the scale of the GC's past jobs, including cost and total square-footage. You don't want to be the job stuck below the radar screen of a commercial-minded contractor, or hook your wagon to a little guy who can't muster the horsepower.

You want the GC to be fluent in the code requirements and logistical considerations of your locale. Negotiating the elevators, union regulations, and neighbors of Upper East Side high rises is very different from negotiating landmark restrictions on historic brownstones. The city permitting and inspection processes, co-op boards, and building management companies are notorious instruments of delay. Also, nail down your GC's availability. If he can't commit to a target start date, you cannot depend on his ability to stick to a completion date, and chances are you'll be living in a construction battle zone for an indefinite time.

Finally, you wouldn't let a stranger in your door, so before you invite a platoon of workers brandishing power tools and sack lunches, get references. The GC's listed in this section are certainly among the most reputable, but talk to clients and inspect jobs in progress yourself to get a feel for a GC's abilities and current slate of jobs. Also talk to those clients with jobs completed to get a reading on how a GC maintains his word and work. More than 30 states now require licensing or registration for GCs. In New York City a GC shouldn't be able to get a permit without.

## On Cost

Typically, three bids should suffice for a clear and fair comparison of estimates of project cost. The market may be cooling down, but it still may mean approaching twice that number just to get a telephone call returned. The more established GC's may bid only for architects with whom they have a relationship, or referrals, or on particularly plum projects. In some cases, you may need to pull strings in order to approach them to consider the project and negotiate a fee.

Cost is a reflection of material and labor (as provided directly or through subcontractors), bonding and insurance, the general conditions (overhead to keep the job running) and the fee. General conditions and the fee are calculated as percentages of the total hard-construction costs, approximately 18 to 25 percent in New York City these days, though the percentage will vary depending on the cost, size and location of the job. Bonding offers insurance against a GC's failure to perform or pay subcontractors. It's a protection against negligence and liens—claims of debt that can be attached to the title of your property and prevent it from being sold until all liens are settled. Insurance covers full liability and Workman's Compensation. Any and all associated permit fees (calculated archaically by the city as a percentage of total job cost), deposits or taxes also figure into the cost.

For the most part GC's come close with their overhead and profit costs, and the degree to which prices vary depends on the quality and cost of their subcontractors, internal resources, their ability to interpret plans accurately and honestly, their ability to meet the schedule, how conservative they wish to estimate, and of course, you. At the end of the day your choice of materials and methods of construction, as well as change orders, determine where the chips are likely to fall. In *The Franklin Report* a 3 Cost reflects a contractor typically charging 20 percent profit and overhead on $50,000 to $500,000 projects that involve standard high-end technical or decorative work.

## Negotiating the Bids

Jumping on the low bid may be tempting, but don't take the bait. If a bid is enticingly low, it almost assuredly signals that the GC doesn't fully grasp the scope or has value-engineered without your consent.

A good GC doesn't lowball, he negotiates. Don't be shy about requesting a thorough cost breakdown. If the GC's numbers come from subcontractors, you may ask for the subs' bid sheets. Remember, the more subcontractors are employed, the more overhead and fee markups will inflate the bottom line. In-house carpenters, for example, are a plus, giving the GC direct control over a trade many consider the engine that drives the job. Any top GC draws from a small, consistent stable of subcontractors. These prices tend to be higher due to lack of competition and constant demand for the subs' service. While loyalty speaks for standards of quality, it's always your prerogative to ask the GC for an alternative sub. Just don't be surprised if he refuses.

You may be able to shave a few dollars off the bid by entertaining the possibility of service contracts. These are typically maintenance agreements that plug the gaps in the basic warranties. Many subs will try to snare you into buying one at the end of the job, but beat them to the punch and inquire about them at the outset. Use the prospect of your entering into a service contract as a tool to negotiate for a reduction in the cost of a bid. It offers contractors the incentive to forego dollars today for the chance of a service contract deal in the future.

## Commissioning Your General

Cost is always a factor, but at the end of the day personality is at least as important. Can you work together? Don't settle for anything less than a principal of a contracting firm who expresses interest in the status of your job both at the outset and throughout. The tone is set from the top. You should feel like you can trust not only your GC with the keys to your house, but also enjoy having him around. Goodness knows he'll be spending enough time there.

Once the job begins, he should dispatch an on-site supervisor and assign a project manager. In some cases a working foreman will super on-site, in others it may be the company owner. In any case, these on-site managers will be the ones coordinating with your architect or designer. Weekly site meetings are a must. As with picking the right GC, running a smooth and successful job is all about communication.

## Get It in Writing

About the only thing that doesn't need to be detailed in your contract documents are the middle names of the contractor's children. Otherwise every detail should be recorded on paper. The plans and specs furnished by your designer provide the fundamental outline of the job. This means noting every raw material and product—including brand, model number, color and installation method. Be meticulous. If it's not on the drawings, it's not going to show up in your home, unless of course you're willing to sign the change order.

The change order, you ask? If you make a request that deviates from the project's scope as defined by the contract documents, expect to pay. Some changes may be inevitable, if you are unfortunate enough not to have x-ray vision or if you fall prey to your own whimsical inclinations halfway through the job. But be sure that any charges passed under your nose weren't already in the original contract. Ask your architect or construction manager to investigate each submission to make sure everything's on the level, otherwise its up to you. Spell out in the contract how change orders will be handled. A smart idea is to fix the unit costs for labor and material that were established with the original contract so there are no surprises about price of extras.

Be warned, a GC's obligation to meet code does not shield you from a city's permitting and inspection schizophrenia. Your contract documents must refer to the applicable codes. Because many are open to interpretation, a city official on a bad day can be a major source of change orders. The rub: if it's not on the drawings, the GC will not claim responsibility. Remember, however, that the GC should be absolutely responsible for obtaining the necessary permits for the job. This includes filing your plans and specs with the city for review and approval.

## Decide Upon a Payment Schedule

If your partnership with a GC is a waltz, and contract documents the choreography, then payment provides the music. Your contract should specify the schedule of payment. Nothing will undermine a job more than misunderstandings about money. If payment is expected on a certain date, don't expect workers to show up if you miss it. Commit to what you can do. The most desirable arrangement is progressive payment on a phase-completion basis. Use benchmarks, like pouring the foundation or rocking up the walls, to close the end of a phase. Agree on the amount of each payment beforehand. It's a great incentive to push the GC through each phase.

Monthly payments are an alternative, but this setup commands more attention to accounting and is less of an incentive. A request for bi-weekly payments does not bode well—it may indicate that the GC doesn't have the capital to run the job properly. In any case, if you don't want to be dropped, keep the music going. Be sure to hold on to retention—ten percent of the money owed on the job—until all punch list items have been completed and all warranties, manuals, etc. have been handed over.

With many mortgage agreements mandating higher interest charges during construction, penalties charged for not making move-in deadlines and the cost of renting space elsewhere, you might find a bust schedule more painful than a bust budget. Use incentives to motivate the GC to keep costs low and to make schedule. Bonuses go over much better than "damages clauses" that threaten penalties for blowing a deadline. Most GCs won't go for them, and anyway, they're almost impossible to enforce.

## TIE UP LOOSE ENDS

Punch list items are loose ends such as missing fixtures, polishing finishes and fine-tuning systems. Left hanging, the punch list and warranties are things that will keep your GC in your life much longer than either of you care for. Spell out the procedure and schedule for generating, attacking and revisiting punch list issues. A good GC doesn't need to be handheld through the process, but it should be clear from the outset who's doing what. And give him a break if not everything is perfect at first. Be patient.

Most of the warranties passed on by the GC are from the subs and manufacturers. Many GCs will offer an umbrella warranty. Ideally you want to have one contact person if things go wrong. Some firms have a computerized database for tracking customer warranties. Warranties can range from one year on parts and labor for equipment to ten years on workmanship items. Any decent GC will be attentive to past clients long into the future. No warranty should kick in until the day the certificate of occupation or completion is issued by the city or municipality.

## COVER YOUR BACK

Remember, success is as much about being thorough in your research and preparation as it is about personal chemistry and communication. All this can be wrapped up in a tidy little standard AIA (American Institute of Architects) contract with the usual qualifications attached: plans and specs, the GC's bid proposal, terms and conditions, co-op regulations and anything else you want to include.

### TIPS FOR A PAINLESS JOB

✧ Make contract documents as detailed, clear and complete as possible.
✧ Establish good chemistry and communication between yourself, the GC and the architect.
✧ Have GC hold weekly site meetings with subcontractors.
✧ Make payments on schedule.
✧ Trust the contractor and keep a sense of humor.

## CONTRACTORS & BUILDERS

**3-D Construction Inc./**          4.5     4     4.5     4.5
**3-D Laboratory Inc.**
268 Water Street, New York, NY  10038
(212) 791 - 7070

*Residential and commercial general contracting, construction management*

For old-fashioned craftsmanship on a fast-track schedule, this full-service general contracting firm that provides construction services for commercial and residential clients in prime Manhattan neighborhoods is tough to beat. 3-D works on Park Avenue apartment renovations, Chelsea loft conversions and similar residential jobs with a challenging level of detail throughout the metro area. In addition, for a retainer, the firm also offers preplanning project assistance in site selection, lease negotiation, cost estimation and value engineering. With design assistance capabilities, 3-D likes to get on-board projects early in order to help steer them in the right direction, and clients can't speak highly enough about the results down the road.

The consensus is that the people from 3-D Construction are organized, talented and "true to their word." While most clients are particularly pleased with the staff's professionalism and upbeat attitude, one recounts knocking heads to get the job done to satisfaction. References do talk about the superb quality and the wide-ranging work 3-D does, from artfully laid stonework to creating custom fixtures and furniture, while Architectural millwork, tile and metalwork remain in-house specialties. We're even told 3-D offers a product line that includes medicine chests, stylized radiators and Forster Swiss-fabricated metal kitchens. While clients highly recommend the 3-D experience, they cite the cost can occasionally veer to another dimension.

*"Personable, well-educated and exacting artisans." "They have a very positive, can-do attitude, but are quite expensive." "3-D is always my first choice in any of our projects. The confidence I have in them has yet to be matched." "The company is meticulous about running a clean, efficient site and keeps excellent records, minutes, etc." "My job with another contractor was such a fiasco I couldn't bear to look at it. I brought in 3-D and told them 'I am leaving and not coming back until everything is fixed.' Needless to say I came back soon thereafter and was floored. Now I can't keep my eyes of my apartment."*

**A.E. Greyson & Company**          5     4.5     4     5
180 Varick Street, New York, NY  10014
(212) 337 - 0929

*High-end residential and commercial general contracting*

This widely-published, widely-accomplished large general contractor has undertaken high-end residential and commercial projects in Manhattan for seven years. Principal Joseph Kusnick is an architect by training, so he brings an aesthetic sensibility and interest to his work that clients find comforting and architects find refreshing. The firm takes on projects as large as $10 million—however, Kusnick will not pass up smaller projects that are architecturally significant or represent inspired, challenging design. Clients characterize the quality of A.E. Greyson's work as excellent, and say the cabinetry stands out.

Clients tell us that Kusnick is sweet, very honest and organized. They were "thrilled" at the ease with which jobs progressed, and say the firm does a "super" job at pulling off complex projects "without a hitch." Consistent, knowledgeable on-site management ensures such outstanding results, cementing A.E. Greyson's reputation for meeting deadlines and budgets. We're told the firm is willing to return years later for projects of all sizes to keep clients happy. For this caliber of work, pricing is deemed competitive by Kusnick's well-heeled clients.

*"I would use him again in a minute." "He was dependable, honest and sincere in his predictions of how long things would take to complete." "Things were always under control. There were no surprises." "Great! Took over where other guy didn't finish and was happy to fix whatever wasn't correct. Very detail-oriented." "Very willing to work with you. Very personable. He still came over five years later to do small jobs."*

## ABR Construction                                          3      3      4      4
49 West 46th Street, 5th Floor, New York, NY  10036
(212) 997 - 3840

*Residential general contracting, heavy construction*

Clients turn to ABR for complex gut renovations in New York City and Connecticut on mostly residential projects that require both heavy and precise construction. A professional design shop, consisting of staff engineers and certified architects (among which principal Bolek Ryzinski is one) has the engineering and design capacity to save a crumbling historic brownstone in the West Village or combine a duplex on the Upper East Side. Equally experienced in roofing, masonry, steel and exterior restoration as in historical detail, millwork and moldings, this firm of 30 to 40 employees includes in-house plasterers, painters and carpenters.

*"Honest, helpful, fair, really knows what they're doing." "Decent man. If there are mistakes he'll fix them at no extra cost."*

## Alliance Builders Corp.                                   4.5    4      4.5    5
236 West 26th Street, New York, NY  10001
(212) 463 - 9229

*Residential and commercial general contracting*

High praise for the forward-thinking artisans of Alliance Builders is what we hear from clients and industry pros, who have been recommending this firm to friends and colleagues for years. Performing mostly commercial and high-end residential general contracting, Alliance takes work through architects. The low-key Larry Kahn has been described as dependable, reliable, ethical, and brings an art background as well as 25 years of building experience to the table. The vast majority of clients tell us that Kahn really cares about the work he does and that the firm's scrupulous follow-through results in excellent fit and finish. Weekly meetings, clients report, kept them informed every step of the way.

With in-house people to engineer drawings, Alliance also offers pre-construction service to complement their construction management. Kahn and crew work to clarify the architect's intent in order to identify potential holes in the plans that are inevitable between concept and execution. In this capacity, Alliance presents a firmer, if somewhat on the surface, more expensive estimate that clients appreciate.

*"Very good quality. Detail oriented. Cares about what he does and does a good job." "Low-key open handed approach to estimating process. Came about it in a realistic way. No surprises or questions." "Handled relationship with the neighborhood very well. One old lady had nothing to do but complain every day so to satisfy her, they built a bird-bath." "No part of the job I thought there was something else they could have done." "Definitely five stars! Would certainly use him again."*

| | Quality | Cost | Value | Recommend? |
|---|---|---|---|---|
| | ➕ | $ | ◆ | ★ |

## ARC Interiors
3.5  3  5  5

128 East Broadway, P.O. Box 870, New York, NY  10002
(212) 226 - 9209

*Residential general contracting, millwork and cabinetry*

In select Brooklyn neighborhoods and Manhattan, references familiar with the professionalism of ARC will wait for this restoration and renovation general contractor to free up before considering anyone else.  We hear that principal Gary Wishart is calm, straightforward and engaging, and that his attention to detail and ability to visualize what the customer wants results in "ecstatic" reactions.  The firm employs a trustworthy stable of subcontractors, and specializes in providing custom millwork and kitchen cabinetry described as "precisely and beautifully" finished.  ARC concentrates on jobs that typically range from $300,000 to just under a $1,000,000, but will take smaller bathroom and kitchen remodels if the job strikes a cord.

During the job and years after, we hear Wishart is wholly accommodating and always on hand.  Clients have included prominent area hotels, celebrities and interior design firms.  For a cost that's never the highest or lowest, clients say the final product is always "so much nicer than I imagined."

*"Gary really stayed on top of things." "Nice guys, extremely conscientious. I miss them coming in the morning." "Gary has an excellent eye for detail, good taste and a good personality." "I really trust Gary.  When he says it's going to look good, it'll look good." "One of the most professional contractors we've worked with.  Organized, on-time, and genuine."*

## Arthur H. Jussel Inc.
4.5  3.5  5  5

227 West 29th Street, New York, NY  10001
(212) 239 - 6860

*Residential general contracting*

Lauded by clients and industry vets as thorough, complete, and extremely professional, this firm, helmed by Arthur Jussel, has been doing high-end residential contracting jobs for a predominantly Upper East Side clientele for more than a quarter of a century.  We hear the consistency of their work is enhanced by strong, long-lasting relationships with a talented group of subcontractors.  Designers and clients alike are effusive about Jussel's integrity and professionalism.  We hear he and his team plan, prepare and execute all projects with the highest quality and care, precision and timeliness, assembling each project team with superior skilled persons who provide leadership and outstanding client and consultant support.  Architects remark working with Jussel makes life easy.  He asks the right questions and addresses issues before they walk on site.  Designers even trust him with their own apartment renovations.

The firm undertakes a wide range of jobs, from $75,000 bathroom remodels to intimidating gut renovations that run into the millions of dollars, but retains a focus on quality regardless of a project's scope, according to references.  Like quality, not all contractors are created equal, therefore Jussel's services come at a premium, but client's insist it's worth every penny, because "Arthur is heads above the rest."

| | Quality | Cost | Value | Recommend? |
|---|---|---|---|---|
| | ✚ | $ | ◆ | ★ |

*"Arthur Jussel sets the tone for his managers—well educated and intelligent." "Their architects love them, their clients love them, their subcontractors love them." "Always honest and forthright & upfront—a big advantage in a contractor." "Runs a tight ship. Doesn't make a lot of mistakes." "Arthur Jussel is a wonderful man. His staff and sub-contractors clearly respect him. Each person is professional and caring in their attitude toward the client and the task they perform." "Always get a bid from Arthur."*

## Bauhaus Construction Corp.

**4.5    4    4.5    4.5**

347 Fifth Avenue, Suite 1304, New York, NY 10016
(212) 779 - 3450   www.bauhausny.com
*Residential and commercial general contracting*

There's "no muss and no fuss" with this full-service construction management and general contracting firm in business since 1989. Their thoroughly professional execution has been tapped by internationally-acclaimed architects, blue-chip private clients and high-profile retailers. Based in New York and working throughout the country, Bauhaus collaborates in residential projects that tend to be large, and often exploit its management's expert knowledge of commercial applications. Clients tell us the firm's work, performed mostly by a strong and dependable group of subcontractors who carry out plans with strict precision, measures at the highest quality. Despite the Bauhaus commercial bent, private clients say they don't feel distanced from the company, remarking that it responds very well to their more specific, residential needs. They tell us if something is wrong "the boys at Bauhaus" fix it.

*"Museum-quality work. Pure class!" "Top of the heap." "Great, Bauhaus talks the talk and walks the walk." "Honest and honorable. One of the best."*

## Beech Associates

**3    3.5    3.5    3.5**

145 East 94th Street, New York, NY 10128
(212) 876 - 6554   www.beechassociates.com
*General contracting and kitchen design*

Kitchens are the main attraction at Beech Associates, a design/builder of interior residential renovation. The company tackles projects consisting of one room to a multi-million dollar apartment. Since the mid-sixties, Raymond Beech has worked for owners in the top buildings in New York City, as well as on properties in Westchester and Long Island. Clients tell us his professionalism, dedication to the job, responsiveness and soft-spoken, honest nature are hard to beat. Beech's kitchens feature clean lines and top-quality materials, often showcasing unique space-saving elements. A New Jersey workroom produces the firm's custom cabinetry.

Clients commend this company's work, noting that attention to detail helps set it apart. However, some say the oversight isn't what it once was, and the quality since Raymond Beech has played a less active roll in day-to-day operations is not the same. KB1990.

*"Ray is a real professional. Goes the extra mile." "High quality, very good guys, one step up from a good kitchen contractor." "The quality has disappeared." "He is a gentleman and his staff is excellent. As much attention is paid to detail as quality."*

## Bel Air Interiors

**3.5    3    4.5    4.5**

61 Java Street, Greenpoint, NY 11222
(718) 389 - 2300
*General contracting, millwork*

A family-run general contracting firm for 40 years, references say they have never seen anything like Bel Air's architectural woodwork. The firm creates custom libraries, kitchens, built-in units and even mahogany doors. Their work ranges

| | Quality | Cost | Value | Recommend? |
|---|---|---|---|---|
| | ✚ | $ | ◆ | ★ |

from renovating small bathrooms to entire brownstones, with budgets from $30,000 topping $600,000. Much work brings them to celebrated buildings on the Upper East Side, and they are known to occasionally make it to the Hamptons.

Customers find Michael Abatiello a "nice, gentle guy," and he and his son a joy to work with. Nearly everything is done in-house, from carpentry to electrical, always a plus they say. Bel Air's staff is helpful, professional, experienced, respects building hours and keeps clean. While it's said Bel Air produces a finish product that is "unparalleled," they do it for a price that's right down the line.

*"They've done six to seven apartments in my building. One better after the other." "An excellent company for any job." "Great medium sized GC. The best I've used in 25 years." "They produce such top-notch woodwork, it's like old-world."*

### Bernsohn & Fetner      5    5    4    5
625 West 51st Street, New York, NY 10019
(212) 315 - 4330 www.bfbuilding.com
*Residential and commercial general contracting, construction management*

Over the course of 17-plus years, Bernsohn & Fetner has proven themselves to an A-list roster of clients and industry insiders to deliver the finest work available when time is of the essence. The bulk of the company's work is large, very high-end, very custom Manhattan residential projects, occasionally undertaking unique smaller projects and notable corporate and retail build-outs. B&F is called upon exclusively by some of the city's most distinguished buildings for renovation work and on-going maintenance.

References report B&F heads projects with go-get-em, efficient supervision, and that the firm's affable, easygoing principals offer hands-on assistance in all undertakings. We hear the B&F team sees all projects through to the end, leaving no detail outstanding. While this firm subcontracts much of its work, clients remark the workmanship of these trades is "amazing." Top decorators often recommend the firm to many of their clients. While some follow the advice, others deem the "wonderful" experience of Bernsohn & Fetner lacking pricing options, and ultimately too expensive.

*"They deliver museum quality." "We can give them the work and not have to worry about them getting it done, and done right." "This is the very best at top, top prices." "Very blunt about cost." "Few change orders." "Big outfit, a competitor on highest possible tier." "Very nice. Randy is low key." "They have to do good work, their clients demand it."*

### Bohn Fiore Inc.      4    3.5    4.5    4.5
30 West 26th Street, New York, NY 10010
(212) 929 - 3610 www.bohnfiore.com
*Residential and commercial general contracting*

It is reported this professional, organized, details-oriented ship "makes the job easier" for design professionals and clients alike. Established by Richard Fiore and his son 15 years ago, they currently employ 40 professionals and offer general contracting and construction management services for a broad array of projects, regardless of size—from retail to commercial to landmark, a depth of knowledge that we hear translates particularly best for larger residential projects in New York City. Most references say that Fiore is an educated, "wonderful" gentleman whose soft touch and over 35 years of experience make the building process go smoothly. Whether navigating co-op boards or punch lists, it's said Fiore is easy to get a hold of and supportive. He often teams with his wife, interior designer Laura Bohn, a pairing clients applaud. The firm is very quality-conscious and delivers work as good as anyone, while pricing work fairly.

*"He doesn't let things fall through the cracks." "Top-notch guy, does what he says he'll do. I've spent a year trying to get co-op approval. If it wasn't for Richard, I'd go crazy." "Upper quality work. Good personality, good craftsmanship." "The site was organized, neat and clean."*

## Burr Graal Glass Inc.

54 Leonard Street, New York, NY 10013
(212) 925 - 1016

*General contracting*

With a masters in sculpting and experience in carpentry, principal Howard Burr brings more than a conceptual instinct about building his residential projects, he knows how to fashion beauty with his hands. This general contracting firm renovates loft to uptown penthouse projects that range from $100,000 to $800,000—and is pushing for even larger projects. Flexible and accommodating, we hear Burr and staff click with even the most demanding personalities. They are known to be transparent in their approach, breeding trust and team work. Arts-educated foreman and an in-house "anything-falls-through-the-cracks" crew round out the firm's assets. Burr also holds a business degree, and subs respect the firm's practices as much as the clients. We're told Burr prefers to walk through drawings with the architect beforehand to give everyone a greater picture of the project's proportion, instead of bidding on plans that are already over budget.

## Cayley Barrett Associates

4    3.5    4.5    5

238 East Grand Street, Fleetwood, NY 10552
(914) 667 - 4527

*General contracting and project management*

For a construction management firm that deals with all the issues before they become issues and provides an uncompromising level of quality, clients recommend Cayley Barrett. Specializing in interior renovation, architectural restoration, kitchens and baths, this firm does many projects without architects, working in a design/build capacity. Projects typically range between $65,000 bathrooms to $600,000 gut renovations and beyond. There are no true minimums, but if the budget is unrealistic for Cayley quality they will tell you.

References find principal Joy Licht a "pleasure" to work with, and "marvelous" at coming up with practical solutions. We hear that Licht always cheerfully available, whether it's the weekend or a call before bed to put a client's mind at ease. Sources point to the winning combination of Licht's crew (encompassing in-house carpenters and decorative finishers) and her "great" subs as key ingredients to the firm's success, as well the attitude if they got something wrong they'd fix it. Working in New York City area for eight years, Cayley Barrett knows the "ins and outs" of many prestigious Upper East Side buildings, and garners kudos from building supers. Licht specializes in celebrity clients. For workmanship delivered, clients say this firm is entirely fair-priced.

*"Joy is a delight to work with—reliable and always there." "All around a thoroughly professional operation. If Joy gave you a price it was all encompassing." "What ever it took, she did it." "Really vets the issues beforehand. Made good suggestions." "Complete renovation of a twelve room apartment. Things worked out just great." "Absolutely would use again."*

| | Quality | Cost | Value | Recommend? |
|---|---|---|---|---|
| | + | $ | ◆ | ★ |

## Chilmark Builders Inc.          4.5   4   5   5
1 Vanderbilt Avenue, Pleasantville, NY  10570
(914) 769 - 3416

*High-end residential and commercial general contracting*

Praised as a "finisher" by clients, Chilmark has garnered accolades as a high-end residential general contractor both inside and out of New York City.  The firm produces in-house millwork for current projects, which includes large-scale renovations and new construction in Westchester and Greenwich.   Chilmark is especially praised for its skill replicating "old-world" craftsmanship.  The firm also offers construction management and consulting services for commercial developers.  References cite the firm is small enough that owner John Ginsberg puts in a personal effort, yet large enough that a skilled and efficient management team also takes care of business.

Clients are impressed by the intelligent, professional and thoughtful approach Chilmark takes and are satisfied with the firm's dedicated execution of each project.  We hear Ginsberg is a personable "stand-up guy"—professional, honest and reliable.  His recommendations to improve the quality of the job both before and during the process, and the results these efforts are wholly appreciated by clients.  The work receives very high marks for quality, and we hear Chilmark is a preferred builder for many prominent New York architects.

*"Extremely professional.  Chilmark goes the extra mile." "Top of the line." "Got the sense that no matter what the cost, I was getting big quality." "Contributed a lot of ideas that enhanced the value of my house and the look I was going for." "Absolutely fantastic."*

## Clark Construction Corp.          4.5   4.5   4   4.5
117 Hudson Street, Suite 2, New York, NY  10013
(212) 219 - 1783

*High-end residential and commercial general contracting*

Sources tell us that everything about Chris Clark and Clark Construction is big—big projects, big budgets, big personality and big recommendations for what we are told is truly top-of-the-line, museum-quality work.  The firm has grown rapidly in reputation and scope, doing very high-profile residential and commercial work for clients in the New York City.  We hear that this committed professional, armed with a stable of A-list subcontractors, is worth every nickel he charges (and, we understand, the nickels add up quickly).

While some find Clark's personality charming, others say he "shouldn't believe all the press," especially architects, who aren't heartbroken that this company prefers to work directly with clients.  That seems to be perfectly fine with Clark's clients, who often go to this "classy operation" first when a complicated project demands unsurpassed finish work.

*"This is an extraordinary operation—BIG projects—it can handle anything." "Top of the heap." "Clark is the second coming of Donald Trump."*

## Collins Contracting Inc.          3   3   4   4.5
319 East 75th Street, Suite 2C, New York, NY  10021
(212) 734 - 7895  www.collinscontracting.com

*General contracting*

The solid reputation of this small, father-and-son-run general contracting firm is footed on 20 years of unreserved recommendations in and around the city.  Clients tell us that while the painting (including specialties like glazing and faux finishes) and millwork are done with expertise in-house, the firm also adds "honest and able" subcontractors to the mix.  Residential jobs range from $20,000 bath-

| | Quality | Cost | Value | Recommend? |
|---|---|---|---|---|
| | + | $ | ◆ | ★ |

room remodels to million-dollar penthouse guts. Collins will take any work that measures up to the company's professional practices, but purposefully limits its docket of new projects in order, we hear, to cater better to existing clients.

Michael Collins Jr. supervises many projects first hand, while it's said Senior provides thoughtful advice and informed recommendations from afar. Clients appreciate the family touch, which they characterize as both thorough and accountable, and call Collins and crew a treat to work with. Several clients who traveled while their renovations were under way said they returned home to be astounded at the degree of care taken with their personal belongings. It's this integrity, as well as Collins' level headed estimating, that "sets them apart."

*"What could have been a protracted and difficult project was instead a relatively simple and very successful renovation." "Great attention to detail. Gave me informed opinions."*

## Cupelli Construction                3.5    3    4.5    4.5
1800 Hunt Avenue, Bronx, NY 10462
(914) 879 - 0040
*Residential general contracting*

Cupelli Construction offers services for jobs ranging in size from a small renovation to an entire apartment gut to building a brand new home. Almost all projects are residential and in Manhattan, yet Cupelli does work in Westchester and Connecticut, including spec homes. He does most everything in-house, from high-end millwork to floors and framing. References tell us that working with the firm is pleasant and that principal John Cupelli earns high marks for being responsive to client needs, straightforward about money issues and neat and tidy.

*"John was always there for us. Callbacks are instantaneous." "He was cost-effective—no surprises, no additions." "He cares about the client."*

## D.H.E. Company Inc.                3.5    3.5    4    4
37 Canal Street, New York, NY 10002
(212) 228 - 8005
*Residential general contracting, substantial restoration*

Grown from a boutique operation into a medium-sized high-end residential specialist, D.H.E. has undertaken a broad spectrum of work for an equally diverse group of clients, who say the firm is enthusiastic and attentive to every detail. We're told D.H.E. is most attracted to jobs that involve substantial restoration such as townhouses. Sources call principal Douglas Cohen "a gentleman and a pleasure to work with." He's said to be a creative problem solver who communicates well with his clients, his crews and others. These skills combine to ensure construction proceeds smoothly and meets deadlines.

Some references particularly noted that D.H.E. works quickly through punch lists. In fact, the team of fine craftsman D.H.E. provides reportedly does such a good job, clients are willing to wait for the company to free up instead of turning to another contractor. D.H.E. has been in such high demand, however, these fans might be waiting for some time. While its fees may be a bit higher than the norm, clients say D.H.E. has a knack for cost shaving measures. The company's work has been featured in such publications as *Elle Decor* and *Martha Stewart Living*.

*"Cohen is a very organized, thorough, nice person." "I really enjoyed working with him." "The crew is unbelievable—always available to come and make adjustments." "Fine craftsmen for extraordinary value!"*

## Davenport Contracting Inc.                4    4    4    5
78 Harvard Street, Stamford, CT 06902
(203) 324 - 6308
*High-end residential general contracting*

| Quality | Cost | Value | Recommend? |
|---------|------|-------|------------|
| ✚ | $ | ◆ | ★ |

In the business of delighting customers, sources say Davenport Contracting has been taking care of business in residential construction projects for over 20 years. Davenport jobs typically approach seven figures, and consist of high-end apartment renovations and tear downs in New York City and surrounding Westchester and Connecticut suburbs, as well as showpiece restorations. We hear the thoughtful project management and strong execution characterizes the firm's projects, keeping the budget under control. Davenport professionals reportedly take a team approach in working with architects and others on a project, and everyone is kept well informed. Customers appreciate the partners' great attention to detail, follow-through and customer service.

Davenport boasts its own coveted mill shop, creating libraries or remaking kitchen cabinets with efficiency and expediency that contributes to what references say is the company's reputation for completing projects on time. For quality that flirts with the best out there, this firm provides excellent results.

*"These are excellent, wonderful people!" "Davenport is a very professional operation." "A thorough understanding of complex detail." "They finished a large project on time and the quality of work was very good." "Excellent communication with the client and subcontractors."*

### Designers Home Improvement Inc.    3.5    3    4.5    4.5

160 East 84th Street, Suite 3E, New York, NY 10028
(212) 249 - 5696

*Residential general contracting*

This small, six-year-old firm renovates kitchens and guts apartments in New York City, Southampton and Bridgehampton. Clients are reportedly very pleased with principal Charles Guarino's personal involvement from concept through completion. They say Guarino is a very creative problem solver, and we hear his devotion to each job shines through in the superb management of the details. Designers Home Improvement does in-house painting, carpentry and millwork, and it's reported his friendly crews "show responsibility" and are "always on the job." Clients say Guarino delivers a unique job on time and on (a usually moderate) budget, with very good quality. If all this "sounds too good to be true," clients say don't fret, "it's true."

*"Charles gets my highest recommendation. He combined two apartments and redid my baths and kitchen. We give him constant thanks for a job extremely well done." "What impressed me the most was anything that popped up these guys took care of in orderly fashion." "Very nice to deal with overall." "I could not ask anything more from a contractor."*

### DiSalvo Contracting Company Inc.    4    3    5    5

4214 Third Avenue, Brooklyn, NY 11232
(718) 832 - 9400

*Residential general contracting, wood and paint finishes*

Clients say they wouldn't change a thing about their experience with Vincent DiSalvo and his company, which has focused on the renovation and restoration of luxury residences in the New York area since 1977. Sources tell us the mid-sized, family-run company does a lot of work in prewar buildings, specializing in painting, carpentry and laying marble.  We hear that DiSalvo—a serious, personable man who demonstrates commitment to every job from the gate—is always "above the board" about any issue and never a salesman.  References report his crew is polite, very respectful and are good craftsman.  One client went so far to say DiSalvo is "probably fussier than I am."  That might explain why so many architects and building supers are DiSalvo converts.  They say DiSalvo delivers tremendous quality on time and on budget. Clients agree, noting DiSalvo standard fees reflect a value that is anything but.

*"Vinnie DiSalvo is a true gentleman.  Stays with issues until he gets them right."  "Easy to work with, honest, does incredible quality."  "When we put it out to bid, Vinnie picked up drawings from the architect himself. He was the only one who sat down with our architect and asked questions to make sure he understood everything and gave a good bid."  "Incredibly responsive. A year later he'll get a guy here in 20 minutes."  "Very eager to do things at his cost if he thinks it's the right thing to do. And Vinnie is not an aggressive biller."  "My super commented how thorough he is. He never had to pester him."  "Can't give him higher grades. We will absolutely use him again."*

## DSA Builders Inc.                     4    3.5    4.5    5
31 West 27th Street, 9th Floor, New York, NY  10001
(212) 684 - 4307
*Residential general contracting*

The two very professional partners of this full-service company specialize in high-end residential work, and customers tell us that they consistently deliver. DSA works primarily in substantial renovation on the Upper East Side, has a stable, talented group of subcontractors and office staff of three.  Projects are notable for their "meticulous" attention to detail, intelligent design and excellent craftsmanship (especially on cabinetry).  We hear the firm prepares a thorough "all-inclusive" bid, keeps clients up on project status, and is very accessible.

The partners, Mitchell Dennis and Carrie Salter, make an extremely effective and balanced team, the former executing well in the field and the latter meeting the needs of clients.  Salter also coordinates with the architects, her experience as a designer and senior project manager at a firm making relations painless, and in the case of younger architects, even instructive. Clients say they deliver an on time job of the highest quality, and are only getting better and busier.

*"Made me feel like I was their only client. Cared for my apartment as if it were their own."  "I highly recommend them. I may be the only person in New York City who has redone an apartment and still loves to say nice things about her contractor!"  "Carrie is the Ying to Dennis' Yang."  "Very good job, nice guys."*

## Duce Construction                     4    4    4    5
91 Moultrie Street, Brooklyn, NY  11222
(718) 383 - 3605   www.duceconstructioncorp.com
*Residential and commercial general contracting*

Sources are often "impressed them from the start" with Duce Construction, a high-end general contractor and construction management firm that comes equipped for soup to nuts design.  The firm is known for renovation, restoration and large addition projects in New York City, Westchester County, and the Hamptons where unearthing the right materials to blend and complement the existing structure makes all the difference. Generous with his time and friendly, principal Rory McCreesh is also known for being patient, accommodating and open to working within a client's budget.  We hear all the efforts McCreech puts in at the outset like talking to the clients and versing himself on all the ins and outs of the property and plans pay off in a "bid that was by far the most detailed" most clients had ever seen, and in long-lasting work of excellent quality.

Clients have also expressed delight with the team he brings to work on his projects, noting their responsiveness and skills. They remark the on-site job-foreman was an amazing trouble-shooter, who always makes suggestions to improve the project or tame the cost. We're even told Duce will create mock-ups in order to help a client understand something in the drawings better. Duce's expensive projects are fairly priced, and with work that has garnered accolades from prominent New York designers and been published in magazines such as *Architectural Digest* and *Metropolitan Home*, clients "only have the best things to say."

*"The effort he puts into do the littlest thing is incredible." "I strongly recommend Rory for the high-quality work and wonderful working relationship he develops with clients." "Before Rory even had the job he came in with an armada of all the trades. We meet everyone and heard what they had to offer. No one knew our 1928 stone Tudor better. Including us!" "Trades outstanding—magnificent at seamlessly matching the old to new. Especially with stone."*

## Edward R. Kraft Construction LLC 💼          4     3.5     4.5     4.5
1435 First Avenue, New York, NY 10021
(212) 988 - 5667   www.kraftnyc.com

*General contracting, millwork and finishes*

Edward Kraft has been involved in high-end interior renovations in New York City since 1985. His 22-person firm focuses on gut renovations of apartments in pre-war and postwar high-rise buildings. He is also experienced with major townhouse renovations, and specializes in providing design consultation services for millwork. Custom doors, cabinets and architectural woodwork are manufactured exclusively for all his projects in an Upper East Side shop. We hear Kraft is a favorite of co-op board presidents, deemed one of the cleanest contractors around. If fact, Kraft's regimen of putting big fans in windows to suck out the dust has been adopted by savvy buildings as the regulatory norm.

Clients comment that Kraft is easy to work with, citing his agreeable personality and reliability. They say Kraft takes an active role in his jobs and can be reached anytime. In-house tradesmen can do everything from carpentry and plaster restoration to high-end spray finishes and stonework in bathrooms and kitchens. We hear the quality is "absolutely excellent" and prices reasonable. Still, it's the millwork that keeps them wowed.

*"Ed can turn rubble into a mansion." "Just goes to show that you don't have to pay insane dollars to get a great job done if you know who to call." "Antiqued doors that were really spectacular." "He still comes back after two years." "I was away 96 percent of the time and trusted him with everything." "Very good at what they do. Better than 90 percent of those who work in our Fifth Avenue building."*

## Euro Struct          3.5     3.5     4     3.5
33 South 8th Street, Brooklyn, NY 11211
(718) 599 - 0031

*General contracting*

High-end residential is the "bread and butter" of this large firm, and clients find the results a treat. Drawing on a staff of 50 that includes an in-house labor pool and a cabinetry shop, Euro Struct also accommodates commercial work. Architects tell us they appreciate Euro Struct's diligence and initiative. Its crews are honest, smart and thoughtful, and we hear "every guy along the chain takes ownership" for the project. Accommodating and amenable, this company "pays attention" and "questions everything" until its work is done correctly. However, for those planning to live-in through the renovation, we're warned Euro Struct's crews don't exactly like to tip toe around the space. While "more expensive than the average bear," clients say it's understandable considering the quality projects Euro Struct considers, and that in the company of other outstanding general contractors, the firm is very reasonably priced.

*"The guys are always thinking about how to do a better job." "Interested in getting it right. Will do things over again." "Hardly had to follow with a punch list." "Good for architects. Smart. Proactive. They see something that's not quite right they will question it." "Superlative."*

## European American Carpentry

|  | 4 | 4 | 4 | 4 |

72 Hawthorne, East Islip, NY 11730
(631) 581 - 0678

*High-end commercial and residential general contracting*

Clients swear this general contractor is more prompt and efficient than anyone else in New York City in delivering impeccable work. We're told European American can do anything, from swank Manhattan office spaces for production companies to Hampton residences or Upper East Side penthouses. This firm can execute work of any caliber, reportedly excelling at custom and reproduction carpentry work. Those who count on them say they deliver, and do things right the first time. In fact, word is they are "far superior than many number one designers at overseeing a job," which may explain why this firm is a favorite of top decorators and real estate agencies. A legacy of very pleased clients say they would recommend European American to anyone anytime.

*"Redid my whole office with a very short time lead." "Made the whole thing easy." "Nothing but good things to say."*

## Fort Hill Construction

|  | 5 | 5 | 4.5 | 5 |

200 Riverside Drive, Suite 1C, New York, NY 10025
(212) 665 - 1583   www.forthill.com

*High-end residential general contracting*

Clients are awed by the museum-quality work and ceaseless attention to detail of this 30-year-old construction management and general contracting firm. Headquartered in Los Angeles, with offices in Boston and New York, Fort Hill focuses mostly on residential work, regardless of location, from custom new home building to historic restoration that ranges from $100,000 to $8 million. This family-run business offers a range of services, including cost analysis prior to construction, project management and permit expediting. The New York office takes on a select number of projects each year and is said to have a particular understanding of the challenges of remodeling Manhattan apartments.

Original partners Jim Kweskin and George Peper still run the show with the same "perfectionism" they waged on their own home renovations, which were their first jobs decades ago. A job supervisor stays on the project until work is completed, then we hear Fort Hill's service department takes care of any small problems that might remain. References report the firm is professional and easy to work with, and can get along with even the most self-described "difficult" of clients—attributes that have helped win the firm a star-studded client list. Fort Hill might steer expensive projects, but its fee is modest compared to other five-star contractors.

*"Top-top notch. Among top four in NY history." "They are a wonderful group—organized, detail-oriented. We had a great project manager on site." "They would make great recommendations." "We liked Fort Hill so much that we are doing phase two of our project with them." "Have been around a long time. Does extremely good work."*

## Godwin Inc.                    4.5    3.5    5    5

215 East 58th Street, Suite 503, New York, NY 10022
(212) 308 - 0558

*Residential general contracting, kitchen and bath design, gut renovations*

At the conclusion of projects, we hear neighbors often end up bearing thankful gifts to this residential construction company's well-heeled clients for making the street or building more beautiful. Godwin Inc. is known to be capable and skillful in a wide variety of areas, specializing in kitchens, baths and gut renovations, and has served clients from Connecticut to Aspen to the UN Plaza. The firm partners with McIver-Morgan Interior Design to offer interior decorating services, and a number of top decorators in the city reportedly also call on Godwin. They say it's solid, on-site project management brings cost in "exactly as projected."

Customers are pleased with the intelligence, insight and initiative owner Steve Godwin brings to a job. Some say they find the consistency of Godwin's presence in the project a personal surprise. They tell us his suggestions lead to a better overall product, and his explanations invite them into the process. In the end sources say they learned a lot, and felt like they had a partner who cared how they were going to live and what their house would look like. References continue to be impressed with the results, remarking that even years after the job walking through their Godwin house wells a sense of "awe and pleasure."

*"Steve gives constant attention to detail, and has enough vision make his perfectionism cost effective." "Very professional and extremely talented." "I give Godwin a lot of credit for positively contributing to the job." "Someone from the contractor on the job at all times." "The job he did altered the course of my life. Wouldn't have embarked on the home if it weren't the success of the apartment project. I have to say I would never think of doing anything with anyone else." "The quality difference is so outstanding that friends who came to visit after the renovation thought I moved."*

## Graphic Builders Inc.              3.5    2.5    5    5

45 West Fort Lee Road, Bogota, NJ 07603
(201) 488 - 8638

*General contracting, custom cabinetry*

This small general contractor "thrills" clients with its dedication and attentiveness. We hear the firm is as comfortable and diligent taking care of odds and ends jobs as overseeing major renovations for its mostly Upper East Side clientele. Graphic's woodworking headlines its many talents. Clients are consistently impressed by the way owner Martin McElroy "doesn't just listen, but hears" their wishes. From the first meeting they tell us Martin and Co. could not have been more responsive and understanding, often presenting several different budget options for projects. From the back office to the painters, references report every one is friendly and eager to help. Their commitment to always make things right for each client, regardless of who's responsible, results in a chain of referrals. Graphic works hard to make its pricing agreeable, work we hear that really pays off for the client.

*"Martin and his staff are a pleasure. They are fair, honest and good." "GREAT woodworker." "Fixed things out of the contract just because he knew they should be done." "We had a tight deadline and large demands, and everyone at Graphic was patient and did their best to please us. They worked hard (early and weekends) to get everything accomplished." "I complained that the magnet on the keyboard drawer was too short, and they came to fix it the next day, a Saturday!" "A real find passed among friends."*

## Gryphon Construction
17 West 17th Street, New York, NY 10011
(212) 633 - 9586

**4    2.5    5    5**

*Residential general contracting*

We get nothing but glowing reports about Gryphon Construction and its approach to the contracting business, which we understand is very customer-focused, honest and straightforward. The size of the job is not as important to Gryphon as the assurance that the firm has gained a lifelong devotee. Gryphon apparently achieves that goal—since clients tell us they "walk on water." Owner Jerry Leiken takes only a selective number of larger jobs a year to insure they get his full personal attention. Clients say he is "amazingly helpful" in terms of ideas and problem solving. While the staff is limited, every job site has a foreman and is worked on by a consistent group of subcontractors, who we're told, possess a one on one old time craftsmanship appeal in which "they want you to love their work as much as they loved making it."

Clients tell us that the firm is serious about getting details exactly right. References recommend without qualification the firm's intelligence, integrity, skill and "all-around great guy way of working." With quality some compare to certain New York contracting titans, we hear Gryphon's costs are considerably less.

*"Best experience in the world, sent them tons of my friends." "I suggested they raise their prices, but they said they just wanted to make a decent living." "The best way to describe them is to say they make a situation inherently fraught with anxiety a pleasure." "Best hiring relationship I've ever had—exact opposite of nightmare you usually hear about. One example: the day they were to remove a fireplace mantle they called me in Vermont just to double-check." "I almost don't want them to leave. I feel like I'm going to mess up their great work."*

## Hanjo Contractors
104-31 Jamaica Avenue, Richmond Hill, NY 11418
(718) 805 - 4731

**4    3.5    4.5    5**

*General contracting, specialty millwork*

Hanjo Contractors is a reflection of its owner Hans Maricher—a thoughtful, sincere and gifted European woodworker. The firm helms complete Manhattan apartment renovations and kitchen and bath remodels, and specializes (of course) in custom millwork and cabinetry. Clients say working with Maricher and his helpful, likeable crew "is a blast." Maricher, who hails from a small farm in the province of Salzberg, Austria, keeps jobs running like glockenspiels via weekly meetings with the client and architect. We hear he always asks intelligent questions and gives good advice. Several references are also very impressed with the firm's followup after jobs are complete. Building managers also love Hanjo, and even co-op board presidents who live down the hall from construction were happy to see they kept things "neat as a pin." While Hanjo is neither the most or least expensive in its class, its estimates are as on target as its schedule.

*"It was fun how everyone worked together." "Honorable and fair—so accommodating and nice." "Definitely going back to them. Really does excellent work." "I was pregnant at the time so it was important Hans had everything done in time so I could move in with my newborn child. They managed everything just right so it was done on time." "Good at solving problems and asking questions." "Nine times out of ten I took their advice and they were right." "Hanjo is about to start their sixth job in our building. The super has confidence not only in the crew's competence but also in their ability to be responsible and sensitive to neighbors' concerns."*

| Quality | Cost | Value | Recommend? |
|---------|------|-------|------------|
| + | $ | ◆ | ★ |

## Hite Construction Inc.

| | | | |
|---|---|---|---|
| 3.5 | 3 | 4 | 4.5 |

700F Lake Street, Ramsey, NJ 07446
(201) 934 - 8899

*Residential general contracting*

Reliability and responsibility are hallmarks of this smaller operation, sources say. Hite Construction has concentrated on interior renovations and restoration work in the New York metropolitan area for about nine years, and does design work itself for smaller projects. We hear the firm produces out of this world quality for real world clients. References commend John Hite for his trustworthy and attentive nature, saying he is a professional who takes his job very seriously and is willing to go the extra mile. One customer was amazed by Hite's skill in finishing an architectural plan abandoned by the original architect. Clients also appreciate the flexibility and respect he and the crews of the subs he partners with show, particularly when renovating a home that is still occupied by a family.

We're told either Hite or a field supervisor is on every site daily, and overall there are always four layers of supervision—a job foreman, sub supers, a project manager and the owner himself. Clients enjoy the hands-on devotion of Hite, who they say walks them through material selection. The resultant excellent workmanship and positive experience at a manageable price has set the stage for customers to call on this firm for multiple projects.

*"John has done three projects with me and each has been absolutely great." "One hundred percent trustworthy. Good manager in terms of paperwork." "I was very impressed with the time he took to help me choose plumbing fixtures and marble." "He was also great around my three kids." "Nice, trustworthy, a really good guy." "John's help and input throughout was invaluable."*

## Horacio Mercado Associates

| | | | |
|---|---|---|---|
| 3 | 3 | 4 | 4 |

345 West 22nd Street, New York, NY 10011
(212) 929 - 4117

*General contracting and restoration*

This firm has undertaken restorations, landmark work and custom jobs for private clients in notable New York City apartment buildings and apartment public spaces, for over a decade. Whether its a smaller job or a $2 million project, the firm is capable of performing at the level demanded by any budget. Much of its work is on the Upper West Side. Owner Horacio Mercado maintains his own millwork shop that specializes in reproducing windows, doors and architectural features for prewar buildings. With a degree in architecture, we hear Mercado brings a developed design sense that offers practical solutions to his projects. Customers feel that Horacio could be charging more for the "incredible work," but that there is no price to be put on Horacio's comforting personality and dedication.

*"I spent every waking moment with Horatio." "If it wasn't for him I would have had a nervous breakdown."*

## ICI Construction Corp.

| 4 | 3 | 5 | 4 |

38-17 54th Street, Woodside, NY 11377
(718) 335 - 1893
*General residential contracting*

Clients give ICI, a general contractor known for accommodating Park Avenue residents, the highest marks "in every regard." Owner Stephen Moy is said to be extremely helpful, charming and open. We're told Moy is calm under pressure, meticulous, a good problem solver and willing to go the extra mile for his clients. Many rave about his honesty and reliability. Clients say Moy engages each job with entire armies of hardworking craftsmen, who are lauded as exceptionally neat, even in the midst of demolition. Satisfied sources told us the cost was very reasonable and the high-end work a great value.

*"Unflappable! If he doesn't know how to do it, he'll figure it out soon thereafter, and do it well." "Hands down the best ever. You would trust your children with him." "Extremely generous by nature." "Steve is an attentive, focused, responsive individual. A pleasure to work with."*

## Integkral Design & Construction LLC

| 3.5 | 3 | 4.5 | 5 |

26 John Street, Derby, CT 06418
(203) 735 - 2798   www.integkral.com
*Residential general contracting and design/build services*

Careful planning, strong management and exacting standards are IntegKral to this small firm's success, references report. The firm takes on all interior renovation work, from small Park Avenue apartments to monster guts in Westchester and Greenwich, interspersing larger jobs with little ones, like bathroom remodels. Principal George Kral, who himself has a master's degree in architecture, works with a client's favored architect or can facilitate design/build services, and we hear client's often implement the agreeable and knowledgeable Kral's creative suggestions throughout the job. They tell us the firm is dependable and highly responsive, in part because someone (if not Kral) is on-site every single day to move the project along, and in part because they add calls to Kral are literally responded to instantaneously, day or night, weekends, whatever. We hear that Kral and his professional staff are extremely pleasant and very accommodating of clients' needs, as well as those of their neighbors, an attribute that impresses building management. Clients say they're very pleased with the timeliness and quality of work of Integkral, and would use the evenly priced firm again in a flash.

*"Nice beyond description—I loved working with George." "Very reliable." "Start to finish, I had a purely pleasant experience" "We have found Integkral to be very responsive, on time and accurate in estimating costs." "Very careful planners. Super quality." "It's George's attentiveness that keeps things on track."*

## Interior Management Inc.

| 4.5 | 4.5 | 4 | 5 |

403 East 62nd Street, New York, NY 10021
(212) 750 - 3700
*Residential general contracting*

As much as the finished product, the relationship with this father-son general contractor is something that clients say they will "always treasure." Interior management specializes in renovating traditional Manhattan residences that boast heavy plaster molding and classic detail. They undertake about ten projects a year, settling between $500,000 and $2.5 million, and predominately on the Upper East Side. The company can do a big job without an architect, and also provides decorating services (their style, we hear, however, may be a bit over the top.) Most patrons found the firm helpful, highly skilled, speedy and extraordinarily tidy. They say the management and the trades people are all delightful to work with, especially the company's principals.

Clients call son Mark Martinez—who has picked up the reins from his well-liked father Al—"a rising star" in the field and a "can do" terrific guy who gets the job done with professionalism and a real knowledge of the whole renovation and construction process. Newly renovated homes are turned over in "move-in condition" (Interior Management will even move in furniture and make beds), and clients are welcomed with champagne and flowers. We hear clients' concerns after the move-in are addressed by a full-time maintenance staff. In no small part because jobs already cost a chunk of change, there's no nickel and diming at Interior Management, clients say, only jobs executed with a skill and talent level that was "beyond any other in their field."

*"The only contractor who even comes close to doing what he says he will do." "Very expensive but worth it. They can get anything done." "They were so helpful, above and beyond the call." "The job site was always clean enough to eat off the floor." "I can't say enough to express the wonderful experience I had with Al." "We call him 'Mr. No Problem'—whenever there is an issue, he says 'no problem.'" "On the design side, however, there are one too many layers of trim and a bit too much gold leaf." "We were lucky to work with Interior Management. They have a positive attitude, amazing follow through, and friendly management." "Finished the work in record breaking time. I was so impressed with every aspect of the company and staff."*

## Izzo Contractors        3    2.5    4    4.5
80 Morningside Drive, New York, NY 10027
(212) 662 - 5695

*Residential general contracting*

Clients express satisfaction beyond expectations with the level of service and quality of work performed by this third-generation general contracting firm, a New York fixture since 1944. Described as down-to-earth, the firm's professionals respond quickly and are attentive to clients' needs. Izzo handles both large and small jobs for clients, with an emphasis on high-end interiors. About 90 percent of the company's work is in Manhattan, although it does take on choice Westchester and Long Island projects. We're told that Izzo drives the pace of its jobs with a team of 45 to 50 people, who do in-house custom cabinets, woodworking, tile, masonry, painting and wallpapering. The company's high-quality work is said to come at a good price.

*"Michael is very responsive, never hesitates to send a worker over for small jobs." "They renewed my faith in general contractors." "A fabulous contractor, very accommodating." "The tile work was very good and the crown molding work outstanding."*

## J.E. O'Donnell Construction Company Inc.    3.5    3    4    4.5
173 Waterside Avenue, Northport, NY 11768
(631) 754 - 1144

*General contracting*

Clients tell us this Northport-based contractor, who works in Manhattan, Long Island and Connecticut, does large and small projects with grace and good humor. Focusing on high-end residential interiors, we hear O'Donnell has an affinity for classic or traditional styles, and is experienced in historical renovations (he recently completed a 200-year-old Brooklyn brownstone renovation). Customers appreciate Jim O'Donnell's easygoing, frank demeanor and flexibility and are genuinely pleased with his high-quality work. We hear these results are due to O'Donnell's hands-on approach, from estimating everything himself to strapping tools on when necessary—just don't expect to be drowned in paperwork. He's said to be a very good liaison between high-end architects and demanding clients, and values each relationship. O'Donnell employs in-house master carpenters, plasterers, and tile and marble installers. The firm produces classic quality at mid-range prices.

*"Jim O'Donnell is a very talented, hard working individual. We were very pleased with the outcome of his excellent work." "Takes direction very well. Great personality. Doesn't fly off the handle." "He's very responsive. We had lightning strike our house and damage our chimney and he came right over."*

## J&J Carpentry & General Construction Corp.

|       | Quality | Cost | Value | Recommend? |
|-------|---------|------|-------|------------|
|       | 4       | 3.5  | 4.5   | 4.5        |

14 Madison Street, Newark, NJ  07105
(973) 578 - 2622

*General contracting and millwork*

J&J Carpentry is known as a secret source for old-world craftsmanship by some of the very best architects in New York.  This 30-year-old company can be found on residential remodeling projects and new home construction, and we hear produces highly touted cabinetry and millwork.  Jobs range from $50,000 to $1.2 million in Manhattan and New Jersey.  The firm also undertakes some commercial work, including assignments in Donald Trump's buildings.  The lead J in this outfit is John Sintra, who clients say is principled, calm and collected on the job and an overall "dream to work with."  Clients tell us the firm succeeds in providing excellent customer service, and for those having worked with the firm on multiple projects (which are many), we hear it is always "a repeat performance."

*"They are astounding. My apartment has become a show place in our building." "Very good people. Do great work. And I'm not even related to them!" "Knows how to get it done at a great price.  Unflappable."*

## John Petrocelli

|       | Quality | Cost | Value | Recommend? |
|-------|---------|------|-------|------------|
|       | 4       | 3    | 5     | 5          |

7E Abbott Avenue, Palisades, NJ  07650
(201) 945 - 5600

*Residential general contracting*

Clients say it doesn't get any better than John Petrocelli Construction, which offers general contracting services ranging from small jobs to gut renovations. Petrocelli splits work between Manhattan and New Jersey.  In-house specialties include tile work, millwork, painting and carpentry.  Renovators tell us this firm exhibits a "work ethic rarely seen today" on projects both large and small, produces outstanding workmanship and insures everything comes in on time and within budget.  They call Petrocelli and crew professional, meticulous, extremely honest and overall a pleasure to work with.  Clients like Petrocelli so much we hear they have never even felt the need to even consider other contractors.  We also hear you won't have to break the bank to experience a Petrocelli project.

*"The highest level of integrity." "I have worked with John Petrocelli Construction on two major gut renovations of prewar apartments in New York City in the last five years. Suffice it to say, I am one of the few people in the city who enjoyed this process and that is due, in large part to John and his crew." "They all take pride in what they do.  John was extremely responsive and reliable.  We highly recommend him."  "The crew did everything possible to make us comfortable and respect our privacy—as we lived in the apartment during the project."*

| | Quality | Cost | Value | Recommend? |
|---|---|---|---|---|
| | + | $ | ◆ | ★ |

## Larson Construction Corp.

**5  4.5  4.5  5**

36 Cooper Square, New York, NY  10003
(212) 420 - 1544

*Residential, retail and commercial general contracting and design/build services*

A veteran of over a quarter century of high-end New York residential, gallery, corporate and retail construction, clients tell us Alfred Larson is "true partner" in the building process.  Larson's background is in design and fine art, and his mostly residential clientele includes a number of celebrities and top-name decorators who use him for their own homes.  We hear he chooses clients carefully, and only works on a few large-scale jobs per year (of course he will do smaller jobs for existing clients.)  References tell us Larson loves to work closely with clients and promotes a pleasant, congenial atmosphere.  They say the firm prides itself on being flexible and meeting customers' needs.  Examples include facilitating design/build services and counseling clients on the purchase of materials.  When Larson isn't present on-site—a rarity we're told—a full-time project supervisor can respond quickly to any detail.  We hear his foremen are excellent and the subcontractors marvelous.  Some references say his work is museum quality and all consider it worth ever penny.

*"He has a hands-on approach.  Works with discretion and flexibility." "Very good guy, everybody loves Fred." "He was very involved. Went shopping with me for hardware and marble. Even designed a closet space for me." "Subs very neat and tidy. The craftsmanship was excellent."*

## Lennie Construction Corp.

**4  4  4  4**

458 81st Street, Brooklyn, NY  11209
(718) 833 - 9634  www.lennieconstruction.com

*Residential general contracting*

With a reputation for expert plasterwork, Lennie Construction has built and renovated high-end residences in and around New York City for over thirty years.  Principal Joe Leone and his small staff undertake jobs in a wide range of sizes, from $25,000 to $5 million, and we hear competes with some of the best contractors in the city.  The majority of references are impressed by the firm's speed and reliability, and say Leone is quite accommodating, while others were "not overwhelmed."  Lennie Construction's work has appeared in major design publications, not a surprise to clients, who label it as outstanding.

*"Joe is fast, really fast. The quality is there and it looks great."*

## Lico Contracting Inc.

**5  4  5  4.5**

29-10 20th Avenue, Astoria, NY  11105
(718) 932 - 8300

*High-end residential general contracting*

Clients are "thrilled" with this full service family-owned firm.  With 45 years in the business, Lico has built a reputation as one of the top contractors in the city.  The firm performs mainly large gut renovation projects in Manhattan, Long Island and Greenwich for a roster of blue-chip clients in a diplomatic and timely manner. A "very helpful" staff upwards of 85 performs millwork, tiling and plumbing services in-house, and produces what we hear are beautiful shop drawings.  Industry sources say Lico has good relationships with the best subcontractors in New York City.

We're told that principal Rich Bruno and his professionals aim for, and deliver, "impeccable" customer service.  Clients, co-op staff, management and architects are all clearly impressed.  Many clients report that Lico's workers take care with details and communicate well about all aspects of a project.  Staff managers are always on site, orchestrating what clients deem Lico's museum-quality work.  Dollar for dollar, they tell us Lico stacks up well against the cities best—a tall order of both service and dollars.

*"Mindful of everything that involves the clients and their home comfort." "Bruno is the Daniel Boulud of contractors." "Strives for strong customer service." "We have had them work on two of our apartments and they have always been extremely professional, conscientious, fair and, most importantly, very proud of what they do."*

## Mastercraft Carpentry & Renovating  3  3  4  4
48 Bayview Avenue, Amityville, NY 11701
(631) 691 - 0630

*General contracting and renovations*

This small, decade-old general contracting firm earns compliments for its low-key work style, dependability and responsiveness to clients. Mastercraft specializes in gutting and renovating upscale apartments in Manhattan and homes in Westchester County and Long Island. The firm has also completed a number of commercial projects. Clients tell us Mastercraft's professionals are pleasant and easygoing. Satisfied customers feel they get their money's worth and say they would refer Mastercraft to others.

*"We were very happy and recommend them."*

## Matilda Construction Inc.  4  3.5  4.5  5
641 West 59th Street, New York, NY 10019
(212) 586 - 5794

*Residential general contracting*

Tim McKenna of Matilda Construction comes recommended as a personable and accommodating man whose detailed, "very enthuiastic" approach to the construction business "doesn't leave a stone unturned" and delivers great results. He does large and small residential projects, working with members of his own dedicated crew, who we're told take great pride in their work and stick to the schedule. McKenna is described as a straightforward businessman who doesn't waste time or money and doesn't produce surprises. Clients comment on his keen eye for design, insightful recommendations and courage to disagree with a client when he thinks they are wrong. They tell us McKenna is honest about what his crew can and cannot do, and is not unwilling to share his great contacts to get the right person for the job. We hear McKenna always honors his responsibilites, whether its picking up a designers slack during the project or following up to repair another's work long after the close of a project himself. Word is the quality of Matilda's work, especially its millwork, plasterwork and wizardry with floor renovation, is really something to write home about without paying too much for the postage.

*"Tim has an answer for everything." "He has an incredible workshop where he keeps everything for old jobs. He came up with planks that matched our 100 year old floor for no extra cost." "He is more detail-oriented and demanding of quality than the architect. I was glad to have him on my team." "Exactly the same great service, whether its a $5,000 job or a $100,000 job." "Not only did he do great work, but I would be happy to have him as my dinner partner." "A superb value."*

## Maverick Builders Inc.  4.5  4  4.5  5
148 First Street, Jersey City, NJ 07302
(201) 610 - 9999

*Residential general contracting*

We're told this construction firm's stock in the industry is rising as it gains a reputation for extraordinary work. Maverick specializes in residential projects and generally works on mid-sized to large jobs in Manhattan, Long Island and Westchester County. Operating it's own mill shop, this self-described "power-house woodworker" garners many compliments. Client's tell us the top gun at Maverick, Michael Ostroff, is a charming gentleman. They say that Ostroff is

refreshingly straightforward in his approach to any problems that arise and never belittles them or their questions. We hear his crews are equally pleasant on the job, and Maverick's office staff returns calls promptly and handles administrative work with competence.

*"Well-crafted product. Terrific woodwork!" "A responsible professional to the highest degree." "This excellent wonderful company does museum-quality work."*

### Mead & Mikell Inc.                4.5    4.5    4    5
150 West 80th Street, Suite 8A, New York, NY 10024
(212) 874 - 3300   www.meadandmikell.com
*General contracting*

Whether its combining duplexes in Manhattan or adding to a historic Greek Revival in Westchester County, we hear Mead and Mickell "does everything just right." The small firm achieves the highest quality work, producing brilliant results for even the most complicated of projects. All references confirm that principal Pinkney Mikell is one of the nicest people they have ever met. They say he will readily admit if there is an issue and do whatever is necessary to fix the problem. Several clients who do not live in New York tell us they trust Mikell to make all the decisions for projects in their absence. Some, however, mention that his desire to "do it right" can string out the schedule. After a project is completed, clients still call on him to manage any subsequent issues.

The company attracts a dedicated group of top echelon subcontractors and architects. They praise Mikell's project management skills and respect the firm's extraordinary standard of work. Clients couldn't recommend Mead and Mikell more highly, particularly for "rich friends with lots of time."

*"The ultimate literate contractor." "Pinkney takes care of people." "Just the right person for a highly demanding client who loves the renovation process." "Loved him. Wants to get it perfect." "Many fewer problems than I would have expected given the scale of the renovation." "Couldn't be nicer. A real family man who understands life on the Upper East Side." "He only knows one way—exactly right."*

### Miller & Raved                    4.5    4.5    4    4
2 Hamilton Avenue, Room 207, New Rochelle, NY 10801
(914) 632 - 3555
*High-end general contracting*

References offering recommendations for Miller and Raved read like an all-star list of the design world. Mostly active in Manhattan, the 40-year-old "extremely reliable" company does residential and institutional jobs both nationally and internationally, from $500,000 apartment guts to $50 million hotel developments. Clients tell us Miller & Raved weave knowledge, staunch professionalism and planning expertise into a tapestry of overall outstanding project management. We also hear partners Charles Miller and Roy Raved are personable and gentlemanly, and exhibit intense dedication to each project. This is an expensive outfit, clients say, but there's no doubt it delivers "really exceptional quality."

*"If 100 is the highest quality, then they are 101!" "Really exceptional." "High end, great guys. Very reliable." "Their timing is terrific!" "They are smart and know exactly what to do and how to put it together."*

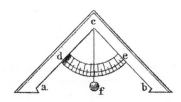

## Myriad Construction

| 4 | 3.5 | 4.5 | 4.5 |

497 Roung Lake Road, Monroe, NY  10950
(914) 774 - 7661

*General contracting, high-end finishes*

Among the myriad skills of this mostly institutional general contractor is doing high-end large-scale residential work for well-heeled Manhattanites.  We are told the firm and its subcontractors are dedicated to doing excellent work, and they're communicative, thoughtful and easy to work with.  Customers say Myriad's familiarity with coordinating complex commercial applications and applying specialty finishes proves a major asset when it comes to more ambitious residential projects.  They are particularly impressed by principal Eric Schonhur's ability to solve somewhat knotty technical and mechanical issues while still demonstrating an aesthetic sensibility.

*"Myriad especially shines in difficult situations.  They are used to doing very high-end stuff."*

## New York Craftsmen's Collective

| 3.5 | 2.5 | 4.5 | 4.5 |

13 Avenue A, New York, NY  10009
(212) 477 - 4477

*Residential and commercial general contracting*

The Collective is a group of expert craftsmen in a variety of home services fields who work together to produce results that thrill residential clients in Manhattan, Long Island, Westchester County and the Hamptons.  We hear the firm brings the idea of a "hands-on" general contractor to a whole new level.  The Collective is described as a hip, talented team that listens and communicates well with customers.  It is as adept performing a smaller apartment remodel as it is serious upstate restoration work, which has been likened to as the perfect showroom for acclaimed antiques.  Clients say principal Norman Sukkar has a great sense of humor and, like all the crew at the Collective, really cares about his projects.  He is known for being honest and able to resolve any issues to make sure clients are satisfied.  Construction hiccups are given immediate treatment, even if the cause was the occasional lapse in oversight.  We also hear Sukkar is the kind of guy a client "can call back five years after a job and he will come and fix or touch up gladly."

Architects appreciate the Collective's sensitivity to design while understanding "the big picture."  While we hear this firm can deliver a caliber of quality as high as any budget demands, it can also make a budget go farther than most.

*"Very professional company.  They finished on time and on budget and were great with any glitches."  "Guys who can take old walls and turn them into mirrors."  "He is a man of his word."  "They stay with it, and keep going back until they get in perfect."  "Clientele is high end. Norman's boys are used to that, so there is no worries leaving them alone."*

## O'Brien-Egan Construction Inc.

| 3.5 | 3 | 4.5 | 5 |

6121 Fieldston Road, Riverdale, NY  10471
(718) 796 - 5497

*General contracting and renovations*

Customers applaud this friendly and dependable family run business, which we're told treats each client like a new member of the family.  The firm does a wide variety of general contracting and renovation work, from painting and plasterwork to gutting apartments, working in Manhattan and Westchester County for thirteen years.  Sources count on O'Brien-Egan's prompt, neat service to meet not only their specifications, but their expectations.  These qualities have helped the firm become a regular in some area apartment buildings.

| Quality | Cost | Value | Recommend? |
| ✚ | $ | ◆ | ★ |

Client's say partners Martin O'Brien and Pat Egan are always courteous, willing to listen to concerns and try their best to accommodate them. Phone calls, it's said, are returned promptly. References trust O'Brien and Egan's good word, which they say is backed up with the help of an "incredibly talented" group of craftsmen, who add to the firm's honest and trustworthy reputation. Millwork seems an oft-cited specialty. The firm offers free on-site estimates. No matter what the size of the job or the budget clients say, this firm always provides fine quality work.

*"Martin is amazing" "Attentive, reliable, detail oriented, doesn't take the scope of work lightly." "Pat and his crew were perfectionists." "When we knocked out a wall in our apartment they searched our building and found an apartment that was putting in a new floor. They got the pieces of the old flooring from them to fit in where we knocked out the wall. Matched up beautifully." "They did such a spectacular job. I already have friends that are using them." "They were pleasant to have in my home and finished ahead of schedule."*

### O'Byrne Construction Services    3.5    3    4    4.5
52-49 73rd Street, Maspeth, NY 11378
(718) 429 - 7476
*General contracting*

Clients in Manhattan, Long Island, the Hamptons and Westchester are all delighted with the O'Byrne experience. Whether it's a bath remodel scheduled between two larger projects or a larger project like creating two duplexes in a 160 year-old townhouse, the small firm can handle everything, literally. O'Byrne's craftsmen paint, plaster, install millwork and even full kitchens. Clients say the firm is cooperative, skilled, professional and most of all, pleasant. They tell us principal James O'Byrne, who takes them through the project himself, is smart, quick and kind. We hear his practical sense is as keen as his aesthetic sense. Sources also say they are impressed with the caliber of O'Byrne's workers, who are always on site in force. The reliable O'Byrne team is reputed to wrap the job up on time and on budget, and come recommended by clients without hesitation.

*"Jim is a gentleman and so are his workers." "He did a gorgeous, perfect job." "Good man who does a good job at a good price." "Would definitely use him and his team again." "We had to have the job fast-tracked. My daughter was about to have a baby and was moving in from Boston. O'Byrne came through."*

### Peter Di Natale & Associates    4    3.5    4.5    5
33 Main Street, Cold Spring, NY 10516
(845) 265 - 3101
*Residential general contracting*

We hear this "extraordinary" decade-old firm prefers to stay small because its owner, Peter Di Natale, values a personal touch. His focus is on high-end residential interiors, with jobs ranging from kitchen renovations to full rebuilds for clients in the New York City area. We hear Di Natale and crew treats clients like partners and their apartments as if they were Di Natale's own home. It is said his patience in learning a client's needs and determination to make a project fun make Di Natale a natural for self-described "more difficult" clients who say the firm is very responsive to their input and questions and offers excellent supervision of projects. Despite having a job foreman, Di Natale is always present to usher the job forward, and even makes living through a renovation a bearable experience. This firm will not come in with lowest bid, sources say, but will come in on budget and on time with work of the highest caliber and no unfair or unexpected add-ons.

*"Peter is a gentleman who gets the job done right." "One-of-a-kind contractor." "I am the one person I know who actually enjoyed my relationship with my contractor." "Doesn't have his fingers in too many fires."*

## Profile Renovation

|  | 4 | 3.5 | 4.5 | 4 |

433 West 260, Riverdale, NY  10471
(718) 796 - 1582

*Residential general contracting, interior renovations*

References tell us this "eager to please" general contracting firm is "on the up and up."  In it's seventh year, Profile tackles both small and large jobs, focusing on interior renovation up to $1 million.  We hear the company's "young and reassuring" principals and consistent skilled crew never overextend themselves, and are considered a steal by designers. Many repeat Manhattan and Westchester County customers tell us Profile cares for everything they throw at it, without knocking their budgets out of the ballpark.

*"They work REALLY HARD and have rewarded us time and time again." "Always see the same guys on a job—not who they picked up at Janovic that day!"*

## Pros From Dover

|  | 4.5 | 4 | 4.5 | 5 |

548 West 28th Street, 5th Floor, New York, NY  10001
(212) 967 - 5033

*Residential general contractors, restoration and renovation*

These might be the Pros from Dover, but clients tell us their work is out of this world.  This "extremely client-oriented," "serious" contractor specializes in the residential restoration or renovation of high-end lofts, townhouses and penthouses all over Manhattan.  Jobs start at a half million.  All carpenters by trade, the three principals formed Pros in 1984.  They are described as "smart, resourceful and fun to be with," and we hear the three are excellent, creative problem solvers. We're told the firm develops long relationships with clients, and that if the clients aren't happy, neither are the Pros.  The firm offers expeditors (to push plans and permits through bureaucracy faster) and engineers on staff, and while it quite often is called in to do engineering for architects and designers, the firm encourages all clients to employ an architect.  It also believes the more involved the client the happier, and welcomes clients into the process, which reportedly goes off "smooth and easy."

The firm fronts a staff of 35 that clients find " a pleasure to deal with," including in-house carpenters, laborers and tile-layers.  Highly-regarded subs tell us they choose to work for Pros for its "quality work, good coordination and satisfied customers."  We hear the Pros doesn't bid jobs, but works on a cost plus open-book basis.  While clients agree the firm is expensive, they say estimates are "sensible" and "realistic," and the finish-quality and service is so stellar "there are no words to describe the Pros." Okay, maybe only 253.

*"I've used the Pros from Dover twice.  Their workers are immaculate and every one of them is skilled."  "Cost is never a surprise.  Everyone shows up when they say they will."  "Tony and Michael were excellent—responsive, helpful and professional."  "Bright, well-informed no-nonsense contractors."*

| | Quality | Cost | Value | Recommend? |
|---|---|---|---|---|
| | + | $ | ◆ | ★ |

## R.C. Legnini Company Inc.                    4      4      4      4
46 Pennsylvania Avenue, Malvern, PA  19355
(610) 640 - 1227

*Residential general contracting and millwork*

This Pennsylvania-based firm stands shoulder to shoulder with some of top local contracting firms for high-end residential work, which it performs in the New York City and Main Line Philadelphia areas.  Legnini undertakes both small and large jobs, and considers millwork, which the firm produces at its own 8,000-square-foot facility.  Clients tell us that David Legnini is professional, helpful and considerate.  They compliment him for finishing jobs on time and on budget and for providing excellent followup service when needed.  We hear this firm is not inexpensive, but you get what you pay for, which Legnini's customers believe to be a superb end result.

*"Excellent people.  They create the very highest-quality product."  "I would highly recommend them."*

## R.C. Metell Construction Inc.              4.5    4    4.5    5
198 West Haviland Lane, Stamford, CT  06903
(203) 968 - 1777

*High-end residential general contracting*

We hear that Ron Metell of R.C. Metell Contracting is a personable man with a great sense of humor, but he is serious about the quality of his work and the integrity of his business, which consists of very high-end residential interiors and new construction.  Most of his clients are in New York City and Fairfield County, with the average Metell project falling between $2 to $4 million.  We are told that he is a team player, whether he is working with a client's restricted schedule or with a top designer, and especially skilled in solving timing issues.  Committed clients who have worked with Metell on multiple projects (including one whose project he rescued after another contractor dropped it) appreciate his dedication to their interests.  Examples of the firm's work have appeared in top publications, including *Architectural Digest*.

*"A class outfit."  "Ron was very considerate of summer hours and got the job done before school started."  "Museum-quality work, and he came in on budget."*

## R.D. Wright Inc.                          3.5    3.5    4      4
527 West 29th Street, New York, NY  10001
(212) 971 - 7501

*General contracting*

A game competitor for large high-end residential projects in the city, clients say that the quality of this firm's work is quite good and has been steadily improving over the years.  They note that the painting and cabinetry are particularly excellent.  We hear principal Doug Reetz is a character—a charming personality who is a pleasure to interact with.  Reetz has "very good guys" working for him, references report, including a job foreman at every project.  All appreciate his straightforward and helpful attitude in resolving any concerns, but some wish it remained as strong during the punch list phase.  We hear Reetz also works well with sensitive neighbors and co-op boards and is extremely honest and fair, especially when it comes to budget. In addition, appreciative clients mention that Reetz always volunteers ways to manage costs and improve efficiency.

*"Doug is a marvellous guy."  "He came through with exactly what he promised."  "Doesn't avoid issues, will admit anytime he has a problem."  "A gentleman with very good quality, attitude and workmanship."  "We negotiated a flat fee and he stuck to it, even when the job and certain materials cost more*

than we expected." "He can communicate well with the client and the architect." "Final punch lists have been problematic. Getting the last two percent finished was a big effort on my part on all three projects. However he has always come in on time and on budget for the lion's share of the jobs." "I find him to be a finisher. I never have to chase him."

## RD Rice Construction, Inc.     5    4.5    5     5
532 West 30th Street, New York, NY 10001
(212) 268 - 1414   www.rdriceconstruction.com
*High-end residential general contracting*

Began in earnest six years ago by Doug Rice with an aim to become the best general contractor of mainly high-end residential work in Manhattan, a number people say the firm is well on its way to succeeding. Clients describe Rice, who got his start buying and refurbishing old Victorian homes in San Francisco, as delightful, quick-witted and a wonder to work with. He now has two partners and 65 employees at work on two-dozen projects each year for some of the most high profile clients in the city. Each job gets a project superintendent, and Rice himself is reportedly on top of everything. Millwork, produced in the firm's 25,000-square-foot shop, is considered an in-house specialty.

We hear customer service is of the utmost importance to Rice: maintenance personnel on staff make sure clients move into a clean home, often complete with fresh flowers and champagne. After the job is complete, if any work arises, they oversee other trades to make sure "the hammer doesn't go through the Picasso." Rice has built a stellar reputation on his commitment to "service, service, service," and plays an active role in each job, jobs that seem to be getting larger and larger. He can even be found assisting a client's selection of marble from an Italian quarry. Whatever his itinerary, there's no dispute the company's finished product is ready for prime time. RD Rice has been featured in *Architectural Digest* numerous times, *Elle Decor* and *New York Magazine*, and it's celebrated services are priced accordingly.

"This is like working with investment bankers in their professional attitude and expectations." "Highest possible quality." "He says that he is the largest purchaser of surgical booties for his men to wear (so as not mess up the house), and I bet he is right."

## Renotal Construction     3     3     4     4
524 West 36th Street, New York, NY 10018
(212) 268 - 8488
*High-end residential contracting*

A civil engineer of 34 years, principal Ronnie Tal has made high-end residential construction in high-rise apartments and townhouses his forte, while maintaining a presence in commercial work. Complete with carpenters, woodworkers, and painters among Renotal's 30 employees, they take on both interior and exterior work around Manhattan. References gush that Tal is the "only contractor with a heart."

## Richter + Ratner Contracting Corp.    4.5    4     4     4
55-05 Flushing Avenue, Maspeth, NY 11378
(718) 497 - 1600   www.richterratner.com
*High-end general contracting*

According to its clients, Richter + Ratner has mastered intricate high-end construction, and its work spans high-end retail stores and offices to luxury homes and apartments. The firm has been in business nine decades and its impressive client list includes such names as Gucci, Cerutti, Armani and Donna Karan, as well as various celebrities. Licensed to work in nearly every state, Richter + Ratner's superb execution can be seen from coast to coast. Particularly noted by some customers is the talent in woodworking displayed by craftsmen who apprenticed

| Quality | Cost | Value | Recommend? |
|---|---|---|---|
| + | $ | ◆ | ★ |

in Europe. We're told the firm is attentive to details, efficient and professional, making it perfectly suited not only to challenging projects but tight deadlines. Clients urge checking out the company web site, saying it speaks for itself.

*"They use only the best for each job." "Top dollar, but you get what you pay for." "A bit less sensitive to a demanding housewife's residential needs, as they often deal with commercial clientele.*

### Silver Rail Construction      4.5    4     5     5
113 Reade Street, Suite 2, New York, NY 10013
(212) 285 - 9500
*High-end residential general contracting*

Silver Rail Construction garners nothing but accolades for it's "superb crafts-manship" on large, high-end residential projects for Manhattan clients, mostly on the Upper East and Upper West Sides. Orchestrated by "outstanding" project managers and construction supervisors, whose superior attention to detail extends to attention to clients, the firm creates an overall cooperative spirit. Weekly status meetings keep projects moving along schedule and costs in-line with budget, contributing to a very positive and "gratifying" experience. References say the folks at Silver Rail are serious, thorough, dependable and promise only what they can deliver, which is often good enough for many of the very top decorators in the city.

We hear that ongoing relationships with clients are important to the firm, and the staff promptly attends to customers whose work was completed a decade ago, when even the smallest issue arises. Clients go so far as to recommend Silver Rail to their children, who often get the same show-stopping results at box seat prices.

*"The all time best ever!" "The office staff is fabulous!" "An amazing man who does only very high-end work for all the important people in town." "He is smart enough to figure out how to creatively implement the unique specifications of exacting decorators." "People of their word." "Professional, organized, efficient, responsible, on time, courteous and responsive." "Always want to do the right thing, good people, great subs." "Not only is the quality of their work outstanding but five years later they are still available to assist us with any difficulty or repair in our apartment."*

### SilverLining Interiors      4     4     4     5
2112 Broadway, Suite 402, New York, NY 10023
(212) 496 - 7800  www.silverlininginteriors.com
*High-end general contracting, decorative finish specialists*

Clients say everyday on a project with SilverLining is productive, and that each person working for the company is helpful and proud of his or her contribution to an elegant and original finished product. Originally focused on painting and decorative finishes, in 1986 the firm evolved into a residential general contracting company that has since become established as a bright, professional, well-run and reliable organization. Still true to its beginnings, SilverLining maintains in-house finishing crews, including painters, tile installers, carpenters, plasterers, stainers, paperhangers and glazers (custom plasterwork is also a specialty). We're told the integrated painting is a big scheduling advantage. Many describe principle Joshua Wiener as attentive, confident and quite a salesman—some say too much so. They remark he has a strong understanding of the aesthetics and quality a client is looking for. Maybe that's because Wiener's wife is Eve Robinson, an interior designer—the two of whom reportedly work well as a team. Indeed, SilverLining often works with top architects and designers in Manhattan.

Clients say this firm ranks in the upper echelon of high-quality bidders when it comes to cost, but "are by no means the highest bidders on jobs." However the overall size of these jobs average $800,000 to $1 million. Whatever the job, we're told the result remains "fantastic" work and "amazing" followup.

*"The work went without a hitch. Very smooth operation." "A class act." "Did a creative and artistic job with multiple glazings and very unusual patterns." "They work toward the same goals as we do. Our client's are comfortable and appreciative of how SilverLining conducts themselves professionally." "They are intelligent, never disappear, and usually get things done on time."*

## Simply Elegant Ltd.

         3.5    2.5    4.5    3.5

191 Newel Street, Brooklyn, NY 11222
(718) 389 - 6546

*Residential general contracting*

Anthony Wala of Simply Elegant concentrates on residential contracting projects in New York City that range from $30,000 to $3 million. Wala is known for his quiet demeanor and close project management. Clients tell us he visits each of the several jobs he has going at once on a daily basis. Clients tell us Wala is a trustworthy and very competent builder who employs extremely talented crafts-people. Firm specialties include millwork and cabinetry, both done in-house. The quality of this company's work is very strong, according to references, who are impressed that Wala and his crew see every detail through to the end. We hear Simply Elegant works with many prestigious New York designers, in addition to private clients, for a very reasonable fee.

*"Tony is dependable, he's there and he follows through like a pro." "Excellent, quality work."*

## Soho Custom Interiors Inc.

         4    3.5    4    4.5

12 White Street, New York, NY 10013
(212) 219 - 0444   www.sohocustom.com

*Residential general contracting*

References tell us Soho Custom Interiors defines what contracting should be. Specializing in New York City townhouses, lofts and penthouse apartments that range from $250,000 to $5 million, we hear the firm makes helpful suggestions, looks out for clients' costs and delivers the product to perfection. Clients tell us owner Sandy Friedman is sophisticated and they are charmed by his personal demeanor. They also appreciate his "fanaticism" about keeping projects on track. Friedman enjoys lending his expertise at the beginning of the project, and working throughout as a team with the architect and client. Clients say he makes sure to explain what is happening every step of the way.

The company has a large group of in-house finish carpenters, painters, plasterers and tilers that clients say insure on-time, high-quality performance. We're told Friedman and crew are excellent problem solvers that can meet the detail and progressive needs of both designer and client. Friedman's background as cabinetmaker also means he's very comfortable with tight specs. Architects recommend Soho to clients, and customers tell us they suggest Soho to friends.

*"I love working with them." "When I need some good carpenters I can count on to build on a tight deadline, I give Sandy Friedman a call." "Excellent work and very professional." "Very nice people who are entirely trustworthy and don't play games." "Brought the work in as promised." "Despite adversity they were always willing to listen and do whatever it took to get the job done right."*

| | Quality | Cost | Value | Recommend? |
|---|---|---|---|---|
| | + | $ | ◆ | ★ |

## Steve Mark Inc.
**4.5 4 4.5 5**

43-15 Dutch Kills Street, Long Island City, NY 11101
(718) 937 - 0300   www.stevemarkinc.com
*General contracting and construction management*

This general contractor is reportedly hot among the uptown "rich and famous." Grown from its millworker roots over the course of nearly twenty years, the firm now builds high-end residential interiors in townhouses and apartments. In addition to being capable of fine in-house millwork, the firm does its own tiling, plastering, general carpentry, and offers construction management services, all of which we hear adds efficiency. Sources tell us that owner Steve Mark is top-notch in both his service and his talent. They report being thrilled with Mark's attention to getting things right, his pleasant, direct personality and his honesty. Customers rely on Mark to deliver and he often comes through, finishing jobs to a level above expectations in quality, timing and budget.

*"Steve is a finisher. He never leaves anything halfway." "A straight shooter." "A very good builder." "We sent out six bid packages. Only two contractors bothered to respond in any detail. Steve Mark was at the apartment the next morning with six subcontractors to make sure the numbers in his bid would be accurate. They were. He came in on budget and very close on time. Did a six month job in four!"*

## Sweeney + Conroy Inc.
**5 4.5 5 5**

33 Great Jones Street, New York, NY 10012
(212) 995 - 5099

Clients tell us this "straight-talking" general contracting firm "doesn't just build a design, but gets involved and cares about what it is they are building." They mention Sweeney + Conroy as one of the "finest" contractors in the city. The firm specializes in gut townhouse and penthouse renovations typically tipping the scales over seven figures. While the lion's share of its work consists of high-end homes, a quarter centers around commercial jobs that have a residential nature. The company will consider taking on unique, design-based little jewels down to $500,000 that incorporate challenging material and installations. A network of respected interior designers and architects often recruit Sweeney + Conroy to execute their spotlight work. While entrenched professional relationships often guides this contractor's output, they aren't necessary for Sweeney + Conroy to headline a successful project. We're told the company is capable of shepherding the development and value engineering of drawings, and offers consulting services along with its general contracting title. It is said the main idea at Sweeney + Conroy is "to have everyone understand the plan."

Principals Sean Sweeney and Jim Conroy deliver decades of construction experience between them. They are described as "hardworking guys" with "no pretension." Clients say one of the two is "totally active" in every project and familiar with "every single" detail. We hear weekly meetings keeping the firm "always in touch with the subs" and reams of paperwork keeping clients always in touch with the project mean "nothing is left to chance." We hear the firm is patient with architects "who tinker" but can "sternly" tell them when it needs the drawings so as not to delay the job.

The firm fields an all-star rotation of superintendents (whose pitches are tailored for each client) and count in-house carpentry, tile, drywall, framing and even their own punch-out team among 60-plus employees. Clients compliment the staff, reporting the "foreman made it all happen" and the "wonderful office girls" were "right on the spot" for calls and questions. In addition to taming Sweeney + Conroy's monster projects, its talented team is kept busy servicing minor items for past customers, who end up customer's for life. Sweeney + Conroy has been featured in *The New York Times, Metropolitan Home,* and *New York Magazine.*

*"Best contractor I ever saw. Five stars." "Very frank. They say what they mean." "Over a two year project, never one day of arguement." "Almost per-*

*fect. And I was a contractor." "Very precise. Asks a lot of questions about minute details." "A lot of integration. Exceptional coordination. Headed things off before they were a problem." "I had two huge notebooks of backup materials." "My only criticism is that they can be overwhelming at times. I don't want all this information and he forces you to deal with detail. Or maybe that's a compliment?" "The fact I can focus on minute things like the shade of one green tile being not quite right says a lot about their job." "My other contracting experience was a joke compared to this one."*

## Taconic Builders Inc.     5    4.5    5    5

125 Spencer Place, Mamaroneck, NY 10543
(914) 698 - 7456   www.taconicbuilders.com
*High-end residential general contracting*

This custom builder of residential projects began working fourteen years ago for patrons in the New York metro area and has established a reputation as one of the top outfits in the business. Architects, decorators and other industry professionals praise both the quality of the work and the ease of teaming with Taconic. They say the firm likes to get involved in a job from the get-go. Projects take Taconic from Westchester County to Greenwich to Manhattan, and average squarely at the $2 to $3 million mark, with $250,000 the minimum for new clients when the firm is available. While much of the work is performed by subcontractors, owners Gerry Holbrook and James Hanley hire well and manage projects very closely, judging from rave reviews. We hear they work equally as well with clients who want to keep plugged into the minutiae of a project as those who are away in Paris for the duration. References also tell us that Taconic Builders has an additional service staff available for project followups and fine-tuning long after a job is complete. Its work has been published in *Architectural Digest.* Fees are standard.

*"I recommend them for very high-quality work." "Everything they did for us was fabulous." "We were delighted and surprised that our relationship with a New York contractor could be so positive."*

## Tal-Design Construction Corp.    3    2.5    4.5    4.5

757 Harrison Street, West Hempstead, NY 11552
(877) 825 - 3374
*Residential general contracting, interior renovations*

A midsize general contracting firm operating in Manhattan, Westchester County and Nassau County, clients tell us Tal-Design is knowledgeable, efficient, timely, and understands the special dynamics involved in interior alteration work involving high-end residences. Clients compliment soft-spoken, hands-on principal Ezra Green as a pleasure to work with, and say "there was simply no neglect" of their needs. They describe his crews, which include in-house woodworkers, as true old-world craftsmen—considerate, professional and of course competent. The company offers ongoing maintenance services long after the job is complete. All seem to agree that Tal-Design offers very good quality work at reasonable prices.

*"A lot of personal attention was given." "I would consider Tal-Design first over all contractors I know. Ezra's integrity is number-one." "Wonderful man. Nothing was ever a problem for Erza." "Excellent, reputable contractor who is affordable."*

## Taocon, Inc.          4    3.5    4.5    5

110 Madison Avenue, 2nd Floor, New York, NY  10016
(212) 689 - 7799   www.taocon.com

*Residential and commercial general contracting*

Dubbed a "dream contractor" by grateful clients, Taocon has been completing gut renovations in Manhattan for high-end residences and commercial clients such as *Time Out* magazine and Shiseido since 1988.  We're told partners David Schlachet and Steven Lamazor maintain their sterling reputation by not over-committing.  What they do commit to, we hear, is top detail, quality and communication with customers and designers, who describe the duo as "craftsmen, businessmen, gentlemen."  A circle of architects report they always look to this firm to drive a job, especially concerning tricky projects when layouts, schedules and budgets are a challenge.  The firm has 55 employees, including its own drywall, framing and carpentry crew.  Clients tell us everyone they dealt with was patient, efficient and nice.  They say phone calls are returned immediately and everything is in writing.

*"Top quality" "They deliver." "The ultimate professional." "Have worked with Taocon on three projects.  They are the best.  Total integrity." "Absolutely use them if they will take your job!"*

## Temple International Construction          4.5    3.5    5    4.5

7 East 27th Street, New York, NY  10016
(212) 691 - 8032

*General contracting*

A "stunning experience," is what Manhattan customers have to say about working with this small firm on their high-end residential gut renovation, or multi-room renovation.  Typical Temple jobs range $250,000 to $750,000 and are characterized by enormous attention to detail and service.  We hear owner Jim Tribe brings 30 years experience, as well as five of the utmost professional, talented, multi-disciplined craftsmen clients have ever seen to each job.  Tribe's tribe does much of the work themselves, and displays great problem-solving skills and higher standards than most contractors.  We're told Tribe's subs are as interested in doing perfect work as he.  Regardless, there's "no monkeying around" when Temple's on the clock, references tell us, due to the fact that one of Tribe's fellows acts as on-site foreman and Jim is always available.  This dependable firm is known to land projects on budget and on time, the near museum-quality work taking off for a fair price.

*"It appeared as if a team of professors were coming into my apartment. They looked neat and academic and blasted classical music while they worked. They're absolutely wonderful." "Not an extra cost added to the contract every time you turn around." "Meets deadlines. Close to the highest possible quality."*

## The I. Grace Company Inc.          5    4.5    4.5    4

403 East 91st Street, New York, NY  10128
(212) 987 - 1900

*Commissioned private residences*

Clients and competitors all agree I. Grace is committed to the highest-end residential work in the regional area.  With offices in New York City and Greenwich, this large, full-service construction company offers end-to-end building and renovation services for spaces ranging from apartments to lofts to country estates.  In addition to the large-scale museum quality projects for which the company is best

known, I. Grace maintains ongoing relationships with clients by completing small projects through a service arm. References tell us the firm's management, headlined by David Cohen, is knowledgeable, educated and very professional. We hear they are particularly great about working under summer work rules.

While Cohen and company encountered "growing pains" in the mid-90s, client's confirm it has now hit stride. The firm's impressive roster of clients includes celebrities, and its work has been published nationally. For those who can afford it, I. Grace can deliver the highest possible quality.

*"They are a pleasure to work with. That's difficult to say when it comes to contractors!" "Fabulous. Did what ever had to do to get the job done."*

## The Renovated Home
1477 Third Avenue, Suite 2, New York, NY 10028
(212) 517 - 7020   www.therenovatedhome.com
*Entire apartment renovation, kitchen and bath design and installation*
See The Renovated Home's full report under the heading Kitchen & Bath Design

## Tom Law & Associates
202 West 78th Street, Suite B, New York, NY 10024
(212) 362 - 5227
*Residential renovation, kitchen planning, design and general contracting*
See Tom Law & Associates's full report under the heading Kitchen & Bath Design

## Traditional Line Ltd.                        4.5      4      5      5
143 West 21st Street, New York, NY 10011
(212) 627 - 3555
*Residential and institutional interior restoration*

The traditional line we get from references is that this restoration and preservation specialist is among the top in the country. The principals, Jim Boorstein and Anthony Lefeber, founded the firm sixteen years ago in New York City after completing the restoration of the new American period rooms at the Metropolitan Museum of Art. The company now works in and around the city on museums, private residences and public buildings, and clients tell us its astonishing talents include the refinish and restoration of complex woodworking details as well as reproduction of panels, mantles, stairways and period hardware. It even does furniture restoration. Clients say the principals are fluent with a broad range of historic periods, styles and materials. Their extensive knowledge and skill is best applied to landmark houses and apartments dating from 1830 to 1930. We hear Traditional Line's staff is a joy to work with. With a crew described as neat, meticulous and mindful of a client's space, references recommend Traditional Line for detail-oriented work and live-in renovations. Despite the highly specialized work, the firm's costs don't require a Louisiana Purchase.

*"They can do magic!" "Top of the heap for what they do." "Nobody at Traditional Line I wouldn't work with again. The best thing out there. I recommend them to EVERYBODY." "Honest hardworking and dedicated to what they do." "We went through four contractors before we found Traditional Line."*

## Uberto Construction                          5      4.5    4.5     5
129 West 86th Street, New York, NY 10024
(212) 874 - 4100
*Residential general contracting*

The depth of this organization's resources, its savvy management and terrific foremen put Uberto on top of designer's wish lists. Given the tricky task of a high-rise penthouse addition or extremely detailed finish, we hear the company's dedicated professionals deliver fantastic work. Uberto has been serving customers on the Upper East and Upper West Sides for two decades. Clients tell us principal Pierre Crosby, a graduate of the University of Virginia School of Architecture, is an intelligent, soft-spoken man who brings an attention to detail and a measured manner to his work. Consultants compliment Crosby's deft political skills and keen sense of a project's critical points. One client noted that even when Crosby encountered delays that were not his company's fault, he worked to remedy the situation and still meet deadlines.

We're told Uberto's crews are polite, honest and friendly. First-rate cabinetry is produced in a 9,000-square-foot shop, located in the historic Red Hook piers in Brooklyn, overseen by a graduate of the Lycée des Metiers de Bartiments Auguste Perret in Poitiers, considered the finest woodworking school in France. No wonder we hear such high-praise for this high-priced general contractor.

*"Pierre Crosby is a gentleman. A real man of his word." "His French craftsman are a goldmine—an undiscovered treasure trove." "The company reflects its people, trustworthy." "Pierre and his crew are obsessed with getting it perfectly right." "We certainly received value for our money and excellent follow-through." "Stand behind everything, by reputation, will fix any imperfections." "Get a price from Uberto first."*

### Urban D.C.    4    4    4    4
970 Grand Street, Brooklyn, NY 11211
(718) 599 - 4000   www.urbandc.com
*Heavy exterior restoration and waterproofing*

What makes this firm more Urban than most is its specialty in exteriors, particularly masonry restoration and waterproofing for stonework, limestone and brownstone. It also performs structural work and restores cast iron sidewalk vaults. About 20 percent of its clients are homeowners—the majority of its jobs are for commercial clients, including the Roger Williams Hotel, Shoreham Hotel and New York Studio School. The company's restoration of Old Navy's Sixth Avenue flagship store won a Landmarks Preservation award in 1996.

Urban D.C. founder and president Daniel Wacks wins praise for being pleasant, relaxed and a great ally to have on a project. Clients tell us he works well with other professionals on a job. Due to their engineering backgrounds (Wacks and others on staff are licensed engineers) we're told that they bring precision and careful thought and execution to any job.

*"A really good guy to call on, careful and conscientious." "Daniel has a certain class in his operation and this reflects in his work."*

### Watters Construction Inc.    3.5    2.5    5    5
3512 Oxford Avenue, Bronx, NY 10463
(718) 543 - 5774
*Residential general contracting*

Clients adore Martin Watters of Watters Construction. His firm performs mid-sized and small high-end residential contracting jobs in Manhattan—mostly on the

Upper East and Upper West Sides. Sources say the company's small size means they get personal attention from the friendly, flexible Watters, who we hear knows what he's doing and gets it done. Clients tell us he is very professional and lays projects out in advance, often informs clients of a cheaper way to work, and gives them cost-saving information. One was delighted by Watters' demonstrated commitment to customer satisfaction and willingness to solve issues left behind by another, less exacting contractor. The company also does all its own millwork, and even designs cabinets. Working closely with renowned architects, references tell us the quality of the firm's work is very high. For those world weary about general contractors, Watters delivers a rare positive experience at a price that keeps his clients' heads above...well, you know.

*"Not only did the contractor respond to our phone calls and keep appointments, we found that there were no hidden costs whatsoever." "He fixed another contractor's mess and did an excellent job." "He is an excellent communicator and is always there when you need him." "A door fell off a cabinet two days before Christmas and Martin came right over to fix it." "My dog ate a corner of a radiator and he fixed it—no problem." "We highly recommend Watters. He is worth every single penny."*

## Wildes Inc.      4    3.5    4    4
127 East 61st Street, New York, NY 10021
(212) 702 - 8706

*Residential general contracting, interior renovations*

Clients tell us the Wildes of New York City renovations are a walk in the park. Wildes Inc. is known for exceptional finishes and assured execution of bold, complicated, singular design in interior renovations of apartments, townhouses and commercial spaces in the $300,000 to $3 million range. The firm also operates in a construction management capacity. Clients tell us this builder is really in tune to the design intent of the architect, and has the resources to fabricate anything. Timothy Wildes toplines this firm, notable for its woodworking tradition. It operates Duke Woodworks, a mill shop in Redhook. Clients say this means Wildes can better control lead times, and deliver product—ultimately jobs—on a tighter timeframe. Finish carpenters perform all rough carpentry.

We hear the firm works closely with many architects and designers, who appreciate that Wildes Inc. often fleshes out and fashions its work by doing mock-ups. The firm boasts a client roster of supercelebrities, media giants, CEOs and others who value discression as much as they do fine workmanship.

## William Paster Inc.      4    3    5    5
153 West 27th Street, Suite 1001, New York, NY 10001
(212) 242 - 3403

*Residential general contracting*

More than the name on the marquee, William Paster rolls out the red carpet. Doing mainly residential work in Manhattan, and he can and will handle both large and small jobs. Paster often works closely with architects, who praise both the quality of his work and his skill in executing finely detailed, complex projects. The firm specializes in complete renovations but can also build houses from the ground up or take on just a few rooms. Noted as charming and amenable, Paster wins applause for his smoothly run jobs. His twenty-person shop has been in business for fifteen years, building a reputation for high-quality workmanship. Paster has assembled a consistent, skilled and good-humored crew over the years, and we are told that he manages projects closely, visiting sites daily. On-site project managers are present from start to finish, and a punch-list team diligently follows. The firm also has its own woodworking studio for custom work. Clients tell us Paster's beautiful work doesn't have to break the piggy bank.

*"Really good people." "Bill is very personable. He can even resolve any issues with the apartment building staff." "He gets things done on time and gets them done right." "We would not think of using anyone else! The quality and detail were impeccable." "Always left my house clean." "Redeemed the profession for me after a bad experience." "We have now gone through two major prewar renovations with William Paster in the past seven years—we would not think of using anyone else!"*

### Xhema of New York           4    4    4    4
160 East 56th Street., Suite 402, New York, NY 10022
(212) 752 - 0270
*High-end residential contracting*

This 30-year-old firm now has a Manhattan outpost at work on projects for some of New York's highest-end decorators. We hear that Xhema is one of the world's top-quality contractors, and the company serves loyal clients building French chateaus or renovating Park Avenue duplexes.

### ZMK Group, Inc.           4    4    4    4.5
192 Lexington Avenue, 5th Floor, New York, NY 10016
(212) 252 - 1400
*High-end residential renovation*

With "unparalleled customer service" this firm executes "flawless" full-scale renovations of prewar and postwar apartments, conversions of lofts and complete structural overhaul of brownstone townhouses, as well as commercial work. We hear principal Zakery Kaplan's project management experience in urban development for the city and his education in architectural and urban history are evident in his knowledge about working here. A native New Yorker, we hear "he knows everybody." Clients say he is very cooperative, highly creative and competent, with a sharp eye for detail. They tell us the patient and polite Kaplin always shows clients ways to save money. Whether working in modern glass and steel or traditional dyed plaster and custom plaster crown, references applaud the "spectacular workmanship," and say any other result must be an aberration.

This mid-sized firm has in-house rough and finish carpenters, who we hear can assuage any clients concerns with a wealth of good information, endless options and great quality. We hear Kaplin's staff is reportedly available, friendly, neat and responsive. Overall, clients tell us ZMK dove into projects thoroughly prepared and took each lap on schedule.

*"Never been unhappy for a moment." "Patient and polite." "Always show me ways to save money." "My family has completed numerous residential projects over the past fifteen years. I only wish we had found ZMK Group sooner. We will never work with anyone else again." "I thought Zack was kidding when he described his attention to details, but you should see the gorgeous custom work— crown and base moldings, doors, stone fireplace, cherry cabinets. Well worth it!"*

### Zoric Construction Corp.           3.5    2.5    4.5    4
21-44 Harman Street, Ridgewood, NY 11385
(718) 386 - 7141
*High-end classical residential renovation*

This "self-motivated" general contractor gets singled out for its efforts renovating upper-end residences—more precisely brownstones where classical-traditional woodwork, plaster and ornamental painting is most prominently on display. The company's smaller projects are also crafted notably. With over 20 years in the trade principal John Zoric, who carrys an engineering degree from Europe, rides a wave of recommendations. We hear the combination of his uber-professional approach to the task at hand coupled with an aesthetic sensibility that has designers buzzing is marvelously novel. The result is Zorich offers design acumen that

many other contractors can't match.  References are especially impressed by the fact that he performs a lot of the work himself.  They tell us Zorich is known to discourage change orders, pinning down the price beforehand so he doesn't have to pin the client down to every penny.  In fact, client's think so much of Zorich they're afraid to tell him how inexpensive he really is.

*"Really good taste. Thinks similarly to me." "A real contractor, all business."*

## ZZZ Carpentry Inc.       4     3.5    4.5    5
547 West 27th Street, Suite 635, New York, NY  10001
(212) 239 - 0403

*Residential general contracting*

It seems ZZZ couldn't throw a stick down Broadway without hitting someone with a good recommendation.  Described as fun and great to work with, ZZZ has delighted residential clients throughout New York City since 1984, in jobs ranging from $300,000 to $5 million.  Customers applaud Derek Huntington and his team for their earnest desire to do the best work in a decent and straight-forward, collaborative fashion.  On-site project managers are considered to be helpful and on top of the details.  To a letter (probably a Z) clients say Huntington is a person of outstanding integrity, professionalism, and capability in every respect.  We're told he gets his priorities straight from an architect's point of view and is inventive with solutions, making the firm a "perennial first choice" with professionals.

Although they excel at performing their own finish carpentry, we've heard that ZZZ's craftsmen produce top-quality work at a good value in all areas.  References report there were virtually no cost overruns and always felt Huntington was looking out for them.  For a reasonable cost, clients say ZZZ Carpentry's "professionalism, perfectionism, fairness and caring exceed all expectations."

*"The most honest and reputable contractor in New York—and I have seen a lot of them." "Never pulls any punches, you always know exactly what they are thinking." "They are also fun and open-minded and will build weird stuff without batting an eyelash." "They are fair, calm and communicative. We hope to continue working with them for years to come." "We've had four separate projects with ZZZ. After our first, we didn't even bid out the following jobs."*

# Hiring an Electrician

Dealing with electricity and wiring is intimidating, and with good reason—you are placing your family and home at risk if it is not handled properly. This is not the area for cutting costs by doing it yourself, or by choosing the lowest-priced service provider. Think of Chevy Chase putting his Christmas light cords into one giant, sagging cluster of adapters in National Lampoon's Christmas Vacation. Hilarious, but a little close to home. Quality, reliability and experience should be the determining factors in selecting an electrician for your needs.

Most electricians do both commercial and residential work, small repairs and large renovations. This versatility means that once you have found a professional that you like and trust, he can help you with all of your electrical needs over the years.

## How to Choose an Excellent Electrician

Of course, recommendations from friends and contractors can be very useful in deciding which electrician to hire, but the final decision rests with you. Whether you are having an outlet rewired for a larger appliance or rewiring an entire renovated wing of your residence, quality and service should be your first priorities.

A good start is to contact each electrician you are considering. Do they return your calls promptly? Are they willing to provide references? Do they listen well? If they take days, even weeks to return your calls, this may be a good indication of the level of professionalism and attention you will receive once they are on your project.

Ask how long they have been in business and in what types of work they specialize. Many electrical professionals working in high-end are very active in commercial projects, and do both large renovations and smaller repairs. Others focus exclusively on "designer" electrical work such as the lighting of artwork and retrofitting museum quality finishes.

## Check the References

Since an electrician's work is virtually invisible, the best way to get an idea of quality is to speak to others who have had electrical work done. When asking the electrician for references, inquire as to whether they have worked on any projects similar to yours, particularly if it is a large and complex project. Most will be happy to provide you with these.

When you are speaking with the actual references, a few areas that are useful to discuss are timeliness, cleanliness and reliability. Were they respectful of surroundings while they were there? Did they clean up when they left, or did they leave their tools everywhere until they came back the next day? Did they show up when they were expected or always arrive late? Did they finish the project on schedule? Did they come in on budget? Did they place safety first? These are good questions to ask of an electrician's references.

## Important Pre- and Post-Project Considerations

Many times electrical work requires cutting into a wall to gain access to the wires. There are two issues to think about here—cleanup and repair. Sheetrock debris and plasterdust are very difficult to clean up, so the electrician should either inform you of this at the time or put up protective plastic sheeting to keep dust from infiltrating your entire house. Some will repair the wall with plaster, but it is unlikely that they will sand and repaint it. Be sure to discuss this beforehand, clearly identifying the extent of the electrician's responsibility—and get it in writing.

When doing renovation or installation work, your electrician may suggest adding additional wiring for future use. This may sound like he's just trying to charge you more, but it's actually a very good idea. It is easier to add wiring and setups in the beginning for that dreamed-of central air conditioning system or six-line phone system or computer network you envision in your future. This avoids the headache of having to tear up walls and floors several years down the road, and saves a great deal of money, too.

It is very common for your electrician to work closely with your A/V specialist, telephone system analyst, computer consultant and security company when installing wiring. Your GC coordinates all of this, but you will need to think about exactly what you may require before everything starts.

Also, before your electrician leaves, make sure you know what switch controls what and that all circuit breakers are labeled properly. Do not let him disappear without doing this because he is the only one who knows. You want the electrician who wires your entire residence to be the professional you use for general maintenance and repair work in the future because he will establish warranties and gain familiarity with your residence.

## Licensing, Insurance and Permits

You should only consider a full-time licensed professional for your electrical needs. A license from the Department of Labor is required for any electrical work, and all work must be filed with the city. This includes any installation related to light, heat and power.

Upfront, you should ask your electrical professional to provide you with an estimate describing the work to be done, the price and the payment, the contractor's guarantee as well as proof of worker's compensation and liability insurance.

Your electrical contractor should always be responsible for obtaining all permits necessary for your job.

## On Cost

When hiring an electrician for a larger project, each electrical contractor submits his bid to the GC, who will then incorporate it into an overall bid which is submitted to the client. All of this should be available to you upon request.

For smaller jobs and service calls, which include repair and maintenance, most companies will charge an hourly fee. Hourly fees in New York these days range from $55 to $115, with around $80 per hour for a master electrician (not including transportation or materials) being the norm, reflected in a baseline rating of 3 for Cost in *The Franklin Report*. However, please remember, a company's standards in relation to product and safety, the depth of its resources and the demand it's in can all affect cost on top of hourly rates, and are factored into the rating. Some companies charge a set fee for a visit, or a higher rate the first hour, then have flat-rate charges for each task performed, such as per outlet relocated or fixture installed. Others insist on doing a consultation to provide you with an estimate before any work is started. This is a must for larger jobs. Fees for contract renovation work are typically higher than those for new construction per hour and per square foot. In the end, it should come down to the company with the best reputation for quality and service, not just the low bidder.

Before any work is begun, request a written estimate. Keep in mind that it is easier to estimate the cost of an installation than a repair. Even seemingly simple electrical repairs may require extensive labor and troubleshooting procedures.

## Guarantees and Service Agreements

Your service provider should always stand behind all work that is done. Be sure to ask about service agreements. Many electrical professionals provide regular "checkups" and inspections. It may seem like wasted money at first, but over time these measures can prevent an emergency.

## Save Money by Saving Time

With a little preparation, you will be able to save money by saving the time of the service provider. Many times an electrician will need to cut into walls to gain access to wires or to replace fixtures. This is something you should think about before the workmen arrive. You may want to move or cover up that priceless antique sideboard near where the sconces are being installed rather than leaving it to the electrical crew.

Consolidating working hours will save time and money, too. Think about any jobs that may need to be done throughout the house and compile a list. Present the list to the service provider upon arrival so he can prioritize the various tasks, allowing his team to work simultaneously, if possible. This prevents having to call the professional back in several weeks for another minor repair.

If the electrician needs access to the electrical panel in a closet or a fixture above the sideboard, clear out the area beforehand to avoid wasted time and possible damage to any objects that may be there. By taking care of these little things in advance, you allow your electrical professional to get right to work, you will not have to worry about the safety of various objects and your billable time will be less.

By following these general guidelines, you can help any future electrical projects run smoothly. And remember, an electrician's work—if truly successful—is invisible.

## The Buzz on Circuit Breakers

It's tripped. What now? Check the breaker in the panel and reset. All breakers should be labeled, marking the locations of the outlets, light fixtures and other energy users on the circuit. If it trips again, you can troubleshoot for:

- ✧ **An overload:** Unplug or turn off the circuit's big energy users. Some users may have to be split onto a different, less crowded circuit.
- ✧ **A short** caused by connections that have pulled loose in electrical boxes.
- ✧ **A short** caused by frayed or nicked insulation that exposes wires (can be repaired with electrical tape).
- ✧ **A short** caused by using a lightbulb with higher wattage than required for the fixture (this melts the wire insulation).

## ELECTRICIANS

### A.C. Green Electrical Contractors Inc.   3   3   4   4
412 West 48th Street, 2nd Floor, New York, NY 10036
(212) 541 - 4100
*Commercial and residential electrical installation and service*

### A.C. Morgan   4   2.5   5   5
(917) 257 - 2768
*Commercial and residential electrical installation and service*

Once Petri Electric, now A.C. Morgan, clients still give this small firm terrific reviews. The company performs residential and commercial work, mostly in Manhattan and is said to be extremely talented. Clients say A.C. Morgan tends to do more large jobs than small, but makes an effort to accommodate everybody, even if it's hanging a fixture. We are told that principal Ray Morales is a skilled problem solver who searches for the long-term solution, which he then executes with efficiency and competence. Customers enjoy Morales' sense of humor and feel he is very fair in making contract adjustments, if necessary. We hear his staff of fifteen is careful not to poke holes in walls unless absolutely necessary.

Morales has recently brought in two partners, a move that accounts for the name change. We're told each of the three focuses upon his expertise, which is divided up between high-end residential, commercial and smaller service and repair-oriented work. Clients tell us A.C. Morgan "doesn't mess around" when it comes to giving it all on service, and that all they ask in return is a sensible price.

*"Especially good at problem solving. He took a lot of initiative with regard to the overall picture." "Gets right to work and did a great job." "Extremely diligent and competent."*

### A.S.M. Electric   3   3   4   4
353 West 39th Street, New York, NY 10018
(212) 695 - 0498
*Commercial and residential electrical installation and service*

A.S.M. can be found mainly on commercial projects and larger, high-end residential installations, but we are told its technicians will pick up smaller jobs and service work when available. We hear that clients appreciate the firm's high-quality service and extensive experience, spanning 40 years in and around Manhattan.

### Altman Electric   3.5   2.5   4.5   4
283 West 11th Street, New York, NY 10014
(212) 924 - 0400
*Residential and commercial electrical installation and service*

Clients tell us "what a relief" it is to have this small, family-run electrical contractor in their corner. We hear principal Richard Altman is known for delivering high-quality work in a courteous, efficient and cost effective manner. The firm has cared for Manhattan and Westchester County residences and commercial clients like New York University for over 50 years, taking on large-scale soup-to-nuts renovation projects to smaller repairs and maintenance for homeowners.

*"Mr. Altman came on time, efficiently evaluated the problem, and solved it when he promised, at a fraction of the expense quoted by several other contractors." "Top notch service and quality workmanship. Richard Altman is very personable, knowledgeable and is a true testament to the company's success. Look no further!"*

## Barth-Gross Electric Company Inc.     4.5    4    4.5    5
110 West 26th Street, New York, NY 10001
(212) 929 - 0446

*Commercial and large-scale high-end residential electrical work*

In business since 1919, we hear this 35-person firm performs "textbook perfect" electrical work for some of the best locations (fancy hotels, commercial buildings, Fifth- and Park-Avenue residences) and architects around the city. We hear Barth-Gross concentrates on commercial assignments while diverting itself with an occasional large top-tier residential project. One of only a handful of companies endorsed by Lutron for installation, Barth-Gross often gets the first call for a complex project that requires sophisticated engineering and coordination.

Owner Roy Barth is an electrical engineer himself. As a result, clients tell us the firm is both more thorough and expert in design than others at the outset of a project, which means it can price a job more accurately. We hear any changes in cost, a rarity, are notified to the client immediately. Barth is widely respected and liked in the industry, not only for the depth of his knowledge and character, but for the fact that he makes the rounds to all his jobs to keep on top of things. While no one we talk to hedges around the fact that this firm is quite expensive, they all say the cost is warranted.

*"One of the best in the business." "There was never a person from this company that wasn't good. And that's pretty much because of Ray. I can't think of a better man."*

## Cammarata Electric Company     3    3    4    3.5
1673 Unionport Road, Bronx, NY 10462
(718) 409 - 0743

*Commercial and residential electrical installation and service*

Anthony Cammarata and his small staff focus on commercial work and large residential projects in Manhattan, but supplement these efforts with a dash of repair work and smaller jobs when time permits. In operation now for 20 years, we hear the company holds building maintenance contracts with established management companies throughout Manhattan and is well-versed in providing full electrical support and service to the gut renovation of penthouses and brownstones. Clients are thrilled with this firm's performance.

## CJJ Inc.     4.5    3.5    5    5
187 Willow Avenue, Bronx, NY 12545
(718) 401 - 6588

*Lighting control design and installation*

Geared primarily for accomplishing major high-end renovation work under the direction of A-list industry professionals, CJJ's highly regarded expertise is only available to homeowners for design and installation of sophisticated lighting control systems. We hear owner Chris Jones knows being a craftsman has as much to do with what clients don't see as what they do. Clients agree, and say this attitude makes this small company a natural for upgrading lighting systems in residences where a high degree of finish and cleanliness is required. They tell us Jones is a joy to work with, and his price as handsome as his work.

*"Chris is a great guy. Does great work, is honest, reliable, and so nice."*

| | Quality + | Cost $ | Value ◆ | Recommend? ★ |
|---|---|---|---|---|

## Coachmen Electric

4    3    4.5    5

256 West 38th Street, New York, NY  10018
(888) 398 - 3635

*High-end residential electrical installation*

Caring for clients primarily on the Upper East Side, and occasionally folks across the park, we're told this small company hangs its hat on customer service. Coachman makes service calls only to current customers in order to ensure them greater availability and front-running quality, a policy clients say they appreciate. We understand Coachmen's stable doors have been open nearly twenty years, and owner Stephan Tate's electrical expertise spans three decades. The bulk of the firm's muscle is reined on high-end residential projects, with restoration (think a 19th-century brownstone) figuring a particular specialty, clients report. They also single out Coachmen's personable, attentive crew.

## Decora Electrical Company

3.5    3.5    4    4

135 Lincoln Avenue, Bronx, NY  10454
(718) 585 - 3800

*Commercial and high-end residential electrical installation and service*

With a pedigree steeped in over 25 years experience in some of the most prestigious addresses in the city, its no wonder knowledgeable contractors highly recommend and often turn to this 40-person firm. Providing electrical support in both residential and commercial spaces, we hear Decora's projects are consistently managed with care and attention. We're told the firm takes on mostly high-end assignments, where its premium prices are more competitive.

*"Reasonable personalities, reasonable quality." "A little expensive but good project supervision."*

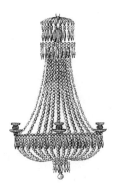

## Gabe's Works

4.5    3.5    5    5

94-49 50th Avenue, Elmhurst, NY  11373
(718) 699 - 6333

*Installation and repair of specialty lighting fixtures*

Gabe's Works in the highly specialized craft of light fixture repair and restoration. Whether its Manhattan residences, notable public spaces, or other parts of the country, Gabriel Valasquez has been practicing his trade for close to twenty years, preferring direct relationships with decorators, designers and architects. Clients tell us he performs assembly, installation and repair work on elaborate chandeliers, antique fixtures and custom sconces. The spotlight is on one-of-a-kind high-end fixtures here, handled, clients say, with exceptional care. Some go so far to report they wouldn't let anyone else near their priceless fixtures. Clients also appreciate his practice of charging on a per-project basis, giving an estimate before the work begins. Valasquez is not a licensed electrician.

| | Quality | Cost | Value | Recommend? |
|---|---|---|---|---|
| | ✚ | $ | ◆ | ★ |

## Gunzer Electric

| | 4 | 4 | 4 | 5 |

36-08 34th Street, Long Island City, NY 11106
(718) 392 - 2219   www.gunzerelectric.com

*Commercial, industrial, institutional and residential electrical work*

Over the course of nearly thirty years, this prime electrical contractor has kept customer satisfaction in its sights. While Gunzer works with a handful of high-end contractors on large-scale renovations or restorations, both residential and commercial, we hear the firm mostly enjoys working directly with homeowners, often on smaller jobs. Clients applaud Gunzer's excellent customer service, and say the firm treats even the little tasks with a high degree of importance. Gunzer's expertise extends into all areas of industry trouble-shooting and maintenance, as well as specialty areas like fire alarm installation, structured cabling for audio/video and computers and lighting control design and installation. We hear that the company's response time to service calls within Manhattan is a mere 30 minutes. While it is said Gunzer's price quotes might cause a client to cover his ears, there's no debate as to whether the quality of the firm's work is on target.

*"They are fabulous!"*

## Jet Pak Electric Inc.

| | 4.5 | 3.5 | 5 | 5 |

341 East 90th Street, New York, NY 10128
(212) 410 - 6000

*Residential electrical services and specialty lighting design*

Clients, decorators and contractors all agree that Jet Pak electric has launched itself into the stratosphere of superior electrical contractors and lighting design professionals. With a reputation as "service-oriented problem solvers," Jet Pak specializes in complete electrical renovation and new construction for luxury residences and commercial clients in and around Manhattan, as well as expert repair and maintenance. Many of New York's top designers and architects choose Todd Rosencrans and his highly skilled team for their projects, describing them as extremely knowledgeable and very responsive. Clients are also impressed with Rosencrans' enthusiasm for his work and his eagerness to educate his clients and partners on such things as the intricacies of complex lighting systems. They add he is a person of creativity and good faith, and that his follow through is out of this world.

Jet Pak has over ten years of experience in the design and installation of whole home lighting control systems. References tell us during this time the firm has gained an impressive client list which includes celebrities and top Manhattan restaurant and retail establishments. Its Upper East Side office offers an interactive lighting technique and lighting control showroom. Jet Pak also works in structured wiring, electronic architecture, system integration, engineering and communication systems and equipment. The company provides an estimate for each job at what we hear, measure to others delivering the highest quality, is competitive.

*"Very responsible, great personnel. Responded promptly to all our needs." "Terrific staff! Loved every single one of them—so knowledgeable and professional." "Todd is wonderful. It is always a pleasure working with him." "One of the best contractors we dealt with in New York City."*

## K&G Electric Co. Inc.

| | 3.5 | 3 | 4.5 | 4 |

3925 Broadway, New York, NY 10001
(212) 923 - 2550

*Residential electrical installation and service*

K&G Electric is "a rare find" according to clients. This firm has the expertise, knowledge and willingness to take on any job in any of the five boroughs. Whether its installing a fixture, maintenance work for some of the most prestigious buildings in Manhattan, or conducting an electrical overhaul on a major renovation, this firm comes highly recommended by industry insiders and clients alike. While we hear the crews are all business, most clients say they are more than willing to forego the pleasantries for rock solid, high-end service.

*"They have been around a long time, know what they are doing, and can do it all."* *"Absolutely dependable, highly skilled employees who know what they are doing."*

## Levy Lighting
371 Broadway, 3rd Floor, New York, NY 10013
(212) 925 - 4640

*Lighting design and installation—custom fixture creation*

Owner Ira Levy tapped his experience in theatrical lighting to energize this small company. Levy Lighting engages in design, consultation and installation of lighting systems for residential, commercial and institutional clients. Whether programming for dimming, integrating with media systems or manufacturing custom fixtures, we hear Levy's work is both functional and architecturally enhancing. The firm can specify lighting packages and produce plans for entire projects. It also offers a division for on-site lighting adjustment and service. Pricing depends on the job, tabulated per hour or per project.

## LLE Inc.                                    4      3      4.5     4.5
236 West 26th Street, New York, NY 10001
(212) 924 - 6787

*Residential electrical installation and service*

This reliable small shop that specializes in residential electrical work is "definitely one of the better ones" in the city, according to references. We hear clients appreciate the advantage of calling on the same expertise and "nice" crew members that bring in LLE's larger high-end gut renovation projects for their smaller jobs. Run by Vince Lalomia, who has eighteen years of lighting design experience, LLE also provides lighting design and consultation services to architects, as well as installation of complex Lutron lighting control systems. Peers compliment Lalomia's professionalism and dedication to the job and to clients. His clients tell us Lalomia's thoroughness and dependability keep them confident and assured that the job will be done right. We hear Lalomia's crews are punctual, "very affable," active problem solvers who get the work done quickly and always pick up after themselves.

*"Vince is a great guy that does really good work." "Incredible. Came out at a last minute situation and fixed everything." "If left to my own devices I'm always on-time, so I appreciate LLE's guys showing up when they said they would." "It's difficult to get a great electrician for a smaller job. Thank goodness for LLE."*

## Mage Electric Inc.                         3      2.5    4.5     4
158 Perry Street, New York, NY 10014
(212) 462 - 0010

*Residential electrical work*

## Manteo Electric Inc.                        4      3      4.5     4
11 Ocean Avenue, Staten Island, NY 10305
(718) 981 - 6500   www.manteoelectric.com

*High end electrical installation and service*

With over four generations and 75 years under its belt, this modest-sized multi-talented electrical contractor designs and installs large-scale top-of-the-market penthouse and brownstone renovations and also takes regular service calls. We hear the firm's lighting design and engineering capabilities are often called upon by industry professionals. References say Agrippino "Pino" Manteo, grandson of the original Manteo, keeps himself, his son Mike and the rest of the staff on top of cutting-edge technologies. In addition to structured cabling, "smart houses" and home theater systems, the company is also familiar with fiber optic lighting and remote lighting control systems that require no wires or cutting into walls during a renovation.

We're told Manteo fields a dedicated, knowledgeable and conscientious crew— kept small to reflect only the best of the company. Customers confirm Manteo does everything he can to retain their business. It's even printed on the back of their shirts: "Whatever Lola wants, Lola gets." The firm's service is so consistent, landmark buildings use it for general maintenance.

### Maximum Electric Corp.      3      3      4      4
36-21 10th Street, Long Island City, NY 11106
(718) 937 - 7555

*Commercial and residential electrical work*

This electrical firm has been doing residential and commercial electric work for ten years, offering maximum services in all five boroughs. While the bulk of its business involves larger projects, the company is willing to do residential jobs of all sizes.

### Michael J. Dotzel & Sons      3.5      3.5      4      3.5
402 East 63rd Street, New York, NY 10021
(212) 838 - 2890

*Light fixture restoration, antique restoration and art metal work*

Since 1943, Dotzel and family have been rewiring and restoring chandeliers and other fine antique lighting fixtures. We are told he repairs and restores most antiques by reproducing old hardware, recasting metal parts and restoring finishes. While experts such as antique dealers and auction houses recommend Mike Dotzel for his skills and service, some customers find Dotzel's prices and persona over the top. He is not a licensed electrician.

### Mistretta Electric      3.5      2.5      4.5      3.5
35-07 Riverdale Avenue, Bronx, NY 10463
(718) 548 - 1649

*Residential electrical installation and service*

This father-son shop takes on anything electric dealing with light, heat and power. In business over twenty years, Mistrella's work ranges from small repair jobs to complete electric rehabs in gut renovations. We hear the firm can even rewire antique fixtures and will install structured cabling for computers, A/V and control systems. References recommend Mistretta Electric because the company can be counted on to get the job done. We are told that all at Mistretta are pleasant to work with, producing a solid product for a fair price.

*"Very nice man, with good abilities." "Gets the job done in a reasonable manner."*

### New York Electrical Management Co.      ▱  ▱  ▱  ▱
222-17 Jamaica Avenue, Queens Village, NY 11428
(718) 217 - 7740

*Residential electrical work and energy-conservation lighting*

## Ostroff Electric

|  |  |  |  |
|---|---|---|---|
| 4 | 3 | 4.5 | 5 |

102-14 159 Road, Howard Beach, NY 11414
(718) 323 - 5200   www.ostroffelectric.com
*High-end residential electrical installation*

This firm, with over 70 years of experience and 30 electricians on staff, has built an impressive reputation among a roster of the top decorators, contractors and architects in Manhattan—we hear many call on the Ostroff team for their high-profile projects. Clients tell us the professionals at Ostroff Electric are incredibly helpful and reliable. They particularly value the accommodating management team, which thoroughly grooms its staff members before they are sent out on call. We're told the firm has superintendents on staff whose knowledge of dimming systems and high end residential work is "second to none." While clients note Ostroff electricians do come back after the main job is done for upkeep, they warn the firm has not been found to sprint over to care for minor items.

*"Good, dependable, helpful."*

## Pell Artifax Co.

|  |  |  |  |
|---|---|---|---|
| 4.5 | 3.5 | 4.5 | 5 |

511 West 33rd Street, 2nd Floor, New York, NY 10001
(212) 563 - 9656
*Trade only—Light fixture restoration*

This firm works exclusively with the trade, who tell us that Pell Artifax does an incredible job with the intricacies of rewiring and restoring chandeliers, sconces and other decorative and antique light fixtures. We hear its knowledge and skills make Pell Artifax a useful entry in any decorator's Rolodex, and just the type of firm savvy customers highly recommend.

*"They know their stuff."*

## Peterbilt Electric Inc.

|  |  |  |  |
|---|---|---|---|
| 4 | 3 | 4.5 | 4 |

87-44 Barrington Street, Jamaica, NY 11432
(718) 229 - 9555
*Commercial and residential electrical contracting*

Run by sixth-generation electrican Peter Gargiulo, this firm primarily teams with a small cadre of top-tier contractors and architects on very large, sophisticated projects. With a star-studded client list, sources tell us Peterbilt is usually found working on Upper East and West Side duplexes and townhouses, or in the Hamptons. We hear the firm has also completed some very impressive commercial projects throughout the city. Clients say Gargiulo facilitates lighting design for complex dimming systems, and offers structured cabling for A/V and computer enthusiasts in conjunction with its major renovation work. For big jobs with big electrical budgets, customers insist on using Peterbilt.

## Polyphase Electric Inc.

|  |  |  |  |
|---|---|---|---|
| 4 | 3 | 5 | 5 |

41-20 38th Street, Long Island City, NY 11101
(718) 392 - 0885
*Commercial and residential electrical installation and service*

The most customer-conscious contractors and discriminating building managers call on Polyphase for residential work throughout Manhattan, from downtown lofts to uptown brownstones. We hear the firm's professionals work on projects varying in size and cost, from maintenance calls to major renovations. References tell us they do good quality work, and are very personable and accommodating. These features, along with very reasonable prices, may be why many clients have asked Polyphase to work on their second homes outside the city as well.

*"Great team. A real family feel."*

| | Quality | Cost | Value | Recommend? |
|---|---------|------|-------|------------|
| | + | $ | ◆ | ★ |

## RHR Electric Co. Inc.

155 East 26th Street, 1st Floor, New York, NY 11010
(212) 689 - 5474

*Residential electrical work*

We hear this big firm is "good and thorough," and considered by those in the industry to be an A-grade electrician. Word is RHR is one of the best electricians in town.

## Salzman Electric Company Inc.            4.5    3    4.5    4.5

208-05 35th Avenue, Bayside, NY 11361
(718) 229 - 5520

*Commercial and high-end residential electrical installation and service*

Clients tell us over and over that this full-service electrical contractor is the most reliable outfit in New York. Salzman has been serving both residential and commercial customers in the high-end market here in Manhattan for over five decades. Contractors, architects and designers all agree that Salzman's staff is made up of consummate professionals—attentive and responsive. We hear the firm turns around estimates quickly, completes jobs on or before schedule, and is great in emergencies. Client's also find Salzman's crew courteous, clean and "very knowledgeable in every aspect of our electrical installation needs."

References mention that with three partners—John Van Blerkom, Pete Danielsson and Larry Zassman—an owner will always show up on the job. Clients say they all strive to make Salzman a "leader in luxury residential contracting" by providing personal attention and a high standard of quality workmanship at a price less than you'd expect.

*"Highly reliable. I only use Salzman." "They do excellent work!" "Working with Salzman Electric was a great experience. They were always responsive and professional." "The job was completed on time, looked good and every detail was attended to. I would highly recommend them." "Job well done."*

## Shahon Electric Corp. Inc.              3    2    4.5    5

137 King Street, Brooklyn, NY 11231
(718) 625 - 1995

*Residential electrical work*

## Vintage Electric Service Inc.            4    3    4.5    4.5

137 18th Street, Brooklyn, NY 11215
(212) 966 - 5580

*Residential electrical installation and service*

Just the right vintage to go with renovation work for high-end residences and prime commercial clients, we hear this veteran electrical contractor accomplishes both big jobs for the biggest names and small jobs for the no-names. In his more than twenty years in the business Jim Kruger and his small but exemplary crew has installed lighting for galleries, intercom systems for Park Avenue penthouses, restored fixtures for churches and dressed up schools for the internet. Clients say Vintage does work right the first time with no short cuts on safety or quality. The firm's rates are fairly standard.

# Hiring a Flooring
# Service Provider

More than any other element of your home, flooring creates the most basic ambiance of a room and gets the steadiest use. Does your personal style call for wood floors or carpeting in the living room and bedrooms? Do you prefer a marble bathroom floor or a softer vinyl tile? In the kitchen, do you make clean-up a priority and prefer function over form? Your floors should be attractive as well as durable, and it's important to do some research so that you do not invest in flooring that scores high marks on looks but low points for practicality.

## Where Do I Start?

Take note of your needs before you speak to any flooring professionals. What type of flooring exists in these rooms now, and what lies beneath them? How much traffic will be in the room you want to recover? Is the subfloor suitable, or will it cost you money to fix it before installing the new floor? If you have children and/or pets, do you want to select a floor covering that is more practical than exotic? Or do you want to invest in imported hard tile to complement your new state-of-the-art gourmet kitchen? To get ideas, look through home furnishing magazines and pay a visit to a flooring showroom or two. Internet sites that will help you learn more about flooring options include Floorfacts, a consumer site filled with links and information (www.floorfacts.com), the National Wood Flooring Association's site (www.woodfloors.com) and the Carpet & Rug Institute's site (www.carpet-rug.com).

## Service and Warranties

The flooring company as well as the flooring material manufacturers should have warranties for your new floor coverings. Before you sign a work agreement, find out exactly who will be installing your floor: will your contact from the firm be doing the job himself, or bringing in a different crew? Check the work agreement to make sure that the firm will supply nails, glue and other installation accessories.

## Know Your Floor

Insist upon receiving written information about the care and maintenance of your new flooring. What cleaning products should you use, and what should you definitely avoid? Is there a standard timetable for cleaning your hardwood floor or carpeting? Does your carpet warranty come with a consumer hotline for stain emergencies? Who can you call for advice about stains and/or damage?

## What Are My Choices?

There are many options in flooring, each falling into five basic categories: wood, laminate, vinyl, carpet and hard tile (see section introduction to Tile, Marble and Stone). After considering the following descriptions of the basic floor types, you should be able to choose flooring that best meets your specific demands for beauty and maintenance.

## Wood

A real wood floor never goes out of style. It complements every decor, from minimalist to Louis XIV, and generally ages gracefully. The most popular woods used in flooring are oak and maple, which can be stained or color washed to your exact specifications. Wood flooring can be designed in numerous patterns, limited only by your imagination (and budget). Some of the most popular are parquet, plank, strip and herringbone. When choosing a stain color, have your contractor apply a few color samples and look at them in different kinds of light. Think of the ambiance you are trying to create in the room—traditional or modern, casual or formal, spacious or cozy. Wood floors can also be bleached for a light and airy look or painted. Hardwood floors can be customized to satisfy every taste and personality and installed in any room regardless of what type of flooring—concrete floors, existing floorboards or particleboard subflooring—is already there.

Aesthetically, a wooden floor is stunning. But consider a few issues before you make this your final choice. How much traffic does the room get every day? Hardwood floors can be dented and scratched, especially from high-heeled shoes. Although a variety of urethane finishes provide excellent protection (and shine), they do not completely prevent dents and scratches. These same finishes, however, make wood floors much easier to clean and maintain than previous generations of wood flooring. Humidity is another factor to consider. If the humidity in your area varies from season to season, a wood floor may expand and contract with the rise and fall of moisture in the air. Storing the wood on site for a period of time before installing will allow the wood to acclimatize to the specific humidity level in the home. The service provider should consider whether the floor is being installed in a particularly humid or dry time of the year, and make his measurements accordingly.

## LAMINATES

If you love the look of real wood but have an active household, laminate flooring may be the perfect choice for you. Laminates are plastic- or wood-based products that look like hardwood. They come in various textures, are durable and easy to maintain. Laminates can also imitate the look of stone, marble or tile, offering a wide variety of creative looks you may not have imagined. A wood-patterned laminate floor has some significant advantages over the real thing—for example, it will not be discolored by sunlight and is very scratch-resistant. Laminate floors wear well and usually come with a guarantee of ten years or more.

Cleanups are also a breeze with laminate flooring. Laminates repel liquid and do not allow stains to set in. This point alone saves your floor, your time and your psychological well-being. Design snobs will, however, look down their noses at laminate as as imitation.

Both hardwood floors and laminates, while possessing the great qualities of longevity and beauty, are quite expensive. If you are looking to invest less money, you may want to explore vinyl or carpet floor coverings.

## VINYL

Vinyl floor covering (linoleum) is the least expensive choice and offers more options than any other type of flooring. Patterns range from classic black-and-white squares to brick, stone, abstract shapes, animal prints—just about anything you can dream up has already been manufactured in a vinyl print. Vinyl is a very popular flooring, but it's important to consider that this material is vulnerable to cuts, rips and scratches from furniture that may be moved across it or sharp objects that fall to the floor. Although it resists moisture, vinyl can stain, so spills need to be handled quickly and carefully according to the manufacturer's directions.

## CARPETING

A cozy, lush floor covering, carpeting adds warmth, soundproofing, texture, color and insulation to a room. When considering carpeting, inquire about the carpet's durability and consider whether it will receive light, medium or heavy duty use. Industry experts suggest light duty for occasionally trafficked areas, medium duty for the bedroom or office, and heavy duty for hallways, stairs and other high-traffic areas. Carpeting requires extra maintenance as stains are more difficult to remove and general cleaning is more work. Wool is a whole lot easier to deep steam clean than nylon, but more expensive. Also, a protective sealant may be applied for future spills and stains. Lastly, if you or someone in your home is allergy prone, carpeting is not a good option because it retains dirt, dust and other particles.

## HARD TILE

Ceramic, quarry (stone, including marble) and terra cotta make up this premium category of floor covering. The look and feel of a hard-tiled floor is unlike any other, with grooves and textures that can be felt underfoot. Often used in kitchens and baths, tile flooring can give a distinct look and originality to any room in your home. In light colors, these materials do take on stains, so it is important to keep this in mind when choosing hard tile for particular rooms. Tile may be one of the most expensive kinds of flooring, but its remarkable beauty and longevity make it a good investment.

## ON COST

Some floor installers charge by the square foot and others by the job. Most providers charge by the hour for cleaning and repairing. If your service provider charges by the hour, confirm whether this fee is per person per hour or for the whole team. Will they charge for moving furniture around? Make sure your order includes extra quantities of flooring in your dye lot to replace broken, worn or stained parts in the future. This is especially crucial with hard tile which can crack if something heavy is dropped on it, and any material which stains easily.

### QUESTIONS TO ASK YOUR FLOORING SERVICE PROVIDER

Does the company have its own workshop? If so, it will have more control over the product than one that purchases its materials from another supplier. Ask the company if it does repairs as well as installation. If you need repairs done at a later date, you will probably have more clout if you also had the same contractor install your flooring.

### FLOORING COMPARISON CHART

RATINGS: Very Poor *    Poor **    Average ***    Good ****    Excellent *****

#### BASIC FLOOR TYPES

|  | VINYL | WOOD | LAMINATE | HARD TILE | CARPET |
|---|---|---|---|---|---|
| Ease of Maintenance | **** | *** | **** | **** | *** |
| Damage Resistance | ** | *** | **** | ***** | *** |
| Moisture Resistance | **** | * | *** | ***** | * |
| Stain Resistance | *** | ** | ***** | ***** | ** |
| Fade Resistance | *** | ** | ***** | ***** | *** |
| Scratch Resistance | ** | *** | **** | **** | N/A |
| Ease of Repairing | * | *** | ** | ** | * |
| Softness Under Foot | ** | * | * | * | ***** |
| Design/Color Selection | ***** | ** | ** | *** | **** |
| ✧Price Range (sq. ft.) | $.50 - $4.50 | $2.50 - $6.00 | $2.50 - $5.00 | $2.50 - $8.00 | $.50 - $5.00 |

✧The price range is for material only and is to be used as a general guideline. Prices will vary from supplier to supplier.

## Flooring Installation & Repair

### 800 Rug Wash
20 Enterprise Avenue, Secaucus, NJ  07094
(800) 784 - 9274   www.800rugwash.com
*Rug and upholstery cleaning and repair—flooring installation and maintenance*

See 800 Rug Wash's full report under the heading Rugs: Cleaning, Installation & Repair

### All Boro Floor Service                    3      2.5     4.5     4
135 East 233rd Sreet, Bronx, NY  10470
(718) 231 - 6911
*Wood flooring installation, refinishing and waxing*

Hardworking, skilled and honest are some of the terms references use to describe this firm. Satisfied clients and well-known contractors have used All Boro for years on multiple jobs. All Boro installs hardwood floors and does scraping, refinishing, waxing and staining. Its workmen also do custom floor projects, and specialize in white pickled floors. This firm also supplies floors, but only if they will install them. In business for eleven years, this residential and commercial firm works mostly in Manhattan and some parts of Westchester and New Jersey. The company is open all year round, gives free estimates and sources say prices are moderate to upper end.

*"Honest. They get the job done under difficult circumstances." "Above what I expected."*

### Amarko Marble & Granite                   3      3       4       4
60-14 60th Place, Maspeth, NY  11378
(718) 821 - 0323
*Marble flooring installation and maintenance*

Amarko installs, cleans, polishes and hones marble floors. Though serving mostly commercial clients, this firm also serves some residential clients. Additional services include cleaning and refinishing countertops and other marble and granite surfaces. Amarko's success can be attested through the exquisite stonework in some of the city's top hotels as well as in some residential interiors in the Upper West Side, Upper East Side and SoHo. Clients appreciate their efficient service and the moderate prices that go with it.

*"A pleasure to deal with." "Quick, efficient."*

### American Custom Wood Flooring             3      3       4       4
3615 Greystone Avenue, Bronx, NY  10463
(718) 548 - 9275
*Wood floor installation, cleaning, repair, custom designs and inlays*

American Custom Wood Flooring specializes in the installation, repair, cleaning and maintenance of wood floors only. The company also creates custom designs and inlays. The firm generally takes on commercial projects in Manhattan, working with contractors and architects, but will occasionally work with homeowners directly for residential projects. In business for fifteen years, the firm usually charges by the job and works on new construction and existing structures. Licensed, bonded and insured, this five-man company will move furniture if requested, but customers will be charged extra.

Clients say that the firm is very professional, prompt, neat and adheres to budget and deadlines.

*"Understands their business." "Performed professionally." "Have used them for several years."*

### Architectural Flooring Resource Inc.   4   3   4.5   4
151 West 28th Street, Suite 2W, New York, NY 10001
(212) 290 - 0200
*Flooring Installation, Refinishing & Maintenance*

Sources say that Architectural Flooring is an architect's dream resource for flooring needs. The firm supplies, installs, cleans and maintains wood, tile, cork, rubber, vinyl, laminates and wall-to-wall carpets. Sources tell us the majority of the firm's work is commercial. Residential projects, which constitute a small portion of the company's workload, are most often sourced from architects, designers and contractors, although owner Cathy Leidersdorff and her team will also work directly with homeowners. Established in 1993, this company serves all of New York, New Jersey, Philadelphia, the Hamptons and Westchester County.

Enthusiastic clients tell us this company has a great work ethic, is extremely responsive and that Leidersdorff can accommodate almost any budget because she has a huge amount of resources available to her. We hear that pricing is moderate to upper end and definitely worth the efficient service.

*"One of the few I really trust." "Excellent installation team."*

### Architectural Wood Flooring   3   2.5   4.5   3
8441 261st Street, Floral Park, NY 11001
(718) 347 - 8306
*Wood flooring installation, refinishing, maintenance, repair and retail*

This firm, which handles mostly residential projects, was established in 1988 and continues to serve most of Manhattan, some areas in the Hamptons and parts of Westchester. Architectural Wood Flooring specializes in all kinds of wood flooring services. The company sells, installs, repairs, restores, refinishes, sands, stains, cleans and maintains. We are told that the company believes in proper prepwork for every project and ensures that all subfloors are correctly done and firmly glued. The company also takes pride in its antique restorations and custom designs and inlays, such as the herringbone, one of their popular patterns.

Sources say the firm takes pride in giving personalized service and attention to detail in every endeavor it undertakes.

### Aronson's Floor Covering Inc.   3.5   2.5   4.5   5
135 West 17th Street, New York, NY 10011
(212) 243 - 4993   www.aronsonsfloors.com
*Flooring installation and retail*

Who says flooring has to be boring? One of the oldest flooring companies in New York doesn't think so. Aronson's believes flooring shouldn't be stodgy and dull, but fun and cool and its showroom certainly reflects this with their "action figures" (i.e. Vinyl Vixen, Carpet Cowboy, Tile Temptress) representing each floor type. Licensed, bonded and insured, this firm has been serving clients in Manhattan, the Hamptons, Westchester and other areas in the regional area since its founding in 1867 by Samuel Aronson. The company is now owned and run by his great-nieces, Laura and Carol Swedlow. This residential and commercial institution sells, installs, creates custom designs and does some repair on wood, cork, rubber, linoleum, area rugs, wall-to-wall carpets and mats. This eighteen-man business works with architects, contractors and designers as well as directly with home-owners. Insiders say the firm has a wide selection of flooring products and a trip to their showroom is a treat in itself.

Clients are delighted with this firm's efficient service. They say that Aronson's is very responsive, fix any problems promptly, are punctual and are tidy workers. Pricing is per square foot. The firm has very fair prices which are definitely worth the efficient service.

*"Customer satisfaction is important." "Crews are self supervising." "Lovely work." "Personalized service." "Not the highest quality in town—but reasonably priced and good attitude."*

## Atlantic Hardwood Flooring                    3.5    2.5    4.5    4.5
3265 Johnson Avenue, Bronx, NY  10463
(718) 601 - 4082
*Wood and laminated flooring installation and repair*

Since its establishment in 1980 by Jerry Plunkett, Atlantic Hardwood Flooring has been installing and repairing hardwood and laminated floors for residential interiors. The company serves mostly Manhattan's Upper East Side and some areas of the Bronx. Impressed clients tell us that the workers are always on time, neat, courteous and conscientious. Satisfied customers appreciate the capable service Atlantic provides and the reasonable prices that go along with it.

*"Extremely well carried out." "Very impressed with workers." "Work executed professionally from beginning to end."*

## C&C Flooring                    3.5    3    4.5    4.5
4276 Oneida Avenue, Bronx, NY  10470
(718) 994 - 1496
*Wood flooring installation and refinishing*

For standard flooring needs at a reasonable price, C&C is your best bet. Founded in 1995, it is managed by brothers Bryan and Keith Chapman. The company does flooring for new construction and existing structures. C&C works mainly in Manhattan and does some projects in Westchester and Mamaroneck, and serves both residential and commercial clients, including a number of high-end management companies, Columbia University, decorators and architects. With a full-time staff of eight skilled workmen, C&C can handle large projects and is small enough to give personal attention to each client. The firm specializes only in wood floors and will clean, repair, restore, refinish, create custom designs and install.

Insiders say the Chapmans are perfectionists and are on the site all the time to ensure that everything goes along smoothly. Clients tell us that they are responsive, prompt, polite and courteous.

*"Absolutely superb work—and fast." "Bends over backward." "Extremely reliable."*

## Chelsea Floor Covering                    4.5    2.5    4.5    5
139 West 19th Street, New York, NY  10011
(212) 243 - 0375   www.chelseafloors.com
*Retailer—flooring installation, refinishing, waxing and cleaning*

Clients tell us they appreciate the personalized service given by this family-owned Manhattan flooring business which has served the area for more than fifty years. Chelsea installs, repairs—and sells—carpet, linoleum, vinyl, laminates, pre-finished wood, cork and rubber flooring. Clients are also pleased with the firm's floor refinishing services. Managed by Bosco brothers Kenny and Dennis Junior, this company produces fine floors for both residential and commercial clients in all areas of Manhattan, many of which have come back time and time again. The company works mostly with architects, designers, contractors and building management firms, but will occasionally work directly with homeowners. Pricing is typically by the job and estimates are free.

References say they are pleased with the service provided by this company and describe them as neat, punctual and organized. They also appreciate that Chelsea Flooring adheres to the budget and meets the scheduled deadline effortlessly.

*"Experts in their field." "Delivered floors the day before and installation was done right on schedule." "They were on time. They stayed on budget. They were perfect." "Flexible with scheduling. Responsive."*

### Cordts Flooring Corp.                    3.5      3      4.5     3.5
111 Route 9 South, Fishkill, NY  12524
(914) 737 - 8201

*Wood, rubber and cork flooring manufacturing and installation*

Cordts Flooring manufactures and installs wood, rubber and cork floors. Established in 1986 by Thomas Cordts, this firm serves mostly residential clients across Manhattan and Connecticut, as well as some areas in Long Island, including the Hamptons. Though the company generally coordinates with architects and decorators, it also works directly with homeowners. Cordts specializes in creating custom designs and inlays, and we are told the company creates authentic-looking antique reproductions. Whether you prefer a Normandy-style home or an old Parisian look, sources say Cordts can create both with quality and ease. This firm also manufactures floors—both modern and antique reproductions—and is very proud of its full-service manufacturing facility. Though they don't install, they can do this service for the client by contracting other installers and manufacturing the floors for them.

Clients say the company is very accommodating, easy to work with and claim the work is rugged—and of high quality. Pricing is per square foot, estimates are free and they also give a ten-year warranty for the wood itself.

*"My floors are holding up after several years." "Neat and punctual. They get the job done."*

### Country Floors Inc.
15 East 16th Street, New York, NY  10003
(212) 627 - 8300   www.countryfloors.com

*Handmade and imported tile sales and installation*

See Country Floors Inc.'s full report under the heading Tile, Marble & Stone

### Curran's Floor Service                    3      3      4      4
4297 Martha Avenue, Bronx, NY  10470
(718) 446 - 9123

*Wood flooring installation, refinishing and repair*

Curran's has real fans among its customers, who compliment the company for the quality of its work and service. We hear that the work is done by skilled, careful and dependable professionals. Curran's specializes in all types of wood. The company installs, repairs and refinishes wood floors for both residential and commercial clients around Manhattan and in some areas of the Bronx and Long Island.

| | Quality | Cost | Value | Recommend? |
|---|---------|------|-------|------------|
| | ✚ | $ | ◆ | ★ |

## Dezel Building Services
767 Lexington Avenue, New York, NY 10021
(212) 751 - 3005

*General cleaning and flooring services*

See Dezel Building Services's full report under the heading Window Washers

## Eastside Floor Services
129 East 124th Street, New York, NY 10035
(212) 996 - 1800  www.eastsidefloors.com

**4    3    4.5    5**

*Wood flooring installation, refinishing, repair, cleaning, custom designs and retail*

Established by Gerry Flynn in 1985, Eastside is one of the city's largest distributors and manufacturers of wood flooring. The company specializes in installing, repairing, refinishing, cleaning and maintaining wood floors and will do both standard jobs and custom-milled flooring in local and exotic woods. Eastside also deals in unfinished wood such as strip, parquet and herringbone of all sizes and types. This firm has the ability to create custom designs and borders in its workshop. Additionally, Eastside distributes prefinished wood flooring from all leading manufacturers. This commercial and residential company serves all New York boroughs, the Hamptons and other parts of the regional area. This company boasts such commercial projects as Barney's New York and Macy's.

Clients praise this company's quality of work and describe them as professional, punctual and neat. Though scheduling is often difficult due to the company's busy timetable, sources say the moderate to upper-end prices and excellent service are worth the wait.

*"The only people who touch our floors." "They're very good at what they do."*

## Elite Floor Service Inc.
12 Saratoga Avenue, Yonkers, NY 10705
(212) 228 - 1050

**3.5    2.5    4.5    4.5**

*Wood flooring installation and refinishing*

References are impressed with this ten-year fixture in the Manhattan flooring business. Many praise the politeness and workmanship of Elite craftsmen, while others told us that the Elite staff is helpful, prompt and efficient. Clients say that this company is conscientious about following up and the prices are reasonable. Some references expressed minor concerns about neatness, but others said projects were carried out in a tidy manner and most would hire Elite again or recommend the company to friends.

Elite specializes in all types of wood floors. The company installs, refinishes, sands, repairs, creates custom designs and inlays and does a lot of staining and pickling. The firm works mostly in Manhattan, the surrounding boroughs and some parts of Westchester. The company has a large number of clients that need standard floor installation and refinishing service. This mostly residential company works with designers, architects, contractors and directly with homeowners. Pricing is usually by the job and estimates are free.

*"Unbelievably polite, considerate. They do a great job." "I was very pleased. There were no surprises." "Fabulous work ethic."*

## Flooring Manhattan LLC
34-49 Irwin Avenue, Bronx, NY 10463
(866) 356 - 6776  flooringmanhattan.com

**3.5    3    4.5    4.5**

*Wood, vinyl, laminate, bamboo, tile and stone installation, cleaning and repair*

Personalized service and customer satisfaction are this company's strongest assets, sources say. It certainly works, for Flooring Manhattan has built a growing list of loyal clients since its establishment two years ago. Though relatively new, the firm's founders have had a long history in the flooring business, one as long as fifty years. Flooring Manhattan installs, repairs, cleans and maintains hardwood, laminates, vinyl, tile, marble, granite, ceramic and bamboo floors. They also specialize in producing floors with custom designs and inlays, such as the herringbone, one of their most popular patterns. Utilizing traditional methods of installation created by European artisans, the firm develops these and applies today's technology to produce new and more advanced techniques. Their laminate installation is first done and patterned through computers, their custom vinyl comes in large strips that ensure longevity and for wood installation, they use special patented pads placed underneath the floor to minimize squeaks and leaks. The company serves most of Manhattan, some parts of Westchester and the regional area, producing floors for mostly residential and some commercial interiors.

Clients report they appreciate such attention to detail as applying protective sealants, buffing between coats and the choice between water or oil-based polyurethanes. Sources tell us that owner Mayan Metzler and his team are very businesslike, efficient, on time and will accommodate even the budget-conscious homeowner.

*"Very pleasant to deal with." "I recommend them to everybody." "Was on top of things."*

## H&K Hansen Flooring     4     3     4.5     5
580 Old Stage Road, East Brunswick, NJ  08816
(732) 251 - 0989
*Wood flooring refinishing and sanding*

A family-run business established thirteen years ago, H&K Hansen specializes in sanding and finishing wood floors only. The firm, run by Kurt Hansen and his uncle, serves only residential clients in Manhattan and parts of the Hamptons, Westchester and Connecticut. The firm works with decorators, contractors and directly with homeowners. Pricing is usually per square foot, unless the project is really small, then H&K charges by the job.

The majority of the sources told us that H&K's work is excellent—some say the best in the city—and that some amount of artistic attitude may go along with getting this top-quality work.

*"Best finisher!" "The best in town. Must treat like a king, though." "Found the experience less than enjoyable." "Reliable and pleasant."*

## Haywood Berk Floor Company Inc.     4     4.5     3.5     4
180 Varick Street, New York, NY  10014
(212) 242 - 0047
*Wood flooring installation, refinishing, custom designs, and repair*

As one of the oldest flooring companies in New York, Haywood Berk is now on its third generation of Berks since Otto Berk established the company in 1921. It is now managed by his grandson Roger, who is described by sources as a knowledgeable craftsman—dedicated and very professional. Indeed, references are quick to say good things about this firm and praise its attention to detail and commitment to offering a high-quality service. Though some residential clients feel that the company's responsiveness to inquiries are not its strongest point, most agree that Haywood staff members are efficient and are experts in this field. In fact, many top tier designers would not consider anyone else for their discriminating clients.

The firm deals only with wood, and performs services such as installation, restoration, custom designs, staining, pickling, refinishing and repair. Most of their projects are in Manhattan and they do a fair amount of work in the Hamptons, Westchester, Connecticut and Los Angeles. This residential and commercial firm has worked on museums and with top architects and designers. They are also a member of the Maple Flooring Manufacturers Association.

*"Good job. Do it until they get it right." "Hard to get through to them as they often did not return phone calls, but I know that their work quality will always be excellent." "As a decorator, I can schedule their work within two weeks on a consistent basis." "Roger understands his products, but more importantly he understands his high-end client base."*

### Hoboken Wood Floors      4    3    4    5

979 Third Avenue, New York, NY 10022
(212) 759 - 5917   www.hobokenfloors.com

*Wood floor distribution, installation, maintenance, custom design and repair*

Hoboken Wood Floors started out as a small company in Hoboken, New Jersey and is now one of the nation's largest flooring distribution and installation companies. It has nine distribution centers and two design centers. The company's New York Offices and showroom are located at the prestigious D&D Building in Manhattan. This business, with 500 full-time employees, serves both high-end residential and commercial clients. Established in 1932 by Jospeh Sakosits, the firm is now run by his grandson Brian Sakosits and his partners. Hoboken installs, repairs, restores, sands, finishes, stains, bleaches and creates custom designs and high quality borders for wood floors. Hoboken works directly with homeowners in addition to designers, architects and contractors. Pricing is by the job and estimates are free. The firm also has branches in Georgia, Florida, Delaware, Connecticut, Massachussets and Maine.

Customers say they appreciate the company's efficient service, excellent work ethic and promptness. Although prices are upper end, clients say it is a good value for the service they provide. Decorators often call on their services, knowing they will do an excellent job at a respectable price.

*"My floors are beautiful." "One of the best in the New York area." "Very reliable quality without killing you on price." "They are a professional company, not three guys and a truck."*

### I.J. Peiser's & Son      3.5    3    3.5    3

475 Tenth Avenue, New York, NY 10018
(212) 279 - 6900

*Wood flooring installation and refinishing*

Known for its handscraped and handfinished floors, I.J. Peiser's is one of New York's oldest flooring companies. Owned and managed by Stephen Estrin, the company was established by his great grandfather in 1909. The company installs, cleans and repairs all types of wood floors. The firm also takes pride in its custom designs and inlays, which are created in Peiser's own workshop. This mainly residential company serves most of Manhattan, some areas in the Hamptons, Westchester, Connecticut and even as far away as Palm Beach and Oklahoma. Estrin also has a strong commercial following, some of which includes prestigious hotels (the Palace, the Carlyle) and some of the top contractor and architectural firms in the city.

Sources describe Estrin as very professional, honest, reliable, easy to work with and a great craftsman. Delighted customers also say that the firm meets deadlines, adheres to budgets and is willing to fix any problem that arises. Although a few expressed minor concerns on the efficiency of their service. Though Peiser's prices are on the upper end of the bracket, clients say the excellent service and the quality of the floors are well worth the cost.

*"Absolutely excellent." "Extremely cooperative." "One of the finest craftsmen around." "Honest." "Been here a long time." "On schedule. Reliable."*

| | Quality | Cost | Value | Recommend? |
|---|---|---|---|---|
| | + | $ | ◆ | ★ |

## Isaiah Johnson Floor Sanding
| | Quality | Cost | Value | Recommend? |
|---|---|---|---|---|
| | 4 | 3 | 5 | 4.5 |

62 Maple Road, Amityville, NY 11701
(800) 734 - 8575

*Wood flooring installation, refinishing, repair, custom designs and inlays*

Sources say this polite, committed craftsman has been delighting and satisfying clients for 35 years. The firm installs, repairs, sands and finishes all types of wood floors. It also does custom designs, pickled floors and can imitate any type of oak. Known for being able to handle difficult jobs and for giving particular attention to detail, Isaiah Johnson established the company in 1966 after training with his brother. Johnson does all the work himself and serves mostly residential clients in Manhattan, as well as some areas in the Hamptons and around the regional area.

Sources say that Johnson is honest, efficient, reliable and remains within the set budget. We also hear that he takes obvious pride in his work and will go the extra mile to make sure the results are perfect. Clients appreciate the personalized service and the reasonable prices that go along with it.

*"The floor still looks brand new." "A true craftsman in the old school style." "Working with him was a really positive experience." "Excellent. Very neat and tidy."*

## Janos P. Spitzer Flooring
| | Quality | Cost | Value | Recommend? |
|---|---|---|---|---|
| | 4.5 | 4 | 4 | 4 |

133 West 24th Street, New York, NY 10010
(212) 627 - 1818   www.janosspitzerfloor.com

*High-end wood flooring installation, custom design, repair and restoration*

Serving high-end clients and satisfying their discriminating tastes are not easy tasks, but clients say Janos Spitzer does both flawlessly—the same way that he creates his exquisite wood floors. Established in 1962, Spitzer installs, restores, repairs, sands and finishes wood floors for mostly residential and some commercial interiors. Preferred by contemporary architects and decorators, but also used by some traditionalists, this company is known for producing exquisite wood floors with low grain definition—floors that look like "shields of glass"—which are more suited for modern, cutting-edge designs. The firm serves most of Manhattan, some areas in the Hamptons, Westchester and California. Samples of Spitzer's work can be viewed at his 2,400-square-foot showroom, which is regarded by insiders as a "must-see" in the city.

Spitzer works with high-end designers, architects and homeowners. His impressive roster of clients include Mark Hampton, Inc., The Getty Museum, The Four Seasons, David Anthony Easton and Philip Johnson, to name a few. Known as one of the best in the country by clients and industry insiders alike for his custom designs and inlays, Spitzer works with local, imported and exotic woods. His company has been featured in such prominent publications as *The New York Times* and *Architectural Digest* where his woodworking skills and floors are highly praised. This firm is also a member of The National Wood Flooring Association.

We hear that the Spitzer team is prompt, attentive, accommodating and very professional. References say that Spitzer himself is honorable, honest, a "hands-on dedicated businessman" and generally, "just terrific to work with." Although some say that his talent is matched with an artistic temperament, the majority agrees the firm's extensive knowledge, commitment to excellence, elegant designs and attention to detail are definitely worth the expensive prices.

*"The top man in the business." "No one can quite match his ability." "He really understands how to make the perfect wood floor." "Excellent work ethic." "Very, very good—not the cheapest in the world, but worth every penny." "Great people." "A genius with a temperament." "A wonderful old-world craftsman."*

## Kirk Window Cleaning Co.
123-25 82nd Avenue, Kew Gardens, NY  11415
(212) 353 - 7780

*Commercial and residential window cleaning, flooring services*

See Kirk Window Cleaning Co.'s full report under the heading Window Washers

## Lane's Floor Coverings & Interiors Inc.    3    2.5    3.5    4
2 Park Avenue, New York, NY  10016
(212) 532 - 5200   www.lanes-carpets.com

*Retail, installation, cleaning, and repair—Vinyl, linoleum, carpets, rubber, cork, tile, marble and wood*

Most clients found Lane's excellent to work with and praised the company's high quality.  Lane's supplies, installs, cleans and repairs vinyl, wall-to-wall carpets, wood, linoleum, tile, marble, granite, cork, rubber and laminates.  Established in 1965 by Lane Brettschneider who comes from a family of experienced flooring people, this firm does projects around the regional area, the Hamptons, Westchester and along the West Coast.

In business for more than 35 years, Lane's has built a strong reputation not only among residential clients, but in the trade as well.  The company works with designers, general contractors and noted architects.  Some of the company's notable projects include providing Pope John Paul II's carpet during visits to New York City in the 1970s and 1995—and the floors for the Reuters building in New York. Lane's has a showroom on Park Avenue which is open to the public and the trade.

*"On time. Responds quickly." "Reliable. Worked out issues well." "Superb service."*

## Manhattan Hardwood Floors Inc.    3.5    3    3.5    4
2147 Second Avenue, New York, NY  10029
(212) 876 - 8100

*Wood flooring retail, wholesale, installation and refinishing*

Manhattan Hardwood Floors offers wholesale and retail flooring and supplies to both commercial and residential customers.  Sources say some of its more specialized offerings include prefinished and unfinished medallions and custom borders.  The company carries such names as Bruce, Robbins and Pergo flooring. According to references, Manhattan Hardwood will install and refinish if they supply the floor, depending on the scope and complexity of the project.  The firm's showroom and warehouse on Second Avenue is open to the public and to the trade.

## New Wood    4    3    4.5    4
22 East 105th Street, New York, NY  10029
(718) 665 - 5400

*Wood floor installation, finishing, sanding, restoration and repair*

Since its founding in 1982, New Wood has been installing, repairing, restoring, sanding, finishing and creating custom designs, inlays and borders for wood floors.  Owner and founder Peter Downs also does full-service consultations and works with domestic and exotic woods.  The firm serves a predominantly high-end residential clientele, rarely working on commercial projects.  Most of the company's projects are on the Upper West Side of Manhattan and some areas in Westchester County and Connecticut.  New Wood is a member of The National Wood Flooring Association and The National Trust for Historic Preservation.

We hear that these craftsmen are very professional, have excellent work ethics and are considerate of the client's home and belongings, are well organized and responsible.  Though prices are high-end, customers delight in the beautiful floors and efficient service that go along with it.

*"Personalized service."  "Works well with other tradesmen in the business." "Excellent at mixing stains and matching floors."*

| | Quality | Cost | Value | Recommend? |
|---|---|---|---|---|

## New York Floor King
2.5   2.5   3   4.5

300 East 96th Street, New York, NY 10128
(212) 410 - 3392

*Wood flooring refinishing, sanding and waxing*

New York Floor King was established in 1984. It specializes in wood floor refinishing, sanding, repair and waxing. The firm serves most of Manhattan, other New York boroughs and some parts of Westchester. Sources say the company rarely does any installations and has mostly residential clients. Pricing is generally per square foot and the firm has a modest minimum amount to do a project. The business also gives a six-year warranty on their floors.

## New York Flooring ▣
4.5   3.5   4.5   5

129 East 124th Street, New York, NY 10035
(212) 427 - 6262   www.newyorkflooring.com

*Wood flooring installation, refinishing, maintenance and repair*

Residential clients and experts in the home services trade report being delighted by their experiences with New York Flooring. Some references tell us that they swear by the company and will use none other. We are told the firm is prompt, attentive, respectful of clients' wishes and extremely dependable. The quality of its work is some of the best in Manhattan, according to clients. We're told its workers are craftsmen who take great care and pride in their work, use only the best materials and exceed expectations. While most clients feel New York Flooring is worth every penny, others say it is a bit pricey for more standard jobs.

New York Flooring works only on wood floors and performs a wide range of services such as installation, refinishing, maintenance, creation of custom designs and inlays and repair. This family-owned firm will also do custom work in its in-house workshop. In business for over 60 years, the company works with many well-known architects, contractors and designers as well as residential clients. New York Flooring has done projects at the White House and Gracie Mansion and for a number of celebrities.

*"I recommend them highly." "They are a good value. Always accommodate. There's no question, they can handle any job."*

## Norwegian Wood
3.5   3   4.5   4.5

174 Ninth Avenue, New York, NY 10011
(212) 929 - 3853

*Wood flooring installation, refinishing, custom designs and repair*

A specialist in installing, repairing, refinishing and creating custom inlays, Norwegian Wood has been satisfying customers since its founding in 1989. With fifteen full time employees, this company handles residential and commercial projects, including new construction and remodeling existing structures around Manhattan and Westchester. Estimates are free and pricing, normally by square foot or by the job, is negotiable. Norwegian Wood is a member of The National Wood Flooring Association.

Clients were enthusiastic about their experience with Norwegian Wood—they say Norwegian is easy to work with, pleasant and dependable. The company's work is described as top quality and lasting. Satisfied customers say they have used the company again and again, and have recommended it to friends.

*"My floors look great!" "Good quality and service." "Reliable. Easy to work with."*

## Pat Pellegrini Floors     3.5    2.5    5    4.5
29-12 39th Avenue, Long Island City, NY 11101
(212) 533 - 2600   www.pellegrinifloorscorp.com

*Wood flooring installation and refinishing*

In business since 1960, Pat Pellegrini works only on wood floors, doing installations, repairs, sanding, bleaching, staining and refinishing and produces standard inlays and designs. He works with decorators, architects and homeowners mostly in Manhattan, Queens, Long Island and the Hamptons.

Pat Pellegrini is lauded as a wonderful man and a great floorer. Clients say he and his workmen are polite, prompt and committed to doing a good job. Clients say that if there is a problem, Pellegrini is more than happy to come back and fix it. In addition to praising the great service, references tell us the work is high quality and very reasonably priced. Satisfied customers have used him more than once and recommended him to friends and family. Sources also tell us that Pellegrini will stand behind his work 100 percent.

*"He laid a beautiful floor: hire him." "Prompt, professional, neat." "Beautiful job, I highly recommend Pat." "Very positive experience. He comes when he says he will." "The floor looks better than what I expected." "It's been three years— the floors are holding up well."*

## Scerri Quality Wood Floors     4.5    3.5    4.5    5
426 East 73rd Street, New York, NY 10021
(212) 472 - 0671   www.gonefinishing.com

*Wood floor retail, installation, refinishing, custom designs and repair*

"Top-notch" is the consensus among patrons of Scerri Quality Wood Floors. We hear that they enjoy working with Scerri and his professional, neat and courteous workmen. Two strong points of the company that clients note is its willingness to listen to customers' ideas and its accommodating approach to the projects they take on. Some clients tell us they have used Scerri for years and recommend it to friends and family.

The firm focuses on wood flooring, particularly custom work, installation, restoration, retail and repair. Scerri will design, manufacture and install all of its work. A large part of the firm's business is working with medallions, borders and inlays. The firm also produces wooden stairways and handcrafted barnyard furniture. The firm's showroom also sells flooring maintenance products. Sources tell us the company serves trade architects and designers as well as high-end residential clients. While most of its work is on the Upper East Side and in second homes in the country, Scerri also does some smaller projects for more budget-conscious clients.

*"There are almost no contractors I've used that I can recommend, and I recommend him highly." "Very efficient—superb work." "Can do any finish you want." "Meticulous. Incredible attention to detail."*

## Walsh Flooring     4    3.5    4.5    4.5
177 Battaglia Lane, 2nd Floor, Fairview, NJ 07022
(201) 945 - 9014

*Wood flooring installation, refinishing and repair*

This New Jersey-based firm caters to a high-end residential and commercial clientele throughout the Northeast. They supply, install, refinish, sand, create custom designs and repair wood floors. This firm is an upstanding member of The National Wood Flooring Association and sources say Walsh Flooring takes pride in its excellent client relations and high levels of workmanship—and top notch materials.

Most references gush with praise about Walsh Flooring. They tell us they love dealing with the craftsmen of this firm, who work with skill, attention to detail and a sense of humor. Some mentioned that Walsh's workers put in extra effort to get any job done perfectly. We've heard that in one instance, a client thought one part of her floor looked dull. She was hesitant to speak up, but did anyway, and Joseph Walsh and his workmen came back and graciously redid the floor. The quality of Walsh's work is roundly hailed as some of the best in the area.

*"Really good work, their herringbone design is gorgeous." "May cost a bit more, but gets it done right." "Floors are fabulous!" "My floors still look good after four years."*

## William J. Erbe Company Inc.

| | | 5 | 4.5 | 4.5 | 5 |
|---|---|---|---|---|---|

560 Barry Street, Bronx, NY 10474
(212) 249 - 6400

*High-end wood flooring installation, refinishing, sanding, custom designs, restoration and repair*

Flooring as art? At the William J. Erbe Company, it certainly is. Erbe is considered by clients, architects, designers and even acknowledged by other high-end flooring companies as being the best and most expensive producer of hand-made and handscraped wood floors. The company installs, repairs, refinishes, sands, restores and maintains wood floors for residential and commercial interiors and designs some of the most intricate floor patterns. Its workmen are few and in demand, and Erbe himself or one of his sons supervises each project.

Though based in New York, Erbe's projects are mostly out-of-state or outside the country. The firm enjoys an impressive roster of local and international clients such as top designers David Easton and Mark Hampton, Inc., the Metropolitan Museum of Art, the White House and the Royal Family in Kuwait, to name a few. Known for his custom designs and antique restorations, Erbe scours France looking for chateau owners parting with their antique parquet floors, imports them and meticulously restores the exquisite pieces for clients. Called by *The New York Times* as "the Rolls-Royce of flooring companies," this family business was founded by Erbe's great grandfather in 1907 and was incorporated in 1968.

Sources say that this company can reproduce and create any kind of floor, and that they are dedicated, professional and "the most amazing craftsmen around." Indeed, whether it be Erbe's famous parquet de Versaille, antique or modern finish, with inlays or without, flooring at the William J. Erbe Company has been elevated to an art form.

*"As an architect, I would not consider risking a clients' floors with anyone other than Erbe—no one can compare." "Seriously the best floor company around." "Exquisite craftsman. Exceeds my expectations." "If there was a New York God for Wood Floors, William Erbe would be it."*

## Hiring a Furniture Repair & Refinishing Service Provider

Does your prized baroque chair need restoration? Do you refuse to get rid of your comfortable thriftstore couch but admit it needs sprucing up? Will your bedroom finally be complete with the addition of a twin reproduction of your favorite antique bedside table? Or perhaps you have a piece that has survived fire or flood damage, a teething puppy, climate changes or just general wear and tear. Before surrendering it to the hands of a professional, you should know a few things about it and the artisan who will repair, restore or conserve it.

### Where Do I Start?

Before locating a professional, take the time to verify that your thrift shop bargain isn't a priceless antique in disguise and your heirloom isn't actually an ordinary reproduction. Inappropriate restoration of an antique can greatly compromise its value. Sometimes a seemingly simple repair can actually cause further, irreparable damage. So be sure to have your piece's history and condition closely examined before allowing any work to be done on it.

Research on your piece should go beyond a consultation with the encyclopedia. Consult a professional—preferably several. Most professionals will visit your home to provide a price estimate and a detailed explanation of how your piece should be treated. Some charge fees for on-site verbal and written estimates; others don't. Estimates should include the cost of labor, materials and transportation. You should also discuss how your piece will be insured and whether or not a warranty will be provided for the work and under what conditions.

Knowing the value of your piece is important not only in determining the type of work that it needs and how well it should be insured, but also how much to invest in the work. If your thrift store table simply needs its broken leg replaced, you may not want to pay top dollar for labor fees. However, if you're concerned about transporting your original Louis XIV dining room table, you may opt to keep it at home and pay for a specialized professional to work on site.

### On Cost

Many professionals base their fees on an hourly or daily rate that is subject to increase, depending on the condition of your piece, the work it needs and where that work takes place. As a general guideline, hourly rates can range from $45 to $150. Be sure you receive a written contract for the amount of work agreed upon and the cost. If additional work is needed, the professional should notify you before taking action and a new fee should be agreed upon.

### Choosing the Right Specialist for You

No licensing bureaus or governing boards regulate furniture restorers, so it is crucial that you take the time to find the right professional for your particular piece. Although furniture restorers tend to be well versed in all styles and periods, each has a specialty. You wouldn't take a broken toe to an allergist, nor would you want to take your japanned armoire to a caning specialist. Inquire about the professional's area of expertise. For example, if your dining room table needs to be refinished, be wary of a craftsman who wants to use French polish and says you'll be eating from your table within a day or two. French polish is typically saved for show pieces such as game tables and armoires and not used on surfaces that are prone to spills or burns. It is also a time-consuming process that requires numerous layers of shellac and alcohol to be applied, dried and rubbed before being reapplied. Keep in mind that moisture captured between the layers can cloud the surfaces irrevocably, so humid weather will prolong the process. Be patient because a good professional will not want to rush the job.

Also, be wary of someone who is eager to refinish your Federal bureau, or any of your antiques. Much of the value of any antique derives from its rarity, quality and condition, and an original finish is an important part of this. Be sure to find a professional who is as interested in preserving the unique qualities of your piece as you are.

## QUESTIONS TO ASK A FURNITURE PROFESSIONAL

Although your main contact will most likely be the firm's principal, most firms have numerous employees, each with a different area of expertise. Be sure you know who is working on your piece and what they will be doing. The person who re-creates the leg of your table may not be the person who finishes it.

Don't be afraid to ask about the firm's expertise, including whether individuals have been trained in a particular style or period. Ask where they've worked and with whom. Also, ask to see their portfolio and to speak with numerous references. Make a point of speaking with the references. They know the work, and will tell you if actual fees exceeded the estimate, if the work took twice as long as expected or—the best scenario—if the work was beautifully done.

## FURNITURE CARE TIPS

- ✧ Protect furniture from direct sunlight, which fades colors, bleaches wood and clouds polished surfaces.
- ✧ Avoid exposure to excessive heat, such as placing furniture near a radiator or setting hot objects upon the piece, as this damages surface coatings, veneers and underlying adhesive.
- ✧ Place coasters on surfaces to protect them from liquids, which can stain.
- ✧ Wipe up water-based spills with a towel, but dab alcohol spills carefully to prevent spreading the spill—alcohol breaks down finishes.
- ✧ Invest in a humidifier/dehumidifier to minimize large fluctuations of humidity.
- ✧ Use a buffer when writing on a table top, as pens and pencils can cause unsightly indentations.
- ✧ When moving furniture, lift by the strongest units or rails—never drag!

## FURNITURE REPAIR & REFINISHING

### Anatoli's Restoration               4      3.5     4.5     4.5
555 Eighth Avenue, 2nd Floor, New York, NY  10018
(212) 629 - 0071

*Furniture repair and restoration*

Anatoli has been in the furniture repair and restoration business for most of his life, studying inlays, carving and design at art school in his homeland, the former Soviet Union. Insiders say Anatoli has a unique niche restoring antique globes and also repairs upholstery, working with all materials, except metal and glass.

Many high-end decorators rely on Anatoli, but he sees only a select few private clients. Calling him clever and versatile, these clients appreciate Anatoli's warm personality and the long-running relations he cultivates. However, while existing clients may feel their relationship is strong, we hear Anatoli is less interested in taking on new customers. Anatoli's work has been featured in *The New York Times*, *New York Magazine*, and *Elle Decor*

*"I give him carte blanche. I trust him completely." "Anatoli refused to come visit my Park Avenue triplex to see a piece I wanted restored. He said I had to bring it to his workroom—a twelve-foot armoire." "He is a reliable professional. Once he is on your team, you do not need anyone else."*

### Anglo-Inscape ■
2472 Broadway, Suite 368, New York, NY  10025
(212) 924 - 2883

*Custom furniture and high-end finishes*

See Anglo-Inscape's full report under the heading Millwork & Cabinetry

### Antiquariato                    4       3      5       5
150 West 28th Street, Suite 1605, New York, NY  10001
(212) 727 - 0733

*Gilding and French polish, French-inspired interior design*

Hicham Ghandour has been in business for eight years since studying in Florence and with the Fashion Institute of Technology's Restoration Program. Specializing in restoring gilded furniture, Ghandour has earned a niche in the trade for traditional water gilding, oil gilding and French polish.

We hear this reliable craftsman is a pleasure to work with and delivers a beautiful product. Sources say he works mainly for the trade—including antique dealers, major art museums and top designers—but he will take on a small number of private clients. Ghandour works both on site and in his workroom, depending on the piece. Some clients have drawn on Ghandour's knowledge of French furniture to employ his services for their decorating. For his interior design work, he charges a modest design fee and retail on products. Ghandour's work has appeared in *Design Times*, *New York Magazine*, *House and Garden* and the *French Designer's Showcase*.

*"He's a real artisan." "All I know is that when we gave him the chair it was a mess. When we got it back, it was beautiful." "Very high-quality work for a great price."*

## Antique Furniture Workroom

▭ ▭ ▭ ▭

210 Eleventh Avenue, 9th Floor, New York, NY 10001
(212) 741 - 2224

*Antique furniture repair*

High-profile clients call upon principal Bill Olson for his restoration expertise. We hear that this sizable list of celebrity clients comes with an equally sizable attitude.

## Antiquity Preservation Network

4.5    2.5    5    5

By Appointment Only, (201) 261 - 8147

*Antique restoration, refinishing and reproduction*

Dennis DeCarlo earns praise from both professionals and private clients for his wealth of knowledge and kind nature. DeCarlo specializes in 18th- and 19th-century English furniture, and works on Continental and Eastern pieces as well. The Merchant House Museum entrusts its collection of American antiques with DeCarlo and even had him teach a seminar on antique restoration. Sources praise DeCarlo's work in structural repair, marquetry, carving, turning, water and oil gilding and French polishing, as well as reproduction and metalwork. Labeled an "expert" with veneers, DeCarlo is said to be completely honest and reliable.

Besides running Antiquity Preservation Network for the last nine years, DeCarlo has twenty years of experience, including serving as Senior Furniture Conservator and Quality Control Manager at Sotheby's and working with the Metropolitan Museum of Art.

*"As a museum professional, my goal is to preserve the furniture for future generations. I choose Dennis to do that, which should tell you a lot." "He knows his stuff, and his qualifications and credentials are incredible." "Top notch, no question about it." "I couldn't recommend anybody any better." "Dennis is the nicest person in the world—he's a lovely man."*

## Baggott Frank Conservation

4    3    5    4.5

361 Stagg Street, Brooklyn, NY 11206
(212) 226 - 6244

*Furniture restoration and conservation*

Clients praise Baggott Frank Conservation for achieving top-quality luster and accommodating their restoration needs. Principal Tom Frank has been in the business for 20 years, working for museums, antique dealers and private clients. References tell us he's extremely knowledgeable and loves his work. Frank specializes in aesthetic furniture, especially Rosewood Herter furniture from the 19th-century. Clients enjoy his personable demeanor and gracious attitude.

*"Top, top quality." "I have no hesitations about giving them any work I have."*

## Budd Woodwork Inc.

54 Franklin Street, Brooklyn, NY 11222
(718) 389 - 1110

*High-end historic restoration and preservation*

See Budd Woodwork Inc.'s full report under the heading Millwork & Cabinetry

## Carlton House Restoration

3.5    3    4.5    4.5

40-09 21st Street, 4th Floor, Long Island City, NY 11101
(718) 609 - 0762

*Antique restoration and refinishing, custom furniture design*

Principal Kenny Dell is described as an antiques expert who truly loves what he does. Dell specializes in the repair and refinishing of wooden furniture, as well as veneers and French polish. Clients laud his abilities with 18th- and 19th-century fine antiques, particularly English, French and Continental. Since the firm moved to a larger space in Long Island City, Carlton House is also designing its own line of furniture.

The city's top designers and antiques dealers rave about Carlton House, saying the qualified staff of nine can handle bigger projects than most. Insiders particularly praise the staff's fidelity to traditional restoration methods. In addition to working for the best in the interior design trade—they have done restoration work for the Ian Schrager hotels—Carlton also works for private clients. We hear Carlton House is competitively priced and extremely reliable and organized.

*"They're the best—that's why we've continued to work with them over the years." "We recommend them wholeheartedly." "There aren't many good restorers in New York City, and we recommend Carlton to all our customers, so that tells you something."*

### D. Miller Restorers Inc.                4.5      3      4.5      4.5
166 East 124th Street, New York, NY  10035
(212) 876 - 1861

*Furniture restoration and sculpture mounting*

D. Miller is a third-generation family business. Loyal clients describe principal Robin Miller as reliable and attentive, her work "brilliant and superb." The three-person firm restores European antiques and mounts sculpture for private clients, the trade, dealers and museums. The company's French polish and gilding draw praise, as do the reasonable prices. We hear Miller is extremely accommodating and will tailor the restoration job to the quality of the piece, so no job is too small. Over the years, the firm has done work for some of Manhattan's most famous residents.

*"Always on time. Great attention to detail." "Everything they've done for me has been quite first class. No one else can compare." "I have worked with two generations of Millers and am now on the third. Obviously I am more than satisfied with their work—in fact, ecstatic!"*

### D. Vitanza Repair & Service                4      3      5      5
728 East 136th Street, New York, NY  10454
(718) 401 - 1022   www.vitanzafurniture.com

*Furniture restoration, particularly Art Deco, upholstery*

Founded in 1930, D. Vitanza is known to be dedicated to the restoration of fine wood furniture using hand-crafted, traditional methods. Since then, the firm has been involved with some extremely high-profile jobs, including the chair of Pope John Paul and the Sotheby's auction for Jacqueline Kennedy Onassis. Principal Michael Maytel has gained a reputation for being one of the premier experts in the restoration of 20th-century modern design, specializing in Art Deco and 1950s furniture.

We hear the firm's craftsmen excel in both contemporary and antique restorations and are adept with lacquer, polyurethane, antique white, French polish, custom color and custom finishes. Clients also praise the line of custom-built furniture. Clients say D. Vitanza uses only the finest materials to reupholster furniture, from fabrics appropriate to the period to horsehair stuffing and coil springs. Sources call Maytel the top in the business and say he works closely with clients, designers, architects and showrooms on both large and small projects.

*"Michael is simply the man for the job. I've had nothing but good experience with him." "Michael is fabulous. The best."*

| Quality | Cost | Value | Recommend? |
|---------|------|-------|------------|

## Daniel's Custom Upholstery
422 East 75th Street, New York, NY 10021
(212) 249 - 5015

*Retail and trade—Slipcovers, recaning and antique furniture restoration*

See Daniel's Custom Upholstery's full report under the heading Upholstery & Window Treatments

## David Linker, Ebeniste          5      4      4.5      4.5
300 Observer Highway, 4th floor, Hoboken, NJ 07030
(201) 653 - 2860   www.davidlinker.com

*Ebeniste—Antique restoration and reproduction*

David Linker is an ebeniste, probably the only one in New York. Named for ebony, an important element in marquetry, the practice of ebenisterie (designing and creating custom furniture for French royalty) arose in the service of French kings in the mid-17th century. Linker's prestigious training and passion for restoration draws awe and affection from his clients, who can hardly articulate their admiration. We hear that Linker dazzles in American, English and Oriental restorations, and can also build reproductions. Despite his capabilities, Linker isn't at all snobby—he respects each piece and reveres its history, no matter its worth. Insiders describe Linker as committed to preserving the integrity of the materials. He works exclusively in methods true to the period, drawing on his encyclopedic storehouse of oils, woods and knowledge.

David Linker appeared twice on Martha Stewart's television show this year. In 1999, *New York Magazine* profiled him for its edition. He has also been featured in *Traditional Home, To the Trade, Time Out New York* and *Atlantic Monthly*.

*"David's the best I know of in the country, and I know them all." "He is absolutely one of the most reliable people I know." "You can't be an ebeniste without being a 5. David is a 10." "David is so charming—my husband and I enjoyed daily breakfasts with David during the months that he assembled French brasserie paneling in our home library."*

## DF Conservation Inc.          4      3      4.5      4
361 Stagg Street, Brooklyn, NY 11206
(718) 381 - 3548

*Antique restoration and refinishing*

Decorators and antique dealers praise principal David Fuentes for his gorgeous finishes and commitment to the project, period and style for all types of restoration. Fuentes, who started the firm seven years ago, is an expert in Nakashima furniture restoration, having reconditioned Columbia University's Nakashima collection. We hear Fuentes enjoys the challenge of researching and working with rare pieces, but he does not do replications. Insiders praise his extraordinary French polish and authentic finishes, calling him conscientious, professional, communicative and timely. DF Conservation charges a fee for estimates for new clients, but once you are an established customer, the estimates come free.

*"David works extremely carefully—not at all mechanically." "He was the only man for the job—he did his research and respected the furniture as much as we do."*

## ECR Antique Conservation Restoration          4.5      3      5      5
515 West 29th Street, 5th Floor, New York, NY 10001
(212) 643 - 0388   www.ecrios.com

*Reconditioning of existing finishes, repair and reproduction*

Principal Eli Rios specializes in the reconditioning of Great American and Regency English furniture in particular, but also of French and Italian antiques. We hear he shuns the word "refinish," saying antiques are so delicate that to strip them down to refinish would devalue the piece. Instead, Rios relies on his 30 years of experience carving, replacing veneers, reconditioning and polishing antique furniture. He can also deliver appraisals. Sources say Rios' reproductions are indistinguishable from the originals, particularly his japanning skills which have been featured by Martha Stewart.

Rios can boast an impressive resume. After training under a German restorer, he was the first employee hired by Sotheby's Restoration, heading that department for six years. He earned a conservator degree from Smithsonian University and taught applied chemistry of historic materials at FIT for seven years. He continues his involvement with FIT by taking on student apprentices. Also on staff are gilders, french polishers, a japaner and carver with refined chairmaking skills and a metalworker who does extensive Boulle work, lock and key repair and metal inlay.

*"Mr. Rios is always very accommodating, professional and competent. It is a pleasure doing business with him." "Eli Rios has been one of our most informant vendors for the past five years. An outstanding restorer, Eli also produces the highest quality reproductions."*

### Fred Agrusa                                   3.5    2.5    4.5    4.5
42-13 162nd Street, Flushing, NY 11358
(718) 961 - 5984

*Furniture restoration and refinishing*

Fred Agrusa opened his business eighteen years ago after training with his father. Currently, Agrusa works with all types of furniture and specializes in antique restoration. We hear he excels in polishing, tightening, refinishing and veneer, and that in addition to hand caning and inlay, he will do custom cabinetry on occasion. Antique dealers say Agrusa responds well to their instruction and accommodates their tastes. Clients praise Agrusa for being very reliable and timely with competitive costs.

Depending on the work to be done, Fred can work in clients' homes or in his studio. He travels to clients' homes to provide estimates, for which he charges between $50 to $100, a fee that is deducted from the final cost of services. Fred has worked with Christie's East for fifteen years, and those in the trade describe his work as very good.

*"They pick up, drop off, it's family owned, they're very reliable and they're very good." "When Fred does it, it's done right."*

### John Kondras                                   4      3      4.5    5
129 West 29th Street, 11th Floor , New York, NY 10001
(212) 564 - 0675  www.kondrasantiques.com

*Antique furniture restoration and reproduction*

John Kondras earns accolades from clients for his superlative finishes and patinas. Insiders call his reproductions unbelievable, saying clients are unable to distinguish his copies from their original antiques. Sources praise Kondras' attention to detail and ability to meet deadlines and budgets without a problem.

Kondras has been in business for 23 years after training with a German cabinetmaker and employs old-world methods for restoration. Kondras works mostly for the trade, including some of the city's top designers, who tell us he delivers 100 percent satisfaction—and then some. Kondras will work for some private clients and prices on a piece-by-piece basis.

*"John is my buddy. I go to him for everything." "If a 5 is the top, John is a 6." "Our business goes to John Kondras."*

## Joseph Biunno Ltd.

| | | | |
| --- | --- | --- | --- |
| 4.5 | 4.5 | 4 | 5 |

129 West 29th Street, New York, NY  10001
(212) 629 - 5630   www.antiquefurnitureusa.com

*Furniture restoration and custom drapery hardware*

A third generation business, Joseph Biunno Ltd. is known for its immaculate reproduction and expert restoration.  Additionally, principal Joseph Biunno makes custom furniture, mostly for architects and designers, many of whom call his works masterpieces.  In recent years, Biunno has expanded the family business into a diversified workroom offering custom drapery hardware, custom legs and antique locks and keys.  Sources marvel at his staff of artisans, experts in carving, cabinetmaking, turning, gilding, metal work, polishing and painting—and say a visit to the workroom is truly worthwhile.

Clients compliment Biunno's professionalism and reliability, as well as his good-natured personality.  He draws respect for his perfectionism and highly analytical mind, which allows him to solve tricky problems.  Biunno works extensively with some of the top designers and architects in the city, and also works with some private clients. Joseph Biunno was recently featured in *House Beautiful* and *W Magazine*'s "Black Book" for the best of the best.

*"He can do anything from Art Deco to 17th-century Flemish bureaus."  "He's enormously creative with special finishes and creates the most marvelous valences and architectural details."  "Extremely high quality for an extremely high cost, but worth it."  "Joe restored a 17th-century European inlayed cabinet that looked as if it had been in a basement for 300 years, and he brought it back to life."*

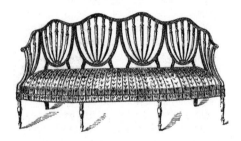

## Lore Decorators

2201 Third Avenue, New York, NY  10035
(212) 534 - 2170   www.loreupholstery.baweb.com

*Retail and trade—Custom window treatments, upholstery and restoration*

See Lore Decorators's full report under the heading Upholstery & Window Treatments

## Mary Ann Miles

| | | | |
| --- | --- | --- | --- |
| 4.5 | 2 | 5 | 5 |

226 East 70th Street, New York, NY  10021
(212) 988 - 6691

*Furniture restoration and repair*

Clients praise Mary Ann Miles as much for her unwavering character and charming personality as for the outstanding quality of her work.  Working in the homes of the most pedigreed clientele, Miles has proven herself polite and personable with everyone on the job, right down to the roughest mover.  We hear the British government relies on Miles for furniture restoration in its offices and ambassador residences, as do many Park Avenue clients.

Insiders say Miles has a genuine interest in history and antiques but can also repair modern pieces.  She will repair anything, whatever its worth, to the satisfaction of the client.  Though she doesn't do gilding, caning or cast iron welding, we hear she'll offer references for those jobs. The obvious pleasure she takes in her work strikes a cord with customers, who value her open lines of communication and flexibility.

*"She's an invaluable resource. She knows who to recommend and where to go to find things, and she'll match a handle or latch because she's just so resourceful." "She fixed a very tricky piece of mine—I don't even know how." "She never fails."*

### Midtown Antiques Inc.

| | | | |
|:---:|:---:|:---:|:---:|
| 3 | 2 | 5 | 4 |

814 Broadway, New York, NY  10003
(212) 529 - 1880

*Antique center—dealership, retail, restoration*

In their 61st year of business, Mort and Violet Ellis at Midtown Antiques are known to be extremely charming, honest and kind.   Besides offering retail antiques with an in-house dealer, we hear Midtown loans antiques to publications and movie studios to create a period look.  Midtown also has a restorer on the premises who reportedly does it all—from refinishing and painting restoration to cabinetry repair, japanning, gilding and gesso.   This third-generation restorer trained in South America under his father and sources call his work exquisite.

*"A magnificent restoration job." "Such nice people with so much integrity." "They restored our family blackamoor collection that was damaged in an earthquake back to its original state."*

### Miguel Saco Fine Furniture & Restoration

🗁    🗁    🗁    🗁

37 East 18th Street, 6th Floor, New York, NY  10003
(212) 254 - 2855

*Furniture restoration*

### Olek Lejbzon & Co.

| | | | |
|:---:|:---:|:---:|:---:|
| 4 | 3.5 | 5 | 5 |

210 Eleventh Avenue, 11th Floor, New York, NY  10001
(212) 243 - 3363

*Furniture conservation and historic building preservation and restoration*

This group of 30 European master craftsmen has been working in the New York area for 50 years, servicing a variety of furniture restoration and conservation needs.  We hear they offer reupholstering, caning, leatherwork, metalwork, marquetry, inlay, water and oil gilding, turning, carving and pietre dure.  They also restore and repair chandeliers, lead cames, glasswork and ceramics. Sources say Olek Lejbzon can design custom furniture and build replications, cabinetry, architectural millwork, paneling and windows and doors in a wide variety of styles, from Medieval to Rococo to postmodern, and everything in between.

Everyone praises principal Peter Triestman's down-to-earth and friendly demeanor, though some have trouble with his temper.  Olek Lejbzon's outstanding quality of work extends to such impressive projects as Grand Central Station, Madison Avenue Presbyterian Church, Prince George Hotel, Jules Bistro and the Cooper Hewitt Museum.  Much of the firm's work has been for locations on the National Building Register of Historic Places.

*"I would highly recommend their expertise."*

### Richard Moller Ltd.

| | | | |
|:---:|:---:|:---:|:---:|
| 4.5 | 3 | 5 | 5 |

178 Upper Shad Road, Pound Ridge, NY  10576
(914) 764 - 0121

*Antique furniture repair and refinishing*

Clients call Richard Moller efficient and conscientious.  They appreciate Moller's ability to work on site, which protects pieces from travel damage and means clients don't have to go without their furniture.  Having trained with European craftsmen in

New York, Moller specializes in 18th- and 19th-century European pieces. Trade professionals rely on Moller, but we hear he also takes on new private clients. After 30 years in the business, Moller has a loyal following—sources say many long-term clients' children employ Moller for their collections.

*"He is always available and is completely reliable."*

### Richomme Inc.       4       4       4       5

27 Vestry Street, New York, NY 10013
(212) 226 - 4706

*Furniture restoration, reproduction and refinishing*

Clients praise Richomme for its customer service and attention to detail. The company is said to deliver an exquisite French polish and finishes that are authentic to the period. Clients call principal Ian Nicolson extremely reliable and personable, praising his ability to meet deadlines. We hear those in the trade use Richomme to restore paneling and build custom furniture as well as restore antiques. Insiders consider Richomme's prices comparable to other high-end restorers but say Richomme's customer service goes way beyond the competition. Our sources tell us Ralph Lauren uses Richomme to build custom furniture and refinish antique and new furniture both in their stores and in private homes.

*"Richomme is a small company that is able to fit clients' needs, budget and timeline." "My business is very deadline-oriented, and they always come through for me."*

### Robert F. Rohr       4.5      3       5       5

310 West 73rd Street, Suite B, New York, NY 10023
(212) 787 - 5420

*Furniture restoration and repair*

Robert Rohr earns praise for his skills as both an artist and an expert furniture restorer. He specializes in inlay, French polish, veneering, lacquering and the restoration of hand paintings. Clients say Rohr does not reproduce entire pieces but reproduces parts essential to restoration. Rohr is respected for being communicative, as well as completely trustworthy.

Customers welcome him warmly into their homes, where he does all of his work in order to eliminate transportation damage and minimize disruption. Clients tell us that Rohr's work never takes more than a few days and is priced very fairly. They describe him as a highly principled and knowledgeable man who will take the time to teach his clients how to care properly for the pieces that he meticulously restores and repairs. Most of Rohr's work is for private clients, many referred by Sotheby's. Rohr's work has been reviewed in *The New York Times*.

*"His workmanship is a joy to behold!" "As usual, he has created perfection." "I'm just so thrilled with the way each piece looks!" "It was a pleasure to meet a craftsman in this materialistic world who cares about his work." "He's an antiques doctor—he doesn't leave anything unattended."*

### Scottie Donohue       3.5      3     4.5     4.5

P.O Box 1368 Cooper Square Station, New York, NY 10276
(212) 477 - 0519

*Chinoiserie, lacquer, coromandel screens and inlay*

In business for over fifteen years, Scottie Donohue specializes in restoring 18th and 19th-century antiques. Clients praise Donohue's gracious demeanor and accommodating service—she delivers free estimates and works in clients' houses, saving them moving fees and inconveniences. In addition to French polishing, veneering, lacquering, gilding, woodcarving and structural repairs, Donohue works on chinoiserie, coromandel screens and inlays in brass, mother of pearl and ivory. We even heard of a case where she did some decorative painting on a chair, turning an otherwise worthless piece into a room-stopper. Clients repeatedly cite Donohue's perfectionism and meticulous attention to detail.

Private clients and those in the trade value Donohue's versatile skills and extensive knowledge, and she has worked with some of the most noted designers in the city. We heard of several occasions on which Donohue transformed pieces that others had deemed "beyond repair." Sources describe Donohue as communicative, informative and absolutely trustworthy. While all agreed that she was honest, some confessed that she takes a long time. Others insisted that perfection cannot be rushed and Donohue's timetable was reasonable.

*"She prices by the hour—an incredibly fair rate—but she's a perfectionist and won't stop short, so everybody might not want to pay for that." "Anything I have asked her to do she has done to perfection. She gives you first-rate stuff, but she works at her own speed, and you can't rush her. If you're looking for perfection, that's what you'll get." "Her commitment to perfection might be her only flaw, if it can be called that."*

## Sheelin Wilson                          3      3      4      5
315 East 19th Street, 2nd Floor, New York, NY 10128
(212) 722 - 2089

*Antique gilding and refinishing*

Trained in London and apprenticed at the Loughcrew Studio in Ireland, Sheelin Wilson specializes in the restoration and conservation of gilded and painted surfaces. In the business for twelve years in the United States, including a term at Sotheby's Restoration, Wilson has built a following among major museums, antiques dealers, designers and private clients. Sources tell us Wilson loves the challenge of 17th- and 18th-century Italian restoration jobs, and clients compliment her inlays. We hear Wilson also offers expert lacquering, japanning and painted finish jobs.

Clients marvel at how Wilson can restore almost anything back to its original state. They add that Wilson is easy to work with and has reasonable costs. We hear reports of her wide array of accomplishments, from restoring a Dutch metal piece to creating Art Deco tiles. Insiders tell us Wilson does much of her work for the trade and has taught traditional gilding at FIT. Clients enjoy her witty sense of humor and find her entertaining and reliable.

*"No hesitation. I recommend her 100 percent." "She is very personable, conscientious and not inexpensive, but she takes care of it and I can count on her." "She finds the original finish and restores it and gildings. She's very good, and she knows her stuff."*

## Sonrise Woodcarving Studio
111 Hurley Avenue, Kingston, NY 12401
(845) 331 - 8692   www.sonrisewoodcarving.com

*Master carver—decorative work, interior millwork, replication*

See Sonrise Woodcarving Studio's full report under the heading Millwork & Cabinetry

| | Quality | Cost | Value | Recommend? |
|---|---|---|---|---|

## Sotheby's Restoration

4.5     3.5     5     5

1334 York Avenue, New York, NY 10021
(212) 894 - 1597   www.sothebys.com

Sotheby's Restoration has greatly reduced its furniture repair and refinishing workload to primarily serve Sotheby's auction house and not those from outside clients. Heading up this reduced service is Brian Stair. We are told Stair, along with his staff of five, is handling the repair and refinishing of Sotheby's purchasers and consignors who find that valuable pieces of furniture have been damaged in transit. Although the firm is only taking on 15-20 extremely high-end pieces per month, we are told Stair welcomes inquiries from those who feel they may have exceptionally high-end or valuable pieces for repair or refinishing.

## Spiegel Fine Framing & Restoration

4     3     5     5

42-22 Orchard Street, Long Island City, NY 11101
(718) 609 - 0750   www.spiegelframes.com

*Antique frame restoration, art conservation, period furniture, glass and Venetian mirrors*

In 30 years of operation, Spiegel Fine Framing and Restoration has established a reputation for quality, taste and attention to detail within a warm, family business. Clients say the firm is best known for dealing and restoring antique frames, with a collection ranging from 17th- to 20th-century European and American frames. The firm's craftsmen also restore period furniture and art, we are told, with an emphasis on preserving the integrity and value of each piece. We hear Spiegel can ably restore sconces, chairs, consoles, torchiers and other small period pieces.

Insiders describe Daniel Spiegel, the company's founder, as a quintessential old-world frame master and artisan with more than 40 years of experience. We hear Spiegel employs a small crew of gilders, art conservationists and master craftsmen, who have a deep appreciation of antiques. Spiegel's services also include relining of canvases, in-painting, reverse painting on glass, glass and mirror beveling, Venetian mirror restoration and mirror antiquing. Clients especially praise the company's beautiful gilding capabilities.

*"What sets them apart is that they are an old-world-style, family business."*
*"Spiegel is extremely attentive—the workers care about what they do very deeply."*
*"A friendly family operation with hands-on service and fair pricing."*

## Stair Galleries & Restoration

4.5     3.5     5     5

33 Maple Avenue, Claverack, NY 12513
(518) 851 - 2544

*Furniture reproductions and restoration and fire and water damage repair*

Stair Galleries and Restoration was created in 2001 after Sotheby's Restoration (see review) was consolidated to take on only a small number of projects each year. Colin Stair left Sotheby's to create his own firm, which is located in Upstate New York but welcomes inquiries from the city. This firm is currently taking on numerous projects referrals from Sotheby's.

Clients laud Stair for his professional demeanor, friendly disposition and quality workmanship. His firm handles fire and water damage, repairs and refinishes for all styles and periods of furniture and also does interior woodwork, paneling, veneering and polishing. According to references, Stair will also make expert furniture reproductions that clients say can't be distinguished from the originals. One customer tells us that when her young daughter's favorite doll bed broke, a call to Stair was all that was needed. He made a house call, whisked the bed away and within two weeks, the bed was delivered "in perfect condition," for a surprisingly small fee.

Stair will assist clients at auctions, providing advice on the worth and restoration potential of pieces. References say Stair performs expert custom work with the highest caliber of integrity and skill—at a price that is considered reasonable.

*"When it comes to finishes, he's the best around—and the finish is the most important and difficult task to undertake." "A really nice guy who really is amazing at what he does." "The service is not cheap, but it's not nearly as much as it could be, given the quality."*

### Timothy G. Riordan Inc.                3.5    3    4.5    5
50 Webster Avenue, New Rochelle, NY  10801
(212) 360 - 1246

*Antique furniture restoration*

Timothy Riordan has been restoring, gilding and polishing fine antique furniture for over seventeen years. He has an enviable background, having worked at Sotheby's during the early years of its restoration program. Over the years, American, French and English antiques have become his areas of specialty. He works on an hourly basis and does a considerable amount of work on the Upper East Side.

### Yorkville Caning                4    2    5    5
31-04 60th Street, Woodside, NY  11377
(212) 432 - 6464

*Furniture refinishing, caning and wicker repair*

New York's top designers and the Metropolitan Museum of Art rely upon principal David Feuer for his restoration abilities. A family business, Yorkville Caning has been recaning chairs, repairing wooden and wicker furniture, refinishing and reupholstering for 102 years. We're told Yorkville works with genuine rush—a service fast becoming a lost art. Insiders gush that Yorkville gives life to pieces deemed irreparable by others, using a special glue from NASA. Yorkville's staff of twelve earns praise for wicker repair and restoration and has also found the time to become expert upholsterers and refinishers.

*"Everyone loves them." "Yorkville saved my chairs."*

# Hiring an Interior Designer or Decorator

The decoration of homes has captivated people throughout recorded history. In 67 B.C., Cicero commented, "What is more agreeable than one's home?" Interior designers put their style, creativity and experience to work to help a home reach its full potential—be it a studio or a multi-million dollar spread.

Despite recent press clippings questioning the integrity of the profession, *The Franklin Report* has uncovered over 150 design firms that clients adore and revere for their abilities and professionalism. Clients believe that these firms saved them considerable time and money by finding unique objects and avoiding costly errors. Each firm has its own style and personality, which is described on the following pages. For our second print edition we have tended to highlight the most prominent designers, which often translates into higher costs and minimums. Additional firms may be found on our website (www.franklinreport.com) which is updated regularly.

## Finding a Match

After you fully assess your needs and your budget (see What You Should Know About Hiring a Service Provider, page 5), we recommend that you gather photographs from magazines and books to share with potential design candidates to communicate your preferences. Through our research, we have found that the best interior decorator-client bonds are founded on common ideas of style and taste. Even the best designers can falter and lose interest in a project if they are not excited by the end goal. So as you gather potential names from *The Franklin Report* and from friends, focus on the preferred style of the designer—even if they say they can do anything.

As you narrow down your list and begin the interview process, think about your working relationship with the interior designer, who, for better or for worse, will become a big part of your life. Will you be seeing the principal on a regular basis or the project managers? Are you interested in a collaborative process or looking for strong direction? Will you be offered a wide range of budgetary choices? Finally, the prospect of working with this person should feel positive and enjoyable. Given the amount of time and money you are about to spend, it ought to be fun.

## On Cost

Only a client can determine the worth of an interior designer's services. The "great masters" of interior design are considered exceptional artists who may charge whatever the market will bear. No one ever valued a Picasso based on a markup over the cost of materials. That said, the vast majority of designers are not masters, but competent professionals looking for a reasonable profit.

Interestingly, very few designers earn huge sums, due to the inherent unscalability of the process. Since clients generally want to talk to the Name-on-the-Door and not a senior associate, a name designer can only handle so many projects a year, usually about eight. Therefore, even with an average job size of $300,000 and a markup of 33 percent, net annual profits to a designer working with eight clients equal only $90,000—a good living but not a fortune (especially compared to their clients).*

---

*Assumes net cost of products of $225,000 with a designer markup of 33 percent, totaling $300,000 of cost to the client and $75,000 of gross revenue to the designer. With a 15 percent profit margin (after all operating costs) net profit to the designer is only $11,250 for a client, or $90,000 for eight clients (before tax).

Just a handful of designers have the clout to make serious money. This can be done by charging unusually high markups or hourly fees, employing multiple senior project managers, selling custom products (which carry very high, undisclosed markups) and/or accepting only clients with very expensive purchasing habits. While you should know standard industry pricing practices, many clients are willing to pay more for additional service or amazing talent.

## Standard Industry Pricing

There are three fundamental services for which interior designers receive fees: 1) up-front design plans, 2) the purchasing of products (new and antique) and 3) the oversight of construction and installation. The pricing indications described below are what you can expected from a very competent, experienced professional—neither a part-time designer nor a grand master.

Up-Front Design Fees: Most interior designers will charge an up-front, non-reimbursable design fee or retainer of about $500 (for a cosmetic rehab) up to $1,200 (for an architectural transformation) per major room, or about $5,000 to $10,000 for a typical three-bedroom, prewar apartment renovation. The extent of these plans can range considerably, from loose sketches to extensive architectural drawings with coordinating furniture memos, swatches and a detailed electrical plan. Qualify these expectations before you sign on.

Most designers will calculate the design fee as a flat rate and others on an hourly basis (both should fall into the cost range above). Occassionally half, and rarely all, of this fee is reimbursable against future product fees. Certain designers will not charge repeat customers a design fee. Some, but not many designers (especially in a robust economic climate), will operate on an hourly consultation basis, with the client doing all the subsequent shopping, purchasing and implementation.

New Product Fees by Percentage: Designers earn most of their fees by delivering products such as upholstery, case goods, window treatments, rugs and accessories. The vast majority charges clients a markup over the net (or wholesale) price. Designers who search high and low for the lowest-cost materials might charge a substantial markup, but still offer a very good value to clients.

✧ **Product Markup Over Net:** Over half of designers charge a flat 30 to 35 percent markup over net on all new products, including workroom costs. This pricing is considered "reasonable" in The Franklin Report's designer reviews (as it is about 11 percent below the suggested retail price on fabrics).

✧ **New York Retail:** Many established designers charge "New York Retail," or 50 percent above net cost on fabrics, 66 percent on new furniture and 33 percent on new rugs. These percentages are based on the discount the decorators receive off the manufacturer's suggested retail price. For example, if the decorator were charged a net price of $100 per fabric yard, the client's New York Retail price would be $150. Workroom costs are usually marked up 25 to 50 percent at New York Retail (this is a very squishy number that should be clarified). This overall New York Retail pricing is considered "standard" in The Franklin Report's interior designer reviews.

✧ **Retail Outside New York City:** Fabric and other showrooms ticket the suggested retail price as 100 percent over the net price, 50 miles outside New York City (vs. 50 percent within the area). So be extra sure to discuss what "retail" means if you are decorating a vacation home.

✧ **Pricing Structure:** Remarkably, virtually no one charges under any other price structure—it is either Retail or about one-third up for new products. This is an interesting unifying principle in an industry that contains so many variables.

ANTIQUE PRODUCT FEES: Antiques are much trickier. First, the retail and net prices are usually negotiable with the dealers. Once retail price is established, most dealers offer designers a further discount of 10 to 20 percent. This presents a conundrum. For the designers to make their normal 33 to 50 percent markup, they may have to charge the client substantially above new retail price (which could be above or below the original retail price). This is further complicated by the fact that most antique dealers are happy to sell directly to the public.

The most satisfactory solution used in many successful client-designer relationships seems to be full disclosure with a sliding scale. These designers charge a markup over the new price, with their usual 33 to 50 percent markup for lower priced items and a much smaller markup for larger items (often a lower percentage for items over $50,000, etc.). Many designers further guarantee that clients will never pay over the original or new retail price. The most prominent designers appear to be able to hold to a set markup and/or not disclose the net prices. For expensive antiques, an independent appraisal may be warranted (see our listings of Appraisers).

There is an additional point that needs clarification between a client and the designer on antique purchasing. If a client happens to walk into an antique dealer on Madison Avenue or an auction at Sotheby's and finds the perfect sideboard that has been eluding the decorator for months, should the decorator get a fee? Arguments may be made both ways, especially if that piece has been specified in the design plans, the decorator has spent time shopping for that piece (educating the client along the way) or the client seeks approval from the decorator before making the purchase.

Most decorators have a strong enough client bond to withstand these issues, and the client will not balk if, in fact, the designer deserves the fee. But specific contracts help in these times. An elegant solution that some of the more sophisticated designers use is to charge an hourly consultation fee under these circumstances or to take a much larger up-front design fee to cover all antique and auction purchases.

HOURLY PRODUCT FEES: A small but growing minority of designers charge clients on an hourly basis for all product procurement, including antiques, and pass the net prices through to the client. This methodology eliminates confusion and uncertainty on pricing, but introduces debates on how long it can take to order all the trims and fabrics for a sofa (it takes longer than you think). Hourly fees are particularly popular with architecture-trained designers (as that is how architects usually charge). These fees generally range from $75 per hour for a design assistant to $250-plus per hour for a grand master, with $150 to $200 as the typical, well-established Name-on-the-Door designer rate.

OVERSIGHT FEES: Most designers charge a 15 to 20 percent oversight fee for the management of the subcontractors from whom they are not already making a profit. Usually these are the subcontractors who work with design elements such as bathroom and kitchen design, architectural woodworking, etc. Other designers will ask for 15 to 20 percent of the general contractor's net product costs to coordinate the artistic direction of the entire project. Or the designer can bill hourly for these consultations. This service may be unnecessary if you are using an architect who takes on the project manager's role. Some designers will also charge for every meeting and "look-see" outside of their immediate responsibilities, so this should be clarified in advance.

FLAT FEES AND OTHER NEGOTIATED TERMS: A limited but increasing number of designers will consider a flat fee for all of the services listed above. This fee would remain stable within a specified expenditure range, and go up or down if the product costs far exceeded or came in significantly lower than the estimates. But the key lesson here is that most interior designers are fairly negotiable on pricing and other terms, within reason.

## CONTRACTUAL AGREEMENTS

Given the wide variance of markups and methodologies, it is highly recommended that you and your designer agree upon an explicit price scheme for each type of product and service before embarking upon a renovation. While not normally necessary, it is not unreasonable to ask to see all bills and receipts.

Also, before you sign, it is customary to speak with of one or two past clients (and occasionally, see the projects first-hand). Once the contract is signed, a retainer will be paid, the design plans will be drawn and purchases will be made. Timing expectations should also be addressed in the contract, but in many cases the timing of materials is out of the control of the designer. Therefore, if you have specific deadlines, the designers should be directed to order only in-stock items.

## LICENSING OF INTERIOR DESIGNERS

The debate over the potential licensing of interior designers has been spirited. Currently it is not necessary to hold any type of degree or license to legally practice interior design in New York State. While the American Society of Interior Designers (ASID) and the National Council for Interior Design Qualification (NCIDQ) administer qualifying examinations, only a minuscule percentage of the top residential interior designers have complied. Most designers describe these tests as having more to do with health and safety issues (generally handled by architects) than with design competency. In fact, the tests do include sections on space planning, historical styles, fabric selection and all the necessary algebra, but do not really test creativity.

All this may change with a bill that is expected to be introduced in Albany shortly. The bill would limit the use of the interior designer title to those with certain educational, experience and testing credentials (including the passing of the two-day NCIDQ exam). Those who are not certified would be classified as interior decorators rather than designers.

From a residential consumer viewpoint, there seems to be little correlation in *The Franklin Report* data between the passing of the NCIDQ exam and the satisfaction of the customer. However, so few designers in our list of top 150 have taken the exam that the sample size is just too small to judge. As discussed in What You Should Know About Hiring a Service Provider, it is incumbent upon the homeowner to do a thorough investigation of the competency of any potential service professional through extensive interviews, referral information and a competitive analysis.

## FINAL CONSIDERATIONS

As further described on the following pages, an overwhelming majority of the countless clients we talked with had very positive feelings toward their interior designers. While it may be possible to purchase "trade-only" fabrics and furnishings in other ways, truly successful decorating is about creating an intangible upgrade in mood and lifestyle that only an expert can accomplish. Professional designers also have the creative energy and resources to manage projects in a cohesive manner from start to finish, realizing clients' dreams more effectively and efficiently.

### WHAT YOU SHOULD NOT EXPECT FROM
### YOUR INTERIOR DESIGNER OR THE DESIGN PROCESS

✧ That the designer will maintain interest in the project if you cannot make any decisions.

✧ That you attend each shopping trip or be shown every possible fabric in the D&D building.

✧ That the designer can read your mind.

✧ That there will be no misunderstandings or mistakes along the way.

✧ That the designer will bid out every subcontractor. There is a reason that the designer has been working with the same upholsterer and decorative painters for years. On the other hand, if you have a favorite supplier, the designer should be accommodating.

✧ That the designer will supervise other's work without an oversight fee. (The designer should be there, however, to oversee the installation of their products at no additional fee.)

✧ That the designer becomes your new best friend.

### WHAT YOU SHOULD EXPECT FROM
### YOUR INTERIOR DESIGNER

✧ The sense that your interests and opinions matter.

✧ That some of your existing furnishings will be integrated into the new design, if you wish.

✧ Being shown a full range of options and products—creative ideas well beyond the D&D building. However, you should not feel forced to take whatever they purchased on their last worldwide jaunt (and pricing is really fuzzy here).

✧ Assurance that the designer will stick to a budget (and not tempt you with "the best" unless you insist).

✧ A full understanding of your lifestyle and use of your living space.

✧ The ability to see the net cost of every item, if you desire.

✧ An accessible and proactive effort, taking the initiative to complete the job to your satisfaction.

## INTERIOR DESIGNERS & DECORATORS

### A. Michael Krieger Inc.          3.5   3.5   4.5   5
45-17 21st Street, Long Island City, NY 11101
(718) 706 - 0077
*Updated, traditional interior design*

Michael Krieger is described by clients as creative, smart and knowledgeable. With over 20 years experience in design—including associations with Kevin McNamara, Mark Hampton, Melvin Dwork and Donghia—Krieger can address a wide range of clients' design interests. Supporters remark that his designs are unique and do not have the stamp of a decorator. Krieger is known to favor both classical and eclectic styles, and is often asked by clients to do English country without the chintz. The owner of an antiques shop in Hudson, New York, it's no surprise he's noted for his strong use of antiques.

Krieger charges a flat fee within the standard range, half of which is deductible against future purchases. Retail is charged on products. He is happy to start with just a few rooms so long as the budget can support good quality work. Living rooms are generally in the $75,000 to $100,000 range. Clients are very pleased with Krieger's detailed design plans, contracts and back office. Furthermore, he seems to have great patience, whether escorting clients to the D&D or to London. We hear if the client is not satisfied, he will "go back to the drawing board." Most of his work is in Manhattan and the surrounding areas. HB Top Designers, 1999, 2000.

*"My husband resisted hiring a decorator, but is now begging Michael to review everything, including our landscape plans." "He can do trendy modernist in a traditional background or vice versa, but everything is different and client-specific." "He turned our big vanilla box of a new house into a warm, comfortable home." "He's able to find a beautiful object in what looks like a pile of junk to me." "I purchased some antiques five years ago on Michael's advice. I now realize they were a steal." "We learned so much in the process." "Michael has a Yankee cost mentality which we really appreciated. While he will sometimes use the very best, he will often have an excellent secret source." "He is a gentleman and a living doll."*

### Aero Studios/Thomas O'Brien        5   4.5   4   5
132 Spring Street, New York, NY 10012
(212) 966 - 4700    www.aerostudios.com
*Contemporary, comfortable and refined interior design*

Thomas O'Brien delights clients by creating distinctive, refined environments that start with a Moderne aesthetic style but are saturated with neoclassical warmth. A master creator of mood, O'Brien studied architecture at the Cooper Union and then worked as the director of the Ralph Lauren Home Collection. At Aero, he has created his own comfortable modernism that fuses bold architectural furniture with serene backgrounds, shots of color and bargain finds. This look, which is the envy of his peers, is also available at Aero's SoHo retail store or through Hickory Chair.

O'Brien wins accolades from his clients for being extremely loyal—he reportedly went to the "ends of the earth" to finish a project before a big wedding. His projects range from an apartment for Giorgio Armani to large-scale houses in Greenwich to major commercial undertakings (Donna Karen showrooms, David Barton gym, Soho Grand Hotel). Satisfied clients testify that he is very involved in the initial design concept and then hands the projects over to strong project managers.

The firm's fees reflect its stature in the marketplace. Up-front charges are substantial, and products are generally offered at retail or above. Hourly fees are charged for oversight, varying considerably based on the seniority of the designer. Despite the chic, relaxed result, patrons say that well over half of the contents are custom made, from furniture and fittings to fabrics and carpets. HB Top Designers, 1999, 2000, 2001. KB 1999.

*"I have the greatest respect for Thomas and his vision. He has taken design to the next level." "He was very good about integrating a modern design sensibility into my more traditional home. He would use chintz, but in a fresh way." "He is extremely expensive, but you get the best." "His rooms are modern, yet brushed with a nostalgic, silver-hued patina." "Thomas's designs are both beautiful and functional." "He often does an exaggerated Jean-Michel Frank in neutral shades, but can also do a more traditional look with unexpected pizzazz." "He can make a suburban Georgian manor house look hip and now." "Aesthetic restraint with a passion."*

### Ageloff & Associates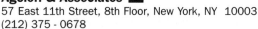
57 East 11th Street, 8th Floor, New York, NY 10003
(212) 375 - 0678

*High-end residential interior architecture and design*

See Ageloff & Associates's full report under the heading Architects

### Albert Hadley Inc.         5    4.5    5    5
24 East 64th Street, New York, NY 10021
(212) 888 - 7979

*Masterful, high-end interior design*

Albert Hadley is a disciplined master whose incredible creativity has always found that perfect balance of "just-so" and leading edge. He is considered by many to be one of the most illustrious figures in 20th-century American design. His signature rooms offer a knowing sophistication based upon classic furnishings with a modern edge, complementing the architecture and the setting. Hadley composes with everything from contemporary zigzag tables to historical, tufted chaises to aubergine painted walls. His edited looks herald luxury, quality and comfort, with a nod to innovation.

Originally from Nashville, Tennessee, Hadley studied and taught at Parsons School of Design. He worked at McMillen Inc. for many years before starting the famous design firm Parish-Hadley with the late Sister Parish, where young designers such as Mark Hampton, Bunny Williams and David Kleinberg got their start. His masterly design is not all that is praised—he is extremely conscientious of his clients, involving them in the process and always taking their personalities into account. Past clients have included Brooke Astor, Happy Rockefeller, Al and Tipper Gore and Oscar de la Renta. While he closed the eigtheen-person office of Parish-Hadley, stating his intention to retire last year, Hadley continues to work independently with longstanding clients and take on a select few new patrons.

He remains very involved in the design industry, extremely generous with his time and inspiring to new designers and contemporaries alike, who agree Hadley has permanently shaped interior design. ASID. HB Top Designers, 1999, 2000, 2001. ID Hall of Fame. KB 1992, 1997.

*"A true master—a genius." "I have never known anyone more generous with their time or their vision. He keeps me thinking and creating." "His designs have never aged, and are always current. Everything he has designed for me is still fresh." "He is extremely generous with his time for clients, friends and young designers alike." "A true gentleman who always knows just how to treat his clients and to treat a room." "He saved many an old-line family from looking like white-shoed snobs." "He abides to his mantra—never more, never less." "He now leads the ultimate design couture experience."*

| | Quality | Cost | Value | Recommend? |
|---|---|---|---|---|
| | ✚ | $ | ◆ | ★ |

## Alison Spear, AIA           4   4   4   4
131 East 70th Street, Suite 3E, New York, NY 10021
(212) 439 - 8506  www.alisonspear.com

*Iconoclastic, colorful and bold interior design and architecture*

Alison Spear is daring, fashionable and fun, according to clients. With an MS in architecture from Columbia and training with Molyneux, she is able to seamlessly combine form, function and design. The firm usually performs both architecture and design roles. References say that she is at ease whether building large-scale houses or refreshing one-room lofts. She often clothes traditional furniture and walls in shiny patents, recycled cotton or aluminum, paralleling current fashion trends. Other projects incorporate just a few high-styled elements into more traditional backgrounds.

With a main office in Miami, and a second in New York City, Spear has a cadre of clients in the surrounding area. When engaged, she is known to take complete control and efficiently meet budgets and deadlines. Some mention, however, that Spear is heavily in demand, and can become over-committed and less available, especially for less challenging and innovative projects. Recent commissions include a 2,600-square-foot loft conversion in Soho, a house in the Hamptons and several residential projects on the Upper East Side and downtown New York City. Additionally, Spear is working on several major commercial projects in New York and Miami.

The firm is known to charge a very reasonable percentage over net on products and low architectural oversight fees. Materials costs can range widely depending on the scope and budget of the client. Jobs can range from under $40,000 for a living room to way beyond. Spear is considered a master of her creative aesthetic and highly recommended by supporters for adding spirit and warmth to their homes. HB Top Designers, 1999, 2000, 2001.

*"I never had to explain the importance of quality to Alison." "She is the Jimmy Choo of interior design." "She is brilliantly creative, with the skills of someone way beyond her years." "While I never envisioned that pony-skin bar stools would fit into my lifestyle, I now just adore them." "We got along so well she was finishing my sentences." "She was clearly impatient with our renovation—pushing me to the point of obstinance. It was not a good match." "She can do one room in a blitz of energy." "I think that she really enjoyed my project because she had stylistic carte blanche: leather floors, pieced-cashmere rugs, aluminum walls." "She was not cheap, but stuck to a budget." "She is amazing, without a big ego. Alison completely upgraded my life."*

## Aman & Carson Inc. ▮          4.5   4.5   4   4.5
85 East End Avenue, New York, NY 10028
(212) 794 - 8878

*Updated, classic, American interior design*

Championed by clients, Aman & Carson is considered to be insightful, resourceful and attuned to the clients' greatest design aspirations. Jim Aman and Anne Carson started their careers in interior design as store designers for Ralph Lauren, and their first clients were friends and employees impressed by the creative pair's polished classic vision. They are known for bringing glamour and elegance to the home without "overdoing it." Clients say that they focus on every detail and gracefully incorporate the owner's viewpoint and surroundings.

Established in 1994, clients now include members of the Upper East Side establishment, Santa Fe ranch owners, Palm Beach traditionalists and downtown modernists in search of a contemporary interpretation of timeless elegance. References are convinced that this pair is skyrocketing to stardom, and they are trying their best not to let the word out too quickly. The firm is so busy with repeat business (including at least one family with six commissions), that very few new clients are brought into the fold (and the few that are, must often wait).

The team tends to have a classically elegant, more formal design approach, much appreciated by patrons not interested in monochromatic minimalism. The firm charges a standard+ design fee, retail on products and standard oversight fees. Living rooms are generally in the $100,000 to $200,000 range. Supporters commend the firm's resourcefulness in locating high-quality products at good prices. HB Top Designers, 1999, 2000, 2001.

*"Jim and Anne were happy to work with my existing furnishings." "They are capable of museum-quality work but are willing to stay within a budget." "They are wonderful businesspeople, having succeeded under the demands of commercial pressures." "Jim has amazing vision, a very quick wit and is such a pleasure. I loved spending time with him." "While offering extraordinary results, they are not really into low maintenance fabrics or the most functional lamps." "They can sometimes forget the little people." "They are good about working things out between the upholsters and the clients." "Jim and Anne love what they do, and the result shows." "They offer the preppy look taken to a modern level of ultra-refined luxury."*

### American Design Company 🛍      3.5      3      4      5
636 Broadway, New York, NY  10012
(212) 598 - 4254

*Funky colorful meets classic modern design*

Established in 1984, American Design Company is known for its modern style and comfortable and practical designs. Customers praise the firm for its innovative finish materials and fearless use of color, as well as the staff's attention to detail. American's interior design work often mixes mid-20th-century furniture with classic modern pieces to create a fun and dynamic atmosphere. Clients laud this innovative use of space and the company's ability to adjust the style to suit customers' individual tastes.

Partners Corinne Calesso and William Hellow both have wide experience in commercial and residential interior design, founding the firm in 1984. Their commercial clients include the Jack Lenor Larson showroom, Robert Marc Opticians, Dawn Mello & Associates, New York Botanical Gardens and Bristol-Myers Squibb. The back office is said to be excellent and professional, with a great client-service attitude. The team is also applauded for its ability to respond well to any client requests, including major design changes.

Residential projects range from lofts to townhouses, with budgets supporting products from industrial catalogs to luxuriously high-end showrooms. Clients say the firm sticks to budget and is financially accommodating. The principals are also reputed to be extremely flexible and caring and take full responsibility in solving any mishaps.

*"They can introduce new, fresh ideas that really spice up anyone's imagination." "Although modern decor is often considered somewhat cold, they have the ability to make it warm with natural woods and polished glass." "The work is exciting without being theatrical." "They are professional, have excellent taste and are easy to work with." "While there were no issues, I would not say budgets are a strength." "AmerDesCo is attuned to clients' preferences and help them articulate their interests." "Every detail is extensively discussed." "They use many bright colors, but in a restrained, sophisticated way." "When guests admire my apartment, I am reminded just how much I love it."*

| | Quality | Cost | Value | Recommend? |
|---|---|---|---|---|
| | ✚ | $ | ◆ | ★ |

## Anderson Papachristidis, Raeymakers     4    4    4    5

300 East 57th Street, Suite 1C, New York, NY 10022
(212) 588 - 1777

*Eclectic, luxurious and traditional interior design*

Creative, intelligent and witty are terms often used to describe Anderson, Papachristidis, Raeymakers. Alex Papachristidis started the firm twelve years ago and Toni Raeymakers joined in 1995. The pair now has an established roster of clients including many young investment bankers and money managers. Recent projects include downtown lofts, country homes, a beach cottage and numerous Park Avenue apartments. Clients laud the firm for its excellent work in a broad range of styles and enthusiasm for mixing bargains with rare antiques.

The team's style is tailored to individual clients' interests and budgets, but most often is classically based with whimsy and full of rich details. Supporters also speak very highly of the designers' focus on service and back-office capabilities. The firm charges a standard design fee (more if it is involved in architectural plans), retail on products and standard oversight fees. Living rooms are typically in the $100,000 area. Clients say the pair is as adept with smaller projects as with large ones. While sensitive to budgets the firm encourages the use of highest quality products (but can often source them inexpensively). Patrons highly recommend this firm, which works for many families year-by-year. KB 1997, 2000.

*"Alex and Toni bounce ideas off one another, and do not box you in." "They always create something interesting and beautiful." "The first thing they ask about is the budget, then they achieve an extraordinary result within the agreed-upon framework." "They embraced my concept of Greek antiquity, came up to speed quickly and, together, we found some wonderful examples." "Not only creative, ingenious and fun, but most of all intelligent." "They are honest and sweet, but have recently gotten much more expensive." "The process could have been scheduled better, but the end result was terrific." "After they did my New York apartment, I did not consider anyone else for my Connecticut country home."*

## Ann Le Coney Ltd.    3.5    3    4    4.5

241 East 78th Street, New York, NY 10028
(212) 472 - 1265

*Traditional, layered interior design (or a trimmed-down version)*

Ann Le Coney specializes in a heavily detailed, layered English country interior design style or, more recently, a trimmed-down version thereof. Most of her clients reside in Manhattan, but she is often asked to decorate their second homes, taking her to Nantucket, Bedford, Palm Beach and Mexico. She is happy to undertake projects of any size. Often there will be multiple phases, accommodating clients' budgets and developing styles. Le Coney also has a "cheap and cheerful" subsidiary business appropriate for the apartments of her clients' children and she is available on a consultation basis.

While she is known for her signature traditional English style, Le Coney will adapt to a client's interests and the environment. Patrons say that she sticks to budgets and can offer a "turn-key" service, with clients making few decisions. Clients appreciate that she does all the decorating herself, however her small staff limits her to just a few projects at one time.

Living rooms usually are in the $100,000 to $500,000 range. Contractors admire her work as thorough and high-quality. She has many repeat customers, including one family with three generations dressed in Le Coney style.

*"No detail is too small for her to think about—even the switch plates are well-treated." "She takes her job very seriously and professionally." "She was happy to brighten up the job she did for us five years ago." "Even the accessories have accessories." "She has weekly meetings to make sure all stays on schedule." "After doing the New York house, the Southampton cottage and the Palm Beach residence, we asked her to do the motor yacht." "She does a complete job for her clients. It is comfortable and elegant, and makes us feel as if we have lived there forever."*

| | Quality  | Cost $ | Value ◆ | Recommend? ★ |
|---|---|---|---|---|

## Antine Shin LLC

200 East 61st Street, New York, NY 10021
(212) 838 - 5006

*Luxurious, developed interior design*

| | 3.5 | 3.5 | 4 | 4 |
|---|---|---|---|---|

Trained in couturier at FIT, Anthony Antine employs luxurious fabrics and rich colors to clothe clients' homes. He often focuses the design plans around a specific stylistic or environmental theme. Projects range from a Mediterranean-style New Jersey villa to a beach-style house in Jeddah to Robert Redford's mountaintop retreat in Japan. The eighteen-year-old firm is currently undertaking the ongoing restoration of The Point Hotel in Saranac Lake. Designer Ho Sang Shin joined the firm ten years ago after graduating from Antine's alma mater. Shin manages projects both locally and abroad. KB 1994, 1998, 2001.

## Antiquariato

150 West 28th Street, Suite 1605, New York, NY 10001
(212) 727 - 0733

*Gilding and French polish, French-inspired interior design*

## B Five Studio

160 Fifth Avenue, Suite 702, New York, NY 10010
(212) 255 - 7827

*Classic, progressive high-end interior design*

| | 4 | 4 | 4 | 5 |
|---|---|---|---|---|

Offering a heightened sensitivity between interior and architectural design, B Five Studio offers a unique and integrated approach applauded by clients. This large firm is made up of five senior architects and decorators well-versed in numerous styles and techniques. Consequently, the firm has a wide perspective and a disciplined, yet open attitude to any given project. Clients describe the firm's signature style to be "classic progressive" with a fusion of strong modern gestures and classic, historically referenced furnishings. The firm is known for its effective use of strong sweeps of color, luxurious fabrics and the incorporation of modern art.

The vast majority of B Five's work is residential, and more than half of all its projects take place in Manhattan. The firm was established in 1981 and currently employs 30. The five partners of the firm are Ronald Bentley, Victoria Borus, Charles Capaldi, Salvatore La Rosa, and Franklin Salasky. The firm accepts approximately 40 projects each year, most of which are done on substantial budgets. B Five is said to quickly provide detailed sketches that truly reflect the client's input. Clients praise the designers for creating many original pieces by hand using imported materials, typical of the firm's highly customized approach.

In addition to its Manhattan work, B Five also does work around the rest of the regional area, as well as Philadelphia, where the firm has another office. We hear the firm generally works with clients of discriminating taste, who share its long-term view of a project and its methodical, patient approach to interior design. We are told the firm provides high-end services for a high-end fee. HB Top Designers, 1999, 2000.

*"They did everything from top to bottom. One stop shopping." "Their resources are amazing, particularly their relationships with unusual and fine craftsmen." "The work they did is elegant, approachable and bathed in beautiful pale gold's, olives and lovely shades of contrasting greens." "No fussiness, but beautiful, luxurious fabrics that speak for themselves—mohair's, damasks, silks." "They certainly don't rush the job and I appreciate the time and care that went into my home." "Their subcontractors are great and easy to work with." "They always show up and get the job done." "B Five brought fun and life to my boring Park Avenue apartment."*

| Quality | Cost | Value | Recommend? |
|---------|------|-------|------------|
| ✚ | $ | ◆ | ★ |

## Barbara Ostrom Associates

| 3.5 | 3.5 | 4 | 4 |

55 East 87th Street, New York, NY  10128
(212) 465 - 1808

*Traditional with a modern flair interior design*

With designs of cheer, warmth and comfort, Barbara Ostrom has been integrating clients' interests and interior visions since 1972. Combining traditional French and English motifs, she adds character and substantially proportioned furnishings to many custom homes. Ostrom's references say that she is a master with colors and uses her skills to add flare to the traditional feel.

Ostrom holds a BFA from the New York School of Interior Design, an MA in Interior Design from Pratt Institute, and a graduate degree in classic european interior design and interior architecture from the Sorbonne. Her extensive client list features many prominent residences including that of former President and Mrs. Richard Nixon, New Jersey State Senator Gerald Cardinale and cinematographer Owen Roizman. She has also been awarded for her work with the North Star Mall in San Antonio and the Citizens Bank in Ridgewood, New Jersey.

Ostrom charges a standard design fee, product fee and oversight fee. The firm will take on a few rooms, but usually does complete renovations. Clients praise her for her excellent quality of work, but some expressed concerns regarding her subcontractors' reliability. Friends recommend Osborn to friends, particularly in the decoration of large, new homes in the suburban area. ASID. KB 1990, 1993.

*"Ostrom's work is beautiful and her ideas inspiring. She pays a lot of attention to details and is concerned with historical correctness too. However, some of the workers she hired did not focus, resulting in a more frustrating process than I had expected." "Every aspect is well-considered. Even the ceilings are painted with integrated designs." "Country French or Tuscan is a love and specialty of Barbara's." "I fear that she make take on a few too many jobs at one time." "She is very involved in the selection of the furniture and finishing's. We spent days together going to furniture markets and kitchen showrooms." "She was very interested in how I lived and incorporated my personality into the decoration."*

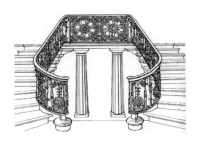

## Benjamin Noriega-Ortiz 🛍

| 4 | 3.5 | 4.5 | 5 |

75 Spring Street, 6th Floor, New York, NY  10012
(212) 343 - 9709   www.bnodesign.com

*Edited, eclectic, elegant interior design*

Benjamin Noriega-Ortiz is admired by clients and industry insiders for his charming and outgoing demeanor, modern design outlook and affinity for rich finishes. With two master's degrees in architecture and six years as head designer for John Saladino, Noriega-Ortiz's distinctive color-saturated forms highlight his work. Clients describe the spaces he has created as open, clean, serene and coherent. He is happy to mix Crate & Barrel finds with the finest antiques. While project managers are employed to run day-to-day operations, he is a self-described "control freak" involved with all major decisions.

| | Quality | Cost | Value | Recommend? |
|---|---|---|---|---|
| |  ✚ | $ | ◆ | ★ |

Noriega-Ortiz works mostly in Manhattan, but has a round of other projects throughout the country, especially Palm Beach (he has a house in Florida). He is willing and able to design a bathroom or a 30,000-square-foot house from the ground up. All fees are by the hour, including consultations. Products are purchased at net. HB Top Designers, 1999, 2000, 2001.

*"Benjamin is the perfect example of what professionalism should be." "Is so sensitive to the client's needs and is happy to walk you through the process." "He has such a lovely personality and he's so easy to talk to." "He enjoys leaning toward the funky side of modern, but always exquisitely well done." "Benjamin has a complete absence of ego, yet he carries himself with a quiet confidence." "We so appreciated his hourly billing system, which gave us complete purchasing freedom." "Uses his architectural training to create really exciting spaces, well beyond the status quo of today's typical interior design."*

## Beverly Ellsley Design Inc.    3.5    3.5    3.5    4

179 Post Road West, Westport, CT  06880
(203) 454 - 0503   www.beverlyellsley.com

*Kitchen design and interior design, custom handmade cabinetry*

See Beverly Ellsley Design Inc.'s full report under the heading Kitchen & Bath

## Bilhuber Inc.    5    4.5    4    5

330 East 59th Street, 6th Floor, New York, NY  10022
(212) 308 - 4888

*Clean, classic, bold, modern interior design*

Jeffrey Bilhuber is creating a new modern classicism by fusing traditional and contemporary elements with fresh, young colors and counterbalancing elements. He is regarded by both clients and peers as one of the great talents of his generation. Clients tell us he is extremely professional, returning calls quickly and working efficiently. Bilhuber is said to be excellent with details, repeatedly checking an upholsterer's progress and looking underneath for perfection. While some may say he is a marketing machine with a very distinctive point of view, his work remains respected by all.

The design firm, established fifteen years ago, takes on about ten projects at one time. Clients include Randolph Duke, Anna Wintour, Elsa Peretti, Peter Jennings and Iman and David Bowie. But Bilhuber is also open to doing less prominent projects. Bilhuber has taught at Parsons and lectures frequently on the influence of interior design. His office is said to be very professional and responsive, even for the smallest request six months later.

Known for his broad range of stylistic tastes and interests and openness to new ideas, Bilhuber also designs with respect for the dogs and children. He is said to pre-shop effectively, but is not the kind of guy to spend the day at the D&D with clients on a daily basis. Living rooms generally run in the $250,000 neighborhood, but Bilhuber has also won the hearts of those clients with much lower budgets. The architecture standards are also very much appreciated. HB Top Designers, 1999, 2000, 2001. KB 1991.

*"He has a very large personality but is always very professional." "He has an amazing ability to be innovative, drawing upon the traditions of masters— Billy Baldwin, Thomas Jefferson." "He can turn my concepts into timeless, classic designs." "While our budget was miniscule compared to others, he made us feel like his only client." "He takes your personality and turns it into a design vision. But you have to appreciate his perspective to start." "Not the guy for traditional chintz." "He listens and then pushes the envelope." "We have done sixteen houses with Jeffrey, and would not consider any other way." "His spirit is contagious."*

| | Quality | Cost | Value | Recommend? |
|---|---|---|---|---|

## Birch Coffey 🛍

4  3.5  4.5  4.5

206 East 63rd Street, New York, NY 10021
(212) 371 - 0100

*Streamlined, international-style interior design*

Clients report that Birch Coffey collaboratively develops thoughtful designs that often incorporate a restrained, international style and architectural presence. He receives kudos for taking initiative, delivering jobs with fine detail and building upon clients' visions. In addition to residential projects, the firm undertakes commercial work, including hotel and building lobbies and cruise ships (Royal Caribbean).

Most residential patrons are business professionals living on the Upper East and Upper West Sides of Manhattan. References appreciate Coffey's professional thoroughness, including strong upfront presentations, excellent documentation and great followup. Clients say it is often unnecessary to hire a separate architect, as Coffey received a BA and an MS in architecture. The firm does 90 percent of the drawings for its projects. While Coffey is occasionally out of touch on commercial assignments, clients say he always is involved in the design phase. Project managers fulfill the day-to-day duties, and we understand Coffey's office staff makes a point of answering all questions within 24 hours.

The firm works on an architect-type fee schedule with relatively high oversight fees billed over the course of the project but with low markups on products. However, the firm's fee schedules vary depending on the scope of the assignment. Living rooms generally run in the $75,000 to $100,000 range. Clients praise Coffey for offering product alternatives, for staying on schedule and for respecting budgets. ASID.

*"Birch offers the unexpected within a traditional framework—but it is always in good taste." "He orchestrates the entire project: the plans are detailed and they make sure the contractors finish the job." "My husband and I not only like Birch, but we also respect his business acumen." "He has an amazing eye. He offers a mix of limited antique and mostly repro to ease the wallet." "When there were issues, he worked them out directly with the contractor, saving me untold headaches." "If he cannot find the perfect piece, he gets it made. I love that can-do attitude." "He was so patient even when I changed my mind a hundred times."*

## Branca Inc. 🛍

4.5  4.5  4  4.5

1325 North State Parkway, Chicago, IL 60610
(312) 787 - 6123   www.branca.com

*Luxurious, stylistic, exuberant continental interior design*

Peers and clients roundly laud Alessandra Branca for her lavish continental design style, intense creativity and stylistic flourish. Recognized as among the very best in Chicago, she has recently completed a few east coast projects. Credited with extraordinary flair, she tends to work best in the classical genre, updated with exhilarating color and a multitude of details. Upholstered walls, multiple patterns, rich glazes and exquisite millwork often factor into the design plans. Italian-born, fine arts-trained and a mother of three, Branca uses all skills and experiences to develop her characteristic design creations.

Branca begins with a physical inventory and plan, and much is retrofitted to the new composition. Clients range from the most established to the young, who may begin with just a few rooms, but usually have high quality expectations, classical views and healthy budgets. Very often these clients continue with Branca, finishing the house, expanding to multiple locations and then to the yacht. European shopping trips often factor into the picture.

Most of the products are custom, with many unusual European sources, creating a relatively expensive, but unique setting. There are eleven people at the firm, including three project directors. The firm's hourly rate ranges from low to high, depending on seniority, and a high markup on product (none on millwork). Typical living rooms are in the $25,000 to $125,000 range. Clients tend to be quite loyal, albeit exhausted, and clearly enthralled by the end result. HB Top Designers 2000, 2001.

"Alessandra has the temperament of an artist, and she produces design masterpieces." "I think that you are born with great style and Alessandra has more of it than anyone else I know." "She gives new life and vibrancy to historical spaces, while retaining their original character." "While there were times when I wondered if we would ever make it to the end, I would not consider using anyone else." "As an architect, I applaud her ability to add multi dimensional, detailed, layered warmth to the architectural renderings. While it is not always easy, her undeniable talent makes me want to do it again." "I have become a great friend of Alessandra's through this crazy, exciting and rewarding process."

### Bray-Schaible         5    5    4    5
80 West 40th Street, New York, NY 10018
(212) 354 - 7525

*Inspired, contemporary, sleek interior design*

Robert Bray and Michael Schaible are roundly recognized for their comfortable, sumptuous minimalism. They have been creating crisp, yet comfortable interiors for over three decades. Clients report a mastery of architectural perspective, clean decoration and effective execution. The two principals trained at Parsons, and Mitchell Turnborough joined the team in 1998. Their design talents range from modern-with-soul to streamlined traditional to 70s-style rejuvenated. Often, they fundamentally reconfigure spaces to achieve their trademark clean lines, incorporating large-scale silhouettes and clever details such as hidden storage space.

Projects range from the transformation of an ordinary two bedroom on the Upper East Side to a living, contemporary art gallery, to the rejuvenation of a worn-down farm in the country to a magical, classically imbued family compound. Clients include Jasper Johns, Faith Popcorn, business moguls and younger enthusiasts. References appreciate the small, old-school couture nature of the firm, feeling that they are working day-to-day with design legends. Bray-Scable take on only a few major projects at a time.

The firm often takes a strong architectural role, and looks to the finest quality construction and products. Most projects easily exceed $500,000. Clients say that there are no surprises and that Bray and Schaible are excellent listeners. They are consistently recommended as dependable, accommodating, diligent and professional. AD 100, 2000. ID Hall of Fame.

"Bob Bray continues to amaze me. I have worked with him for 20 years and appreciate that he can do a large Greenwich home as well as a modest Hamptons oceanfront." "They realize that bones dictate, and follow with decoration that is not fussy." "The masters of sleek." "Incredible, quality people, great to work with." "They are one of the few who can make simple look strong and becoming." "They offer flawless execution even under the most trying of circumstances." "Others often take their lead, but Bray and Schaible never run out of creative breakthroughs."

## Brian McCarthy Inc.

| | 4.5 | 4.5 | 5 | 5 |

1414 Avenue of the Americas, Suite 404, New York, NY  10019
(212) 308 - 7600

*Stylish, strong, edited, traditional interior design*

Clients of Brian McCarthy quickly become advocates.  Noted for his depth of knowledge, clarity of design and warm personality, McCarthy pushes for perfection.  Admired for his innate desire to create rooms of unique character and grace, many are filled with special treasures coherently placed in classic frameworks. Trained by master designer Albert Hadley, McCarthy displays both Hadley's professionalism and skill in combining the expected and the traditional with elements of more modern protocols.

McCarthy's clients are generally very well established, many with large Park Avenue apartments, in search of the extraordinary.  Recent projects outside the city include homes in Pebble Beach, Fresno, San Francisco and washington, DC. Supporters say the firm's client service is outstanding—issues magically disappear and bills are clearly presented.

References consider his work quite expensive, but worth it.  Living rooms are generally in the $250,000 to $400,000 range, before fine antiques.  On the other hand, he is said to be quite practical in children's rooms, using $15-per-yard fabrics that are washable.  Supporters are protective, considering McCarthy a friend and a fabulous secret source.  Customers cannot wait to embark upon another project with him.

*"Everyone who walks in here is blown away by the warmth and details." "He strongly encourages you to find your own design viewpoint." "The best part about working with Brian is having a drink with him at the end of a long day. He is such delightful company." "We hired him just to do the public rooms, but fell in love with his work and did the whole house." "While you spend more than you care to think about, you are always investing in pieces of quality." "Three years later, Brian is more than gracious about finding just one little lamp." "He is the voice of reason in an extravagant process, always with an eye towards market value." "My curtains rival any of Marie Antoinnette's dresses." "We couldn't recommend him more highly."*

## Bruce Bierman Design Inc.

| | 4.5 | 4.5 | 4 | 5 |

29 West 15th Street, New York, NY  10011
(212) 243 - 1935   www.biermandesign.com

*Classical, modern high-end interior design*

Bruce Bierman wins accolades for his practical skills, refined aesthetic and warm nature.  Trained in architecture and interiors at RISD, Bierman brings both skills to a project.  While he is known as a modernist, clients also appreciate his ability to do traditional work with a lighter touch.  Spaces typically feature a few shapely focal points instead of an overwhelming number of objects.  Projects include a Normandy-style house on Long Island, a large clapboard in Greenwich, a country home upstate, a townhouse and a duplex on the Upper East Side and a Midtown pied-a-terre.  This work—no matter how large or small the project may be—offers comfort, strong details and clever storage space, all of which are Bierman's specialties.

Started in 1977, the firm now employs fifteen people, ten as architectural and design project managers.  Clients happily report that they have a wonderful rapport with Bierman and the staff.  The firm charges a design fee depending upon the scope of the work, a reasonable percentage over net for product and standard oversight fees.  Products reportedly are of high quality, including intriguing electronics, but not over the top.  Antiques may be purchased on an hourly consultation basis or percentage, depending upon the involvement of the firm.  Budgets are meticulously detailed, with living rooms generally in the $75,000 to $200,000 range.  Clients strongly recommend Bierman for his sympathetic approach to their lifestyle. HB Top Designers, 2000. ID Hall of Fame.

*"I have used many well-known designers over the years, and I felt that Bruce was the only one committed to the project and our family for the long haul." "I have never been to our construction site because Bruce really represents our interests." "Bruce is a very special person—mature, calm and generous. I am happy to say that he is now a friend." "There is a clarity and straightforwardness about what Bruce is trying to accomplish." "What a professional—he never gets flustered." "Our cookie-cutter apartment now magically looks like a glamorous loft." "I am a very opinionated client. I interviewed 30 people for this job, and I will definitely go back to Bruce for the next one." "A gentleman and a man of his word."*

## Bunny Williams                4.5    5    4    4.5
306 East 61st Street, 5th Floor, New York, NY 10021
(212) 207 - 4040   www.bunnywilliams.com
*Lovely, traditional interior design*

Bunny Williams is roundly known for rooms deliberately fashioned in an undeliberate manner—unpretentiously looking as though they evolved over generations. She combines traditional elegance with extraordinary professionalism, talent and energy. Clients report that she can expertly execute a range of styles but gravitates toward a refined, welcoming English sensibility. More recently, though, she has tended to trade needlepoint pillows for larger-scale furnishings dressed in vintage textiles.

Raised in Albermarle County, Virginia (home to Nancy Lancaster), Williams carries on the craft of gracious Southern living. Trained at the venerable Parish-Hadley, she opened her own firm in 1988. Her organizational skills and strong back office allow for excellent efficiency and quick project development. The firm has four integrated design teams, headed by a Design Associate. Williams is said to travel extensively, but be the design inspiration behind each project.

Most projects are quite substantial, ranging from Manhattan penthouses to large homes in California, Palm Beach, Atlanta, Maine, Texas and a house in the South of France. Clients confirm William's "ladylike nature" and her ability to "do it all," saying that she is a woman of her word. Prices are reportedly extraordinarily high, but can be brought under control. Williams also has a great passion for gardening. She is a partner in Treillage, a garden furniture shop in Manhattan and is the author of the book *On Garden Style*. HB Top Designers, 1999, 2000, 2001. ID Hall of Fame. KB 1990, 1998.

*"You tell her how much you want to spend, and she develops a design plan very quickly." "We hired Bunny for a relatively modest project and she totally got it." "She treats design like a cottage industry—she has an amazing array of specialists at hand who she can dispense at a moment's notice." "She also did my friend's apartment, and I was surprised to see some of the same elements as in mine." "We have meetings every three weeks, and she is always very prepared." "She even showed us how to make the beds in the correct manner." "She is not a prima donna and was very thoughtful in her allocation of our budget." "Her rooms have extraordinary style and grace." "I would not change a thing." "She is dazzling in a quiet kind of way."*

## Celeste Cooper/Repertoire        4.5    4.5    4.5    4.5
325 East 57th Street, New York, NY 10022
(212) 826 - 5667   www.repertoire.com
*Crystalized, modern high-end interior design*

An engaging woman with a strong modern view, Celeste Cooper has many fans. She is known to have a clear, philosophic preference for functional modernism. Adherents revel in her interiors, admiring her creativity with space, luxurious taupe-based furnishings and dramatic detailing. She has recently completed a range of New York and Boston residences and several commercial projects in Boston (three restaurants and XV Beacon, an exclusive hotel). Cooper professes to create her designs like a musical composition with repeated and related liet motifs, to which clients respond "bravo!"

As the design director at Repertoire (a design atelier and reseller of imported contemporary European furnishings—currently in New York and Boston), Cooper encourages clients to incorporate leading-edge pieces. The designer charges an hourly design fee and standard markup on product. Clients note that Repertoire is quite reasonable in addressing any issues.

Cooper received a BA in Architecture, history and art history from Tufts and a degree in interior design from Harvard Graduate School of Design, where she also studied hotel planning and design. She previously ran her own design firm for thirteen years. References highly recommend Cooper for potential clients who buy into her specific vision. ASID. HB Top Designers, 1999, 2000, 2001. ID Hall of Fame. KB 1996.

*"The Armani of interior design." "While all the public rooms of my apartment are in neutrals, she was quite accommodating with my daughter's request for purple walls in her bedroom." "She has created a new kind of classic elegance, rooted in today, not in Chippendale and chintz." "I did not know there could be so many discrete variations on beige. Cocoa textures, coffee walls, buckwheat linens." "A delightful, warm, but direct iconoclast." "She makes brushed steel, bronze tables and leather ottomans speak to refined Georgian side chairs." "Luxury and the latest sound and internet technologies are inherent to the whole." "If you are quite committed to the modern sensibility, Celeste is the best. She makes Modern elegant, warm and soothing."*

### Christopher Coleman 👜      4     3     5     4.5

70 Washington Street, Suite 1005, Brooklyn, NY 11201
(718) 222 - 8984

*Colorful, bold, witty, contemporary interior design*

Clients appreciate Christopher Coleman's confident mix of geometric shapes, clean lines, exuberant colors and warm undertones. They also applaud his enthusiasm, wit, warm personality and willingness to take design risks. Following five years with Renny Saltzman, Coleman founded his design practice in 1993.

Recent projects include a traditional Park Avenue duplex, a Westchester retrofit, a country Hamptons home, a plantation bungalow in Key West and a large shingle-style home on Nantucket. Clients include *Harper's Bazaar* editor Kate Betts, established professionals and many young couples decorating their first apartment, loft or weekend house. Many credit Coleman for taking time to educate them about the design process—including classical historic styles, economic alternatives and timing. Other strengths include a sensitivity to family living, mixing the old with the new, and ties to creative artisan resources. Clients say Coleman is very available and attentive.

Coleman works with a design fee, a reasonable percentage over net for products and reasonable oversight fees if no architect is involved. Coleman is known for his ability to make the most of less with some living rooms costing in the $45,000 range. Clients report that Coleman is highly professional and straightforward: all bills and the background paperwork are presented on a regular basis. HB Top Designers, 1999, 2000, 2001. KB 1997.

| | Quality | Cost | Value | Recommend? |
|---|---------|------|-------|------------|
| | + | $ | ◆ | ★ |

*"He finds the most unique furnishings. Whatever he cannot find at a reasonable price he gets made. His upholstery people can do the highest quality sofas for half the price of what we expected, and deliver in half the time." "We so enjoy his creativity—anything can become an interesting design motif to him—country, ethnic, old maps." "He is the only guy in the business who can do red vinyl successfully." "He is overtly modern without being rehashed-retro." "When I was after a particular very expensive Italian look, he found a very good match at Crate and Barrel." "He has a wicked sense of humor and a hip design sensibility to match."*

## Clodagh Design International

| | 4 | 4 | 4 | 4.5 |
|---|---|---|---|---|

670 Broadway, 4th Floor, New York, NY  10012
(212) 780 - 5300   www.clodagh.com
*New age high-end interior design*

Clodagh is known for her innovative use of form, lighting and harmonizing materials to create life-enriching environments. To this designer, a job is complete only if it involves all of the senses and the elements. This often translates into the use of natural, low maintenance and environmentally friendly materials. Her young and spirited team take great care to understand clients' interests, a process that can include lively discussion of energy fields or astrological signs. Clients also appreciate Clodagh's strong ties to many artisans worldwide.

Clodagh began her career as a highly successful fashion designer in her native Ireland. Moving to Spain and finally New York City, she shifted her focus to architectural and interior design, opening a New York City firm in 1983. Residential projects include smaller Chelsea lofts and larger uptown penthouses. Recently she has expanded into landscape architecture, commercial projects (Elizabeth Arden's spas, Felissimo), lighting design, furniture and textiles.

The firm charges by the hour for consultations (design, feng-shui, environmental) or can work on a retainer. Clodagh is recommended by clients and peers for her creative and sensitive design approach. HB Top Designers, 1999, 2000, 2001. ID Hall of Fame. KB 1992, 1995, 1998.

*"We respect and adore Clodagh." "She was totally available." "She has a magical touch. The cement floors glow a rich taupey gold, but it is still very subtle." "She completely upgraded our life by adding a sink area in the bedroom, so my husband and I can get dressed in the morning at the same time." "Clodagh fixed all the idiotic things the contractor did, and was extremely fair about the costs." "She asks you to close your eyes when choosing a fabric, to experience the textural." "I am very fussy, and she captured exactly what I wanted by asking careful questions." "While she is clearly expensive, there were never any issues." "My home is now a work of art."*

## Connie Beale Inc.

| | 4 | 4 | 4 | 4.5 |
|---|---|---|---|---|

6 Glennville Street, Greenwich, CT  06831
(203) 532 - 4760   wwwconniebeale.com
*Traditional personified*

Connie Beale is known as a focused professional with fine taste who settles for nothing but the best in quality materials and products. Beale is described as extremely hands-on to the point of carrying around a hammer and screwdriver to demonstrate to contractors how something should be done. Beale's design style has been called "casual elegant," with an absence of excessive chintz and tailored directly to the client's needs. References tell us each project is a unique work and hail Beale as extremely collaborative with the client, yet resolute in her overall vision. The vast majority of Beale's products are custom, with higher-end retail product, for the nonpublic.

Beale, a native of Louisiana, holds a degree from Louisiana Tech and established this twelve-person firm in 1979. The firm's staff consists of three project managers, one draftsman and decorators and administrative staff. The vast majority of Beale's work takes place in Manhattan and Greenwich, Connecticut, although her firm has found itself in Bermuda and Texas. We hear Beale discusses budgets up front and with great detail, establishing a standard starting budget that can greatly increase, as the project evolves.

We're told the firm has excellent followup practices and that Beale has a confident back office who understands fine design and can answer most questions. Clients who have used Beale for numerous projects say they completely trust her uniquely creative ideas, and let her take the ball and run with it. The firm charges standard hourly rates and product markups. HB Top Designers, 1999, 2000. KB, 2001.

*"Never used the same fabric twice." "Enormously talented and creative." "Doesn't think she knows everything." "She doesn't make a fuss if you buy on your own." "She is no-nonsense and doesn't play games. Says is like it is with no fluff, but she's not a prima donna or a diva." "There were some tricky situations with the architect. It took longer than we expected because they were both fairly adamant." "I can't put my finger on it, but she knows immediately what is the best. But it is usually quite expensive." "I am at a point now where I just give her the keys and tell her to do it." "She comes up with ideas—panels, moving panes and color schemes that I never would have considered. Now there is nothing but compliments and raves."*

## Constantin Gorges Ltd.

26 East 63rd Street, New York, NY 10021
(212) 753 - 3727

| | | | |
| --- | --- | --- | --- |
| 4 | 4 | 4 | 4.5 |

*Traditional, yet stylishly modern interior design*

Constantin Gorges is credited for his creative use of luxurious materials, selective use of fine antiques and exquisite results. While rooted in the traditional, he incorporates an updated "here-and-now" sensibility. According to supporters, Gorges enjoys conjuring "truly beautiful" spaces that combine the client's interests and the surroundings (funky 50s on the West Side, New Age on the 77th floor, classical elegance with spunk on Park Avenue). He has completed a number of large-scale projects, and also enjoys working with younger clients on smaller projects.

Gorges is sympathetic to budget constraints, expertly integrating clients' existing furnishings into the design plan. While he knows and offers the best, he seems always to have a well-priced alternative "up his sleeve." Because of his excellent and varied training—Parsons, Noel Jeffrey, Peter Marino and Parish-Hadley's architecture department—Gorges often becomes the project manager, according to appreciative clients. While he wins accolades from clients for delivering exquisite architectural details (including lighting schematics) and intelligent design elements, some say he has less interest in selecting the detailed accessories (books, picture frames, etc.).

Gorges is known to be very fair with his fees, waiving charges for things that are redone even if he originally followed a client decision. He charges a standard design fee and a reasonable percentage over net. Oversight fees may be charged by the hour or on a percentage basis. Clients highly recommend Gorges for his cohesive vision and fabulous project management skills. KB, 2001.

*"He has an amazing work ethic—if the client is not happy then Constantin feels he has not done his job properly." "He will find or make a knock-off if you can't afford the real thing or he can take it as high as the imagination." "The living room can be a Bentley and the kids rooms attractive VW Bugs." "He pre-shops and doesn't waste your time" "He is the kind of decorator that your husband would also like, but he not going to take the place of your best girl friend." "Constantin is 100 percent dependable and particularly effective at getting suppliers to deliver." "He is always available and has no attitude, but your apartment will have tons of personality."*

| Quality | Cost | Value | Recommend? |
|---|---|---|---|
|  ✚ | $ | ◆ | ★ |

## Courtney Sloane/Alternative Design

|   |   |   |   |
|---|---|---|---|
| 4 | 3.5 | 4.5 | 4.5 |

334 Barrow Street, Jersey City, NJ 07302
(646) 230 - 7222

*Holistic, progressive modern interior design*

From Sean "Puffy" Combs to football pro Levon Kirkland, interior designer Courtney Sloane has built a loyal clientele who admire her cross-cultural, multi-dimensional style with a modern twist. Sloane undertakes about a third of her projects with large, commercial entertainment and marketing companies (Sony Recording Studios, Fila showrooms) and much with younger, hip downtown clients, all of whom share her global and progressive perspective. This firm of five was established in 1993, and takes on three to five projects of substantial size and budget each year. We are told the entire firm collaborates on each project, dividing responsibilities into phases, although Sloane is directly involved in each endeavor.

The cost of a typical living room can range from $70,000 to $125,000, and approximately 75 percent of the firm's work takes place in Manhattan. Budgets tend to evolve with the design process. Insiders tell us the firm employs high-tech design software and creates 3-D animated walk-throughs for clients. The firm charges standard design and retail on product. Clients say Sloane inherently understands their design objectives and delivers a comfortable and unique product. HB Top Designers, 1999.

*"Really unique spaces with some imaginative elements—it can be over the top funky or twisted traditional." "Courtney melds numerous cultures and styles into her design. It really is a reflection of how modern, edgy American design is evolving." "You have to see her work. Words do no justice to this kind of imagination." "She forced me to focus on the important elements of the structure upfront, so there were no surprises." "Courtney breaks out of the box, offering much more than design, but a new identity."*

## Crain & Ventolo Associates

|   |   |   |   |
|---|---|---|---|
| 4 | 4 | 4 | 4 |

215 East 58th Street, New York, NY 10022
(212) 223 - 2050

*Lovely, detailed, traditional interior design*

Gary Crain and Robert Ventolo are recognized as solid, knowledgeable veterans of design with a proficiency for the traditional. They are known for their delicate and classical use of soft chintzes, hand-painted walls and floors, imported crystal lamps and intricate trims. Rooms often include a mix of English and French antiques, and look as if they have existed for generations.

Crain began the firm in 1977, with Ventolo joining more recently. The business is said to be organized yet personalized. Multiple family members often follow each other's lead, and they tell us the firm responds appropriately to their various needs and interests. While most living rooms are in the $275,000 to $300,000 range before antiques, younger clients may do Shabby Chic, with an eye to upgrading over the years. As a testament to the longevity of the firm's design style, the FDR Presidential Library and the Maidstone Club have been clients for years.

The company charges a small retainer and retail on products. While a good number of its clients appreciate the principal's calm design style and comfortable approach, others have ventured away toward a modern look. Nevertheless, many families have been loyal clients for decades and warmly recommend this firm. ASID. KB 1992.

*"The rooms are classically beautiful and not overdone." "Lighter than the 80s traditional look, but not fashion-forward." "They are so easy to work with." "We have used Gary for over 25 years, as have both my sons and my sister." "You have to make them aware of your budget and stick to it." "They take care of all the details and are always available." "They are so patient and can always deliver a well-heeled look."*

## Cullman & Kravis Inc.

4.5    5    4    4.5

790 Madison Avenue, New York, NY 10021
(212) 249 - 3874

*Exquisite, formal, traditional interior design*

Cullman & Kravis is roundly credited for its exquisite taste, versatile design skills and a client list to die for. Founded in 1985 by Elissa Cullman and the late Heidi Kravis, the firm is often called upon to design around superb collections of fine art and antiques. Clients are consistently impressed by the firm's unusual sources and fabrics, project management acumen and extreme attention to detail. The team is also known for creating exceptional wall finishes and other opulent backgrounds.

Clients have included the CEOs of Philip Morris, Goldman Sachs, Paramount, Salomon Brothers and Miramax, as well as the estate of John Singer Sargent. While the firm may have as many as 25 projects at any one time (in various stages), a full staff of "super competent" project coordinators help manage the day-to-day project operations, and reportedly deliver the highest caliber of service. Cullman's supporters see her as the design inspiration, based on clients' interests.

Customers consider pricing top of the market but worth it. The firm charges a standard design fee, retail on product and workroom, a standard markup on antiques and an hourly fee for oversight. While "no expense is spared," the contract is said to be followed to the line. Supporters highly recommended the firm for those who appreciate superb management skills and the highest caliber quality. AD 100, 2000.

*"The firms incredible organizations skills are very comforting." "If she could not find the perfect antique, she would find a really good substitute." "You may pay more but the level of detail is amazing." "They seamlessly worked with the architects." "Even though slipcovers are not Ellie's thing, she did what I asked, and made it look great." "Ellie personally vetted every antique and kept a close eye on the associates assigned to us." "I did not want to be involved on a detailed basis, and I certainly did not need to." "My husband is crazy about Ellie—it amazed me that he got involved at all." "Ellie's knowledge of antiques and rugs is extensive and central to her stately decorating." "The designs are less predictable than you would have thought." "She delivers an American original—extraordinarily luscious designs that withstand the test of time. It is classic opulence meets livable comfort."*

## D'Aquino Monaco Inc.

4    3.5    5    5

180 Varick Street, 4th Floor, New York, NY 10014
(212) 929 - 9787   www.DAquinoMonaco.com

*Unique, vibrant, warm interior design and architecture*

Clients recommend D'Aquino Monaco with warmth and joy. The firm is said to take a personal investment in each project, creating vibrant and unique interiors. Carl D'Aquino has been in the profession for over two decades, and was later joined by architect Francine Monaco. Clients appreciate the full-service capabilities of the partners, and also mention their unusually calm and kind nature. The firm is known for its remarkably varied styles, from Italian modernism to resonant color to High Victorian, driven by client preferences.

The firm's recent projects include large houses built from the ground up, chic downtown lofts, Upper East Side apartments and a penthouse in Knightsbridge. Clients include a wide range of professionals—artists, fashion designers, actors and Wall Street. Bringing charm and character to newly built large-scale homes is a specialty recognized by clients. The firm also is developing a furniture line and recently designed the La Prairie commercial offices. Clients benefit from the unusually close ties the firm has established with its suppliers.

Generally, a standard up-front design fee is charged and products are acquired at a reasonable percentage over net. Oversight fees are in the typical range, and

the firm is quite sensitive to budgetary constraints, often shopping outside normally traveled paths and offering creative alternatives. D'Aquino Monaco will also do consultations by the hour. The partners have many repeat customers who think the world of the firm. ASID. HB Top Designers, 2000, 2001.

*"Francine and Carl will go the extra mile for their clients—we undertook an exhaustive auction hunt together for the perfect antiques for our house." "They were instrumental in advising me on the purchase of my new apartment." "Carl and Francine are very cost conscience, offering several alternatives." "I did not want a traditional, refined apartment, but a fresh breeze. They got it." "We were amazed at how they created a room of multiple functions, with folding furniture that looked just fabulous." "They work by instinct, not rule." "All the firm's interiors make a thematic personal statement, and are tied together with fully comfortable upholstery." "I admit to being a skeptic at first, but they did an incredible job." "Carl and Francine have brought expression and joy to all six of our projects. We are dedicated clients."*

## D'Urso Design Inc.                        4      4.5      4       4
39 Cooper Lane, East Hampton, NY  11937
(631) 329 - 3634

*Modern residential interior design*

Widely praised for his incorporation of neutral colors, smooth textures and naked, raw materials, Joe D'Urso's continually updates the definition of modern. His minimalism is rooted in the 1970s, yet is said to be neither cold nor harsh. Clients feel like they are working with a legend of great vision. D'Urso is credited for instituting the "High-Tech interior movement," using furnishings intended for the industrial environment placed in the domestic landscape. D'Urso currently has collections of furniture manufactured by Donghia and Knoll. His style stays on the forefront, while retaining an unmistakable signature. HB Top Designers, 1999, 2000, 2001. ID Hall of Fame.

*"As a designer he was unquestionably one of my early influences. Even today, his innovations push the edge of the envelope." "Living in his interiors is an honor—it is like living in a museum." "The first class expenses to Mexico did me in." "I felt as if nothing I owned was good enough to keep." "He singularly envisions solutions where everyone else only sees difficulties." "He is a designer's designer."*

## Dana Nicholson Studio, Inc. 🛍              3.5     3      4.5     4.5
515 Broadway, New York, NY  10012
(212) 941 - 6834

*Spare, luxurious interior design*

A classicist and modernist at once, Dana Nicholson is praised for his cultured and opulent designs. Frequent references to antiquity and unapologetically decorative furniture often reside in clean and restrained backgrounds. Born on Canada's Prince Edward Island, raised in Germany and rural Maine, Nicholson is able to capture an elegant, yet peaceful harmony of cultures and styles. This aesthetic beauty is said to be functional and comfortable. All customers, especially those unsure of what they are trying to articulate, applaud Nicholson's confident direction.

After graduating from Northeastern University, he spent five years with Melvin Dwork, mixing interior design with jewelry, photography and fashion. In 1992, he opened his own studio. Clients include young bohemians and the uptown chic with loft-like aspirations. Some commercial projects have been completed as well, including the Sean clothing store and the advertising offices of Grey Entertainment. Nicholson is said to be very adept at designing complementary lighting fixtures, custom carpets and intricate hardware. No detail is said to be too small for Nicholson to improve upon its design.

Pricing is said to be quite reasonable, with Nicholson providing a multitude of economic choices. Return clients say they would recommend him to anyone. HB Top Designers, 2000, 2001.

*"Dana is so imaginative. He will let you go as far as you want to go." "After he did my loft twice, I recommended him to my mother. She just loved his minimal elegance." "All my friends use him." "I don't know how he does it, but his rooms are both luscious and spare." "I would not recommend him for traditional spaces, it would be a mismatch." "While my new Florida apartment was supposed to be top quality, Dana redid all the bathrooms and the kitchen because I knew he could do it so much better." "Dana has strong taste and loves strong colors. You have to be equally strong to change his mind, but it will be glorious." "Dana's follow through is his biggest strength." "He is the master of meticulous perfectionism."*

## Dara Stern LLC

11 East 78th Street, Suite 2A, New York, NY 10021
(212) 734 - 3744

*Traditional, American classic interior design*

## Darcy Damgard Interiors          3.5      3      4.5      4.5

580 North Sea Mecox Road, Southampton, NY 11968
(631) 283 - 2525

*Updated, traditional high-end interior design*

Clients appeal to Darcy Leeds for a classic, genteel, timeless look that is both reliable and functional. They warmly mention Leed's practical good sense and ability to work professionally and effectively. While paying homage to the great traditional masters, Leeds uses her creativity and the input of her clients for a less predictable, more livable, individual look. Leeds will incorporate much of clients' existing furnishings and leans toward moderate pricing.

As a sole practitioner, Leeds only takes on a few clients a year, however she is said to accomplish more in a month than complete firms have done in six. She has been in the business for over 20 years, first as a hobby for friends in Washington, DC. Current clients include young law partners, young entrepreneurs and more established supporters in Manhattan, Palm Beach and Southampton.

The firm will work on a consultation basis at a reasonable hourly fee. For full projects, Leeds will charge a minimal design fee, a reasonable markup on products and a substantial oversight fee. Living rooms can range from $50,000 (if clients bring a lot to the party) to about $100,000. Leeds has strong relationships with excellent, but not outrageously priced subcontractors. Clients laud her honesty and "can-do" attitude, further commenting on her sensible judgment and inherent understanding of the interests of her "carriage trade" audience.

*"She definitely jumps right into the job, taking on the most intricate design tasks as well as the mundane—like helping me hang pictures." "Darcy really has a talent for walking into a room and salvaging a good percentage of my current furnishing which she retrofits into a refreshing new look." "Not only talented in her vision, but also efficient in her execution." "Is happy to do something over if it's not exactly to my specs." "Really does a great job managing subcontractors." "She just gets it and gets it done!"*

| | Quality | Cost | Value | Recommend? |
|---|---|---|---|---|

## David Kleinberg Design Associates

|  | 5 | 5 | 4 | 4.5 |

330 East 59th Street, New York, NY 10022
(212) 754 - 9500

*Bold, luxurious, contemporary-inspired interior design. HB Top Designers, 1999, 2000, 2001. KB 1998.*

## David Scott Interiors Ltd.

|  | 4.5 | 4 | 4.5 | 4.5 |

120 East 57th Street, 2nd Floor, New York, NY 10022
(212) 829 - 0703

*Client-oriented, updated, traditional interior design*

David Scott is described as exceptionally knowledgeable, accommodating and practical. His style is often an updated traditional view that is deemed "elegant but approachable," serene but luxurious, and always in sync with the client.

The majority of his clients are in Manhattan, while the rest are spread throughout the suburbs and Florida. Clients tell us Scott is a "design psychologist" who makes a great effort in accessing their needs and desires and delivers a highly customized product. He is said to create rooms that fulfill his clientele's objectives, both physically and spiritually. Scott teaches residential design at the New York School of Interior Design, and previously was in the business end of real estate.

The firm charges standard hourly fees for design plans and oversight, and reasonable markups on products with a sliding scale for more expensive antiques. Scott offers a variety of economic alternatives and is said to meet timing deadlines. Most living rooms are in the $100,000 to $200,000-plus range. Patrons comment that Scott is very professional, but has a lean back office. The vast majority of clients come back for additional projects.

*"David's aesthetic sensibilities are superb." "I enjoy my home as much today as I did three years ago when it was finished." "He is as nice as he is talented and professional." "David always returns phone calls the same day." "He became like a member of the family." "He maintained a wonderful sense of humor throughout." "We reap the benefit of his wonderful relationships with vendors." "As a businessman, he relies on his contract, to the letter." "David listened to our dreams and wishes and turned them into a wonderful reality." "He is as nice as he is talented, with real star potential."*

## Denning & Fourcade Inc.

|  | 5 | 5 | 4.5 | 5 |

111 East 56th Street, New York, NY 10022
(212) 759 - 1969

*Opulent, classical interior design*

As a venerate connoisseur of late 19th-century design, Robert Denning's expertise is not questioned. Founded in 1960 with the late Vincent & Fourcade, the firm has fiercely loyal clients. Denning & Fourcade has decorated eight houses and a boat for one couple and four homes for Jean Vanderbilt. Other clients include Oscar de la Renta and Henry Kissinger. For all his success, Denning is noted by clients to be delightful, self-effacing and intensely involved with his projects on a day-to-day basis. According to patrons, he can often be seen urging the architect and the contractor to improve their attention to detail to match his own.

While Denning often uses damask from Tassinari and Chatel (the oldest fabric house in the world and purveyor to Marie Antoinette), he also specifies the appropriate fabrics for children's rooms and can work within a budget. We are told that he is a genius with color and has great vision, encouraging clients to move walls or use fabrics they might otherwise not consider. Reportedly, Denning is "always right." He mixes Regency, Empire and Biedermeier, considering it boring to hold to one style. Clients say he can't look at modern design without flinching but considers it great fun to find a bargain in a flea market.

The firm is quite small, and Denning takes only a few clients at a time, giving each his utmost attention. He charges an up-front design fee and then can work on a percentage or on a flat-fee basis for product. AD 100, 2000.

*"He still maintains this great enthusiasm for his work after all these years. It's such an inspiration." "I fully trust the man in every aspect of interior design." "He sees things well beyond the imagination of mere mortals." "He is a madman in a flea market, finding the most interesting objects. But by the time you have these objects in their proper place, they look fabulous, but are no longer necessarily a bargain." "Don't make the mistake of questioning his methods or vision because in short time he'll just prove to you how right he was." "He does things one way— the right way." "His work and reputation speak for themselves."*

## Dennis Rolland Inc.

405 East 54th Street, New York, NY  10022
(212) 644 - 0537

4    4    4    5

*Sumptuous, traditional, European and American interior design*

Clients continue to laud Dennis Rolland for his cultivated eye, exacting standards and warm personality.  He ably mixes charming objects of less value with important antiques to assemble an atmosphere of saturated color, layered elegance and timelessness.  Clients report that they receive great personalized attention, and that he can do "over-the-top" classical grandeur, "perfect suburban" and "funky-exuberant-charming" equally well, but that he does not like to compromise quality.  Suppliers also respect Rolland, enabling him to deliver the highest quality to clients.

Rolland started his own business in 1987 after six years with mentor Mark Hampton.  Clients currently include world-renowned businessmen, European dowagers, Greenwich establishment and some second-generation young couples with high standards and healthy budgets.  He is willing to do a few rooms at a time, knowing that the initiated will come back for more.

Most clients do not have a set budget, with many living rooms in the $250,000-plus range, before antiques. The firm has an excellent business reputation. There is no design fee and products are purchased at retail. KB 1990, 1994.

*"I can't say enough about Dennis.  He will come to your house to hang the pictures himself and puff the pillows before a big party." "He arrives at my house with five or six shopping bags to see how I will react. If I don't like them, he goes back and does it again." "My husband is an antique furniture collector, and very much respects Dennis' knowledge and sophisticated eye." "He is never pushy, and would never tempt the young with choices that are too expensive for them. He always puts the money in the right place." "He is perpetually hired in our house and a real friend."*

## Dessins LLC

787 Madison Avenue, New York, NY  10021
(212) 288 - 3600

4    4.5    4    4.5

*Detailed, thoughtful, traditional interior design*

Known for her traditional European style, clients applaud Penny Drue Baird's insight, taste and talents.  Her skills with details and standards of quality are also cited.  Often offering a unique perspective, Baird is said to take great pains to match the interiors to the architecture of the house and the personality of the client. Multiple layers of stripes, piques and taffetas are often highlighted with contrasting trims, shown against bright and patterned walls.  Most everything is custom and top of the line.  While thought to be very highly priced and outside of many budgets, clients consider her worth every penny, often returning for later projects. KB 2000.

*"She came into my living room and did five things, transforming it from a frumpy, grandmotherly look to the hip and now.  My friends and I were amazed." "She is so busy.  It would help if she hired a few more office people to leverage her time and answer the phone." "She does not clamor to work on a budget." "She had wonderful resources in Paris and London." "I think her work is amazing.  We have used her in the past and love what she did. If I won the lottery, the first thing I would do is hire her again."*

## Diamond Baratta Design    4.5    5    4    4.5

270 Lafayette Street, Suite 1501, New York, NY 10012
(212) 966 - 8892

*Exuberant, colorful, American interior design*

Principals William Diamond and Anthony Baratta employ a distinct, energetic and playful take on the Americana aesthetic with multilayered fabrics, vibrant colors and an unconventional twist to the traditional. While the indelible signature of the firm is based on this American vernacular (bright, oversized chintzes, classic-shaped furniture updated with exuberant color, contrasting millwork, plaid rugs), they have also designed the interiors of stately homes and finely refined East Side townhouses with dignity and flair. Clients praise their "extraordinarily innate sense of the appropriate" and their leanings toward the highest quality materials.

Diamond Baratta was established 28 years ago. References praise the firm's sources for imported furniture that ranges from 18th-century English to 30s vintage. The firm charges high fees, but clients are very satisfied with the total outcome. HB Top Designers, 1999, 2000, 2001

*"They restored and added dignity to our house with fine interior architectural details. Then they added charm with fresh colors and bold chintzes." "They do traditional with merriment, really adding joy to our lives." "Their creativity is beyond compare." "The pair were very willing and very able to adapt to my desire for a classic house with understated decoration. They are first-rate designers." "They have an extraordinary eye for architectural concepts, but let someone else draw the blueprints." "It was amazing how they could come up with a solution right then and there. Then they would draw it freehand on the wall for the contractor to implement." "They are not great about babysitting the subs." "They pretty much lost interest at the end of the job." "We could not be happier with the result."*

## Drake Design Associates Inc.     4    4    4    4.5

140 East 56th Street, New York, NY 10022
(212) 754 - 3099   www.drake_designassoc.com

*Bold, quirky, colorful interior design.*

Jamie Drake is heartily endorsed by clients for his inventive contemporary style, attention to detail and warm personality. Well known for an invigorating palette of vibrant color, fashion infusions and over-the-top embellishment, Drake also works well with more moderate customers. Clients report that he is happy to take their lead, while gently nudging them in a coherent direction.

Drake graduated from Parsons and established his firm in 1978. Currently there are two senior designers and a registered architect who work with Drake. While there is a good-sized minimum for new clients, Drake will work with a client in phases, and can be very budget-minded. His clientele range widely in age and design interests. Recent commissions include Madonna's lush, dramatic LA residence, Michael Bloomberg's Manhattan townhouse and Victor Gramm's retreat on Martha's Vineyard. References all conclude that Drake offers wonderful customer service.

A standard design fee is charged, with all products (including antiques) at a reasonable markup. Oversight usually falls under Drakes purview at higher rates. Younger clients often do living rooms in the $100,000 range with more established clientele in the $500,000 range. A number of clients are repeat customers, including one who has done nine projects with Drake including two planes, a helicopter and a boat. ASID. HB Top Designers, 2000, 2001.

*"His designs tell creative, fashion-based stories." "Jamie has an infallible eye and a great sense of humor." "They have given me the best service imaginable." "He is an original with very high quality standards." "Jamie transposed my estate sale apartment into something absolutely fantastic with creativity and color." "I follow his lead without question." "In all the years I have dealt with Jamie, I can not remember a single lapse." "A perfect match of wondrous creativity and a well-run business." "Decorating with Jamie is like FAO Schwartz for big kids."*

| | Quality  | Cost $ | Value  | Recommend?  |
|---|---|---|---|---|

### Easton-Moss & Company

|  | 5 | 4.5 | 5 | 5 |

72 Spring Street, 7th Floor, New York, NY 10012
(212) 334 - 3820

*Extraordinary, timeless, elegant interior design*

The joining of Charlotte Moss with David Easton has created one of the undisputed design powerhouses of our time. With Easton as an accepted master of the baronial manor house (or apartment) and Moss's renown warmth and genteel style for interior detail, they are the dream team of classic English interiors. As of now, projects are either Easton- or Moss-directed, but references say that there are plans for joint-inspiration. Moss is ably overseeing the merging of the process management and back office, particularly billing (having spent a decade on Wall Street, herself). The firm continues to use Eric Smith for architecture, offering seamless project coordination.

Easton's stellar reputation was built upon his striking ability to instantly visualize the perfect solution, acquire masterful product and manage (with a large support system) a comprehensive process. Supporters also say he is brilliant, funny and friendly. Most projects have been exceedingly large and expensive (Patricia Kluge, Carol Petrie), and many references report that much of their contact with the firm is through project managers working with extraordinary, "Easton-approved" materials (with custom markups). Moss had historically taken on a few number of quality projects a year, but was known for her brilliant ability to combine fabrics and heirloom antiques with bargain finds to create fabulously elegant interiors that did not "bankrupt the client." While Moss travels extensively, she is reportedly still the primary client contact. Easton is launching a line with Lee Jofa and Moss is a consultant with Colonial Williamsburg.

Both designers have a devoted following. While Easton's clients generally acknowledge that costs are over the top (reportedly, living rooms of $600,000 to $1,200,000 are the norm), most say the firm's extraordinary results and overall client service are worth every penny. Moss was known to be relatively reasonable on cost and very generous. Clients are keenly awaiting the result. AD 100, 2000. HB Top Designers, 1999, 2000, 2001. ID Hall of Fame. KB 2000.

*"I so enjoyed my time with David—he instantly connects with people and I learned so much from him. He has a masterful touch, and his spaces are extraordinary, livable and timeless." "While we liked our project manager, I only saw David about once a month and he was always about to fly somewhere else. While we were very pleased with the end product, we did not enjoy the process." "David's unique products and superior client service are unmatchable."*

*"Charlotte's Virginia-bred charm and hospitality illuminate her interiors." "She is warm, but a sharp professional." "Charlotte allows her clients vision and taste to shine through" "I can not imagine her working with an indecisive client, it would drive her crazy." "She continues to design because she is passionate about it." "The day after I finished my house I was offered twice what I put into it." "Charlotte is focused and fun."*

| | Quality | Cost | Value | Recommend? |
|---|---|---|---|---|
| | ✚ | $ | ◆ | ★ |

## Elaine Griffin

☞  ☞  ☞  ☞

150 West 123, 4th Floor, New York, NY 10027
(212) 665 - 7189

*High-end residential interior design. HB Top Designers, 2000, 2001.*

## Eric Cohler Inc.

| 4 | 3.5 | 4.5 | 5 |

872 Madison Avenue, Suite 2B, New York, NY 10021
(212) 737 - 8600   www.ericcohler.com

*Updated, traditional, ingenious interior design*

Clients laud Eric Cohler for his helpful, reliable and diplomatic nature, saying that he quickly understands and incorporates their interests. Most of his projects are classically based with a more modern twist. Appreciated for his architectural inventiveness as well as his design skills, Cohler effectively works with architects from inception, adding significant architectural detail. He received a BA in art history and an M.S. in historic preservation and design from Columbia University. On his own since 1990, he comes recommended by more established designers, trades people and product vendors as a rising star in the industry. While Cohler himself is not a licensed architect, his associated project architects prepare the firm's drawings.

Cohler is consistently described by his clients as gifted, hardworking and intelligent. They also rave about his design sense, resourcefulness and creativity. (He is privately known as "Mr. Answerman.") Cohler gravitates to the best quality the budget will allow, but he is perfectly willing to mix this with the client's existing furniture and Crate & Barrel items. His client service is said to go beyond the normal call of duty, and he is also "lots of fun."

The firm works with a reasonable up-front design fee and a reasonable markup over net for products. Alternatively, they can work on an hourly fee basis when shopping for product. Standard oversight fees are charged on a percentage basis. Cohler is noted by clients as being very professional, businesslike and generous. HB Top Designers, 1999, 2000, 2001. KB 1994, 1999, 2001.

*"Eric is so easy, quick and has so much range. He is as good with his left brain as his right—so creative and yet so practical." "When my architect and I were perplexed as to how to treat the walls adjoining the three floors in our apartment, Eric envisioned the solution with just one look." "Eric willingly and lovingly helped design our Christmas decorations last year, and never asked for a fee. He did the same for my friend's Rosh Hashana dinner." "His compositions, mixing centuries and continents are unifying and uplifting." "He could even make items purchased at Ethan Allen sing on Park Avenue." "I am so glad that Eric is pursing a career in design. It is in his DNA—this is what he was meant to do in life. It is a joy to see." "Eric is my insurance policy because I know everything he suggests will be correct." "There is no question that Eric's decoration was the reason I was able to sell my house so quickly and profitably."*

## Erica Millar Design

| 4 | 3.5 | 4.5 | 4.5 |

16 East 65th Street, 5th Floor, New York, NY 10021
(212) 439 - 1521

*Upscale, understated, serene interior design*

Dealers and clients, alike, applaud Erica Millar for her deft design, creating rooms of unassuming beauty and refined elegance. The designer is also noted for her ability to make rooms comfortable, welcoming and appropriate for the lifestyles of her clients. We hear Millar often teams up with her architect/husband Russell Riccardi, resulting in a very successful, collaborative effort between the professionals and the client.

After graduating with a painting degree, Millar worked for some of the finest designers of our time—Frank Gehry, Robert Stern and Ward Bennett. The firm was established in 1988 and does mostly substantial renovation projects for clients residing in Manhattan. While there is a good amount of staff support, Millar is the primary client interface and does most of the shopping herself. Clients further appreciate that she is quite demanding of the dealers, having them restore every little scratch before delivery. Sources also appreciate that what funiture is not readily available, Millar has the capability and resourcefulness to create. This is an extension of her furniture partnership with the manufacturer, Walter P. Sauer.

Millar charges a low design fee, a reasonable markup over net on product and an hourly consultation fee for oversight. Living rooms are generally in the $150,000 range, before major antiques and carpets. All patrons cite her efficiency and professionalism. Many customers have done several projects with Millar, and recommend her "whenever they can."

*"Erica's designs work perfectly for both toddler playdates and for highbrow cocktail parties." "Her sense of style, color, detail and scale is impeccable" "You feel as if Erica cares as much about the outcome as you do." "She has done three large residences for us as well as offices. What more can we say?" "My friends are always struck by the calm simplicity of the apartment." "She is not afraid to put Crate & Barrel along side the finest antiques—and it works." "She feels that her job is not done unless the client is totally satisfied." "Our homes are a source of great comfort and pride."*

### Eve Robinson Associates

| | 4 | 4.5 | 4 | 4.5 |
|---|---|---|---|---|

2112 Broadway, Suite 403, New York, NY 10023
(212) 595 - 0661

*Clean, comfortable, modern interior design*

Eve Robinson is appreciated for her creative use of natural materials, client collaboration and cohesive compositions of "forward-thinking" interior elements. Clients also report that she very accessible and thoughtful. While Robinson generally favors the modern aesthetic, clients say she makes their homes warm and comfortable by adding traditional elements and accent colors. In addition, she is known for her use of high-quality fabrics and workmanship.

Robinson studied art history at Vassar, worked in fashion for Polo/Ralph Lauren and then studied interior design at Parsons. After a year with Victoria Hagan, Robinson founded her firm in 1990. Recent projects include a New York City residence for actress Marisa Tomei, a villa in Kent, New York, and a kitchen and bath renovation in Manhattan. Robinson presents lots of options to clients, who happily report that she will also accompany them shopping. They feel they can rely on her to create "perfect" rooms, on time and without any surprises. She often works with her husband, the owner of the contracting company SilverLining, a teaming that effectively increases the collaborative approach.

To start a project, Robinson's firm charges an hourly rate for design concept and shopping, with a commission for product. Oversight fees are in the standard range. Robinson stays to the reasonable side in her product selections and no hourly product fee is charged if a client is paying for oversight services. Living rooms generally run in the $70,000 to $80,000 range, but can be much more. Clients say they continue to come back to Robinson for livable interiors that are simple yet elegant. HB Top Designers, 1999, 2000, 2001. KB, 1998, 2001.

*"Eve is amazing in her ability to choose objects that look 'overly funky' to me in the showroom, but when she places them in context, they look just right." "When the tile layer had a problem matching a pattern Eve came right up and straightened it out." "She finds furnishings that tread that fine line between unusual and livable." "Everything she did for us we think we will keep our entire lives." "She was very patient about working with us in multiple phases, one project at a time over four years, and we are still going." "Eve has great vendor relationships and sources that I would never dream of." "I've never made a mistake when I have used Eve. I have worked with other decorators to save money, but will not do so again."*

| | Quality  | Cost | Value | Recommend? |
|---|---|---|---|---|

## Fox-Nahem Design

4.5   4.5   4   4.5

82 East 10th Street, New York, NY  10003
(212) 358 - 1411

*Modern, sumptuous high-end interior design*

Industry insiders and clients praise Joe Nahem and Tom Fox as much for their accommodating nature as for their "exceptionally elegant and interior compositions with wit." The firm receives acclaim for a wide range of looks, from traditionally-based townhouses to Americana farmhouses to more tailored, even minimalist beach houses. Nahem and Fox are regarded as first-class professionals who work integrally with clients as well as architects and painters, "without the attitude of a big designer." With an architect on staff, the firm is also adept at creating spaces that are in balance and sensitive to the architectural perspective.

This firm of five was founded in 1975 and currently takes on five to twelve projects annually. Both Fox and Nahem are graduates of Parsons and are said to have substantial involvement in each project. Clients tend to have a open outlook and a healthy budget.

A typical living room is usually in the $150,000 to $250,000 realm. Standard design fees are taken up front with reasonable product markups. Clients say the firm is wonderful about switching out any furnishing that doesn't strike a cord, and highly recommend them to friends. HB Top Designers, 1999, 2000, 2001.

*"They strike that perfect balance between the sumptuous and the seriously hip." "Certainly not cheap but their work is so beautiful while being completely functional and comfortable." "They created some really bomb-proof designs with my kids in mind—but it's still fun and incredibly attractive." "Cool and down to earth." "They are not primadonnas, but honest and easy to work with." "They are little pit bulls with suppliers. If anything is late they will make it happen." "We did not have one disagreement throughout the whole process. Very much a joint effort." "I asked for 'Chanel with combat boots' and they more than delivered."*

## Fraser Associates

4.5   5   4   5

133 East 64th Street, New York, NY  10021
(212) 737 - 3479

*Luxurious, elegant, updated, classical interior design*

Generations have depended upon Clare Fraser for her ability to create traditional laced with glamour, well before becoming the style of the moment. Patrons say that her taste is absolutely faultless, her creativity unique and her execution impeccable. Every project is uniquely dramatic, employing rich color, exquisite details and many custom elements. Fraser is very involved with each project. She is good at listening and involving the client, but is said to show resolve when necessary to keep the project on track. Clients completely trust her design judgment and defer to her good taste.

According to clients, Fraser and her assistants handle every last detail. About ten assignments are taken on at any one time. Residential commissions are generally centered in Manhattan's Upper East Side and Greenwich, CT, with Hobe Sound/Palm Beach as another focus. Commercial projects include suites at the Waldorf Towers and the Plaza, the Lyford Cay Club and the Hudson National Golf Club.

The firm operates with no up-front fees for current clients and charges retail on products, a reasonable markup on labor, and a negotiated oversight fee. Fraser reportedly prefers job with budgets that can support the highest quality fabrics and furnishings. Living rooms are often in the $150,000 to $200,000 range. While clients clearly appreciate her high standards, some felt that Fraser went "a bit too far," urging them to replace moldings and doors that looked just fine to them. Clients highly recommend Fraser for a timeless, yet remarkable statement of personal style. KB 1993.

*"She metaphysically puts your signature in the room. It looks just like you." "I never feel as though she is giving me the cookie-cutter approach." "With Clare, you die when you get the estimate. But when the furnishings arrive, you are always floored by the look and happy with the investment." "She can do the ultimate Waspy-calm for the country and super-chic for the city." "She can do a guy's apartment with perfect taste, and without it looking too fussy." "I know that Clare Fraser's clients are mostly wealthy or well known. I am neither, but my home looks like it now." "Simultaneously functional and drop-dead gorgeous." "I frequently see the retail prices as we have shopped for years, and that is what I am billed." "She inherently knows how to create that 'je ne sais quoi' that is stunning, but always in good taste."*

### Frederic Jochem                 3.5    3.5    4.5    5
240 Central Park South, New York, NY 10019
(212) 956 - 1840

*Updated, refined, Continental interior design*

Frederic Jochem has been acclaimed for his calm continental style, excellent oversight capabilities and care for the client. Described as traditional with a twist, Jochem's decorating incorporates his client's tastes and personality with his own confident and open-minded style. Jochem is said to have a particularly good sensitivity for patrons heralding from his native France.

With extensive experience in planning, architecture, landscape and interior design, Jochem has worked for a range of well-known families from the Rockefellers to the Cartiers to the Hermes. Commissions range from Beekman Place to Casa del Campo to Bermuda and the Left Bank. Commercially, his work can be found in Fifth Avenue lobbies, showrooms and high-end office spaces. Jochem holds a BA from the Paris law university, Rue d'Assas, and from the Ecole d'Architecture de Paris as well as an MBA from the Paris business school, Ecole Des Cadres. He also attended the New York School of Interior Design.

Jochem charges a reasonably priced oversight fee, a standard product fee and a standard designer's fee. All of Jochem's clients report that he is honest, clear and precise with his contractual agreements and that the quality is superb. Jochem is consistently noted by his clients for his troubleshooting capabilities and his managerial abilities. Clients praise Jochem for his extensive knowledge, innovative tastes and exemplary professionalism. ASID.

*"He made my home express my personality and reflect my multinational interests and background. He makes sure the client is totally satisfied." "Frederic is meticulous in his round-the-clock supervision of multiple teams, including some highly sensitive European craftsmen." "On the human level, he proves his honesty, loyalty, patience, tenacity and flexibility of mind. On a professional level, Frederic brings a wealth of experience and talent to any job." "Our requirements were exacting, if not strenuous, but Mr. Jochem totally stayed on the program." "He handled substantial funds in a manner which inspired our utmost confidence." "Every phase of the project was completed in advance of the original schedule." "I am delighted to have the opportunity to positively recommend him."*

### Geoffrey Bradfield                 4    4.5    4    4.5
105 East 63rd Street, Suite 1B, New York, NY 10021
(212) 758 - 1773

*Opulent, modern interior design*

Known for his unique perspective, Geoffrey Bradfield brings opulence, quality and verve to his projects. He often bases his designs on 1930s glamour with a contemporary lilt, highlighted with antiques and objects from different centuries and continents. Art Deco often factors into the picture. Art collectors often

become clients and clients often become art collectors, owing to Bradfield's passion and knowledge of contemporary art. Clients say he is particularly adept at designing a room around a single piece of art.

After working with McMillen for a brief period, Bradfield joined the late Jay Spectre in 1978 to pursue his more contemporary style. Recent projects include spacious Park Avenue apartments (including several in the Pierre Hotel), substantial apartments in Chicago, grand private homes in Palm Beach, private jets, yachts and offices with character. Clients appreciate his responsiveness, and say Bradfield makes it very easy to have a long-distance relationship.

The firm charges a standard+ up front design fee, standard product markups and hourly rates only for hours where no commission is otherwise received. Bradfield tends to work with only the highest-quality materials, including elegant silks and sateens. Living rooms tend to be quite well over $100,000, although sisal can also be used with style. While many enjoy Bradfield's fulsome personality, others say he can be a bit overwhelming. Overall, clients roundly praise Bradfield for his attention to detail, resourcefulness, accessibility and style. ASID. AD100, 2000. KB, 1993.

*"Geoffrey has endless imagination and a riotous sense of humor. This makes for wildly amusing interiors." "He took a shell of a house, my dream concept and my color scheme, and transposed the property into something magical." "While always respectful and professional, he was not thrilled when I pushed the aesthetic line toward practicality." "I feel as if I am happily floating on a cloud in my high-rise living room." "Jean Harlow would be at home in one of his interiors." "As a fine furniture dealer, I can say that he has an excellent eye." "We were a team and I loved the experience." "I cannot tell you how many people are dying for a dinner invitation just to see the house." "I have never enjoyed working with anyone as much as I did with Geoffrey."*

## Glenn Gissler Design

4    3.5    4.5    5

36 East 22nd Street, New York, NY 10010
(212) 228 - 9880

*Calm, considered, edited interior design*

Hailed for his cool, clean, sophisticated rooms in cohesive colors, Glenn Gissler is equally noted for being hot on design details. It is said that nothing escapes his scope and that he is a "finisher." Additionally, sources report Gissler goes out of his way to understand clients' needs by examining their lifestyles and interests, and to educate them throughout the process. Knowledgeable about antiques and passionate about design history, Gissler places objects with historical significance in new contexts. Clients feel privileged to work with Gissler and say that his Midwestern roots make him appealing and approachable.

Gissler is known to start as the designer on a job and evolve into the project manager. While primarily an interior designer, Gissler has a degree in architecture from RISD, and often designs and supervises complete renovations. Before striking out on his own, he worked with Rafael Vinoly and Juan Montoya. Projects range from small to large apartments in the city to houses in the Hamptons, the Vineyard and Naples. Clients range from first time homeowners to curators' apartments full of fine art. Most clients continue to seek this designer's advice well after the project is formally completed and hire him again.

A standard design fee is charged and the firm then works at a reasonable percentage over net. Oversight fees run in the standard range. Any issues (all small) are reportedly handled very professionally and with Gissler taking full financial responsibility. Living rooms generally are in the $100,000 to $150,000 range, and he sometimes works on a consulting basis. ASID. HB Top Designers, 1999, 2000, 2001.

*"While my architect was only so-so, and my contractor left me high and dry, Glenn was a dream." "Glenn distinguished himself by asking really good questions about how we lived and worked, not about which Louis we preferred." "He can make objects with great historical significance dance with purchases from Pottery Barn." "His subs are of the very best quality." "He took on the project as if it were his own." "He was exceptional at creating a quality background that had personality, yet highlighted our artwork." "He kept the rooms open enough for us to enjoy the luxury of space." "I don't know how he did it, but he took my sketchy concept and translated it into an apartment of clarity and beauty."*

## Gomez Assoc./Mariette Himes Gomez 💼  5  5  4  4.5

504-506 East 74th Street, 3rd Floor, New York, NY 10021
(212) 288 - 6856   www.mariettehimesgomez.com

*Modern, elegant interior design*

Mariette Himes Gomez is considered a master by peers as an innovator of today's warm modernism, infusing beige linens and oatmeal raw silks with exquisite dressmaker details. While she has a healthy respect for tradition, she is known as a master editor who refines spaces with clean upholstered lines, solid textiles and jaunty 30s French or English showpieces. Best known for her trademark colors of whites and creams, she will incorporate soft hues at the client's request. References say that Gomez is not, however, the person to hire for flounces or frills, and that she has a very specific view of what she believes will work.

Gomez graduated from RISD, the New York School of Interior Design, and began her design career with Parish-Hadley and then-architect Edward Durrel Stone. The firm is quite large by industry standards. Senior Manager, Dominick Rotondi is noted as gracious and extremely accommodating, running a tight organizational ship with excellent follow-through. Historically, demand has far exceeded Gomez's available time, especially since about a third of her time is spent in London. More recently, the firm is only taking on a handful of large, new projects each year to meet client service expectations. High-profile bankers and a large number of entertainment moguls count among her clients, including Harrison Ford and director Ivan Reitman. Over the last year, Gomez opened a 2,000-square-foot showroom, The shop, at the address above, showcases hand-picked antiques, a custom furniture line and intriguing accessories.

Clients seem to be very pleased with Gomez's fee structure, which is somewhat unique in the industry. A substantial design fee is charged, based upon anticipated hourly reviews and a standard flat fee is taken for the product purchases, based on the estimated budget. Clients speak lovingly of her designs, and if imitation is the sincerest form of flattery, she wins the prize. ASID. AD 100, 2000. HB Top Designers, 1999, 2000, 2001. ID Hall of Fame. KB 1991, 1994, 1996, 1999, 2001.

*"She is the champion of minimalism, yet hearteningly eloquent." "Mariette is particularly good at solving functionality challenges, every room is used to the maximum potential." "It is not easy to get Mariette on the phone." "She was amazing with my major new house, collaborating with me and our serious architect. But when it came to renovating my Manhattan apartment, she was less interested." "Our house is a youthful vision of traditional." "She finds the most sublime furniture in England that is grand without being presumptuous." "Dominick is the backbone of the office, always helpful and always straight-forward." "Her rooms delight the senses and warm the soul."*

## Greg Jordan Inc. ▉

| | | | |
|---|---|---|---|
| 5 | 5 | 4 | 5 |

504 East 74th Street, Suite 4W, New York, NY 10021
(212) 570 - 4470

*Lavish, traditional, colorful interior design*

Firmly established as one of New York's finest designers, Greg Jordan has won the allegiance of clients with his ability to fulfill their design aspirations and exceed clients' service expectations. Jordan intricately combines historic backgrounds with superluxurious, eclectic ingredients to create texture and movement. This melange creates a relaxed yet stylish environment steeped in historical reference. Clients report that the firm can also develop more traditional interiors and produces sumptuous chintz-laden environments that do not look overdone or fussy. Architecture is now integrated into the mix, creating coherent visions.

Raised in Louisiana, trained by Robert Stern, clients describe Jordan as a true "Southern gentleman" with a clear mission. The business was established in 1984 and has cultivated a very impressive roster of clients including Blaine Trump, Libbet Johnson and various banking moguls. The firm operates like a family, which the clients feel like they join. There are generally ten to twelve projects active at any one time.

The designer's own line of furniture is now available at Scalamandre, with accessories and antiques available in his retail shop. Most all fabrics, furnishings and trims are custom, according to Jordan's grateful, but well-heeled patrons. Most jobs are between $750,000 and $2 million. Clients roundly acknowledge Jordan for his verve, flourish and commitment to the very best. AD 100, 2000. HB Top Designers, 1999, 2000, 2001. KB 1992, 2000.

*"Greg absolutely wants to please, the rest of his office follows up." "Greg is a wonderful listener who not only hears what I am saying, but also what I am not saying." "He envisions how our family works, making sure all of us are comfortable, and that each room is used." "He has the ability to make any complication or issue disappear, by either fixing it or underplaying it." "He is a master with design details, color and timeless design." "Greg is filled with energy—he hammers nails in a wall or moves furniture about himself." "I have worked with many decorators and Greg is a breath of fresh air." "We have complete faith in him." "He has become a great friend through this engaging process."*

## Harry Schnaper Inc. ▉

| | | | |
|---|---|---|---|
| 4 | 3.5 | 4.5 | 5 |

692 Madison Avenue, New York, NY 10021
(212) 980 - 9898

*Streamlined, traditional interior design*

Upholding very high design standards while maintaining a practical sensibility, Harry Schnaper continues to impress clients and peers. He ably incorporates French, Regency or Deco furnishings with clean lines into classic spaces, creating interiors that are "breathtakingly appealing," livable and timeless. Schnaper is said to favor schematic design themes, translating into artful consistency. Clients also praise Schnaper's intent client focus, expedient intelligence and amusing sense of humor. Many note that he is particularly adept at maximizing the living space in New York apartments.

Equipped with a degree in clinical psychology and schooled at the Chelsea School of Art, Schnaper worked with Gay Matthaei and Robert Metzger. He opened his eponymous firm in 1989. While most of Schnaper's work is in Manhattan, recent projects have taken him to Southampton, Philadelphia, Washington, D.C. and New Jersey. A small boutique, generally only three to four major projects are undertaken at a time. The firm's fees are considered to be very fair. Some say that Schnaper can be very economical, while others indicate budgets are not a strength. Project costs have varied, from $40,000 to well over $1 million, with recent living rooms falling between $200,000 to $300,000.

Many clients are repeat customers, crediting Schnaper's handsome designs, solid implementation skills and charm. AD 100, 2000. HB Top Designers, 1999, 2000. KB 1996.

*"Everyone loves Harry and his designs. I keep expecting him to become huge, but he is not a self-promoter." "He successfully worked with John McEnroe, so I knew that he could handle my husband. He is delightful and charming." "While his love is more modern, he has a great range of styles that he does so well." "He has flair without being flashy. He is all substance." "His work astounds the eye." "He works really well with architects, but should not be allowed outside without one." "I would never consider purchasing an apartment unless Harry had seen it." "I found Harry through my cabinetmaker. He has an amazing group of vendors who admire him and his work." "Harry was always there to supervise." "While I know he can be expensive, I did not have the budget for that and he was amazing." "You only buy once with Harry." "He is rock solid."*

### Housefitters Inc. 🛍      4    2.5    5    4.5
57 East 93rd Street, New York, NY 10128
(212) 348 - 2417

*Classical, warm interior design*

Ruth Ann McSpadden is lauded by clients for designs with old-world comfort that incorporate strong classic architectural details and warm palettes. She mixes fine antiques with excellent reproductions to create environments that appear to have evolved over generations. Mindful of the budget, she offers a range of fabrics and furnishings, but always creates the highest quality ambiance. She personally prefers lively colors and a mix of patterns, but we're told that McSpadden is very accommodating. She has completed at least one highly successful monochromatic apartment that sold weeks after redecoration at 20 percent over the asking price. Clients say that McSpadden is especially good with family environments, choosing practical and inviting fabrics.

McSpadden officially opened Housefitters for business in early 1999, after undertaking numerous personal projects for herself and her friends. Recent projects include the gut renovation of a large Upper East Side town house, a penthouse duplex apartment, several houses in the Hamptons and various Park Avenue redecorations. Extremely reasonable in her pricing, she will do just one room or a whole town house. Due to lean staffing and a full schedule, the firm limits the number of jobs taken during any particular period of time. Clients highly recommend Housefitters for enhancements or for a complete renovation.

*"Ruth Ann is a delight to work with. It was as if I were redecorating with my best friend." "She was also incredibly helpful mediating style issues between my husband and me." "Ruth Ann encouraged me to become much more involved that any other decorator—and the end result was so me." "She has an uncanny sense of color, distinguishing shades that elude me to this day." "She has a clear view, that she will tailor to your needs." "Ruth Ann has to be the most honest decorator in New York—she spent an inordinate amount of time talking me out of unnecessary purchases." "A generous and kind person with a classically refreshing sense of design."*

### Hoyt-Levasseur LLC      3.5    3.5    4    4.5
208 East 60th Street, New York, NY 10022
(212) 688 - 0900

*Au courant interior design*

Heather Hoyt and Alison Diamond Levasseur artfully, gracefully and dramatically design for just a few clients each year. While meeting the objectives of the clientele, the pair often adds the flair of couture fashion to their compositions. French 40s with jaunty color, glamorous silk taffetas, Lucite furniture and textural mohair often fit into the montage. They have been known to use $3-per-yard fabric for walls and window treatments, finished off with J. Mendel sable trim.

Hoyt received a masters in decoratives arts from Cooper-Hewitt/The New School, worked in antiques and then in interiors with William T. Georgis. Levasseur received a BA in painting from Cornell, spent a year with Sotheby's London and worked with Sills Huniford for several years. Their collaboration in the 1999 French Designer Showhouse led to a partnership. Recent projects include several Manhattan apartments, a house in Delaware and commission on Staten Island.

References commend the team for staying within budget and time expectations. Bills are detailed to the fabric yard. A standard design fee is charged up front with reasonable markups on product. Living rooms often total in the $75,000 to $125,000 range. Quality is said to be excellent with very good attention to detail. Clients hail the pair's au courant style for the young and young at heart. HB Top Designers, 2000, 2001.

*"There were so many highlights of the project it is hard to pick my favorite." "Nothing is expected. My antique chairs were covered in gorgeous gold pigskin." "They have very good listening skills, and would give us time to find the right balance." "There were no surprises. Everything was in the budget." "Even the most complicated, large scale patterns were seamed exactly right." "They have so much fun, but they are not yet a full-scale office." "They would only suggest items that they would like to live with themselves." "I never would have picked these colors on my own in a million years. But they are beyond fabulous."*

### Irvine & Fleming Inc.                    4.5      5      4      4.5
327 East 58th Street, New York, NY 10022
(212) 888 - 6000

*Traditional, English interior design*

For the last 41 years, Keith Irvine and Tom Fleming have maintained the standards of traditional English style with rich fabrics, warm colors and 18th-century formal-to-bohemian classicism. They have the highest standards of quality, and are regularly praised for their knowledge and effective design process. Clients will often give them carte blanche to design, implement and detail a new home, though Irvine & Fleming can also take cues from their clients' preferences. The firm successfully mixes exquisite antiques with vernacular straw rugs and paint-chipped furniture to create a home with a history.

During their partnership, Irving & Fleming have decorated historic homes, ranches, airplanes and railroad cars, mostly in the New York area, but also throughout the world. While they are known to be fond of the highest-priced fabrics and furnishings (with living rooms generally well above the $150,000 level), the partners encourage clients to reuse existing furniture in new settings or with a different covering. Their efficiency pleases most customers, but some find the process overwhelming and too hurried. AD 100, 2000. HB Top Designers, 1999, 2000, 2001.

*"When my friends walk in they always say, 'Wow!'" "Their effective process and the gorgeous results earn them superstar status in our minds." "They deserve a place in the design annals, but are fairly set in their ways." "I really wanted to choose the rugs first, but they were focused on the fabrics and on getting the project done quickly." "They are the only choice for the English Belle Epoque look, and can do so much more." "While upholding the traditional standards of the 70s and 80s, we were ready to move into the 21st century." "old-world charm at it's finest with clients that are in the very upper echelons of old, quiet New York Society."*

| | Quality | Cost | Value | Recommend? |
|---|---|---|---|---|
| | + | $ | ◆ | ★ |

## J.P. Molyneux Studio Ltd. ∿∿

29 East 69th Street, New York, NY  10021
(212) 628 - 0097

**4.5    5    3.5    4**

*Lavish residential interior design*

With artistic flourish, architectural support and stylistic detail, J.P. Molyneux is known for insisting on the very best quality.  Clients say he has brilliant vision and can shape a room with just one look.  He has many enthusiastic clients who extol his "stunning" taste and exquisite design skills.  Many creations are an imaginative amalgam of fantasy and opulence, combined with the comfort and richness of neoclassical traditions.  Grand entryways are said to be important to Molyneux's strategic thinking, and often are "beyond the imagination."

Born in Chile, educated in modernist architecture in Santiago and in classical design at the Ecole des Beux-Arts in Paris, Molyneux is a man of many continents and influences.  After working in Santiago and Buenos Aires, he settled in New York in 1987.  Commissions include many impressive Park and Fifth Avenue apartments, and sumptuous homes in Hobe Sound, Lyford Cay, Palm Beach and other major vacation spots.  Most of his satisfied clients do not need to think about budget and do not become overly involved in the design process.  The results, they say, are spectacular, and can be seen in the Rizolli monograph of his work published in 1997.

Others say that his strong vision is a bit overwhelming.  He often chooses and delivers furniture or a rug to a client without much discussion.  While this is a blessing to some, others find it difficult to say no to Molyneux and find it hard to resolve any design issues.  All clients lavishly praise Molyneux's talent, charming personality and the quality of the end results, but some characterize the design process as exhausting.  AD 100, 2000.  KB 1992, 1995.

Clients express caution: *"J.P. is worth every penny if you can control him or completely buy into his vision." "I thought he could have made my house just as beautiful without redecorating quite as much as he did." "If ever I disagreed with his vision fully, I became distressed because I did not want to upset him." "He is the type to say, 'Take the roof off and move it up three feet,' without much regard for cost."*

Still others are full supporters: *"I never worried, as he has the most refined eye of anyone I have ever met." "He created the most lavish and spectacular rooms— better than I ever imagined."  "Everything is done correctly, nothing is ever makeshift."  "His design choices can be audacious or more subtle, but are never boring." "We are so happy and would absolutely hire him again."*

## Jane Gaillard Inc.

167 East 74th Street, New York, NY  10021
(212) 988 - 3356

**3.5    3    4.5    4.5**

*Classic-to-Updated Old-School interior design*

Gaillard is highly recommended as a calming, clear influence in a world of possibilities.  Admired and appreciated by many a Park Avenue resident, Jane Gaillard has been practicing interior design since 1976.  Designs are said to be "toney" and appropriate, with the English and French 18th-century as major influences.  Lately, some clients are asking for a more tailored and structured look, and Gaillard is happily taking their lead.  While she is noted to be a helpful confident and excellent second opinion for customers who are actively engaged in the design process themselves, she also offers complete solutions for others who don't know where to begin.

A small operation, Gaillard is the clear client contact and very accessible.  Only a few major projects are undertaken at any one time, keeping Gaillard perfectly-whelmed and schedules in line.  Gaillard often starts with the public rooms, and at the request of the satisfied client projects often escalates from there.  The designer can work on a consulting or project basis.  For defined projects, a mini-

mal design fee is charged with reasonable product markups. Living rooms tend to be in the neighborhood of $100,000 but can move uptown. Ethan Allen is considered for the children's rooms.

*"We started with just the living room, and ended up doing two apartments and the country house." "Jane was amazing at breaking the deadlock my husband and I had over the last two years." "She never assumes that the sky is the limit—she is reasonable and practical." "We attended her 20-year anniversary party at the Colony five years ago, and met the loveliest group of past clients." "Not the decorator to use if you are trying to make a statement. Perfect for the low-key, just-so couple." "She never nickel and dimes you." "I thought that I knew a lot, but Jane brought the apartment to a new level." "Jane can guide you, but it is good if you have a direction." "There is a tremendous comfort level in using Jane."*

### Jed Johnson & Associates     5    5    4    4
211 West 61st Street, New York, NY  10023
(212) 489 - 7840

*Thoughtful, edited, exceptional interior design*

Design director, Arthur Dunnam, continues to set standards in the industry. Clients, peers and vendors consistently and wistfully speak of the firm's impeccable taste, inspired style and remarkable quality. Dunnam worked closely with the late Jed Johnson for ten years, and reportedly has maintained the ideals and forward-thinking design momentum of the firm. Known truly as a full-service operation, Jed Johnson & Associates will provide architectural, as well as design services, patrons praise the firm's ability to shop and install its product to the very last detail.

Seventeen members strong, the firm is said to professionally and diligently deliver a finished product. Buzz Kelly and Christine Cain, each with over eight years of experience at the firm, are noted as exceptional designers in their own right. While, certain clients say that they would have liked to have been more involved in the design process, all applaud the firm's efficiency. References compliment the team's color sensibility and knowledge of all sources, especially antiques and lighting.

The firm asks for an up-front design fee, retail for new products and net plus a percentage for antiques. Cost-conscious clients caution that the firm much prefers couture products which are very difficult to return, but will present less costly alternatives if urged. Living rooms may start at $150,000, but can run as high as the imagination. This design team is highly recommended for the latest in thoughtful, modern-edged, classic design. HB Top Designers, 1999, 2000, 2001. ID Hall of Fame.

*"They made it incredibly easy. Poof and it was done—I did not have to do a thing." "They do everything to the point of perfection. Mundane drawer handles become an opportunity to create artistic, interior jewelry." "Their first instinct is to create custom product. However, if I insist on pret-a-porter, they usually can find an excellent alternative." "Even their design peers are inspired by their creativity." "While inordinately expensive, they put in a very full effort, tweaking and retrofitting until just so." "The only complication was when some of the pieces did not seem right to me (although I had approved them). We never came to a final conclusion." "It is all or nothing with these guys." "They are the cutting edge of classic design." "We travelled together for nine days in Europe, and then Arthur created my dream."*

### Jeff Lincoln Interiors Inc.    4    3.5    5    5
675 Madison Avenue, New York, NY  10021
(212) 588 - 9500

*Classical, comfortable interior design*

With an innate ability to synthesize the best of the classical past with the allure of edited chic, Jeff Lincoln has built a loyal clientele. He is a favorite of many Park Avenue families who would not consider a minimalist look. Warm and resonant col-

| Quality | Cost | Value | Recommend? |

ors, refined fringes, old-world craftsmanship and surprising details are revisited with a modern eye, resolving to a sophisticated presence. References also praise Lincoln for his knowledge of fine antiques, period design and creative sources.

Clients include many of New York's young sophisticates, who relate to Lincoln's easy manner, genteel sensibility and business approach. Supporters love his vision and his artistic sketches. While some clients express concern that he starts slowly, he always wins client's hearts with the outstanding end result.

The firm charges a reasonable up-front design fee, a reasonable percentage over net and standard oversight fees. Lincoln is capable of going as high as a client would like in the quality spectrum but is equally open to less costly alternatives. Living rooms are generally in the $200,000 realm. He is highly recommended by many of the most discerning shoppers in New York for timeless comfort. HB Top Designers, 1999, 2000, 2001. KB 1995, 1998, 2001.

*"Jeff is so accommodating and such a pleasure to be with. He was never pushy and knew just the right look that I was hoping to achieve—not too traditional but not too contemporary." "His rooms are full of happy luxury without being over the top. And he can add a bit of whimsy, which we really appreciate." "The rooms are never pretentious, but beautiful." "An emerging talent who is just coming of age. While prone to a few bumps, the outcome was fabulous." "I have only positive things to say about Jeff. He has great taste and is a great guy." "His balance of the comfortable and the formal exactly matches our lifestyle." "He really listens and responds appropriately."*

## Jennifer Post Design 🛍                           4        4        4        4.5
25 East 67th Street, Suite 8D, New York, NY 10021
(212) 734 - 7994

*Polished, classical progressive interior design*

Clients say that Jennifer Post "possesses an unfair share of talent." For those seeking a transformation, she is applauded for her ambitious ability to convert boring or staid apartments into streamlined visions of classical contemporary. References are enchanted by her spatial insights and ingenuity translating into the raising of doorways, lowering of floors and elimination of superfluous details. Post environments are also commended for their strong bias toward comfort and livability. Historically, Post favored a white palette juxtaposed with dark floors and accents. Lately, she has judiciously added vibrant color to the mix, but works with clients to incorporate their vision. Clients admire her can-do attitude and tenacity with contractors and suppliers, describing her record-breaking project timing. Post can also be adamant regarding the cohesive nature of a design.

Post's clients include a number of celebrities (Jennifer Lopez, Matt Lauer), high profile executives (Homestyle Editor, Suzy Slesin) and other progressive, high-end homeowners. While most clients applaud her ability to give you a great look at a "decent price" and within budget, others say the price can be high. Living rooms generally range from $60,000 to $150,000-plus. Post holds a graduate degree in fine arts and design, and a minor in architecture. Supporters recommend Post for a specific, sleek and polished contemporary look. HB Top Designers, 1999, 2000, 2001. KB 1999.

*"Jennifer is a master at both concept and craft." "She annihilates the notion that modern is minimal." "Jennifer represents the beginning of the next generational wave in interior design." "I fell in love with her upon our first meeting. She is committed and is a ball of fire." "She is very dedicated and energetic—she would call me back immediately whether she was in Italy or Paris." "Jennifer tends to keep the design details in her head instead of on blueprints. But everything worked out beautifully." "She did my entire apartment in two months." "She took my staid, box of an apartment and created an environment of excitement, polish, refinement and warmth." "Her designs elevate the spirit."*

### John Barman Inc.     3.5    3.5    4    4

500 Park Avenue, New York, NY 10022
(212) 838 - 9443   www.barman.com

*Distinctive, stylistic interior design*

John Barman has staked out an iconoclastic design niche with resonant colors, lush fabrics and courageous appointments. Vibrant arabesque taffetas meet hot pink custom carpets, vivid red walls exaggerate linear space and French modern furniture converses with acrylic. Drawing from mid-century design emblems or the historically referential, Barman intensifies and enlivens. More discretely, Barman can do a modified version by using bright or distinct colors to freshen a more traditional construct. To his clients' delight, Barman builds such themes upon their interests and then retrofits to their lifestyles.

This firm of seven was established by Barman more than fifteen years ago. It takes about 30 assignments annually, six or eight of which are major. Clients say Barman is backed by a "first-class" support staff that keeps meticulously detailed budgets and status reports. Additionally, Barman is said to work extremely well in collaboration with architects and contractors to ensure the final product is the client's true vision.

Barman conducts the majority of his business in Manhattan, but also works in the Hamptons and will not hesitate to take on unusual decorating products— including boats. A typical living room runs about $100,000 to $150,000, with the firm charging standard design fees and standard markups on product. Budgets can be set or evolve, but Barman is trusted by clients to stay sensible. ASID. HB Top Designers, 2000, 2001. KB 2000, 2001.

*"His rooms are always dazzling compared to other designers." "You have to see his portfolio to believe it. We love him, but he would not be for everybody." "His style is so varied—he's able to do whatever the project called for, but he works really well with themes." "He rescued the architect and the contractor from what could have been a disaster on the house we built in the country." "Timing can be a issue, especially if the project is not focused." "John is an earnest and straightforward character with a bottomless pit of untapped creativity." "After wondering in the design forest, John has really found his groove." "He respected issues of economics and authenticity, and was very understanding about my choices." "As long as it looks good, he will go to Crate & Barrel." "He selects fabrics and furniture with such character. He would not settle for anything less."*

### Josef Pricci Ltd.     4    4    4.5    4.5

249 East 57th Street, Suite 2R, New York, NY 10022
(212) 486 - 2530

*Sumptuous high-end interior design*

Known as a decorator for the highly layered English look, Josef Pricci has many fans even in this era of restrained and minimalist design. Clients love his multiple flows of colorful chintz, silks and accessories. Many consider him to be one of New York's secret decorating sources, and have such confidence in Pricci that they often leave everything in his hands, returning only after the job has been completed. This suits Pricci who very much enjoys the responsibility and the autonomy. The firm is quite small but clients always get Pricci, who does all the design work himself.

Pricci began his design career in jewelry, selling his creations to Cartier, Van Clef & Arpels and Tiffany & Co. Vera Wang's father was his first interior design client. Eighteen rooms later, his interiors career was launched. Clients include many of the well-established ladies of New York and Palm Beach who cannot imagine living without needlepoint pillows. He is thought to be very reasonable by clients, as he is very resourceful at finding products and fabrics outside the standard channels. He is also very generous with his time—while he charges retail, there are no oversight fees or hourly bills. Many clients consider him a dear friend and a necessity, highly recommending him. KB 1990.

*"He is of the old-design school, saturated in luxury and comfort. I cannot imagine living any other way." "He is attentive but not overbearing." "Every detail has been considered." "You can smell the potpourri from the photographs." "I totally trust and depend on Josef for his thoughtfulness, energy and thoroughness." "Josef plans everything, chooses everything and oversees it all." "He worked as if this was his very own apartment, with extraordinary care and attention." "He encouraged us to start a collection of blue-and-white porcelain, which we just adore." "Josef creates refuges from the real world with plush, down-stuffed, ornate English furnishings and matching cascading curtains."*

### Juan Montoya Design      4.5    5    4    5
330 East 59th Street, 2nd Floor, New York, NY 10022
(212) 421 - 2400   www.juanmontoyadesign.com
*Neoclassical and contemporary interior design*

Juan Montoya is highly respected by clients and peers for his exquisite juxtaposition of cultures and periods, dramatic yet restrained taste and exceptional good manners. His contemporary design work is seen by past clients as sleek and eclectic, often merging bold South American and Asian elements into a neutral palette. More recently, he has developed a neoclassical design sensibility that integrates exquisite fabrics, fine antiques and rich colors. Clients applaud his ability to offer sophistication to any design construct, be it idealized cowboy or an Art & Crafts yacht.

The son of a Columbian diplomat, who worked in Paris and Milan before settling in New York, Montoya tends to have an international following. Many clients are very well-established New Yorkers or South Americans with impressive collections. Many are loyalists—at least one client has completed fourteen projects with Montoya over two decades. Montoya and his office are commended as highly professional. Experienced project directors are assigned to each commission, yet Montoya makes all design decisions down to the buttons on every cushion. A detailed 380-page monologue of his work was published in 1998.

The firm will work on a percentage basis or for a flat fee. Costs are said to be on the very high end of the range, with most living rooms well above $100,000. Patrons report that there is a healthy respect for schedule and budgets, and that Montoya is always happy to discuss alternatives. Most clients consider Montoya to be a master and continue to use him whenever possible. ASID. AD 100, 2000. HB Top Designers, 1999, 2000. ID Hall of Fame. KB 1992.

*"Juan is a total gentleman with a joyful outlook." "I was amazed how he integrated Aztec, Art Deco and Egyptian in an artfully masculine way." "I wish that I was still a priority client for him. When he is focused on your project, no one can match that richness and complexity." "I feel as if he would spend all the time the world with me walking up and down Madison Avenue, until we find the perfect solution." "He has done an excellent job, evolving over the years with my changing lifestyle and design interests." "Definitely not a primadonna, he's happy to discuss every detail with you." "I gave him my mish-mash of a priority list and he delivered a gorgeous, coherent product." "For my out-of-town project, Juan did commendable due diligence, visiting two to three possible contractors and woodworkers."*

## Julia Durney Interiors Ltd.

| | Quality | Cost | Value | Recommend? |
|---|---|---|---|---|
| | 3 | 2.5 | 4.5 | 4 |

79 Putnam Park Road, Bethel, CT  06801
(203) 798 - 7110

*Traditional interior design with a modern flair*

Julia Durney is said to have a natural flair for traditional designs imbued with a modern empathy. Many applaud her easygoing manner, great listening skills and attention to detail. We are told that Durney's skills can take you to excellent levels and that her creativity also expands to accommodate those of more modest means. All clients say Durney takes pleasure in incorporating their design interests and vision.

Durney began her career as a bond trader, attended Parsons and then started her design business in 1990. Her work is split between upscale clients in New York City and country homes in Fairfield County. The Nightingale-Bamford School recently commissioned Durney to redesign their boardroom. While the firm is quite small, clients note that Durney is very accessible and quite reliable.

The firm charges no design fee and very reasonable markups on product. Hourly consultations are also reasonably priced, and fully reimbursable against product fees if Durney is subsequently hired on retainer. Many of her clients are repeat customers.

*"She is a one-woman show and a pleasure to work with." "While Julia has no formal training, she is very pragmatic and accommodating." "Julia's ideas are well formed—bright and imaginative." "She is very considerate and patient, happily incorporating our family pieces into the design plans." "She was so good about doing our apartment on a project-by-project basis, over time, as the budget allowed." "I love working with her." "She goes with the flow and will wait all day for the carpet men to arrive." "Great ideas without interfering with your personal style."*

## Katie Ridder Design & Decoration

| | Quality | Cost | Value | Recommend? |
|---|---|---|---|---|
| | 3.5 | 3.5 | 4 | 4.5 |

1239 Broadway, Suite 1604, New York, NY  10001
(212) 779 - 9080   www.katieridder.com

*English meets eclectic interior design*

Katie Ridder is acclaimed for her striking balance between style and discretion. Clients say that she takes care to preserve the integrity of classic elements while incorporating the unexpected. Innovative hues, whimsical accents and eclectic objects are often layered on to more traditional backgrounds, making spaces more comfortable and friendly. References say she is very conscience or their lifestyles, and is interested in making the most of each room.

After working as a decorating editor at *House & Garden* and *House Beautiful*, and establishing a retail home furnishings store on the Upper East Side, she founded the firm in 1993. About fifteen projects are taken each year, half of which are of substantial size and scope, but sometimes consist of just a few rooms. Most commissions are in Manhattan and the surrounding area. It is said that Ridder's affable, organized, helpful manner really puts clients at ease, and that she is the primary client contact.

The design firm has a unusually strong computer capability, using CAD to map out every project to a budget beforehand. Charging standard design fees and retail on product, a typical living room costs around $100,000. Ridder is highly recommended for her updated classical style and intelligent view. HB Top Designers, 2000, 2001.

*"She worked very well under tight deadlines and she did it with a smile." "We immediately connected. She's so intelligent, compassionate and talented. What more can you ask?" "She had just the right approach to get me to try out new and interesting things. Never pushy, no ego." "Her colors were so unusual and so perfect." "Katie's organizational skills are phenomenal." "Furniture placement is definitely a strength." "She turned our unused den into a thing of beauty that the kids now love to use." "She breathed new life into our traditional Tudor home."*

## Kenneth Alpert 🛍        4    4    4    4
30 East 76th Street, New York, NY  10021
(212) 535 - 0922
*Traditional yet colorful, detailed interior design*

Kenneth Alpert is said to approach each project as having its own custom style dictated specifically by the client's need and vision. While best known for his traditional-to-the-max style, bedecked with chintzes, toiles and elegant trims, Alpert is also fluent in Art Deco, minimalist and formal French. Distinguishing his work is the firm's high levels of service and client relations, bringing attention to detail to a new level. We're told Alpert takes each job very seriously, and is extremely upfront and honest with his clients.

Alpert holds a BS from Wharton and an MBA from NYU. While attending classes at the New York School of Interior Design, he founded the firm 27 years ago. Currently with 15 members on the team, about 40 projects are undertaken annually, 10 of which are of substantial size and scope. Most of Alpert's work takes place in Manhattan and Long Island, with additional client bases in New Jersey, Westchester and Fairfield counties, and Florida.

Alpert's formal presentations are appreciated by references, who comment on his excellent budget layouts and strong professionalism. Clients express equal confidence in the back office. The firm charges standard design fees and standard product markups, with a typical living room baselining at about $150,000. Clients say Alpert looks to very high quality but is practical.

*"He has a sense of what is good, fun and economically appropriately." "There is no dilly-dallying." "He's a real straight-shooter." "They were very receptive to using the furniture that I already owned." "He is in his office from seven in the morning to seven every evening." "The project managers did a really efficient job day-to-day." "I turn to Ken for so many design situations well beyond the decoration of my home— from what to wear to vacation choices to dinner party options." "They are always willing to listen." "It was definitely a collaboration." "Excels in every aspect."*

## Kevin McNamara Inc.        4    3.5    5    5
41 West 25th Street, New York, NY  10010
(212) 462 - 0055
*Traditional, detailed, luxurious interior design*

Practicing for more than three decades, Kevin McNamara is considered by all to be one of the most experienced classic designers of our time. He is known for an elegant timeless style that evokes the charm of bygone days. His rooms are always comfortable, infused with Louis XVI furniture, quality seating in joyful colors and luxurious detailing. Clients praise him for his skills in taking ordinary rooms and setting them apart with dignified crown moldings and luscious background colors. McNamara's fabric, furniture and lighting designs are available in the Christopher Norman showroom in the D&D, where McNamara is creative director and cofounder.

He began his career with extensive training, first at McMillen (by Albert Hadley) and subsequently with Parish-Hadley. He founded his namesake firm in 1975.

McNamara is noted as very respectful of his clients, who confirm that he listens well and has reasonable pricing. Only about four major projects a year are undertaken, assuring excellent response time. He is well known in the antique dealers' world, and these professionals confirm that he is very knowledgeable and fair on pricing. Peers and clients highly recommend McNamara, saying that he can do it all. ID Hall of Fame. KB 1992, 1995, 1998.

*"I am addicted to his designs—they are opulent and sophisticated, but so livable." "He has the highest standards in his design work and his practice." "He just gets that understated, genteel thing, but backs it up with eons of experience." "If a piece is of good quality, Kevin would rather use it than replace it." "A professional businessman. While certainly not cutting edge, he delivers timeless designs that feel as it they has existed forever." "As a designer myself, I think that Kevin is one of the unsung heroes in the industry."*

### Kitty Hawks Inc.            4    4    4    5
136 East 57th Street, Suite 702, New York, NY 10022
(212) 832 - 3810

*Classic, tasteful, eclectic interior design*

Kitty Hawks is extremely well regarded by clients, peers and other industry professionals. She designs rooms using classic fundamentals that gracefully meld with eclectic accents. Clients speak glowingly of her work as beautiful, inviting and calm. Her designs very much speak to the function of a room and the lifestyle of its inhabitants.

Most of Hawks' work is done on a substantial scale with healthy budgets, but markups are quite reasonable. Many clients are entertainment moguls looking for a comfortable classic elegance. Most living rooms are in the $150,000 to $250,000 range. She is known to work hard and is noted to be very approachable, gracious and warm. Clients appreciate her businesslike manner and her wealth of experience. Sources extend way beyond the D&D. Her friends are often clients, and her clients often become friends. HB Top Designers, 1999, 2000, 2001. KB 1998.

*"Very professional with loads of experience." "For a woman of her stature, I was surprised that she had no attitude." "More upright than Sister Parish, and more relaxed than Albert." "She is respectful of the client and every subcontractor." "She works consistently with the same teams, which makes everything go smoothly." ""She has that rare ability to add glamour, and yet maintains warmth and old-world dignity." "More design oriented and architectural." "Nothing is formulaic, it all meets the clients realm of comfort and focus." "We were in it together." "While more expensive than I would have liked, the quality was well worth it." "It was an extremely happy journey that began with just a few minor adjustments and ended up a complete renovation." "I would not dream of using anyone else."*

### Larry Laslo Designs           3.5    3.5    4    4
135 Central Park West, Suite 2NC, New York, NY 10023
(212) 873 - 6797

*Contemporary, lively residential interior design*

Loyal clients return to Larry Laslo for his clean lines, vibrant colors and dedicated nature. He is said to be excellent at restraining clients when "necessary" and also encouraging them to stretch beyond their general inclinations. Even plain white is developed into more painted shades than the imagination can contemplate. Clients say Laslo incorporates a wealth of historical information into his work, from ancient classical Egyptian to Italian 1940s. They say nothing is off-limits.

Laslo began his design journey as a oil painter and fashion illustrator. After working with Bergdorf Goodman for several years in store design, he worked with Mikasa and Takashimaya developing their United States look. His interior design firm was founded in 1985 and remains small, with Laslo doing all the shopping. Clients tend to be the young and less conservative in Manhattan and the regional area. Laslo also likes to be involved with the architectural details and spends a good deal of time with clients understanding their lifestyle before anything is purchased.

The firm charges a typical design fee and reasonable product fees. Depending upon the client's interests, living rooms can range from $50,000 to $300,000-plus. He is said to much prefer just a few pieces of higher quality than a full room. Clients are shown all invoices and often pay directly. His own furniture products may be purchased through John Whitticomb, Directional and Interior Craft, with a new pottery line in the fall via Haeger. HB Top Designers, 1999, 2000, 2001. KB 2001.

*"While gold was not something I would have thought of, Larry advised me to go for the ultimate gold dining room—walls, chairs and skirted table all in gold. We absolutely adore it." "He places furniture in a room like jewels in a necklace." "He is a visionary. He found treasures in dusty antique shops in London that looked like nothing to me." "Larry is really a team player." "He took our historic mansion and added modern life and great cheer." "He offers a broad range of economic alternatives, pointing you to Bloomingdales if that makes sense." "You don't have to worry about the architect, because Larry will provide all the inspiration." "He is always there when you need him and is so much fun."*

## LBDA/Laura Bohn 🛍   4   4   4   4.5

30 West 26th Street, 11th Floor, New York, NY 10010
(212) 645 - 3636

*High-end, contemporary interior design*

Clients applaud Laura Bohn's unpretentious, intriguingly calm style and helpful attitude. They also appreciate her extensive design background which includes a degree from Pratt, training with John Saladino (leading to the senior designer position) and over 20 years of practice in her own firm. References report that she is most comfortable doing a few complete renovations of substantial size per year, working with a full budget. However, we understand that she is mindful of the customer's expenses, and is willing to combine expensive antiques with the latest from IKEA.

According to clients, Bohn's taste tends toward clean contemporary lines mixed with antiques and brushed in layered, muted neutral hues. References say that she is very flexible and practical, with "form following function" and comfort ruling all. There is said to be a strong back office that can answer most any day-to-day questions. Bohn often works with the contracting firm of Bohn-Fiore, owned by her husband, a pairing that members say works like a charm.

Bohn charges a design fee of approximately 10 percent of the budget and then charges a reasonable markup over net on products. Living rooms tend to run in the $125,000 to $175,000 range. Clients report that they would happily work with Bohn and her team again. HB Top Designers, 1999, 2000, 2001. ID Hall of Fame. KB 1992.

*"She is a seasoned professional—what she sketches is exactly what you get, and it is always perfect." "She is very good at making the space comfortable and functional for family use." "She has an extensive library of resources at the office that makes most decision making a breeze." "She uses the unexpected, but in a relaxed way." "Laura is not afraid to use a bargain and knows how to make it work." "I paid most vendors directly, so I knew exactly were we stood financially." "She is strong enough to voice her opinion but good about listening to the client." "I was hysterical when she used six different shades of green in a single space, but she was absolutely right—it looks rich, yet homogeneous and peaceful." "Unbelievable sense of color, every room is gorgeous and exciting. She delivers the highest quality."*

## Leta Austin Foster

|  |  |  |  |
|:---:|:---:|:---:|:---:|
| 3.5 | 3.5 | 4 | 4.5 |

424 East 52nd Street, New York, NY 10022
(212) 421 - 5918

*High-end, traditional interior design*

Sally Giordano heads up the New York location of this Palm Beach firm, began by her mother, 25 years ago. While 90 percent of the work is traditional, clients are very pleased by the creativity, quality and broad range of styles Giordano can expertly execute, including 1930s Art Deco and pure modern. Supporters also mention that the firm is very well-organized, fun to work with and willing to take stylistic cues from the client.

The firm has recently completed a spate of projects, including first apartments for young New Yorkers, regional homes and several vacation homes across the country. The firm's work can be found in L.A., Greenwich, Shelter Island, Texas and elsewhere throughout the United States. The company works with no design fee, but charges retail on products and standard oversight fees. Clients mention that Giordano will offer a variety of quality product choices, allowing the client broad economic and stylistic latitude. It has been mentioned, however, that she can be quite adamant that her clients make sound design choices, and that she would rather go back to the proverbial drawing board than settle for anything less.

*"They have traditional design down pat, with sparkle." "They are not form-over-function decorators, like the last group I dealt with." "Sally is phenomenal. She will bring 20 to 30 fabric samples and will have an elaborate discussion about them. But if we do not agree, 30 more will be here the following week." "Helped to guide me in the right direction despite my initial reluctance. Now, I'm so glad she was persistent." "Together we created an Italian Modern apartment that was 10 times better than I ever had imagined." "They are incredibly well organized."*

## Letelier & Rock Design Inc.

1020 Madison Avenue, New York, NY 10021
(212) 288 - 2287

*High-end residential interior design*

Sheryl Asklund Rock and Jorge Letelier are known for their versatile approach to interior design and the melding of an array of styles into their work. We are told the firm is just as adept at creating historically accurate design as it is in the contemporary vocabulary. Letelier, a Chilean-born architect creates the layouts and clients tell us his drawings portray a certain exotic feel. The duo designs and builds much of the furniture for clients who say this is a much appreciated service.

Rock and Letelier take on about twelve projects each year, half of which are large in scope and scale. Approximately half of the firm's projects take place on the Upper East Side of Manhattan, but the firm also works in the Hamptons, Connecticut, Florida and Montreal. The firm charges a lower flat fee and standard markup on products.

## Libby Cameron

|  |  |  |  |
|:---:|:---:|:---:|:---:|
| 4 | 4 | 4 | 4 |

24 Ervilla Drive, Larchmont, NY 10538
(914) 833 - 1414

*Lively, friendly, eclectic American interior design*

Supporters appreciate Libby Cameron for her eclectic, colorful, comfortable designs that lean toward casual traditional. While Cameron is better known for easy, natural fabrics geared toward family living, clients recount her excellent abilities with more formal English traditions. Much of the work is done in Manhattan and the surrounding areas, and she also has a loyal group of clients up and down the East Coast, many of whom consider her to be a "secret source." As a single practitioner, patrons say she has certain timing limitations, but works hard to please clients, some of whom date to Cameron's years as a senior partner at Parish-Hadley, where she worked closely with Sister Parish. She struck out on her own about seven years ago.

The firm charges a relatively small design fee and charges retail for products. Cameron favors complete renovations over more fragmented work. While project cost and budgets are considered, this is not the focus of the work (but clients say they are informed and feel comfortable with charges). Sources range from the top-quality Alessandro mantels to Pottery Barn, to whimsical secret sources in the South. Living rooms can be as low as $30,000, going to about $100,000, not including any major antiques. Supporters have often completed numerous projects with Cameron and look forward to doing more. HB Top Designers, 1999, 2000, 2001.

*"She understood that we wanted a comfortable home, not a showpiece." "She is very dependable and efficient, and her staff is always there when she is not." "While she will not sit around and watch the painter, she goes out of her way to give me peace of mind." "She is very easy to deal with. No pretentious ego." "Her schemes tend to lack a detailed master plan or meticulous measurements, but turn out beautifully." "She is the only decorator in New York that understands that pedigreed threadbare or chintz-on-chintz look." "Waspy with flair." "People come into the house and exclaim in delight. I still pinch myself when I wake up—I can't believe how gorgeous it all is."*

## Lichten Craig Architects LLP 🛍
6 West 18th Street, New York, NY 10011
(212) 229 - 0200
*High-end residential architecture and interior design*

See Lichten Craig Architects LLP's full report under the heading Architects

## Lisa Jackson 🛍                4    3.5    5    5
235 East 60th Street, New York, NY 10022
(212) 715 - 0726
*Coherent, polished interior design*

Patrons are consistently impressed Lisa Jackson's ability to seamlessly meld the patina of traditional with the delight of the modern. Architectural detail and calming color tones are also said to be her strengths, forming the underpinnings of a coherent and sophisticated result. With a proclivity for handsome and daring furniture, rooms are admired for their understated, yet distinct personalities. With measured professionalism, Jackson's supporters say that she listens well and always makes the most of her clients' spaces.

Jackson and her partner Catherine Aaron also run Blanc, an antique furniture and furnishings store at the address above. Many high profile designers frequent the store, allowing an easy exchange of design concepts that often surface in Jackson's private client work.

Clients report that the firm charges standard design fees, reasonable product fees and retail on antiques. The bills include vendor paperwork. We understand Jackson is good about working with the client's existing furnishings, finding alternatives and staying on budget. While the firm is quite small, it is said that the partners endeavor to not take on more than they can handle. Supporters highly recommend them for their creativity, grace and commitment to quality. HB Top Designers, 1999, 2000.

*"Lisa completely understands the look and world in which we live, and what we are trying to accomplish." "She keeps the strategic design on target, while being practical about the costs and the children's rooms." "I completely trust her design judgment." "Over the summer, there can be timing lags, but nothing major." "Even though I hate the process of decorating, Lisa made it fun." "She was able to create something grand from a boring classic seven, using her creativity and thoughtfulness. My friends are truly amazed." "We have worked with some of the major brand name decorators, and the experience with Lisa was such a pleasure in comparison."*

## London Bridge Interiors

3.5    2.5    4.5    4.5

1111 Park Avenue, New York, NY  10128
(212) 426 - 6167

*Timeless, English, traditional interior design*

Clients praise London Bridge Interiors for high-quality work that "perfectly fits the Park Avenue lifestyle." Heather Harper and Jenny Emlinger, sisters with an eye for timeless designs and excellent details, run the firm. Supporters say they work effectively and efficiently to achieve the client's vision, be it traditional English with a twist or stark white modern, all in good taste.

Many clients are Park Avenue families turning to their first "real" decorator. Clients report that one of the firm's great strengths is an understanding of family traffic patterns and interests. The team will undertake a wide variety of projects, from home "facelifts" to gut renovations. While scheduling is usually not an issue, these partners are moms who do have ceratin limitations, according to clients.

London Bridge charges a low design fee and a very reasonable markup on product. Oversight fees or consultations are being billed at reasonable rates. Living rooms fall in the $75,000 to $125,000 range. The firm taps only the best suppliers and has fostered great industry relationships. This team can also work on a phased approach or a consulting basis. Clients say they feel no pressure to purchase items they do not love. Harper and Emlinger are reportedly very professional and many repeat customers highly recommend them.

*"They are so special and incredibly pleasant. You want to sit down and have tea with Heather and Jenny." "I was a little worried that their family obligations might hinder the progress of my renovation, but their efficiency compensated for any scheduling conflicts." "I was so grateful that they found an excellent contractor for us, and stayed on top of him." "They solved any misunderstandings, and absorbed the cost." "They work together as a team, so that one of them is always accessible." "A great strength is that they have great empathy for my life with kids." "They are very practical, suggesting the highest for certain pieces and keeping the rest of it under control." "They opened my eyes to the possibilities for my apartment and made it happen."*

## Lulu DK

136 East 64th Street, Suite 2E, New York, NY  10021
(212) 223 - 4234   www.luludk.com

*Decorative painting, hand-painted fabric and interior design*

See Lulu DK's full report under the heading Painters & Wallpapers

## Lynn Morgan

19 Hill Top Road, Wilson Pt., S. Norwalk, CT  06854
(203) 854 - 5037

*High-end residential interior design. HB Top Designers, 2000, 2001.*

## M (Group)                    4.5    4.5    4.5    5
152 West 88th Street, New York, NY 10024
(212) 874 - 0773   www.mgrouponline.com
*Chic, urban, classic interior design and architecture*

Clients have expressed only the warmest feelings toward Carey Maloney and Hermes Mallea, partners of the M (Group). This collaborative team is wellknown for strong architectural details, complex layering of classical effects, good manners and wit. With Maloney (an MBA) focusing on design and business and Mallea (AIA) focusing on architecture, clients report a seamless exchange of ideas and no production hassles.

Mallea was raised in Miami and Maloney in Beaumont, Texas. The subtleties of classic Southern taste and charm are evident in both their work and their relationships with clients. They win accolades for interpreting patrons' visions into beautiful, tangible products, be it bohemian or high neoclassical. Clients report that the team uses their strong regional connections to find excellent quality at excellent prices well outside normal paths. Going well beyond the call of duty, references report that the team makes sure clients "never commit any social or design faux pas."

The firm is in high demand and only works on a few projects each year. Clients include Barbara Warner (of Warner Bros.), illustrious entertainment players and notable businessmen. About two-thirds of the projects are in Manhattan and the rest worldwide. Supporters say that the partners spend quite a lot of time upfront on design plans, and that there are no surprises concerning budgets or timing. While noted as extremely expensive, clients believe the result to be well worth the cost. AD 100, 2000. HB Top Designers, 1999, 2000, 2001. KB 1993.

*"Carey and Hermes can redefine spaces. I bought an ugly new house in the suburbs with absolutely no character. They made it look wonderful with gorgeous colors and subtle detailing." "They are with you from the very beginning to the bitter end." "While they might use eight coats of paint for an effect on my living room wall, it does not look ostentatious. You can feel the quality, but you cannot identify it." "When I asked them to slow down due to the uncertain economic environment, they could not have been more gracious." "They run their practice like a business." "They know when to push and when not to, in their quest for serious excellence." "Not a cheap date." "They believe that good architecture and good bones are essential, which transformed my apartment." "It is like working with dear friends."*

## MAC II                       4.5    5    4.5    4
125 East 81st Street, New York, NY 10028
(212) 249 - 4466
*Memorable, comfortable, high-styled interior design*

Mica Ertegun has been recognized over the last several years for her panache and spare design sensibility. With the late Chessy Rayner, Ertegun founded MAC II on a whim in 1967. The firm's design approach combines simple fabrics and sparse yet substantially sized furniture, carefully edited with a flash of glamour. MAC II insists on several high-quality antiques for each room, though not everything has to be of the utmost provenance. This translates to serene, uncluttered yet opulent environments. The firm has followed this model of mixing modern and traditional elements for over 30 years, and it continues to serve them well.

Clients are predominantly the very well established, including many top echelon businesspeople and commercial enterprises including Bill Blass, Warner Communications, Kenneth Jay Lane and the Carlyle Hotel. Many of the firm's clients have multiple homes, all decorated by MAC II. About fifteen projects are ongoing at a time. More recently, certain clients have mentioned less attention to detail and follow up. The large staff is reportedly quite professional with strong project managers. Pricing levels are said to match the firm's commitment to the highest quality products. AD 100, 2000. HB Top Designers, 1999, 2000, 2001. ID Hall of Fame.

*"As an architect, I have admired the structural beauty of her work for years."* *"Clients tend to be the well-heeled and well-traveled."* *"She delights in finding the most unusual furniture specimens, from unexpected sales markets in Europe to the world's finest antiques dealers."* *"When the work is unsatisfactory, not enough is done to rectify the situation."* *"Consistent with her reserved demeanor, Micca designs are reserved in a comfortable sort of way, with clean lines and an opulent sparsity."*

## Marc Charbonnet Associates

| 4 | 3.5 | 4.5 | 4.5 |
|---|---|---|---|

222 East 46th Street, New York, NY 10017
(212) 687 - 1333 www.mecaproductions.com

*Updated, classical comfortable interior design*

Marc Charbonnet has cultivated a group of dedicated clients by offering a highly individualized look. Much of his design inspiration is rooted in early 19th-century Continental interiors, updated with modern comfort. Supporters consider him to be a highly knowledgeable social and design historian, and they enjoy the education he provides along the way. Charbonnet often commissions the design of high-quality custom furniture, rugs and imaginative decorative painting for his clients. We hear he is very attentive and allows the client to be as active as they wish in the design process.

Charbonnet was raised in New Orleans, worked for Peter Marino and started his own firm in 1991. Current clients include Michael J. Fox and other prominent New Yorkers. Many former New Yorkers have subsequently brought Charbonnet with them to other parts of the United States. Marc leads all design decisions and is bolstered by a reportedly excellent back office.

The firm charges reasonable up-front and product fees, with additional hourlies for the design of newly created product. It is said the firm will work endlessly to find a client well-priced alternatives. Nonstructural architectural design details are also well incorporated, with clients noting that Charbonnet works quite well with architects. References applaud Charbonnet for his incorporation of their existing furnishings, and for the use of Crate & Barrel, when appropriate. Living rooms can range considerably, from $30,000 to $300,000. He is consistently known to be funny, fair and honest, delivering a very high-quality product at an excellent value. AD 100, 2000.

*"Though he did my apartment seven years ago, my friends say how beautiful it is every time they see it."* *"While he is extremely knowledgeable about antiques, he is not a snob. He will scour all parts of town to find the most cost-effective solution. He even identified an estate sale the week before it went to Sotheby's and we had a field day."* *"He offers comfort that can be enjoyed in diamonds and high heels or barefoot."* *"No one can beat Marc on value—he has incredible resources."* *"He is really flexible, and loves to design creative, integrated pieces."* *"I always have a good time with Marc, and will use him wherever I go."*

## Marcy V. Masterson Inc.

| 4.5 | 4.5 | 4 | 4.5 |
|---|---|---|---|

140 West 57th Street, Suite 12D, New York, NY 10019
(212) 541 - 6076

*Tailored, considered interior design*

Noted as a perfectionist and a connoisseur of fine furnishings, Marcy Masterson is held in great regard by clients. Though interiors may be Russian neoclassical, slick moderne or Nantucket American, all are said to be carefully studied, intellectually focused, yet user friendly. As an expert on 18th- and 19th-century English and continental furniture, Masterson is said to passionately research and pursue the penultimate. Clients have a lot of confidence in Masterson, usually taking her design lead.

After a year with McMillen and ten years with Jed Johnson, Masterson established an independent firm in 1995. A full-service organization of six, Masterson dispatches project managers but is reportedly very much on top of every shopping, installation and architecture detail. About seven very large renovations are taken on at a time, with most in the New York area. Many clients have very large collections of antique furniture or important art, but not all clients are collectors. She is said to listen very carefully to requests, but can be persistent in her quest for design integrity.

A reimbursable, standard+ design fee is charged upfront with retail on product. Living rooms are typically well over $100,000. While there are no surprises and careful consideration is given on all fronts, projects tend to evolve as new possibilities are recognized. Patrons appreciate the masterful framework and the great effort to purchase components of value.

*"Dealers are her biggest fans as she expertly appreciates every piece." "Marcy will work herself into the ground to get it just right." "After dinner, she insisted upon seeing my apartment one more time, rearranging everything in her high heels." "Marcy is a real professional—extraordinarily competent, but not pushy." "Only Marcy could find a 1580s Milinese table and an 1820s Russian Tula piece that worked together in perfect sympathy." "I wouldn't second guess Marcy, she will get frustrated, and you will be wrong." "She is seriously brilliant at composite connections. A refined motif or subtle hue will become the basis of a interwoven design masterpiece." "If anything, I think she under bills given the vast amount of time she dedicates to each project." "My interiors positively glow with quality and warmth."*

### Mario Buatta Inc.    5    5    4.5    4.5
120 East 80th Street, New York, NY 10021
(212) 988 - 6811

*Elegant, classical residential interior design*

For classical, traditionally based interior design, Mario Buatta continues to be the gold standard. Amazing clients with his joie de vivre and "design genius," he adds luster and the most refined glamour to every setting. Buatta is noted as the consummate colorist, mixing colors that no one else would have imagined, to create the ultimate look that lasts more than a lifetime. Buatta can make a fabulous room from pieces clients would have otherwise discarded, and add "a small accessory or trim to tie it all together." Clients further report that he can, with just one look, regularly solve the issues that confound architects and contractors.

While Buatta does not have a consistent office staff or any design associates, clients appreciate that this "one-man maelstrom" is involved in all the design decisions himself. Getting Buatta to focus, however, can be an issue according to his patrons. To that end, Buatta generally limits the number of his new clients to just a few of very substantial means. Former clients include Barbara Walters, the Forbes family, Mariah Carey and the White House guesthouse. Interestingly, he can also play a much more limited role, especially with family of past clients, acting as a consultant.

Buatta works with a significant retainer that is fully reimbursable against product purchases. Products are acquired at retail and there is a 25 percent oversight fee. His out-of-town daily rate is $3,500. Bills are reportedly always late, but quite clear. He is recommended by clients for the ultimate look at "whatever cost." AD 100, 2000. HB Top Designers, 1999, 2000. ID Hall of Fame. KB 1990, 1997, 2000.

*"Mario is the most gifted decorator of our generation." "Once you get him going, there's no one better. He was molded from the great masters." "While Mario's fees are relatively reasonable, project costs can get out of control." "While the project took much longer than expected, Mario is incredible under deadlines. Once I sent out invitations for a large party, he magically finished." "He is clearly a genius, but will drive you to drink." "He hangs Peale portraits and field hockey sticks with equal skill and enthusiasm." "Mario believes that a house grows like a garden, and is never completely finished." "Mario is a true friend, taking client relationships well beyond the business level." "He is not for the faint of heart, but well worth it."*

| | Quality | Cost | Value | Recommend? |
|---|---|---|---|---|
| | ✚ | $ | ◆ | ★ |

## Mark Gaudette

| | 4 | 3.5 | 5 | 4.5 |
|---|---|---|---|---|

320 East 23rd Street, New York, NY
(212) 260 - 4210

*Timeless, classic high-end interior design*

In addition to being highly sought for his elegant, classic design, Mark Gaudette is in demand for his helpful nature and confident execution abilities. Gaudette spent fourteen years with David Easton (including time as lead designer) and now incorporates much of Easton's timeless warmth in his own practice. Clients say he has a great heart, exquisite taste and a sure hand, often transforming existing furnishings in a masterful way.

Recent projects include various city apartments, smaller homes in the regional area and mansions in Greenwich, Florida and Greece. He is said to be extremely accommodating and patient, willing to shop at the D&D with clients, but is not frivolous with their time. Supporters praise his willingness to work within a budget and decorate their home in phases. They report that the quality of the firm's products can be as high as you want to take it, but don't have to be astronomically priced.

Gaudette takes on only a few projects at one time, and current clients would like to keep him as a "secret source." Timing can be an issue—current clients and potential customers have found him quite hard to reach. Fees are said to be reasonable and flexible, depending upon the scope of the job.

*"He is as thrifty or high-brow as you want him to be." "David [Easton] could trust him with entire projects of the top clients." "Mark is making the proverbial silk purse from the sow's ear of my apartment." "While we used him for our country house, I wasn't sure he could do our very formal city apartment." "He is always saying, 'you have to like it, not me.'" "After two housewife decorators, I thought he was worth every penny. Although still quite expensive, everything was just perfect." "I wish he could take over my life. I would never consider using anyone else."*

## Mark Hampton Inc. 🛍

| | 4.5 | 4.5 | 4.5 | 5 |
|---|---|---|---|---|

654 Madison Avenue, 21st Floor, New York, NY  10021
(212) 753 - 4110

*Classical, detailed, high-end interior design*

Clients are consistently impressed with Alexa Hampton's innate design sensitivity, commitment to quality and range. But beyond the design notebook, Hampton is also credited for her attention to detail, flexibility, professional demeanor and charming personality. Hampton assumed the reins of Mark Hampton Inc. after the death of her father in 1998. Hampton has ably gained the confidence of past clients and built a base of her own, reflecting her spirited approach and broad design knowledge.

Hampton graduated from Brown and studied at the Institute of Fine Arts at NYU. At the age of thirteen she began working in her father's office, honing what clients say are her remarkable design instincts. Hampton's versatile capabilities are reflected in her recent projects. These include a new Louis XIV-style home in Atlanta, a Balinese-style Florida retreat, a formal Anglo-French home, a traditional boat with modern backgrounds and several New York apartments, ranging from modern eclectic to streamlined traditional. Clients say that the common thread is a desire to steer the project to the highest standards, given the budget.

The firm works with a fairly high design fee (but this includes oversight services and auction consultations) and standard markups on products. Hampton is known to mix it up to meet budgets—De Angelis for the living room and Classic Sofa for the playroom (with some unique tweaks). While most projects are large, the firm is happy to work on smaller assignments. HB Top Designers, 1999, 2000, 2001. ID Hall of Fame. KB 1997, 1999.

*"I have been in the real estate development business for over 30 years, and I have not seen anyone with the project management, skills Alexa has brought to the table." "Walking through the D&D with Alexa is like being with royalty, everyone rushes to her side." "Over the last year, Alexa has built an excellent team." "Alexa has a unique eye. We will go through 200 samples at the D&D and she will know exactly which blue will work. It is amazing." "I am not of the rich and famous, and got great attention from Alexa and the firm." "While not cheap, Alexa is quite fair. Getting it right is a matter of pride and family tradition."*

### Mark Zeff Consulting Group
601 West 26th Street, 17th Floor, New York, NY 10001
(212) 580 - 7090

*Eclectic, hip-to-traditional interior design*

| | 3.5 | 3.5 | 4 | 4 |
|---|---|---|---|---|

Zeff has intrigued and attracted New York-area clients since 1984 with his worldly style of interior design that exudes a "subtle fortitude" clearly influenced by his frequent travels around the world. A native of South Africa, scholar from the U.K. and long-time New Yorker, Zeff is a skilled furniture maker, decorator and architect. We are told he has an uncanny ability to blend airy colors with exotic textures in an eclectic amalgamation of various periods and styles. Often seen existing together are handsome woods, custom ironwork, English antiques and 1930s French modern. With his pared-down, exotic style, Zeff tends to work with a younger clientele looking for a unique and romantic aesthetic.

Insiders tell us Zeff runs a full-service design agency with a wide spectrum of services that range from residential, retail and commercial architecture design to furniture and accessory design. Zeff also has his own line of spa and scent lines—available at his Southampton boutique, ZeffStyle. Clients say the firm is quite professional, and that the design process is enjoyable. HB Top Designers, 1999, 2000.

*"What he created was a unique and inviting space that is comfortable to live in and a joy to look at." "Mark can do anything—and he's been successful at every endeavor he's taken on." "While Mark is a bit stretched between the retail ventures and the interior design, the project was very professionally managed." "He takes a holistic view of design, thinking about the mind and the spirit as well as the look."*

### Markham Roberts Inc.
P.O. Box 839 Murray Hill Station, New York, NY 10156
(212) 532 - 8822

*High-end residential interior design*

### Marshall Watson Interiors 🛍
105 West 72nd Street, New York, NY 10023
(212) 595 - 5995

*Classical interior design with a twist*

| | 4 | 3.5 | 5 | 5 |
|---|---|---|---|---|

Marshall Watson has a strong group of clients who are fans of him and his work. His interiors are favored for their classically elegant bones, elements based on historical reference and a hint of surprise. He often employs soft flowing fabrics, stately, yet comfortable seating areas and a welcoming palette of warm colors. Customers say he is a very engaging man who tries to please them by matching his designs to their lifestyles and interests. Younger clients on a budget, as well as more established patrons with very substantial projects, give the firm high marks.

Watson originally studied design at Stanford University and currently has his own line of furniture produced by Lewis Mittman. Resources applaud him for his dedicated philanthropy work, particularly in the area of the design arts.

The firm is based in New York, and many of Watson's clients are in Manhattan and Chicago, with others in the Hamptons, Nantucket, St. Louis, London and Spain. While certain clients suggest that Watson's followup could be a bit better, most find him highly effective. They consistently report that Watson is fair, honorable and helpful until the end. His up-front design fee and product and oversight fees are very reasonable, and he finds unusual and interesting pieces to fit a budget. Projects range greatly from $100,000 to $2 million. The firm is highly recommended for the beauty and comfort of each design.

*"He has the warmth of a Midwesterner and the sophisticated design sensibility of a New Yorker." "He quickly understood what we wanted and became part of our family." "He designs for the real world, not for* Architectural Digest *photo shoots. There is good reading light near every sofa." "Many a Goldman partner have commented that we have the most stunning dining room they have ever seen." "We love every single room." "He has excellent ideas, but does not take himself too seriously." "As we gutted our big, old house, he carefully instructed the contractors to place every A/C duct and every light switch correctly." "He delivers great quality without killing you on the budget." "I am very fussy and we take great pride in his work." "He listened well and delivered. A+"*

### Martin Raffone

10 East 16th Street, New York, NY 10003
(212) 532 - 8822

*High-end residential interior design, HB Top Designers, 2000, 2001.*

### Mary Meehan Interiors

| | | | |
| --- | --- | --- | --- |
| 3.5 | 3.5 | 4 | 4 |

157 East 72nd Street, New York, NY 10021
(212) 772 - 6644

*Opulent, layered, continental, eclectic interior design*

An innate ability to fuse classic functionality with modern undertones is what sources say is Mary Meehan's greatest draw. Clients appreciate Meehan's ability to recreate the feel of classic, aged elegance without making interiors appear renovated. Meehan takes advantage of open architecture by incorporating grand windows, mirrors and exaggerated openings to create an airy, yet livable space. With textured and layered luxurious design details, Meehan tastefully incorporates clients' ideas. Furthermore, they know she is willing and able to guide the implementation process effectively.

Customers have included notable writers Jay McInerney and William Goldman, as well as several upscale Park Avenue and suburban families. Patrons typically say Meehan is honest, fair and gracious, though some suggest she could use a slightly larger staff to better leverage her time. Meehan charges retail for products and a reasonable workroom markup. For hourly and oversight work, a standard+ rate is charged. AD 100, 2000.

*"Extends herself to make sure she's available to the client any day, any time." "Displayed an enthusiasm for the project that matched my own—and it's my house." "It doesn't matter if something needs to be done over and over, she'll do it until it's done to my fickle taste." "Some more support staff would be a big help." "I wanted the house to look old, not redone. She delivered beautifully and with great integrity."*

### Matthew Patrick Smyth ▮

| | | | |
| --- | --- | --- | --- |
| 4 | 3.5 | 5 | 5 |

12 West 57th Street, Suite 704, New York, NY 10019
(212) 333 - 5353

*Classic, sophisticated, delightful interior design*

Clients speak of Mathew Smyth with affection. He is known for his classic design judgment, original thinking and organization skills, with great affection. He is most appreciated for the joy he radiates when incorporating clients' specific interests and personalities into a project. His architectural aptitude is also said to be strong—references do not usually employ an architect when working with Smyth, and his design plans are said to be very clear and helpful. The firm is small and clients appreciate that they receive Smyth's full attention. While he personally tends toward the modern, clients report that he is successful with any style including highly traditional. His own line of furniture can be found at Hinson.

After spending five years with David Easton, he started his own firm in 1989. Most of his work is in New York, though clients are based worldwide. He often decorates second or third residences, and many of his new customers are family referrals. He is willing to do small projects for interesting new clients but usually undertakes complete renovations. Smyth charges a standard design fee and a reasonable markup on product. Living rooms are in the $75,000 to $125,000 range. All bills include the net costs. He can work within a budget and offers a wide range of product possibilities. HB Top Designers, 2000, 2001. KB 1995, 1998, 2001.

*"I can not fully describe his respect and concern for his clients." "I completely admire and trust Matthew's design sensibility. He is involved in everything right down to the last trim selection." "His demeanor and his billing is so straightforward." "Dealers are always surprised that he speaks of the net price in front of the client." "His architectural talents are better than any architect I have ever known." "He is unique within the industry. He always makes it right." "His friendly countenance belies his determination." "I just love being with Matthew. He is tons of fun and has a wide range of interests." "He not only understands peoples design interests, but also their values." "He can deal with any circumstances. I had to move in a week, and Matthew made it happen."*

## Maureen Wilson Footer Interior Design 🛍  3.5  3.5  4  4.5
177 East 87th Street, Suite 506A, New York, NY 10128
(212) 427 - 0601

*Classic, bold, clean high-end interior design*

Combining her penchant for French 18th-century design and a offsetting modernism, Maureen Wilson Footer is gaining an increasingly admiring audience. Fine art and antique textiles are playing a more prevalent role in her designs, offering a layered warmth against spare, yet bold backgrounds. Footer is also applauded for her efficiency and her sincere desire to please the client.

Drawing upon her Northern California upbringing, a degree in French and English literature from Wellesley and an MBA from Columbia, Footer brings a lot to the table. After working in banking for several years, she trained with Pam Banker and then McMillen, and studied in Paris before starting her own firm in 1995. Supporters respect both her design skills and business judgment. Clients often are established collectors of fine art or younger homeowners involved with their first big decorating project. While most clients are relieved that she limits design choices and presents a polished view, others occasionally would have preferred a bit more presentation scope. All say Footer absolutely has the client's design interests at heart and will continue on until it is just right. She also wins accolades for her accessibility, communication skills and design continuity.

The firm charges a reasonable hourly rate plus a small markup on product. Clients say that she suggests ways to remain within a budget and is very committed to delivering an excellent product. Most living rooms run in the $80,000 to $100,000 range. ASID.

*"Maureen has real abilities to create quiet drama. It is amazing what she can do with a can of paint and a few pictures." "She pores over every detail with such care." "My teenage daughter just loved Maureen's work." "When the headboard I had chosen arrived, but wasn't what I had thought it would be, Maureen had it remade at her expense. She is so responsible." "She would always suggest ways to bring down costs when asked." "I had analysis paralysis and she got me right on track." "She does what she says she will do. I am incredibly pleased with the process and the result." "My husband keeps on thanking me for the job well-done by Maureen." "I feel that we were really lucky to have found Maureen before she rises into the stratosphere."*

## McMillen Inc.      4.5   4.5   4   4.5
155 East 56th Street, 5th Floor, New York, NY 10022
(212) 753 - 6377

*Extraordinary high-end interior design*

McMillen is regarded as one of the most established in the business, as generation after generation of discreet old-money clients celebrate the firm's timeless design. Founded in 1924 by Eleanor McMillen Brown, the firm's guiding light is now Betty Sherrill and Louis Rey, who lead a strong team of experienced senior designers. McMillen can deliver a surprising range of styles (way beyond just chintz) and undertakes most of the related architectural work. They focus on the highest quality product available, often cultivating unique sources. At a client's request, they will even provide the books on your shelves.

McMillen's list of highly satisfied customers is enormous. Many have a habit of owning several homes over time, all decorated by McMillen. The firm takes great pride in retrofitting clients' old curtains and upholstery to new venues. The company is open to new clients, especially ones that will grow with the firm. The very professional office staff is said to deliver the ultimate in customer service, exchanging items until the client is satisfied.

The firm charges a standard design fee (for an average sized project), standard oversight fees and retail on products. Patrons say that the net product pricing is unknown to them, but that perfection is worth any price. AD 100, 2000. HB Top Designers, 1999, 2000. KB 1993, 1997.

*"McMillen functions seamlessly. A senior designer was always on-site, and they faxed my office with any decisions I had to make." "So gorgeous yet so livable." "Managing to a budget is not really their thing past the major pieces." "We had to choose between a new car and the McMillen curtains. Thirteen years later, the curtains still look fresh, and the car would have been dead." "Not decorators, but true interior designers." "They are embarking upon a new phase of the McMillen story." "McMillen represents a system which works, but they are not the most innovative designers." "These are schooled professionals that are not worried about invitations to the South of France." "They are never condescending or haughty. These are practical people who get the job done without an attitude." "It would never occur to me or my family to think about using anyone else."*

## Meg Braff Interiors, Inc. 🏠      4   3.5   4.5   4.5
162 East 55th Street, Suite 6C, New York, NY 10022
(212) 355 - 2482

*Warm, tailored, traditional interior design*

Clients gratefully turn to Meg Braff for her engaging and "uplifting" design style and business manner. While she takes her cue from the client, Braff usually favors an updated traditional style with "happy yet sophisticated colors" and creative details. Alongside partner Robert Lindgren, she will do two rooms or a complete redecoration. References appreciate the firm's unusual secret sources, many from the South where Braff was raised. Braff is a favorite of many young uptown families, more established suburban clients (Locust Valley, Greenwich, Bronxville) and the hip downtown crowd.

The partners are noted to be sensitive to cost constraints and can work with a budget. They are further commended for their professionalism and "quick and appropriate action" if any issues arise, despite a relatively small office. While Braff is sometimes over-committed, her clients say that she always comes through. Fees are based on a standard design charge and retail on products the company sources. Living rooms often are in the $75,000 range. The firm is referred from friend-to-friend with the strongest commendations.

*"I can always count on Meg, especially for that just-so 'Town & Country' look." "They have many less expensive, creative options." "We were so impressed that they took our very fine Oriental rug (to which we were attached), and had it magically transformed to fit our new apartment. We are so appreciative of their resourcefulness, willingness and the quality of the work." "I actually think they are too cost-conscience. Sometimes you just have to go for it." "They are really team players, working with the architect and the contractors without a hitch." "Meg is so professional and gracious, she can even work with friends." "The rooms turned out exactly like the pictures they drew." "Meg is amazing with fabrics and Robert with hard goods. They make a very well-matched pair." "In the dealing with any issues, they make it right, design-wise and financially." "It is like working with a good friend."*

## Michael Christiano       4    4.5    4    4.5

215 East 58th Street, New York, NY 10022
(212) 371 - 9800

*Luxurious, imaginative interior design*

Michael Christiano is well regarded for his array of sumptuous baroque, Georgian, neoclassical and deco designs. Well-heeled clients adore Christiano for his attention to detail and his inability accept anything less than the best quality. He is noted for a penchant for large-scale design statements, which are based upon toned, thoughtful, contemporary backgrounds. Luscious satins, saturated colors and handsome lines often play a role.

Christiano majored in architecture at Berkeley, worked in the interiors department at Skidmore, Owings & Merrill and then partnered with the late Robert Metzger. While about twenty projects are ongoing with a third in major stages, clients say Christiano is very accessible, and reliable. The firm produces computer-aided drawings architects and contractors applaud.

The firm takes a design advance, charges retail on product (including antiques) and a standard hourly fee. Living rooms are often in the $250,000 to $300,000 arena, with lots of clients interested in fine antique rugs. Christiano is highly recommended by references for potential clients seeking an exquisite interior with no budget constraints. AD 100, 2000.

*"Michael can fulfill your individual design fantasies." "He has a kind heart and a wicked sense of humor." "He can do drop-dead Deco and over-the-top Ocean Mediterranean with equal ease." "While known for color, our home was exquisitely done with a neutral palette, and touches of color." "We adore him as a friend and think he deserves more press." "As a contractor, I was impressed with his detailed drawings and the client's respect for Michael." "When we said that the console was just too costly, he found an alternative we liked a thousand times more." "We nervously bought several pieces based solely on photographs send by Michael from Paris. Each piece was sheer perfection." "He is a one-armed paper hanger, working so hard for his clients." "He is so gracious, and really there for you."*

| | Quality + | Cost $ | Value ◆ | Recommend? ★ |
|---|---|---|---|---|

## Michael Formica Inc.

| | 3.5 | 3 | 4.5 | 4 |
|---|---|---|---|---|

95 Christopher Street, New York, NY 10014
(212) 620 - 0655  www.michaelformica.com
*Contemporary, mid-century, modern interior design*

Michael Formica is known for his edited "cool and hip look" with quality furnishings and neutral backgrounds. Formica works in restrained colors, clean surfaces, serious mid-century furnishings and "moments of folly," creating a modern view. Clients say Formica is also skilled at drawing inspiration from the 40s and 50s to create a happy marriage of contemporary living and the simplistic functionality of yesteryear. Sources applaud Formica's intelligent juxtaposition of furnishings and colors to maximize ambient light that reflects on open spaces. He is also reportedly adapt at using clients' existing possessions—particularly artwork—into refreshing and inspired interiors.

Trained at RISD and now a resident of downtown New York, most clients are in the metropolitan area. Recent projects include a Park Avenue penthouse, a TriBeCa loft, a Cobble Hill town house, a North Shore residence and a Sands Point shingle cottage. His enthusiasm for his work is said to be appreciated by clients, dealers and vendors. HB Top Designers, 1999, 2000.

*"He is not a slave of period architecture. Regardless of the exterior, the interiors are edited and light as if fill by a breeze." "He really came up with an effective use of lesser, yet larger pieces of furniture to dramatize the space." "I never thought 'groovy' could be of such quality."*

## Michael La Rocca

| | 4.5 | 4.5 | 5 | 5 |
|---|---|---|---|---|

150 East 58th Street, Suite 3510, New York, NY 10155
(212) 755 - 5558
*Opulent, fresh, elegant interior design*

Michael La Rocca has one of the finest reputations in the business for his classic design sensibility, quality products and strong client service. He often weaves different time periods and provenance, creating rooms with personality, character and wit. Clients say his vast experience allows him to make the "absolute most" of their spaces, often transforming the fundamental disposition of the home. It is said that his interiors are very "balanced," creating highly livable environments with serenity and a highly personalized feel.

After thirteen years as David Easton's partner, La Rocca has been on his own for about twelve years. He focuses on just a few very well-heeled clients each year, mostly in the New York and Chicago areas. Patrons say that he listens well, is quite accessible even for out-of-town projects and delivers a complete package. Patrons also comment on the strong back office.

The firm charges a standard design fee, retail on products and workroom, and standard oversight fees. Projects start in the $300,000 range and head north from there. He is reportedly a stickler for schedule and a bit more flexible on budget. He is said to focus on very high quality and is considered well worth the cost by clients. KB 1991.

*"He is a gentleman and a scholar." "He can always find the perfect solution, even when there may have been a difference of opinion between my husband and myself." "He likes creating magic for his clients." "They develop constant checklists and punch lists, and really fight for their clients." "Michael has an unbelievable memory for design—almost like Dustin Hoffman's Rain Man." "He is a finisher." "I have worked with Michael for over five years, and we have never had a disagreement." "A master at scale and proportion." "He makes you feel as if you are the most important person in the world." "He has lasted way longer than my husband."*

### Michael Simon Interiors Inc.    5   4.5   4   5
180 West 58th Street, New York, NY 10019
(212) 307 - 7670
*Historically derived, 18th-century French interior design*

Michael Simon's passion for quality French design is apparent to all who view his work. Clients extol his encyclopedic knowledge of Louis XIV to XVI design, unique resources and ideas beyond anyone else's imagination. Peers cite his creativity, attention to detail and meticulous execution. He is also noted for intricate planning, highly developed backgrounds (wall paneling/floors/ceilings) and comprehensive project management skills. While his interiors certainly have a historical point of view, clients mention that they do not appear stuffy due to cleverly reformulated motifs. Patrons also report that he can also do English country rooms extremely well.

Trained as a musical composer, Simon then worked in the design group at Citibank for eleven years. Most of his clients are well established, have traveled widely and have been exposed to important homes and museums. While Simon is accommodating and realistic about his clients' interests, he has been known to be adamant about certain design decisions. There is a small but strong back office, with Simon on the front line.

The firm charges a substantial percentage-based, reimbursable design fee, reasonable percentages over net and standard oversight fees. City living rooms generally run in the $150,000 to $300,000 range, before serious antiques. Country home living rooms can be developed for far less. Clients say that Simon offers many alternatives, and his years in commercial design enable him to meet timing and budget schedules. However, the inherently detailed nature of these undertakings, most of which incorporate elaborate custom fabrics, can result in very expensive projects that take up to two years to complete. KB 1998, 2000.

*"Michael's detailed craftsmanship and quality is as good as David Easton's at half the price." "He was very understanding about the fact that we are at the mercy of our children and dogs and designed with them in mind." "He brought fabrics in all price ranges from $49 to $300, all of which were great choices." "His design plans are amazing—each page, room, object and light socket is keycoded to each other and to a price schedule." "While a knowledge bank, he is not a snob." "He has an army of world wide artisans on call." "There are no surprises and I did not need an architect." "He is the most honest, lovely person you can possibly imagine." "Vendors in the D&D will pull you aside to exclaim how much they admire Michael."*

### Miles Redd LLC    4   4   4.5   5
300 Elizabeth Street, New York, NY 10012
(212) 995 - 1922
*Elegant, updated interior design with panache*

With exuberant style and an enthusiastic manner, Miles Redd has developed a devoted client base. With an original sense of design wit, flair and color as applied things once traditional, Redd has reconfigured the concept of updated neoclassical. Clients say Redd's signature style is layered and full, with intricate detail and perfect placement, resulting in a balanced and open feel. While more modest projects are artfully arranged thrift-store stunners, others are more Fendi-meets-F. Scott Fitzgerald.

Redd, in a partnership with his sister, Sarah McCain, created the firm in 1999 after he spent five years with Bunny Williams. Redd is said to take on a wide scope of projects, from small downtown apartments to large uptown town houses and single-family homes in the surrounding area. Redd has done work in New York as well as Montana, and has worked with a diverse clientele that includes empty-nesters, young professionals and families. Redd and his small, yet strong office of four, is said to have excellent communication and organizational skills.

The firm charges a flat design fee and low markup on product. Sources tell us Redd has as much appreciation for flea market finds and forgotten closet items as he does for exquisite Louis XV antiques. A typical living room will run the gamut from $50,000 to $150,000. HB Top Designers, 2000, 2001.

*"Preppy version of new millennium glamour." "Miles is open-minded and finds something special in everything that you have." "He has exquisite taste, imagination and wit as well as a beautiful sense of color." "He can take others' throwaways and make them grand in the right setting with the right fabric." "He took the 18th-century-style curtains that I refused to get rid of and incorporated Indian gossamer fabric with sequins, adding spice to a tired concept." "He is such a gentleman—suave and sweet." "He's 100 percent responsible, great a returning phone calls and would always keep us in the loop."*

### Milly de Cabrol Ltd.     3.5    3    4    4
150 East 72nd Street, Suite 2C, New York, NY 10021
(212) 717 - 9317

*Stylish, comfortable, colorful interior design*

Milly de Cabrol is praised by her mostly young and chic clientele as being masterful in combining styles and ideas to fulfill their imaginative visions. While ably using a diverse palette of textiles and colors, her editing skills are said to be as strong as her versatility. Clients appreciate the fact that Milly is the sole contact and inspiration for projects.

Born into an aristocratic and artistic Italian family, she lived in London for ten years and traveled extensively in the Far East. She moved to the United States in 1984, and started her career in interior design. She most enjoys unusual design projects, according to her clients. Recent projects have included an Indo-Portuguese duplex on the Upper West Side, a chateau-like house in Westport, an Indian-Swedish apartment on Fifth Avenue, an Upper East Side townhouse and a pied-a-terre filled with modern art. She is known to possess a particularly good touch with collections.

The firm charges a standard design fee and low product markups. She is lauded by supporters for her hardworking attitude and helpful nature. HB Top Designers, 2000, 2001.

*"I am so impressed by Milly's skill at combining so many styles into a livable, tasteful composite that I call my home." "She is the complete opposite of stuffy, but at the same time classy—just what we was looking for." "She has a very strong ability to choose just the right amount of 'ethnic style' to give a room verve without it looking overdone." "I love Milly and would absolutely use her again, but she really could use a bit more support." "As a peer, I can vouch that Milly has a really good style and is a really good person." "Her clients are the young nobs and swells of New York."*

### Muriel Brandolini Inc. 🛍    3.5    3.5    4    4
167 East 80th Street, New York, NY 10021
(212) 249 - 4920

*Idiosyncratic, exuberant interior design*

Muriel Brandolini is hailed for an abundance of creative exuberance, colorful sweeps of fabric and dramatic details. Her high-energy interiors are inspired by her heterogeneous heritage—born in Saigon, raised in the Caribbean, educated in Paris, married to an Italian aristocrat, she brings a unique perspective. Brandolini is known for her bold new ideas, unusual combinations and strong point of view. Client's interiors reflect their families needs, and become warm cocoons of joyful, comfortable elegance.

While Brandolini's business is small, her clients are large, including Crown Prince and Princess Pavlos of Greece, Christopher and Pia Getty and several media moguls. She is known to show clients a plethora of opulent fabrics, much to their amazement and delight. While most happily remark that she often beats their deadlines, others suggest she is more about the overall look than the details.

Many of her clients are the young and very chic, and they appreciate Brandolini's designing talent and ardent love of color. They say she can bring fantasy and fun to otherwise boring Upper East Side apartments. Some, however, find her a bit overwhelming. Supporters recommend her for exhilarating projects incorporating the Brandolini style. HB Top Designers, 1999, 2000, 2001.

*"Muriel's range is mind boggling—she can go from the smallest loft to the grandest Park Avenue apartment, and have great fun with both." "Nothing intimidates Muriel, either stylistically or process-wise." "Muriel thinks decorating should be fun and does not take herself too seriously." "She can visualize many different uses for a room which is amazingly helpful for New York City living with kids." "Her antique sources in Paris are unbeatable." "She is a whirlwind of style, opulence and the unexpected."*

### Nannette Brown Ltd. 📱                          4       4       4       4.5
41 East 57th Street, Suite 1406, New York, NY 10022
(212) 756 - 0110

*Handsome, grand, minimalist interior design*

With a style that spans from modern to traditional Hamptons, Nanette Brown is lauded by clients for her meticulous detail and purist approach to interior design, which generally results in minimalistic with historic character. Clients say no matter what the style, Brown can be relied on to uphold the highest integrity and respect to the project and customer. Brown is said to be an excellent purveyor of fine antiques from across Europe and London in particular, where she lives and works half of each year. While in London, Brown often works with an expatriate clientele who seek her ability to meld elements of American living peppered with a European vernacular. Sources tell us Brown is superb at selecting materials and unique decorative objects for their artistic and aesthetic value. Clients praise Brown's handsome monochromatic palette and neutral tones.

Tenesse-born Brown is known as approachable, kind and an excellent listener, developing clients' ideas collaboratively. In addition, we hear Brown takes a highly intellectual approach to design, and carefully plans out every detail right down to the exact placement of every piece creating continuity. Clients say they are willing to wait for up to six months for Brown, and that once she commits to a project, it is done with great precision and care. Brown started the firm in the mid-90s and in 1999 partnered with architect Stephen Miller to create Brown Siegel Design Associates. She recently reverted back to her solo practice, keeping offices in New York Ciy and London. We are told Brown's services are not cheap, but the quality of work exceeds all expectation. HB Top Designers, 1999, 2000, 2001. KB 1999.

*"The finished product is a work of art." "Her work really exudes quality and luxury, but is not precious." "She selects decorative pieces for their sculptural qualities." "Her interiors are incredibly well-edited." "The juxtaposes add flow and life to the rooms." "Not one for ruffles and flourishes but includes an element of surprise and depth of intellect." "Expensive, but that's a reflection of the quality." "She stayed within budget, but we had a big budget." "She got to know exactly what we wanted—so I felt like we were designing the place with her guidance."*

| | Quality | Cost | Value | Recommend? |
|---|---|---|---|---|
| | **+** | **$** | **◆** | **★** |

## Naomi Leff & Associates

| | 4.5 | 5 | 4 | 4 |
|---|---|---|---|---|

12 West 27th Street, New York, NY 10001
(212) 686 - 6300   www.naomileff.com

*Sumptuous, high-end interior design*

Innovative, detailed and intense are all words that clients and peers use to describe Naomi Leff. She is known for her ability to set a mood, as she did with the design of Ralph Lauren's flagship store in New York, where luxurious fabrics and sumptuous materials intensify the setting. Other retail successes include Georgio Armani and Ferragamo. She will often spend a great deal of time studying the geographic or historical perspective before embarking upon a project, much to the delight of the client.

We hear Leff is very good about listening to customers' dreams and expectations, though some say she has a hard time "calling it a day" to meet budgets. For one project with a Native American theme she impressed the clients with exceptional finds at a local museum. Her talent to procure the highest quality antiques is a strong draw. Residential customers include Steven Spielberg and Kate Capshaw, Tom Cruise and Nicole Kidman, as well as many others in the entertainment industry. In New York she has worked on several Park Avenue and Hamptons homes over the last year. Leff has proved very accessible while in the middle of a large project, but less reachable otherwise. Her extreme intensity can be fabulous, but can be an issue if the client has a different vision. Nevertheless, most clients appear delighted with the end result.

Naomi Leff charges no design fee, but does have an initial consultant fee. She is generally acknowledged to be over the top on cost, but worth it for a very special project. AD 100, 2000. ID Hall of Fame.

*"The project we undertook together absorbed the better part of my life for a year. It was an amazing process. I learned so much from Naomi." "While obviously outstanding as a set designer of retail projects, she did not focus on our (very large) home. I ended up finding all the fabrics and furniture, and she just procured them." "Finding economic alternatives are not a strong suit." "Naomi understood exactly what to feature, and did not overwhelm the antiques with unnecessary draperies or details." "She goes way beyond decorating—raising ceilings, changing floors, completely rejuvenating a space." "There is no one better at decorating your once-in-a-lifetime project."*

## NDM Kitchens Inc.

204 East 77th Street, Suite 1E, New York, NY 10021
(212) 628 - 4629   www.nancymullan.com

*Gourmet kitchen design, interior design, complete renovation and contracting*

See NDM Kitchen's full report under the heading Kitchen & Bath

## Nile Inc.

| | 4.5 | 4.5 | 4 | 5 |
|---|---|---|---|---|

38 East 64th Street, New York, NY 10021
(212) 688 - 8860

*Neoclassical, detailed, luxurious interior design*

Clients speak in the most glowing terms about Nile's imaginative design capabilities, superb project management skills and meticulous attention to detail. Parners Terese Carpenter and Patrick Naggar continue to delight clients with their ability to draw inspiration from antiquity and integrate these foundations of classicism to the modern landscape. With Naggar based principally in Paris and Carpenter in New York, the firm combines the best of these worlds into creative solutions for its patrons.

As a small firm offering a boutique service, clients rely on the principals to play an integrated, hands-on role. Clients completely trust Nile with every aspect of their homes and compliment the firm for its skill in navigating the complexities of the process. Only a few new commissions are taken on each year, and they tend to be a substantial size. The firm was founded in 1987.

Nile charges no design fee, a reasonable percentage above net for products and high oversight fees. The firm often takes on much of the architect's role with its architectural design capabilities. Products are only of the highest quality, with much of the upholstery done in Paris. Living rooms are generally in the $200,000-plus realm. Nile is highly recommended by its clients, all who report that they would not consider using any other designers, and many of whom always have something going with Nile. HB Top Designers, 1999, 2000, 2001.

"She's designed one boat and two home interiors for me and all three were executed with the highest level of professionalism." "Terese is just bursting with positive energy and has an enviable work ethic." "The level of detail of their work is visible right down to the weave of the rug." "No detail is unimportant and the overall result is extraordinary." "The follow through is impeccable." "I completely trust Terese. She knows my taste, I love hers and she gets things done." "The most creative team in design today."

**Niven Scully Designs**                    3.5    3    4    4.5
160 East 72 Street, New York, NY 10021
(212) 452 - 1175

*Modernized, traditional interior design*

Clients and peers highly recommend Eugenie Niven for her distinct traditional aesthetic interwoven with contemporary flair. Rooms are said to be dignified and livable, highlighted with charming versions of traditional motifs brought to a modern age. We are told that she is an excellent listener and works in a constructive and collaborative manner with her clients to create a personalized, young and vibrant style. The results range from updated traditional to bold, exciting drama, depending upon the clients interests.

As the granddaughter of actor David Niven and daughter of Sotheby's Jamie Niven, Eugenie has inherited a graceful elegance and characteristic design panache, "well beyond her years." After studying at the New York School of Interior Design, she started the firm three years ago. Niven is the sole practitioner, generally takes on about sixteen projects each year, ranging from one sofa to a complete renovations. Clients say she is not shy about demolition, intent upon establishing a good flow and ambience, but definitely takes her clue from the customer.

The vast majority of Niven's work takes place in Manhattan, although she has completed projects in the surrounding metro area. Her clientele tends to be younger singles or newlyweds. Niven will take on projects that range from just one or two furnishings to entire apartment renovations and project budgets typically start at or below a modest $20,000. Niven charges low hourly rates and standard markups on product. HB Top Designers, 2000, 2001.

"Her rooms are full of charm and life, but are still classically based." "We had just gotten married and she gave us a fantastic product that was forward thinking enough to grow with our family." "Not too fancy, not too chintzy, just perfect." "The best choice for a classy, low-maintenance bachelor pad." "Eugenie could probably use a bit more support staff." "Our dining room is just amazing—blue-purple lacquer with a silver ceiling and a Chinese red chandelier. What imagination, yet still so distinguished." "She actually came in under the budget." "A really talented woman at an incredibly reasonable cost."

| | Quality | Cost | Value | Recommend? |
|---|---|---|---|---|
| | + | $ | ◆ | ★ |

## Noel Jeffrey Inc.

4.5  4.5  4  4.5

215 East 58th Street, New York, NY 10022
(212) 935 - 7775  www.dir-dd.com/noel-jeffrey.html

*Substantial, comfortable, traditional interior design*

Noel Jeffrey is consistently described as a gentleman and an expert creator of upscale luxe. He began his design career 30 years ago, studying design at Pratt and architecture at Columbia. While he is now known for a strong classical-to-eclectic look, his early preference was for the Bauhaus. This broad range lends Jeffrey a fluency of stylistic interests, meeting clients' various desires, all with punch. Even traditional has intrepid colors and modern juxtapositions to surprise the eye.

The firm usually undertakes complete renovations of substantial size, with budgets large enough to maintain the highest quality. Given his large staff of resident designers and architects, the firm has the capability to manage every aspect of a project and to keep it synchronized. Jeffery offers customers economic choices in the up-front design stages (e.g. reproductions vs. antiques), and quickly assesses the budget. Clients compliment him for taking complete control of their projects and for staying within budget. Supporters agree that he is very accessible, and that his staff is excellent, and all watchful of other vendors' work.

Jeffrey charges a standard design fee and standard markup over net. Clients feel that he is very expensive but quite worth the cost. He recently published *Design Diary: Innovative Interiors* (Rizzoli). ASID. HB Top Designers, 1999, 2000, 2001. KB 1991, 1994, 1998, 2001.

*"Noel is the consummate professional." "He offers a guiding hand, to shape our style with his strong vision." "Not a Crate & Barrel type of guy." "He would always be there for you, constantly in touch." "He even faxed things to me from Paris for approval." "I felt that he took a strong personal interest in our project." "Noel has an amazingly positive attitude." "No one can do curtains like Jeffrey—full, rich and dramatic." "Noel offers a historic dialogue without seriousness." "I was impressed by the entire office's desire to please the client." "We so appreciated the generous proportions of the design." "Very exciting process, we had a ball."*

## Olsen & Ayers

📁  📁  📁  📁

60 East 66th Street, New York, NY 10021
(212) 988 - 9003

*Classic high-end interior design*

## Orsini Design Associates 🛍

4.5  4.5  4.5  5

330 East 59th Street, 3rd Floor, New York, NY 10022
(212) 371 - 8400

*Updated-traditional, high-end interior design*

Susan Orsini is commended for her acute attention to detail, professional manner and excellent client service. She leans toward updated traditional designs, reflecting the interests of her client base. The firm also has successfully completed Art Deco and more contemporary projects. All designs are appreciated for their defined, tailored lines and livability. The majority of the firm's work is residential, mostly for prominent business executives (including their boats and planes), though Orsini is open to smaller projects with new clients. The firm also delves into office, commercial and hospitality work, including projects for Chanel, GTE, Goldman Sachs, NYNEX and Disney's first two cruise ships.

Orsini is reputed to deliver exactly on budget and on schedule. New clients are charged a design fee and products are purchased for a reasonable percentage over net. The firm spends a great deal of time with clients doing research and planning, and often recommends complete reconfiguration. All types of products are considered, from the finest French silks to Crate & Barrel. The firm often implements winter and summer maintenance programs for its customers, and has embraced new home technologies such as home theaters.

While there is a "very capable" staff of 27, with offices in New York and Los Angeles, Orsini oversees all client relationships. Many of her first clients of 22 years ago are still clients today. HB Top Designers, 1999, 2000. KB 1996.

*"Susan's style reflects the ease and comfort necessary for very busy people, who often have several houses to keep up." "She has a strategic plan for everything, which was very appealing to my husband who is used to that sort of thing." "She was the first designer in New York to understand our interest in a California, modern comfort." "They are open 24/7, and can make things happen faster than a speeding bullet, even if Susan is out of town." "Her designs work. There is always an electrical outlet where you need one." "She has gotten to know my design preferences so well that she will send me the same photo in this month's AD that I planned to send her, before I get to it." "Susan checks every penny the contractor spends and will always win any debates with them." "The details overseen by her office are remarkable: right down to placemats and paper napkins."*

## Pamela Banker                    4.5    4    4    4.5
136 East 57th Street, New York, NY 10022
(212) 308 - 5030

*Formal, traditional, old-school interior design*

Pamela Banker is wellrespected by clients and the trade for her efficient, capable professionalism and her strong, clean designs in the Parish-Hadley tradition. With a calm hand, she will mix classic traditional designs with comfortable, crisp contemporary. Clients say that she makes a particular effort to save and restore the architectural bones, and then trims away any unnecessary embellishments. Room identities are then created with color, design themes and functionality. She wins accolades from clients for her structured approach, although some say she could be a bit less focused. Patrons remark favorably upon her excellent commitment to budgets and schedule, as well as her helpful back office. Customers are also most appreciative that they get Banker directly as their point of contact.

In the late 1960s, Banker started her own firm. After 20 years, she joined McMillen at a senior level, and then went with Parish-Hadley after Sister Parish died. With the quasi-retirement of Albert Hadley, she recently went out on her own again. Many clients and families have followed Banker wherever she goes. Now younger generations have followed suit.

Retail is charged on all product, with a standard design fee covering hourly costs. While her many clients appreciate her timeless approach, others say that much of her inspiration dates back to her days at Parish-Hadley. But the work is said to always be completed accurately and meticulously. Many devoted clients and families would not consider using anyone else.

*"After 30-plus years, she has seen it all. She is the consummate professional." "Sister Parish without the ruffles." "Bold contemporary jungle prints at the beach and more rarified, traditional silks on Park Avenue." "Pam is an excellent listener upfront, but once you are in the implementation phase—watch out! She gets on a roll." "There is no nonsense with Pam." "She will inspect the upholsterer's work on her hands and knees to make sure he has it right." "She is one of the few designers out there that understands what 'classy' means. Trendy is not in her vocabulary." "I interviewed a handful of other decorators, and she was reasonably priced." "She was on budget to the dime." "What you see is what you get." "Our family has depended on her for years."*

## Pauline Boardman Ltd.             4    4    4    4.5
44 East 67th Street, New York, NY 10021
(212) 288 - 8379

*Livable, luxurious interior design*

| Quality | Cost | Value | Recommend? |
|---------|------|-------|------------|
| ✚ | $ | ◆ | ★ |

## Pierce Allen

4     4     4     4.5

80 Eighth Avenue, Suite 1602, New York, NY 10011
(212) 627 - 5440

*Eclectic, fun, colorful interior design*

With Michael Pierce on architecture and DD Allen on interior design, many clients feel that they have found the "dynamic duo" of leading edge style radiant with character and warmth. The pair are said to be particularly creative with color (eggplant, lime ice walls) and original materials (leather floors, pony-skin chairs, stainless steel tables), taking the edge off with antiques. They take pleasure in incorporating the client's view, and are said to be easy to work with and "not stuffy."

While they are known for a roster of high profile clients, including many Hollywood superstars (Matt Damon, Tommy Tune, Ellen Barkin, Tracey Ullman, Ben Affleck), "regular" clients also sing their praises. Pierce holds an MA in architecture from Harvard and Allen holds an MA in architecture from Columbia. Founded in 1986, about half its clients call on Pierce Allen for both disciplines. The back office is said to be very professional and committed.

The firm works with a standard design fee, a reasonable markup on products, a lower markup on antiques and a standard architectural fee (which eliminates the need for an oversight fee). References report that they are not "exactly budget conscience" but not outrageous either. City living rooms run in the $250,000 to $350,000 range with beach houses at less than $100,000. Bills are sent periodically with no surprises. Patrons say that the partners have the pulse of every secret source in New York and recommend them highly. HB Top Designers, 2000, 2001.

*"A New York treasure—they have superb taste and follow through flawlessly." "Fabrics in the $400 per yard area does not faze them. They are committed to the highest possible quality, yet mix it up." "They are real people who will artfully handle normal jobs." "While I first engaged them before they were 'known', they are happily updating just one room for me now, and are very responsive." "DD is a true artist." "Ordinary apartments become dashingly dapper." "They should be on the American Team (of architects and designers) at the 2004 Olympics." "Thoughtful, relaxed and very, very smart." "Discrete and protective of their clients. I appreciated their intuitive balance." "I recommend them to everyone." "Fun with a capital 'F'" "I have used them on six projects over six years, and have always been thrilled with the results."*

## Ralph Harvard Inc.

🗁    🗁    🗁    🗁

177 East 70th Street, New York, NY 10021
(212) 535 - 0707

*Timeless, traditional interior design. HB Top Designers, 1999, 2000, 2001. KB 1992, 1996, 1999.*

## Randall A. Ridless 🛍

4     4     4     4.5

315 West 39th Street, Suite 1504, New York, NY 10018
(212) 643 - 8140

*Exquisite, chic, high-end interior design*

Randall Ridless has the complete confidence of his clients who speak glowingly of his businesslike manner and design elan. His stylistic interests are noted to be unbounded—from Federal to Swedish, African to Country Folk—but all reflect Ridless's knowledge and passion of defined historic periods. Conventions honoring the hallowed past are twisted, with a heartened sense of the new.

Ridless draws upon his extensive training—first at RISD, then in the corporate world at I. Magnin (prototype stores) and Macy's (antique buying), two years with David Easton and most recently at Saks (store design). His residential design firm was founded quite recently with VP Elizabeth Martell, but his clients are numerous, many dating back to his days with Easton. While Ridless still devotes about half of his time to corporate endeavors (lead designer for Burberry's revamped stores), patrons find his residential design skills extraordinary, citing his chic, comfortable detailing. References say that you feel as if yours is his only project.

Ridless reportedly understands clients' desires very quickly, and works hard to fulfill their vision. He can collaborate with clients or assume all angles, which he often does for vacation homes. The firm works with clients to determine a fee construct that works for both parties. This could include a percentage over net or a flat fee. Customers remark upon Ridless's willingness to always offer "another option" to satisfy expense or style inclinations and highly recommend the firm. HB Top Designers, 2000, 2001. KB 2000.

*"I interviewed six potential decorators, but Randy was the obvious choice." "He takes a vision and puts it on paper so fast. Then he executes just as fast." "We did a six-story townhouse together. He caught on right away. Did the same thing for my sister." "I've worked with other decorators, but he is such a professional." "He will make your old ABC chair look as if it came from Kentshire." "Randy's sense of value is excellent." "He is brilliant at mixing expensive and not." "Even when he offers me choices, he always knows which one I am going to pick." "He is the only one I would trust to go Italian Neobaroque." "He is so open and enthusiastic, yet executes with confidence and class."*

### Richard C. Carpenter Interiors     🗁    🗁    🗁    🗁
114 East 32nd Street, New York, NY 10016
(212) 686 - 6851

*Luxurious interior design*

Richard Carpenter, the longtime associate of the late Renny Saltzman, is maintaining the commitment to design excellence and thorough execution of the partnership. Many clients are continuing with the firm, which specializes in luxurious and graceful high-end design. They report that Carpenter is charming, very talented and open to new design approaches. Others add that he is committed, earnest and dependable. The firm charges standard design fees, percentages over net and oversight fees. ASID.

### Richard Keith Langham Inc.      5     5     4     4.5
153 East 60th Street, New York, NY 10021
(212) 759 - 1212

*Lavish, colorful, inventive interior design*

When Richard Keith Langham is dedicated to a project, nothing can stop him. Customers say he adds sparkle, over-the-top creativity and imagination. Langham has been living the extravagant English-toned sensibility for over 20 years—first at Parsons and FIT, and then with Mark Hampton and Irvine & Fleming. He began his own firm in 1990. While he can be humble with clients, he has worked with some of the most fabled, including Jacqueline Kennedy Onassis, who said to him, "You have a sorcerer's eye. How lucky I am to be a beneficiary." While Langham is open to new clients and can keep to a budget, the budgets tend to be capacious.

His back office is quite large and reportedly strong, though clients who demand Langham's eye are generally satisfied with his accessibility. Supporters say that he is very demanding of himself and of the quality of his work. While he may willingly use less expensive fabrics, they are always cut and sewn to exacting specifications. Strong primary colors, saturated cashmeres and exquisite trims are usually part of the program.

The firm charges a standard design fee, a percentage over retail for products, and hourly oversight fees. The public can get a taste of Langham's timeless designs by visiting his newly opened upholstery and antiques showroom (at the above address). Patrons strongly recommend Langham for potential clients with significant and alluring projects. HB Top Designers, 1999, 2000, 2001. KB 1998.

*"I feel privileged to work with Keith. In time, I feel that he will be recognized as one of the world's legendary designers." "He is a control freak and can be very adamant about certain choices. But I trust his taste." "If you draw a line in the sand, he will flex and do it your way." "He can do less expensive country houses, but the detail work is still remarkable. Anything less kills him, and he loses interest in the project." "His dedication to the projects he loves is unbelievable. My builder vanished from the job site a week before a big party. Keith took paintbrush in hand for six straight days." "He is the definition of fun. I am sad it is over." "He is not a small potatoes kind of guy. Big projects, big clients are his forte." "My curtains are nicer than any of my couture clothing." "He does not like to talk about money, but all the proposals and bills are clear." "I absolutely trust and adore him beyond measure."*

### Richard L. Ridge & Roderick R. Denault 💼    4    4.5    4    4.5
903 Park Avenue, New York, NY 10021
(212) 772 - 6091

*Old guard-to-modern interior design*

Richard Ridge and Rod Denault are highly regarded by a devoted group of well-heeled clients for creating elegant, traditional interiors with an emphasis on clear colors and comfort. Historically, their focus was more English with horse prints and Georgean silver, but they have recently forayed into more contemporary designs. We are told Ridge and Denault are flexible in terms of the size of projects they will take on—anything from the design of a few rooms to the renovation of large suburban homes. Clients appreciate their "incredible organization," careful advance planning and excellent accessibility.

Taking on an average of twelve projects each year, we are told this duo is extremely knowledgeable and organized—Ridge brings 30 years of decorating experience to the firm, which was created more than 20 years ago when Denault joined. Manhattan is the scene for half of the firm's work, the rest completed across the globe, including France and England. Insiders tell us the firm is expanding its reach beyond a base of loyal, established emptynesters who make up the majority of its clientele. All say the pair are extremely patient, but some mention that they could benefit by some additional back office personnel.

Standard design fees are charged to cover drawings, floor plans, furniture or new designs. Budgets are developed room by room, and standard product and oversight fees are taken. Living rooms generally range from $150,00 to $200,000, but clients say they are very understanding and flexible on budget. KB 1992, 1995, 2000.

*"They get the big picture." "They are very practical and will guide you step-by-step." "You can see that they are always thinking two paces ahead, but are happy to answer any questions." "I was involved in the project, but they took the lead, and that really made me feel at ease." "Very caring people." "I am so happy with our choices, even years later." "Delightful, wonderful human beings." "They have all the ladies at the Club enthralled." "Very responsive and responsible. Tremendous follow up on every level and detail." "They are willing to work with what you have and will create a style for any price range."*

| | Quality | Cost | Value | Recommend? |
|---|---------|------|-------|------------|
| | + | $ | ◆ | ★ |

## Richard Lee Interior Design Inc.

| Quality | Cost | Value | Recommend? |
|---------|------|-------|------------|
| 4 | 3.5 | 4 | 4 |

205 West 57th Street, Suite 2AD, New York, NY 10019
(212) 765 - 3197

*Memorable, high-style, American residential interior design*

A keen eye for proportion and the creative assemblage of furniture with Asian or French antiques is what sources tell us distinguishes Richard Lee. Clients praise Lee for his exceptional taste in color schemes, furnishings and textures, and also credit him with the ability to create interiors that are equal parts client input and Lee's vision.

In addition to his design skills, we are told Lee understands the vagaries of construction and is effective in communicating with the client. Lee's ability to identify with the clients' view and effectively oversee a project leaves no doubt in references' minds he will get the job done on time and on budget. He enjoys a loyal clientele who refers him to friends and family. HB Top Designers, 1999, 2000, 2001.

*"A never-ending flow of energy and great pride in his work." "Most importantly, he sublimates his design interests to those of his clients." "A mature designer who knows what needs to be done—and does it." "As a major dealer in New York, I have seen it all. He is creative, professional and a pleasure to work with." "He takes responsibility for the project. A lost concept with most people today." "I was always at ease knowing he was overseeing the project. That's why I've hired him for the third time."*

## Richard Mishaan Design

🗁    🗁    🗁    🗁

750 Fifth Avenue, Suite 1303, New York, NY 10019
(212) 265 - 5588   www.homerdesign.com

*Contemporary, residential interior design. HB Top Designers, 2000. KB 1998, 2000, 2001.*

## Richard's Interior Design

1390 Lexington Avenue, New York, NY 10128
(212) 831 - 9000   www.richardsinteriordesign.com

*Retail—Custom upholstery and window treatments*

See Richard's Interior Design's full report under the heading Upholstery & Window Treatments

## Robert Couturier Inc. 📷

| Quality | Cost | Value | Recommend? |
|---------|------|-------|------------|
| 5 | 5 | 4 | 4.5 |

69 Mercer Street, Third Floor, New York, NY 10012
(212) 463 - 7177   www.robertcouturier.com

*Dramatic, stylish, lush interior design*

Customers are captivated by the style and grace of Robert Couturier's work. They find him innovative, creative and an attentive listener. The French influence of years spent studying in Paris often finds its way into his work, usually in a fanciful tone. He is known with awe for creating visions that relate to historical moments, infiltrated with the presence of today.

While many projects are undertaken for the international elite (huge houses in Mexico, chateaus in France), younger clients also enjoy working with Couturier. He is willing to begin just one room at a time, knowing that the budget-constrained will return when they are able. Alternatively, he is capable of constructing an entire village of workers in a remote location to get the job done correctly.

While some balk at his prices and uncompromising taste in expensive fabrics, all find him honest, and his staff helpful and responsive. Living rooms are typically in the $100,000 to $300,000-plus realm. Well-heeled references commend Couturier for helping them to make wise design investment decisions. He readily admits and absorbs mistakes, and most feel the high costs are clearly worth it for the ultimate in upscale chic. AD 100, 2000. HB Top Designers, 1999, 2000, 2001.

*"Robert captured exactly what I wanted even though I didn't know how to express the thought myself."* *"We hired him after not being pleased with our former decorator—what a difference. Whatever he touches is extraordinary. He is very service-oriented."* *"Works with the most influential people in the world and with my friends who own rather small apartments."* *"He brought cheer and wit into our dreadfully boring Park Avenue digs."* *"He is a ingenious master who knows every historical reference, but he does not take himself too seriously."* *"If ever there is an issue, he says, 'Don't worry about it,' and magically finds a solution."* *"He could not be more delightful, and is a gentleman through and through."* *"Robert provided a heart for my home."*

## Robert Schwagerl
📁 📁 📁 📁

119 West 57th Street, New York, NY 10019
(212) 315 - 1744
*Residential interiors, kitchen and bath design*

## Roderick N. Shade Interior Design
3.5    3    4.5    4.5

PO Box 1797, New York, NY 10026
(212) 681 - 7942  www.roderickshade.com
*Eclectic-to-traditional, high-end interior design*

Clients applaud Roderick Shade for his ability to add urban elegance and sensible functionality while successfully integrating family heirlooms, contemporary lines, ethnic crafts and thrift-store finds. Many projects combine warm, natural fabrics and woods with bold, clean lines in a neutral color palette. Other are highlighted by swags of bold, colorful fabrics. His stylistic range includes his recent uses of African looks to more traditional English and French designs. Sources report that he is eager to work hand-in-hand with his clients, respecting their stylistic choices and taking care of the nitty-gritty details.

After working with designers like Roger Franks and Ed Terntine in Los Angeles and Jane Gaillard in New York, Shade has been on his own for six years. He founded the Harlem United Show House, the first African American interior design showcase and has developed a custom furniture line in the deep colors and smooth shapes of African design. Most projects are currently in the New York area. We are told that Shade uses elegant, clean designs, while remaining flexible and patient, to ultimately produce comfortable and stylish rooms.

Shade is flexible with his design fee, charging a flat fee or reasonable hourly rates. He works within his clients' budgets, offering a reasonable markup on products and a range of styles and prices to choose from. Clients describe working with Shade as educational and inspiring. His unique blend of cultures and looks creates an elegant, unmistakable style. KB 2000.

*"This is definitely not your usual, run-of the-mill designer. He goes beyond the box to find really exciting, intriguing ideas and new uses of traditional (and untraditional) materials."* *"Really listens to your interests, and creatively formulates a personalized vision."* *"He's highly ethical and a kind, good man."* *"Rod was so sensitive to my budget constraints, yet kept me focused on buying a few high end pieces."* *"I was so insecure about decisions. He gave me confidence and got me to the end game."* *"He has the patience of Job."* *"I took huge design risks with Rod, and was thrilled by the result."*

| | Quality | Cost | Value | Recommend? |
|---|---|---|---|---|
| | + | $ | ◆ | ★ |

## Roger de Cabrol Interiors 💼    3.5    3    4.5    4.5
121 East 24th Street, 8th Floor, New York, NY  10010
(212) 353 - 2827   www.rogerdecabrol.com

*Modern-edged, European-enhanced interior design*

Conversant in both Continental elegance and modern chic, Roger de Cabrol mixes it up with harmony and delivers on time and on budget. Many projects begin with a traditional European background that de Cabrol accents with playful and elegant modern pieces, offering a result that is modern, affordable and livable. His clients report that he works closely with them, listening to what styles they prefer, yet remaining very practical, especially with families.

Educated in France at L'Ecole des Roches and L'Ecole des Beaux Arts in Paris, de Cabrol has worked with such names as Baron Fred de Cabrol (his uncle), Valerian Rybar and Jacques Granges. He started his own firm in 1987 and works with a mostly Manhattan clientele. Clients very much enjoy the design process with de Cabrol and note that he strives to produce a comfortable, gorgeous living environment. We're told de Cabrol keeps his practice small to focus on client relations and to have an active role in every project. He has been known to call repeatedly while on vacation to check up on items as small as a doorknob.

The firm charges a standard design fee with a lower markup on product or de Cabrol can work on a consultation basis at reasonable hourly rates. A typical living room starts at $75,000. The designer will take on a few rooms for new clients and is known to offer a wide range of product selection and price ranges. Clients say that he is patient, honest, never pushy and offers a stylish look that is practical and affordable.

*"Roger's scope is really remarkable. We did three projects with him—one French traditional, one contemporary and one modern. My friend did ultra-traditional with him." "His European background is evidenced in his biases regarding furnishings and fabric—not a lot of chintz here." "He's able to visualize a room and make it happen." "Roger de Cabrol is an ideal decorator for people who are time deprived." "While not the pinnacle, he gets it done to great satisfaction." "In an amazing short three months and just three shopping trips with Roger, my apartment was on the cover of* Architectural Digest.*" "Roger is not hindered by architecture, creating rooms that the client envisions." "He made each room warm and inviting. We now use them all." "I have no hesitations recommending him to others or hiring him again."*

## Ronald Bricke & Associates Inc. 💼    3.5    3    5    5
333 East 69th Street, New York, NY  10021
(212) 472 - 9006

*Innovative, chic, refined interior design*

Ronald Bricke is best known for a "fabulous unfused modernism" that borders on funk. He is also said to be quite facile with 18th-century period spaces with an affinity for English and French antiques of that period. The common thread, reportedly, is Bricke's painstaking attention to detail and his strong desire to please the client. Clients say that Bricke is simultaneously adept at creating luxurious, eye-pleasing interiors, and taking into account the overall comfort of the space.

Bricke, the sole principal of this three-person firm, is a graduate of Parsons and started his practice in 1972. We are told he is extremely hands-on and has excellent followup practices—always returning phone calls and making himself available to his clients. Bricke is said to quickly come up with drawings and usually formulates five plans for the client to choose from. The firm generally takes on about five major projects each year (about twenty overall).

Projects start around $75,000 and clients say Bricke is excellent at working within strict budgets. In addition to his many New York City clients, Bricke has taken on work in London, Florida, Texas, California and Maine. Brick charges a standard retainer applicable to the last bill and retail on products. Clients trust Bricke to creatively incorporate their clients' existing furniture and save money in the process. HB Top Designers, 1999, 2000. KB 1994.

*"He is just so creative and knows how to get things done on budget." "He has the patience of a saint. Never talks down to you or scoffs at ideas or questions." "Great quality for a price that was less than it could have been." "Absolutely delightful in personality and design." "Creates the most whimsical updated French that knocks your socks off." "He is a big fox terrier in personality. He wants to do a good job and will bring you the bone."*

### Russell Bush        4    3.5    4    4.5
4 Park Avenue, New York, NY 10016
(212) 686 - 9152

*High-end residential interior design*

Clients praise Russell Bush for a discerning eye, highly personalized design and gentlemanly demeanor. He is further complimented for having a highly educated view of a wide array of styles, and a strong ability to incorporate clients' collections. English country chintz is said to be done as well as Japanese or Chinese, taking the cue from the client. Whether it's providing museum quality decor or quickly assembling a stylish, inexpensive guest room—clients say Bush is equally detail-oriented and handles himself in a most professional manner.

After working under Diana Vreeland at the Costume Institute for seven years, Bush joined Peter Marino for ten years, leading projects with Ann Bass and Valentino, and leaving as head of the interiors department, Bush went on his own in 1997. The firm of three generally takes on about six projects each year. It is said that no job is too small, and no job is too big. He has been known to take up a needle himself to get the curtains to flow just so. Most clients are in and about New York City.

Budgets generally evolve throughout the course of the project and are always dictated by the client. The firm charges a relatively high retainer and lower product markups. ASID. HB Top Designers, 2000, 2001.

*"He is extremely honest, and genuinely cares about providing a home that is both beautiful and livable." "His interest in providing an individualized look set him apart from all the others I interviewed." "So organized, professional and gentlemanly." "He respects any budget and always remains calm—both such rarities in this business." "He is very considerate of special requests." "He does not feel a need to blow out your walls to dramatically improve your space." "He is a perfectionist, and will rob Peter to pay Paul to make sure he sticks to the budget." "His sense of style is amazing."*

### Russell Piccione       4    4.5    4    5
131 East 71st Street, New York, NY 10021
(212) 288 - 3033

*High-end residential interior design*

Russell Piccione has developed a discreet group of loyal patrons who appreciate his attention to quality and detail, strong knowledge base and client focus. Piccione takes on only a few clients a year, and takes an extremely hands-on approach. He is known to advise on every kind of design-related family decision, including helping husbands choose jewelry for their wives. Most of his clients are on Manhattan's Upper East Side, with a few downtown and in the region. Piccione's clients are generally quality-biased, traditional-minded and often appreciate fine art and antiques. This works well for Piccione, who is known for his encyclopedic understanding of continental furniture and art.

The firm asks for a small design fee, but a substantial retainer. Products are purchased at standard markups with a sliding scale for higher-priced antiques. He reportedly favors higher-quality/cost fabrics and furnishings. Piccione has been in interior design for about ten years, seven on his own, but has developed an established group of dedicated supporters.

*"Client relationships are so important to him that he interviews you, not the other way around." "His patience is limitless, he will take me to the D&D all day just to find the right trim." "He doesn't fool around with lower quality fabrics and is not one to focus on price tags, but he does not spend money stupidly either." "He takes great care to understand and appreciate his client's particular interests and needs." "He is a maniac for quality, but will use Crate & Barrel for the beach house." "Anyone that uses him loves him."*

## S. Russell Groves
210 11th Avenue, Suite 502, New York, NY 10001
(212) 966 - 6210   www.srussellgroves.com

*Open, practical residential and retail architecture and interior design*

See S. Russell Grove's full report under the heading Architects

## Saladino Group          4.5    4.5    4    4
200 Lexington Avenue, New York, NY 10016
(212) 684 - 3720

*Graphic, contemporary interior design. ASID. HB Top Designers, 1999. ID Hall of Fame.*

## Salon Moderne Inc.      3.5    3    5    5
281 Lafayette Street, New York, NY 10012
(212) 219 - 3439

*Hot, colorful, modern interior design*

Sabrina Schilcher amazes clients with creative furnishings and attention to detail. We understand that she is a great listener and very savvy about evoking mood without spending a fortune. She has an up-to-date flair that mixes easily with stately (but not expensive) antiques. Her background in fashion allows Schilcher to weave fashion trends through interiors (think Prada). Translucent panels, pendant lighting sculptures and vintage Knoll happily co-exist with sleek custom wood cabinetry.

Many customers are the young and hip on Wall Street—often single guys who do not want a polished designer look. Others include young families decorating their first apartments or lofts, businesspeople with glamorous pied-a-terres, and fashion and Internet companies with commercial spaces. Those who have given her carte blanche have been very pleased with the results. The firm charges a standard design fee and a very reasonable markup over net for products. She has been known to do wonders with $200,000 budgets for entire projects. Customers feel that they always get Schilcher's attention.

She also designs her own furniture, which may be purchased at the above address (for soft modern) or at 14 Wooster Street (for edgier pieces). Many of today's pre-eminent modern interior designers purchase furniture at her stores. Schilcher studied at the Viennese Academy in her native Austria, worked in fashion and has been in the furniture business for fifteen years. She began to design interiors nine years ago.

*"She did everything for me—from soup to nuts. I arrived and it was done." "She is a great listener and has an incredible flair at such reasonable prices." "While she is not the person to go to for chintz and toile, she did my bedroom in the softest, most feminine manner, without being fussy." "Groovy artwork, cement floors, stylish furnishings and fun." "She utilizes every inch of space, in a thoughtful and exciting way." "I was amazed that she was able to tone it down to make it work in the suburbs, while still being fun and sexy." "She has grown with us, developing a more refined palette." "We would not think of hiring anyone else."*

## Sam Blount Inc.
21 West 58th Street, New York, NY 10019
(212) 888 - 0515

*English country style, high-end interior design. ASID. HB Top Designers, 1999, 2000, 2001.*

271

| | Quality | Cost | Value | Recommend? |
|---|---|---|---|---|

## Sandra Nunnerley Inc.

**4    4.5    4    4**

595 Madison Avenue, New York, NY 10022
(212) 826 - 0539

*Timeless, crisp, modern interior design*

Sandra Nunnerley is known for her tailored and eclectic style creating functional and fashionable interiors, as well as her ability to solve quirky architectural challenges through design. Patrons also praise her creation of rooms that incorporate unique and unexpected elements, and that also work for clients' lifestyle, attitude and needs. Most layouts integrate a subtle interplay of textures and quiet colors, often highlighted by juxtapositions of objects from the East and the West, and the old and the new. Nunnerly's professional capabilities and attentiveness is said to be very high, while in the midst of a project.

After studying architecture for three years in Sydney, working with several NY art galleries and then beginning a career in interior design with the contract firm L.S.K., Wellington-born Nunnerley opened her firm in 1984. She reportedly takes control of projects from the start, having a hand in most details—from the moldings to the furnishings. Sources say that Nunnerley is a great buffer between the client and subcontractors, demanding of the subs and collaborative with clients and the architects. Additionally, the back office is noted to be strong and knowledgeable.

Sources say Nunnerley is intense, organized and, once developed, completes projects swiftly and accurately. In addition to her Manhattan clientele, Nunnerley also works in the Los Angeles area. Projects costs tend to be standard and start around $75,000. Clients remark on her excellent relations with antique dealers, who often show her the crème of the crop before going retail. HB Top Designers, 1999, 2000. KB 1992.

*"Classic, timeless, modern and smart design. It still looks up-to-date many years later." "Sophisticated, not sentimental rooms." "I am fairly wishy-washy when it comes to these sort of things, and Sandra was just what I needed." "Her follow up is superb and her support staff is amazing." "She is a professional; she is not looking to become your best friend." "Sandra is a tough taskmaster with the subs, taking the proverbial ball and running with it." "As an architect, I was impressed with her clear and honest communication." "While Sandra would only ever give us four fabric choices, one was always perfect." "Has expensive taste, but her rates are fair." "I dream of using Sandra again to redo the apartment when the kids are older." "Her designs take your breath away."*

## Sara Bengur Associates

**4    3    5    5**

525 Broadway, Suite 701, New York, NY 10012
(212) 226 - 8796   www.sarabengur.com

*Exotic-tinged classical interior design*

Taking delight in the successful melange of unexpected, old-world objects and gallant cosmopolitan furniture, Sara Bengur has bisected the avant-garde. Drawing upon her Turkish heritage, Bengur creates a highly customized look that is fresh and original, yet comfortably appropriate for some of the most patrician neighborhoods. Antique textiles, custom mid-19th-century upholstery and lots of detailed decorative painting often are seen. Clients report that Bengur initially invests a great deal of time understanding their interests, and takes great pride in creating something uniquely suited for each situation. Many clients have young children which we hear are a special sensitivity of Bengur's.

After working on Wall Street for a few years, Bengur studied at Parsons, then managed large projects for Stephen Sills. She struck out on her own about nine years ago. Current projects include homes in Manhattan, Washington, D.C., New Canaan, Boston and Mt. Desert Island, Maine. Clients praise Bengur's close attention to every little detail. Living rooms tend to be in the $75,000 to $150,000 realm. The firm generally charges a standard design fee, a reasonable percentage over net on products (same on antiques) and hourly fees for oversight. HB Top Designers, 2000, 2001.

*"She has a unique perspective, and can assemble a beautifully coherent composition that works." "You get the highest possible quality without the headaches and at half the cost." "Sara will never do the same thing for any two clients, right down to the last lampshade." "She tirelessly searches up and down the eastern seaboard to find unique antiques and objects." "While she does not push, she will encourage us to go for the highest quality we can afford without spending a fortune." "Sara would never purchase mass market, preferring small shop treasures at the same cost." "She has a wonderful sense of human scale and a delicate understanding of propriety, especially for someone so young." "Sara insisted upon going to my attic to see if we could reuse any of my family pieces. That meant so much to me." "She designs comfortable, serene rooms of unassuming beauty." "She is the only person who has consistently bought me Christmas presents I love."*

## Scott Salvator

4    4.5    4    4.5

308 East 79th Street, New York, NY 10021
(212) 861 - 5355

*Pretty, lavish, classic interior design*

Scott Salvator and Michael Zabriskie win accolades from customers for their businesslike manner, elegant-yet-updated formal, classical style and personable nature. Clients often praise the firm for refined use of color and intricate layering of fabrics and coordinated trims, saying that they construct the ultimate "traditional-but-not-stuffy" home. Salvator is noted to be accommodating, detail-oriented, professional, deeply tied to his work, intense, smart, practical and fun. While some say that his detail and legal background can, at times, slow progress, all are effusive about the end results.

Salvator received a BS in accounting and a JD in law, and then studied interior design at FIT and Parsons. Before starting his firm in 1992, Salvatore worked for Mario Buatta, Gary Crain and Robert Metzger. Zabriskie, an associate at the firm, graduated from Parsons and worked with Mario Buatta, McMillen and Parish-Hadley. Clients tend to live on Park and Fifth Avenues, and often have the firm do their country home. Homeowners interface directly with Salvatore or Zabriskie, who do all the shopping themselves. The back office is said to be quite small.

The firm asks for a standard design fee that is deductible against future purchases. Products are purchased at retail. Clients have strong opinions about the firm, with most lifelong devotees and a few that just don't click. HB Top Designers, 1999, 2000, 2001. KB 1994, 1999.

*"From city house to country house and back again. All were lovely and appropriate." "I never used a decorator before and he was very sensitive to that issue." "For that kind of money I did not want to talk to an assistant, and I never had to." "While Scott can talk up a storm, the end product is just right." "I would not use him for my country house, but love his urban vision." "They are traditional, but not frumpy." "Scott's glamorous couture product stands out in a sea of neutral sameness." "It was rare when I said no, but if I did, he was good about finding an alternative." "We went through several possible schemes with Scott, but we never really connected." "I did not have to interfere because he totally understood. He is great for people with limited time." "A well organized system of estimates and billing." "Great sense of dry humor." "Scott has a real flair for living and livability. We continue to go to the movies together."*

## Scott Sanders LLC ▪

3.5    3    4.5    4.5

302 A West 12th Street, New York, NY 10014
(212) 627 - 5816

*Classic Americana with a Twist*

Who do you call when your postwar white box apartment needs serious help? Clients say Scott Sanders, who can magically transform it into an urban farmhouse, and so much more. Sanders brings a consistently calm, traditionally based and comfortably nostalgic, yet fresh sensibility to his interiors. Clients turn to Sanders for his expertise with a range of classic, fresh designs from the metamorphosis of an elegant Fifth Avenue apartment with limestone and camel hair to a 400-square-foot West Village jewel with vibrant red and plaid.

After graduating Parsons and nine years at Polo Ralph Lauren, where he created the Interior Design Department (interior design for outside clients), Sanders opened his eponymous firm in 2000. A design boutique, clients receive the full attention of Sanders. They tell us he is amazing at follow-up both during and after the project. Projects have included residences in New York, Palm Beach, Greenwich, Palm Springs, Paris and London. Sander's redesign of the Albion, a South Beach hotel, to New England understated genteel from typical Art Deco beachside, received much attention.

The firm's unusual methodology of pricing is welcome by clients. Sanders charges a flat fee, based on a reasonable markup of estimated project costs. Living rooms can be as low at $15,000, demonstrating Sanders strong creativity and insider resources. Sanders is said to be equally adept at redecorating few rooms as working with architects on new construction. Clients highly recommend Sanders for addressing the practical needs of clients while simultaneously creating manifest design moods.

*"I really am grateful for Scott's inherent understanding of my traditional view." "It is like living in a Polo fantasy, with patina." "I use Scott as an example to my staff as to what good customer service means." "He finds a solution even under tight budget situations." "Scott has a distinct 'well-groomed' style which is organized, but unpretentious." "Scott really loves what he does and is an absolute pleasure to work with."*

### Scott Snyder Inc.                                 4      4      4      4
12 East 80th Street, New York, NY  10021
(212) 288 - 1511

*Luxurious, continental interior design*

A true traditionalist, Snyder favors interiors with an acute sense of symmetry, scale and perfect proportion. He is best known for his classical and neoclassical decor of numerous sprawling estates in the Palm Beach area. Snyder has recently opened a Manhattan office and is adapting to his metropolitan clientele by incorporating a more contemporary feel to neoclassical backdrops. Sources tell us Scott Snyder has an instinctual eye for design, deciding upon the layout and general direction he will pursue after just a few minutes of observation.

Snyder is noted by insiders as "making the most" out of New York's tight living spaces by utilizing grand mirrors and crafty color schemes to greatly enhance the perception of open space. We are told Snyder is excellent at melding the interior of any given home—be it in the subtropics of southern Florida or the concrete jungle of Manhattan—into the existing landscape to create a harmonious balance.

Clients appreiciate the firm's customer service, and say that while the prices are high, they are not outrageous. Snyder is known to highlight one or two major pieces in a room and keep the rest in line. References say Snyder is a "safe bet" and a will do all he can to make the client happy. KB 2001.

*"It's amazing—the rooms appear to have a grandeur and symmetry, even though they began as fairly odd shapes." "He knows where to draw the line. I had wanted a more updated look, but Scott made sure we stayed true to the architecture of the house." "Scott very much gets involved with the architecture as well as the design, to make sure it all flows." "He is excellent at understanding the*

| Quality | Cost | Value | Recommend? |
|---|---|---|---|
| ✚ | $ | ◆ | ★ |

*just-so Palm Beach look, and will take care of you." "While the furnishings are indeed traditional, he encouraged us to break it up with some amusing contrasts." "Even after several years, I am so comfortable in his beautiful classical work."*

### Scott-Ulmann Inc. 🛍          4    4    4    4.5
71 Hill Street, Southampton, New York  11968
(212) 755 - 4306
*Robust, classical, English-hued interior design*

Known for her thoughtful designs reflecting a classic English sensibility with all-American comfort and zest, Pricilla Ulmann has built a steadfast clientele. Strong, warm hues of reds, greens and yellow are often featured on traditional silhouettes with continental flair. Quirky pieces with personality may also be seen, with few perfectly matched pairs. Ulmann is said to work with the customer to realize their design goals, within the framework of "classical with patina."

After graduating from the New York School of Interior Design and working as a fashion editor, Ulmann ran her own design firm for over twenty years before joining McMillen in 1995 and Parish-Hadley in 1997. In 1998, she revived her firm with a team of three. About 20 projects are underway at one time, ranging from the recovering of a few chairs to substantial new construction. Most all projects are in the New York area, with much in the Hamptons, where her new office is located. Celebrity names seek her designs as well as the most socially prominent. Clients are delighted to receive excellent attention from Ulmann who they describe as "very buttoned-up" and smooth.

The firm charges a standard retainer and retail on product. Products are said to range appropriately in price, depending upon the setting. Ulmann is highly recommended for an updated traditional look that is always "in good taste."

*"She absolutely opens your thinking and vision, but is very sensible on budgets and timetables." "She would not consider showing you a piece unless she likes it enough to use it herself." "I would highly recommend her for all classical motifs, but she does not like modern design." "Pricilla will look forever for you in the antiques shows to build up a collection of accessories that look as if they were created by you over time." "Pricilla likes things in order but recognizes the reality of everyday living." "She can decorate as well for men as women." "She will creatively work with you to make a great effect with less money." "Pricilla took the time to really learn how we used the space. She earned our trust and confidence."*

### Sharon Simonaire Design          📁  📁  📁  📁
216 West 18 Street, Suite 1102, New York, NY  10011
(212) 242 - 1842
*High-end residential interior design. HB Top Designers, 2000, 2001.*

### Sheila Bridges Design          4    3.5    4.5    4.5
1925 Seventh Avenue, Suite 8M, New York, NY  10026
(212) 678 - 6872   www.sheilabridges.com
*Luxurious, contemporary interior design*

Sheila Bridges has been recently lauded by clients and peers for her deft use of vintage furnishings artfully placed in minimalist settings. While focusing on the comfortable, she fuses bold, richly-colored upholstery, weathered sideboards and soothing backgrounds of creams, taupes and white. Recently chosen by *Time Magazine* as the only interior designer in their People to Watch issue, Bridges reports that she designs "low-maintenance homes for high-maintenance people." Clientele include former President Clinton, software designer Peter Norton and novelist Tom Clancy. Other clients include bankers, artists and entrepreneurs. Bridges is recognized for being flexible and open, while introducing clients to interesting new options.

Educated at Brown and the Parsons School of Design, Bridges worked with Shelton Mindel and then with Renny Saltzman, each for two years. Bridges formed her own firm in 1994 and it remains small, with Bridges as the clear client contact herself.  While most work is in New York, other projects have taken her to Boston, New Orleans, LA and London.  Bridges' first book, *Furnishing Forward*, is to be released in 2002, and a retail store is soon to be opened.

The firm charges a standard design fee, reasonable product fees and strong oversight fees.  A wide variety of sources are cultivated from the Upper East Side to upstate New York to Paris.  Patrons recommend Bridges for her functional, beautiful designs that accommodate busy lifestyles.  HB Top Designers, 1999, 2000, 2001.

*"Your learn so much from Sheila. She always has a new thought and a new historical reference." "Design is not a mystery with Sheila, but an evolving practical process." "She offers comfortable, livable spaces which are lovely, but not pretentious." "Shelia is clear, reasonable, professional and smart." "She knows how to persuade you without being overbearing." "While at first I thought the budget was outrageous, I now think every penny was worth it. I would have made costly mistakes and she did it just right." "I am always able to reach her and the two projects came in right on budget." "Sheila took us from a college black leather sofa-look to an eclectic, sophisticated style that looks better every year."*

### Sherrill Canet Interiors           3.5    3.5    4    4.5
171 East 62nd Street, New York, NY  10021
(212) 308 - 5193   www.sherillcanetinteriors.com
*Updated, traditional interior design*

Clients praise Sherrill Canet for her personalized design abilities, knowledge of fine English and French antiques and for her accommodating nature.  Designs are said to start with the architecture and to develop based on the clients' interests and lifestyle.  While offering a range of choices, the interiors are generally based on a clean, traditional style with unique objects and details.

Canet is a veteran of the London antique scene, as she studied in the city at the Inchbald School of Design.  She also holds an economics degree from Fordham University.  Beginning her business on the retail side with Bellwethers Antiques in Locust Valley, interior design was a natural evolution. The firm currently fields eight and accepts approximately a dozen projects annually, many of which are substantial in scope and budget.  While the bulk of Canet's work takes place in Long Island and Manhattan, she has also completed commissions in Fairfield County, Colorado and Las Vegas.

The firm charges standard design fees and reasonable product markups, with lower hourly rates for drawing and drafting.  Living rooms are typically in the $75,000 to $100,000 neighborhood.  Discrete clients commend Canet for her designs of understated elegance and practicality.

*"A total professional with a unique view on traditional design." "She was amazing at finding a compromise between my husband's taste and mine." "She kept us on the straight and narrow, focusing on classic, workable designs that made sense for our family." "Sherrill found some really interesting, chic pieces that distinguished our apartment but were in good context with the rest of the plan." "She is a real professional, executing the job with a great eye." "She understood that we did not have an unlimited budget." "My husband likes to get involved with every single design decision, but after a while he has such confidence in Sherrill that he let her run with the project. That says a lot!"*

### Sills Huniford Associates          5    5    4    4
30 East 67th Street, 4th Floor, New York, NY  10021
(212) 988 - 1636
*Luxurious, neoclassical interior design*

On the forefront of the harmonic integration of classical antiquity into early 20th-century modern, Stephen Sills and James Huniford operate at the highest levels of quality.  Known as grand yet restrained, their interiors evoke ages past with the comforts and flourish of today.  Architectural backgrounds are said to exceed any seen before, with intricate painting, strong moldings and elaborate floors. Contractors and architects remark that the firm maintains extraordinary control over jobs, making sure that every subcontractor knows just what to do and exactly how to do it. Patrons say the firm always develops highly customized design plans that incorporate customers' particular interests.

The firm's long and exceptional list of clients includes Tina Turner, Vera Wang and Nan Swid. On the other hand, not all clients are among the "rich and famous." The partners are known to make frequent worldwide shopping trips in search of unique furniture, storing the items in their large warehouse for current and future clients. Given the firm's large volume of clients with large residences to fill, they also are well known among New York antique dealers.

According to clients, Sills and Huniford stress the importance of strong client relationships based on "understanding and trust." Apparently, if client and firm are not on "the same wavelength," Sills and Huniford will turn down a potential assignment.

The partners are loved by many of their clients for delivering the very best product available, usually in a very timely manner. For years, however, peers and dealers have asked about the firm's ambiguous fee structure in which certain products are purchased at an "agreed upon price" instead of a set markup, but clients say they are comfortable with this structure and can always say no. Supporters recommend the pair for the ultimate, innovative design journey. AD 100, 2000. HB Top Designers, 1999, 2000, 2001.

*"Head and shoulders above anyone else, if you can afford them." "Sometimes the craftsmen's work is so painstaking, I wonder if it is worth it. But it looks amazing." "Editing is their credo." "They are fearless in their innovative approach." "They are uniquely able to construct magnificent settings, combining various objects from different periods in a cohesive and beautiful manner. When others do this, it just looks like a mish-mash." "Even their cottons are custom dyed." "While they do love objects of serious provenance, they are good about mixing it up." "I am so grateful I found these guys—they have completely upgraded our lifestyle." "I am spoiled by working with these two, but they are beyond expensive."*

### Siskin Valls, Inc.　　　　　4　　4　　4　　5
21 West 58th Street, New York, NY 10019
(212) 752 - 3790

*Luxurious, contemporary interior design. HB Top Designers, 1999, 2000, 2001. KB 1994.*

### Snook Studio　　　　　👝　　👝　　👝　　👝
10 Greene Street, New York, NY 10013
(212) 343 - 2420

*High-end residential interior design. HB Top Designers, 1999, 2000, 2001.*

### Stedila Design　　　　　4　　4　　4　　4
135 East 55th Street, 5th Floor, New York, NY 10022
(212) 751 - 4281

*Classical, creative high-end interior design*

Stedila Design, led by John Stedila and Tim Button, is applauded for thematic classical elegance infused with spirit and whimsy. Supporters say that they are incredible with creative clients who are interested in design adventures. Button and Stedila have different modus operandi. Stedila is known to be less engaged in ordinary decorating projects, and Button takes on a wide range.

Recent projects include a mansion on the northern shore of Long Island, a 16th-century chateau, a Southampton tudor oceanfront, a Palm Beach Venetian palletiza, and a contemporary Victorian house in New Jersey, with clients such as Perry Ellis, Calvin Klein and renowned jewelry designers. Stedila has done seven different houses for at least one client. Button's stamp can be found on

Clinton's home in Chappaqua, finishing less than a year before it was sold to the former President and New York Senator. We are told both principals are adept at building extensive and valuable collections for clients, and at mixing reproductions with antiques. Supporters maintain that both are accessible and freely admit and correct any concerns.

The firm charges a standard up-front design fee, reasonable percentages over net for products and a significant oversight fee. Hourly fee arrangements can also be made (though are not preferred). Stedila clearly gravitates toward more expensive fabrics and furniture, but can offer a range of options. Button is more flexible, but also favors excellent quality. Supporters highly recommend them for unique, exciting projects. HB Top Designers, 1999, 2000. KB 1993.

*"Tim and John offer all the best in interior design." "John is a passionate decorator. Not the guy to use if you want a neutral palette." "He is best with clients who have a specific point of view. If you are wishy-washy or uninspired, he loses interest." "If you click with John and capture his imagination, together you can create something truly extraordinary. I would never consider using anyone else." "Tim went along with our program, with the greatest integrity and quality. We enjoy mixing unusual and quirky objects and he did it with grace." "Tim orchestrated our project like a symphony!" "Tim's sketches are so good they are a virtual reality." "Tim has many celebrities and dignitaries as clients, but gives you the same level of service." "Tim was great about coordinating all the construction details." "They are world class, but a real personality."*

### Stephanie Stokes Inc.                    3.5      4      4      4
139 East 57th Street, New York, NY 10022
(212) 756 - 9922

*Understated, elegant, traditional interior design*

Stephanie Stokes receives kudos for her inherent sense of the classically traditional with a strong nod to the here and now. Clients say that she quickly develops a design vision that is pursued with focus and energy. Designs are often have an English heritage but are said to be brought to life with unexpected, intricate patterns, thoughtful accents and rich complementary colors, based upon customer preferences. Patrons include those from the more prominent neighborhoods of Manhattan, as well as Long Island, Westchester County, Washington DC, Colorado and Florida.

The majority of clients enjoyed the design process and are very happy with the results—particularly when their style interests were embraced by Stokes. Many mention her efficient professionalism, strong ownership and sensible, clever choices. We're told Stokes can take complete leadership, bringing the project to final move-in condition for out-of-town clients. However, clients with less design experience or less-formulated views, can feel a bit overwhelmed by the process.

Stokes charges a standard up-front design fee and retail prices for products. Oversight charges are in the typical range. Her experience, knowledge and organizational skills often allow for expedited design decisions, and she is personally involved with every client. She is also commended for incorporating the clients' existing furnishings. Many clients use the firm repeatedly, and recommend it to family members.

*"Seeing Stephanie's work is what made me hire her." "She has extraordinary vision." "Stephanie guided me to discover my own taste." "Brought me many choices to review. We even shopped in the D&D together." "To her credit, Stephanie has a lot going on, but she can be hard to reach." "She took care of every detail for me." "When the chair in the bedroom was too large, she worked with the upholsterer to find an excellent solution." "Though mistakes are always make on a project, we had a hard time coming to conclusion." "I would describe possible concepts with her, and miraculously they would appear. She is a mind reader." "I have known Stephanie since I was fifteen and would never consider anyone else in New York."*

| | Quality | Cost | Value | Recommend? |
|---|---|---|---|---|
| | + | $ | ◆ | ★ |

## Stephen Shadley
144 West 27th Street, New York, NY 10001
(212) 243 - 6913

| | 4 | 4 | 4 | 5 |
|---|---|---|---|---|

*High-end, residential interior design. AD 100, 2000.*

## Studio Sofield
380 Lafayette Street, New York, NY 10003
(212) 473 - 1300

| | 4.5 | 4.5 | 4 | 4.5 |
|---|---|---|---|---|

*Stylish, modern design and architecture*

William Sofield confidently and uniquely stimulates the senses with interiors that look hip, glamorous and slightly decadent all at once. Columns with gilded fluting, floating ceilings, polished concrete floors and a maximization of the natural lighting are signature elements. Sofield is best known for his interior design of the SoHo Grand Hotel and many other "boutique" hotels, the worldwide redesign of the Gucci, Boucheron and Yves Saint Laurent stores and the executive offices for Disney. Sofield Studios is about 30-people strong and takes on a wide variety of residential projects, ranging from metropolitan apartments to expansive estates with extensive landscaping, including Ralph Lauren's personal residences. He reportedly is just as happy working on the first apartment of young newlyweds as for the most esteemed. But for all, we understand that every detail must be precisely designed and executed.

Sofield graduated Princeton with a degree in architecture, urban planning and European cultural studies. After receiving a Whitney Museum fellowship, he apprenticed with a variety of architectural firms and craftsman, forming his own practice in 1989. In 1992, he cofounded Aero Studios, and in 1996 he established Sofield Studios with a strong interdisciplinary approach. Sofield Studios is known for its original looks that redefine the structural underpinnings and combine historical and modern materials. Project costs can range greatly as the firm often mixes pricey artifacts with a client's existing collections. Clients speak glowingly of the resulting decor. HB Top Designers, 1999, 2000, 2001.

*"He rises to all challenges with commitment and the ultimate execution." "He is dedicated to bringing the finest craftsmanship to interior design—inlaid leather, Italian carvings—nothing is too much to pursue." "Sofield's main interest is the successful marriage of functionality and fine detailing." "Bill is the only one that can make loft-chic look grand."*

## Susan Zises Green Inc.
475 Fifth Avenue, Suite 1200, New York, NY 10017
(212) 824 - 1170

| | 3.5 | 3.5 | 4 | 4.5 |
|---|---|---|---|---|

*Warm, layered, traditional interior design*

Clients turn to Susan Zises Green for her consistently tasteful design, three decades of experience and knowledgeable, professional staff. Many of Green's clients repeatedly seek her services and in some cases have had a working relationship with Green for a decade or more. We are told Green is exceptional at incorporating refreshing combinations of strong painted hues, clear patterns and rich chintzes with a nod to the English cottage or manor house. Clients applaud Green's warm and cheerful updated takes on traditional design.

She will take on a variety of projects, from those with modest budgets of $50,000 to larger full-scale design endeavors in large single-family homes. Many of Green's own staff members have been with the firm for more than fifteen years. The firm is reputed to be very organized and takes on around seven or eight projects each year. Most of Green's work takes place in Manhattan, but she has designed for clients in Palm Beach and elsewhere.

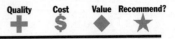
Green generally charges standard design fees and markups on products, and will also work on a consulting basis. Clients say Green truly loves her work and looks to connect both stylistically and practically with her clients. ASID. HB Top Designers, 1999, 2000, 2001. KB 1990, 1993.

*"Such a refined and elegant look, but amazingly comfortable and inviting." "I can always look to her for solid, tasteful design." "Everything was organized— from the initial design consultation right down to the itemized invoices." "She brings all the comforts of home." "Susan is impervious to fashion, much to our delight." "Susan's designs make you think of a more relaxed era."*

### T. Keller Donovan Inc.        4    3.5    5    5
325 West 38th Street, Suite 1101, New York, NY 10018
(212) 760 - 0537

*Fresh, colorful, traditional interior design*

Clients are enchanted with T. Keller Donovan for his good humor, livable interiors and traditional design sensibility infused with flashes of contemporary whimsy. He favors crisp lines, comfortable furniture and geometric shapes. Donovan studied at Parsons and then held apprenticeships with Barbara D'arcy, Tom O'Toole and David Easton. His client base is centered in New York and the southeast (his second residence is in Miami).

Donovan is noted for creating fresh interiors, many with jaunty colors that either coordinate or juxtapose. He is known to be resourceful, with an eye toward economical solutions, successfully mixing Hyde Park or Pottery Barn with clients' existing furnishings. He also enjoys finding wonderful objects in Europe. Donovan does everything himself and would have it no other way, focusing intensely on client service, according to his many supporters. He can start with just a few rooms or coordinate an extensive renovation.

The firm works with a design fee and a reasonable markup over net on products. Living rooms are often in the $70,000 arena. References say Donovan is very professional in his business dealings and is a good listener. Even other decorators say they would happily hire him. HB Top Designers, 1999, 2000, 2001. KB 1993, 1998.

*"Keller is such a sweetheart. I love his use of color and bold patterns." "I appreciate the way he mixes high style with comfortable living. He had very appropriate ideas, given the way we live." "He never guilds the lily." "The key to his decorating success is that our house does not look 'decorated'" "Keller's rich colors are so simple, yet so compelling." "He taught us everything, including how to arrange the books on the shelves." "He works 24/7. When he is not working, he is dreaming about improvements." "Any questions would be answered or fixed immediately." "He honored our economic priorities." "From the storyboards on, he knew exactly where we were headed." "We call him 'our Keller,' taking great pride in his success."*

### Thad Hayes Design        4.5    4.5    4    5
90 West Broadway, Suite 2A, New York, NY 10007
(212) 571 - 1234  www.thadhayes.com

*Classic, modern interior design*

Thad Hayes is considered to be at the top of his game, fueling a new group of younger designers with his leit motif of rigor, restraint and elegance. He favors calm backgrounds, spare and serene furnishings, intimate settings and warm, neutral colors. Often he will maximize the space in New York City apartments with a good deal of high-caliber, built-in furniture embellished with clean wood-toned trims. Accents of classic mid-20th-century furniture, fine art and wit distinguish the work.

Clients are often art collectors, the young establishment seeking the new classic style or modernists in search of the very best quality. Though Hayes is in high demand, he aims to please every client. He is described by customers as a warm and engaging man who is helpful until the end. Many applaud his drawings, including several architects of great note. Clients say he often will completely transform the character of their living space, including the artwork. Born in Louisiana with a modernist heart, he began his career with Robert Bray and Mike Schiable, and then started his own firm in 1985. The office includes eight and is said to be highly efficient.

Considered expensive but very fair, the lowest project cost is around $500,000 and can easily go into the millions. He is highly recommended for clients that share his essentialist, modernistic vision. AD 100, 2000. HB Top Designers, 1999, 2000, 2001.

*"Historic provenance meets the machine age." "The minute that I saw his work I knew that I wanted to live in it, and I was right." "He completely revitalized the utility and atmosphere of our apartment." "A forward-looking modernist with warmth." "Thad is very concerned that every welt and every hem are exactly correct." "Thad is philosophically devoted to the aesthetic melding of disparate notions that meld exquisitely in his hands. But you have to be on that program." "The amount of thinking that goes into each design is staggering, especially given the minimalist outcome." "He is perfectly suited to his line of work—very disciplined yet a delight to be with."*

### Thierry W. Despont Ltd.                    5    5    4    5
335 Greenwich Street, New York, NY  10013
(212) 334 - 9444

*Extraordinary, opulent interior design and architecture*

Thierry Despont's name is only spoken with awe. As the interior designer to Xanadu, Bill Gate's $50 million house, and to The Getty Center, the world's richest museum, he is in a class by himself. Other recent projects include the homes of Calvin Klein, John Gutfreund, Leslie Wexler, Oscar de la Renta, the Frick mansion and Ralph Lauren's flagship store in London. Lauded for his interior design, Despont often takes on the architect's role as well. He is recognized as one of the few architects or designers who can orchestrate the building of a gargantuan new home to look as if it had existed for generations. Despont's attention to detail is legendary. He is said to receive the greatest pleasure from fulfilling his clients' dreams.

Classically inspired and stylishly forward-thinking, Despont is said to worship the work of Palladio. Rotundas are Despont's favorite design element, which to him are "spaces with magic poetry." Despont's genius lies in his ability to make use of the most current technology to produce timeless masterpieces. His presentation skills are legendary. For Wexler's review of the plans for his 64,000-square-foot Columbus, Ohio home, Despont placed the large scale model in a blackened room. Upon Wexler's arrival, a simulated sun rose over the house, complete with mist and George Gershwin music.

While he maintains a residence in Paris, most of Despont's time is spent in New York, where his firm was established seventeen years ago. He studied design at the Ecole des Beaux-Arts in Paris, urban design and city planning at Harvard University, and then worked on the redesign of Tehran for the Shah of Iran. References say that he is extremely charming—dressing, speaking and decorating with the grandeur that only the French can summon with grace. We are told that he can decorate equally well in the English tradition and in contemporary styles. Patrons say that the net cost of the products and the corresponding fees of the firm are "inordinately" high, but worth it. ID Hall of Fame.

| | Quality | Cost | Value | Recommend? |
|---|---|---|---|---|
| | ✚ | $ | ◆ | ★ |

## Thom Filicia Inc.

| | 4 | 4 | 4 | 4.5 |

270 Lafayette Street, Suite 1001, New York, NY 10012
(212) 736 - 6454

*Modern, hip with warmth. HB Top Designers, 1999, 2000, 2001.*

## Thomas Britt Inc.

| | 4 | 5 | 4 | 4.5 |

136 East 57th Street, Suite 701, New York, NY 10022
(212) 752 - 9870

*Imaginative, colorful interior design*

Thomas Britt wins accolades from clients and peers for his creative twist on classical symmetry on a grand, glamorous scale. Large marble or stone entranceways, deep velvet upholstery, oversized arched facing mirrors and exuberant colors often factor into his aesthetic. References report that he particularly enjoys transforming ordinary spaces into spectacular showplaces with unexpected colors and eclectic groupings of artwork and furnishings. Clients say that he has a very distinctive personality, and hardly thinks twice before suggesting the removal of walls or the raising of ceilings. All describe finished rooms with wonder and delight.

Britt freely mixes reproductions with fine antiques and pieces from different geographic styles and various historical periods. Dhurrie rugs are often juxtaposed with silk curtains or Dutch marquetry, and many of the larger pieces Britt incorporates into his designs are purchased during his extensive worldwide travels. A native of Kansas City, Missouri, Britt studied at Parsons in New York and in Europe, and established his namesake firm in 1964. Britt has a loyal base in New York and in Kansas City, and has completed interiors worldwide. Clients have included Her Highness the Raj Mata of Jaipur, Princess Priya Ransit of Thailand, Ambassador Charles Price, the Frederick Woolworths and the Seymour Milsteins.

Clients say his prices are very high, but worth it for those without budget constraints. ASID. AD 100, 2000. HB Top Designers, 1999, 2000, 2001. ID Hall of Fame. KB 1995, 1997, 1999, 2001.

*"He marches to his own drummer. His work is interesting and spectacular." "He drives the bus." "If I won the lottery I would definitely use him." "He is neither short on imagination nor gusto." "He developed our unique, personal statement." "He operates on another level." "As a contractor, I must say that he is not easy to work with. But the results were dramatically impressive."*

## Thomas Hays Interiors 🛍

| | 3.5 | 3.5 | 4 | 4.5 |

248 West 23rd Street, New York, NY 10011
(212) 741 - 8548   www.thomashaysinteriors.com

*Eclectic-to-modern interior design*

Clients praise Thomas Hays for his clever transformations and his "out-of-the-box" creative thinking. Turkish carpets and Indian camel carts may make appearances in his work. Other projects incorporate a cleaner palette, evocative of a more natural setting. Hays uses line and form to distinguish his work, usually incorporating a range of eclectic elements and a splash of color. Clients note that there is often a focus in each room, highlighting a unique and creative object. Hays blends clients' interests and existing furnishings with his own design sensibilities to conjure a balanced result.

Hays received an MBA at Northwestern and was a banker in New York and London before becoming a designer. His design training includes study at numerous international institutions including London's Chelsea School of Design and the National Academy of Art in New York. His design firm was founded in 1996. Clients laud Hays for his unusual resources, both local and international. He is said to be just as skilled at doing a few rooms as an entire renovation.

Design fees are based on a very reasonable hourly rate and products are purchased at a very reasonable markup over net. While clients say that Hays encourages them to purchase high quality products, they also say that he is also sympathetic to economic constraints. Living rooms are generally in the $75,000 to $150,000 realm. Clients believe that he saves time and money with his "extraordinary" coordination skills.

"I have used Thomas for three projects in three years. He has that rare blend of a clear passion for design and financial savvy." "He's professional and a very good value, even though not cheap." "Well-balanced with an artistic touch." "He's fantastic with colors and found truly unusual pieces for my kitchen and bathroom." "He remains calm and professional at all times, and keeps the project running without any hoopla." "Thomas went out of his way to find some really stunning pieces." "One area floats into the next—people are amazed." "He stuck to the budget and the timeline." "He was on call like a doctor." "He capably managed the contractor and the architect as well." "A perfectionist who will never rest until the job is done right."

## Thomas Jayne Studio Inc. 🛍        4.5    4.5    4    4.5

136 East 57th Street, Suite 1704, New York, NY 10022
(212) 838 - 9080   www.thomasjaynestudio.com

*Historically-based, spirited American interior design*

Heralded for his preservationist expertise in all things American and appreciated for his design integrity, Thomas Jayne has won the respect of his clients and peers. While retaining a historic mood, he adds whimsy with high-spirited colors and modern accents. His designs run from fun to serious, but all references say they are gorgeous. Most clients note that Jayne is captivating company, highly focused and charmingly intent.

Jayne received a master's degree in American architecture and decorative arts from the Winterthur Museum. He then trained at the Cooper Hewitt, Christie's and Parish-Hadley. Clients say he takes his training seriously and believes in "period-pure" rooms without "gimmicks" or reproductions, though he will mix styles and give these rooms a comfortable, sophisticated touch.

His clients are generally well-funded art and antique collectors, often from the South and ranging widely in age. Projects include uptown townhouses and apartments, as well as homes in the metropolitan area, the Hamptons, Virginia, Maine and Palm Beach. Many clients are repeat customers—one or two own five residences all decorated by Jayne. By the time the fifth house is completed, it's time to do the first over again. Jayne reportedly has a hard time saying "no" to a client, sometimes accepting more jobs than he can handle. All, however, remark that he meets the important deadlines and is very conscientious.

The firm charges retail on products and a standard markup on antiques. Customers say Jayne has a strong preference for high-end fabrics (some quite over the top) and expensive rugs. Living rooms can start at $50,000 for "guerrilla decorating," but usually are $150,000-plus, and can go as high as the imagination with serious antiques. All believe that Jayne is quite earnest and honest. He is highly recommended by serious collectors of American antiques who are looking for intelligent quality with a modern twist. HB Top Designers, 1999, 2000, 2001. KB 1996.

| | Quality | Cost | Value | Recommend? |
|---|---|---|---|---|
| | + | $ | ◆ | ★ |

*"No one knows how to make formal Americana sing more joyfully than Thomas." "Working with Thomas is like a really good addiction, it is hard to stop once you get going." "He knows when he is right, but patiently waits for you to come around." "Timing used to be an issue, but now he has a hyper-efficient back office." "As a small client, he is clearly worth waiting for—he is always direct about timing and treated us with the utmost respect." "He has a passion for doing things the right way starting with the architectural bones." "When the rectory of his church was in disrepair, he took it upon himself to refurbish." "He has amazing common sense, great judgment and an original dry wit." "He is so calm, yet so specific and clearly a genius."*

### Todd Alexander Romano Interior Design     3.5     3.5     4.5     5
1015 Lexington Avenue, New York, NY 10021
(212) 879 - 7722

*Classical, high-end, residential interior design*

Todd Romano has a loyal set of clients who relate to his easy design elegance and helpful nature. Much of Romano's settings are founded upon classical American motifs highlighted with unexpected colors, inherited furnishings and rich details. He is known to interweave fine antiques with quality reproductions, creating a finished product at a reasonable price. Romano often works with architect Patrick Carmody, and clients say the two make a terrific team.

The firm works with standard design fees, standard percentages over net and reasonable hourly oversight fees. Romano is also available for hourly consultations. Most clients are the young carriage trade of Park Avenue and the suburbs referred by friends to their first real decorator. Other clients include more established homeowners who appreciate Romano's breadth of product choices. References report that Romano never pushes and has many interesting sources. Project costs average in the $250,000 to $500,000 neighborhood.

He recently opened a shop at the above address with furniture ranging from 18th-century English to 1970s Lucite. He is highly recommended by clients for the "right look" created with good humor, thoughtfulness and high-quality workmanship.

*"He took my inherited English and funky Victorian, and created something beautiful." "He has great Texas warmth." "He was able to do a great job with our first apartment, and then he created a whole new, more sophisticated and polished look for our Park Avenue apartment. I can't wait to see what he will do with the country house." "The cost of the children's beds were more that I expected, but they looked great." "He is a real gentleman. While my project was not very large, I got lots of attention." "He does not need to reshape the apartment to make it look good." "Todd even considered what colors I look best in, and flooded the house with those tones." "If I didn't like it, he would take it back." "Todd oversaw the entire operation really well." "He has a great group of custom vendors. The light fixtures were particularly fabulous and changed the whole construct of the apartment." "I would use him again in a heartbeat."*

### Todd Klein Inc.     4     4     4     4.5
48 West 20 Street, 4th Floor, New York, NY 10011
(212) 414 - 0001   www.toddklein.com

*High-end residential interior design. HB Top Designers, 2000, 2001.*

### Tom O'Toole     3.5     3.5     4     4.5
145 East 92nd Street, New York, NY 10128
(212) 348 - 0639

*Coherent, classic, warm, traditional interior design. KB 1994.*

### Tom Scheerer     3.5     3.5     4     4.5
18 Irving Place, Suite 1504, New York , NY 10003
(212) 529 - 0744

*Detailed, traditional-to-modern interior designs. HB Top Designers, 2000, 2001.*

| | Quality + | Cost $ | Value ◆ | Recommend? ★ |
|---|---|---|---|---|

## Tonin MacCallum Inc.

**3.5   3.5   4   4.5**

21 East 90th Street, New York, NY  10128
(212) 831 - 8909

*Fresh, color-saturated, traditional interior design*

With professional verve, a classic sensibility and strong integration skills, Toni MacCallum has been working with high-end interior design clients for over thirty years. Designs are often traditionally-based with a dynamic twist, but she very flexible in delivering a wide range of design styles. Clients say MacCallum spends a great deal of time upfront, learning about their lifestyle and interests. Reportedly, contemporary is executed with the same flair as traditional.

Clients range in age and in the scope of their projects. There is no minimum and MacCallum is acknowledged for her willingness to take a project in stages. While most of the work is in the New York area, past clients have enticed her to journey to Florida, California, New Orleans, London and Venezuela for second homes. Clients report that MacCallum is very much in control of the trades people, who know to remove their shoes before entering a cients' home. ASID. KB 1991, 2000.

Budgets have been known to be specific or to evolve. Pottery Barn is used as well as fine custom upholstery, and the client's own furnishings are often incorporated into the plans. MacCallum's frequent travels often lead to unique resources and "jeweled finds." A design fee is charged at higher hourly rates, with retail on products and a standard oversight fee. ASID. KB, 1991, 2000.

*"She really gets the laid-back old-world look, that does not have that decorator feel." "While the preppy look has just come back in style, it is something that never went out of style in Toni's designs." "My tired, old apartment has become something remarkable under Toni's guidance." "She is on the case daily." "Toni's style expands to meet the clients' desires." "While her focus can be a bit overwhelming to others, I love that can-do attitude." "I think I have the most extraordinary apartment in New York, thanks to Toni."*

## Tori Golub Interior Design

**3.5   3.5   4   4**

26 East 63rd Street, New York, NY  10021
(212) 583 - 9570

*Modern, classic interior design*

Drawn to her clean, modern aesthetic, clients are gravitating to Tori Golub for "great design" that is also comfortable, reasonably priced and functional. Supporters say Golub leans toward an edited style with a felicitous juxtaposition of period decor alongside more modern furnishings and thrift store finds, creating a look with an edge. Sources tell us Golub generally favors muted hues, with shots of color. Although her designs are simple and clean, they are not cold and very much speak to the wishes of the client.

Golub has been on the forefront of style for many years, first in the fashion business, then as a freelance stylist and then with Andrew Frank in interior design. Golub struck out on her own in 1996, and currently takes on about seven major projects each year. Many clients are young singles or young couples with families who appreciate her sensible budgets and fabrics. Golub is said to have an open view on the clients' existing furnishings, and exhibits an excellent touch with thrift-store finds, reinventing them into "works of art."

The firm charges standard design fees and reasonable product markups. A typical living room ranges from $60,000 to $100,000, and is based on a detailed budget, after presenting several design alternatives. Clients highly recommend Golub for understanding their design needs better than they do. HB Top Designers, 2000, 2001.

*"Tori grabbed the essence of what I was trying to accomplish very quickly and worked with me hand-in-hand to get it done." "She was really sensitive to the fact that it had to be safe and functional for the kids, but still stylish for us." "A very comfortable, homey version of modern." "Flea marketmania with a gorgeous touch."*

*"Tori was great with some architectural details, designing millwork that worked as a bar, bookshelf and entertainment center." "She adds a bit of glamour to all her work." "She is so hip and now—she totally transformed my space into a joyful refuge."*

## TW Black                                       4      4      4      4.5

33 Riverside Drive, New York , NY   10023
(212) 875 - 0014

*High-end residential industrial design.  HB Top Designers, 2000, 2001.*

## Vanderpoel Schneider Group              3.5    3.5     5      5

79 East 79th Street, New York, NY  10021
(212) 472 - 0405

*Warm, traditional, English interior design*

Sandra Schneider and Barrie Vanderpoel have been a mainstay of Park Avenue for decades.  Schneider joined Vanderpoel (her first cousin) two years after the firm was started.  They are described as masters of the authentic English-traditional look, classical but not overdone.  Clients say that the two principals are elegant and gracious, yet efficient and dependable.  Clients applaud the partners' strong design sensibilities and their sincere interest in developing the clients' ideas.

The firm is expert in executing complete renovations including the purchase of antiques, and is also willing to take on smaller projects.  Vanderpoel handles much of the City and Hobe Sound/Palm Beach clientele, while Schneider tends to cover the suburbs of New York.  While the partners accommodate a wide range of budget choices, they lean toward high-quality products.  Clients are particularly pleased with the planning stages, which takes into full account the client's traffic patterns and lifestyle.  A standard up-front design fee is charged—and products are purchased at retail.  Living room generally run in the $125,000 to $150,000 realm.  Clients note that while costly, the firm's expense is clearly worth the investment and that the timeless designs will always appear fresh.  KB 1996.

*"They deliver the perfect English country manor house reinterpreted for Park Avenue—not the scary chintz look.  This is not the American version of the English look, but the real thing." "Elegant, but completely livable for the children and the dogs." "They were incredibly accommodating—using lots of the curtains and furniture from our old house and taking me to the D&D to help choose the new." "They design for comfortable and happy living. The rooms are built around at least one fabric that I absolutely adore and there is always good lighting." "Opinionated, but plenty of room to for your taste." "They worked with my concept and cultivated it."  "Their designs stand up to the test of time and family wear." "They have good manners, an excellent attitude and will finish the job."*

## Vicente Wolf Associates                  4.5    4.5    3.5     4

333 West 39th Street, 10th Floor, New York, NY  10018
(212) 465 - 0590

*Dramatic, contemporary interior design*

Vicente Wolf is known for his distinctive design style, which includes handsome, strong lines and a noticeably lean palette.  Clients appreciate the drama in his work that is created with sophisticated monochromatic fabrics, compelling background textures, sculptural furnishings and careful editing.  Supporters note that he is a passionate designer with a true love of the creative process.  The firm usually brings its architectural talents to the table as well.

Wolf was raised in Cuba and moved to Miami during the revolution.  He started his design career by folding samples in the D&D showroom, eventually working with Bob Patino and starting his own business in 1988.  While Wolf is clearly the guiding light on each account, there are eight capable members of the firm and project coordinators on each job.  Customers include major entertainment executives, investment bankers and appreciative suburban homeowners.  While many embrace and praise Wolf's signature style, others say that he did not incorporate family character.

A well-known traveler and insatiable collector of eclectic furnishings, Wolf has recently opened a 3,000-square-foot retail space near Hell's Kitchen that showcases these purchases and his line of custom furniture. Many of these products are incorporated into his clients' designs at retail prices set by the firm. His sleek design sensibility can also be seen in licensed products manufactured by Hendredon furniture, Sasaki flatware and L.S. Collection dishes.

The firm charges a standard design fee, standard markups on products and higher oversight fees. Sisal rugs and over-the-top originals are used with equal aplomb, but greatly affecting pricing. AD 100, 2000. HB Top Designers, 1999, 2000, 2001. ID Hall of Fame. KB 1990.

*"The rooms offer a fresh, balanced tranquility with European flair." "Is the Richard Gere of interior design. He has the charm and spirit of an artist." "He works best if you walk away and let him create." "There is often one dark room which he thinks is mysterious and sexy." "He will clearly state that he is the professional and should hold the painter's brush." "While some of the fabrics are impractical and way expensive, they look amazing." "You basically know the look he will deliver, only it was 100 times better that I expected." "He orchestrated a metamorphosis of my home from a jumble of small rooms to something magnificent."*

## Victoria Hagan Interiors     4.5    5     4     4.5

654 Madison Avenue, Suite 2201, New York, NY 10021
(212) 888 - 1178   www.victoriahagan.com

*Cool, cerebral, edited yet elegant interior design*

Known for her sculptural, harmonious modern designs and her professionalism, Victoria Hagan stands out among the new set of contemporary designers. Clients praise the quality of her workmanship, her handsome and subtle neutral forms and her nod to modern comforts. Warm velvets and cashmeres enhance spare, clean, cerebral lines. Hagan's work is further distinguished by a generous use of fine antiques, architectural enhancements, natural materials and distinguishing eclectic embellishments. Designs are thoughtfully integrated into environments or settings. While references say that she is firm in her design opinions, they also acknowledge that she is determined to make her clients happy. Hagan reported presents clients with several possible scheme options, and works with the client to lead them through the process.

A graduate and Board Member of Parsons, Hagan founded her own firm in 1991. She accepts only a few projects per year and devotes significant attention to each one. Clients include Revlon head Ronald Perelman, movie director, Barry Sonnenfeld and the Bronfmans. While lesser knowns are taken on, projects scopes remain large and serious, and none are undertaken without a specific commitment. Recent commissions include a Greenwich manor house, a bucolic South Carolina retreat, a Westchester country home and several Manhattan apartments. An exclusive architectural consultant often works on projects with Hagan.

Clients are often repeat customers. It is said that the cost of her work is quite high (with budgets usually in the generous six figures), but well worth the expense and on budget. AD 100, 2000. HB Top Designers, 1999, 2000, 2001. KB 1990.

*"She is a pleasure to deal with and has a very good office." "Victoria is thoughtful, smart and interesting to work with, but she is not a pussycat. She gets it done." "I totally trust her design judgment and her process." "Her designs flow with continuity. Nothing distracts from the whole." "Everything is comfortable, with mostly neutral shades, yet there is still drama." "While the look is modern, most of the objects have a qualified and quality heritage, some old, some more contemporary." "While a model of restraint, her designs have energy with the unexpected in scale or form." "We asked Victoria to come look at the historic restoration of an important building, but she would not even talk to us without a consulting contract." "She makes a conscience effort to have a small, select clientele as to not spread herself too thin." "He designs are so livable, full of sunshine with room to breathe."*

# Hiring a Kitchen & Bath Designer

The perfect kitchen won't make you a great cook, and an all-marble bathroom will still need cleaning. But the fact remains that a kitchen or bath remodel can make your life at home enormously more pleasurable on a daily basis. They are often the two rooms that see the most use, and so their planning and construction deserve careful thought. A good kitchen and bath designer will listen attentively to a client's desires and incorporate them into rooms that are as functional as they are beautiful.

## Finding a Designer

Some architects, interior designers, space planners and certified remodelers dabble in kitchen and bath design. There are even "designers" who work for manufacturers and home improvements stores. But if your sights are set on a specialist, you'll want to look for a Certified Kitchen Designer/Certified Bath Designer (CKD/CBD). To get certified, the designer needs at least seven years of hands-on experience in addition to coursework, and must pass a series of tests administered by the National Kitchen and Bath Association (www.NKBA.org), the field's main professional organization. Remember, it's not a bad idea to inquire about your designer's involvement in trade organizations or whether he or she frequents trade shows. Even after certification, continuing education will enable a designer to stay abreast of current styles and the latest advances in equipment.

Most designers have either a showroom or portfolio to give you a sense of their particular style. You may think that you are on the same page when you talk on the phone, but when you see the ideas embodied in a room you may find that you have very different ideas of what a word like "contemporary" or "traditional" means. You'll be a giant step closer to getting what you want if you can find a designer whose style is similar to your own. Take a look at your prospective designer's recent work history while you're at it. At the very least, a designer should be able to produce three current references, and a history of two or more projects per month shows a healthy demand for the professional's work.

Finding someone you feel compatible with will make the whole process more pleasant and productive—especially if you see eye-to-eye on budgetary considerations. It will also help alleviate some of the inevitable stress. With the right designer, you'll be able to openly discuss such issues as project cost, time frame for completion, product information and warranty issues. You should feel comfortable asking for advice on the logical and functional placement of appliances, how to make cabinets childproof, lighting alternatives, your storage needs, personal preference for gas or electric stoves, the upkeep involved in tile kitchens vs. stainless steel and other design considerations. Also, do you want to work with the appliances you have or completely replace them? If you want new appliances, the designer may or may not coordinate their purchase. Don't assume that a designer can read your mind and know that you will not—under any circumstances—part with your matching canary yellow refrigerator and stove.

## On Cost

There are generally two ways in which designers can charge for their services. The first type of pricing structure is a percentage—about 10 percent—of the project's total cost. This type of fee schedule is common when the designer coordinates the entire project as well as supplies the artistic template. Coordinating the project includes ordering all materials and finding and managing the workers to install everything. This approach is often a good value. It also relieves you of having to find someone else to carry out the project, or of immersing yourself in the hassles of ordering and overseeing.

The second method of pricing is an initial fee called a retainer or pure design fee. If your designer charges a pure design fee, this means that your money buys only the designer's ideas and plans for creating the kitchen or bath of your dreams. The price will depend upon the designer's experience, education and general reputation and generally ranges from $65 to $200 or more per hour. The other possibility is a retainer fee. This usually includes the project design, and often covers the cabinetry deposit and any initial paper work necessary to get the ball rolling. In either case, most designers will deduct the initial fees from the total cost of the project as indicated on the contract.

It is imperative to discuss total cost prior to starting the job, of course, so you know what to expect. If you have your heart set on a new kitchen layout that requires new plumbing and electrical work, for example, know that this will be a more expensive renovation than one that involves existing systems. If the cost of such a renovation is more than you'd like to spend, work with the designer to match your dreams with your budget.

Once you've chosen a designer, you'll need a contract to protect both parties. No professional will be offended if you request one. The contract should spell out the services you are expecting and include a timetable for payment. Expect to part with a down payment of 40 to 50 percent to secure a good designer.

Many designers are sole proprietors, which means that the designer may be the only employee of the company. Others are part of a large firm with designers representing a range of specialty areas. Deciding whether or not to use an individual or a firm is a choice that depends upon your own style and the scope of your project: a firm's diverse collection of talent may come in handy if your project is especially complex. Some clients prefer dealing with one person, while others may feel more confident having a number of designers available. If, after speaking to a few of the vendors in this book, designers from both large and small firms interest you, make some comparisons such as their availability to begin work and how long they anticipate it will take to complete it. Their answers may help you narrow your search.

As with any major home project, you'll go through a period of upheaval when everything—including the kitchen sink—gets overhauled. But the result will be worth the trouble, whether your fantasy is to cook dinner for 20 with ease or to sink into a tiled Roman bath.

### TREND IDEAS

✧ **In the bathroom:** When space is at a premium, installing a bathtub may not always be possible. If you can't go without soaking yourself in relaxation, give your stand-up shower the capacity to be a "steam room." All it requires is the plumbing of the steam device, a tiled seat and sealed glass door. Hint: a frameless glass shower enclosure lends a spacious and seamless look to smaller bathrooms.

✧ **In the kitchen:** Use an open cabinet for storing all your everyday dishes and glassware. This will break up the monotony of all-doored cabinets and comes in handy when washing dishes—you'll duck beneath open doors less frequently. Placing your everyday dishes in open cabinets may also motivate you to clear out any mismatched pieces and to better organize your frequently used tableware.

| Quality | Cost | Value | Recommend? |
|---|---|---|---|
|  |  | |  |

# KITCHEN & BATH DESIGN

## Al & Dave Reglazing 3.5 3 4 4.5
16 Shenandoah Avenue, Staten Island, NY 10314
(718) 761 - 5800
*Bathroom tub and tile refinishing and reglazing*

Clients adore the staff at Al & Dave Reglazing, calling Dave the "teddy bear" of the company. Many report that in addition to great service, this firm offers an affordable alternative to renovating an entire kitchen or bath. The firm specializes in spraying and refinishing tubs, tiles, appliances and wood panels with both synthetic and enamel finishes. This family firm has spent the past 35 years servicing clients in Manhattan, the outer boroughs and lower Westchester County. We hear that their work crew is not only neat and tidy, but also offers friendly and competent service throughout the duration of the project. Some reports say this firm can be expensive, but admit it is a lot less money than replacement. Most clients appreciate the company's free consultation service, and attest to the accuracy of Al & Dave's own motto: "What Al & Dave sprays on, stays on!"

"Realistic and honest about the product." "Would recommend to friends."

## American Bath Company/I.P.R. Inc. 2 1 4 3
P.O. Box 2741, Babylon, NY 11703
(800) 244 - 2850
*Bathroom renovation, design, installation, respraying and regrouting*

We've heard that American Bath prides itself on "economically revitalizing" bathrooms—scoring big points with budget-conscious clients. Whether the project entails complete renovation or simple installation of bathroom fixtures, we hear this firm will cover the job for homeowners and the trade. American's services include installing and reglazing bathroom surfaces, and regrouting work for tub and tile. Clients from Central Park West to Battery Park City report satisfaction with both the service and the reasonable cost, and many comment on the staff's thoughtful handling of special requests.

## American Classic Kitchen Inc. 3 2 4 4
150 East 58th Street, 9th Floor, New York, NY 10155
(212) 838 - 9308
*Kitchen design, installation and appliance sales*

We hear American Classic Kitchen offers clients personal attention from the beginning stages of any project. A knowledgeable design staff works diligently to complete each job according to client's wishes and in compliance with the firm's 60-year standard of quality. Only a few references comment positively on the customer service at the showroom. Yet, many say this firm is thorough, overseeing not only the cabinetry design and installation, but also ensuring accuracy from its flooring and countertop contractors. Should anything go awry during the process, clients call American Classic's staff "great problem solvers."

American Classic Kitchens has a showroom, open to the public, which features four full kitchen displays. This firm is a certified dealer of Wood-Mode and Brookhaven cabinetry, and we hear American Classic retails all appliances at ten percent above wholesale price.

*"They taught us how to make the correct decisions along the way instead of dictating what we 'need' in our home." "When issues came up, they ate the cost."*

## Ann Morris Interiors, Ltd.

| | Quality | Cost | Value | Recommend? |
|---|---|---|---|---|
| | 4.5 | 3 | 4.5 | 5 |

515 Madison Avenue, New York, NY 10022
(212) 688 - 7564

*Complete kitchen and bath design*

Insiders say that Ann Morris designs for every room of the home, but specializes in beautifying kitchens and bathrooms. She has a reputation among clients for working within a range of styles—from ultra-contemporary to the more traditional, and her designs have appeared in a number of national publications. Morris is praised for her ability to transform a homeowner's wishes into her work. We hear she excels in communication and trust-building, especially when working with other members of the industry. Many former clients, now friends, return to her repeatedly for design consultation on outside projects.

*"Ann was responsible and always available during the project. We named her this year's 'greatest find.'" "Her designs have such personality."*

## Beverly Ellsley Design Inc.

| | Quality | Cost | Value | Recommend? |
|---|---|---|---|---|
| | 3.5 | 3.5 | 3.5 | 4 |

179 Post Road West, Westport, CT 06880
(203) 454 - 0503   www.beverlyellsley.com

*Kitchen design and interior design, custom handmade cabinetry*

References laud this mother-daughter interior design team for their expertise in high-end kitchen design and construction. Beverly Ellsley's style of "rustic elegance" is a favorite among clients. Known best for its exquisite custom cabinetry, we hear that Beverly Ellsley, along with daughter, Rebecca Ellsley and their 35 year-old firm will design, build and decorate entire kitchens for clients in Manhattan, Westchester and Fairfield counties. All cabinets are handmade and insiders say Ellsley's firm "builds what they design"—the hallmark of a Beverly Ellsley kitchen.

We hear the Beverly Ellsley design staff incorporates a unique interaction with clients from the beginning stages of wish lists and floor plans all the way through project completion. The staff "leaves little room for mistakes" and offers a lifetime guarantee on all of their work. KB 1992, 1996, 1998, 2000

*"Beverly is so knowledgeable—not only about kitchen cabinets—but about the way her clients will use the space. She takes the homeowner's lifestyle into account and designs a functional kitchen to match."*

## Bloom & Krup

| | Quality | Cost | Value | Recommend? |
|---|---|---|---|---|
| | 3 | 3 | 4 | 4 |

504 East 14th Street, New York, NY 10009
(212) 673 - 2760   www.bloomandkrup.com

*Appliance sales and installation, kitchen and bath products*

Since 1928, this well-established high-end dealer of kitchen and bath appliances, hardware, fixtures and cabinetry has served clients in all five boroughs, often working in concert with architects and interior designers. From their newly renovated showroom—now the largest of its kind in Manhattan—insiders say the company delivers virtually anywhere in the country. The showroom is equipped with everything from Subzero refrigerators to kitchen and bath hardware. Bloom & Krup also features an expanded Viking display and the latest in Miele convenience technology, including the steam oven and the complete coffee system.

While the installation work Bloom & Krup does is limited to appliances, the firm will also recommend contractors for other work. Clients say a knowledgeable staff is always on hand to help them. However, we also hear the Manhattan showroom is often busy, so be sure to make an appointment.

*"I have been using them for fifteen years. It's a great operation."*

| | Quality | Cost | Value | Recommend? |
|---|---|---|---|---|

## Broadway Kitchens & Baths Inc.

**3    2    4.5    4.5**

819 Broadway, New York, NY 10003
(212) 260 - 7768  www.broadwaykitchens.com

*Kitchen and bath design, installation and appliance sales*

No, the UKW is not an industry association. Rather, it stands for the "Ultimate Kitchen Warrior"—a client-dubbed nickname given to manager Jeff Chinman for his quality kitchen creations. Since 1995, Chinman and his staff at Broadway Kitchens have been servicing the New York City area in everything from custom kitchen design to supplying faucets and plumbing fixtures. We hear Broadway's 2,000-square-foot showroom is a manageable resource for clients, equipped with a knowledgeable staff, computer-aided design technology and a unique selection of "New York City-friendly" appliances. Broadway Kitchen's cabinetry lines include Canac by Kohler and Plain & Fancy.

*"Once everyone moved into their condos, we gave Jeff a punch list of minor repairs or adjustments. The residents were so impressed with the quality of the kitchens and service that they began ordering additional cabinetry." "Aces across the board." "I was so pleased with their work for my construction firm, that I'm hiring them to do my kitchen at home."*

## Bulthaup Kitchen Architecture

**4.5    5    3.5    4**

578 Broadway, Suite 306, New York, NY 10012
(212) 966 - 7183  www.bulthaup.com

*Kitchen design, German cabinetry and home furnishings*

This German company has been in operation overseas for 50 years, having arrived in New York only recently. Bulthaup views its high-end work as distinct from that of other kitchen companies in that it employs the European approach of designing the kitchen as the "center" of the home. According to clients, there is more to Bulthaup's design principle than one may realize. In fact, many admit to being surprised upon discovering Bulthaup's broad selection of styles—from the ultra contemporary almost industrial look to muted kitchens with a more traditional appeal. Bulthaup works mostly with architects and designers and the firm's contemporary-style cabinetry has been described as "the Mercedes of kitchens."

*"Totally apart from other kitchen companies—they have much more in furnishings and free-standing units." "They really have captured that sharp European look that I wanted for my client's new kitchen, and the space remains warm and inviting."*

## Cardinal Kitchens Inc.

**3.5    3    4    4.5**

301 East 58th Street, New York, NY 10022
(212) 888 - 8400

*Kitchen and bath design, installation, flooring, lighting and electrical work*

We hear that at Cardinal, quality kitchen design and installation is not just any business—it's a family business. For more than 50 years, the third-generation staff at Cardinal Kitchens has been serving residential and commercial clients in Manhattan and the surrounding area. These craftsmen perform a wide range of services from design to gut renovation. Working as contractors for larger projects, the staff does flooring, countertops, lighting and electrical work in addition to its standard services. At the Cardinal showroom, there are four full kitchens on display and several smaller vignettes. We also hear the firm has its own manufacturing facility.

Cardinal is a certified dealer of CE cabinetry. Clients remark on the company's friendly showroom staff, and compliment the work, calling it "good quality" at reasonable cost. References appreciate that the foreman is an owner and is always present for client assistance.

*"They promised completion of the project within 60 days and finished in 52!" "Throughout the entire job, they always kept me updated." "The most friendly staff. We are so pleased."*

| | Quality | Cost | Value | Recommend? |
|---|---------|------|-------|------------|
| | + | $ | ◆ | ★ |

## Christians of New York

| | 4.5 | 4 | 4 | 4 |

1020 Madison Avenue, New York, NY 10021
(212) 570 - 6371

*Luxury kitchen and bath design and custom cabinetry*

Internationally esteemed by clients and members of the industry, Christians has a reputation for delivering top-quality design and installation of kitchens, bathrooms, bedrooms and dens reminiscent of the English Country tradition. Clients include many high-profile media and entertainment figures, top designers and architects. Sources say Christians' professional and knowledgeable staff will introduce clients to a variety of stock designs, which are of custom-made quality and detailing—at a lower price than most custom work. References praise the entire process of working with Christians, calling the overall experience "luxurious."

*"The perfect English look with excellent quality." "A Christians kitchen is an exquisite kitchen—I recommend them for my best clients." "The staff works with you to perfection . . . A surprisingly good resource for issues outside of cabinetry design."*

## Christopher Peacock Cabinetry

34 East Putnam Avenue, Greenwich, NY 06830
(203) 862 - 9333   www.peacockcabinetry.com

*Highly-detailed, custom cabinetry*

See Christopher Peacock Cabinetry's full report under the heading Millwork & Cabinetry

## Culin & Colella Inc.

632 Center Avenue, Mamaroneck, NY 10543
(914) 698 - 7727

*Custom millwork and furniture*

See Culin and Colella Inc.'s full report under the heading Millwork & Cabinetry

## Custom Design

1388 Lexington Avenue, New York, NY 10128
(212) 410 - 0634

*Kitchen and bath design and installation*

We hear that Custom Design sells and installs cabinets, appliances, electric plumbing and HVAC—specializing in all aspects of kitchens and bathrooms. A large public showroom offers a wide selection of products including Wood-Mode, American Best, Dynasty, Viking, Fridgidaire and Kitchen Aid. The staff charges for floor plan and estimate service, but that fee is ultimately deducted from the cost of the client's project. Custom Design works mostly in Manhattan and has been doing so for more than 20 years.

## Custom Spraying and Reglazing      3.5    2     5     5
232 Sand Lane, Staten Island, NY 10305
(718) 556 - 5996 www.sprayingandreglazing.com

*Porcelain and kitchen appliance reglazing, wet electrostatic refinishing*

After twelve years of service to both residential and commercial clients in all five boroughs, James (Jimmy) White and his staff claim that years of experience is what led them to expertise. Insiders say this small operation handles a very large list of prestigious clients including Lincoln Center and the Waldorf Astoria. Custom Spraying and Reglazing offers a strictly cosmetic service, refinishing both porcelain and metallic surfaces for tub, tile and major appliances. This firm specializes in wet electrostatic refinishing, which is said to be safer and more efficient than traditional methods and is often requested by clients. Fees are based on labor and cost, with a two-year conditional warrantee. Over-the-phone quotes are available.

*"Jimmy and his staff are experienced and reliable. I've been using them for years." "For a guy with a small operation, he does a very good job."*

## Dura Maid Industries      3    2.5    4     4
130 Madison Avenue, 6th Floor, New York, NY 10016
(212) 686 - 0246

*Kitchen and bath design and installation and complete renovation*

Flexibility is what clients say draws them toward Dura Maid Industries for their renovation projects. We hear this firm works with every type of style, designs everything from kitchens and bathrooms to entire apartment renovations, and can accommodate budgets ranging from middle market jobs to the more exclusive. Clients remark that even more pleasurable than the high quality service is the firm's cleanliness and efficiency.

Dura Maid carries Wood-Mode, Brookhaven, Craftmaid, Merit, Cabico and several lines of appliances including Viking, Subzero and Kitchen Aid. The firm works primarily in Manhattan, but will accept jobs in the Hamptons and Westchester and Fairfield counties. Dura Maid's clients often pass on the business by way of personal recommendations.

*"I was very pleasantly surprised at Dura Maid's cleanliness both during and after the renovation—it was one less thing for us to worry about." "Guita is really on top of her projects. She took me shopping around town for the products I had in mind and made great suggestions, especially for my flooring."*

## Elgot Sales Corp.     3.5    3     4     4
937 Lexington Avenue, New York, NY 10021
(212) 879 - 1200

*Kitchen and bath design, installation, renovation and appliance sales*

Elgot is a family-owned company in business since 1945. Insiders say the firm works strictly in Manhattan with the trade as well as retail customers. Specializing in the design and installation of kitchens and baths, we hear Elgot's strengths include a solid understanding of how to navigate some of this city's unique renovation obstacles (difficult neighbors, traffic issues, late deliveries, narrow apartments, etc.). Clients appreciate the variety of options available at Elgot's showroom, but we are told that some occasionally feel a bit pressured in deciding which products to use.

Contemporary, Mega and Plato cabinets are among the lines Elgot carries. We hear that many architects and decorators depend on Elgot for appliance purchases and installations at "decent prices" with a great upper-end selection.

*"Coordinated every phase of a total gut renovation of my kitchen without a hitch." "It lasted one month, start to finish, with every detail carefully executed." "There was very little hand-holding and guidance throughout the process, which is fine for most, but my husband and I were very indecisive."*

| | Quality | Cost | Value | Recommend? |
|---|---|---|---|---|
| | + | $ | ◆ | ★ |

## Euro Concepts Ltd.

|  | 4.5 | 3.5 | 3.5 | 4 |

1100 Second Avenue, New York, NY 10022
(212) 688 - 9300   www.euroconceptsltd.com

*High-end kitchen cabinetry design and installation*

Top tier and budget-friendly, insiders say that this firm creates kitchens for the "decorator's decorator." The professionals at Euro Concepts offer design and installation services, in addition to dealing a variety of high-end appliances. After 30 years in business, this firm has gained quite a following among clients who are quick to praise its innovative kitchen designs. Now with two show-rooms—one in Manhattan and another in Huntington—we hear this company carries Downsview and William Ohs cabinetry, and offers every style spanning country, modern and classical.

*"Their design team is ingenious—they were actually able to harmonize my husband's and my wacky taste with something more simply-stated." "Were able to create a classic, yet modern space, timeless and elegant."*

## Gracious Home

|  | 4 | 4 | 4 | 4.5 |

1220 3rd Avenue, New York, NY 10021
(212) 517 - 6300   www.gracioushome.com

*Kitchen and bath design*

Gracious Home's service department provides repair services for all small household appliances, such as vacuum cleaners, toaster ovens, toasters, irons, blenders, etc. They are factory-certified to perform repairs on Hoover and Miele products and offer a three-month parts and labor warranty on all their repairs. While they don't respond to round-the-clock service calls, Gracious Home is open seven days a week.

Patrons suggest Gracious Home as a terrific place to shop for kitchen and bath appliances as well. With a "no hassle" return policy, Gracious Home enables you to bring home different bathroom fixtures and accessories so that you can really see what looks the best in your own home. However, the store does not offer any design or installation services.

## Hanssem Intelligent Kitchen

|  | 3 | 2 | 3.5 | 4 |

157 West 72nd Street, New York, NY 10023
(212) 501 - 8000   www.hanssem.com

*Exclusive Korean kitchen cabinetry, design and installation*

A recently expanded product line, paired with what sources call semi-custom capability, enables Hanssem Intelligent Kitchen to accommodate a broad spectrum of client budgets and special requests. This firm's exclusive Hanssem cabinetry line has been industry-renowned since 1970 as the first Korean kitchen furniture exporter. Hanssem offers full design services for all of its products and is an appliance dealer as well. However, the firm does not do any installation work.

Sources call the Hanssem design staff flexible and patient, although the same may not always be said for a handful of its subcontractors. The majority of their work is done in Manhattan and the outer boroughs, with occasional jobs in surrounding areas.

*"The showroom staff was responsive. Although, lack of communication with the contractors led to a few minor problems with my cabinet specs." "The staff is patient and professional."*

## Homeworks

|  | 3 | 2.5 | 3.5 | 3 |

132 West 17th Street, New York, NY 10011
(212) 620 - 7070

*Kitchen and bath design, marble, stone and tile installation*

With more than ten years at its Manhattan location, Homeworks has earned a multitude of affluent clients including homeowners and the trade alike. The firm offers full design and installation services and its showroom carries product lines such as Brookhaven, Richmade, Paris and Yorktown. Although Homeworks does not sell tile, the firm does install all kinds including marble, granite, limestone and ceramic, among others.

*"Handle design through installation of full kitchens and floors at a good price."*

## Kitchen Solutions Inc.
4.5     4     4.5     5

1086 East Gun Hill Road, Bronx, NY 10469
(718) 547 - 6100   www.kitchensolutionsinc.com

*Custom kitchen and bath design, countertop and cabinet sales and installation*

Kitchen Solutions has been in business for 42 years and has done multimillion-dollar jobs in some of the toniest neighborhoods in New York City. Clients report that even more impressive than the firm's high-end work is its extraordinary ability to customize and "make any project work." Specializing in high-end cabinetry such as Rutt and Siematic, insiders say they constantly add to their showroom, and now feature Pyrolave—an illustrious form of French lava stone. Satisfied customers tell us how much they enjoy working with the group and are impressed by how well the staff can "anticipate a client's needs." Even though the company does not install, its staff is willing to recommend people who can.

*"They act as liaison between architect and client . . . so all facets of design are accounted for." "The Rutt looks beautiful—I never thought the design would work as well as it does." "I return again and again because they really bend over backwards to customize for my clients."*

## Kitchens Etc.
149-42 Cross Island Parkway, Whitestone, NY 11375
(718) 352 - 8818

*Kitchen remodeling, architectural detailing*

In business since 1959, Kitchens Etc. designs and installs kitchens and baths for clients in Manhattan, the outer boroughs and Nassau and Westchester counties. The firm also does custom architectural work and we hear these professionals can accommodate all styles of cabinetry. For most projects, the shop design and some of the installation work is done in-house, with the remainder of the work assigned to a team of outside subcontractors. The staff at Kitchens Etc. encourages clients to visit the company's new showroom in Whitestone, which features cabinet lines such as Wood-Mode and Brookhaven, as well as a selection of kitchen appliances.

| | Quality | Cost | Value | Recommend? |
|---|---|---|---|---|
| | ✚ | $ | ◆ | ★ |

## Krup's Kitchen & Bath

| | 4 | 2 | 5 | 3.5 |

11 West 18th Street, New York, NY 10011
(212) 243 - 5787

*Exclusive kitchen appliances and bathroom fixtures*

The staff at Krup's deals in high-end appliances sold to the trade and public, and has been doing so for almost 25 years. Although there were reports of some delays, most customers praise the company's ability to take the necessary steps in preventing or correcting any issues. Many award the company a high quality rating, with reasonable pricing to boot. Krup's showroom is open to the public, and features both European and domestic lines. This firm has a reputation for staying on top of current trends by constantly attending trade shows and keeping the latest product lines in stock.

Krup's carries a wide selection of appliances, domestic and international, including AGA (England) and La Cornue (France).

*"When our stove delivery was held up, they promptly tracked it down for us and had it brought to our home." "Any and everything they carry is state-of-the-art." "They're on time and on price . . . I use them for all my kitchen jobs."*

## Leesam Kitchen & Bath

| | 3 | 3 | 3.5 | 4 |

124 Seventh Avenue, New York, NY 10011
(212) 243 - 6482   www.leesamkitchens.com

*Kitchen and bath design and installation*

Family owned and operated, Leesam has been designing kitchens and baths in the New York Metro area since 1932. Insiders say this firm uses computer-generated designs at its showroom to work up stock, semi-custom and custom plans for its clients, who are mostly residents of the Upper East and Upper West Sides. We hear Leesam's showroom also features kitchen displays and smaller vignettes, vanities, bathroom fixtures, shower enclosures and more. Clients value the guidance and insight offered by the company's professional staff saying that Leesam's unique service "enhances the experience."

Leesam carries several lines of kitchen cabinetry products available at retail and to the trade, including Raywal, UltraCraft and Adelphi.

*"David masterminded the whole project. He sat down with me for an hour and created a computer-generated design for my kitchen and I hired him because of this special attention. His guidance really made the project a pleasure." "Our granite countertop broke while they were moving it into the kitchen area and David replaced it—free of charge!" "Their subcontractors are well-versed craftsmen."*

## Linda London Ltd.

200 East 62nd Street, New York, NY 10021
(212) 751 - 5011

*Comprehensive home and office organization*

See Linda London Ltd.'s full report under the heading Closet Designers

## NDM Kitchens Inc.

| | 5 | 2.5 | 5 | 4.5 |

204 East 77th Street, Suite 1E, New York, NY 10021
(212) 628 - 4629   www.nancymullan.com

*Gourmet kitchen design, interior design, complete renovation and contracting*

Clients call designer Nancy D. Mullan a "traditional New York Lady." Reports show that she will design any room of the home (although kitchens are her forte) and will do so with great care and attention to homeowners' needs. From the culinary novice to the professional chef, Mullan begins each project by interviewing her clients and having them complete a ten-page questionnaire. By doing so, this expert has a more accurate idea of her clients' lifestyles, and can proceed accordingly with her "inventive" designs. One client, a caterer, used Mullan to transform her family kitchen into a professional one and told us she could not have been more pleased. Another hired Nancy to renovate an entire apartment and reports reflect that they are elated with the result. References show that Mullan oversees all aspects of a job, and her sub-contractors and craftsmen receive stellar reports as well. We are told she manages the project with strict attention to detail. Clients laud her ability to finish on time and on budget, and say that during the project she's flexible, easily accessible and fun to work with.

Mullan studied at Parsons School of Design and has been practicing for eighteen years. We hear the bulk of her clientele is in New York City, New Jersey, Connecticut and Long Island, and is quite high-end. She handles projects across the United States as well, and has done some as far afield as the Bahamas. In reference to her work, sources say she "designs rooms that people are drawn to." KB 1992, 1995.

*"Nancy and I worked as a team. Planning with her made me feel as though I had my best friend's opinion on everything!" "She is very eclectic in her abilities. I was most impressed with her hat-changing from designer/decorator to general contractor extraordinaire."*

## Neff by Design Concepts International Inc.    4    3.5    3.5    3
150 East 58th Street, 8th Floor, New York, NY 10022
(212) 308 - 9674  www.neffweb.com
*Fine Canadian designs for cabinetry, free-standing units and built-ins*

For more than 30 years, this company has been in business designing kitchens and baths, and shipping their products to clients worldwide. As its name suggests, it is an exclusive dealer of Neff cabinetry—a Canadian collection—on display in the company's showroom. We hear that when it comes to style, they design everything from country to contemporary. Further, customers marvel at the product's ability to adapt to a range of tastes, while still incorporating the unique space dimensions and "Z-cut" design that is exclusive to the Neff line. Satisfied customers comment on the firm's exceptional success in creating cabinet interiors, including drawer lining and interior shelves made of glass, steel, aluminum and exotic woods. Some say that, given its high-end pricing, Neff could improve upon customer service.

*"At first I was apprehensive about the option to paint my kitchen cabinetry, but when a staff member handed me the Benjamin Moore sample palette, I went to town choosing my colors." "Neff has a lot of options, and seeing the showroom helped me understand just how much is available."*

## Northernlight Saunas    4    3.5    4    4.5
167 Clinton Avenue, Kingston, NY 12401
(800) 344 - 0513  www.northernlightsaunas.com
*Luxury saunas and steam enclosures—custom and pre-fabricated*

Northernlight receives rave reviews from clients spanning New York City to Dutchess County. For twelve years, this company has specialized in the design and installation of custom and pre-fabricated saunas and steam rooms. Sources say the firm can integrate its products into any style home—from rustic to contemporary, while adjusting to specific client needs—therapeutic or otherwise. Although construction work is subbed out, Northernlight offers maintenance and repair on all equipment and includes a two-year warrantee on its products.

Northernlight uses soft steam technology and is a certified dealer of Finlandia, Helo, Amerec and Heartmate. Clients say the staff is polite and helpful, offering guidance during the challenging stage of choosing an ideal design.

*"Excellent. In fact, I'm hiring them again for another project of mine." "They were courteous when dealing with my clients and for me, that really stands out." "Personal and polite customer service."*

| | Quality | Cost | Value | Recommend? |
|---|---|---|---|---|
| | ✚ | $ | ◆ | ★ |

## Nu-Facers Kitchens & Baths

3    2.5    4.5    4

1368 Lexington Avenue, New York, NY  10128
(212) 426 - 4160   www.nufacers.com

*Cabinetry refacing, addition and installation*

Many clients say they were pleasantly surprised with the quality of work done by Nu-Facers and expressed enthusiastic satisfaction with their choice to reface kitchen cabinets rather than renovate.  More than a decade in the business has taught Nate Nowygrod and his staff that sometimes a facelift is more suitable for a galley kitchen than gutting and new construction, not to mention that it's easier on the wallet—and clients wholeheartedly agree.  The company does offer additional services including installation of new countertops, sinks, faucets, appliances, floor tiles and custom cabinet additions.  We hear that the Nu-Facers showroom has full kitchens on display and there is a fabrication shop on location.

*"They are honest and stand by their word." "The quality is par with the promise . . . It's not a brand new kitchen, but it looks and serves its function as one."*

## One to One Studio

6037 Fieldston Road, Riverdale, NY  10471
(718) 432 - 5986

*Decorative and straight painting, color consultations and kitchen and bath design*

See One to One Studio's full report under the heading Painters & Wallpaperers

## Poliform USA

150 East 58th Street, 9th Floor, New York, NY  10155
(212) 421 - 1220   www.poliformusa.com

*Closet design and installation, kitchen and doors sales and installation*

See Poliform USA's full report under the heading Closet Designers

## R.G. New York Tile

225 West 29th Street, New York, NY  10001
(212) 629 - 0712

*Tile installation and marble countertop fabrication, kitchen and bath design*

See R.G. New York Tile's full report under the heading Tile, Marble & Stone

## Rutt Kitchens of New York

4    3.5    3.5    3.5

150 East 58th Street, 9th Floor, New York, NY  10155
(212) 583 - 0638

*Kitchen design and installation, cabinetry, countertops and flooring*

We hear that Rutt of New York has made some significant changes over the past year due to corporate ownership.  However, aside from any internal restructuring, insiders report that they are continuing sales and design of Rutt cabinetry, in addition to product lines such as Plain & Fancy and Katherine Gabrielle.  This twelve-year-old firm has a Manhattan showroom, which references refer to as an excellent "source of ideas."  One client was thrilled to learn that the Rutt staff offers extensive services, which include providing countertops and flooring through the firm's affiliates.

| | Quality | Cost | Value | Recommend? |
|---|---|---|---|---|

## Siematic Corp.

Quality 4.5 · Cost 4 · Value 4.5 · Recommend? 4

150 East 58th Street, 8th Floor, New York, NY 10155
(212) 593 - 4915   www.siematic.com

*High-end German cabinetry, kitchen design*

When it comes to innovation, clients say Siematic is renowned for the unimaginable. In addition to a range of kitchen cabinetry styles, this firm has gadgets galore to insure convenience and product durability—while maintaining the design function and aesthetic. Sources say the showroom is spacious and features large-scale kitchen displays in a broad range of styles. The company specializes in high-end kitchen cabinetry and furniture, but also sells kitchen and bathroom fixtures, and offers some contracting services. Reports reflect that the Siematic reputation for quality is what keeps customers returning for multiple projects.

Although Siematic is a global operation based in Germany, the Manhattan location is praised by clients for its personal customer service. Clients say the staff is extremely helpful, asserting that more than 30 years in the business has earned Siematic true veteran status among industry insiders and homeowners alike,

*"They've thought of everything . . . the workers even attached tiny soft-rollers to my drawers so they won't scratch the cabinet interiors!" "At first I disagreed with my contractor, thinking Siematic was too contemporary for our taste, but it turns out they had exactly the traditional look we were going for on display in the showroom."*

## Smallbone of Devizes

Quality 4.5 · Cost 4 · Value 4 · Recommend? 4

105/109 Fulham Road, London, UK  SW3 6RL
(207) 838 - 3636   www.smallbone.co.uk

*Fine hand-painted English cabinetry, custom design and installation*

High-quality painted cabinetry is the hallmark of Smallbone of Devizes, a London-based firm with an elite following in New York and other hubs worldwide. This firm claims to allow clients to choose "any color from the 20 or so the human eye can detect" and will paint each piece by hand according to client-specified painting techniques. Smallbone uses a variety of woods for its cabinet construction, the most popular choices being: oak, olive ash, sycamore, pine, teak, maple and chestnut. Smallbone also designs custom furniture and wall-paneling.

Smallbone operates from overseas, and so, choosing its services can be a big commitment. To insure optimum client relations, the firm assigns a personal design team consisting of designers, a draftsperson and a professional installation manager to each project. Some clients report that the quality is not quite up to the price, while others are completely satisfied, praising the designs as "free-flowing, stately and elegant." KB 2001.

## St. Charles Kitchens of New York Inc. ∿

Quality 2.5 · Cost 4 · Value 2.5 · Recommend? 3

150 East 58th Street, 8th Floor, New York, NY 10155
(212) 838 - 2812

*Complete customized kitchens*

Located in the A&D building for almost 30 years, St. Charles Kitchens is a design firm that states it "solves design issues and caters to the millworking needs of clients." Many clients support this claim, referring to the firm's performance as consistent, efficient and professional. While a number of references report satisfaction with the quality of the work, they are reluctant to praise the customer service.

St. Charles works mainly in Manhattan but will also do kitchens outside of the city. We've been told that the company's 3,000-square-foot showroom is one of the only locations in the city where clients can find more exclusive brands such as La Cornue. Recent projects include Martha Stewart's studio kitchen and eleven test kitchens for *Gourmet* magazine.

| | Quality | Cost | Value | Recommend? |
|---|---|---|---|---|
| | + | $ | ◆ | ★ |

*"Always the first place I take my clients when we begin to tackle the kitchen design." "Great suggestions." "In hindsight I am very pleased with the quality of my cabinets, but communicating with the contractors during my project was a bit of a struggle."*

## St. James Kitchens 〰                3.5    3    4    4
102 East 19th Street, New York, NY  10003
(212) 777 - 4272  www.stjameskitchens.com
*Kitchen design and installation*

We hear St. James carries a broad spectrum of cabinetry styles from traditional to contemporary. After ten years in the business, the firm is a dealer of products such as Wood-Mode and Leicht, all of which come with a lifetime guarantee. Most references claim that a visit to the showroom is what led them to choose this firm. Some reported that showroom stock and samples are limited, but assert that the prompt customer service is "a big plus." Some expressed skepticism concerning the subcontractors used by St. James.

*"The style and quality of the showroom cabinetry is what led me to choose St. James." "The staff made really good suggestions." "Paul came to my home years later to do some repair work. I really appreciate that."*

## The Renovated Home             3.5    3    4    4
1477 Third Avenue, Suite 2, New York, NY  10028
(212) 517 - 7020  www.therenovatedhome.com
*Entire apartment renovation, kitchen and bath design and installation*

Since 1985, The Renovated Home has worked in Manhattan, primarily for an Upper East Side clientele. Well known by clients for kitchen and bath design and installation, this family-operated design and build firm is also experienced with full residential renovation. Numerous clients laud the firm's ability to meet time and budget requirements. In addition, customers comment on the high quality of both product and service, although a few express reservations about follow through. The Renovated Home has a 3,000-square-foot Upper East Side showroom. All services are provided in-house, prompting many to praise this firm's "one-stop" convenience.

*"They were very respectful of our home—and us." "Renovating in Manhattan is scary. Lee and Toby made things easy."*

## Tom Law & Associates                4    3    4.5    4.5
202 West 78th Street, Suite B, New York, NY  10024
(212) 362 - 5227
*Residential renovation, kitchen planning, design and general contracting*

Client reports describe this firm's work as "Park Avenue quality for the smaller space and tighter budget." Specializing in the design and renovation of kitchens and bathrooms, Tom Law and Associates have been renovating apartments in New York City for more than 20 years. Owned and managed by a husband-and-wife team, these professionals oversee all projects from conception to completion. The firm offers architects, interior designers and its clients a diverse blend of professional services including design and planning, general contracting and project management. The showroom is located in a historic brownstone near the Museum of Natural History on the Upper West Side, and is accessible by appointment only. Clients recommend Tom Law and Associates without reservation and say that Tom and Caroline really plan each project to perfection.

*"I love working with Tom—he's a real New York design professional." "Very reliable." "Tom likes to do high-end work—he takes pride in it. Regardless of the project size or cost, you are guaranteed great quality."*

| | Quality | Cost | Value | Recommend? |
|---|---|---|---|---|
| |  | $ | ◆ | ★ |

## Whitney Interiors Ltd.

| | 4 | 3 | 4.5 | 4 |

537 Broadway, 5th Floor, New York, NY 10012
(212) 219 - 9654   www.whitneyinteriors.com

*Kitchen and bath design, interior design and total project management*

Whitney Interiors has a lot to offer NYC homeowners seeking complete designs for kitchens, baths or other rooms of the home. References report that Colette Whitney excels in anticipating client needs and designs to accommodate them. We hear that the firm's home design review is helpful to those clients who are in the primary stages of project development and are in need of educational and creative guidance. Working with homeowners and in concert with architects and designers, the company is flexible in its style and is reputedly able to satisfy most tastes. Customers say that Whitney herself is easy to work with and that her friendly, professional staff strives to understand and deliver on client preferences. Whitney is the President of the Manhattan Chapter of the National Kitchen and Bath Association.

*"Colette Whitney has an excellent eye." "Listens to your requests and understands." "Colette put us in touch with the city's most professional product suppliers and retailers . . . great contacts!"*

## Yves-Claude Design

| | 5 | 3.5 | 5 | 4.5 |

199 Lafayette Street, Suite 4B, New York, NY 10012
(212) 625 - 9612   www.kanso.com

*Stainless steel kitchen design and home furnishings*

The word "adventurous" is a client favorite in describing Yves-Claude and his professional quality stainless steel kitchens. Insiders tell us Yves-Claude coined the term "essentialism," meaning that he creates only what a client needs—a philosophy apparent in his clean, sharp and industrial looking designs. We hear that although his work is contemporary and creative, it is far from over-the-top. In fact, Yves-Claude's designs are said to reflect his firm belief in mobility, longevity and adaptability. In addition to kitchens, Yves-Claude now features a new line of stainless steel furniture. Sources say that his creations are functional and stylish, and his work has piqued the interest of some big names in the industry.

Clients rave about Yves-Claude's select designs and warm-nature, calling the designer himself dependable, personable and inspired. Yves-Claude won the 1997 Food & Wine "Kitchen of the Year" Award.

*"Can a designer be too attentive? That would be my only complaint." "He never says 'it's impossible' and he has great manufacturers behind him."*

# HIRING A LANDSCAPE
# ARCHITECT/DESIGNER

Along with the hustle and bustle of living in New York City comes the need to be able to escape the concrete and bright lights and return to nature. The ultimate refuge is your very own green space where sunlight, plants, flowers, walkways, trellises—or simply a colorful flower box in the window—creating a delightful escape. The artisans who turn these dreams into reality are garden designers, horticulturists and landscape architects. Experts in both art and science, these professionals create natural havens in any type of space. Garden and landscape designers use plants and masonry to plan, design and construct exterior spaces—in the city, the suburbs or the countryside.

## MORE THAN PLANTING

Planning a garden paradise for your surroundings is a job for professionals, as many technical elements are involved. Garden designers create water and soil systems that are unique to city landscapes, and their craft requires a complex blend of botanical knowledge, construction expertise and creativity. Suburban or country projects can be more or less involved, incorporating large trees and bushes, masonry and rock formations, ponds and streams. In contrast, Manhattan landscape architects and designers are faced with the everyday challenge of creating an outdoor paradise in limited spaces that often sees little not have a great deal of sunlight due to the tall buildings in the city.

Service providers included in *The Franklin Report* reveal a common thread—artistry combined with a passion for creating the ultimate natural space to suit each client's unique habitat.

## WHERE DO I START?

The most general decision to make about your city garden or country landscape is what type of purpose it will serve. Are you a cook who loves using fresh ingredients and would like to build an herb, vegetable or cutting garden? Have you discovered the joy of exotic plants and wish to install a greenhouse for your orchids? Or are you dreaming of a superbly designed terrace with benches and several layers of growth? With your overall purpose in mind, take stock of the space available in and around your home. If you want to create a balcony or rooftop garden, are you primarily interested in shrubs, trees, vines or particular colors and species of flowers and plants? Is privacy—building a hedge to separate your yard from your neighbor's—an important issue? Do you prefer the informal charm of an English cottage garden or the elegance of a neoclassical French one? Keep in mind that the more complicated the design, the more maintenance of it is involved. Nurture your ideas by looking through home, garden and architecture magazines before you contact a garden designer.

Foremost in a landscape designer's mind is building a setting that can be enjoyed year round. The designer will have many ideas for you, but if you have done some research and fallen in love with specific plants and flowers, you will be a step ahead in designing your perfect oasis.

## ON COST

The pricing system for landscape design varies from firm to firm. Some designers charge an hourly rate—others determine a flat fee after analyzing the job. The average hourly rate in Manhattan is between $50 and $75, translating into a baseline of 3 for Cost in our book. Like other professional services, garden design companies will produce a written agreement for the client that lists what will be done and at what cost. It is not unusual for these agreements to leave room for flexibility in scheduling and pricing, should unforeseen circumstances, such as bad weather delaying the work, affect the job.

## WILL A DESIGNER ALSO MAINTAIN MY GARDEN?

Services provided by garden designers vary from firm to firm and depend on the scope of your project. Many companies provide a complete package of design, installation and maintenance, and thus establish a long-term relationship with the client. Other professionals are limited to design and consulting, and subcontract for installation and maintenance. Landscape projects can vary drastically in size and detail and therefore in degrees of maintenance. Discuss these aspects with your designer and make sure you're aware of the amount of attention your yard or garden will require. Like interior designers, garden designers, horticulturists and landscape designers work closely with clients on a one-to-one basis to bring their creative ideas to fruition.

## PERMITS AND PROFESSIONAL CONSIDERATIONS

A garden-design project may require a permit from your building management if you live in a downtown city apartment. Designers are well-schooled in this process and some will even intervene with a super-strict co-op board to get your plans set in motion. No license is required to be a garden or landscape designer, and these green specialists come from a variety of educational backgrounds, including degrees in horticulture, study programs affiliated with arboretums and botanical gardens, degrees in sculpture and other studio arts and lifetime experiences with plants and nurseries. Landscape architects, many of whom focus primarily on the hardscape aspects of garden design rather than on horticulture and maintenance, have degrees in the field and are licensed.

There are organizations such as the Association of Professional Landscape Designers (APLD) that continually educate the landscaping field by offering classes and conferences. Although it is not necessary for the landscape architect or designer to be a member of such an organization, it certainly enhances their qualifications. All the those drawn to the garden design profession, especially those devoted to the challenges of city landscapes, undoubtedly share the view of Thoreau, who wrote, "In wildness is the preservation of the world."

### HERBACEOUS PLANTS FOR ALL SEASON INTEREST

- ❖ **Asarum europaeum "European Wild Ginger"** An excellent ground cover for the woodland garden. The heart shaped leaves are glossy, dark green and it is evergreen in most places. This is a very hardy and lovely woodland plant.
- ❖ **Helleborus orientalis "Lenten Rose"** One of the finest early flowering plants in cultivation. The flowers begin in March and go through May. It also has semi-evergreen foliage and so it stays attractive during much of the winter. It needs to be cut back in early spring.
- ❖ **Liriope muscari 'Silvery Sunproof' "Lily Turf"** A sturdy member of the Lily family, the Liriope also bears very attractive lavender flowers in the fall. It can grow almost anywhere and is very easy to get established.
- ❖ **Pennisetum alopecuroides "Fountain Grass"** Great all season grass. Has attractive flowers during the summer and fall. This grass has great winter interest. Very handy, but can be slow to get established.
- ❖ **Sasa veitchii "Low Bamboo"** Summer foliage is a solid green and in the fall the leaf margins develop a tan to white border. The characteristic marginal stripe gives an attractive variegated appearance for outstanding winter foliage. It spreads slowly and grows well in the shade.
- ❖ **Vinca minor 'Ralph Shugert' "Myrtle"** Very pretty low variegated ground cover that is covered with purple flowers in the spring.

## LANDSCAPE ARCHITECTS/DESIGNERS

### Barbara Britton                    4.5    3    4.5    5
314 West 77th Street, New York, NY  10024
(212) 799 - 0711
*Garden design and consulting*

Clients say that Barbara Britton is a real professional and a phenomenal garden designer.   After designing, Britton will coordinate installations and maintenance.  She tells us she enjoys "working on gardens because they are, in a sense, public even though they're private," for ground-level co-ops, rooftop gardens and other shared spaces.  Many comment on her considerable talent and experience, flexibility, lovely manner and concern for clients.  Britton works primarily in Manhattan.

Sources rave that Britton delivers great value and can help clients maximize a budget— if you need to keep costs down by purchasing and installing plants yourself, she will happily design and advise.  Clients say that Barbara's hourly rate of $75 is a price that they would pay again and again without hesitation.

*"She listens and then she makes her suggestions and she is very cooperative. I've felt as though I'm working as part of a partnership." "Really a lady. Extremely polite." "I don't know where I would be without her. I can go away for weeks without worrying about this project." "Barbara is a true gardener's gardener."*

### Canyan Antiques & Design              4    4    4.5    5
9 East 97th Street, New York, NY  10128
(212) 722 - 0030
*Garden design and antiques*

Canyan Antiques is known by fans to offer the most stunning turkish marble stone garden containers in the city.  They also say that Ani Antreasyan's love of gardening can clearly be seen in the firm's beautiful landscaped terraces. Although Antreasyan has only been in business since 1996, she has been fascinated with gardening since she was a little girl.  Her love of ancient stone comes from accompanying her mother on archeological digs in Turkey.

Pleased customers and well-known interior decorators say that Antreasyan and her team of three create the most unusual and gorgeous urban gardens and rooftop terraces in Manhattan.  Her fees are calculated on a per project basis and the firm will not only design, but maintain its work.  The work of Antreasyan has been published in *House and Garden*.  KB 2000.

### Chelsea Garden Center Inc.          3.5    4.5    3    4
435 Hudson Street, New York, NY  10014
(212) 727 - 3434  www.chelseagardencenter.com
*Nursery and garden center, landscape design and contracting*

In addition to offering a huge array of trees, shrubs, plants, fountains, furniture and other accessories, clients report that Chelsea Garden Center provides a wide range of "green services," including landscape design and contracting, tree service and general horticultural consulting.  Owned and operated by David Protell, Chelsea Garden Center is one of the most widely recognized New York City nursery and gardening centers.

| Quality  | Cost $ | Value ◆ | Recommend? ★ |
|---|---|---|---|

Though sources caution that it may be more expensive than most, we hear that Chelsea Garden Center's agreeable staff, wide selection of unusual plants and easy accessibility within Manhattan makes it worth the cost, particularly for smaller jobs.

*"They tend to be a little pricey, I think, but they have unusual plants and I have good luck with them."*

### Cole Creates                                    5      4.5    4.5     5
126 5th Avenue, 8th Floor, New York, NY 10011
(212) 929 - 3210   www.colecreates.com
*Container garden design, installation and maintenance*

Clients enthusiastically support Rebecca Cole's low-maintenance, naturalistic gardens. Drawing on her experience as a passionate gardener and antique collector, Rebecca Cole opened her much-publicized Greenwich Village store, originally named Potted Gardens, approximately six years ago. Cole designs, installs and maintains rooftop and terrace container gardens around New York City—she also designs floral arrangements for festive events. Using just about any primitive or antique container, from washtubs to watering cans, iron sinks to wooden boxes, Cole advocates an organic, wild effect. We hear that although carefully designed and planned, Cole's gardens often look as if they were planted by nature itself.

Cole has even written two books on her carefree garden style: *Potted Gardens: A Fresh Approach to Container Gardening* and *Paradise Found: Gardening in Unlikely Places.*

### Corlett Horticultural Design       📁    📁    📁    📁
230 East 79th Street, New York, NY 10021
(212) 535 - 6759
*Landscape design*

### Dagni Senzel                                   4      4      4       4
101 Central Park West, New York, NY 10023
(212) 496 - 4107
*Landscape design*

### David Vaucher Garden Design & Care    4.5    3      4.5     4.5
185 West End Avenue, Suite 29P, New York, NY 10023
(212) 769 - 0724
*Urban Gardens—design, installation and maintenance*

Sources comment that David Vaucher's sensitivity and attention to detail is a combination that creates wildly beautiful urban gardens. Because David Vaucher Garden Design & Care is a small company, we hear Vaucher is able to pay close attention to and develop an ongoing relationship with each client. Vaucher founded his company in 1992, but he has been in the landscape architecture profession since 1987. Clients say he likes to be on site to oversee every step of the process, whether it's a city terrace or a country home. Believing that it takes more than one season to have a successful garden, he prefers working on projects where he will have long-term involvement.

Vaucher charges a design fee that is based on the extent of the project as well as an hourly fee. His passion for the field and interest in tending the gardens over time reportedly stem from the fact that he comes from a family of avid gardeners.

*"Simply the best!!" "I now have the most beautiful rooftop garden in Manhattan." "I never had to worry that the project would not go well."*

### Deborah Nevins         5    4.5    4.5    5
270 Lafayette Street, Suite 903, New York, NY 10012
(212) 925 - 1125

*Landscape design, installation and maintenance*

Interior designers and clients from all over the United States rank this firm at the top of the compost heap, which, in the world of horticulture, is a high honor. This small company of six designs and installs gardens in New York and has worked as far as Chicago, Texas and California.

According to clients, Nevins creates gardens that are not only spectacular in the spring, but in the winter as well. Paying close attention to the structural elements of rooftop terraces and gardens is one reason that sources say Nevins and her team is one of the best in the industry. Nevin's interest in gardens and horticulture began in childhood, and she founded her company in 1983. She personally visits the company's gardens, regardless of location, to oversee maintenance plans and procedures.

### Devore Associates       4    4    4    5
2557 Burr Street, Fairfield, CT 06430
(203) 256 - 8950

*Landscape architecture*

### Dimitri Nurseries Inc.       3    4    3    4
1992 Second Avenue, New York, NY 10029
(212) 876 - 3996

*Nursery and garden center, landscape design and contracting*

A family owned and operated business for over 42 years, Dimitri Nurseries carries a variety of products, including indoor and outdoor plants, trees, shrubs, soil, pottery, fertilizer, garden furniture, statuary, fountains, window boxes, baskets and irrigation systems. Open seven days a week, the company also offers on-site landscape design, contracting services and ongoing maintenance. Customers say that the quality of service at Dimitri Nurseries is not effected by the fact that they are one of the largest garden centers in Manhattan.

The firm charges hourly anywhere from $75 to $150, depending on the amount of people used for the project. Although the prices are high, customers are pleased with their gardens by Dimitri and rave that they always receive professional and personable customer service.

*"We have used Dimitri for three years and Dimitrios and his team always gives great advice regarding our rooftop garden." "My flowers always coordinate beautifully with one another. I don't know how they do it." "They showed me all of my options, and I knew exactly what to expect."*

### Distinctive Gardens       4    3    4.5    4
250 West 27th Street, Suite 6H, New York, NY 10001
(212) 414 - 0290

*Landscape design, installation and maintenance*

Robert O'Keefe of Distinctive Gardens has already made a name for himself among Manhattan landscape designers. Sources say that although O'Keefe has only been in business for six years, he is considered to be "a young gardener who

really knows his stuff." He prides himself on designing, installing and maintaining gardens that thrive in the city's harsh environment. Sources affirm that the talented O'Keefe has excellent horticultural knowledge and strong design skills.

O'Keefe studied Islamic courtyard gardens in Spain, while pursuing his degree in horticulture. Though he admires and enjoys working in that style, he is not restricted to it in his design abilities and garden creations. "I design gardens that work within a client's space and are conducive to his or her lifestyle," O'Keefe says. Clients are more than satisfied with the results, praising O'Keefe and Distinctive Gardens for their careful work, attentive service and attractive arrangements.

Robert O'Keefe will see his clients by appointment only.

*"Robert made the process entirely enjoyable and the end result was magnificent." "Their work is beautiful, just beautiful." "If you have something specific in mind, Robert is willing to search the country to find the right plant or garden accent." "I recommend him without reservation."*

## Edwina von Gal & Co.    5   4.5   4.5   5
11-17 43rd Avenue, Long Island City, NY  11101
(718) 706 - 6007   www.edwinavongal.com
*Landscape design, installation and maintenance*

Clients hail landscape designer Edwina von Gal for her elegant, simple designs that capitalize on the habit and nature of each plant she uses. She has been designing, installing and overseeing the maintenance and production of gardens for approximately fifteen years. While the firm is known to work primarily in the Hamptons, they will venture to the city.

Von Gal's talents, described as "prodigious" and "considerable" by her peers, have earned her an international following and an illustrious clientele. Though some of her designs incorporate flowers, von Gal also appreciates the clean line and texture of leaves, stems and pods, which gives her gardens a minimalist, modern quality. She has done a variety of residential and commercial projects throughout the United States and abroad, including the topiary animals of Rockefeller Center's Channel Gardens. Customers not only appreciate von Gal for her talent as a landscape designer, but say that working with the firm was a pleasure.

*"Working with Edwina and her team of landscape designers and architects was a fabulous experience." "She created a garden design that far exceeded my expectations." "Fantastic, fantastic, fantastic!"*

## Elsa Williams    4.5   2   5   4.5
1364 Lexington Avenue, New York, NY  10128
(212) 348 - 2794
*Landscape design, installation and maintenance*

Clients commend Elsa Williams for her great design and patient personality. Williams has over two decades of horticultural experience, and has earned a reputation for being thoughtful, knowledgeable and responsible. Williams designs, installs and maintains backyards, rooftop and terrace gardens, street trees and planters throughout Manhattan. Clients appreciate that Williams is a registered architect, adding to her talent as a fabulous designer. Sources praise her great taste, flair with color, the way her "arrangements thrive despite the challenges of the city environment" and her extremely reasonable pricing.

We're told that she listens well and tries to accommodate client preferences as much as possible. Clients also report that Williams is very experienced and flexible regarding budgetary constraints, particularly with co-op boards—as one put it, "She figures out how to deal with them in a satisfactory manner, despite how ridiculous the Board may be." Though some report that Williams can be hard to reach, particularly in the busy season, they are quick to add that they highly recommend her.

*"Elsa has great taste and flair for lovely bulbs." "Williams has a pleasant countenance that makes her easy to work with, especially in stressful situations." "Came*

*back time after time to teach me how to properly water." "Great feel for Park Avenue—delivered the most amazing and distinguished pair of spiral cut trees for our front door." "My window boxes are wonderfully color coordinated thanks to Elsa."*

## Estelle Irrigation Inc.          4.5   3   4.5   5
262 West 26th Street, New York, NY 10001
(212) 243 - 7209

*Garden irrigation systems and decorative garden lighting*

If you don't want your garden to suffer during your regular escapes to the Hamptons, you must either hire a firm to water and maintain your greenery, or install an irrigation system and handle the weeding and dead-heading yourself. Many of those who choose the latter consider Estelle Irrigation an essential Rolodex entry. We hear that most top Manhattan landscape designers call on Declan Keane and his team at Estelle Irrigation to customize, install and service irrigation systems for their clients' gardens. Keane was formerly a school teacher who watered plants for other people in his spare time. In 1990, he started his firm, and clients are grateful that he did.

Estelle Irrigation is geared toward urban, terrace gardens and the vast majority of its clients are in Manhattan. While the firm is most commonly contracted by a landscape architect or designer, about one fifth of its clients are private residents looking to purchase irrigation systems on their own. Estelle Irrigation handles almost every kind of system, from micro-sprays and sprayheads to drip-irrigation, customizing each setup to the site requirements and the clients' needs. Keane and his crew also can be contracted to provide troubleshooting and regular system maintenance. Clients and other garden professionals praise their excellent and dependable service.

*"They are clearly the best there is for your Manhattan garden." "Among landscape designers, everybody knows and uses him." "Low-key, good guy." "Due to Declan, I have the healthiest plants in Manhattan."*

## Florence Boogaerts Garden Design 🛍   4.5   4.5   4   4.5
316 Valley Road, Cos Cob, CT 06807
(203) 629 - 1297

*Landscape design and installation*

Since 1988, Florence Boogaerts has been the landscape designer at Sprainbrook Nursery in Scarsdale, New York, where she designs and supervises the installation of gardens and landscapes. According to clients, Boogaerts strives to create landscapes that are maintainable and beautiful. "I like it when clients have something specific in mind, then I can give it to them in a tasteful, practical manner," Boogaerts shares. While she does not offer long-term maintenance of her work, clients have been thrilled with her creations.

Boogaerts received her Certificate in Landscape Design from the New York Botanical Garden, where she has lectured since 1994. For the past eight years, Boogaerts has also worked independently for clients, primarily in Westchester and Connecticut, though she does do some work in Manhattan. In addition to a flat design fee, Boogaerts charges an hourly fee that ranges anywhere from $85 per hour to $150 per hour. Sources comment on her warmth, dry wit and intelligence, and call her designs and installations "appropriate" and "exactly what I hoped for."

*"No matter how many times I ask Florence the same question, she always answers with patience." "She really understands her clients." "Very talented designer."*

## GardenWorks

|  | 4.5 | 3 | 4 | 4.5 |
|--|-----|---|---|-----|

208 East 7th Street, New York, NY 10003
(212) 677 - 3920

*Landscape design, installation and maintenance*

According to experts in the industry, Gardenworks is a landscape design firm on the rise. The company is owned and operated by Brem Hyde, who has been designing, installing and maintaining landscapes primarily within Manhattan for the past seven years. Though Hyde and his small staff of six do it all, they especially like to work with grasses and full-flowering annuals. Hyde uses a variety of hardscape garden accessories in his creations, including rare hardwood containers and custom-designed pergolas. Hyde was recently quoted in an article on window gardens in *Martha Stewart Living* (April 2000), but his clients are quick to say that they discovered him first.

*"He's a very good person and a good gardener." "He and his work are just great." "Outstanding." "Whether Brem and his crews were working for me in the downtown Manhattan area or at my homes in Oyster Bay and East Hampton, they have been great to work with."*

## Glorietta Group

| 4 | 3 | 4.5 | 4 |
|---|---|-----|---|

720 Fort Washington Avenue, New York, NY 10040
(212) 928 - 4946

*Landscape design, installation and maintenance*

Clients are unanimously pleased with J.J. Brennan's designs and impressed with the personal attention he devotes to their gardens. Since 1996 Brennan has been designing, installing and maintaining rooftop and terrace gardens for the Glorietta Group. He prides himself on working with his clients to "bring their ideas to fruition." Sources confirm that Brennan and his assistant "listen very well," "work hard to design and install beautiful, lush gardens" and "take care of everything."

Despite the small size of the firm, Brennan has a total of about 20 regular clients. Regularly praised by customers for the high quality of work at a great price, Brennan charges a flat hourly rate of $45. We also hear Brennan takes a great deal of time with his clients to instruct them in light garden maintenance, if they wish.

*"J.J. is prompt, reasonably priced and has an unbelievable imagination that allows him to design gorgeous gardens." "He's really understanding." "He really takes care of the garden as if it were his own." "I love him. He's just great." "Very responsive to requests and pleasant to work with." "I liked his work, attitude and service orientation so much that I hired him to service my business facility as well."*

## Grass Roots Garden

| 4 | 4 | 4 | 4 |
|---|---|---|---|

131 Spring Street, New York, NY 10012
(212) 226 - 2662

*Landscape design, installation and maintenance*

In 1970 Larry Nathanson of Grass Roots Garden bought a house in Brooklyn and began to fill the attached greenhouse with plants, where we're told a passion for gardening sprouted. Nathanson, a graduate of NYU business school, started a career in advertising before spending more time doing research at the Brooklyn Botanic Library than at his work, and soon left to establish Grass Roots Garden. Today, Nathanson wins clients respect for his skill in designing, installing and maintaining residential and commercial landscapes and plantscapes throughout the city.

We hear he has two goals in mind when designing and creating gardens—they should be attractive, and the plants should grow over a long period of time. Clients say Nathanson hand-selects the best plant materials from his growers and in designing his landscapes he often forgoes planning on paper so that he can leave himself "open to the possibilities" presented by the availability of unusual plants. Resources comment on Nathanson's precision, commitment to quality and his artistic eye. His talent and attention to detail have earned him a number of notable clients—he recently finished a two-year project creating the largest private garden in the Caribbean.

Grass Roots Garden also is a retail store that carries a variety of plants, fertilizers, insecticides, orchid supplies, pottery from all over the world, garden books, gifts and more.

*"A truly talented artist." "A great guy."*

## Green Earth Gardens

**4    4    4    4.5**

7005 Shore Road, Suite 2F, Brooklyn, NY 11209
(718) 836 - 1754

*Landscape design, installation and maintenance*

We hear the Green Earth Gardens client list includes the most demanding Manhattan elite and upscale boutiques, and the firm takes on a range of projects, large and small. The company, owned and operated by James Johnson, is a small landscape design firm that can handle very big projects. Creating gardens in every style, clients tell us Johnson and his crew design, install and maintain landscapes throughout New York City and beyond. In his effort to realize his clients' dreams, Johnson has, since the firm's inception in 1994, reportedly designed and installed everything from a rain forest (which actually rains) to a Zen dry landscape garden. Sources say he also oversees the Narrows Botanical Gardens in Brooklyn. There he has installed a variety of gardens, including a sandbox that he converted into a water garden and a native plant garden. At 4.5 acres, it is the largest community garden in the New York City area and is visited by hundreds each year.

Johnson finds designing for ten acres or a terrace equally challenging—he claims, "I can create just as much surprise and intrigue in both spaces." Sources completely support his assertions, calling his designs "truly exciting."

*"Very skilled." "Adaptable."*

## Greg Yale Landscape Illumination

**4.5    4    4.5    4**

27 Henry Road, Southampton, NY 11968
(631) 287 - 2132

*Landscape lighting design, installation and maintenance*

Sources praise Greg Yale's careful planning and the balanced, subtle effects and absence of glare in his lighting schemes. A nationally recognized expert in the landscape lighting field, it is said Yale has been working to inform and reshape the landscape architecture and design world through lighting. Landscape lighting has been steadily growing as a significant niche within the lighting design world and an important part of landscape architecture and design. We find private residents are discovering that carefully planned illumination of the natural environment can beautify their properties, extend hours of garden use, and contribute to home security.

*"A master." "His lighting reshaped our property. At night, looking out, we can still enjoy our garden. It's just beautiful."*

## Halsted Welles Associates Inc.

**4    3.5    4.5    4.5**

287 East Houston Street, New York, NY 10002
(212) 777 - 5440

*Landscape design, installation, maintenance*

Halsted Welles is commended by customers for his ability to do it all when it comes to landscaping. The firm brings together engineering, architecture, horticulture, construction and maintenance all under one roof. Welles, the owner and main designer, came to landscape design through a background in sculpture. Involved in "a little of everything," the firm does fireplace planning, masonry and

metalwork, from ornamental iron to elaborate aluminum gazebos. The company has over 30 years of experience and includes a multitalented crew of architects, horticulture designers and artisans.

Clients appreciate the way Halsted Welles Associates handles every aspect of garden design, including hardscape features like arbors and pergolas, garden lighting, irrigation systems, pools and fountains and all plant design and installation. According to Welles, the firm's current passion is "the design of gardens and garden processes that are ecologically sensitive, including water nutrient recycling, water tables to limit the need for irrigation and nontoxic pest control."

*"They are reliable and respectful of working in a co-op building and not a townhouse." "Amazing maintenance team." "Totally in-depth service, one-stop shopping." "I have great respect for Halsted and his company—they are extremely talented, reliable and thorough."*

## Higher Ground Horticulture     3.5    3    4.5    4
470 West 24th Street, Suite 14E, New York, NY 10011
(212) 691 - 3633

*Landscape design, installation and maintenance*

Supporters of Higher Ground Horiculture say that the firm creates gardens that clients can truly be proud of. Mark Davies started Higher Ground Horticulture five years ago, and has been designing large and small gardens throughout New York ever since. As well as designing, he also installs and maintains plantscapes and landscapes. Davies brings years of experience with indoor plantings, which clients consider this to be his specialty.

## Holly, Wood & Vine      4    3    4.5    4.5
212 Forsyth Street, New York, NY 10002
(212) 529 - 7365

*Landscape design, installation and maintenance*

Industry leaders say that Peter Diffly and Bill Meyerson are owners of one of the hottest landscape design firms in New York. They design, install and maintain gardens throughout New York for the city's elite, including John Leguizamo and Lee Bailey. Despite the client list, we hear that Holly, Wood & Vine will take on jobs as small as a window box and as large as an entire garden. Peers in the industry comment repeatedly on the firm's well-known reputation as talented, top designers who provide excellent care and client coddling.

Customers rave that the firm's prices are a phenomenal deal. On average a rooftop terrace runs anywhere from $15,000 to $20,000. Maintenance is around $50 per hour. Diffly and Meyerson work with eight employees, and the company takes on twenty to thirty new projects each year.

*"I have used Peter and Bill for a number of years and they have yet to let me down."*

## J. Mendoza Gardens Inc.      4    4    4    4
18 West 27th Street, 11th Floor, New York, NY 10001
(212) 686 - 6721

*Landscape design, installation and maintenance*

Pleased customers say that Jeff Mendoza is fluent in numerous garden styles, from English to Japanese gardens and beyond, and that he draws on his international travels and extremely wide plant vocabulary. Recognized as a "master" by his peers, Mendoza is known for his skillful color combinations in creating landscape designs. In business since 1987, he designs, installs and maintains gardens and grounds throughout New York and the Hamptons.

Adept at balancing plants of the correct hue and value in his landscapes, Mendoza also works expertly with texture and form in his plant compositions to create soothing or energetic arrangements. Mendoza recently spoke about the

| Quality | Cost | Value | Recommend? |
|---|---|---|---|
| **+** | **$** | **◆** | **★** |

issue of color in plant and flower selection at the New York School of Interior Design. References comment on Mendoza's professionalism, expertise, excellent service and calm demeanor.

*"I am in love with my galvanized metal flower boxes." "His passion for gardening is so inspiring." "A true artist." "Remarkable."*

### Jane Gil Horticulture                    4.5    3    5    5
290 Riverside Drive, New York, NY 10024
(212) 316 - 6789

*Landscape design, installation and maintenance*

Sources praise Gil's talents as a horticulturist and designer, and say that her client care and attention to detail are top-notch. We hear Gil designs, creates and maintains many gardens, including for several illustrious clients in Riverdale. Overseeing all aspects of garden creation and care, Gil and her three-man crew are said to install all plants, supervise tree maintenance and take care of all irrigation and grounds issues. She tells us, "When I take on a new client I first determine their particular needs and preferences. Then, using my suggestions, we work together to create a garden that is unique to them." Though most of her work centers around these Riverdale properties, Gil also does Manhattan terrace gardens.

After leaving her position as the plant buyer with Surroundings, an established New York City plant supplier, Jane Gil embarked on extensive horticulture training at the New York Botanical Garden. Gil does not design in any particular style or restrict herself to any particular types of plants. She strives to create variety for her clients to enjoy throughout the four seasons. According to clients, Gil has done just that.

*"My experience with Jane has been fabulous in every way. She has worked for us responsibly, creatively, intelligently and energetically for 20 years." "The most wonderful aspect of her work is the full, unending palette that's always changing." "Jane is great to work with and has incredible taste."*

### John Merryman Landscaping                3.5    3.5    4    4
278 Mulberry Street, New York, NY 10012
(212) 925 - 6808

*Landscape design and installation*

### Judith Maniatis Garden Design ■         4.5    3    5    4.5
101 North 3rd Street, Brooklyn, NY 11211
(718) 782 - 5731

*Terrace gardening—design, installation and maintenance*

Clients agree that Judith Maniatis marries beautiful containers with coordinating plants in a wide range of colors and textures. The company specializes in container gardening, particularly terrace gardening, in and around the New York area. Sources say she draws on an extremely wide plant vocabulary in creating her designs and is known for her use of exotic annuals.

Maniatis and her staff of two install and maintain gardens all around the city. Clients comment on Maniatis' "meticulous" garden maintenance and her friendly demeanor. The firm is also respected throughout the landscaping community and has worked alongside top landscape architects, planting their designs. Maniatis charges a design fee of $125 an hour and she charges $45 per man per hour— a price that clients say is a steal. Sources only hesitate to recommend Maniatis because they are reluctant, as one client says, to share her.

*"Judith has an amazing ability to arrange the most stunning color combinations." "Tremendous sense of color." "I was impressed not only with her designs, but I found her fees to be extremely reasonable." "Always cleans up afterwards." "She is a marvelous gardener. What will happen when the word gets out?"*

### Kevin Lambert                 4.5    4    4.5    4.5
2025 Broadway, New York, NY 10023
(212) 877 - 2297

*Terrace design, installation and maintenance*

Clients are impressed by Kevin Lambert's imaginative solutions regarding landscape design and tell us he is unbelievable with penthouse gardens. Throughout the years, Lambert's landscape business has narrowed its focus to terrace design and maintenance. Lambert has a small circle of clientele that he works with for years at a time. According to Lambert, he tries to concentrate on the seasons that his clients are most likely to use their terraces. They say he specializes in flowery extravaganzas with vines, flowering tropical plants, shrubs and interesting containers.

Although clients remark that he is not the cheapest man in town, they all believe that he is well worth it. Lambert has an extensive background in landscape architecture and has worked alongside many well-known landscape architects and floral designers.

*"Kevin is expensive but about the same as competitors. He creates fabulous outside gardens and also parties and Christmas decorations." "Imaginative solutions given with diligent care."*

### Landgarden Landscape Architects        3.5    3.5    4    4
215 Park Avenue South, New York, NY 10003
(212) 228 - 9500

*Landscape architecture*

We hear this firm is particularly noted for its strong use of rocks and plantings, and touted for its "fine designs" and "true expertise." Since its founding in 1991, Landgarden, led by David Harris Engel, Dennis H. Piermont and Michael Spitzer, has designed public and private projects throughout the United States and abroad, earning the respect of clients and peers alike. This firm's design philosophy "to promote a partnership between the natural and the built environments" contributes to an end result that clients say is an original and economically sound landscape.

### Laurel Hill Farms                4.5    4    4.5    5
2 Laurel Hill Drive, Valley Stream, NY 11581
(516) 791 - 5676

*Landscape design, installation and maintenance*

We hear that Sherry Santifer is consistently ahead of trends when it comes to landscape design. For example, she has been incorporating tropicals into her work for the past six years, while others are just beginning to add them to their plant palette. With roughly 20 years experience, Santifer of Laurel Hill Farms has a very impressive track record of designing, creating and maintaining a wide variety of gardens in, around and above the urban landscape. Her considerable talents have not gone unnoticed, as her client list includes an international elite that Santifer is too discrete to indentify.

Santifer also specializes in forcing bulbs. She draws on this talent to create designs with a wide variety of texture, color and interest, references report. Her work has been extensively recognized at the Philadelphia Flower Show.

Sources report that Santifer and her small staff of five provide the same impressive level of excellence in customer care as they do in garden design. If clients wish to be involved in light garden maintenance, Santifer is more than happy to train them. If, however, clients want the garden oasis without the work, the Laurel Hill Farms crew will take care of absolutely everything. Clients could not be more pleased with Santifer and highly recommend her.

"Meticulous." "Great client coddling." "Very knowledgeable horticulturist and a very impressive person."

### Madelyn Simon & Associates Inc.     3.5   3.5   4   3.5
510 West 34th Street, New York, NY 10001
(212) 629 - 7000

*Landscape and plantscape design, installation and maintenance*

References claim that this firm stays on top of everything. With a staff of 80-plus employees, Madelyn Simon & Associates (MS&A) provides a dizzying variety of "green services" to commercial and residential clients throughout Manhattan and beyond. MS&A offers fresh and silk flower arrangements, outdoor furniture and accessories, seasonal displays, irrigation systems, as well as complete landscape and interiorscape design, installation and maintenance. Uniformed, experienced field personnel go to clients' homes for regularly scheduled maintenance and pride themselves on offering top-quality, ongoing garden care.

While references caution that they "do not have the same attachment to MS&A servicemen as close friends have with their personal landscape designers," they insist that they receive variety and interest in design, great plant and garden care and extremely good value for their money. Clients also comment on MS&A's initiative, reporting that the staff "calls ahead to confirm regular appointments," "arrives on time" and leaves sites "neat and well-tended."

"They really take the initiative and call ahead to make appointments to come service my garden." "Madelyn Simon & Associates have made sure I've received a great deal of enjoyment from my garden over the years." "Really, really great."

### Madison Cox Garden Design     4.5   5   3.5   4
220 West 19th Street, 9th Floor, New York, NY 10011
(212) 242 - 4631

*Landscape design*

Madison Cox's work is known, respected and admired in discriminating design circles worldwide. Trained at the Parsons School of Design in Paris in "environmental design," a program which integrates architecture, interior design and landscape design, Cox creates public and private gardens internationally for the most discerning interior decorators and residential clients.

Customers appreciate Cox's academic approach to garden design. While Cox strictly designs, contracting out the installation and implementation of his work to other firms, he prides himself on his ability to "interpret and realize clients' dreams." Though resources caution that his work is expensive, they also say that it is worth it. KB 1991.

"I learned so much about my garden from Madison, he was a great teacher." "If you're considering a project with Madison Cox, it can get quite pricey." "Madison Cox really is among the very best." "He is an absolute darling!"

## Mary Riley Smith Landscape Garden Design  4  4  4  5

200 West 72nd Street, Suite 27, New York, NY 10023
(212) 496 - 2535

*Landscape design*

References are all "just thrilled" with Mary Riley Smith and her work. In New York City circles and beyond, Smith is considered among the best of the best in landscape design. Smith renovated and now oversees the prestigious Cooper Hewitt Museum garden, which is generally recognized as the best gallery garden space on Museum Mile. Smith is known for designing gardens with four seasons of interest, incorporating a wide variety of plants, from shrubs and evergreens to exotic annuals.

Smith also includes pots, urns and trellises in her designs. While she does work throughout Greenwich, Bedford and the Hamptons, approximately half her clients are in Manhattan. Smith contracts out and then oversees all garden installation and is happy to train her clients or their gardeners in maintenance techniques. Concerned by the number of poorly planned and underused front properties, Smith wrote *The Front Garden: New Approaches to Landscape Design,* in which she provides creative ways and detailed plans for making front gardens both decorative and functional.

*"Mary made the planters for the front of my building. She has great carpenters." "Mary is fabulous." "THE ONE."*

## MetroScapes  4.5  2  5  4.5

16 Burnett Terrace, West Orange, NJ 07052
(973) 243 - 5585

*Landscape design, installation and maintenance*

Clients agree that Bill Mitchell not only has great artistic sensibilities, but he is also a pleasure to work with. We hear MetroScapes is a small, up-and-coming landscape design firm owned and operated by Mitchell. Since 1996, Mitchell has been designing, installing and maintaining gardens around New York City. He also serves as a contractor, helping other landscape designers actualize their garden plans. We're told Mitchell has a history of interest in plants and plant design dating back to early childhood—"In the third grade I was the one they looked to to take care of the class plants because they knew I wouldn't kill the African Violet." Years later, after leaving a career in computer design, Mitchell went back to school to study horticulture at the New York Botanical Garden.

New to the field, Mitchell is not yet associated with a particular style of garden design and he is open to client suggestions. His current projects include penthouse, sculpture and terrace gardens, and the owners report that they could not be more pleased with Mitchell's reasonable pricing. Additionally, references comment on his "lush and beautiful design," the pride and enjoyment he takes in his work and his "true artistic sensibilities."

*"Bill takes great pride in his work . . . he brought his parents around to see the garden." "He is a delightful young man, and our garden is just beautiful." "He's the nicest guy, and he does great work."*

## Mingo Design LLC 🛍

| | 4 | 4 | 4 | 5 |

470 West End Avenue, Suite 7D, New York, NY  10024
(212) 580 - 8773

*Landscape design, installation and maintenance*

Kari and Andrew Katzander and their small team at landscaping firm Mingo Design have a reputation for offering brilliance on a budget.  The firm designs, installs and maintains a variety of gardens and grounds throughout the New York area.  Kari Katzander brings a strong family background in contracting, having gained experience with her father's company restoring farms and farmhouses.  After fifteen years of owning her own landscape maintenance and design company on Fishers Island, she brings considerable practical construction and installation knowledge to her position as the creative director of Mingo Design.  Andrew Katzander contributes a design and contracting skills gained at both the New York Botanical Garden and the Pratt Institute.

This partnership strives to "bring the outside in and the inside out" in their designs.  Sources mention the firm's commitment to designing with four seasons of interest, its use of color and the trust they have developed in the Mingo Design team and its contracted staff.  Mingo Design's commitment to finding the best craftsmen to implement its designs has led to the firm's evolution to include contracting work, bringing the Katzander's full circle.  In addition, a request that Kari Katzander use her eye for color to coordinate her clients' interior decor with their newly installed Mingo Design garden has led her to expand the firm's repertoire.  Having recently established the firm in the worlds of contracting and interior design, they have arrived with their latest venture in designing the rooftop terrace for MTV's The Real World.

*"Kari cared passionately about the design both in terms of the large concepts and the small details that make the project sing."  "Kari and Andrew were both extremely professional."  "Tremendous talent at excellent value."  "They took a great deal of time to assess our needs, learn our tastes and resource contractors who could work within our budget."*

## Nadine C. Zamichow Inc.

| | 4 | 4 | 4 | 4.5 |

205 East 69th Street, New York, NY  10021
(212) 517 - 9317

*Landscape design, installation and maintenance*

Resources admire Nadine Zamichow for her flexibility, efficiency, horticultural talents and agreeable nature.  If you've walked around Washington Square Park or NYU, you have probably admired the work of Zamichow.  For the past 20 years she has designed, installed and maintained gardens throughout Manhattan—her largest long-standing client is NYU.

With a large base of private residences as well, Zamichow has long enjoyed designing and executing a variety of projects for a very disparate client base.  "I love the diversity of my clients," she declares, and insists she is not restricted to big-budget projects or gardens of any particular size.  She is willing to "do anything in any style."  Clients rave that she is great at sticking to a budget.

*"Nadine is a good listener and is able to imagine what the client is thinking about and then plan and develop the idea into a wonderful reality."  "Nadine is the only woman in the history of commerce who sticks to an estimate."  "I look forward to her work every spring."*

## Patricia S. Ouderkirk Landscape Design

| | 4 | 3 | 4.5 | 4.5 |

49 West 70th Street, Suite 3, New York, NY  10023
(212) 799 - 4870

*Landscape garden design—backyard*

Patricia Ouderkirk is hailed by clients as being detail-oriented and always listening to their needs.  Ouderkirk has been designing gardens in both New York and the Hamptons for ten years. We hear her successful career evolved from years of loving gardening and plants and completing the program at the New York Botanical Garden.

Ouderkirk is not only a member of the APLD but she is also on the board. Clients and professionals say that her expertise is in designing backyard gardens. While Ouderkirk subcontracts the installation of the project, references say that she is "hands on" and stays involved with every aspect of the process.

*"What we got is a garden worth waiting for. She included many of our old favorites in the planting plan and also chose some new ones that we like very much but would have never thought of ourselves." "Patricia was imaginative, thoughtful, patient and considerate of our budget."*

## Peter East                                    4        3       4.5      4.5
310 East 49th Street, Suite 11D, New York, NY 10017
(212) 832 - 2899
*Terrace design, installation and maintenance*

Englishman Peter East has over eighteen years experience in designing and maintaining rooftop gardens and terraces throughout Manhattan. East is recognized among clients for a pleasant demeanor and congeniality that makes him a joy to work with. East's passion for gardens came when he was working on his own Manhattan terrace. Aside from designing and maintaining the actual terraces, he also sets up watering systems for the gardens and terraces. He works with his clients from start to finish, and we're told they appreciate his weekly visits to keep the plants fresh. They say limiting his engagements only in the city allows East to spend more time with each client. Despite the individualized attention that East gives his clients, they all say that his prices are quite reasonable.

*"Peter's arrangements on our private rooftop garden are balanced and interesting and combine privacy and openness. Plus Peter and his assistants are responsive, courteous and always pleasant." "When it comes to aesthetic concept and design, Peter East is an absolute genius."*

## Plant Fantasies                               3.5      3       4.5      4
224 West 29th Street, 7th Floor, New York, NY 10001
(212) 268 - 2886
*Landscape design, installation and maintenance*

Owner of Plant Fantasies, Teresa Carleo and her team of fifteen have been landscaping around Manhattan and the Hamptons for fourteen years. Both residential and commercial clients remain pleased with the customer service and the high quality of work this firm offers. We hear Carleo handles everything from the design to the irrigation for the project. Resources say that the company also does a fabulous job with Christmas decorations.

Considering herself to be self-taught, Carleo began her landscape design career working for other landscape design firms. Clients say she makes sure to use plants that compliment the environment and are also considered to be quite maintainable. The firm charges reasonable rates on a per project basis and monthly for maintenance.

*"Teresa is great to work with because of her enthusiastic but not overbearing personality." "Not only is Teresa a gem, but everyone at the company is so responsive to my needs."*

## Plant Specialists 🗂                           4        3.5     4.5      4
42-25 Vernon Boulevard, Long Island City, NY 11101
(718) 392 - 9404   www.plantspecialists.com
*Indoor and outdoor garden design, installation and maintenance*

Despite the large size of Plant Specialists, clients enthusiastically approve of the specialized attention they receive. Founded in 1973 by Timothy and Dagny Du Val, Plant Specialists is the only top-quality firm in New York that personally designs, implements and maintains all aspects and areas of landscape design, from flooring and furniture to irrigation and decorative lighting systems. The team consists of 50 talented landscape architects, designers and horticulturists. We hear, in fact, that over the years some of Manhattan's most talented gardening experts have worked for Plant Specialists and later "graduated" to their own independent firms.

Though Plant Specialists provides a wide variety of services, including fresh floral contracts and firewood delivery, clients tell us a majority of its work involves installation and maintenance of Manhattan rooftop gardens. We hear its decades of experience have contributed to the firm's mastery in designing and implementing gardens tailored to the location's existing conditions and clients' needs. Timothy studied at both the New York Botanical Gardens and the Royal Botanic Gardens in Kew, England. We are told that Plant Specialists is so well regarded that the firm regularly serves as contractor to other top-name landscape designers, installing gardens of its competitors' design. References praise the professionals at Plant Specialists for combining "ease and elegance" and are amazed by their ability to do it all.

*"Tim was responsive and he always promptly returned my phone calls." "Amazing rooftop gardens." "With them, it's top-quality, one-stop shopping."*

## Roger Miller Gardens                     4      4      4      4.5
771 West End Avenue, New York, NY 10025
(212) 662 - 6142

*Rooftop and terrace garden design, installation and maintenance*

From shady first-floor patios to sunny rooftop container gardens, references report that Miller's 20 years of experience and expertise enable him to create pleasing gardens in challenging sites. Clients comment on Roger Miller's flexibility, attention to detail, charming personality and strong ability to correct and respond to site problems through skilled design. With his staff of ten, he also serves as a contractor for others' designs.

He is known to individualize his designs from space to space and client to client, creating gardens that work well with their surroundings and that meet his clients' tastes. Appreciative clients say that his respect for their budget is a breath of fresh air. We also hear that Miller strives to design with a wide variety of plant materials from year to year so his clients can always experience something new and enjoy an assortment of greenery. Miller's clients applaud his painstaking efforts and enjoy his amusing sense of humor.

*"His design is wonderful. Despite the constraints of the space, he found ways to give me a lot of choice . . . Roger is very willing and diligent." "I couldn't be happier. I have nothing negative to say about him." "His manner is lovely. He's very trustworthy and accessible." "He ALWAYS answers his cell phone." "Roger is terrific." "He's ethical, responsible and he listens."*

| | Quality | Cost | Value | Recommend? |
|---|---|---|---|---|
| | ✚ | $ | ◆ | ★ |

## Rosedale Nurseries Inc.

3.5     3     4.5     4

51 Saw Mill River Road, Hawthorne, NY  10532
(914) 769 - 1300

*Nursery and garden center, landscape design and installation*

Well known among its peers, Rosedale Nurseries has a sizable client base in Manhattan.  Rosedale offers a full range of landscape design and contracting services.  References verify that the firm carries a considerable selection of high-quality, unusual plants and that the staff is comprised of helpful, knowledgeable horticulturists.  From street tree service to terrace garden installation, sources report that Rosedale Nurseries is a reliable choice.

## Semperflorens Inc.

4     4     4     4

223 West 14th Street, Suite 1B, New York, NY  10011
(212) 627 - 1477

*Rooftop, backyard and terrace gardening*

Customers commend Beverly Perkey and her small staff of three for creating gardens using organic techniques.  Semperflorens has been in business since 1994, known for design and installation of rooftop terraces and gardens through-out Manhattan.  Perkey, however, will only maintain the gardens that she installs.  The company charges on a per project basis and also charges, according to clients, a reasonable flat design fee.

## The Metropolitan Gardener

4     3     4.5     4.5

344 West 23rd Street, Suite GLF, New York, NY   10011
(212) 675 - 7588

*Landscape design, installation and maintenance*

Clients and peers highly recommend Karen Fausch for her excellent skills, strong knowledge base and accommodating nature.  In 1989, new to urban gardening and frustrated by the lack of information on the topic, Fausch began to publish a newsletter, *The Metropolitan Gardener*, based on her backyard experiences.  As her interest, knowledge and experience grew, friends recommended her to other friends, and soon Fausch stopped publishing her newsletter to concentrate on her burgeoning business.  With the help of her small staff, Fausch designs, installs and maintains gardens, primarily in Manhattan.  Fausch also wrote a book called *The Window Box Book,* based on her teaching experiences with three- to five-year-olds at the New York Botanical Garden (NYBG).

While Fausch prefers "a little wilder style" in gardens, particularly in Manhattan, we're told she tailors her creations to suit each client's lifestyle, plant preferences, favorite colors or home decor.  We hear Fausch also serves as a general contractor on garden projects, enlisting and overseeing a small team consisting of a freelance irrigation specialist, carpenter, mason and the like to create gardens that meet clients' needs and specifications.  References across the board are thrilled with Fausch's work.

*"So, so talented." "Her work is simply wonderful." "Intelligent, capable, gifted and overall, the nicest woman."*

## The Window Box

4.5     4.5     4     5

217 East 27th Street, New York, NY  10016
(212) 686 - 5382

*Landscape design, installation and maintenance*

Clients throughout Manhattan agree hands down that Maggie Geiger is not only creative, but also collaborative.  Since 1975, Geiger has been offering clients creative suggestions that have been right on the mark, clients say, without ever imposing her view.  Trained at the world-renowned Wave Hill Gardens in the Bronx,

Geiger has designed and installed gardens and greenery for a variety of elite clients, such as Richard Avedon and the Carlyle Hotel. We hear that prospective clients shouldn't be intimidated by her pedigreed training and work history, however, because she doesn't restrict her herself to elite clientele.

As her firm's modest name indicates, Geiger handles small projects, but her work varies in scope from front door planters to extensive rooftop and terrace gardens. We're told Geiger also handles indoor plantscapes and floral arrangements. Geiger and her team take on around 20 new projects annually. The firm charges per project and sources say that they always work within budget. Geiger's designs have been featured in *The New York Times*, *New York Magazine* and *House and Garden*.

"*Maggie and Window Box are beyond excellent. They are talented, responsible and sensitive to the many requests we might make.*" "*She has turned a moderate-sized New York roof garden into an informal paradise.*" "*Our building management has gotten calls from neighbors who can see our terrace and want to know who the landscaper is.*"

### TLC Plant Care Service Inc.    4    3    4.5    4.5
410 East 6th Street, Suite 15H, New York, NY 10009
(212) 475 - 5399

*Landscape and plantscape design, installation and maintenance*

Peter Michael Rosenzeig has earned the respect of both the landscape industry and clients. TLC Plant Care Service is a small landscape design firm owned and operated by Peter Michael Rosenzweig. Specializing in both residential and commercial work, we hear Rosenzweig designs, installs and maintains both interior plantscapes and rooftop or terrace container gardens. He also sets up drip irrigation systems for his clients.

Rosenzweig got his start in the "green industry" in the 1970s working with various gardeners and plant stores, including Larry Nathanson of Grass Roots Garden. After a number of years, Rosenzweig established his own independent firm. A well-kept secret, Rosenzweig has never had to advertise. Instead, all of his clients have come to him through word of mouth, impressed with his service and the work he has done on their friends' gardens. Shortly after Rosenzweig's work on a new garden is complete, he's used to hearing, "When will I see you again?"

"*I trust Peter completely. He has been in the business so long and he really knows his stuff.*"

### Tree Care Consultancy of New York Inc. 💼    4    3    5    5
310 Park Place, Brooklyn, NY 11238
(718) 638 - 8733

*Master arborist*

Sources call Bruce McInnes of the Tree Care Consultancy of New York "The King of Trees." After working for a tree maintenance company in the 1970s, McInnes started his firm in the 1980s when it became impossible to "get advice that wasn't tied to a buzzsaw." McInnes offers consultations on "trees and tree issues." He is also a member of the American Society of Consulting Arborists (ASCA).

Though much of his work involves overseeing tree rescue, McInnes works with landscape architects or retail clients, advising on overall design or the installation of attractive site-appropriate trees. He also performs site analysis and sets up proper tree maintenance programs for his clients. McInnes will visit a site in Manhattan for $160 to $200. He then charges an hourly rate of $75 to $80. He says, "I try to be available for any tree situation." References verify that he more than meets that objective, however, if a tree falls in the forest and nobody hears, we wonder—where's Bruce McInnes?

*"Reasonable rates, VERY reasonable, but don't tell him." "Bruce McInnes is incredibly knowledgeable. He works very hard to do the best work possible, be helpful and act as a resource to his clients." "Goes out of his way to be excellent to people. I always recommend him." "Thumbs up. He's a fine man and certainly a qualified arborist." "Bruce is a pleasure to work with, a very easy-going man." "Nice guy. Fun to work with. Knows his stuff. Well regarded in the business."*

## Urban Forest & Backyard Tree Care     4    2.5    5    4.5
41 West 82nd Street, New York, NY 10024
(212) 799 - 7926

*Tree and shrub pruning and maintenance*

Bob Redman's entry into the tree maintenance business is legendary in New York gardening circles. Defying authorities, Redman built twelve different tree houses in and around Central Park from 1978 to 1985. When police and park officials found a treehouse and ripped it down, Redman would simply move on and build another in a different area of Central Park. When asked why he persisted in spite of the risks and threat from the law, Redman replied, "I like to be up in trees." When Redman was finally caught in his five-floor treehouse in a beech tree off 78th Street, members of the Central Park Conservancy intervened to harness his unique talents.

After working with the park for several years, Redman began offering his services to private residences through his one-man firm, Urban Forest & Backyard Tree Care. Specializing in tree and shrub pruning, he serves clients exclusively in Manhattan. Resources comment favorably on Redman and his work, noting his easy nature, the interest he takes in his work and his "incredible tree talent."

*"Bob is concerned about safety, aesthetics and proper pruning techniques." "He is professional and very easy to work with." "Remarkable man."*

## Zamora & Co. Inc.     4    4.5    3.5    5
338 East 5th Street, Suite 16, New York, NY 10003
(212) 254 - 4604

*Landscape design and installation*

Sources are continually impressed with Lonnie Zamora's organic gardening to promote healthier conditions and more vibrant gardens. Clients who use Zamora are convinced that he's the best. Zamora favors a naturalist style, telling us he "strives to work with or manipulate nature as opposed to forcing it with a heavy design."

Zamora was in school getting his fine arts degree in sculpture when he took a job with a florist tending gardens on the Upper East Side. Now, eighteen years later Zamora is well established in a career in which he has "encountered every kind of situation and designed every kind of garden." He designs and installs gardens throughout New York City and also serves as a contractor for others' designs. Though he does not maintain the landscapes he creates, he is affiliated with gardeners who do. Sources love Zamora's skillful use of rich color and texture and his willingness to listen. They express complete trust in him and his staff.

*"I'm very pleased with the work he's done for us." "Trustworthy." "Top-quality craftsmanship." "Really an artist and it shows." "The most thorough person I know." "His designs are excellent."*

# Hiring a Lead & Asbestos Service Provider

If like most New Yorkers you live in a building or home constructed before 1978, there may be sleeping beasts in your walls. Lead could be lurking in your copper piping or interior paint, and asbestos hibernating in textured paint, patching compounds on your walls or ceiling joints, vinyl floor tiles, window caulking, linoleum or glue that attaches floor tiles to concrete or wood. Homes built between 1930 and 1950 could have asbestos in piping or wall insulation. Before you embark on a search-and-destroy mission, however, you should be certain it's necessary—often it's better to let sleeping beasts lie. While it's disconcerting to know that you're cohabiting with lead or asbestos, the fact is that trying to remove them could release toxic fibers. On the other hand, if the beast has already been disturbed in its lair, you'll need to call in the handlers. The vendors in this chapter fall into two main categories: those who will inspect for lead and asbestos, and those who will remove it. Some do both.

Even in a pre-1978 home, lead and asbestos are unlikely to pose a threat if the home has been well maintained and has escaped damage. Painting interior surfaces regularly and washing the woodwork help keep the lead or asbestos where it can't do any harm. But once insulation or flooring has been damaged or paint chipped, particles can be disturbed and fibers released. Have a professional assess the area if you see any of these signs or if you are planning renovations. Inspection fees are typically charged by the hour, but may vary, based on the condition and location of the area to be inspected.

## Who Is Qualified to Do This Work?

Be aware that not all inspectors are licensed to assess both lead and asbestos, as these require separate licenses. Asbestos inspection and removal companies, as well as their handlers (those who work directly with the toxic material), supervisors, inspectors, project designers and limited handlers (plumbers, electricians, contractors who work on a contaminated site) must be licensed by the state. Asbestos investigators (as inspectors are called in New York State), handlers and supervisors must be licensed by New York City as well as the state. Note that city licenses expire every two years, while state licenses must be renewed each year.

The Environmental Protection Agency (EPA) issues licenses for companies and professionals who work with lead control, including removal, inspection and risk assessment. In addition, everyone on the work site must be certified. Although the city does not issue licenses, the Department of Environmental Protection (DEP) must be notified when lead abatement work is taking place. This is the responsibility of the contractor and compliance should be included in the written contract.

## What Should I Expect from an Inspection?

Be sure that your lead and/or asbestos inspector does a complete visual exam and takes samples to be analyzed at a laboratory. If results indicate contamination, the inspector should provide a complete written evaluation, describing the location and extent of the hazard and suggestions for correction or risk prevention. With asbestos, the best remedy is often to do nothing. If action is required, a simple repair will often suffice. Repairs tend to be cheaper than removal, but there's a risk: they may make later removal more difficult and costly. Removal is typically a last resort for asbestos control because of the risk of fiber release, but if you are planning a major renovation that could disturb and release fibers, it might be necessary. Then you will need a professional contractor to manage the job and minimize potential hazards.

The most advanced testing for lead utilizes X-Ray Fluorescent (XRF) technology. Not all companies have this equipment because it is expensive and requires extra licensing from the state and certification for its users. Some lead inspectors, however, will contract another provider who has XRF technology to do the job. This technology is more expensive than taking paint samples from the home because it does a more thorough job, inspecting every inch of space, and it does not damage surfaces. On the other hand, chipping—the most standard lead-testing procedure—is invasive. Chip sampling requires taking four-inch squares of paint from walls, ceilings, door jambs, moldings, etc., then examining these pieces in the lab. The recommended sampling method for lead dust is the surface wet wipe. Dust samples are collected from different surfaces, such as bare floors, window sills and window wells. Each sample is collected from a measured surface area using a wet wipe, which is sent to a laboratory for testing.

## CONTRACTS, COST AND COMPLIANCE

Although it is fine for an inspector to recommend a contractor, never hire one connected with the inspector's firm. You want to avoid any possible conflict of interest. Fees are generally based on an hourly rate, but vary according to the condition and location of the area to be treated. Ask for an on-site estimate, and get a contract in writing. You should also have the inspector visit the work site frequently to make sure that the contractor is following the proper procedures. Many inspection firms are also licensed to monitor the air quality of work sites, which is a wise precaution to take throughout the repair or removal process. When the contractor's job has been finished and before you sign off on the written contract, it is wise to have the same inspection or air monitoring firm do an assessment of the job site to ensure that no particles have escaped into the air. Again, this firm should not be connected with the contractor.

You should also obtain copies of each worker's licenses and certificates as well as a written contract that guarantees compliance with all state and local regulations and clearly defines the work plan and cleanup process. When the job is completed, make sure that you receive written assurance that the terms of the contract were met and that all local and state procedures were followed.

## WHERE TO LEARN MORE

Good resources for more information about lead and asbestos include the American Lung Association (www.lungusa.org), the US Consumer Product Safety Commission (www.cpsc.gov), the Environmental Protection Agency (www.epa.gov), the American Industrial Hygiene Association (www.aiha.org), the Department of Housing and Urban Development (www.hud.gov) and the Occupational Safety and Health Administration (www.osha.gov).

## FACTS ABOUT LEAD POISONING

- ✧ Lead paint was banned in US residential paint in 1978.
- ✧ According to the Department of Housing and Urban Development (HUD):
      90 percent of pre-1940 buildings have lead
      80 percent of pre-1960 buildings have lead
      62 percent of pre-1978 buildings have lead
- ✧ Lead poisoning is a serious disease affecting many organs and the central nervous system, which, when affected, causes learning and developmental disabilities in children.
- ✧ The primary cause of lead poisoning is inhaling tiny particles of lead dust from deteriorated paint.
- ✧ In the US, more than three million children age six and younger—one out of every six children in that age group—have toxic levels of lead in their bodies.
- ✧ Even children who appear healthy can have dangerous levels of lead in their blood.
- ✧ Lead poisoning is preventable—hire a certified inspector and remove any lead-ridden paint or pipes in your home.

| | Quality | Cost | Value | Recommend? |
|---|---|---|---|---|
| | + | $ | ◆ | ★ |

## LEAD & ASBESTOS

### Action Environmental Group      3.5    3    4    4.5

3010 Burns Avenue, Wantagh, NY 11793
(516) 781 - 3000 www.actionhazmat.com

*Lead and asbestos removal and lead inspection*

Specializing in lead inspection and removal and asbestos abatement, Action Environmental Group provides other, more commercial services as well. For more than 20 years, this company of 30 licensed professionals has consisted of three divisions—Fiber Control, Action Remediation and Action Industries. Fiber Control provides asbestos abatement, including around-the-clock emergency response, while Action Remediation provides lead-based paint inspection and removal service. Action Industries focuses more on commercial projects which require demolition services. We hear that Action Environmental is quick to respond to any emergency and that its technicians are always very informative on the abatement process.

### Airtek Environmental Corp.      3     3     4     4

39 West 38th Street, New York, NY 10018
(212) 768 - 0516 www.airtekenv.com

*Lead and asbestos inspection*

Airtek provides extensive environmental consulting services including lead inspection, asbestos inspection, indoor air quality assessment, laboratory services and building inspections. Principals Mike S. Zouak and Benn Lewis along with their sixty employees credit their industry know-how to the almost fifteen years of specified experience in the field. We hear that customer confidentiality is very important to the firm, especially when it comes to the high-profile projects. Although the firm does not remove any hazardous materials, Airtek does work closely with many removal firms and will configure a detailed cost effective plan if a problem is found. Clients say that the employees at Airtek are very informative and dedicated to creating an environment free of harmful substances.

### Anson Environmental Ltd.      3.5    3    4    4

771 New York Avenue, Huntington, NY 11743
(631) 351 - 3555 www.ansonltd.com

*Lead and asbestos inspection*

For more than fourteen years, Anson Environmental Ltd. has offered a variety of environmental services. Specializing in consulting, this firm does not participate directly in the hazardous materials removal process—it inspects, locates, and oversees the abatement procedure. In addition to lead and asbestos, this company also monitors air quality, aids in home inspections for real estate transactions, and monitors site cleanup. Anson is licensed in the regional area, performing residential and commercial consultations. We hear with its small staff of nine employees, President Dean Anson is able to maintain a friendly, yet professional relationship with his clients.

### Dominion Risk Management Inc.      4     3    4.5    5

190 Village Center, Baldwin Place, NY 10505
(800) 735 - 5935 www.dominion-inc.com

*Home Inspection*

This family-run structural engineering firm has a long-standing reputation among its clientele and operates solely on word-of-mouth referrals. We are told staff members are not only knowledgeable about the trade, but are also friendly and interested in educating their clients. Dominion does pre-closing inspections for residential and commercial properties, addressing such concerns as lead, asbestos and radon. The firm is responsible for many of the inspections for some of New York's most reputable law firms' real estate deals.

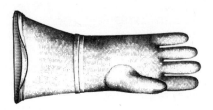

### Emerald Environmental Inc.          3.5      3.5      4      5
P.O. Box 187, Northport, NY  11731
(800) 300 - 3951   www.emerald-environmental-inc.com
*Lead and asbestos inspection and abatement*

This small firm mainly provides inspection services for lead and asbestos as well as indoor air quality testing. President Bill McCarthy and his three employees focus on environmental consulting for both residential and commercial properties, yet the firm also oversees the clean-up process when necessary. Using subcontractors that Emerald has known for years, this company oversees abatement projects, whether it is the discarding of lead paint from a client's home, or the removal of asbestos from a business. Some of Emerald's commercial clients include, Citibank, Exxon, Mobil and the Rockefeller Center Group. Although Emerald does not carry out the actual removal of lead or asbestos, clients say the firm does provide the necessary expertise and managing skills needed for an efficient abatement.

### H.A. Bader Consultants          3      3      4      4
88 Bleecker Street, Suite 4E, New York, NY  10012
(212) 475 - 4122
*Asbestos inspection*

With a small staff, H.A. Bader Consultants has more than eleven years of experience in asbestos inspection and air monitoring. Although this firm works primarily with architects and contractors, H.A. Bader also works with individual clients. With more significant long-term projects, H.A. Bader Consultants hires qualified and licensed subcontractors when needed. Clients say the company's intimate size makes H.A. Bader more approachable without sacrificing expertise in the field.

### Hazardous Elimination Corp.          4.5      3      4.5      5
195H Central Avenue, Farmingdale, NY  11735
(631) 491 - 1515   www.asbestosnet.com
*Lead and asbestos removal*

This well-established firm has offered lead, asbestos, and hazardous waste remediation for over thirteen years. Hazardous Elimination Corporation works on many high profile corporations but will also take on smaller residential apartments. Specializing in asbestos inspection and abatement, this company maintains a 24-hour emergency response team for larger, threatening projects, yet smaller clients still comment on this firm's excellent personalized service. The company's commitment to its customers and the quality job it performs is signified in its ISO 9001 and 14001 registration. Achieving such registration means that this firm has met strict quality assurance and safety guidelines that allow it to perform its operations on an international level. We understand that Hazardous Elimination Corporation is the only environmental contractor in the United States to earn this registration.

### JLC Environmental Consultants                    4    4    4    5
200 Park Avenue South, Suite 1001, New York, NY  10003
(212) 420 - 8119   www.jlcenvironmental.com
*Lead and asbestos inspection*

Concerned with the world's ecosystem and human impact on the environment, insiders tell us owner Jennifer Carey founded JLC in 1987 as a solution to various hazardous problems in the New York City area. The 40 members of this firm offer consulting services, which include lead and asbestos inspection, industrial hygiene and environmental site assessment. Relatively expensive compared to some of the smaller companies, we hear JLC maintains a personal level of communication with the client by educating the client before, during and after the procedure. Even though many commercial customers include large businesses and institutions, this company consults private residential clients as well.

### Lead Safe Inc.                    3.5    3    4.5    5
29 Bank Street, Stamford, CT  06901
(800) 392 - 6468   www.leadsafeinc.com
*Lead and asbestos inspection*

Despite being just five years old, sources tell us this relatively small company manages to provide a vast amount of consulting services. Lead Safe is fully licensed and certified in asbestos consulting and testing, lead consulting and testing, radon testing and air monitoring. This seven-person firm uses state-of-the-art x-ray fluorescence technology to produce floor plans which detail the areas containing hazardous materials. Lead Safe will devise abatement and managing plans for the client's home or business to ensure that a safe environment is established and maintained. Many large firms and institutions such as the New York Housing Authority, The Trump Organization and the University of Connecticut use this company for its safety checkups.

### North Atlantic Laboratories                    3.5    3    4    4
100 Sweeneydale Avenue, Bay Shore, NY  11706
(631) 951 - 0400
*Lead and asbestos inspection*

A division of the larger firm, Windswept Environmental, we are told North Atlantic Laboratories specializes in lead and asbestos inspection. Due to its affiliation with Windswept Technologies, this company is able to employ a copious amount of resources, such as its certified asbestos inspectors, air sampling technicians, industrial hygienists, toxicologists and management planners and designers. North Atlantic uses such methods as XRay Fluorescence technology, to provide on-site detection of lead in paint or in the air. Using its own laboratories (hence the name) this company will analyze the gathered substances and test for various types of hazardous materials. Although most of the firm's work is commercial, North Atlantic will work on residential properties as well, providing consultation services for real estate transactions. Clients praise North Atlantic for the staff's attention to detail and commitment to getting the job done thoroughly and safely. (See Trade-Winds Environmental Restoration for the abatement division of Windswept Environmental Group.)

## Spectrum Environmental

|   |   |   |   |
|---|---|---|---|
| 4 | 3 | 4.5 | 5 |

P.O. Box 550, Nanuet, NY 10954
(914) 472 - 0843

*Lead and asbestos removal*

This family-run business has been fighting lead and asbestos throughout Manhattan and Westchester County for more than thirty years. All fifteen employees are fully licensed to do abatement and demolition. We hear that the staff is knowledgeable, experienced and easy to work with. Fees are based on linear or square-footage, the condition of the structure and the amount of time needed to do the job.

## Trade-Winds Environmental Restoration

|   |   |   |   |
|---|---|---|---|
| 4 | 4 | 4 | 5 |

100 Sweeneydale Avenue, Bay Shore, NY 11706
(631) 435 - 8900    www.interoz.com/wegi

*Lead and asbestos removal*

Trade-Winds Environmental Restoration is the lead and asbestos abatement division of Windswept Environmental Group. One of the larger firms, this eight-year-old company consists of 100 fully-licensed employees, who provide residential and commercial abatement. Technicians are continually trained in new lead and asbestos laws and methods of abatement. Besides lead and asbestos, Trade-Winds also specializes in environmental management including services ranging from soil and water testing to wetlands restoration and oil spill cleanup. Although mainly applicable to more significant corporations and hazardous materials that need immediate attention, this firm maintains a 24-hour emergency response team. Clients say the resourceful nature of the firm makes it very good at what it does.

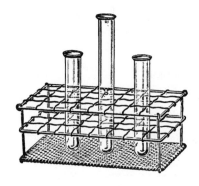

# Hiring a Millwork & Cabinetry
# Service Provider

Transform your den into an elegant library with a mahogany ceiling and walls, lined with matching bookshelves. Add a touch of warmth to your loft apartment with a gleaming spiral staircase, or renew your dining room with oak wainscoting and French doors with glorious beveled glass. From kitchen and bathroom cabinets to custom moldings and wall coverings, millwork enhances interiors with the beauty of finely crafted wood.

## Choosing a Millwork Firm

After making a short list from *The Franklin Report,* you can learn about the process and make a choice by visiting select millwork shops. Surrounded by works-in-progress, you can get a first-hand look at the various qualities of workmanship, look at photographs of finished projects and speak to some of the craftsmen. You should feel comfortable with the woodworker's style and confident that your ideas will be listened to and valued throughout the process. During this visit, ask for references from customers who ordered work similar to yours.

## Three Levels of Quality

Once you've determined the scope of your project, it is wise to determine the caliber of workmanship and quality of wood that is most appropriate for your needs. There are essentially three grades of woodwork to choose from, each with its own standards for materials and craftsmanship.

Economy is the lowest grade of woodwork and may be chosen for projects that will not put a lot of demand on the structure or materials. For example, a built-in desk and shelving in a guest room that gets very little use could be constructed at the economy level. Although the work must be attractive, it need not be made from exotic wood or constructed with intricate joinery.

The next grade is custom woodwork, the level of craftsmanship most frequently requested. Custom woodwork ensures good quality wood and workmanship and is suitable for such popular projects as household cabinetry and moldings. A beautiful kitchen makeover with glass-paneled cabinet doors and a new butcher block island could all be constructed using custom woodwork.

The highest grade is premium woodwork, top-of-the-line millwork that delivers the highest quality of craftsmanship, wood and finishing. Premium jobs include outfitting an entire room with elaborately carved wall and ceiling panels made of top-grade wood, or building a grand staircase using imported wood and marble.

## Major Renovations

Millwork jobs that involve complex structural elements or that will affect your home's electrical or plumbing systems will require a contractor and, in many cases, an architect. The contractor will assure that the job is done properly and on time, taking into consideration any electrical, plumbing or heating issues that arise, and an architect will assist with the design and structural elements. A contractor or architect can also recommend millworkers with whom they've worked in the past, and you can explore those firms.

## ON COST

Due to the specialized, diverse nature of the millwork business, there is no standard pricing structure. Most firms determine their fees based on the materials that are being used and the complexity and scope of the project, which is why it is important to collect several bids for your job. When requesting bids, it is also important to note whether or not the cost of installation is included. Some firms subcontract the installation process. Before you sign a contract, be sure that you know exactly who will install the work you ordered in its intended place in your home.

## WHAT TO EXPECT FROM YOUR MILLWORK COMPANY

If the structure of your home will not be altered by your millwork project (as with replacement kitchen cabinets, for example), the job will not require a permit and can probably be done without a contractor or architect (if the millwork shop does detailed drawings). There are no license or permit requirements for millwork firms, nor are there any trade associations through which millworkers are generally certified. Before you sign a work agreement, request proof of the company's insurance and warranty policies, which vary from firm to firm. If craftsmen will be working in your home, you'll want to be sure that they are covered by the company's worker's compensation policy. You don't want to be held responsible for a misguided nail or toppled ladder.

Like all artisans, millworkers take pride in their work. You'll enjoy working with a wood craftsman who shares your enthusiasm for bringing a rustic, cozy or luxurious new look to your home.

### MILLWORK MASTERY TIPS

✧ It's your millworker's duty to measure! If you do it yourself and give him the dimensions, you're only asking for trouble.

✧ Plan the electrical and plumbing layout meticulously or you may have to rip up fine work, send it to the scrap heap and pay to have it redone.

✧ Don't install millwork too early in a renovation project. Your millworker should be the last person in so that other workers won't scratch your beautiful new wood finish.

✧ Hire excellent professionals for the entire renovation. Millworkers must have a level surface, and shoddy workmanship from carpenters, drywall or plastic contractors will haunt the millwork.

✧ Remember to design backing structures where necessary. You don't want a cabinet that will store heavy cookware fastened to a mere one-half inch of drywall.

✧ Don't be afraid to reject a panel or piece of molding that doesn't match the quality of its brothers and sisters.

✧ Allow at least six and up to sixteen weeks for fabrication and delivery of the materials—and more for installation.

## MILLWORK & CABINETRY

### Anglo-Inscape 🛍                    4.5    3    5    5
2472 Broadway, Suite 368, New York, NY 10025
(212) 924 - 2883

*Custom furniture and high-end finishes*

Clients are so taken with Principal Andrew Rouse's good-looking, British charm that they invite him to houses all over the country to do his exquisite work. Rouse studied in the UK and has been in business for fifteen years. In addition to designing a furniture line, he specializes in antique furniture restoration and refinishing, as well as decorative wall finishes. Rouse's French Polish is reportedly magnificent, and we are told he works in oil- and water-based glazes, graining, marbling and specialty plaster treatments.

We hear Rouse values the integrity of old-world methods and uses only traditional techniques, applying rubs and finishes by hand. Clients praise Rouse's enormous body of knowledge and recommend him for projects that call for preserving the character of a valuable piece. Insiders say that in an industry of divas, Rouse stands out for his reliability and absence of ego.

*"Work is of the highest quality and is completed within the time specified." "Andrew's work is outstanding and his commitment is undaunting." "Some high-end finishers are difficult to work with—Andrew is not one of these. His pricing is fair, he's there when he says he will be and goes the extra mile to make sure the job is done right."*

### Atlas Woodworking                    📁    📁    📁    📁
15 Naugel Street, Closter, NJ 07624
(201) 784 - 1949

*High-end office millwork*

Principal Ken Ewald and his company of ten have been in business since 1994. The firm does high-end custom office setups in any style to fit clients' needs. Sources say Atlas Woodworking's jobs are half residential, half commercial, working with various materials, like Corian and granite with a one-year warranty.

### Breakfast Woodworks                    4.5    4    4    5
135 Leetes Island Road, Guilford, CT 06437
(203) 458 - 8888   www.breakfastwoodworks.com

*High-end custom millwork*

Clients rave about Breakfast Woodworks's exquisite achievements in mahogany, tiger maple, bird's eye, oak, red ash, lace-wood, teak and trellis pieces. We hear the principals are forthright and dependable with no ego. The firm has been known to turn jobs down if they don't have the time. Sources say Breakfast Woodworks uses computer-aided design and executes with superior quality.

Principal Louis Mackall, an architect educated at Yale, co-founded Breakfast Woodworks with Kenneth Field, a master craftsman. Mackall and Field combine age-old skills with high technology to bring complex shapes into three-dimensional renderings. We hear Breakfast Woodworks works on residences, office and commercial interiors, churches and historic preservation. The firm has won ample publicity for the quality of its work, including features in *Architectural Record, Progressive Architecture, House and Garden, House Beautiful,* and *The New York Times.*

*"Exceptional quality, beyond our wildest dreams." "Their work is an art form." "The nicest guys you could hope for."*

| | Quality  | Cost $ | Value ◆ | Recommend? ★ |
|---|---|---|---|---|

## Budd Woodwork Inc.
54 Franklin Street, Brooklyn, NY 11222
(718) 389 - 1110

*High-end historic restoration and preservation*

**4.5    4.5    4    4**

Budd Woodwork's high-end historic restoration and preservation work includes such high-profile jobs as the Louis XIV Room at the Met and the Venetian Room for Mrs. John Hay Whitney. Insiders say Budd Woodwork specializes in a classic French style, especially Louis XV and Louis XVI, and caters to a sophisticated and exclusive clientele.

Founded in 1952, the company employs eighteen. We hear Budd's staff is humble and polite but works only through architects and decorators, not directly with clients. Sources say the firm takes on a limited number of jobs each year, since it only deals in the finest materials and architecture. The firm's work has been featured in *The New York Times* and *Architectural Digest*.

## Building Block
314 Eleventh Avenue, New York, NY 10001
(212) 714 - 9333

*Custom doors, paneling and molding*

**4.5    3    5    5**

A high-profile clientele describes principal Noah Block as an honorable businessman with a genuine love for the work. We hear the 24-person firm offers full-service millworking, specializing in custom doors and moldings, using only hardwoods. Building Block designs shop drawings for moldings, doors and paneling to accommodate customer ideas, and even custom designs tools for the job.

Clients describe Block as a perfectionist, and praise Building Block's attention to detail. This solid reputation has kept Building Block in business for 31 years, with work featured in places like The Guggenheim, The Whitney, Tavern on the Green and a number of celebrities' homes. Although most work is done through contractors, private clients are also accepted.

*"Delightful to work with." "Just sensational." "We love these guys. Would highly recommend."*

## C.F. Woodworking Co.
68 35th Street, 3rd Floor, Brooklyn, NY 11232
(718) 965 - 4241

*Custom interior millwork*

**3    3    4    4**

Gracious, helpful and friendly—that's how our sources describe principal Caesar Florez. C.F. Woodworking has been in business for four years and has four professional employees, including Caesar's brother. The firm specializes in custom cabinetry and interiors, but the craftsmen will also work in aluminum, brass and plastic laminate. We hear C.F. Woodworking enjoys the challenge of artistic designs but does not create its own designs, working instead from architects' plans.

## Cal Michael Woodworking Inc.
225 East 134th Street, Bronx, NY 10451
(718) 402 - 1525

*Custom interior millwork*

📁    📁    📁    📁

## Catskill Fine Woodworking
11 Field Court, Kingston, NY 12401
(845) 339 - 8029  www.catskillfurniture.com

*Custom millwork and furniture*

**4    3    4.5    4.5**

Clients praise Robert Allen for his attention to detail and sense of responsibility. Allen is reputed to have a pleasant personality and a talent for solving millwork problems. Trade insiders maintain an ongoing relationship with Catskill Fine Woodworking, which they say offers high quality at a relatively low price. Sources note, however, that Catskill works primarily with architects and contractors, not directly with the client.

Allen also runs Catskill Furniture Makers, which combines historic reproduction work with contemporary design ideas. The firm's website features an online gallery, and customers can also visit the Kingston showroom. One client was so satisfied with the chair she purchased from Catskill Furniture Makers that she went on to use Catskill Fine Woodworking for a major interior custom-millwork job. Catskill's work has been featured in *Architectural Digest* on several occasions.

*"Not every millworker is ready to throw himself into the job when the contractor is ready. Bob is always ready with the ultimate solution." "Excellent people, excellent work."*

## Christopher Peacock Cabinetry       4.5     4     4.5     4.5

34 East Putnam Avenue, Greenwich, NY 06830
(203) 862 - 9333   www.peacockcabinetry.com

*Highly-detailed, custom cabinetry*

Customers can't wait to show off their cabinets from Peacock. Christopher Peacock Cabinetry opened 20 years ago and has established a reputation for some of the finest cabinetry manufactured in the United States. We're told each piece is carefully constructed with strict attention to the smallest detail. Cabinets are primarily patterned on fine traditional English style and craftsmanship.

Once a customer's cabinets have been commissioned and completed, the company's professional installers make sure that each piece fits perfectly and that moldings and cornices are scribed on site. Peacock offers a wide selection of stains and finishes, and its artists work to achieve the exact shade, including various painterly effects, that each client wants.

*"Extraordinary." "Quality work." "I am so happy with my beautiful kitchen cabinets." "I don't believe people can be perfect all the time, but always accountable. That is Christopher Peacock."*

## Classic Millworks       4.5     4     5     5

2417 Third Avenue, Bronx, NY 10451
(718) 993 - 1200

*High-end millwork and exotic veneers*

High-end clients and architects give unanimous praise to Classic Millworks for its intricately detailed and complex work. Sources say one extremely complicated job baffled contractors with its many specifications and complex shop drawings, but Classic Millworks "did a gorgeous job like they always do." Those in the trade consider Classic Millworks singularly unique in its ability to execute an exotic veneer. On the other hand, we hear the firm is not great at rustic or antique finishes, but will recommend someone for those jobs. Classic Millworks has earned fame for their piece-de-resistance libraries unparalleled in quality and detail.

Principal Charles Dinstuhl is said to have a waiting list to join his staff of 22. Serge, the shop drawer, is well known for his extraordinary artistic genius and detail, with the obsessive personality of an artist to match. Insiders recommend customers do their homework and have good drawings to start (Serge demands it)—then he'll take your ideas and produce shop drawings. While not affecting clients, we have heard that Classic Millworks gives contractors a headache by demanding its (high) payment immediately after a job.

*"When I saw the high prices, I balked, but then I visited their workshop, and I understood." "I don't think you can find higher quality." "There is no limit to what they can do."*

| | Quality  | Cost $ | Value ◆ | Recommend?  |
|---|---|---|---|---|

## Crowned Woodworks    4   3   4.5   4.5
281 Greene Avenue, Brooklyn, NY 11238
(718) 636 - 4402   www.crownedwoodworks.com

*High-end custom cabinetry for kitchens, libraries, bedrooms and bathrooms*

Crowned Woodworks' principal Steven DeSouza draws rave reviews for being honest and dedicated. Clients say he really cares about customer service and is completely devoid of attitude or greed. One client reports that the job turned out to be smaller than DeSouza originally estimated, so he gave her a refund. He is unanimously reputed to be communicative, accessible and thorough.

Insiders call DeSouza a skilled craftsman and intelligent problem solver, adding that Crowned Woodworks's high value comes at a comparably low price. The company specializes in cabinetry, detailed molding work and custom doors, but is also known to completely renovate bathrooms, including tile and marble work. Sources say Crowned Woodworks typically works with decorators and architects but will work with private clients as well. Crowned Woodworks' projects have been featured in *Interior Design* magazine and most recently in *British Vogue.*

*"He really cares about the client—he's a gem!" "Half the cost, twice the quality." "Without hesitation, he's terrific." "Steve was a dream!" "His work is flawless." "He has a vision for the best possible look, and everything he said was absolutely true."*

## Culin & Colella Inc.    3   3   4   4
632 Center Avenue, Mamaroneck, NY 10543
(914) 698 - 7727

*Custom millwork and furniture*

The husband-wife team of Ray Culin and Janis Colella heads up this ten-person staff, keeping it small to maintain control of the firm's high standards. Clients praise Culin and Colella's unquestionable quality and one-of-a-kind furniture designs. Insiders say the firm will work under architects and designers but prefers to work closely to the client to ensure satisfaction. We hear Culin and Colella can incorporate any kind of drawer, slide or finish imaginable. They are reputed to be very reliable and attentive, especially after their recent reorganization.

*"They are fabulous, top quality." "Outstanding quality, workers and execution." "The work they did is the highlight of our house."*

## Donodick Woodwork    4.5   4   4   4.5
3654 35th Street, Long Island City, NY 11106
(718) 361 - 9888

*Highest quality millwork*

## Eisenhardt Mills    4.5   3.5   4.5   5
1510 Richmond Road, Easton, PA 18040
(610) 253 - 2792

*Architectural millwork, specifically traditional and classic revival themes*

Considered the standard for premium millwork, Eisenhardt Mills was founded in 1937 and is a third-generation family business. We hear Eisenhardt Mills works primarily, but not exclusively, in traditional styles and classic revival themes based on architectural or interior designs. The company draws praise for its work in historic preservation, including Independence Hall in Philadelphia, and the prestigious Secretary of State and Deputy Secretary of State offices in Washington DC, featured in *Antiques* magazine.

Clients and very top decorators and contractors praise principal Don Lockard's dedication to meeting their needs. Sources say that Eisenhardt's top-quality work does not include hand-rubbed finishes or ornate carvings, but that the firm collaborates with vendors who can provide those services. Insiders say Eisenhardt's prices are comparable to other high-end firms, but the superior shop drawings, follow-through and dependability Eisenhardt offers makes it a better value. Sources also compliment the firm for meeting very aggressive deadlines without a problem. We have heard there can be some communication problems during installation, but the universal cry is that Eisenhardt is an exemplary firm.

*"They're totally on target." "Eisenhardt is superb, with a long tradition of exceptional service, and Don can handle very complex projects." "Lockard is personable and helpful. They were exceptional in every way. The end result was truly amazing. He does exactly what he sets out to do—there are no surprises."*

### Elli NY Design                                       3      2.5     4.5      4
803 Broadway, New York, NY 10003
(212) 777 - 4071   www.ellicorp.com

*Custom millwork*

Carlo Danesi, the principal at Elli NY Design, draws strong reviews for being personable, attentive and reliable. We hear that at the end of a job, Danesi likes to take his clients out to the workroom before installing their piece, just to make sure the client is satisfied. If not, he'll make changes, often free of charge. Clients admire Danesi's aesthetic sense and reassuring nature. One self-described "neurotic homeowner" could not say enough about his dedication to meeting her stringent needs.

Those in the know differentiate between Danesi and his shop. They say his drawings are excellent and he's very responsive, but at some point the work goes to the shop, which is not quite of of the same caliber. However, sources stress that for the reasonable price, the company provides an excellent value.

*"Carlo is creative, imaginative, an excellent drawer, smart and easy to talk to." "It was almost as if Carlo could read my mind." "Did a great bookcase quickly, based on a rough sketch." "Excellent for mid-tier work."*

### Englander Millwork
2369 Lorrilard Place, Bronx, NY 10458
(718) 364 - 4240

*Windows and doors, millwork, historic replication*

See Englander Millwork's full report under the heading Windows & Doors

### Enjo Architectural Millwork
16 Park Avenue, Staten Island, NY 10302
(718) 447 - 5220   www.enjo.com

*Architectural millwork—restoration of windows and doors to landmark standards*

See Enjo Architectural Millwork's full report under the heading Windows & Doors

### Euro Woodworking                                     3       3       4       4
303 Park Avenue, 8th floor, Brooklyn, NY 11205
(718) 246 - 9172

*Millwork and veneers*

Wolfgang, the principal at Euro Woodworking, is reputed to be very responsible and able to meet deadlines with no problem. Sources say Euro Woodworking specializes in high-end millwork and veneer and can design custom cabinetry but mostly builds to the designs of architects. This company of five has been in business since 1996.

*"Very responsible. Hits deadlines."*

| | Quality | Cost | Value | Recommend? |
|---|---|---|---|---|

## European Woodworking

**Quality** 4.5  **Cost** 2.5  **Value** 5  **Recommend?** 5

167 Sawmill River Road, Yonkers, NY 10701
(914) 969 - 5724

*Architectural millwork*

Loyal clients applaud Joe Lo Nigro, who heads European Woodworking's small shop of three. A fourth generation millworker, Lo Nigro trained under his father, who trained under his grandfather. Sources hold Lo Nigro in esteem for his delightful personality, humility and strong sense of responsibility. We hear that European Woodworking executes custom millwork with exactitude and abundant detail, and that Lo Nigro is obsessive about perfection. Insiders say he is typically done early and tends to undercharge.

*"He's dependable, he comes through and is a real artist. I couldn't recommend anyone more than this young man." "No one is perfect in this world, but Joe is certainly striving for it." "Whenever I need work, I go to him, because I know I'll get the best job at the best price."*

## Greenpoint Manufacturing & Design Center

4  3  4.5  4

1205 Manhattan Avenue, Brooklyn, NY 11222
(718) 389 - 8615   www.gmdconline.org

*Custom high-end woodworking*

The Greenpoint Manufacturing and Design Center (GMDC) is a nonprofit arts and industry facility housing 65 manufacturers, designers, craftspeople and artisans in a century-old complex. GMDC purchased the property, previously Chelsea Fibre Mills, in 1994 and has invested $5 million to rehabilitate the historic buildings.

More than 20 custom woodworkers work within the five commercial buildings at GMDC. Since all the woodworkers at Greenpoint are high-end custom millworkers, customers should peruse the highly detailed website or call Tom Naklicki, one of the administrative principals to find out which millworker is right for the project.

Greenpoint's list of honors and awards is extensive. Among them are the National Trust For Historic Preservation, Architects, Designers and Planners for Social Responsibility, HUD Secretary Award for Urban Excellence, and the Eastman Kodak Award for Economic Ingenuity. GMDC has been featured in *The New York Times*.

*"They are an absolute pleasure to work with."*

## Hamilton Woodworking/AAI

3.5  3  4.5  5

123 Water Street, Norwalk, CT 06854
(203) 857 - 0554

*Custom architectural millwork*

After 27 years, Hamilton Woodworks is under new ownership. Jim Andrews bought the firm and changed the name to Hamilton Woodworking/AAI. We hear Andrews and his team of fourteen skilled employees excel in millwork, custom doors and windows, custom furniture and historic preservation. Clients marvel at the firm's capabilities with tricky jobs like curve work for stairs and casing, turnings and high-end cabinetry.

Sources say Andrews will work with contractors or private clients and happily shows clients around his workroom, which is also a showroom. He earns respect for his personable manner and reasonable fees, but insiders especially cite Andrews' unfailing timeliness on projects. Hamilton Woodworking/AAI was featured recently in *Architectural Digest*.

*"Jim Andrews is very proficient. He is always willing to help us find what we need." "Jim is very easy to work with. He and his staff are very helpful and responsive."*

| | Quality | Cost | Value | Recommend? |
|---|---|---|---|---|
| | **+** | **$** | **◆** | **★** |

## Heights Woodworking Co.

| 3.5 | 2.5 | 4.5 | 5 |

411 Third Avenue, Brooklyn, NY  11215
(718) 875 - 7497

*Custom interior millwork*

Principal Amor Villar works for both clients and contractors, creating high-end residential moldings, doorways, entryways, windows, bookcases and interiors.  Clients say he will work in formica, and will even make tables out of stone and wood.  Villar is known for doing quality work in a timely manner.  We hear Villar is highly versatile, working with equal skill in numerous styles.  Recently, Heights Woodworking participated in the Madison Avenue Presbyterian Church restoration project.

*"He always delivers with no problem and at a great price."*

## Jacob Froehlich Cabinet Works

| 5 | 4 | 5 | 5 |

550-560 Barry Street, Bronx, NY  10474
(718) 893 - 1300

*High-end millwork, varnishing*

Clients speak admiringly of Jacob Froehlich Cabinet Works, noting the firm's exceptional thoroughness.  The company's skills in using stains and varnishes are reputed to be top in the field.  This firm, which has been in business since 1865, services celebrity clientele and is no doubt in the upper price range.  However, sources call the cost appropriate for the product and well worth it to anyone who can afford it.  Insiders say Jacob Froehlich Cabinet Works distinguishes itself with an excellent architectural department, which starts with a conceptual approach, and provides fine shop drawings and follows through with flawless execution and installation.

Jacob Froehlich Cabinet Works draws accolades for its management capabilities and extremely organized team.  Everything is itemized and broken down, so the budget is never an issue, nor are timetables.  Professionals call the company extremely accommodating and flexible and its excellent shop drawings ensure no surprises.

*"They're so communicative and articulate that there are never any problems."*
*"We have worked with Froehlich for 20 years and have tremendous respect for the workers' ability to prioritize and coordinate work in the shop and to produce stellar quality work."*  *"Very sophisticated and familiar with the top-end work of architects and designers."*  *"They're excellent, top of the line—the Rolls Royce of millworking.  They can handle anything—totally unflappable."*

## Jorgensen-Carr

| 4 | 4 | 5 | 5 |

111 First Street, Jersey City, NJ  07302
(201) 792 - 1916

*Custom interior millwork*

Mike Jorgensen and Ken Carr have been in partnership since 1987.  They earn client praise for their feats in stainless steel, wood and leather.  We hear Jorgensen-Carr finds the ultimate solutions to tricky problems.  Insiders say the firm distinguishes itself with its intricate designs, moldings, finishes and veneers.  Clients say they admire the good-natured team and their high-quality work, but worry that the firm is getting too popular and too busy.  We're told that once on the job, Jorgensen-Carr's workers always meet deadlines, but it's sometimes hard to schedule them initially, due to filled appointment books.

*"Mike and Ken are just the greatest guys on the face of the earth.  Working with them was such a pleasant experience."*  *"I can't wait to do another project with them."*  *"They were the one bright spot in my renovation."*

## Juliano Interior Millwork

4.5   3.5   5   4

575 Madison Avenue, Suite 1600, New York, NY 10022
(718) 833 - 8879  www.julianomillwork.com or www.cofferedceilings.com
*Custom cabinetry and millwork*

With 36 years of experience, Juliano Generale specializes in coffered ceilings, libraries, raised panels, decorative architectural ornaments and mantels and custom furniture on occasion. We hear Generale works for top architects and contractors all over the country, and is particularly respected for his magnificent molding.

Sources describe this Egyptian-born, European-trained craftsman as charming, funny and completely honest. One trade insider report that Generale saved a Park Avenue job from disaster after a series of contracting mistakes. We're told Generale works accurately and ably in any style and is described as reliable, conscientious, timely and accommodating.

*"More than fabulous." "His woodworking is wonderful, he is really a craftsman."*

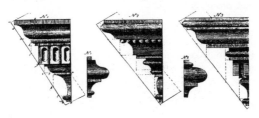

## Keats & Waugh 🛍

4   3   4.5   5

15-19 Pollock Avenue, Jersey City, NJ 07305
(201) 451 - 3911
*Custom cabinetry and millwork*

It's common knowledge among interior designers that there is no better way to build a library than with Keats & Waugh. This small millworking firm creates custom built-ins, armoires, cabinets, bookcases, furniture, children's rooms and entertainment units. It also does some paneling, few kitchens and no molding or decorative carving. We're told the firm excels in complicated work. While the firm can and has worked in the Hamptons and Westchester and Fairfield counties, most of its work is in Manhattan and affluent New Jersey suburbs.

The firm is owned by Bill Keats, who clients compliment as a "nice, chatty" guy who offers honest communication. Keats stepped into millworking after studying oceanography and a stint as a merchant marine, and is self taught. Clients tell us he has clearly taught himself well, as the firm is in high demand. While this means Keats is sometimes backed up with work, he is straightforward about it and reflects this in his initial timetables, which clients say go off like clockwork. They also remark upon the fact that the firm's size means Keats himself can keep control over the quality, which is said to be top shelf. Keats prefers to work through designers and architects and not to facilitate design drawings. We hear Yeats costs are average.

*"Bill is meticulous and reviews each detail so there are no surprises." "If he's available we use him." "He doesn't take on more work than he can do, which means he isn't always available, but he is always true to his deadline." "Returns calls, calls with questions and suggestions, discusses detail."*

## Little Wolf Cabinet Shop

3   3   4   4

1583 First Avenue, New York, NY 10028
(212) 734 - 1116
*Unfinished custom furniture and cabinets*

Little Wolf Cabinet Shop creates custom entertainment centers, bookshelves and cabinets of all kinds. Insiders describe the firm's process as generally cost-effective. First, customers bring in their own measurements, and Little Wolf shows

| Quality | Cost | Value | Recommend? |
|---------|------|-------|------------|
| + | $ | ◆ | ★ |

the clients a number of possible designs with a price. Once the client agrees to the project, the company will send someone to take final measurements. Once installed, Little Wolf doesn't finish the piece but recommends someone. We hear prices are moderate, but be sure to get an estimate on the finishing as well. It can easily be 50 percent of the price of the piece.

Principal John Wolf draws praise from many for solving space issues and doing superb work at a reasonable price. Many others, however, say the firm does not satisfactorily resolve issues.

*"I feel very strongly about his work—I have total faith in him. I can't imagine any reason to go elsewhere." "When I tell you he's unique, I mean it. He makes good on his word and takes honor in his work." "When the kids' desks were six inches too short, they never admitted or fixed the problem."*

## LM Woodworking Inc.　　　　4　　3　　5　　5
238 North 9th Street, Brooklyn, NY 11211
(718) 388 - 6137

*Custom cabinetry and design*

We hear principals Michael Larkin and Lionel Squires go to great lengths to suit clients' needs. One satisfied customer says Michael even built her a model so she could visualize the project and proceed more comfortably. Larkin and Squires are said to be very patient and experienced.

Insiders call the duo incredibly attentive, with realistic estimates and reasonable prices, and say that they finish ahead of time. We hear they are friendly, humble, and easy to talk to, bringing a great sense of humor to the job—one source noted that Michael is a talented cartoonist, drawing hilarious cartoons of the job site. This talent, we are told is second only to his meticulously detailed shop drawings.

*"I recommend them to anyone needing cabinets." "Some of the nicest guys I've had work for me."*

## Manhattan Cabinetry　　　　3　　4　　3　　3
227 East 59th Street, New York, NY 10022
(212) 750 - 9800　www.manhattancabinetry.com

*Custom cabinetry and furniture*

Manhattan Cabinetry, founded in 1976, creates custom furniture in mica and woods. We hear the firm will gladly work with outside designers, or its in-house designers will create what the customer wants, after a visit to the showroom. Designers will also do on-site consultations, but there's a charge, and you will be expected to do your own measuring (which is always dangerous). Manhattan Cabinetry boasts a client list that includes the Hard Rock Café, the Waldorf Astoria, the Palace Hotel, the MoMA, Tavern on the Green and Carnegie Hall. In addition to its location on East 59th Street, Manhattan Cabinetry has showrooms located at 455 Park Avenue South, (212) 889-8808 and 1630 Second Avenue, (212) 772-8870.

*"I know that I'm in excellent hands with Manhattan Cabinetry." "Check the millwork corners at the showroom before you commit."*

## Mead & Josipovich Inc.　　　4.5　　4.5　　5　　5
140 58th Street, Brooklyn, NY 11220
(718) 492 - 7373

*High-end millwork and custom furniture*

Trade insiders rely on this firm for top-quality, specialty jobs on an unlimited budget. Principal Boris Josipovich has differentiated himself with creativity and attention to detail, and clients laud his work as "truly special." Insiders praise the firm's shop drawings and meticulous work and call Josipovich completely reliable, honest and communicative.

We hear Josipovich has done work in the fashion industry and always meets tight deadlines. Insiders praised the firm's unparalleled finishes and veneers, adding that Mead & Josipovich give clients exactly what the client wants, as opposed to many other millworkers who impose their ideas on the client.

*"What differentiates Boris is that perfection is his standard." "Boris is a real guy." "I can't always afford them on my jobs—would my life be a lot easier in terms of getting the right work at the right time if I could? The answer is yes."*

## Michael Gordon Inc.                                     4.5        4        5        5
2 East Main Street, Paterson, NJ 07522
(973) 389 - 1414

*Custom millwork and furniture, trade only*

Clients and professionals praise the father-son team for built-in units, complete paneled rooms and stand-alone furniture. Reported to be personable and cooperative with an imaginative flair, Michael and Eric Gordon transform private clients' conceptual designs into reality, though most of their work is with the trade. With a staff of 26, the most up-to-date technology and more than 30 years of experience, Michael Gordon Inc. is a favorite among clients for building sophisticated offices and fanciful children's rooms.

*"One of the best. Really fun to work with." "Michael is a charming, thoughtful and sophisticated gentleman."*

## Millwork Specialties
189 Prospect Avenue, Brooklyn, NY 11215
(718) 768 - 7112

*Historic window and door replication*

See Millwork Specialties's full report under the heading Windows & Doors

## New York Craftsmen's Collective
13 Avenue A, New York, NY 10009
(212) 477 - 4477

*Residential and commercial general contracting*

See New York Craftsmen's Collective's full report under the heading Contractors & Builders

## Nordic Interiors                                        4        4        4        4
56-01 Maspeth Avenue, Maspeth, NY 11378
(718) 456 - 7000

*High-end millwork for the trade*

We hear that Nordic Interiors works primarily on extremely high-end commercial projects, but that a select few private clients gain access through architects. Sources report that the 28-year-old firm has a 60,000-square-foot shop in Queens with 200 employees who keep it operating smoothly.

## Peter E. Kilroy                                         3.5        3        4.5        5
145 Wyckoff Street, Brooklyn, NY 11217
(718) 802 - 9105

*Custom millwork and handiwork*

Clients report that they depend completely on Pete Kilroy, reputed to be extremely careful, neat and of pleasant disposition. Some customers go so far as to say they call him immediately for wallpapering, bookcases, painting and installations—and refuse to use anyone else. Sources say Kilroy's terrific work lasts, and he's worth every penny. Kilroy earns admiration for his good eye and useful suggestions—insiders say he can solve problems and see things from all angles.

*"I trust him completely."*

## Ralph Di Maio

|  |  |  |  |
|---|---|---|---|
| 4 | 3 | 4.5 | 4.5 |

12 Bright Place, Yonkers, NY 10705
(914) 476 - 1937

*Custom millwork*

Sources tell us top contractors flock to Ralph Di Maio, especially for commercial work, though he has done some residential work in prestigious Upper East Side residences. Clients praise the quality of his work, especially his ability to make poor woods look their greatest.

## Smallbone of Devizes

105/109 Fulham Road, London, UK SW3 6RL
(207) 838 - 3636  www.smallbone.co.uk

*Fine hand-painted English cabinetry, custom design and installation*

See Smallbone of Devizes's full report under the heading Kitchen & Bath Design

## Sonrise Woodcarving Studio

|  |  |  |  |
|---|---|---|---|
| 5 | 2.5 | 5 | 5 |

111 Hurley Avenue, Kingston, NY 12401
(845) 331 - 8692  www.sonrisewoodcarving.com

*Master carver—decorative work, interior millwork, replication*

Self-taught, Stephan Toman has been carving since 1985. Sources call him a kind man with a strong work ethic and high level of integrity. Insiders say Toman's respect for the craft and disregard for the bottom line means he won't rush a job if it will compromise the quality, even if that means turning down work. However, we hear Toman meets all reasonable deadlines. Toman's decorative carving is visible on his website, and we hear he'll also do replication, repair and restoration, though he doesn't have formal training in historic or artistic styles. Toman works through architects, contractors or directly for the client. Insiders say while his intricate carvings are really special, Toman also excels in interior millwork.

*"Stephan's work is totally unique, all hand-done—he is truly an artist." "A guy like Stephan is one in a million—it took me forever to find someone who can do that kind of work." "There are very few people in the country who can do the intricacy or as fine of carving as Stephan."*

## St. John's Bridge

|  |  |  |  |
|---|---|---|---|
| 3.5 | 2.5 | 4.5 | 5 |

25 Railroad Street, Kent, CT 06757
(860) 927 - 3315

*Custom decorative millwork*

We hear Greg St. John brings a special twist to his custom millwork by adding decorative inlays, veneers and professional paintings. Clients say he will work from clients' designs or do period reproductions, but he prefers the opportunity to create his own designs. Reputedly conscientious and personable, St. John brings a fine arts education to his love for creative expression. Insiders praise St. John's skill with metals and exotic woods, calling his bookcases and moldings "beautiful."

*"He's talented, conscientious and plans ahead." "If you explain what you want, he can come up with the design. He's very thorough, and a very nice person." "He uses the best materials and the cost is never a surprise."*

## Techline Studio

|  |  |  |  |
|---|---|---|---|
| 3.5 | 3.5 | 4 | 5 |

35 East 19th Street, New York, NY
(212) 674 - 0551  www.techline-ny.com

*Custom office designs*

Although Techline is a national chain, its team of New York designers including Sera DeMira and Mark Scher draws high praise from customers satisfied with its architect-conceived office systems. We hear the firm specializes in a modular system of "crisp" office materials that can be sized for any space and function, and Techline's designers will work with standard or custom materials to fit a client's budget.  Clients praise the personable and professional Techline team, which services the full range of office design—from field measurements, layout and budgeting, to installation and delivery, including office accessories. Clients say they appreciate Techline's unique five-year warranty and extremely reliable customer service department.

*"My bedroom is now my playground, and I love to spend time there, enjoying the beautiful Techline cabinetry." "I am a happy camper in my Techline office."*

## William Somerville              4.5    4      5      5
166 East 124th Street, New York, NY  10035
(212) 534 - 4600

*Architectural millwork*

For more than 30 years, the Miller family has been running William Somerville, which is respected in the industry as one of the best architectural millwork firms in the country.  We hear William Somerville focuses its top-quality efforts on high-end commercial jobs, but will occasionally take on a residential project.  Principal Lee Miller heads up the company with his mother, and the firm works with some of the top architects in the city.

*"These are very, very good people." "Without a doubt one of the best firms in the country."*

## Wohners Millworkers             4      3      5      4.5
29 Bergen Street, Englewood, NJ  07631
(201) 568 - 7307   www.wohners.com

*Mantelpieces and carving*

Ferenc Wohner founded Wohners Millworkers in 1909 in Europe.  Today, his son Robert Wohner runs the business with his three sons, all trained in the family tradition.  Wohners specializes in doors, goldleaf, corbles, full rooms, carved accents, architectural pieces, mantel pieces and carvings, mostly from the firm's own French-influenced designs.  Sources say Wohners will also work from others' designs but doesn't do much replication.

Besides its custom work, Wohners carries a retail line of imported and domestic mantels to accommodate every price range.  Insiders say Wohners works mostly with private clients, and determines fees by the job's complexity.  Wohners Millworkers has done rooms in the Dakota Hotel and was the subject of a chapter in John Lewmans' book, *Fireplace & Mantel Ideas*.

*"The Wohner touch added elegance and class to my living room." "This family-run company is simply delightful!"*

## Wood-O-Rama                     3.5    3.5    4      4
238 West 108th Street, New York, NY  10025
(212) 749 - 6438   www.woodorama.com

*Custom millwork*

Sources describe Wood-O-Rama as a neighborhood store that provides homeowners with beautifully crafted cabinets and moldings.  Wood-O-Rama's expertise in moldings extends to an extensive stock of 754 moldings from the leading American and European manufacturers.  The company's custom-made cabinets are said to be elegant, versatile, long-lasting and installed with efficiency.

# Hiring a Mover

Whether relocating downtown to a new hip apartment or moving the family and pets to the suburbs, just the thought of moving can bring the most toughest New Yorkers to tears. Even more worrisome than organizing the process is the thought of placing all of one's worldly goods into the hands of a truckload of burly strangers. The less-than-sterling reputation of the moving industry doesn't help either. According to the Better Business Bureau, moving companies consistently make the list of the top-ten industries consumers complain about. Even moving companies themselves admit that three in ten moves result in a complaint against the mover. While those odds don't sound promising, there are several precautions you can take to ensure that you are one of the satisfied customers who end up providing glowing references about your moving company to your friends—and to The Franklin Report.

## Where Do I Start?

Hundreds of moving companies are listed in the Manhattan yellow pages. Consider four main factors in making your choice: reputation, reliability, cost and availability. Begin with an assessment of your needs. According to most movers, if you are a single city apartment dweller you will probably need 15 to 20 boxes for all your possessions. A family of two adults and two children will require approximately 120 to 200 boxes. Most companies will provide an informal verbal estimate based on your description of items, number of rooms, the availability of elevators on both ends of the move, etc. If you're looking for a binding estimate, some movers will provide one after surveying your property and assessing your needs for themselves. Be forewarned that in this industry, a binding estimate is an elusive thing. Be prepared to consider any estimate a rough calculation rather than a binding agreement. In any event, be prepared with the requisite information before you call movers for estimates. Keep in mind that some movers only perform in-town moves while others are licensed to do countrywide and international moves as well.

Most movers provide packing services in addition to transportation. Packing, of course, incurs additional cost. If you choose to have your items packed by movers, you'll need to schedule packing days. Be sure to take inventory of what gets packed into each box, making sure to make a note of any existing damage. Keep a copy of the inventory list handy as you unpack to ensure that all your items have arrived safely. While movers assume liability for damage incurred by any items they packed themselves—they will not accept responsibility for items packed by you. Be sure to get estimates both with and without packing services in order to ensure that you opt for the services best suited to your needs and budget.

The organization that issues licenses to moving companies in New York is the New York Department of Transportation (www.dot.state.ny.us). They have a helpful telephone line (800-786-5368) that can tell you if a company is licensed to perform moves in New York, how much business they did in the past year, and most importantly, how many complaints, if any, a company received in the current year. The DOT claims that one to two complaints in a twelve-month period is "average." While the number of complaints against a firm is definitely a good indication of their reputation, it is always a smart idea to get references and consider all information when making the final choice.

## On Cost

Local moves are generally billed at an hourly rate, ranging anywhere from $80 per hour (a 1 on our Cost scale) to $200 per hour (a 5 on our Cost scale). This rate generally includes a truck and the labor of three men. Usually, moving companies will stipulate a minimum number of hours of moving time, and sometimes also a minimum amount of travel time. You should plan to factor in a gratuity of at least $5 per man per hour. Most movers will supply blankets and other padding material at no extra cost, but anything additional—rope, boxes, packing material, tape, bubble wrap, Styrofoam—will be supplied at a significant markup over retail. So you're better off buying your own packing materials ahead of time.

Weight-rated fees are usually used for long-distance moves. The charges are based on the weight of the goods and the distance they are moved. The truck is weighed before it is loaded with your household items and furniture, and then again after. The difference between the two weights will determine how you are charged. Again, get the best estimate you can before the move, but realize that the actual cost will be calculated after all the goods are loaded on the truck and weighed.

To keep the cost down, budget-minded consumers should consider packing their own books and clothes, but leave the packing of breakable items to the movers. That way the cost of moving can be contained and yet the cost of breakage and any other kind of damage can be absorbed by the moving company.

Summer is the most popular moving season. Not surprisingly, movers are generally over-extended during the summer months. The busiest time of year is generally also the most expensive. Many movers will offer up to a 30-percent discount on moves after Labor Day. Some will also charge less for weekday moves. However, these are options that movers don't readily mention, so make sure to ask about them when you're getting an estimate.

## Contracts, Insurance and Licenses

As with most business relationships, make sure that you negotiate a written contract before you move. Most moving companies have a standard contract form. If it doesn't include every foreseeable detail of the move, insist on adding these details. As with any contract, scrutinize it carefully before signing it. Ensure that any agreed-upon terms such as mileage, packing, standard charges, additional costs and insurance are all included in the contract. The contract should state that the men will stay after 5:00 PM to finish the move if it takes longer than expected. If possible, attach a copy of the inventory to the contract as well. Retain a copy of the signed contract well after delivery has been completed to ensure that all of your possessions are delivered in the manner that the contract dictates. Be aware that most standard contracts require that the movers be paid before they unload their truck at your new home.

For interstate moves, basic insurance usually provides $.60 of coverage for each pound of goods transported ($.30 for local moves). While there is usually no additional cost associated with this kind of coverage, you do need to sign an additional contract to activate it. Unfortunately, the coverage itself is less than adequate: for instance, if your $500 television weighs ten pounds, you can collect only $3. Several other insurance plans are provided at additional cost, and protecting the value of the $500 television might require purchasing one of these supplemental plans. Optional plans come at varying costs and provide different degrees of coverage. The American Moving and Storage Association (www.moving.org) can provide you with greater insights about moving insurance—they also supply guidelines to follow when planning a move.

### COST-SAVING MOVING TIPS

✧ Packing items yourself will save you a bundle. However, movers are only liable for damage resulting from *their* packing, so limit the do-it-yourself items to unbreakables such as books and clothes.

✧ Packing materials cost significantly more when purchased from the moving company. If you're doing your own packing, buy the materials at an office products or packing products store.

✧ Insurance may seem like an expensive frill, but it can save you a lot of money and headaches in the event of damage. There are many types of coverage, so check out all your options before choosing one.

✧ The time of year and/or week during which you move will affect the cost. Since movers are typically busiest on weekends and in the summer, many companies offer discounts on moves that take place during the week and between Labor Day and Memorial Day.

## MOVERS

### Aaron's Relocation          4.5    3    4.5    4.5
223 East 58th Street, Suite 2B, New York, NY 10022
(212) 980 - 6190   www.aaronsrelocations.com
*Residential moving, fine art and antiques*

Aaron's Relocation actually started out as an antique moving outfit in 1996, but now is focused on the business of full-service residential moving. A relatively small firm, clients rave about the attention they receive. Described as the ultimate in personalized service, the company offers wrapping, packing and moving for residential and commercial customers throughout the regional area. Charging either by the hour or a flat fee based on an on-site estimate, references tell us that there are no hidden costs. Sources say the prices are fair, all agree that the level of service makes an Aaron's relocation quite a bargain, and well worth the price.

*"They are like the brothers (or husbands) you wish you had." "They did everything they promised and more." "Whether it is antiques or IKEA—they have an entire team of fabulous movers." "Their professionalism allowed me to sleep at night."*

### AirSea Packing Group Ltd.
40-45 22nd Street, Long Island City, NY 11101
(718) 937 - 6800   www.airseapacking.com
*Packing and shipping of delicate and valuable items*

A family-owned company in business for over 30 years, AirSea Packing Group. specializes in the packing and shipping of art and special items worldwide. With a client list that includes private collectors, commercial customers and museums, this firm has operations in London, Paris and Los Angeles in addition to its New York location. Consulting services include on-site advice on packing, installation, transportation and security. The firm also assists in purchasing and project management and boasts a storage facility offering the ultimate in protection and security. In addition, computerized temperature-controlled facilities, custom designed storage vaults, a viewing gallery and restoration and appraisal services make AirSea Packing a "one-stop-shopping" experience for your fine art needs.

We hear that the 80-person staff is well trained and works with integrity and discretion for the well-heeled and high-profile clients it serves. References say the types of service AirSea Packing offers are expensive, but that "door-to-door" estimates given include everything, and are typically "right on the money."

### All American Moving & Storage ∿          2.5    2.5    3    3
495A Walton Avenue, Bronx, NY 10451
(718) 585 - 4113
*Residential and commercial moving*

Families and businesses have trusted All American Moving and Storage to move them in New York and throughout the nation since 1995. A full service company, sources tell us that this firm has accommodating, flexible crews and streamlined operations, which, they say, allow them to charge reasonable prices. While not all clients, moves were problem free, most agree that the firm got the job done.

*"The men were prompt, respectful and experienced." "A moving company that cares about their customers and takes pride in their work."*

| | Quality  | Cost $ | Value ◆ | Recommend? ★ |
|---|---|---|---|---|

## All American Van Lines
**3  3  4  4**

192 Quality Plaza, Hicksville, NY  11801
(888) 777 - 6683  www.cybermove.com

*Residential and commercial moving*

With a unique approach to pricing, All American Van Lines impress clients with a flat fee move and no hidden charges, we're told. In business for over seventeen years, this company performs both commercial and residential moves locally and around the country. We hear the crews are good natured (a plus when moving day comes), are willing to accommodate special treatment or storage for a particular item and work efficiently within outlined time frames.

*"I was relieved to encounter movers that were prompt, efficient and amiable." "The crew was cheerful in spirit and meticulous in their work." "Your motto On Time, On Budget, On Target is exactly right." "Remarkable skill and strength."*

## All-Star Moving & Storage
**4.5  2.5  4.5  4.5**

88 Sanford Street, Brooklyn, NY  11205
(212) 254 - 2638

*Residential moving and storage*

Described as honest, hardworking and compassionate, clients say owner Rich Barrale sets the tone from the top for the team at All-Star, a full-service moving and storage company in business for over a quarter of a century. While primarily serving the regional area, we hear the firm has moved customers as far as Chicago. All-Star also offers storage services. References report they were treated fairly, and the move went smoothly, as planned. Free estimates are done on-site, and sources tell us that the prices are reasonable given the extraordinary treatment they receive. Barrale's commitment to outstanding quality service sets this company apart, making it truly an All-Star in the industry.

*"All-Star came on time, they were far and away above the rest, and everything worked out to our expectations." "There were no surprises, everything went well." "Unbelievably accommodating crew, they were outstanding!" "The crew took pride in their work and there was a great 'team effort' attitude." "A great experience." "Professional, thorough and accurate estimate."*

## Appeal Moving
**4  3  4  4**

238 Meagher Avenue, Bronx, NY  10465
(718) 931 - 2260

*Residential moving and rigging services*

An excellent choice for small-scale jobs and budget-minded clients, Appeal Moving has been in business for 21 years. References tell us this mid-sized firm is flexible and accommodating and takes the utmost care in handling their belongings. In addition to residential moving, Appeal can handle huge items unable to fit in elevators by offering rigging services.

*"Careful, cooperative, and honest. A good value."*

## Arthur Werner Moving & Storage
**2.5  2.5  3  4**

241 East 86th Street, Suite 2C, New York, NY  10028
(212) 831 - 6789  www.arthurwerner.com

*Residential moving*

Specializing in document, antique and piano moving and storage, we hear Arthur Werner has aided New Yorkers in relocating their precious items for over 90 years. Working primarily in the city, this firm has also been known to work across the country. Fees are calculated on a per-hour, per-cubic-foot rate so there is no contract to be signed ahead of time.

| | Quality | Cost | Value | Recommend? |
|---|---|---|---|---|
| | + | $ | ◆ | ★ |

## Auer's
4.5  4.5  4.5  5

1721 Park Avenue, New York, NY 10035
(212) 427 - 7800

*Residential and commercial moving, fine art and antiques, rigging services*

Admired for their expertise and skill in storing and transporting art, antiques and pianos, Auer's has cared for major auction houses like Sotheby's and Christie's since 1923. The firm works in Manhattan, and specializes in fine art and the rigging and hoisting of oversized pieces, but also does local, long-distance and international household moves as an agent for Wheaton Worldwide Moving. Some references blush at Auer's price tag, but consider the experience of the firm and quality of service to be worth the expensive cost.

*"Best riggers in town." "The only people I would trust to hoist a marble table up 20 floors without damaging anything."*

## August Pensa Modern Movers
3.5  3.5  4  4

1110 Kennedy Boulevard, Union City, NJ 07087
(212) 964 - 2369

*Residential moving*

## Banner
3  3.5  4  4

36-16 23rd Street, Long Island City, NY 11106
(212) 759 - 8330

*Residential and commercial moving, art and antiques*

Banner headlines in moving art and antiques for customers and art dealers in the New York City area. Using a flat-rate, per-truck fee structure, references tell us that the prices are on the higher side, but worth it for the high level of service. In business for over 80 years, we hear the pleasant and professional staff knows how to deliver a good experience along with the goods.

*"Will definitely use them again." "Would certainly recommend them to a friend." "Good value, their prices are fair given the great job they did."*

## Bay Shore Storage Warehouse Inc.
3  3  4  4

One Corporate Drive, Hauppauge , NY 11788
(631) 231 - 1313

*Residential and commercial moving, storage*

This Allied Van Lines agent provides full-service residential and commercial moving and storage services for the New York metropolitan area. We are told that Bay Shore has a league of loyal and pleased customers who appreciate the careful crews and reasonable prices.

## Ben Hur Moving & Storage 〰
2.5  2.5  3  2.5

140 West 83rd Street, New York, NY 10024
(212) 595 - 3000   www.benhur.com

*Residential and commercial moving and storage*

| | Quality | Cost | Value | Recommend? |
|---|---|---|---|---|
| | + | $ | ◆ | ★ |

Handling a full spectrum of services for both small and large relocations, Ben Hur has been in business for over ten years. This company flexes its muscle doing both local and long-distance moves for residential and commercial clients and offers dismantling and reassembling services, crating for fine art and antiques and has short- or long-term storage capabilities.

## Big John's Moving                    4     4     4     4.5
1602 First Avenue, New York, NY 10028
(212) 734 - 3300   www.bigjohnsmoving.baweb.com
*Residential and commercial moving*

Perfecting household moves on a local and national scale, clients say Big John's prides itself on the responsiveness of its staff. They know that moving is a stressful experience and we hear that the crews are patient, compassionate and come equipped with a sense of humor to usher customers through the moving day "jitters." Clients appreciate the guarantee Big John makes on pick-up and delivery times for long-distance moves, and the moving supplies delivered before the scheduled move. For those in need of additional supplies, the company even has a "moving" showroom displaying all types of boxes, which they happily deliver to your door. References say that this firm gives value to its customers by offering really good service. While on the higher end price wise, clients tell us they feel good paying for piece of mind.

*"They could not have been nicer!" "I just asked for boxes, and they delivered them quickly, and at a reasonable price." "From start to finish, an overall excellent experience." "Everything was handled with care and arrived in good condition."*

## Brownstone Brothers                 4.5    4     4     4.5
426 East 91st Street, New York, NY 10128
(212) 289 - 1511   www.brownstonebros.com
*Residential and commercial moving*

Whether the move is large or small, we hear this streamlined company is responsive, accommodating and capable. Serving the New York metropolitan area since 1977, many decorators and the carriage trade have been long-time customers of Brownstone Brothers. Offering packing, moving and storage services as well as an on-site store selling everything one could possibly need to move, references tell us that the quality is particularly good and the prices, while not inexpensive, are worth it for the level of service provided.

*"Efficient and effective. They had a quick response time, and have never broken anything!" "Very reliable." "I was dreading moving day, but in the end everything was just fine."*

## Celebrity Moving                      4.5    3.5   4.5   4.5
440 44th Drive, Long Island City, NY 11101
(212) 936 - 7171
*Residential and commercial moving and storage*

Specializing in local, high-end moving, this firm receives rave reviews from private clients as well as the trade, who say the crew at Celebrity is one of the best in the industry. Working almost exclusively through referrals from top-tier decorators, Celebrity Moving, led by Jim Gomiela, ushers merchandise through many phases of shipping for its clients. In addition to the sophisticated controlling of inventory, services include the crating of art and pianos, as well as storage. We hear Celebrity is famous for their work ethic and high level of customer care. KB 2001.

*"Jimmy and his crew are the best!" "An exceptionally accommodating firm." "They are there for you when you are in a bind." "Celebrity provides the highest quality of service, this company is outstanding."*

| | Quality  | Cost $ | Value ◆ | Recommend? ★ |
|---|---|---|---|---|

## Chelsea Movers

3     2.5     3.5     3.5

300 West 23rd Street, New York, NY 10011
(212) 243 - 8000

*Residential moving and storage*

With a largely local clientele, Chelsea Movers will move New Yorkers at affordable rates. Customers report that this is a solid, middle-ground moving company that "does the trick" for basic moving needs.

*"Accommodating and skilled—these guys know what they are doing."*

## Clancy-Cullen

2339 Cross Bronx Expressway, Bronx, NY 10462
(718) 828 - 3000   www.clancy-cullen.com

*Residential and commercial moving*

Clancy-Cullen combines the resources of a large firm with the intimate and personalized service of a small privately held business. They provide "hometown service" for moves that are local, long-distance or international for both residential and commercial clients. The company demonstrates its commitment to customer satisfaction by requiring its employees to acquire over 40 hours of training and to pass in-field tests.

## Collins Brothers Moving Corp.

4     3.5     4     4

620 Fifth Avenue, Larchmont, NY 10538
(914) 646 - 6316   www.collinsbros.com

*Residential and commercial moving and storage*

In business since 1910, the heart of this large, full-service moving and storage company is its staff. Three hundred strong, Collins Brothers performs local and long-distance residential moves as well as international and commercial relocations. We hear the rigorous training the team at Collins Brothers goes through pays off in the professionalism demonstrated on the job. All estimates are done on-site, eliminating surprises. Clients say a field supervisor monitors each move, assuring an excellent job, we're told.

*"Collins Brothers ensured that everything was done correctly." "What a wonderful job." "Not only are they skilled packers, but gentlemen you will be happy to have in your home." "The crew was very reliable, polite and helpful." "They got the job done with no pain."*

## Dahill Moving & Storage

5620 First Avenue, Brooklyn, NY 11220
(800) 765 - 0905   www.dahillmoving.com

*Residential and commercial moving*

A leading moving company in business since 1928, Dahill is an agent for Mayflower International and can move you locally, across the country or across the globe. With a sizable staff, this firm handles all phases of relocation, from packing, moving to long- and short-term storage for jobs large or small. Local rates are charged by the hour, and outside a 60-mile radius of New York City, rates are based on weight.

## Fred Worden Inc.

4     4     4     5

184-A East 7th Street, New York, NY 10009
(212) 529 - 3072

*Residential moving, artwork*

This is a specialty firm focusing on the moving and installation of art in homes and businesses. References tell us that the crew's packing skills, attentiveness and efficiency are excellent, and while most say they are on the pricey side, the piece of mind in knowing their valuables were well taken care of is by far worth the cost.

*"These guys did a great job." "I will definitely hire them again." "Very good with high-end art."*

| | Quality | Cost | Value | Recommend? |
|---|---|---|---|---|
| | + | $ | ◆ | ★ |

## Gander & White                 4.5    4.5    4    5
21-44 44th Road, Long Island City, NY 11101
(718) 784 - 8444

*Residential moving, art and antiques*

Providing climate-controlled storage, Gander & White are high-end residential movers, packers and shippers of fine art and antiques both domestically and abroad. With offices in New York, London and Paris, this firm is truly an international operation. Clients are quick to note the personalized attention they receive from the professional and reliable staff. Many reported that they are meticulous and accommodating, and although on the high-end price wise, are worth it for the outstanding service provided.

*"A truly professional job." "They are used to the most discriminating clientele, and have foremen that can relate to the clients." "While quite expensive, they stayed until the job was done. It was worth the cost." "They didn't even bat an eyelash when my husband and I had them move a large armoire four times back and forth across the room." "They will even hang pictures on the wall!" "When the platform they promised didn't come on the right day, they sent it later and moved our entire garage onto it at no extra charge."*

## J. Santini & Brothers Inc.       3.5    3.5    4    4
932 Southern Boulevard, Bronx, NY 10459
(718) 542 - 3000

*Residential and commercial moving*

Not to be confused with the similarly named moving firm J. Santini, J. Santini & Brothers has been in operation since 1917 and primarily serves clients in New York but will also service other parts of the country. The company charges an hourly rate for each mover and a fee for the truck. Packing charges are based on carton sizes. References tell us you can expect a fair deal and decent service from this company.

## Liberty Moving & Storage        2.5    2.5    4    4
17 Central Avenue, Hauppauge, NY 11788
(212) 223 - 6440   www.libertymoving.com

*Residential and commercial moving, large objects and art*

Family owned and operated since 1939, Liberty provides local moves or moves "from sea to shining sea" as an agent for United Van Lines. Available to handle small or large projects, they've been known to honor such requests as hooking up major appliances, unpacking household goods, and reassembling furniture. We are told this firm takes special care of art, statues and pianos, and that the helpful crew is responsive, diligent and thoroughly trained in the "art" of moving. References tell us that the rates are reasonable and the service is good.

## Liffey Van Lines Inc.

3    2.5    4    4

229 East 120th Street, New York, NY 10035
(212) 410 - 3500   www.alliedvan.com
*Residential and commercial moving*

Whether it's a one piece cupboard or an entire household, Liffey Van Lines will move anything anywhere. Estimates are always done on-site, avoiding hidden costs later on. Liffy's moving and packing services encompass both local and long-distance relocations (they are Ireland specialists) and we hear that this company offers good value at a fair price.

## Meyer's Moving & Storage

3    3    4    4.5

370 Concord Avenue, Bronx, NY 10454
(212) 688 - 8888   www.meyers-moving.com
*Residential and commercial moving, art and antiques*

With 18 years of local service, this Mayflower agent has a capability to move you across town, across the country or across the world. Specializing in artwork and antiques, Meyer's Moving & Storage can handle a single priceless piece, or an entire museum collection. Clients praise the high quality of service and attention they receive from this professional and efficient moving company, regardless of the size of the job. While the fees depend on the job's size, Meyer's makes a point of clearly stating the prices and not surprising customers down the road.

*"A big thank you." "Even though we made last-minute changes, our needs were accommodated promptly, politely and without hesitation." "Kudos on a job well done." "Thoughtful and careful."*

## Moishe's Moving Systems

3    3.5    3.5    4

449 West 14th Street, New York, NY 10014
(212) 691 - 8681   www.moishes.com
*Residential commercial moving, art and antiques, pianos*

Started as a man-with-a-van business in 1983, now one can't help to often see a Moishe's Moving truck, one in it's fleet of 50. The company proudly claims to perform more than 10,000 moves a year. In addition to household relocations, Moishe's offers moving services for art and antiques, and boasts its own piano-moving division. Client say rates are on the higher end, reflecting the more delicate pieces this company handles, but we hear that rates go down during off-peak moving times, which are any time other than the beginning or end of the month.

## Morgan Manhattan Moving & Storage

4.5    4.5    4    4.5

434 East 91st Street, New York, NY 10128
(212) 633 - 7800
*Residential moving, fine art and antiques, wine storage*

Catering to discriminating, high-end clients as well as celebrities, Morgan Manhattan, an agent for United Van Lines, performs moves locally and nationally. The firm shies away from smaller jobs, but we are told will handle single, priceless pieces. In addition, references report Morgan cares for the storage and inventory control of fine wine collections, housing them in their refrigerated and humidity controlled facility and tracking them with a sophisticated, interactive computer system. While many say this fifth-generation firm charges a generous sum, they say you get generous service back in return.

*"Very careful, very seamless, very professional. I have absolutely no complaints." "The service was impeccable." "I wouldn't trust my valuables to anyone else." "Very personal attention." "I demand the best, and I got white-glove treatment from this company."*

| | Quality | Cost | Value | Recommend? |
|---|---|---|---|---|
| | ✚ | $ | ◆ | ★ |

## Moves LLC
224 Twelfth Avenue, New York, NY 10001
(212) 695 - 0200   www.movesllc.com

2.5    2.5    3    4

*Residential and commercial moving*

From free, on-site estimates and delivery of moving supplies, to storage of your belongings, Moves LLC offers full-moving and storage services to its clients. Customers are comfortable recommending Moves to take good care of their possessions. We hear that the staff is friendly, professional and efficient. If you are looking for basic, no-frills moving and storage, Moves fits the bill.

*"I would happily trust Moves with any move I need in the future—very professional." "Didn't blink an eye at the challenge we presented to them." "Every single item was wrapped and shipped with much care and attention, and arrived just the way it left—in perfect shape. I recommend them."*

## Moving Ahead ▪

4.5    3.5    4.5    5

101 Fifth Avenue, Garden City, NY 11040
(212) 262 - 0600   www.movingahead.com

*Residential and commercial moving and storage*

Sporting an exemplary record up and down the East Coast, Moving Ahead comes highly recommended by both private and commercial clients. Led by John Tarko, the team is described as knowledgeable and professional as well as courteous and flexible. This firm is designated as the only official mover of Manhattan Mini-Storage. From the spotless trucks to the work ethic of their employees, references tell us that Moving Ahead is the only company they will use for both their personal and business relocations. Charging by the hour, estimates are given for really big jobs. While not the cheapest on our list, all agree that a stress-free move is well worth the price.

*"We had relationships with other movers and always had issues with customer service. Five years ago we gave Moving Ahead a shot and we've never looked back!" "They're extremely professional and helpful—our relationship is based on trust." "What sets them apart is that they work with the customers to resolve the few issues that ever arise, instead of simply turning their backs and walking off, as most movers do." "We would never use another moving company."*

## Moving Man Inc.

3    3    3    3

429 West 127th Street, New York, NY 10027
(212) 281 - 4300   www.movingman.baweb.com

*Residential moving, art, antiques and pianos*

The eponymous Moving Man moves throughout New York City, and as an agent for Wheaton Worldwide Moving, is able to handle nationwide and international jobs as well. In addition to standard household moves, the firm takes special care of fine art, pianos, antiques and other more fragile possessions. Rates are calculated by weight for long-distance moves, and by the hour for local moves.

## MZ Movers Systems

3    3.5    3.5    4

543 Tarrytown Road, White Plains, NY 10607
(914) 421 - 9095

*Residential and commercial moving*

This firm comes recommended by private clients as well as the trade who tell us MZ Moving Systems has proven to be a company dedicated to total customer service. The firm handles each customer uniquely, customizing each job based on needs. Visual inspections are done to determine cost, which we hear are on the higher side, but reasonable given the high quality level of service.

*"Honest, fair." "Did a very good job—we had no problems at all."*

## Noah's Ark Moving Co. Inc.
2112 Broadway, New York, NY 10023
(212) 874 - 1313   www.noahsarkinc.com

*Residential and commercial moving*

Surviving almost entirely from the bouyant referrals of satisfied clients, Noah's Ark has been handling clients, two by two, since 1982. This firm works locally and anywhere across the continental United States. In addition to residential moves, this firm offers packing services and storage. We hear that the prices, which are charged by the hour locally and by weight for long distance, are fair.

## Oz Moving & Storage
**2.5   2.5   3   3**

314 East 78th Street, New York, NY 10021
(212) 924 - 4485   www.oz-moving.com

*Residential and commercial moving and storage*

Clients moving somewhere over the metropolitan rainbow seek out Oz Moving and Storage. In addition to local residential moving services, we're told Oz can also do long-distance relocations, and offers mini-storage, warehousing and document storage. Clients like the fact crews travel to their location in order to prepare an estimate, and will wrap and pack items destined for storage, providing them with an inventory list. Hourly fees are the rule locally, while long distance is determined by weight, distance and cubic foot. Clients say Oz understands there is no place like home.

## Pace Moving & Storage
**3   2.5   3.5   3.5**

2107 Borden Avenue, Long Island City, NY 11101
(212) 867 - 4874

*Residential moving, storage*

While some references are impressed with this five-year-old, mid-sized firm and rave to us about Pace's prices and courteous, conscientious and very speedy service, others are less "moved" with the outcome of the inevitable moving-day problems. Pace says it will beat anyone else's prices and promises no hidden costs when you use the company to move your household (it will move single pieces as well). We're told Pace even offers one month of free storage with long-distance moves. For the most part, clients have noted Pace's skill in dealing with the most complicated multi-location moves, carefully handling the goods they have been entrusted with.

*"We would certainly recommend this company highly." "My experience with Pace last month was an absolute pleasure." "Everyone who was involved in the move had nothing but compliments about how everything was handled, packed and delivered." "This firm was professional, courteous, on time and generally a joy to work with."*

| | Quality | Cost | Value | Recommend? |
|---|---|---|---|---|
| | + | $ | ◆ | ★ |

## Padded Wagon

| | 2.5 | 2.5 | 3.5 | 3.5 |

163 Exterior Street, Bronx, NY 10451
(212) 222 - 4880  www.paddedwagon.com
*Residential and commercial moving, fine art*

Judging from the happy trails this large, nationwide firm has left behind with the city's top decorators and auction houses, Padded Wagon proves to be a solid, reliable, middle-of-the-road mover. Offering residential and commercial moving services, the firm also employs a mechanical crew to hang chandeliers, sconces, etc. Customers note the company's reliability and responsiveness, especially for last minute needs. Customers also feel Padded Wagon's crews do a professional job at a fair price.

## Paladin Movers

| | 2.5 | 2 | 3 | 3 |

1633 Woodstock Street, Elmont, NY 11003
(516) 561 - 0959
*Residential moving*

A relatively small firm, Paladin handles residential moves throughout the regional area. In business since 1966, we hear that their prices are reasonable, and their service reliable.

## Personal Touch

| | 5 | 3.5 | 5 | 5 |

78-61 79th Place, Glendale, NY 11385
(718) 417 - 6740
*Residential moving*

Working exclusively through referrals, Personal Touch has developed a reputation for being one of the finest moving companies in New York. Owner, Sal diPiazza takes the name Personal Touch to new levels, meeting with each client to estimate the individual needs of the job and establish a flat fee to cover the entire move. Clients remark there are no hidden costs—the price estimated is the price paid.

Clients report that diPiazza brings to each job far more men than they had ever expected. All involved seem to benefit from this unique "high man power policy"— the customer gets a speedy move and the crew gets in and out in a reasonable time. We hear clients couldn't be happier with diPiazza and his amazing staff and say that the value and service at Personal Touch is truly exemplary.

*"Best mover I have ever used!" "There is no reason to consider another mover." "I was so impressed, they were on time and right on budget." "The entire experience was pleasant from the time they arrived until the time they left." "Efficient, courteous, careful and anxious to please." "Unbelievably efficient, pleasant, and fast."*

## The Packing Shop

| | 4.5 | 3.5 | 4.5 | 4.5 |

89 Leuning Street, South Hackensack, NJ 07606
(201) 342 - 9097  www.thepackingshop.co.uk
*Packing, storage and transportation of fine art and antiques*

The Packing Shop founded in London in 1987, is one of Europe's leaders in the specialized field of the packing, storage and transportation of fine art and antiques. Clients throughout the United States can enjoy all of the benefits of those in Europe, as this company now has a United States operation headquartered in northern New Jersey. The firm serves trade clients including decorators, art dealers, galleries and auction houses, as well an impressive list of private collectors and art investors who laud the efficiency, reliability and professionalism of the 50-strong team. Offering daily collections and deliveries in Manhattan, this full-service organization will unpack and remove your packing materials.

Capable of dealing with large volumes of extremely valuable shipments by land, air and sea, the company boasts high-tech security and tracking systems and state-of-the-art, climate-controlled and secure warehouses in London and New Jersey. We hear that the staff is well trained, and that they constantly strive to remain leaders in the field. References tell us that the piece of mind they get from knowing their precious cargo is in safe hands is well worth the cost.

*"Incredibly reliable and efficient." "Packing is exceptional." "A joy to deal with."*

### The Velvet Touch

| | 4 | 3.5 | 4 | 4 |
| --- | --- | --- | --- | --- |

145-21 23rd Avenue, Whitestone, NY 11357
(718) 742 - 5320
*Residential and commercial moving and storage, art and antiques*

This relatively young company has taken the moving industry in New York City by storm, developing a client list of top decorators and antique dealers who praise The Velvet Touch for being professional, trustworthy and most importantly, careful. With a team in the moving business for fifteen years, the firm handles residential and commercial jobs, specializing in art and antiques. Clients tell us that the crews at The Velvet Touch handle their delicate and expensive items with the utmost care, as if they were their own possessions. Others nod to the personalized service where owner Kimon Thermos personally performed their on-site estimate, as well as stopped by the job to assure things were going as planned.

*"They are always willing to work with clients and agree on fair pricing." "I have confidence in them."*

### Tony's Fine Art Movers

| | 4 | 3.5 | 4 | 5 |
| --- | --- | --- | --- | --- |

13069 224th Street, Springfield Gardens, NY 11413
(718) 949 - 6112
*Art moving*

Not surprisingly, Tony's Fine Art Movers specialized in moving fine art and antiques, which sources say this firm handles with professionalism and care. Clients tell us the crews are pleasant and meticulous in their work, and for the service outstandingly rendered, the prices are worth it.

*"A lovely man who took great care of my art and the interior of my home." "Very thoughtful." "Reasonably priced and the highest possible quality of work."*

### West Side Movers

| | 3 | 3 | 4 | 4 |
| --- | --- | --- | --- | --- |

644 Amsterdam Avenue, New York, NY 10025
(212) 874 - 3800   www.westsidemovers.com
*Residential and commercial moving, art and antiques*

From well-known celebs to the largest businesses, West Side Movers has been relocating Manhattanites (not only West-siders) for over 26 years. Sources tell us this full-service firm specializing in moving fine antiques is professional, reliable and even has a moving supply store. We hear its costs fall in line with industry standards.

*"A good value. They are definitely on my short list."*

### Yorkville Moving & Storage

| | 3.5 | 3.5 | 4 | 4 |
| --- | --- | --- | --- | --- |

1587 Third Avenue, New York, NY 10128
(212) 722 - 3890
*Residential moving and storage, art and antiques*

Serving the New York metro area for over 70 years, this mid-sized firm offers moving services as well as storage for fine art and antiques in two local warehouses.

# HIRING PAINTERS & WALLPAPERERS

You walk into a room painted a beautiful celadon green and immediately your mood changes—you become calmer, more relaxed. By merely changing the color of a room, you can produce a feeling of drama or tranquility. Designers know that painting is one of the quickest, most versatile and cost-effective things you can do to transform a room. But painting can be a messy and hazardous proposition for the novice, so many homeowners opt to hire a professional contractor.

Paint contractors with a wide range of abilities and services abound in the New York City area. Choices range from small start-ups to large established firms, and from straight painters to custom muralists. Depending upon the size of the job and the quality and complexity of the work, there is a paint contractor out there for you.

## WHERE TO LOOK FOR A PROFESSIONAL

Finding the right paint contractor for your job involves some research. It is very important to check references and ask to see a certificate of insurance. Each contractor should have worker's compensation and general liability insurance which protects you from jobsite-related liabilities. Several trade organizations, such as the Painting and Decorating Contractors of America (www.pdca.org), list paint contractors in your area. And of course, *The Franklin Report* offers a range of client-tested choices.

## CONTRACTS

Reputable contractors will encourage using a written contract. Your contract should clearly explain the scope of the work to be performed and include a list of the surfaces to be painted, a time schedule for the project, payment procedures and any warranty or guarantee the contractor might offer.

## PRICING SYSTEMS

When considering the price for painting it is important to know that the cost structure for straight painting is much different than that of decorative work. While some firms do both types of work, it is important to know that your bill will be determined using different factors.

The cost for straight painting in residential homes varies based on such factors as the cost of the materials used and the company's overhead costs. You should invite at least three paint contractors to bid on your paint job, and ask each to submit a detailed written proposal. Painting contractors charge on a per person per day basis, which generally runs in the $425 to $475 range for nonunion jobs (this equates to approximately a 2.5 to 3 on our Cost scale.). Union jobs start at about $500 per-person per-day. The contractor should provide you with an overall cost estimate for the job that is broken down by room. Also ask for a step-by-step plan outlining how the job will be spackled, skimmed and painted. If colors are being matched, ask the painter to apply 24 inch-square samples on the walls.

Decorative painting, which is often considered "art," as in the case of murals or decorative finishes, is much more subjective price wise. There is usually more involved—there are meetings with the homeowner, the decorator and the painter, determining a style or theme and incorporating the decorative work into the overall design plan. Time frames for completing a job are usually longer compared to straight painting. All of these factors contribute to the cost of decorative painting.

When considering the "bottom line" for any painting job, ask for client references. They can provide valuable insight into not only the quality of work and timing, but cost as well.

## How Many Painters Will Be in My House?

The size of the crew needed largely depends upon the scope of the job involved. Some painters listed in this guide are sole proprietors who work on small jobs themselves and subcontract larger jobs—others are larger companies with complete crews. Ask how many men will be working on your job and whether there will there be a supervisor or principal on site.

## The Elements of a Professional Paint Job

Typically, paint contractors offer the services of straight or flat painting (meaning no decorative textures, just one color in any finish, including glossy) and wallpapering. Flat painting a room involves preparing the walls, trim and ceiling surfaces for the paint as well as the paint job itself. To prepare walls, paint crews will do all the taping, plastering, plaster restoration, if needed, and skim coating. This prep work is considered one of the most important elements of a paint job as it provides the foundation for the paint. A primer coat, which prepares the walls for the paint, should be applied to dry walls. Two coats of high-quality paint should be applied to the wall surfaces.

## Which Paint?

The quality of the paint is crucial in determining its longevity. Fine quality paint, properly applied, should last for six to seven years. If you or your contractor skimp on the quality of the paint, you may be facing a new paint job a lot sooner than you would like. The two most common types of paints are latex and oil-based paints. Latex paint is water based and dries quickly, which allows for more than one coat to be applied in a day. Latex paint is better at resisting mildew, easier to clean and lasts longer than alkyd paints, which are oil based. Alkyd paints are preferred by many painters because they are durable and long lived, but they take longer to dry, have a significant odor and can yellow over time. Most experts agree that oil-based paints are best suited for the doors and trim, and latex paint for the walls and ceilings.

## Lead Paint Hazards

The presence of lead paint presents health hazards in many homes. The federal government banned the use of lead paints in 1978, therefore, if you live in an older city building, your apartment is likely to contain a layer of lead paint if it was painted prior to that year. When sanding is done in advance of painting, the sanding may cause lead dust to enter the air in your home. Your contractor should provide you with a pamphlet that discusses lead issues in your home. Ask your contractor what measures he takes to ensure that lead particles are eliminated. If you need to have your home inspected or have lead removed, the Environmental Protection Agency (www.epa.gov) issues licenses for companies and professionals who work with lead control, including removal, inspection and risk assessment. Other good resources for more information about lead and asbestos include the American Lung Association (www.lungusa.org), the US Consumer Product Safety Commission (www.cpsc.gov), the American Industrial Hygiene Association (www.aiha.org), the Department of Housing and Urban Development (www.hud.gov) and the Occupational Safety and Health Administration (www.osha.gov).

## Wallpaper

Wallpaper can add depth, texture and visual interest to a room. Floral or striped wallpaper can make even small windowless rooms cheerful. It can be a costly investment, so it is important to find a qualified, competent professional to install your paper. Finding a wallpaper hanger can be as easy as talking to your paint contractor, as most of them also provide this service. Depending upon the complexity of the job, it may be appropriate to contact a professional who specializes in wallpaper hanging. One source is the National Guild of Professional Paperhangers (NGPP). For their local chapter local, call (516) 433-5701 or visit www.ngpp.org.

Cost for wallpapering is based on a per roll basis with rates averaging about $50 per roll. Most wallpaper is sold in double-roll units, which measure approximately 60 square feet. The price quoted should include trimming the sides of the paper if necessary. Professionals will strip your walls of existing paper and prep it for the new paper for an additional fee. Your wallpaper hanger should calculate the quantity of paper you will need for the room based on the room size as well as the "repeat" pattern on your paper. The larger the repeat, the more paper you will need. The newer vinyl wallpaper comes pre-pasted, while traditional and costlier papers need to be trimmed and pasted with wheat paste.

## Decorative Finishes: The Art of Imitation

Decorative finishes, often called "faux finishes," are used by painters to add depth or to imitate materials such as marble, wood, paper, stone, metal and fabric. These finishes can be elegant, whimsical or dramatic, depending upon the artist and the paint technique utilized. Current trends today include fake wood- ("faux bois") paneled libraries, limestone facades and "washed" finishes. When done by a gifted artist, a faux finish can cost more than the material being imitated. Decorative finishes can customize a space through color and texture and dramatically reflect the owner's style.

## Decorative Painting: A Master Tradition

A wall-sized mural that recreates a Pompeian gallery . . . majestic Greek columns beside the swimming pool . . . famous storybook characters dancing along the walls of a child's room . . . these enchanting effects are the work of decorative painters.

Decorative painting is an art form using techniques that have been passed down by artisans throughout the centuries. Today, decorative painters can come from a variety of backgrounds—some have fine art degrees, many have studied the techniques of the Old Masters in Europe and others have been schooled specifically in decorative painting. These professionals carry the legacy of a tradition that was once passed from master to apprentice. Both artists and craftsmen, many decorative painters have a thorough knowledge of specific historical and decorative styles and have the ability to translate this knowledge in a historically accurate artistic rendering. Others, however, are clearly unqualified to be attempting this work.

There are many forms of decorative painting. Some of the most popular today include fresco, murals and trompe l'oeil. Over time, techniques and materials have been enhanced and improved, allowing artists and artisans to produce works that have lasted—and will last—for centuries.

When you are considering any decorative painting style, ask to see a portfolio of the artist's work and, if possible, visit a home that has work of a similar nature. Decorative showhouses are also an excellent venue in which to witness the artistry of decorative painting. Many decorative painters use these showcases to demonstrate their talents. If working with an interior designer, consult with him or her on the project and how it will enhance your overall room design. If the designer finds the artist for you, ask how that affects fees. Artists should also provide you with renderings of the work being produced.

Fees vary widely for decorative painting and are based on many factors, including the scope and scale of the project and the expertise of the painter. Ask your contractor to provide you with a sample board of the paint technique you desire. Some charge for this service while others include it in the total cost of the project. Decorative finishes can be charged on a per person or on a per day basis but are usually priced per job.

Decorative painting can be a major investment, but certainly one with exquisite results.

### PAINT-CHOOSING TIPS

- ✧ Use oil-based paint for metals and trim; latex for wood and drywall.
- ✧ High-traffic areas need a durable, easy-to-clean paint job. Use delicate paint applications in light-traffic areas only.
- ✧ Use flat paint for base coats; gloss to set off trim and doors.
- ✧ Be alert to the number of coats required. Eggshell paints, for example, take at least one extra coat.

| | Quality | Cost | Value | Recommend? |
|---|---|---|---|---|
| | + | $ | ◆ | ★ |

## Painters & Wallpaperers

### Alatis Painting                                            4.5    3.5    4.5    5
143-11 45th Avenue, Flushing, NY  11355
(718) 358 - 9051

*Decorative and straight painting and wallpapering*

Alatis is a family-run painting company that comes highly recommended by some of New York City's top contractors.  The timely and professional Alatis team does everything from straight residential painting and wallpapering to specialty painting and decorative finishes, and sources tell us they execute a great finished product.

*"They do great work." "Very professional and timely."*

### Alton Inc.                                                  4    3.5    4.5    5
40-19 35th Avenue, Long Island City, NY  11101
(718) 784 - 4230

*Decorative and straight painting and wallpapering*

The painter of choice for a number of high-end building professionals, Alton offers straight residential painting, wallpapering and decorative painting.  We hear Alton excels in faux finishes, trompe l'oeil, graining, gilding, Venetian plaster and stucco.  Unlike many other practitioners of decorative work, this firm does all of its own prep work, which we're told is exemplary.  Alton comes highly recommended for its value, service and outstanding work.

*"Very responsive." "Great prep work." "They did a fantastic job—well worth the money."*

### Andrea & Timothy Biggs Painting 💼                          4.5    4    5    5
279 Sterling Place, Brooklyn, NY  11238
(718) 857 - 9034

*Faux finishes and murals*

We're told "there isn't anything these two better halves can't do."  Andrea and Tim Biggs collaborate to produce a wide variety of decorative paintings and finishes for both residential and commercial clients.  Together they have developed an expansive portfolio that includes trompe l'oeil murals combined with landscape painting to create architectural illusions, large-scale murals with a focus on floral, organic or fantasy imagery and faux finishes that include glazing and marbleizing for ornamental pieces, walls and ceilings.  Clients remark the Biggs' work is consistently completed with "beautiful quality."  Andrea and Tim often produce their own creations, but they also reproduce traditional artworks and create pieces that bring their clients' vision to fruition.  Sources say they collaborate closely with designers and architects to integrate their work into the overall design.

Andrea holds an MFA in painting from Bard College and Tim studied design and painting at Parsons School of Design.  They are described by peers and clients alike as "true artists with a businesslike approach" and "very accommodating and professional."  One architect "can't imagine anyone not being pleased."

*"I love working with them—they're honest, businesslike and reliable." "I think they're terrific and I'm a tough customer." "They're clearly high-level professionals and quality people." "Their faux marble work has held up beautifully for ten years and counting." "They are both extremely talented." "They always do what they commit to." "Flexible and client oriented."*

## Andrew Tedesco

**4.5  4  4.5  4.5**

122 West 26th Street, New York, NY  10001
(212) 924 - 8438  www.andrewtedesco.com

*Decorative painting and murals*

Customers have been very impressed with the quality and creativity of Andrew Tedesco's painting, from the high-end glazing and gold-leaf ceilings to murals, trompe l'oeil and fine art. Tedesco has done residential and commercial work, both on-site and in his studio, for ten years. Clients have been particularly impressed with his ability to take their ideas to another level, adapting the work to fit the space while balancing their taste with his style of painting.  He has also been known to work with the city's top decorators and is routinely seen at Kips Bay and at the French Design Showcase.

Educated at the Parsons School of Design, Tedesco also spent some time working with Broadway scenic artists and has drawn on all of these experiences to create a unique personal style, often using the palettes of old masters.  We hear his impressive results may come at quite a price, but are well worth it

*"Amazing work at a good value."  "An extremely high quality painter."*

## Anne Harris Studio 🛍

**4.5  4  4.5  4.5**

145 East 74th Street, Suite 11B, New York, NY  10021
(212) 794 - 3540  www.anneharrisstudio.com

*Murals and decorative painting*

Delighting both private clients and decorators, Anne Harris's work has been gracing the walls of New York City residences for sixteen years. Painting in a wide range of styles, she is best known for her old master-style landscapes, which are characterized as realistic and tight.  The soft color palettes catch the eye of clients, who tell us that Harris's talent is complemented by her flexible, easygoing personality, as well as her skills as a strong technician.  This firm also does furniture distressing and aging.

*"Incredibly talented—she is in a class by herself."  "Extraordinarily accommodating, adorable person."*

## Anton Sattler

**5  4.5  4.5  5**

466 Main Street, New Rochelle, NY  10801
(914) 636 - 2916

*Decorative and straight painting and wallpapering*

In business since 1891, Anton Sattler has developed a premier, international reputation for the very finest high-end residential painting.  Clients include some of the most prominent businesspeople and most exclusive decorators worldwide. Sattler does straight painting as well as a range of decorative custom work.  With a team of 50, we hear the firm's craftsman are professional, neat, tidy and courteous.  References uniformly judged the quality of Anton Sattler's work to be the very best and, while costly, worth the price.

*"Very beautiful work;—this is as good as it gets."  "A painter's painter."  "They do the highest quality work."*

## Applied Aesthetics

**4  3  5  5**

90 Valentine Avenue, Glen Cove, NY  11542
(516) 759 - 2188

*Decorative painting, gilding and plaster finishes*

Sought after by some of the most reputable decorators and architects in New York, Jennifer Hakker and her team at Applied Aesthetics perform all kinds of decorative and specialty painting.  Specializing in plaster finishes, gilding and wood graining, Hakker also works in trompe l'oeil, painted furniture and fabrics. References tell us that Jennifer Hakker is a marked creative talent, and shows a

| | Quality | Cost | Value | Recommend? |
|---|---|---|---|---|
| | **+** | **$** | **◆** | **★** |

real interest in the ideas her clients bring to the table. Many comment on the firm's professionalism and reliability, remarkable attention to detail and the consistently superior results. KB 2001.

*"A magician with paint!" "Applied Aesthetics are modern-day masters." "The final project is always more brilliant than I imagined." "Jennifer and her crew are the most reliable, focused and talented decorative painters I have ever worked with." "Her work is consistently superior and she is extremely professional." "I would never have anyone else touch my walls."*

## Applied Arts       4     3     4.5     5
174 Nassau Street, Brooklyn, NY  11201
(718) 858 - 2495
*Decorative and straight painting*

This boutique shop of four painters has been doing decorative and straight residential painting in New York and Connecticut for 27 years. Services include wood graining, marbling, glazing, trompe l'oeil and faux molding, for which it does all its own prep work. Professionals in the trade tell us they have built lasting working relationships with principal Jim Sheban and call on his firm repeatedly.

Sheban has a background in fine art, including postgraduate work at the Whitney. Sources praise Sheban, saying he is easygoing and delightful to work with. Similarly, his firm's work wins accolades as clients tell us it is high quality and comes at a surprisingly low cost.

*"Beautiful work. High recommendation." "Sheban is not only professional, but he is easygoing and great to work with."*

## Audra Frank Painting       4     3     4.5     4.5
1118-A North Avenue, Plainfield, NJ  07062
(800) 293 - 2212
*Straight and decorative painting, wallpapering, plastering*

For over 25 years, this midsized, husband-and-wife team-run firm has provided painting, plastering and wallpapering services in New York City and surrounding areas. Employed in some of the city's most prestigious apartments and by top contractors, the firm works for residential and commercial clients, and we are told that its expertise is in special finishes like glazing and color plastering. We hear this duo is said to be helpful, and considering the high quality of work, clients tell us Audra Frank is reasonably priced.

*"Audra Frank and her team are very reliable—they handled the job quickly and professionally." "They will try to accommodate clients needs and try to correct issues." "Excellent service and terrific painting—the team was outstanding."*

## Bernard Garvey Painting       3.5     2     5     5
63-62 78th Street, Middle Village, NY  11379
(718) 894 - 8272
*Straight painting and wallpapering*

Bernard Garvey offers painting and wallpapering services to residential clients who tell us that he is one of the nicest, most accommodating people you could ever have working in your home. One reference toward the end of her pregnancy felt the need to make her apartment as welcoming as possible for the baby's arrival and called on Garvey for help. He arrived the next day with three workmen and transformed her apartment with "the most amazing" paint job. Clients rave about the staff, noting the positive attitude, high character and professional work ethic they possess. They say this company's even-handed price coupled with its hand-holding service provides a phenomenal value.

*"I recommend him to all my friends—the quality is excellent!" "Very organized, kind and helpful." "It is a pleasure doing business with Mr. Garvey." "One of the best!" "The entire team is honest, ethical and professional." "I suggested that he raise his prices, but he said he is just looking to make a fair living."*

| | Quality  | Cost $ | Value ◆ | Recommend?  ★ |
|---|---|---|---|---|

## Bill Gibbons Studio

3.5    4    3.5    4

368 Broadway, Suite 203, New York, NY 10013
(212) 227 - 0039   www.billgibbons.com

*Murals on canvas and tiles*

Bill Gibbons designs and creates traditional murals on canvas in his New York City studio and once painted, the murals are then installed like wallpaper in the client's residence. His work includes classical pieces, architectural renderings, landscapes, trompe l'oeil paintings and decorative ceiling tiles. Clients say they have Gibbons's murals removed and relocated. In business for over a dozen years, he works frequently with New York City interior designers and also with private clients. We understand his prices are slightly bolder than others,' but then so they say is his art.

## Brian Kehoe Wallcovering/BFK Inc.

4    3.5    4.5    4.5

506 West 42nd Street, Suite 5E, New York, NY 10036
(212) 629 - 3040

*Wallpapering*

Strictly a wallcovering specialist, Brian Kehoe Wallcovering/BFK, led by Brian Kehoe, has been serving New York City residents and businesses for 15 years. The firm handles both large and small projects with care. It has been entrusted with the hanging of a mural at the Guggenheim and the wallpapering of designer showrooms. References tell us the team is a pleasure to work with, and praise their reliable, accommodating and professional service. While the firm's expert services are said to be pricey, they are competitive with similar tier professionals.

*"Their work is outstanding." "Willing to be flexible and accommodate our schedule." "Brian has always provided the highest level of professional, reliable service." "I find his prices competitive and his work excellent." "I would recommend Mr. Kehoe and his staff with complete confidence."*

## Bruce Wimbiscus

3.5    2.5    5    5

430 East 63rd Street, New York, NY 10021
(212) 421 - 0687

*Decorative and straight painting and wallpapering*

If repeat business is any indication of a good reputation, Bruce Wimbiscus has achieved it and then some. Clients tell us they use Wimbiscus and his three-person team year after year for straight interior painting and wallpapering for their professional, honest and pleasant approach. This firm performs an array of decorative painting which includes rag, sponge and faux finishes. We hear Wimbuscus makes great suggestions, and is diligent on followup and touch-ups. The sum of these parts exceeds the fair minded cost of the whole.

*"Whatever you need. They are honest and wonderful." "Nothing fancy, great straight wallpaper." "Bruce does a very professional job." "He is very easy to work with and offers great suggestions."*

| | Quality + | Cost $ | Value ◆ | Recommend? ★ |
|---|---|---|---|---|

## Carl Masi
**3.5  3  4.5  4.5**

321 East 12th Street, New York , NY  10003
(212) 475 - 1789

*Straight painting and plastering*

With a client list consisting almost entirely of referrals, one-man-show Carl Masi has been performing interior residential painting and plastering in New York City for over 22 years.  Masi works throughout the city with much work south of 57th Street.  Described as meticulous, professional and wonderful to work with, clients tell us that he offers high-end quality at a fair price.

*"Carl is like an artist—very meticulous."   "Always does excellent work and is a pleasure to work with."   "Carl is honest, reliable—I totally trust him."   "He really cares about the end product and making the customer happy."   "Pleasant, receptive and trustworthy."   Carl is so wonderful—I only have great things to say about him."*

## Carol Cannon
**3.5  3  4.5  5**

32-45 37th Street, Astoria, NY  11103
(718) 956 - 9334

*Decorative painting and murals*

Client's are equally impressed by Carol Cannon's decorative painting, which includes all types of special effect treatments for walls and ceilings, as well as murals in both classical and abstract motifs, and her dedication to the craft.  We hear the "charming Cannon" is not satisfied until she can capture exactly the right color.  References also describe her as reliable, fair and very honest.  Known for her trellis mural at Nicholas Antiques in the D&D Building, Cannon works through-out New York City and the Hamptons.

*"Delivers that dreamy look."   "Can get you exactly the right texture, color and mood."   "Very accommodating . . . works hard to get it right."   "Very consistent and very professional."*

## Chuck Hettinger
**4.5  3.5  4.5  4.5**

208 East 13th Street, New York, NY  10003
(212) 614 - 9848

*Decorative painting and color consultations*

Clients say Chuck Hettinger merges the skills and sensibilities of mixed media and decorative painting with great success.  For the past 21 years, Hettinger has been specializing in decorative surface work, including special glazes, stripes, faux bois, marbling and stenciling.  His mixed media work is shown in New York galleries and sold to patrons locally and around the world.  In addition to his other work, he will do color consultations.  A number of distinguished clients and top decorators recommended Hettinger, labeling him "a true artist" who also has "a sense of humor."  They say working with the witty, friendly and easygoing artisan was a treat.

## Colleen Babington
**3.5  3  4  4.5**

300 West 12th Street, New York, NY  10014
(212) 924 - 4868

*Decorative painting*

With an education in classical, old-school painting and study at the Isabel O'Neil Studio, we hear this soft-spoken, unpretentious artist brings a strong academic background in decorative painting to her work.  Exciting finishes which range from gilding and glazing to stenciling and marbling, clients tell us her work is exquisite.  Working primarily in New York City, Babington takes jobs both in residences and commercial sites, including designer showrooms.

*"She really does exquisite work."   "So easy to work with, a pleasant experience from beginning to end."*

## Donald Smith Design Services Inc.
4     3     5     5
555 Main Street, Suite 1007, New York, NY 10044
(212) 688 - 4537

*Straight painting and wallpapering*

For seventeen years, Donald Smith has done high-end residential straight painting and wallpapering in New York City and the Hamptons. We hear Smith and his staff of six do all the prep work, including plastering, plaster restoration and skim coating, which clients characterize as phenomenal. They tell us the firm is a pleasure to work with and the quality of the work fantastic for the dollar spent.

*"Absolutely fantastic, I think they are great!"*

## Donald Staszyn Painting
4     3.5     4.5     4.5
124 Eastwood Drive, Sholoa, PA 18337
(570) 296 - 5452

*Decorative and straight painting*

Featured in several design magazines, this small firm provides residential decorative and straight painting services for well-heeled clients in New York City, the surrounding area and other parts of the country. We hear the firm's craftsmen are utilized by several top interior design firms and the quality of their work is deemed very good.

*"Excellent quality." "They are real artists."*

## Edward Micca Decorative Painting
4.5     3     5     5
312 Bayport Avenue, Bayport, NY 11705
(631) 472 - 3559

*Decorative painting, cabinet glazing and special finishing*

A one-man operation, Edward Micca keeps tight control of his projects from start to finish making it a priority to do all of his own prep work. Micca will do any paintable surface, creating interesting "leather" walls, tinted and color plasters, wood graining and glazes, as well as trompe l'oeil. A favorite among professionals, the charming and low-key Micca has been creating his decorative finishes in New York and farther afield (in the United States and Europe) for over 21 years. Clients tell us his work, primarily his cabinet glaze, rivals some of the best in the field. They say his expertise comes at a moderate cost.

*"His glazing is absolutely amazing!"*

## Gotham Painting
4     3     4.5     5
123 East 90th Street, New York, NY 10128
(212) 427 - 5752

*Straight painting, plastering and wallpapering*

For top quality workmanship and exceptional service, notable designers and contractors in addition to private clients highly recommend this large, full-service firm. References are impressed with Gotham's skill in straight painting including skim coating, restorative plastering and wallpapering. For the service, you can't beat the price, they say.

*"Gotham painting is perfection."*

## Grand Illusion Decorative Painting Inc.
5     4     4     5
20 West 20th Street, Suite 1009, New York, NY 10011
(212) 352 - 2037

*Decorative painting and special finishing, murals*

We hear Pierre Finkelstein of Grand Illusion produces finishes that are extraordinarily realistic through the use of original 18th- and 19th-century techniques.

His small firm focuses on very high-end residential and museum work and also creates murals. Finkelstein comes to the decorative painting world with an impressive background, including training at the Van Der Kellen Painting Institute in Brussels. He has authored two books on the subject of decorative painting and finishes and teaches classes in his studio. Clients say that Finkelstein is charming and an absolute delight to work with. Finkelstein will hire freelancers if needed to round out his work force.

Grand Illusion works with some of the top decorators and designers in New York, and his private client list has its share of instantly recognizable names. They consider Finkelstein's work outstanding, and while we hear it can cost a pretty penny, there's no doubt about remarkable quality.

*"The best painter of faux bois in the world!" "Best of the best." "For that quality, I was surprised that it was not insanely priced." "The only issue is how to get on his dance card."*

## Ira Smolin Painting      3.5    2.5    5    5
1435 Lexington Avenue, New York, NY 10128
(212) 831 - 0205   www.smolinpainting.com

*Decorative and straight painting, wallpapering and color consultations*

Engaging, straightforward and easy to work with, that's how clients describe Ira Smolin, who has been providing decorative and straight painting and wallpapering for New York City residents for over 25 years. The firms specialties include marbling, gold leaf and trompe l'oeil, and Smolin takes on jobs large or small. Clients appreciate the company's neatness and pleasant approach, and inform us that Ira Smolin is prompt and always at or under budget (written estimates are always provided).

*"Easy to work with—always considerate and neat."*

## James Alan Smith      5    4    4    5
174 Red Creek Road, Hampton Bays, NY 11946
(631) 728 - 1340

*Decorative painting and murals and residential interior design*

Patrons consistently laud James Alan Smith for his superior skills, focus and a wide range of artistic capabilities. Trained in dance at Ohio State University, Smith is known for the lyrical style of his work, which includes complex trompe l'oeil and murals on both canvas and walls. His education in the decorative arts came from his mentor, the late master Richard Lowell Neas, and from time spent learning and teaching at the Isabel O'Neil studio in New York. Clients tell us that Smith's work is phenomenal and his personable and trustworthy disposition make the entire work process a pleasant experience. Smith's parquet patterned floors, hand-painted in Japan oils, round out his skills in all areas of a room. He is "the anointed one" in the world of high-end interior design and clients say deservedly so. KB 1990, 1995.

*"Fabulous. A real gentleman." "James gets the picture and then paints it flawlessly!" "The top and only choice for those that can afford him in the trade."*

## Joe Stallone

| | | | |
|---|---|---|---|
| 5 | 3.5 | 5 | 5 |

75 Riverside Drive, Suite 2R, New York, NY 10024
(212) 787 - 2011

*Decorative painting and finishing*

Joe Stallone's renowned talents, enhanced by his personable and witty demeanor, are in high demand among New York's glitterati. In business for fifteen years, Stallone has developed and refined his skills in decorative painting and finishing, rooted in an extensive education in the arts. He studied in Brussels, attended the Frances Binnington Gilding School and the Leonard Pardon Decorative Painting School and received both bachelor's and master's degrees in art. He does wall glazing, gilding, faux semiprecious stones and pattern painting on floors and furniture, in addition to using rare wood in painted marquetry. Adding to this impressive repertoire, we're told he does "super realistic faux wood graining and a range of different faux marbles." Stallone and his work have been featured on Martha Stewart's Home Show and in numerous publications, including *Town and Country* and *The New York Times*.

## John A. Weidl Inc.

| | | | |
|---|---|---|---|
| 4.5 | 4 | 4.5 | 5 |

379 Huguenot Street, New Rochelle, NY 10801
(914) 636 - 5067

*Straight and decorative painting*

Working primarily through decorators, John A. Weidl is considered by many to be one of the best painting outfits in New York. This large firm, established in 1975 performs decorative painting in the form of glazing, faux finishing and trompe l'oeil, in addition to straight residential painting. Freelancers are brought in for mural work. Some references have told us that the firm's pricing is reasonable, while others feel it is quite high—all agree on the quality of the work and say it is worth the price. KB 2001.

*"You have to go a long way to find a better painter." "The only painter in New York I can trust will go to a client without upsetting a household."*

## Lauren J. Chisholm

| | | | |
|---|---|---|---|
| 3.5 | 3 | 5 | 5 |

669 East Olive Street, Long Beach, NY 11561
(917) 538 - 7684

*Decorative painting, murals and tiles*

Approaching each project with a positive attitude and sincere interest in pleasing her clients, Lauren Chisholm does decorative painting, murals and glazing in New York City and on Long Island. We are told that she does extensive research and planning for her trompe l'oeil and mural projects, making the end result all the more spectacular. Chisholm also hand paints silk pillows with botanical designs, as well as kitchen tiles, bath tiles and sinks.

Impressed with the quality of the work she turns out, her customers often comment on her masterful trompe l'oeil and lovely stroke work. All are pleased with the pricing.

*"A very talented woman who can design and paint almost anything." "Her work is outstanding and her imagination and ideas are endless." "Lauren is an extremely talented trompe l'oeil artist with original and unique ideas." "She is a delight to work with and deserves only the highest praise." "Magnificent painting skills."*

## Lillian Heard Studio

| | | | |
|---|---|---|---|
| 3.5 | 4 | 3.5 | 4.5 |

790 President Street, Suite 3R, Brooklyn, NY 11215
(718) 230 - 8693

*Murals and Venetian plastering*

| | Quality | Cost | Value | Recommend? |
|---|---------|------|-------|------------|
| | ✚ | $ | ◆ | ★ |

Lillian Heard specializes in decorative plaster techniques, including Venetian plastering and traditional lime putty plaster, producing walls that resemble polished marble, stone or fresco. Trained at the Art Institute of Chicago, she is now based in New York City and does work internationally. In addition to her skills in specialty plasters, she is known for the spare style of her "atmospheric landscape" murals. She and her two employees also do painted floors, stencils and glazes. The firm's fees vary with the size and scope of each project, but many have said they are on the "pricey side."

*"Everyone that walks into my apartment comments on the beautiful walls and ceilings she executed." "Her work is elegant yet durable." "Heard is a sensitive and dedicated artist, but quite expensive."*

## Lulu DK                                          4.5      4      4      5
136 East 64th Street, Suite 2E, New York, NY 10021
(212) 223 - 4234   www.luludk.com
*Decorative painting, hand-painted fabric and interior design*

Lulu Kwiatkowski's contrasting styles of geometric and floral designs result from an amalgamation of her studies, travels and ability to embrace both chaos and control. After graduating from Parson's School of Design with a degree in interior design, Kwiatkowski studied trompe l'oeil at IPEDEC in Paris and then traveled throughout Europe under the apprenticeship of Italian trompe l'oeil artist, Francesco Gurnari. Kwiatkowski began her own business five years ago and has recently expanded it to include a line of hand-painted fabrics of her own design. Whether designing a refined pattern of shaded squares that evoke the feeling of light penetrating through the wall, or an exhuberant mix of colorful flowers, paisleys and squiggles, we hear that her use of color, light and style can enliven just about any surface. HB Top Designers, 2000, KB 2001.

*"She can always be counted on to produce." "Lulu is among the most talented people I have worked with." "She has her finger on the pulse of what's 'now,' but also an eye on the classic." "Fresh and certainly hip, but not at all trendy." "A great sense of color and an appreciation of the value of simplicity." "A pleasure to do business with."*

## Maer-Murphy 🛍                                    4.5      4      4      5
420 West 49th Street, New York, NY 10019
(212) 265 - 3460   www.maermurphy.com
*Decorative and straight painting, finishes, murals and wallpapering*

With a star-studded client list and notable projects such as murals at the Bellagio in Las Vegas and renovation painting at the Lunt-Fontanne Theater, Maer-Murphy has become internationally known for its high-end straight and decorative painting work. The firm takes control of the destiny of its projects by doing its own prep work. Clients appreciate the methodical care in preparing for each job, and the end results, we hear, are artistic triumphs. Murals, faux gilding, Venetian plaster, glazing and historic stenciling come at a price not all clients are willing to pay. Those that do get top quality and a respectful, professional crew who will leave their home in a condition better than they found it.

*"Did a great job, very precise." "Their professionalism, creativity and attention to detail make doing business with them a pleasure." "Beautiful work." "So talented—I highly recommend them." "Very patient and flexible."*

## Michael Tyson Murphy Studio

|     | 4 | 3.5 | 4 | 4 |
|---|---|---|---|---|

135 West 20th, Suite 400, New York, NY  10011
(212) 989 - 0180
*Decorative painting and murals*

A multidimensional, multitalented artist, Michael Tyson Murphy extends his painting projects into the fields of architecture and interior design.  His clients note that he approaches the many surfaces of a room the way a fine artist composes a painting.  His stated goal is to create a space that works with the architecture of the room, often incorporating custom-designed or custom-painted furniture, or playing off the colors and patterns of existing pieces of art.  Rooms often are completed by pieces of his own original fine art on canvas.

As a teenager Murphy began with trompe l'oeil painting, then expanded his repertoire through his education at the San Francisco Art Institute and his assistantship with the artist Helen Frankenthaler.  His extensive worldwide travels have influenced the effects he creates, from Russian-inspired faux bois floors featuring mahogany, ebony and walnut to mosaics calling on Portuguese themes.

## Miro-Art Interiors

|     | 5 | 4 | 5 | 5 |
|---|---|---|---|---|

20 Bronxville Glen Drive, Bronxville, NY  10708
(914) 237 - 6306
*Decorative painting and frescoes*

The quality is breathtaking and the projects very high-end (for example, the Blue Room in the White House) when client's mention Roman Kujawa and Miro-Art Interiors.  The team of five is in high demand by some of the most prestigious decorators and architects in New York City and in the country, specializing in decorative painting finishes like gilding and imitation limestone.  These artists are also well known for their frescoes and trompe l'oeil work.  Miro-Art does not do its own prep work, preferring to have a few select firms perform that task.

*"Not just good but great.  A real master."  "Their work is exquisite."*

## Natasha Bergreen & Liza Cousins

|     | 3.5 | 3.5 | 4 | 4 |
|---|---|---|---|---|

35 East 20th Street, New York, NY  10003
(212) 427 - 2928
*Decorative painting and finishing*

In business for thirteen years, sisters Bergreen and Cousins's partnership has benefited from a lifetime of complementing each other's talents.  With two assistants, they provide an abundance of services, including painting stripes, gilding, glazing, marbleizing and other classic and contemporary finishes.  Although their specialty is decorative painting and finishes, the firm has begun to accept some design projects as well.  Both professionals have a background in the arts.  After attending art school, Bergreen studied with Leonard Pardon and Cousins studied decorative painting in London.  We hear their talents are in demand by many of the top designers.

## Old Vienna Painting

|     | 4.5 | 3 | 5 | 5 |
|---|---|---|---|---|

24316 Thornhill Avenue, Douglaston, NY  11362
(718) 428 - 5457
*Decorative and straight painting, wallpapering*

Led by Hans Pavlacka, who has been painting all of his life, Old Vienna Painting specializes in straight and decorative painting as well as wallpapering in New York City residences.  Trained in apprenticeships throughout Europe, Pavlacka's firm handles glazing, faux finishes, plastering and restoration of moldings.  Clients tell us that the small team at Old Vienna restores old apartments back to their original glory through meticulous prep work and with great sense of color.  They say

Pavlacka is the only person allowed near their walls with a paintbrush. Pavlacka always maintains excellent relationships with his clients, which explains why he has sustained a business for 35 years on mostly referrals.

*"Reliable, consistent and top quality." "The only painter I would use." "Consider yourself fortunate if Hans paints your apartment." "His painting is beautiful, his prep work is first rate." "Great eye for color." "Old Vienna is the absolute top end of what a great painter should be." "They produce a very high-end residential product."*

### One to One Studio        3.5    2.5    4.5    5
6037 Fieldston Road, Riverdale, NY 10471
(718) 432 - 5986

*Decorative and straight painting, color consultations and kitchen and bath design*

Formerly a projects editor of a do-it-yourself magazine, we hear Clare Donohue brings a wealth of ideas to projects and takes "one to one" to heart when it comes to consulting clients. This small firm, founded four years ago, offers both straight painting and decorative finishes, including designs on floors. Recently One to One has branched out into kitchen design, specializing in creative designs for space-constrained New York City apartments. Donohue, known for her special ability to assist in color selection, has developed a personal style clients describe as sophisticated and elegant. We are told she has the ability to translate a customer's self-proclaimed "vague ideas" into beautiful results, often suggesting wonderful extras that the client would have never thought of. Her fee structure is fair, and, as many have attested, the bills are accurately estimated from the outset, which clients say makes using One to One a utterly professional and pleasurable experience.

*"Clare is unsurpassed at choosing colors, and the crew was terrific." "Responsive, energetic and neat as the proverbial pin." "I'd never paint any home without her." "Clare Donohue is an intelligent, charming, well-mannered craftsman and artist—with warmth and wit."*

### Optical Grays Inc.            4    3    5    5
300 East 93rd Street, Suite 40A, New York, NY 10128
(212) 686 - 7371

*Trade only—Decorative painting and floor painting*

Reserving its services exclusively for top-trade professionals, the Optical Grays crew brings a background in art and theatrical scenic painting to its decorative painting business. The company is noted for its custom-designed ceilings and stenciled walls and floors, including a unique floor marquetry-design technique. Its craftsmen have also been known to create hand-painted silk panels. We hear that this firm works well as part of a team of architects, contractors and decorators, and that it contributes "buoyant personalities as well as skills." The high-quality work Optic Grays helps produce leaves clients bubbling with appreciation, and has been published in top design magazines.

*"Exquisite floor painting!"*

### Otto Interiors Inc.            4    4    4    4.5
115 East 9th Street, Suite 21A, New York, NY 10003
(212) 982 - 1598

*Decorative finishing, straight painting and wallpapering*

Bert Schuppenies and his crew are determined to do everything it takes to beautify the walls of New York's upscale homes. Beginning with skim coating and canvassing walls, Otto Interiors applies wallpapering, flat painting or one of many decorative finishes such as sponging, stenciling, marbleizing, gold leafing and wood graining.

| Quality | Cost | Value | Recommend? |
|---------|------|-------|------------|
| ✚ | $ | ◆ | ★ |

We hear this witty German native began his career in Berlin where he studied and worked. Upon coming to the United States fifteen years ago, he started his own business and has been in high demand from both private clients and top designers in the city ever since.

## Painting by Picker
219 East 85th Street, New York, NY 10128
(212) 535 - 6380

| 3.5 | 3 | 4.5 | 4.5 |
|-----|---|-----|-----|

*Decorative and straight painting and wallpapering*

Robert Picker and his charming crew are popular with private clients as well as the trade. This small firm offers straight and decorative residential painting and wallpapering services, performs its own prep work and we are told, specializes in faux finishes such as sponging and ragging. References crow about Picker's helpful, funny and easygoing manner, and tell us his crew is fastidiously neat, very prompt and attentive to the furnishings. High recommendations come from clients who say Picker does high quality work at fair reasonable prices.

*"The apartment was cleaner after he left than it was before he came." "He is an artist." "He is flexible and able to work with different budgets—while he did my mother's apartment to the highest standards, he did a terrific but less detailed, less expensive job for me." "The crew is extraordinarily helpful." "I loved working with Robert."*

## Paulin Paris
69 Mercer Street, New York NY 10012
(21)-334 - 6343

| 5 | 4.5 | 5 | 5 |
|---|-----|---|---|

*Decorative painting, sculptures and murals*

For over 15 years, Paulin Paris has catered to an A-list clientele that has brought him from his homeland of Paris to homes of the most elite around the world. With a PhD in philosophy and a degree from the Ecole des Beaux Arts, Paris has been able to take his inspiration from the past, but treat it in a modern way. Paris' versitility can be seen in the broad range of his clientele: from the fashion houses Dior and Valentino, to commissions for private residences and interior designers and the Alsatian fabric and wallpaper studio Zuber, Paris works hard to incorporate his vision with the owners vision, with spectacular results. Clients praise Paris' ability to concieve the space as an artist but also have the ability to work alongside the architect and designer. Paris divides his time between his studios in New York and Paris where he works on murals, paintings and sculptures.

*"A modest man, generous with his clients." "His work is exquisite—he has the ability to take an idea and bring  to life." "There is no finer."*

## Poltime Interiors
99 Newel Street, Brooklyn, NY 11222
(718) 383 - 9402

| 4 | 3.5 | 4.5 | 5 |
|---|-----|-----|---|

*Decorative and straight painting*

Poltime Interiors addresses a range of jobs, from basic straight residential painting to complex, decorative finishes. Working for private clients as well as

some of the city's most respected decorators, principal John Stephanski keeps up with the most recent trends in painting. Many laud Stephanski's ability to duplicate any existing color or find its perfect complement. In addition to his masterful eye, his glazes and faux finishes get great reviews. We hear the mahogany is incredible. References say he produces excellent cloud ceilings, but is not a general muralist.

Stephanski is described as meticulous, dependable and businesslike, arriving with full crews and finishing in record time. While some clients may quibble about how wide they have to open their wallet, they all agree that they get what they pay for.

*"An artist who is amazing with color." "Amazing work, high quality, great value." "European craftsman." "An absolute joy to deal with." "So talented—I couldn't have imagined more beautiful results." "John will work with you until it is right."*

### Renaissance Decorative Artistry   4   2.5   5   5
111 East 14th Street, Suite 202, New York, NY  10003
(212) 252 - 2273

*Murals and faux finishes*

Serving a clientele of celebrities and top designers, some of whom are reluctant to share him with the public, Dean Barger and the small team at Renaissance Decorative Artistry have developed quite a following for their sophisticated murals, multi-layered stenciling and high-end faux finishes. Dividing his time between New York City and Maine, Barger, who has a fine arts background and studied in Europe, is described as pleasant, low key and an absolute delight to work with. We hear his work is inspired and his rates are moderate.

*"Extraordinary work." "I don't want to give him up." "Dean is wonderful, his work, outstanding."*

### Robert J. Braun   4.5   3.5   5   5
104 West 87th Street, New York, NY  10024
(212) 799 - 6282

*Decorative painting and murals*

Working primarily through the referral of designers, Robert Braun flexes his decorative painting muscles for both residential and commercial clients in New York, on both coasts of the United States and abroad. He works on canvas for future on-site installation and focuses on historic period styles which include architectural trompe l'oeil, which we hear is outstanding.

*"One of the best trompe l'oeil artists!" "Robert is extremely talented." "He collaborates with designers for a fabulous product."*

### Robert Roth   4   4   4.5   5
305 East 46th Street, Suite 104, New York, NY  10017
(212) 758 - 2170

*Decorative and straight painting, architectural trompe l'oeil*

Popular with the trade in addition to private clients, the father-and-son team at Robert Roth receives high marks for their decorative and straight painting. The two have been praised for very successful trompe l'oeil work and their dedication to meticulous preparation for flawless straight painting. We hear they are detail oriented and clean up thoroughly every night. One client happily left them the keys to her home when she was out of town, and says she would never do that for anyone else. Providing a wide range of skills, clients say that this firm is best for larger jobs, and that they can be quite expensive, but are wonderful to work with.

*"Brilliant." "I have never written such a large check with such pleasure!" "True European artists." "Impeccable." "The end result is perfection."*

| | Quality  | Cost $ | Value ◆ | Recommend? ★ |
|---|---|---|---|---|

### Robert Star Painting

| | 4.5 | 3.5 | 4.5 | 4.5 |

178 East 80th Street, New York, NY 10021
(212) 737 - 8855

*Flat painting, decorative painting and finishing and wallpapering*

The witty and charming Robert Star and his professional team artfully orchestrate and manage all types of projects—from wallpapering to flat and decorative painting to decorative finishing. With a century-old family history of painting, Star came from England and gained experience in all aspects of the painting industry before incorporating his own contracting business 21 years ago. He is in high demand from an elite client list including architects, interior designers and private clients.

From skin coating walls to hanging paper or applying a decorative finish to the final touch-up, we are told his crew of fifteen produces extraordinary results. Robert Star Painting has been published in such magazines as *Town and Country*, *Architectural Digest* and *New York Magazine*.

*"An absolute joy to work with." "Robert is a cut above the rest." "I couldn't dream of better service." "Not only is Robert fun to work with, he and his team are true professionals and produced results that I am proud to show off."*  ◂

### S.M. Zacko Painting

| | 4 | 3 | 4.5 | 5 |

230 East 48th Street, New York, NY 10017
(718) 278 - 7330

*Decorative and straight painting and wallpapering*

A staple subcontractor of the city's most discerning, high-end builders, S.M. Zacko offers straight painting, wallpapering and decorative painting, including glazing, faux wood graining, trompe l'oeil and Venetian plaster. In business for sixteen years, references tell us that this twenty-person firm provides great quality at a terrific value.

*"Best value out there."*

### SilverLining Interiors

2112 Broadway, Suite 402, New York, NY 10023
(212) 496 - 7800   www.silverlininginteriors.com

*High-end general contracting, decorative finish specialists*

See SilverLining Interiors's full report under the heading Contractors & Builders

### Simonson & Baric

| | 4.5 | 4 | 4.5 | 5 |

847 Lexington Avenue, New York, NY 10021
(212) 570 - 1996

*Straight residential painting and wallpapering*

Knowing that you are only as good as your last job, the team of Simonson & Baric put customer service at the head of the table when serving up residential painting and wallpapering. We hear they can handle anything, and the level of attention exhibited on each job translates into exceptional quality. Of course, this comes at a premium, but sources tell us it is well worth it.

*"Simonson is the best of the best." "Expensive, but you get what you pay for."*

### Skinner Interiors

| | 4.5 | 3.5 | 5 | 5 |

71 First Place, Brooklyn, NY 11231
(718) 243 - 1378   www.skinnerinteriors.com

*Straight painting and wallpapering, plasterwork*

A favorite of both hot young designers looking for exceptional craftsmanship at decent prices as well as old-guard designers who have been pleased with this firm's work for years, Skinner Interiors does straight and decorative painting plastering and wallpapering for some on New York's most demanding clientele. When not working in the city, Skinner and company can be found attending to those very same clients at their weekend homes in Connecticut or the Hamptons. Known for its attention to detail and professionalism, the firm is frequently used for expertise in wallpapering showrooms in the D&D building.

In business for eleven years, principal Mark Skinner carries a "hands on" reputation. In addition to doing all of the prep work, he is said to nurture close relationships with clients during the process, keeping them updated on progress and staying sensitive to their needs and budgets.

*"From the first day of preparation to the completion of the job, we knew we had made the right choice." "They understand quality and were sensitive to our needs." "Great employees with a great attitude." "Skinner Interiors is highly creative and professional." "A true artist." "Truly worth every penny for the most meticulous work."*

## The Isabel O'Neil Studio Workshop
177 E. 87th Street, Suite 302, New York, NY 10128
(212) 348 - 4464
*Referral service for decorative painting and finishing*

The Isabel O'Neil Studio Workshop is an educational institution that provides extensive professional training in decorative painting and finishing. The school has been functioning as an apprentice system since 1955, with an all-volunteer group of instructors. Upon request, the school will refer individuals to a number of professionals from its expansive network in order to meet their specific needs.

## Thomas Lent Painting
3   2.5   4.5   5
414 East 89th Street, New York, NY 10128
(212) 722 - 7312
*Decorative and straight painting and wallpapering*

In business for over 26 years, Thomas Lent Painting has been providing straight painting, decorative painting and wallpapering services to New York City residents and designers. Sources tell us the staff is hardworking, knowledgeable and commit a dedicated level of care to each project. We hear the prices are reasonable given the high quality of work.

*"They are helpful in choosing color and finish." "Wonderful and caring." "They are hardworking and respectful."*

## Tomo
4   3.5   4.5   5
4235 64th Street, Woodside, NY 11377
(718) 426 - 4316
*Decorative and straight painting and wallpapering*

Prestigious real estate agencies and top-tier general contractors call upon this high-end painter, which has operated in Manhattan and Connecticut for over 31 years. Tomo and his sizable staff of 45 do both straight and decorative work, wallpapering, and in-house prep work. A list of clients that include celebrities say this well run and organized company produces a superb finished product, and Tomo himself is a gem to work with.

*"Amazing, flawless work." "Tomo is an excellent painter, very high-end, great quality."*

## Vincent Millette Company
4   3   4.5   5
1040 Bushwick Avenue, Brooklyn, NY 11207
(718) 574 - 1661
*Decorative and straight painting*

In addition to straight painting for residential clients, Vincent Millette and his group handle decorative stucco, Venetian faux-finished plastering, glazing, custom painting, crown moldings and other decorative finishes. Interior designers, contractors and other professionals "in the know" often secure Millette's services. Sources tell us that considering the high quality of work, his fees are well worth the price.

## Walter Shostak Painting       3    1.5    4.5    4.5
124 West 26th Street, Bayonne, NJ 07002
(917) 312 - 5810
*Straight residential painting and wallpapering*

Considered an excellent secret source among top decorators and private clients, Walter Shostak has been painting and wallpapering Manhattan homes for fifteen years. His down-to-earth style, good quality and extremely modest prices have earned him numerous fans. We hear clients value his opinions and recommendations and appreciate his keen interest in the project at hand. Shostak is such a find, clients often ask him to do their second homes outside of the city.

*"He transformed our apartment from average into a place we are just dying to move into." "Walter gives great advice." "He is honest, efficient and ethical." "High quality work at reasonable prices." "I found him to be quite accommodating about scheduling." "Walter gave our home so much attention."*

## Yona Verwer Studio       4    3    4.5    5
336 East 13th Street, Suite C5, New York, NY 10003
(212) 674 - 5015
*Decorative painting and murals*

Lauded as a true artist, Yona Verwer has been doing decorative painting and murals for New Yorkers for sixteen years. While the firm does all kinds of specialty finishes including glazes, gilding, stenciling, plaster effects and faux finishes, it's the murals that particularly charm clients. These pieces, described as whimsical, fanciful and inspiring, are applied on canvas and on walls. We hear Verwer will create contemporary pieces of her own design or will execute any style a client prefers, including classical and trompe l'oeil. She has created an extensive planning process designed to keep the customer involved at every stage of the project, references report.

Verwer, who holds an MFA from the Netherlands, is described by many as patient, understanding and a pleasurable collaborator. Sources tell us that she is extremely ethical, citing the fair prices and exceptional quality that this company delivers.

*"Yona is an excellent artist—her work is truly valuable." "Yona is patient, understanding and will work through anything to make sure the designer and end user are happy." "It's a pleasure to work with her."*

## Zeccodec Painting       4    3.5    4    5
42 Stuyvesant Street, New York, NY 10003
(212) 254 - 1500
*Decorative and straight painting and wallpapering*

Repeat business and referrals make up the majority of Zeccodec's client list, which includes both private clients and the trade. Maybe they just like saying the name, or more likely, as clients report, it's the straight and decorative painting and wallpapering services that this small firm has been offering New Yorkers for sixteen years. We hear principal Glenn Zecco is a straightforward professional who offers good quality for the price. References say his staff of twelve, many of who were trained in Europe, are conscientious, efficient and do a good job.

*"Easy to talk to." "Very professional." "I am very happy with the results."*

# Hiring a Pest Control
# Service Provider

Roaches, mice, rats, termites, carpenter ants, ants, fleas, ticks, spiders and silver fish. These are the ten most common household pests, and according to the National Pest Management Association (NPMA), every house in America has been visited by at least one of them in the past year.

Even though do-it-yourself pest-control kits are readily available, they are not as effective as the services offered by professionals. The application of pesticides is just one part of a total pesticide management program, which typically includes safety considerations, prevention methods and structural modifications. Whereas untrained homeowners may be able to apply pesticides with varying degrees of success, professionals rely on training, expertise and sophisticated techniques to control pesticide infestations in an efficient, economical and safe manner—protecting the long-term interests of the homeowner's family and the environment.

Not all pest control service providers are alike. While most work to eliminate a wide range of infestations, termite abatement requires a different kind of training and licensing and, therefore, a different kind of exterminator than most other pests. In addition to eliminating bugs from your living space, a lot of these professionals also specialize in removing birds and rodents, persuading squirrels to nest elsewhere, etc.

Generally, exterminators advocate that homeowners practice prevention to the greatest extent possible to minimize disease and damage to property. In fact, most reputable firms will happily provide training on standards of cleanliness in order to prevent infestations and mating, as well as counsel on cleanup of eggs and droppings.

## Where Do I Start?

The first step involved in seeking the services of a pest control expert requires that you perform a preliminary inspection of your home yourself. Beware of exterminators who arrive at your doorstep unsolicited and offer free inspections. They tend to prey on homeowners' general ignorance about pests by intimidating them into authorizing immediate and expensive treatments. It has been rumored that some such service providers are known to bring bug specimens with them and release them into the premises of unsuspecting homeowners (a clever variation on the "fly-in-my-soup" routine).

When seeking an exterminator, be sure to have ready a list of the kind of infestation you have or suspect you have, the number of pets, children and adults that inhabit your home, any allergies these inhabitants have and the number of rooms in your home. These factors will determine the kind of exterminator you need to hire and the processes that will ultimately be used to eliminate infestations.

## A Variety of Pest Control Methods

Pest control is a highly specialized industry and its jargon can be confusing. Be sure to ask the service provider for a description of each project and a success-rate estimate for each procedure. If, for instance, an exterminator advises fumigating your home with toxic gas to get rid of termites, ask for a detailed description of the method and its possible hazards. Not every extermination, however, requires you to leave the premises for a few hours and subsequently air out your home. New technology, such as microwave and electro-gun systems, may be safer for families with pets and children. Work with the professional to choose which option best suits your needs.

## ON COST

Once you've conducted a preliminary inspection and suspect the presence of a residential free-loader, contact a licensed pest control service provider. Since large projects are often costly and require skill, expertise and knowledge, it is generally suggested that you get several bids from multiple vendors for large projects.

Different firms charge varied rates, depending on: 1) the scale and nature of the project, 2) the complexity of the infestation, and 3) the potential need to remove walls and other structures. While there are no standard hourly or per-room charges, most exterminators are usually happy to give free estimates when they perform preliminary inspections.

## CONTRACTS AND GUARANTEES

Once you decide on a firm, negotiate a contract and get it in writing. In the contract, specify the nature of the infestation, the extent of the infestation and the resulting damage, the exact services to be provided, description of guarantees, the desired end result (abatement only or continuing control) and how long the treatment is expected to last.

Some exterminators do offer guarantees with their contracts. Be realistic about guarantee provisions that promise a one-time total solution! Cockroach abatement, for instance, needs to be renewed every six months in order to be completely effective. While this may seem a little excessive, remember that roaches are the only living creatures that can survive nuclear holocaust—one electronic or chemical application will only humor them.

## IMPORTANT ISSUES ABOUT THIS HIGHLY REGULATED INDUSTRY

Because exterminators handle highly toxic products, they should undergo rigorous training to practice their profession. A pest control specialist's membership in a national or regional professional association is usually a good indicator that the service provider has access to the most cutting-edge technical information and is committed to ongoing education. Inquire about a service provider's affiliations and follow up by verifying membership with the professional organization. The NPCA is one of the largest and best known national organizations in the field and can be reached online (www.pestworld.org) or by calling (703) 573-8330.

State organizations include the New York State Pest Control Association (www.nyassoc.com (518) 463-6333), New York State Professional Applicators Coalition (516) 399-4541 and the Long Island Pest Control Association (same number (516) 399-4541).

## INSURANCE

Permits and licensing are not the only business issues to verify before hiring an exterminator. It is crucial to find out whether or not the exterminator carries liability insurance to cover potential damage to property and/or to people in the course of the exterminator's work. If the exterminator doesn't carry such insurance, check your homeowners' policy for coverage. In the absence of both, consider buying insurance to protect your belongings and yourself from liability.

## What's Bugging You?
### A few precautions to help prevent pest-nesting in your home

- ❖ **Termites:** Wet wood is every termite's favorite meal. Get rid of old tree stumps, form boards and wood debris around your house and rid your home of excess moisture, making sure gutters are unclogged and all pipe leaks promptly fixed.

- ❖ **Rodents:** Take out the trash. Daily! Garbage is a rat's favorite nesting ground, and they begin to mate at the tender age of five weeks to produce up to 48 spawn a year. Also, be vigilant about keeping all the entry points into your home clean and clear, including ducts, vents and chimneys.

- ❖ **Cockroaches:** While it is very hard to combat a cockroach infestation without professional help, a few tactics will go a long way toward keeping them at bay: proper ventilation, fitting all holes with screens, sealing around pipes where they come through the floor and ceiling and storing and/or covering all food (yours and your pets!).

## PEST CONTROL

### A All Borough Exterminating Co.    3    3    4    4.5
139 Finlay Street, Staten Island, NY  10307
(718) 356 - 1100
*Residential pest control*

Safety is the main concern for this company when it comes to taking care of unwanted pests. With more than 30 years of experience, William Macri and his four employees handle anything—including birds. The company's animal-friendly policy ensures that birds, skunks or squirrels are returned to their proper habitat. As its name suggests, A All Borough services all boroughs of New York, Long Island, Westchester Count, and New Jersey. Clients say the firm's awareness of the environment is what attracts clients A All Borough. Clients commend William Macri for his friendly attitude and concern for the health and safety of all parties involved—both animal and human.

*"He is as friendly as they come." "Honest!" "He's a great guy who does an excellent job."*

### A.C.E. Inc.    3    2    4    4.5
717 East 52nd Street, Brooklyn, NY  11203
(718) 629 - 6660
*Residential, commercial, institutional and industrial pest control*

Clients say that for ten years, A.C.E. has stressed the importance of environmentally sensitive pest control using highly nontoxic, long-term methods. Principal Donovan Glave and his ten employees are known for their creative techniques when dealing with insects, rodents, birds and any other animal that may invade the home or business. Insiders say this small firm prides itself on its specifically devised training program, which helps establish consistency throughout the company. A.C.E. carefully screens customers to ensure that the firm associated by people who share its vision of long-term toxin-free abatement and eradication.

Clients say the continual communication between customer and vendor is strengthened with quality evaluation surveys and independent quality-assurance teams, which inspect recent projects. Clients say that Glave is more than willing to educate them on the process, and even requires that clients become active participants in the elimination of pests. Although A.C.E.'s methods may seem too hands-on for some, many find that its procedures ultimately maintain a safe and pest-free environment.

*"Donovan is one of the most personable people I've met." "He always finds a solution and explains everything to me."*

### Allied Exterminating    3    3    4    5
360 Lexington Avenue, New York, NY  10017
(212) 557 - 1515
*Residential pest control*

Allied's clients find them to be a good solid choice for pest control services, especially for ongoing maintenance contracts. It comes as no surprise that this veteran firm gets a lot of repeat business and has several long-term clients. Allied's staff is reputed to be easy to work with, reliable and responsive to clients' needs.

*"Has been with [our building] for many years. Does a good job."*

| | Quality + | Cost $ | Value ◆ | Recommend? ★ |
|---|---|---|---|---|

## Arrow Exterminating Co. Inc.

| | 3.5 | 3 | 4 | 3.5 |

289 Broadway, Lynbrook, NY 11563
(516) 593 - 7770   www.arrowexterminating.com

*Residential and commercial pest control*

One of the most established pest control companies, Arrow Exterminating has been providing quality pest control since 1947. This diverse firm is equipped to deal with all forms of pests, including all insects, rodents, birds and other animals. Insiders say principal Bernard Stegman requires that his 100 employees complete training and new technology education on a continuous basis—well beyond the state minimum. Bernard himself helped found the Long Island Pest Control Association over 38 years ago. Based in Long Island, Arrow serves all five boroughs and Westchester. Designated "quality circles" provide greater communication among service technicians and clients as well. Many clients highly recommend Arrow, and are very pleased with the overall service—although some clients say the firm's staff is difficult to get in touch with and their fees are higher than most.

*"Extremely polite and professional people." "On the higher side price wise."*

## Broadway Exterminating Company, Inc.

| | 3.5 | 2.5 | 4 | 5 |

782 Amsterdam Avenue, New York, NY 10025
(212) 663 - 2100   www.broadwayexterminating.com

*Residential pest control*

Most references are happy with Broadway Exterminators, and tell us that its work is top quality. They also praise the firm for its reliability. Not surprisingly, a large percentage of Broadway's livelihood is based upon the repeat business of satisfied customers.

*"A good company I have relied on for years."*

## Careful Cleaning Contractors

153 Lincoln Avenue, Bronx, NY 10454
(718) 665 - 8314

*Commercial and residential window cleaning*

See Careful Cleaning Contractors's full report under the heading Window Washers

## Exterminare Pest Control Service

| | 3.5 | 3.5 | 4 | 4 |

430 East 6th Street, New York, NY 10009
(212) 254 - 4444

*Residential pest control*

Although its specialty is rodent proofing and removal, Exterminare Pest Control Service also provides insect, bird and animal eradication as well. For more than 30 years, this family-owned and operated firm has offered pest control services to all five boroughs, Mt. Vernon, New Rochelle and parts of Nassau County. Owner Herb Schnieder is said to have extensive knowledge of the field, and is also on the board of the Professional Pest Association. Consisting of seven people, this small firm handles several high-profile commercial and residential clients. Clients say Exterminare Pest Control Services' child-friendly methods allow for safety and convenience. All technicians have received licensing and training in bird control—another one of their specialties. Customers say that Herb Schnieder and his team offer friendly service accompanied by ample followup.

*"A knowledgeable and thorough group."*

| | Quality + | Cost $ | Value ◆ | Recommend? ★ |
|---|---|---|---|---|

## Knockout Pest Control

| | 3.5 | 3 | 4 | 4.5 |

1009 Front Street, Uniondale, NY 11553
(800) 244 - 7378   www.knockoutpest.com
*Residential and institutional pest control*

Knockout Pest Control is one of the first companies in the New York City area to offer the Sentricon Termite Colony Elimination System—a specific non invasive termite prevention and eradication method. Clients say this 25-year-old firm offers a variety of services for rodents, birds, animals and other insects. Founder Arthur Katz and his 27 employees provide commercial, industrial and residential work in all five boroughs, as well as Suffolk and Nassau counties. Insiders note Katz's commitment to the industry—he has served on the board of directors of the Long Island Pest Association and is currently president of the New York State Pest Control Association. Continual up-to-date employee training is mandated and we hear that Knockout is also dedicated to educating its clients about all areas of pest control. Customers note that although this company prefers bait technology for its value and efficiency, many other methods are available. Clients highly recommend Knockout Pest Control for their prompt service.

*"They are always on time." "Knockout's technicians are very professional and polite."*

## Magic Exterminating Company

| | 3.5 | 2.5 | 4 | 4 |

59-01 Kassena Boulevard, Flushing, NY 11355
(212) 645 - 6191   www.suburbanpestcontrol.com
*Residential pest control*

Magic Exterminating Company provides insect and rodent abatement and eradication in all five boroughs of Manhattan. Founded by Hal Byer, this family-owned and operated firm consists of 30 employees, all of which are fully licensed and insured. Most of Magic's work is residential, but the firm does work on commercial projects as well. Magic offers insect and rodent solutions, but does not provide animal control services. While the firm's work area is limited to the five boroughs, its sister company, Suburban Pest Control, handles all other inquires on Long Island. Clients have commented on this company's dependability.

*"They always respond quickly when I have any bug problem in my home." "I trust them in my apartment all the time."*

## Metro Pest Control

| | 3.5 | 2.5 | 4.5 | 4.5 |

5127 Queens Boulevard, Woodside, NY 11377
(212) 545 - 0888   www.metropest.com
*Residential pest control*

Founded in 1977, this well-established family-owned company prides itself on its friendly relationships with clients. Metro Pest Control offers all standard services and is also licensed to deal with mosquitoes and wildlife such as birds and squirrels. Consisting of 60 employees, this firm serves all five boroughs, mainly working for residential clients, but also handles commercial and institutional clients as well.

*"They are very knowledgeable and always know what they're doing." "Metro gets the job done." "The employees are polite and courteous."*

## Pioneer Exterminating Co. Inc.

| | 4 | 2.5 | 5 | 4.5 |

360 Lexington Avenue, New York, NY 10017
(212) 557 - 7500
*Residential pest control*

Pioneer is a family-owned and operated business that has been keeping New York homes and businesses pest-free since 1936. Pioneer only offers Integrated

| | Quality + | Cost $ | Value ◆ | Recommend? ★ |
|---|---|---|---|---|

Pest Management services, an approach to pest-management that begins with training of the technicians and includes sanitation, structural modifications, inspections and monitoring to achieve optimum levels of pest control and sanitation. Sources tell us the firm probably exterminated over 150 million square feet of residential and commercial space in Manhattan.

"They do several of our buildings and do a great job on each one." "Very satisfied . . . I would have no hesitation in recommending them."

## Sterile Peril      3.5   3   3.5   4
179 Fifth Avenue, Brooklyn, NY 11217
(718) 622 - 0053
*Residential pest control*

Clients say this unique company concentrates its resources on providing health-oriented pest control in all five boroughs. For fifteen years, Principal Shelly Mandell and her three employees have worked mainly with insects, yet they do provide some animal services when asked. The company was established on the idea of servicing those who have cancer, HIV or Aids, where chemicals in the home are of great concern. While some clients may say the techniques used by Sterile Peril don't seem to be the most efficient at first, clients later agree these techniques are the safest and the most thorough in the long run. We hear that Mandell is extremely sensitive towards clients' needs, going out of her way to maintain a healthy environment. Spraying does not take place throughout the home—rather the all-natural pesticides are injected into the problem areas. Customers applaud Sterile Peril for unique and sensitive service.

"She always informs me on what she is doing." "Shelly came over immediately when I had an emergency." "Shelly is good at what she does and really seems to care about her clients."

## Terminate Control      4   3   4.5   4.5
441 East 12th Street, New York, NY 10009
(212) 995 - 0668
*Residential pest control*

This family-run firm is recognized by clients and insiders alike for its personal service and lasting relationships with clients. Principal Gary Packer has over 50 years of experience in the proofing and eradication of insects, birds and animals. Working with residential and commercial clients, Packer and his five employees are fully licensed and insured. Clients say the firm's traditional methods of exterminating are implemented in collaboration with newly developed, more environmentally friendly techniques that use less chemicals. Constantly in demand, Terminate Control still remains attentive to its clients needs and we hear that their fees are reasonable.

"Gary is very trustworthy." "They come to my house like clockwork, even when it's an emergency."

## Tompkins Exterminating      3   2   4   4
360 Lexington Avenue, New York, NY 10017
(212) 557 - 7507
*Residential pest control*

References report that Tompkins delivers excellent service at a good price. The family-owned and operated business provides professional and competent pest eradication in New York and the city's suburbs.

"A good, solid company." "I am happy with their service."

# Hiring a Plumber

Whether it's trimming out a kitchen and bath remodel, installing an entire system for a new home, a routine repair or maintenance call or an absolute emergency, you need a plumber you can count on.

Obviously, you want to hold on to a plumbing contractor that has proved himself over the course of a major project. Handpicked by your trusty GC, he knows the guts of your home better than anyone. Even if you aren't planning a renovation and just need someone to handle more mundane problems like leaky faucets, its worth putting in the effort to build a relationship with a plumber who can offer quality and service, so he'll be there before you're sunk.

Although most plumbers are available for a simple service call, some high-end service providers prefer to limit service calls, especially 24-hour emergency service, to existing customers. This practice ensures that you will receive the highest level of service and quality with a prompt response.

## Where Do I Start?

You will want to ask prospective plumbers how long they have been in business and what types of work they specialize in. Many plumbing professionals do both commercial and residential work, dealing with both large renovations and smaller repairs. Specialties and focuses vary in this industry, so it is best to look to someone that has experience with your type of project.

When you call a plumber's references, you'll want to ask the usual questions about quality of work and whether the project was finished on schedule and on budget. Because plumbing can be a messy business, respect for surroundings and cleanliness are especially important.

## A Job for Professionals

You should only consider a full-time licensed professional for your plumbing needs. Though a license is not required in New York to perform basic plumbing maintenance work, your service provider must be licensed for any jobs that require the filing of a permit. As always, ask about insurance, including worker's compensation and liability insurance. Your plumbing professional should always be responsible for obtaining all permits necessary for your job.

## On Cost

For larger projects, each plumbing contractor will submit its bid to the GC, who will then incorporate it into the overall bid submitted to the client. Often the GC for your project will bring in a trusted plumber for the job, but you are free to ask your GC to include another plumber in the bidding process, which also helps to ensure that bids are competitive. If your renovation is relatively small and a GC is not involved, get several estimates for the proposed work.

For smaller jobs and service calls, which include repair and maintenance, most companies will charge an hourly fee, typically $80 for a single plumber, $115 for a dispatched two-man team. A baseline rating of 3 for Cost in *The Franklin Report* reflects these standards. However, please remember, a company's standards in relation to product and safety, the depth of its resources and the demand of its customer base can all affect cost on top of hourly rates, and are factored into the rating.

Some companies charge a set one-time diagnostic fee to produce an estimate even for smaller jobs, while others will send troubleshooters or technicians to assess the work and come up with a price free of charge. All will work up fixed estimates for larger jobs to be executed in a contract. Fees for contract renovation work are typically higher than fees for new construction per hour and per square foot. In the end, it should come down to the company with the best reputation for quality and service, not just the low bidder.

## Guarantees and Service Agreements

When your equipment is installed, it should come with both a warranty from the manufacturer and a guarantee from the service provider. Be sure to ask about service agreements. Many plumbing professionals provide regular "checkups" and inspections. It may seem like wasted money at first, but over time these measures can prevent an emergency.

## Save Money by Saving Time

If you inventory the state of your plumbing and think ahead about work that will need to be done, your plumber will be able to work more effectively. Check faucets, drains, radiators and fixtures throughout the house and compile a list. Present this list to the plumber upon arrival so he can prioritize the various tasks and work simultaneously if possible. This way, you won't have to call him in again for another minor repair in a few weeks.

If the plumber will need access to the pipes under your kitchen sink, clear out the area to save billable time. Also put away or protect anything vulnerable to damage. Your plumber will appreciate being able to get to work without having to wade through piles of children's toys or rummage around in a cabinet full of cleaning supplies.

Don't wait until your bathroom is flooded with four inches of water. Develop a good relationship with a plumber now, and you'll never have to page frantically through a phone book and throw yourself at the mercy of whatever plumber happens to be free.

### More Than Pipes

Your plumber is trained to do much more than fix clogged drains. A full-service plumber can:

⬥ Provide condensation drains for air conditioning units.
⬥ Install the boiler, lines and radiators necessary for household heat.
⬥ Install hot water recirculation and water pressure booster pumps.
⬥ Hook up major appliances (gas stoves, washing machines).
⬥ Make a gas-meter connection, install gas lines and provide gas shut-off valves.
⬥ Install storm/slop drains for the kitchen, patio, garage, laundry room, greenhouse and roof.

## PLUMBERS

### A.C. Klem Plumbing & Heating
4.5  3.5  4.5  4.5

37-24 33rd Street, Long Island City, NY  11101
(718) 433 - 2400
*Residential plumbing and heating services, pipe and drain cleaning*

One of the city's premier plumbing contractors, A.C. Klem has been a staple plumber for discriminating contractors and well heeled clientele, especially those in the Upper East Side, for over 50 years.  The firm practices its comprehensive plumbing services mostly on renovations, but with 24-hour emergency service and radio dispatched trucks it does handle some smaller repairs and maintenance. A.C. Klem also installs and repairs radiant heating systems, and condensation pipes for A/C units.  We are told they are pipe and drain cleaning specialists. Clients say the firm provides highly skilled and friendly service, delivering "top, top" quality to both residential and commercial clients in New York.  References report the staff is reliable and trustworthy, and that its large size helps to make the company's response times hard to beat.

*"Everyone says best of the best." "Great guys.  Great company."*

### Anchor Plumbing
4  3  4.5  5

449 Graham Avenue, Brooklyn, NY  11211
(718) 383 - 5100
*Residential plumbing services*

We hear the number of this small shop is programmed into the cell phones of some of the most talented residential contractors in the city.  They tell us Steve Einhorn and his team provide excellent workmanship on very high-end projects at prices to call home about.

*"Incredibly well priced."*

### Bradshaw Mechanical
3.5  3  4  4

57-09 59th Street, Maspeth, NY  11378
(718) 894 - 1000
*Residential plumbing services*

Bradshaw Mechanical handles large projects with ease and professionalism, according to clients.  References also point to the firm's great customer service as one of the reasons they keep Bradshaw high on their list for any project.

### City/Suburban Plumbing
4  4  4  4

448 Fifth Avenue, Pelham, NY  10803
(914) 738 - 0894
*Commercial and residential plumbing services*

### Demar Plumbing & Heating Corp.
3  2.5  4  4

235 Mulberry Street, New York, NY  10012
(212) 431 - 9779
*Residential and commercial plumbing and heating services*

This reliable and reasonably priced second-generation Lower East Side-based plumbing and heating company is capable of both performing full-scale renovations and fielding service calls for commercial and residential customers, the latter of whom reside primarily in Manhattan. Led by master plumber Alex Demarines, we hear Demar's crew gets the job done in impressive fashion, fomenting a loyal long-term customer base that includes both management companies and private households. In addition, the firm does gas boiler installation and repair as well as sprinkler maintenance. Two-man teams respond in company trucks.

## Efficient Plumbing & Heating    4    4    4    4

580 Sackett Street, Brooklyn, NY 11217
(212) 877 - 0343

*Residential plumbing services*

Hassle-free, detail-oriented, quality craftsmanship is what makes Efficient true to its title. The 25-person firm boasts over twenty years and two genera-tions in the plumbing and heating business. Clients say the company spends less energy on service calls than small and large renovations of top-dollar, high-end residential, retail, office and restaurant space. We hear Efficient especially excels at and is comfortable working in high-rise co-ops or townhouses, where combining two apartments into one or splitting a single brownstone into two duplexes is common. The firm is also reputed to be a specialist when it comes to gas services. It offers both emergency gas restoration for interrupted serv-ice and restoration, maintenance and installation of gas fireplaces—it can even recommend where to go to purchase new ones. In addition, the firm is also licensed for fire suppression systems. Efficient typically sends two men for service calls at a fairly standard rate.

## Empire Plumbing & Heating    3    3    4    4

3944 Richmond Avenue, Staten Island, NY 10312
(718) 980 - 4073

*Residential plumbing services*

Working exclusively in Manhattan, this firm thrives on performing high-end kitchen and bath renovations. While some say the small, six-person firm is best suited for general repairs and maintenance, Empire has broadened its scope to include complete apartment rehabs. Park Avenue customers and TriBeCa contractors all compliment Empire's crew as very competent and ded-icated. We hear they are meticulous about getting a job done right and will do whatever it takes. The firm, clients say, often teams up with Cardinal Kitchens, producing reportedly "good, but not great" results. Service, call rates for one of the firm's three two-man teams, when they're available, are quite a deal we're told by past customers.

*"They know what they're doing."*

## Fred Smith Plumbing & Heating Co.    5    3.5    5    5

1674 First Avenue, New York, NY 10128
(212) 744 - 1300

*Residential plumbing and heating services*

Widely heralded as the "the rocket scientists of plumbing," we hear this com-pany comes as prepared as NASA to the primarily small and large repairs and alterations on all phases of plumbing for Manhattan residences. Client tell us Fred Smith brings over 85 years of experience and one of its nine field supervi-sors to troubleshoot and assess each job, free of charge, before sending the mechanic and helper. They report the firm can "adjust to anything," consistently delivering efficient, top-quality work. Based right in the heart of the city, we're told Fred Smith keeps servicemen in reserve, on board what is already the largest ship in the city to ensure a quick response time. This is just one more reason Fred Smith's client base, much of which is represented by the luxury co-op market, look no further for their plumbing and heating needs.

While references admit the firm has "A" and "B" crews, clients describe all the Fred Smith's men as consummate professionals—courteous of clients, respectful of space, and highly skilled. Managers of prestigious co-ops and flagship general contractors all recommend Fred Smith without exception. Surprisingly, as a result of economies of scale and the firm's troubleshooting, Fred Smith's prices are competitive with anyone in the city. And considering the fact that about sixty percent of the firm's repair jobs are done with one man, and charged accordingly, the firm may be not only the best overall plumbing contractor, but one of the best values as well.

*"They are fabulous, I found Fred through* The Franklin Report, *and he is great. Tremendous!" "The best of the best—no question." "Does some of the best work in Manhattan. Professional, reliable, knowledgeable." "Has the best response time in town because of the large staff. Does great work."*

## Henry Myers Plumbing & Heating

| | 4 | 3 | 4.5 | 5 |
|---|---|---|---|---|

68-10 Eighth Avenue, Brooklyn, NY 11220
(718) 836 - 1324

*Residential and commercial plumbing and heating services*

Word is this small, family-run business "does great work" serving both residential and commercial clients, and is ranked among the city's finest at the "bottom of top-tier" plumbers. We're told the firm operates with two crews: one focused on working mostly with contractors on major renovations in Manhattan and the other attending to service calls predominately in Brooklyn. References report Henry Myers is at its best in smaller jobs, where the owner's active role on-site is most reverberant. Clients note that the company can solve just about any problem that arises. Typically, free estimates precede most jobs, which clients find a certain source of value.

*"The kind of guy that you call to come in and fix what some other plumber messed up. Owner does work himself, which says a lot!"*

## Jack Lichtenberger & Co.

| | 5 | 4 | 4.5 | 4.5 |
|---|---|---|---|---|

304 Spring Street, New York, NY 10013
(212) 807 - 8811

*Complex industrial and residential plumbing projects*

Started in the late 1800s as a roofing and carriage repair company, this company made its transition to plumbing in 1905 and claims to be the oldest of its kind in the city. Robert Lichtenberger, Jack's great-grandson, now runs this versatile, modest-sized plumbing and heating business which serves both residential and commercial clients throughout Manhattan. References tell us Robert is enthusiastic and engaging, and very mindful of keeping customers in the loop. As a result of Lichtenberger & Co's vast range of experience, we hear the firm displays superior aptitude in tackling high-end residential projects. Clients say the firm's stable of supervisors for these types of jobs enables it to continue to excel.

Dedicated repair and service work round out this company's repertoire. The firm provides a free estimate for jobs both big and small—from a 17,000-square-foot townhouse to a 700-square-foot apartment—jobs clients say Lichtenberg & Co. execute with equal aplomb.

*"The ultimate plumber for true professionals."*

| | Quality | Cost | Value | Recommend? |
|---|---|---|---|---|
| | ✚ | $ | ◆ | ★ |

## John J. Repetti Plumbing
21 Downing Street, New York, NY 10002
(212) 242 - 6232
*Residential plumbing services*

◻   ◻   ◻   ◻

## John Sideris Plumbing
123 West 79th Street, New York, NY 10024
(212) 501 - 0971
*Residential plumbing and heating, emergency services*

3    3    3.5    3.5

Caring for all five boroughs, the team at John Sideris specializes in large residential projects, particularly complete plumbing and heating installations and renovations of co-ops, brownstones and lofts. The firm also scoops up smaller jobs such as routine service and (24-hour) emergency calls for both residential and commercial customers. Whatever size the task, the firm charges at a fixed flat rate.

## Kapnag Heating & Plumbing Corp.
27-16 41st Avenue, Long Island City, NY 11101
(212) 289 - 8847
*Residential plumbing services*

3    3    4    4

This 75-year-old firm comes with heady endorsements by Blue Chip city realty companies. Manhattan residents find themselves just as content with the Kapnag's plumbing and heating services. We hear the company stays as active in smaller repair and maintenance tasks as it does larger installations and renovations, though references tell us the firm's responsiveness lacks the expediency of larger projects. However, all agree that one can expect very competent, considerate service.

## Liberty Plumbing
1 Chantilly Court, Dix Hills, NY 11746
(516) 673 - 4473
*Residential plumbing services*

3    2.5    4    4

Clients say this affable plumber makes a kitchen renovation a bit more bearable. Liberty comes highly recommended by some of New York's top contractors for its installations on larger projects for both residential and commercial clients all over the metropolitan area.

*"Such a nice guy."*

## Mac Felder Plumbing
138 West 83rd Street, New York, NY 10024
(212) 877 - 8450
*Residential and commercial plumbing*

4    3.5    4.5    4.5

References can't help speak volumes about the "incredible" work of this plumbing contactor, in business since 1936. The city's elite building managers, construction companies and private clients all vie for Mac Felder's services. We're told the firm takes on all size jobs almost exclusively in Manhattan, specializing in a large number of complete residential renovations. It also has a number of service contracts with some very prestigious Upper East Side buildings. Felder fields a "friendly and helpful staff" of over twenty, storied to be "very neat," always a feat when working with water. The firm repairs heating systems on occasion. Securing this company's services is a step or two more expensive than most, but that's what it takes to get to get a look from the top tier.

| Quality | Cost | Value | Recommend? |
|---|---|---|---|
| ✚ | $ | ◆ | ★ |

## McManus Mechanical Maintenance, Plumbing & Heating Inc.

| | 3 | 3.5 | 3.5 | 4 |

424 Beach 135th Street, Belle Harbor, NY 11694
(718) 945 - 3966

*Plumbing and heating services and fire suppression systems*

We hear this plumber places a priority on a swift response to clients both old and new in four of the city's five boroughs (sorry Staten Island), mostly in Manhattan. Owner Robert McManus brings two decades of experience to this firm, which performs both small and large installations and repair of plumbing, heating and fire-suppression systems for residential, commercial, institutional and industrial clients. Clients say the firm is very adept at service work. They tell us McManus's small staff is always honest, keeping them 100 percent informed about the status of their job. Rates are fairly standard for both one- and two-man teams, and decline outside Manhattan.

## Metro Plumbing & Heating

219 Johnson Avenue, Brooklyn, NY 11206
(718) 417 - 6008

*Commercial and residential plumbing and heating*

## Midtown Plumbing Inc.

| | 2.5 | 3 | 3 | 3.5 |

102-15 159th Road, Howard Beach, NY 11414
(718) 323 - 5006

*Residential plumbing services*

Midtown Plumbing earns positive reviews for its commercial and residential renovations and installations, which tend to be larger and coordinated through contractors. Half the firm's work is in Manhattan, while the rest is for clients in the other boroughs.

## N. Pagano Heating & Plumbing Contractors Ltd.

| | 4 | 3 | 4.5 | 4.5 |

225 East 134th Street, Bronx, NY 10451
(718) 993 - 7337

*Residential plumbing services*

This small, "very reliable" Bronx-based company is run by Nunzio Pagano and Maurizio Taormina, two master plumbers who we hear "fix everything except broken hearts." In addition to plumbing repair and maintenance, N. Pagano also does full-scale installations and renovations. The firm has been in the business for over fifteen years, though Pagano has been servicing the Upper East Side for the past 25 years.

Clients rave about the "courteous professionals" at Pagano, who they say are thorough, patient and always quick to respond to calls. They tell us the company fosters an atmosphere of familial comfort. Each mechanic is singularly talented, and collectively the firm delivers consistent high-quality work and excellent service. This may be why Pagano, Taormina and company are called on by some of the top contractors in the city, one of which noted that N. Pagano provides "outstanding service in a very busy time." A diagnostic fee accompanies each job.

*"Keep up the good work!" "Every Mechanic has a certain area of expertise, so the work goes together without much trouble through the job." "Good company, good men, very responsible." "Good follow up—I would not hesitate to use them again."*

| | Quality | Cost | Value | Recommend? |
|---|---|---|---|---|
| | + | $ | ◆ | ★ |

## New York Plumbing & Heating Corp.     3     3     4     4
87-71 Lefferts Boulevard, Richmond Hill, NY  11418
(718) 441 - 6800
*Commercial, residential and industrial plumbing and heating*

Members have come to expect professional service from New York Plumbing & Heating—24 hours a day, seven days a week. The company serves commercial, residential and industrial clients, and has offices in Manhattan, Brooklyn, the Bronx, Queens and Nassau County. Most notable is that New York Plumbing charges by the job, not the hour, which many clients seem to favor.

## Ozery Plumbing & Heating Inc.     5     4     5     5
206 East 119th Street, New York, NY  10035
(212) 410 - 6800
*High-end residential and commercial plumbing and heating, fire suppression*

If you have an extraordinary project and need an extraordinary plumber, clients say that this is the guy for you. Ed Ozery and his small, selective and highly skilled team have pleased both residential and commercial clients in Manhattan for 23 years undertaking larger installation and renovation projects. We hear Ozery's expertise is rivaled only by his open demeanor and ability to pin down a client in conversation. Top contractors, architects and designers all look to this firm, citing Ozery's planning and supervisory capabilities. When he's not asked to design the job himself, Ozery often utilizes the firm's CAD capabilities to cross-check the work of engineers, and is always willing to offer advice on system design.

Ozery specializes in high-end residential and commercial plumbing, heating, fire suppression, gas boilers, hydronics and radiant floor heating. We are told that maintaining and servicing his existing clients (a rather star-studded list) is his top priority, so he tends to stay away from all other basic service calls.

*"I'd just like to concur with your evaluation. I've used Ed Ozery for two years now and other than the occupational hazard of over-chattiness, he's just great. Simple explanations to complex problems and a serious can-do attitude. You can consider yourself lucky if he works for you."*

## Pro-Tech Heating & Plumbing Corp.     4.5     4     4     5
150-44 11th Avenue, Whitestone, NY  11357
(718) 767 - 9067   www.protech-plbg.com
*Plumbing and heating services*

Clients tell us this modest-sized, multi-disciplined firm boasts "knowledgeable, good mechanics" who carry themselves as serious professionals. We hear principals Vincent (Vinny) Tolins and Joseph Minarik have positioned this firm among the finest in the city, caring for the smallest to the largest jobs with pride and confidence. In addition to all-encompassing plumbing, hot-water and steam heating, sewer and gas work, the firm also offers HVAC service and repair. Top tier contractors and architects, as well as managers of high-end buildings in New York, choose this team for all of their projects.

Word is most appreciate the high priority the firm puts on speed and customer service with teams "on-call" 24 hours a day. However, reference's "only complaint" is that the firm always dispatches two men, even when the job doesn't demand it, "so you tend to pay more for tiny jobs."

*"They know what they are doing. Definitely among the top three in the city."*
*"Very knowledgeable."*

## R&R Plumbing & Heating    3    3    4    4
2524 Forest Avenue, Staten Island, NY  10303
(718) 981 - 3808   www.rrsc.com
*Residential plumbing services*

You guessed it, R&R is part of the national corporation Roto-Rooter, the Kleenex brand of plumbing services. Is there an actual roto-rooter?  Sure, invented by Samuel Blanc in 1933 with a 1/6 HP Maytag washing machine motor, roller skate wheels and 3/8" cable to turn blades that cut tree roots.  While emergency service is this company's speciality, and drain cleaning the image conjured—the firm's ever-expanding residential services also includes the installation, repair and replacement of whole plumbing systems.  Appointments and service calls can be scheduled online.

## RAM Plumbing & Heating    3    2.5    4    4
707 5th Avenue, Brooklyn, NY  11215
(718) 768 - 6706
*Commercial and residential plumbing services*

Clients of RAM Plumbing & Heating tell us the owner "knows his stuff," but some were slightly less enthusiastic about his staff.  Still, they say not to worry, the owner is "all over" his jobs and his men in order to ensure decent quality at a reasonable price.

## Ranger Plumbing    3.5    3.5    4    4
10-15 48th Avenue, Long Island City, NY  11101
(718) 392 - 6607
*Residential plumbing services*

Ranger is helmed by two 25-year vets of the high-end home renovation front. Principal Tony Ruggi and Peter Aff go to the extreme to deliver not just the quality behind the walls, but in a finely buttoned-up finish.  We hear they and their small staff have the patience and experience to incorporate imported, handcrafted or vintage fixtures into their installations.  Working with private clients as well as contractors, the firm typically takes on small bath fit-outs to apartment guts that include heating and gas work.  It does not, however, deal in sewer or street connection or clean outs. Clients say the firm follows projects through and charges accordingly.

## S. Hoffman Plumbing    3    2.5    3.5    3.5
1775 Broadway, New York, NY  10019
(212) 664 - 0770
*Residential and commercial plumbing and heating*

While clients say this midsized firm's responsiveness is "not going to set the world on fire," we hear it is a competent and caring operation.  S. Hoffman does both smaller repairs and maintenance as well as larger installations for commercial and residential clients in Manhattan.  Nice crewmen and quality work keep customers pleased.

*"They are decent, thoughtful guys that send me a Christmas card every year."*

| | Quality + | Cost $ | Value ◆ | Recommend? ★ |
|---|---|---|---|---|

## Sandy's Plumbing

| | 3.5 | 3.5 | 4 | 4 |

210 Forsyth Street, New York, NY  10002
(212) 475 - 6510

*Commercial and residential plumbing*

This small father and son shop will do anything from a clogged sink to a $10 million renovation.  Sandy's Plumbing serves both commercial and residential clients throughout Manhattan, including some of the city's finest restaurants and management agencies.  We hear the staff at Sandy's is friendly and informative. While they "definitely know what they are doing," clients say their reliability is less than definite. Estimates are given for major jobs, while minor ones are handed to a two-man team and charged reasonably by the hour.

## Sanitary Plumbing & Heating Corp.

| | 2.5 | 2.5 | 3 | 3 |

211 East 117th Street, New York, NY  10035
(212) 534 - 8186

*Residential plumbing services*

A long established, professional organization, Sanitary Plumbing has been family-owned and managed since 1946.  With the benefit of a large staff, the firm serves residential and commercial customers on both large and small plumbing and heating jobs.  Sanitary is known mainly for its skill with alterations and renovations.

## Speedway Plumbing & Heating

| | 2.5 | 3 | 3 | 3.5 |

69-02 51st Avenue, Woodside, NY  11377
(718) 424 - 7863

*Residential and commercial plumbing and heating*

Industry pros tell us Speedway knows its way around the plumbing and heating track.  Working in the commercial and residential sectors on both small and large jobs, approximately 75 percent of which are in Manhattan, this small firm revs its "great skills" to produce "fine" if not first-place work.  The firm's basic rate is slightly above standard.

## The Pipeline of New York

| | 3 | 3 | 4 | 3.5 |

145 Reade Street, New York, NY  10029
(212) 267 - 4241

*Plumbing and heating services*

Whatever clients find in their pipeline, this Pipeline offers the five boroughs 24/7 plumbing and heating service.  The firm services and installs faucets, drains, sinks, valves, radiators, boilers, high and low pressure steam, gas, water meters, sewers, hot water heaters, as well as spearheading gut renovations in apartments and brownstones.  Private clients and real estate companies all place confidence in Pipeline of New York. They especially appreciate that prices are based upon a contract based upon a "fixed price" booklet that lists 100 different jobs that are done at preset prices. Estimates are free.

# Hiring a Rug Cleaning, Installation & Repair Service Provider

Does your heirloom Oriental display a record of your adorable yet hard-to-housetrain puppy? Did Uncle Mike spill a Bloody Mary on your Persian? Did your cat sharpen his claws on that hidden corner of your needlepoint? Or is your rug just overdue for its regular cleaning (every two to four years, according to The Oriental Rug Importers of America)? Not to worry: rug cleaners and restorers can address every kind of need on every type of rug, from museum-quality handmade rugs to inexpensive carpeting.

## Gathering Information

When choosing cleaners or restorers, there are many factors to consider. Ask if they perform free, written estimates. If they make house calls, do they charge a travel fee, and do they have free pick-up, delivery and reinstallation? Before they quote you a price, you may wish to inquire how they set their rate: by the job, the hour or the size of the rug? Do they require a deposit? Will they arrange a payment plan if you need one? Do they offer discounts for multiple rugs or rooms? It's a good sign if they honor their estimate, even if the job overwhelms their expectations. It's an even better sign if they guarantee perfection, and don't consider the job finished until you are satisfied. Such an assurance (especially in writing) may be more valuable than letters of reference or membership in one of the professional associations, though both of these would add further reassurance of competence.

If your rug is handmade and you think it may be valuable, you may want to get it appraised by a rug-care service before having it cleaned or repaired. If it is valuable, you'll need to consider more expert (and expensive) services. On the other hand, you may also discover that the rug isn't worth nearly as much as you believed, and hence may not warrant lavish attention. Either way, a professional appraisal certifies the value of your belonging in case of mishaps—you may want to inquire beforehand whether liability falls in your court or whether the cleaner/restorer's insurance covers any mishaps. Many rug cleaning and reweaving establishments appraise rugs for insurance, estate sale, tax and charitable donation. Watching appraisers evaluate your rug also allows you to preview their professionalism. If their work instills confidence, hire them for the whole job—if not, you can still use their appraisal (and estimate, if they perform one simultaneously) as a first opinion in approaching another establishment. For complicated (expensive) repair or restoration jobs, ask how long it will take. Often the expert restorers have other jobs they must finish before they can get to yours. If your rug is valuable, it is worth waiting for the best.

If the rug needs repair before cleaning, confirm that the restorer knows the techniques of the tradition in which the rug was made: Navajo yarn-dying and rug-weaving methods differ vastly from those of Iran. Ask to see a portfolio of their previous repair work, which often displays side-by-side "before" and "after" pictures. Inspect how well they match colors, recreate designs, and blend repairs into existing weaves. If your rug is valuable, inquire whether an expert or an apprentice will perform the repair work. Also, see to it that all repair work is included in the estimate, from reweaving holes to renapping worn areas; restoring moth damage to rewrapping seams and re-fringing to re-blocking your rug to its original shape. Particularly thorough rug conservationists will even unravel strands and overcast weaving in order to blend repairs into the rug's existing texture and design.

## CLEANING AND DRYING TECHNIQUES

There are many different cleaning methods, each of which addresses different situations with varying degrees of efficacy and expense. Carpet cleaners typically have mobile operations, and will clean rugs in your home with hot "carbonating" systems, steam-cleaning or dry-cleaning. Will they move the furniture to clean under it or do they expect it ready when they arrive? Rug cleaners, on the other hand, usually perform the cleaning at their site. They may expect the rug to be rolled up and waiting for their pick up. Silk rugs, fragile tapestries and textiles with "fugitive" (short-lived) dyes, or bright colors that might "bleed" (run), should be hand-washed—the most delicate and expensive method. Luster cleaning immerses the entire rug in cleaning solutions, and thus achieves a deep clean while minimizing wear on the fabric. Soap washing involves running a vacuum-like machine over the rug; this vigorous method is only for particularly rugged or less-valuable rugs. Discuss in advance what problems the cleaner can and can't fix. For example, excessive wear on a hallway rug will still be there after a cleaning, though it will be much less noticeable. If you are health or environmentally conscious, ask whether the company offers nontoxic cleaners.

Any rug that's washed must also be dried properly to avoid mildew and dry rot. Be sure to ask about the time and drying technique for in-home jobs —you should know beforehand if you need to reroute traffic through the patio for three days. For in-plant jobs, bigger outfits have dry-rooms where they control temperature and humidity levels. In the home, drying basically involves not walking on the rug until it is dry, which depends on humidity and other factors. Some businesses also offer stain protectants, which they apply directly to the rug to shield it from future accidents (should the tipsy uncle return). Other companies may take a purist approach, preferring periodic cleaning to chemical protectants.

## CARPET AND RUG INSTALLATION

Before the carpet or rug is put down, padding should always be laid first. Padding gives more cushioning for your feet and keeps the rug from sliding, which helps prevent slips, falls and spills. Ask what kind of padding the installer will use, as there are generally different quality and price options.

For wall-to-wall carpeting installation, the most common method is to lay wooden tack strips around the perimeter of the room. The tack strips have pins sticking up that grab the carpet and hold it in place. The tack strips are attached to the floor using small nails, which leave holes in the floor when the carpet is removed. The padding also is usually either nailed or stapled to the floor. If you must cover your nice wood floors (for the kids, maybe), you should discuss with the installer how to minimize the floor damage. Unfortunately, there is not that much that can be done if you want wall-to-wall. Some installers may suggest attaching the carpet with double-faced tape, but most say that this doesn't hold well and the carpet shifts and buckles. If your floor contributes to the value of your apartment, it is simply better to stick with area rugs. Remember to ask whether or not there are any potential extra charges, such as for ripping up existing wall-to-wall carpeting before installing the new one or for disposing of the old carpeting and pads if you don't want to keep them.

Some rug cleaners focus on just stain and odor removal services to meet the needs of pet owners, smokers and families with small children (or just klutzes). Many providers offer stain protection for future spills, which, depending on your lifestyle, may be a sound investment. Other companies specialize in emergency services in case of fire, smoke or water damage, and may even be available round-the-clock. If you're moving, remodeling or otherwise in need of storage, look to the larger outfits for mothproofing and storage services. After storage or in-plant services, many companies will reinstall your rug over appropriate padding.

Rug cleaners and restorers also offer many other services for rugs and other furnishings. Many rug cleaners also clean curtains and upholstered furniture. Some businesses prefer to remove the draperies from the home and wash them at their facilities. In-home carpet cleaners are more likely to clean curtains in the house.

Since curtains, upholstered furniture and rugs dominate most of the space (not to mention the attention) in a room, rug cleaners and restorers emphasize the importance of maintaining these items. Their colors will be clearer, they'll last longer, you'll be inhaling less dust—and your home will look more beautiful.

## ON COST

Prices among rug companies vary immensely because each has its own specialties and services. Some rug firms work on standard cleaning and focus on wall-to-wall broadlooms, upholstery and drapery. For this type of cleaning, some charge by the square foot, which could start at $.27 per square foot and could go up to $1 to $1.25 per square foot. Most companies charge $.30 to $.60 per square foot. Then again, some give a flat rate after inspecting the carpet and seeing how much cleaning needs to be done. This usually conforms to their minimum rate, which most companies have. Minimum rates start at $50 and go up to $150 for standard wall-to-wall broadloom cleaning.

Area rugs are a different terrain altogether. New York has numerous experts and "specialized" firms that only deal with area rug cleaning, repair and restoration—those that work mostly with the rare, the old, the valuable and in most cases, only the handmade ones. Most companies who do standard wall-to-wall cleaning also clean area rugs, but the older and rarer the rug is, the more specialized the cleaning, repair and attention it needs. Pricing for area rug cleaning starts as low as $1 per square foot and could go as high as $3 to $5 per square foot, depending on the amount of cleaning needed and the value of the rug. These firms also have minimum rates, and fees start at $100 minimum up to $700. Then again, if your area rug is not a hundred years old and requires only regular cleaning or minimal repairs, you could end up paying a standard $50 to $100 per job or $1.25 to $2 per square foot.

### DON'T LET THE RUG BE PULLED OUT FROM UNDER YOU!

- ✧ Get several bids. Prices among competent cleaners can vary quite a bit.
- ✧ When you have an estimate, ask if it's binding. Ask what factors might cause it to become higher (or lower) when the job is actually done.
- ✧ Is there a minimum charge for a house call? If the cost of cleaning your rug is below the minimum you might want to have them perform another service (such as clean or stain-proof another rug, piece of furniture or curtains) at the same time.
- ✧ Once they are in your house, the rug cleaners will often do another rug for much less money, especially if paid in cash.
- ✧ Some of the larger more commercial cleaners have regular "sales." Get on their mailing list to receive updates. If you're not in a hurry, wait for a sale.

| | Quality | Cost | Value | Recommend? |
|---|---|---|---|---|
| | ✚ | $ | ◆ | ★ |

## RUGS-CLEANING INSTALLATION & REPAIR

### 800 Rug Wash
4    2    5    5

20 Enterprise Avenue, Secaucus, NJ 07094
(800) 784 - 9274   www.800rugwash.com

*Rug and upholstery cleaning and repair—flooring installation and maintenance*

Although 800 Rug Wash's specialty is cleaning, repairing and selling rugs, the firm also cleans upholstery, fabric walls, drapery and fabric blinds. 800 Rug also has a flooring division which handles installation, sanding and finishing of all types of floors. We are told that even before establishing the company in 1980, owner Benjamin Hatooka, a chemist by trade, had a number of rug dealers come to him to change the colors of rugs and make them look old. Today, one of the firm's specialty is still antiquing. The firm has been serving residential and commercial interiors mostly in Manhattan, some parts of Los Angeles, Florida, Boston, Virginia and Canada. 800 Rug Wash is an upstanding member of the Oriental Rug Importers Association and the National Wood Flooring Association.

Pricing is generally per square foot, and sources say that the firm's prices are moderate. Clients have expressed satisfaction with this firm's reliability, promptness and good work ethic.

*"Knows his business." "Prompt—very good work." "Fair prices for efficient service."*

### ABC Carpet & Home
3    3    3    3

888 Broadway, New York, NY 10003
(212) 473 - 3000   www.abchome.com

*Retail—Reupholstery, window treatments, rug cleaning and installation*

See ABC Carpet & Home 's full report under the heading Upholstery & Window Treatments

### Abraham Moheban & Son Antique Carpets
5    4    5    5

139 East 57th Street, 3rd Floor, New York, NY 10022
(212) 758 - 3900   www.moheban.com

*Dealer—fine rug cleaning and restoration*

One of the best in the city that deals with fine antique European and Oriental rugs, clients say Abraham Moheban & Son also cleans, restores, repairs and appraises antique and semi-antique decorative rugs and carpets. All cleaning is done in-house and is heavily supervised. This family-run business is now being managed by a fourth-generation Moheban, David, and has been satisfying clients mainly in Manhattan and some areas in the Hamptons and Westchester County.

The firm was established in 1961 by Abraham Moheban. Born in Iran, Abraham Moheban started working in the rug industry at the age of fourteen and is known as one of the pioneers of the rug trade here in America. Though insiders say the company works mostly with designers and architects, they also have an impressive roster of well-heeled residential clients. The firm is a member of the Oriental Rugs Importers Association and ASID.

Enthusiastic clients rave about this firm's wide array of high-quality rugs and the exquisite repair and restoration work it does. Though prices may be expensive, references agree that the service is definitely worth the cost. Indeed, sources say, this firm's impeccable taste, knowledge of the industry and meticulous attention to detail makes them one of the masters of the rug business.

*"Beautiful repair and restoration job." "Their inventories are just exquisite." "Wouldn't hesitate to go back." "Great eye for quality carpets and rugs. They understand and appreciate the history of the rugs."*

### Action Carpet Cleaners

| | | | |
|---|---|---|---|
| 3 | 2 | 3.5 | 4.5 |

543 West 43rd Street, New York, NY 10036
(212) 757 - 2554

*Rug, upholstery and floor cleaning*

Action Carpet Cleaners has won over quite a solid group of happy clients since opening its doors 21 years ago. The firm's principal, Joe Carilli, has developed a reputation for honesty and reliability as well as for delivering top-quality service at reasonable prices. The firm serves both residential and commercial clients mostly in Manhattan and some areas in the outer boroughs. The firm mainly cleans, installs, repairs and sells rugs and wall-to-wall carpets. Action also provides some flooring services, as well as drapery, fabric walls, furniture and upholstery cleaning. The company is also one of the few in the city who specializes in water damage restoration and offers a 24-hour emergency service. Pricing is usually per square foot and so are the estimates, except for very small jobs. There is a reasonable minimum amount to do a project and the workmen will move furniture within reason. There is also no extra charge for spot cleaning.

Sources tell us that Carilli is a firm believer in personalized service and does most of the work himself. Clients praise the firm's efficient and reliable service and the fair prices that go along with it.

*"Used them for five years. I am thrilled with them." "Trustworthy, reliable and on time." "Bottom line—He satisfies his customers." "I tested him against a few other vendors—Action delivered higher quality and lower cost."*

### All Clean Carpet & Upholstery Cleaning

| | | | |
|---|---|---|---|
| 3.5 | 2.5 | 4 | 4 |

10 Hilltop Place, Albertson, NY 11507
(516) 621 - 0524

*Rug, upholstery, furniture and drapery cleaning*

Sources tell us that since its establishment sixteen years ago, All Clean has been serving notable carpet retailers, celebrities and high-end residential clients. This company cleans rugs, furniture, upholstery, drapery and wall fabrics. The firm also specializes in water damage restoration and does some minor rug and upholstery repairs.

Capable of cleaning the finest Orientals, the firm does only on-site residential work. Clients say they are thrilled with the skill and knowledge All Clean brings to the job. They commend the firm for its willingness to make emergency (read: sick dog) visits for regular customers. Customers also appreciate that the crew moves furniture and puts it back, rather than just cleaning around it.

*"Fabulous, very high standards." "He takes time to find out what stains there are and breaks them down properly." "Very professional." "Neat and responsive. They know what they are doing." "Meticulous." "Saved me from buying new carpets!"*

### Anita deCarlo Inc.

| | | | |
|---|---|---|---|
| 4.5 | 3.5 | 4.5 | 5 |

605 Madison Avenue, New York, NY 10022
(212) 759 - 1145

*Antique rug restoration, brokerage, cleaning and maintenance*

This "one-woman band" has more than 30 years experience in the high-end rug business. Anita deCarlo is known by clients as a rug broker who does accurate appraisals and can locate the finest and rarest pieces for the discriminating tastes of her sophisticated clientele. She also offers cleaning and restoration services for rugs, needlework and textiles. We hear most of the work is usually done in-house, but very large pieces are done on-site. She usually works in Manhattan

| Quality | Cost | Value | Recommend? |
|---------|------|-------|------------|
| ✚ | $ | ◆ | ★ |

but has done projects in the Hamptons and Westchester County. Clients rave about her work quality and entrust her with their most valuable rugs. References also compliment her professional demeanor, outstanding credentials and charm.

*"Excellent, delightful, efficient." "Marvelous—the best." "Knows her business." "Extremely competent and a pleasure to work with." "Her credentials and knowledge are very impressive." "Excellent navigator in the sometimes shady world of carpet dealing."*

### Apple Window Cleaning
305 West 18th Street, Number 3, New York, NY 10011
(212) 620 - 0708
*Commercial and residential window cleaning, general cleaning services*

See Apple Window Cleaning's full report under the heading Window Washers

### Beauvais Carpets        4.5    3     5     5
201 East 57th Street, 2nd Floor, New York, NY 10022
(212) 688 - 2265
*Dealer and fine rug and tapestry cleaning and restoration*

Conveniently located in midtown Manhattan, Beauvais Carpets is primarily a dealer with a "preeminent collection of fine antique rugs and tapestries." The firm also provides high-quality restoration, appraisal and cleaning services for fine antique, semi-antique and contemporary rugs. They also sell and install wall-to-wall carpets. Insiders tell us that their gallery is a haven for rug collectors and dealers since it features an outstanding selection of rugs and tapestries from 16th- through 19th-century Europe and Asia and custom broadloom carpets that allows custom, size and design specifications.

Pricing is generally by the job and there is a charge for pick-up and delivery. Though the firm deals mostly with designers and architects, it also serves an impressive list of distinguished residential clients. With regard to spot cleaning, we hear that Beauvais pre-tests stains and informs the client of the predictable result. All repairs and cleaning are done in their workshops located in Brooklyn and Manhattan. Sources say that the workmen are thorough, polite and knowledgeable.

*"The definitive source for fine antique rugs." "Exceeded my expectations."*

### Beyond the Bosphorus        5     3     5     5
79 Sullivan Street, New York, NY 10012
(212) 219 - 8257
*Antique rug cleaning, retail and restoration*

Aside from the eye-catching name, its impressive credentials, accurate knowledge and vast resources on Turkish and Oriental flatwoven rugs make Beyond the Bosphorous stand out among its peers. The company is owned and managed by Istanbul native Ismail Basbag, who boasts ten years of training and experience working in the Grand Bazaar of Istanbul before founding Beyond the Bosphorous in 1985.

This firm cleans, repairs, sells and restores antique and semi-antique Turkish flatwoven rugs called kilims, Turkish cylindrical pillows (Bolster pillows), trunks upholstered with kilims and other types of Oriental area rugs. Work is done in or out of Basbag's workshop, depending on the type of project. His sophisticated clientele appreciates Basbag's fine taste and shares his knowledge of antique rugs. The firm has clients at some of the city's most elite addresses as well as in California, New Jersey, Connecticut and Texas. Beyond the Bosphorous was also mentioned in *New York Magazine's* Spring Issue of *Manhattan's 1,000 Best Shops.*

Sources describe Basbag as a nice, quiet and polite man, who does a splendid job with a pleasant demeanor and excellent work philosophy. Though prices are a bit high-end, clients say the service is worth every penny.

*"Reliable—excellent at following up." "Did what he should. Excellent work ethic." "Knowledgeable about his work."*

## Bloomingdale's Home Cleaning
3    2.5    3    4

301 Norman Avenue, Brooklyn, NY 11222
(718) 389 - 3500
*Rug and upholstery cleaning*

As one of the departments of Bloomingdale's department store, Home Cleaning provides steam cleaning services for rugs and other household items such as upholstery and pillows. Prices are based on size, with higher rates for fine or antique items. Clients compliment Bloomingdale's efficiency and reasonable prices—particularly its periodic sales—and have found the management professional and reasonable. Workers will clean on site, or pick up and deliver, depending on the job.

*"They get the job done." "Responsive. Fair prices."*

## Brooklyn Carpet Exchange
3    2.5    3.5    4.5

37 West 37th Street, New York, NY 10018
(212) 391 - 7727
*Dealer, rug installations, repair and cleaning*

Brooklyn Carpet Exchange installs wall-to-wall carpets, cleans and repairs area rugs and upholstery. The company is also a dealer in new and used area rugs. The firm serves residential and commercial clients in Manhattan and some areas in the outer boroughs.

## Buff-Away of Manhattan Inc.
2.5    2.5    2.5    3

427 East 13th Street, New York, NY 10009
(212) 477 - 7100
*Upholstery, textile, rug and drapery cleaning*

This company offers cleaning services for carpets, drapery, upholstery and fabric walls. Buff-Away works residentially as well as with corporations. The firm, run by Vincent and Larry Ingenito, works mainly in Manhattan, but also serves the outer boroughs.

Although most clients tell us that the firm is terrific with stains and general carpet cleaning, others are less satisfied with the quality of their work. Despite comments from some sources that they had a "not-so-smooth process" with Buff-Away, the majority maintains that the workmen are polite, thorough and knowledgeable about their business.

*"One of the best upholsterers in New York." "Asked them to redo my carpet— was not satisfied with the result."*

## Carpet Pro Service Inc.
3    2.5    3    4

1717 East 48th Street, Brooklyn, NY 11234
(212) 829 - 9790
*Rug and upholstery cleaning*

A New York old-timer in the rug and carpet business, Carpet Pro has been serving Manhattanites for 27 years now. This firm specializes in water damage restoration and offers a 24-hour emergency service to its customers. The company also cleans carpets, area rugs, upholstery and drapery. Insiders tell us that one can also take advantage of additional services such as fabric protection, pet odor control and spot cleaning. The company also has a decent restoration department. Carpet Pro works with residential and commercial clients mostly in Manhattan but will travel to other outer boroughs.

## Clean Bright Process Co.    3.5    3    4.5    4.5
350 Fifth Avenue, Suite 3304, New York, NY 10118
(212) 283 - 6400

*Rug and upholstery cleaning and repairs*

This firm provides on and off-site cleaning services to high-end residential and commercial clients in the New York metro area, and has been doing so since 1964. Much of Clean Bright's business comes from personal, architect and decorator referrals, and we have heard many of the city's top decorators sing the firm's praises. Several customers say that Clean Bright is well worth the cost for cleanup after a renovation. While its technicians will clean area rugs at your home, you may get better service by having the rugs cleaned at the plant. The company cleans both broadloom and area rugs and we hear Clean Bright is great with upholstery as well as supplying and installing wall-to-wall carpets. The firm will clean blinds, fabric walls and acoustical ceilings, and will pick up and deliver.

*"Definitely worth it." "Recommended by my decorator."*

## Cleantech    4    3.5    4    4.5
350 Fifth Avenue, New York, NY 10118
(212) 619 - 7600

*Rug and upholstery cleaning and other cleaning services*

Decorators, architects, contractors and homeowners all agree that Cleantech does a thorough and efficient job in cleaning their carpets and rugs. The firm also offers a wide range of high-quality cleaning services, some of which are cleaning and installing draperies and carpeting and waxing floors. One client raved about the terrific job this firm did on her sisal rug, which, she said other companies normally decline to address. We hear that top designers also call on the firm for post-construction cleanup work.

*"Great cleaner of rugs, will get out most spots." "Couldn't get over the great job Cleantech did with the tough stains in my rugs."*

## Cleantex Process Co.    4    2.5    5    4.5
2335 Twelfth Avenue, New York, NY 10027
(212) 283 - 1200

*Cleaning and repair of rugs, upholstery and draperies*

Cleantex has been handling the rug, wall-to-wall carpets and drapery cleaning needs of New Yorkers for nearly 75 years. This firm also cleans and repairs upholstery and furniture. References, many of whom have used the company for years find Cleantex reliable, professional and cooperative. We hear that several dealers of fine Oriental rugs refer their clients to Cleantex. Should clients need it, flameproofing is one of this firm's specialties—and provides the service for the curtains at Lincoln Center. The firm also has convenient pick-up and delivery services for fine and standard carpets. The company serves most of Manhattan as well as some areas in Connecticut, New Jersey, Long Island, Westchester County and the Hamptons.

*"Wonderful, cooperative, no-nonsense people." "We know it will be done professionally." "Everything always goes smoothly." "They are getting up there with some of the best in the city."*

| Quality | Cost | Value | Recommend? |
|---------|------|-------|------------|
| ✚ | $ | ◆ | ★ |

## Cohen Carpet, Upholstery & Drapery Cleaning

| | | | |
|---|---|---|---|
| 4 | 3 | 4 | 4.5 |

2565 Broadway, New York, NY 10025
(212) 663 - 6902

*Rug and upholstery cleaning*

Clients across the city say David Cohen personally does most of the work for this firm himself, and has maintained a high level of customer service since he established the company in 1983. Cohen cleans area rugs, wall-to-wall carpets, upholstery, fabric blinds, fabric walls and draperies both on and off site, mostly for residential customers. He doesn't do restoration, but will do minor repairs. Clients tell us that Cohen comes recommended by furniture firms and designers alike, who are pleased with the quality of his work and confident in his professional conduct. They say he is always pleasant, prompt, straightforward about pricing and trustworthy.

*"Easy to work with." "Really great with tough stains: nail polish, cranberry juice, etc." "The rugs look like new." "Not cheap, but very fair." "Great at troubleshooting." "We were ready to get new carpeting, but he somehow managed to repair our old one." "Performed miracles on our carpet."*

## Costikyan Carpets Inc.

| | | | |
|---|---|---|---|
| 4.5 | 4.5 | 4 | 4.5 |

28-13 14th Street, Astoria, NY 11102
(718) 726 - 1090   www.costikyan.com

*Dealer, fine rug and fabric upholstery cleaning and restoration*

Known for its exceptional cleaning and restoration work, we hear Costikyan Carpets has been satisfying discriminating clients since its founding in 1886 by Kent Costikyan. The company is now managed by his great-grandson, Philip. Costikyan buys, sells, cleans, repairs, restores, manufactures and imports fine antique, semi-antique and modern rugs. The firm also cleans fabric upholstery and fabric walls. Prices are high-end, but for valuable pieces, clients say they will trust no other. The firm works on site and off, and in most cases gives free pick up and delivery. Costikyan works mostly in Manhattan, in some parts of the regional area, the Hamptons and Westchester County. This mostly residential company also works with designers, dealers, private collectors, museums and high-end homeowners.

A number of the area's top designers and homeowners go to Costikyan for repairing their most expensive and rare rugs. The highly skilled workmen at Costikyan are described as professional, reliable and trustworthy.

*"When my husband walked all over the carpet just cleaned by Costikyan with muddy boots, they came back and recleaned for no charge." "One of the best in the business. Impeccable credentials." "While excessively expensive, I would trust no one else with my Kerman."*

## Delmont Carpet & Upholstery Cleaning

| Quality | Cost | Value | Recommend? |
|---------|------|-------|------------|
| 3.5 | 3 | 4 | 4 |

217 East 86th Street, New York, NY 10028
(212) 513 - 7500   www.delmontcleanny.com

*Rug and upholstery cleaning*

A top choice for numerous references for cleaning carpets, upholstery and drapes, Delmont Carpet has served residential and commercial clients around Manhattan, Brooklyn, Long Island, the Hamptons and Westchester County since 1973. Sources describe this company's workmen as prompt, courteous and efficient. The firm is also known for its attentive and personalized service. Pricing is usually per rug and we hear the workmen will move furniture, at no extra cost, as long as it is nonbreakable and not too heavy. Appreciative clients applaud the firm's reasonable rates.

*"Fastidious job." "The only company in the city I will use." "I couldn't have imagined a better job. On time and so reliable."*

## Duraclean Service Company of New York

| Quality | Cost | Value | Recommend? |
|---------|------|-------|------------|
| 3 | 2.5 | 3 | 5 |

164 East 86th Street, New York, NY 10028
(212) 289 - 8700

*Rug and upholstery cleaning*

Established in 1958, this company cleans and repairs all types of area rugs and wall-to-wall carpets. Duraclean serves mostly residential clients, but also has a healthy list of commercial customers, mostly in Manhattan. Estimates are free and pricing is usually by the foot.

## Durotone Company

| Quality | Cost | Value | Recommend? |
|---------|------|-------|------------|
| 2.5 | 3 | 3 | 4 |

510 Ogden Avenue, Mamaroneck, NY 10543
(914) 381 - 1167

*Rug and upholstery cleaning*

References tell us that they are satisfied with Durotone's service and describe their quality of work as "just fine," There is somewhat less enthusiasm about the firm's responsiveness, particularly to customer phone calls. Still, the majority agrees that Durotone gets the job done well. The firm cleans area rugs, wall-to-wall carpets and upholstery for residential and commercial clients.

## Exclusive Home Care Specialists

| Quality | Cost | Value | Recommend? |
|---------|------|-------|------------|
| 4 | 3 | 3.5 | 4 |

217 East 86th Street, Suite 177, New York, NY 10028
(212) 795 - 7727

*Rug and upholstery cleaning*

Exclusive Home Care Specialists offers professional cleaning services for fine upholstery, wall-to-wall carpeting, oriental and fine rugs, draperies, custom shades and fabric walls. Sources tell us the firm's staff combines friendliness with professionalism and inspires trust in its services and products. Exclusive Home Care offers emergency stain removal and can provide Seal-Tex lifetime stain protection (its version of Scotchguard) for upholstery, carpeting and rugs. Exclusive Home Care is also are experienced in wood floor waxing and polishing.

The firm, established in 1990 by Tona Athas, serves mostly residential clients in Manhattan as well as the Hamptons, Westchester County, Connecticut and Long Island. Prices are generally by the square foot and most of the cleaning is done on the site. The firm is described by clients as prompt, courteous and responsive.

*"Honest, friendly and reliable." "Top-notch stainproofing."*

| | Quality | Cost | Value | Recommend? |
|---|---|---|---|---|
| | + | $ | ◆ | ★ |

## F.J. Hakimian
**4.5     4     4     4.5**

136 East 57th Street, 2nd Floor, New York, NY 10022
(212) 371 - 6900   www.fjhakimian.com

*Dealer—Fine rug and tapestry cleaning, restoration and conservation*

F.J. Hakimian has earned a reputation of being one of the best in the rug business. Primarily a dealer, retailer and appraiser of fine, antique handmade rugs, this firm also offers cleaning, restoration and conservation of beautiful and rare tapestries, needlepoints and area rugs.

Owned and managed by Joseph Hakimian, the firm has been in business for 30 years and serves dealers, decorators, homeowners and private collectors. The firm's well-heeled references say its craftsmen do excellent work and consider Hakimian the natural choice for specialized jobs. Indeed, hiring this firm wouldn't make sense for those who are looking for an inexpensive company to clean the average rug. In fact, insiders tell us the relatively high cost and high-end focus would make it less suitable for anything but valuable, top-quality antique rugs and tapestries. Although some insiders tell us Hakimian's busy schedule makes him almost impossible to reach, most say it is worth the wait. Sources tell us that top decorators and important collectors will trust no other with their valuable treasures.

*"A gentleman and very honest businessman." "Excellent work." "Very good, but expensive."*

## Fabra Cleen Carpet & Fabric Specialists Inc.
**4     2.5     5     4.5**

P.O. Box 280471, Queens Village, NY 11428
(212) 777 - 4040

*Carpet, upholstery and fabric cleaning and repair*

"One of the nicest people around," is what many clients say about Fabra Cleen. This company cleans and repairs area rugs, carpets, upholstery, leather furniture, fabric headboards, fabric walls and drapery. The company also sells and installs wall-to-wall carpets, does post-construction cleanup, and has been known to handle some minor repairs on carpets and rugs. Established in 1949 by Samuel Kornet, the firm is now managed by his son Brian, and wife Wendy. Fabra Cleen serves both residential and commercial clients in Manhattan, parts of the regional area, the Hamptons and Westchester County. Cleaning is done on location or at the company's facilities, in which case, pick up and delivery is free. Sources tell us Fabra Cleen prides itself on meticulous attention to detail and will move furniture for free in order to clean under it, and not just around it.

Honest, trustworthy, reliable, responsive and punctual are some of the superlatives used to describe this company. Sources say they appreciate the efficient service and the moderate prices that come with it.

*"Excellent." "When I need them they are here at the drop of a hat." "They have my keys and my security codes—they are completely trustworthy." "Courteous."*

## Fiber-Seal of New York
**4     4.5     3.5     5**

214 East 52nd Street, New York, NY 10022
(212) 888 - 1070

*Upholstery fabric sealing*

A force-field against stains? One could call it that. Clients tell us that Fiber-Seal provides an invaluable service to protect upholstery from staining. These professionals spray an invisible and odor-free stain-repellent coating on any home fabric, including upholstery, draperies, lampshades and bedspreads. Fiber-Seal's service comes with an eighteen-month warranty. If the fabric becomes stained and the cleaning products the firm provides won't get it out, Fiber-Seal will return to your home and remove the stain at no additional cost. The expense is not insubstantial, but customers say the service is well worth it to protect their upholstery investment.

*"They must be doing something right, as there was a one-month wait for an appointment." "Quick and painless, but expensive."*

| | Quality | Cost | Value | Recommend? |
|---|---|---|---|---|
| | ✚ | $ | ◆ | ★ |

## Finesse Cleaning Service

| | 3 | 2 | 4 | 4 |

18 Beechurst Avenue, Floral Park, NY 11001
(718) 229 - 3856

*Rug and upholstery cleaning*

Finesse specializes in cleaning rugs, wall-to-wall carpets, upholstery and curtains. Sources tell us the firm also does Scotchguarding and stainproofing to give carpets extra protection from future stains. This eleven-year-old business was established in 1990 by owner Steven Leone and serves residential and commercial clients mostly in Manhattan, parts of Queens, Long Island, the Hamptons and Westchester County. We are told that pricing is per square foot, estimates are free, and so is pick up and delivery. The firm also cleans sisal rugs, fabric headboards, leather furniture and does post-construction cleanup. Clients praise the time and care the staff takes with even the toughest carpet cleaning issues. Sources also appreciate the firm's moderate prices.

*"I was extremely satisfied with how clean my carpets were." "Took his time." "What a fantastic job done by a very competent and friendly staff." "They get the job done right."*

## Hayko Restoration & Conservation

| | 4.5 | 3 | 5 | 5 |

857 Lexington Avenue, Second Floor, New York, NY 10021
(212) 717 - 5400   www.hayko.com

*Antique carpet, tapestry and needlepoint cleaning, retail and restoration*

The buzz among Hayko Oltaci's loyal clientele is that he is a man who understands that rugs are not only decorative and functional pieces—but trademarks of history as well. This is certainly reflected in his work, insiders tell us. Hayko Restoration and Conservation restores, conserves and cleans fine antique, semi-antique and contemporary area rugs, tapestries and needlepoints. He also buys and sells rugs, and even gives consultation for his valued clients. Oltaci established his business in New York nine years ago, but worked in the rug business for ten years prior, in France. Originally from Istanbul, Turkey, Oltaci also worked and trained at the Grand Bazaar there. Insiders tell us his impeccable credentials and industrious nature makes him a favorite of top designers, private collectors, well-heeled homeowners, museums, dealers and auction houses.

High-end clients rave about Oltaci's warmth and charm as well as his exceptional skill and knowledge of rugs. Christie's considers him quite a find and recommends him to their clients. Sources appreciate his efficiency, reliability and the fact that he will go out of his way to serve his loyal clientele. Prices may be top of the line, but clients say this "amazing craftsman" is worth every penny.

*"The most honest man I know." "There's nobody else as good as Hayko." "A wonderful craftsman. I've been using him for at least ten years now." "He goes out of his way for his clients. He came to my aid in an emergency—came to my home in the evening and repaired my rug right there."*

| | Quality | Cost | Value | Recommend? |
|---|---|---|---|---|
| | + | $ | ◆ | ★ |

## Irwin Cohen

| 4.5 | 2.5 | 5 | 5 |

16-10 212th Street, Bayside, NY 11360-1527
(718) 224 - 9885

*Carpet and rug spot cleaning and repair*

When others give up on a stain, sources tell us they call on Irwin Cohen. We hear that he has yet to be truly stumped by a stain—despite being faced with some very stubborn ones. Clients say he will personally come out to tend stains on short notice and always does so with a smile, using little potions from his briefcase. Cohen, whose grandfather and father were also in the business, has been serving clients around Manhattan, New Jersey, Long Island, Connecticut, Westchester County and the Hamptons for 35 years. This firm is a specialist in spot cleaning and will work on area rugs, wall-to-wall broadlooms, fabric walls and upholstery. The company also demonstrates a talent for reweaving and minor repairs. Pricing is by the job and all work is done on-site.

*"Couldn't live without him." "Excellent! Takes out spots that baffle other carpet cleaners." "Works on stains that other cleaners can't get out." "Pleasant and easy to work with."*

## Kalust Barin

| 4.5 | 3 | 4.5 | 4.5 |

1334 York Avenue, New York, NY 10021
(212) 606 - 7896

*Antique rug and tapestry restoration and repair*

"A man of many talents," is what people are saying about Kalust Barin. Clearly Sotheby's thinks so, too, since Barin holds fort in the institution's new building on the Upper East Side, where he does a number of jobs for some of the auction house's famous and distinguished clients. Barin has been in the rug business his entire life, starting with his family's business in Turkey, where he worked in the Grand Bazaar. This soft-spoken man serves mostly residential clients in Manhattan and some areas of New Jersey. The firm repairs, restores and cleans antique rugs, with a specialty in Caucasian, European and Middle Eastern pieces. Barin also conserves tapestries and needlepoint. While most of his work is done at Sotheby's, he occasionally works on-site and has several clients whose rugs he checks on a regular basis. His showroom in Sotheby's is open to the public and the trade.

Sources tell us that this gentleman is a hard worker who is dedicated to his craft. They tell us he is reliable and trustworthy and though his prices are upper-end, references say the service is worth the price tag.

*"An extremely nice and honest man." "Worked for us for fifteen years now." "Extremely skilled. Knows his business." "Best man for the job." "Has such a discriminating eye for repairing and restoring fine pieces."*

## Kermanshah Oriental Rugs Inc.

| 4.5 | 3.5 | 4.5 | 4 |

57 Fifth Avenue, New York, NY 10003
(212) 627 - 7077

*Fine rug and tapestry cleaning, repair, restoration, retail and wholesale*

A name synonymous with rug ancestry, the Kermanshah family has been in the rug business since 1880. Kermanshah has locations in New York, Saudi Arabia, Iran and other parts of the Middle East. Sources tell us the firm's impeccable credentials and rich legacy make them one of the foremost authorities in the rug industry. The firm cleans, repairs, restores, buys and sells fine antique, semi-antique and contemporary handmade area rugs and tapestries. Kermanshah's New York establishment was founded in 1960 and still has a growing list of clients that include private collectors, decorators, dealers, museums and homeowners. All cleaning and restoration is done in the firm's workshop and prices include pick up and delivery. Their showroom is open to the public and the trade.

Sources rave about the efficiency of this firm's services. The staff is described as extremely trustworthy, reliable and responsive. Customers appreciate the fact that the firm is knowledgeable about the product, its history and the business. Though some say the prices are reasonable, others feel it is expensive. But clients across the board agree the service and the product quality are well worth the cost.

*"Wide inventory. Exquisite pieces." "Worked with them for years. Never had a problem with them." "Miracle workers. Took out a stain that proved to be difficult for others."*

### Long Island Carpet Cleaners 〜〜〜            3      2.5      3      3.5
301 Norman Avenue, Brooklyn, NY 11222
(718) 383 - 7000
*Rug and upholstery cleaning*

Sources tell us this Brooklyn-based firm will do wall-to-wall carpet cleaning in the home and area rugs at its on-site facility. While some clients are big fans and say the company is very reliable and able to do quality work at reasonable prices, others have been less convinced. Long Island Carpet specializes in hard-to-clean fabrics and also will clean upholstered walls. The company works with residential and commercial clients in Manhattan and the surrounding boroughs.

*"The only people I know to recommend." "Fair—and they get the job done."*

### Majestic Rug Cleaners            3      2      4.5      3
644 Whittier Street, Bronx, NY 10474
(212) 922 - 0909
*Rug and upholstery cleaning*

This large company cleans wall-to-wall carpets, area rugs, drapes and fabric upholstery. Majestic was established in the 1930s and has been satisfying residential and commercial clients in the greater New York area. This firm has also, through the years, acquired some other rug cleaning companies under its belt. Some of its sister companies are: J&J Williams Rug, Metropolitan, AAA Radiant, Master Craft, Prince, Perfect Carpet and Upholstery, Fibre Guard and Capital Atlantic.

*"Fabulous work done on my Orientals." "Good. Gets the job done."*

### Majik Cleaning Service            3      2      4.5      4.5
443 Park Avenue South, 10th Floor, New York, NY 10016
(212) 545 - 7830
*Rug and upholstery cleaning, household cleaning services*

The Majik employees sent out from the main office are always terrific, sources tell us. Majik offers a wide range of household cleaning services, including carpet and upholstery cleaning, but does not do repairs. The company's main business is office and household cleaning. We hear the firm's technicians do all work on-site and operate almost completely in Manhattan. Established in 1991, the firm works with residential and commercial clients. Sources give the firm high marks for work quality.

*"Reliable and trustworthy." "Emphatic thumbs up." "A great service from great people." "Carpets are always really clean."*

### Marvin Kagan Gallery            4.5      4      4.5      5
625 Madison Avenue, 2nd Floor, New York, NY 10022
(212) 535 - 9000   www.marvinkagan.com
*Dealer, fine rug and tapestry cleaning and restoration*

Sources simply rave about the high quality and excellent workmanship of this high-end gallery. Established 45 years ago, we hear the employees at Marvin Kagan are specialists at restoring, cleaning, conserving and repairing antique and semi-antique area rugs. They also do appraisals and retail. The firm's clients range from museums, designers and dealers to well-heeled residents and private collectors. The professionals at this company are described by reference in superlatives—honest, personable, respectful and knowledgeable about the business. Clients tell us Kagan's primary interest is in establishing and maintaining strong customer relationships based on trust and an impeccable reputation in the field. Most clients agree that the high quality of Marvin Kagan's work makes it an excellent value for the expensive price tag.

*"Astoundingly pleased with the job." "Expensive, though." "Best men for the job." "Gives honest advice."*

## Megerian Brothers Oriental Rugs     4    3.5    4    4.5
262 Fifth Avenue, New York, NY 10001
(212) 684 - 7188   www.megerianrugs.com
*Fine antique rug cleaning and restoration*

One of New York's antique rug specialists, Megerian cleans, repairs, restores, buys and sells (wholesale and retail) antique and antique reproductions to dealers, private collectors, decorators, other high-end residential and commercial clients in the regional area. The firm specializes in Egyptian, Aubussons, Pakistani and Oriental area rugs. The company also manufactures and sells antique reproductions called artex rugs. All cleaning is done at Megerian's Brooklyn facilities and its showroom on Fifth Avenue is open to the public and the trade. The firm was established in 1917 and is now managed by third generation Megerians. Estimates are free and so is pick-up and delivery.

## Metropolitan Carpet Cleaning Co.     3    2.5    3.5    3
644 Whittier Street, Bronx, NY 10474
(212) 354 - 1874
*Rug and wall-to-wall carpet cleaning*

A sister company of Majestic Rug Cleaning, this firm cleans area rugs and wall-to-wall carpets for residential and commercial clients. The firm also provides additional services such as cleaning of fabric walls, draperies and upholstery. They serve most of Manhattan and some outer boroughs of New York.

## Nemati Collection     4    4    4    4.5
1059 Third Avenue, New York, NY 10021
(212) 486 - 6900   www.nematicollection.com
*Dealer, fine rug and tapestry repair and conservation*

One of New York's premier dealers in antique Oriental rugs and European tapestries, Nemati also has a full-service restoration department. One reference who has worked with the firm on a number of projects marvels at its expertise in working with vegetable dyes and in matching yarns. The company was founded by Parviz Nemati in 1963 and he is now the company's acquisitions consultant. Nemati's son, Darius directs the gallery. The firm cleans, repairs, restores, conserves, buys and sells antique area rugs, tapestries and needlepoint. The showroom is open to the public and the trade. Nemati's distinguished clientele hails from all over the world, entrusting the company to restore rare and antique treasures. A knowledgeable staff with low turnover has contributed to Nemati's excellent reputation. All cleaning is done by hand to put minimal stress on the piece. This high-end company is a member of the Oriental Rug Retailers of America and has been featured in prominent publications such as *Town and Country* magazine.

*"They look at a rug as a piece of art, not just a rug." "All the workmen are terrific."*

## Pasargad Carpets                    4    3    4    4
105 Madison Avenue, New York, NY 10016
(212) 684 - 4477   www.pasargadcarpets.com
*Dealer of fine antique rugs—rug cleaning and restoration*

In business in Iran since 1904, Pasargad Carpets has been serving New York for fifteen years. The company buys, sells, cleans, repairs and restores antique, semi-antique and modern handmade area rugs. The firm's 4,500-square-foot showroom in Manhattan is open to the public and the trade—Pasargad also has a showroom in Washington, DC. The company also boasts of a wide selection of rugs, from scatter to oversize—as well as mansion-size rugs. The Pasargad website also allows customers to fill out a form with information on size, color and design. They in turn, will send back a digital photo that most closely matches the request, with no obligation to purchase.

This firm's sophisticated clientele varies from decorators, dealers, homeowners and distinguished private collectors who come from Manhattan, Washington, New Jersey, the West Coast and Canada. The firm's cleaning and restoration is done in-house and is heavily supervised.

*"Widest selection of rugs." "Excellent restoration and repair." "Responsive and cooperative. Nice fellows—easy to work with."*

## Perfect Carpet Cleaning Co.        3    2    4    3
644 Whittier Street, New York, NY 10021
(800) 905 - 9994
*Rug and upholstery cleaning*

Please see Majestic Rug Cleaning's review.

## Rainbow Carpet Cleaning           4    2.5   4.5   4
260-21 Hillside Avenue, Floral Park, NY 11004
(718) 347 - 5560
*Rug and upholstery cleaning*

References say they are thrilled with Rainbow for its excellent work and outstanding customer service. This firm cleans area rugs, wall-to-wall carpets and upholstery. Prices are calculated on a per-square-foot basis, and clients say there are no hidden fees lurking in the contract. Some indicate that while they often turn to specialists for needlepoints and fine Oriental rugs, everything else has been skillfully handled by Rainbow.

*"Four-star service. They are great."*

## Reedway Services                  3.5   2    4    4.5
360 West 22nd Street, New York, NY 10011
(212) 691 - 2431
*Rug and upholstery cleaning*

Straightforward, easy to work with and prompt are some of the things clients are saying about Reedway services. This Manhattan-based rug company cleans wall-to-wall carpets, area rugs and upholstery. The company works mostly in Manhattan and some areas in the outer boroughs. Clients appreciate the firm's reasonable prices and the efficient service that comes with it.

*"Really quick and very neat."*

## Ronnee Barnett Textile Restoration

**5  3  5  5**

(212) 966 - 3520

*Fine antique rug, tapestry, needlepoint and textile restoration, repair and cleaning*

References agree that Ronnee Barnett is a woman dedicated to her craft and passionate about her work. Barnett started her own textile restoration business in 1978 after deciding to give up psychology because she "had an intense desire to weave." She restores, conserves, cleans, reweaves and repairs rare antique area rugs, needlepoints, tapestries and textiles. She also works part-time for the Metropolitan Museum of Art where she restores and mounts medieval textiles.

The firm works mostly in Manhattan, but has clients from all over the United States. This one-woman company works with museums, decorators, dealers, private collectors and homeowners. We are told Barnett believes in in-depth client interviews to discuss the project in advance to determine the specifications of her customers. We're told Barnett also educates clients in the proper way to care for their priceless treasures. Sources consider her work museum-quality, and find her incredibly professional, trustworthy and communicative. Clients say she takes her time, does the job right and treats each piece like a work of art.

*"She is the best—such a find." "Artistic, capable and business-like." "Can't tell it was repaired. Great workmanship." "Fabulous!"*

## Rug Renovating Co.

**3.5  3.5  4  5**

532 North Grove Street, East Orange, NJ  07017

(212) 924 - 0189   www.rugrenovating.com

*Fine rug and upholstery cleaning, repair and restoration*

This large, high-end rug cleaning company has been in business for over 100 years. Rug Renovating does on-site and plant cleaning of rugs for homeowners, area celebrities and leading rug dealers and designers. Sources tell us the firm also cleans, repairs and installs wall-to-wall carpets. They also do furniture cleaning and minor repairs. Clients laud Rug Renovating for its skill with expensive carpets, specialty fabrics and other complex, challenging jobs. In addition, we hear that business is handled very professionally, with excellent scheduling and strong customer service.

*"One of the top for unique repairs." "I love these guys." "A good but not incredible job for on-site spot removal, but always helpful and professional." "Expensive but nice quality work."*

## Safavieh Carpets

**4  4  4.5  4.5**

238 East 59th Street, New York, NY  10022

(212) 477 - 1234

*Fine rug retailer and restoration*

One of New York's prominent retailers, appraisers and restorers of fine antique, semi-antique and contemporary rugs, Safavieh Carpets has been serving well-heeled clients since its establishment in 1914 by Hamil Yaraghi. Now managed by his grandson Arash, the firm continues to provide the same top-notch service to their discriminating clientele. The firm also does some restoration and conservation for museums. Safavieh's wide selection of rugs includes Orientals, Aubussons, Persian, Pakistani, Indian and Tibetan. The company also works with tapestries and needlepoints. Safavieh takes pride in its restoration department, where workmen meticulously do all the work by hand and in the same method that the original weaver used. All cleaning and repair is done in-house and is heavily supervised.

With three showrooms located in Manhattan—one of them exclusively open to the trade—Safavieh also built seven more locations around Long Island, Connecticut and New Jersey.

*"Fabulous. Wouldn't think of going to anyone else." "Meticulous and thorough."*

# Hiring a Security System
# Service Provider

There are those of us for whom turning on the TV when leaving the house is considered a security measure. Of course, with an American home burglarized once every eleven seconds, it could also be considered hospitality. In fact, security systems, the first centrally controlled integrated system to make it into most homes, are branching out into fire/life-safety and the convenience/lifestyle sectors that are now becoming the backbone of home automation. So, if you really think "*Three's Company*" re-runs will scare away potential burglars, you can program your TV's routine, along with the rest of your security system, over your cell phone or the Internet while vacationing halfway around the world. Now if only you could get the vacuum cleaner to pick up your mail.

Like their A/V brethren, security system service providers are marketing themselves as the one-stop shop for your home's central nervous system. No one company may be best at everything yet, but security is a natural place to start to smarten up your home.

## A Host of High-Tech Options

Options once reserved for technophiles, supervillains, museums or celebrities have become available to anyone. Closed circuit television (CCTV) can now be fed through your television or computer to eyeball for trouble and can be monitored online from virtually anywhere. Sensors can be installed that detect motion, change in temperature, smoke and carbon monoxide, fluctuation of sound waves, broken glass or breached barriers. When tripped, they transmit the offended sensor's serial number to a central control panel, which in turn relays the home location and the point of alarm to the monitoring company. The monitoring company will immediately attempt to contact the homeowner to verify that a break-in has occurred. If there is no response, or the respondent fails to give the proper secret password, the police or fire department is notified. In addition, some monitoring companies will dispatch their own personnel to check out the situation, either from the street or, if keys are provided, from inside the home itself.

The explosion of cellular and wireless technology promises further protection and convenience to homeowners. Teamed with battery packs in the event of power failure, communication is fully safeguarded. Wireless modular components (touch pads) can be placed in convenient locations by homeowners themselves, as no cords or wires are needed. This is great for renters, too, who can take the wireless system with them when they move. Alarm devices range from the sounding of a voice wistfully repeating "fire" to the crazed bark of a pack of 100-pound Rotweillers, to the snapping on the lights in your home as if it were Yankee Stadium.

All of these functions are managed through a central control panel, traditionally a keypad and display. But as this industry charges toward the home automation front, touch screens, or a platform on your PC, are increasingly becoming the way to go. This makes it much easier to program and manage your systems. You can keep tabs on the alarm history and security status, play back the sequences of which lights you turn on and off or kick on the air conditioning while driving home from work—and do it all remotely via computer or cell phone.

Choosing the right system for is as much about the logistical characteristics of your location (i.e., apartment vs. house, rural vs. urban) and budget as it is about the degree of system integration you want in your home. The options range from an "I'm Protected" warning sticker on a window to a virtual HAL 5000. How sophisticated do you want to get? How intrusive? A homeowner's personal circumstances and susceptibility must also be considered.

## ON COST

The cost of any security system depends upon the number of devices, the sophistication of the control unit, the degree of integration, the term and service of the monitoring and whether it's wireless or hardwired technology. Basically, the cost reflects the time and material for installation plus the monitoring agreement. The monitoring agreement covers three to five years. Shorter terms are available, aimed at renters, but these agreements may include higher-than-average installation costs. At the end of the term the monitoring agreement should be automatically renewable, with a ceiling for rate hikes spelled out in the contract. Payment can be made on a monthly, quarterly or annual basis. If you break your contract, don't be surprised if you're held responsible for as much as 90 percent of the unexpired term as liquidated damages. If you sell your home, however, you should be able to transfer your monitoring agreement over to the new homeowners.

It is important to know the parameters of your monitoring agreement, before you sign it. Many people are involved in your security, and awkward mistakes will cost you. Security providers allow a familiarization period in which no signal will be acted upon. Use this time wisely. Once you're up and running, you will be charged for false alarms by both the monitoring company and the city for wasting their time. They will also charge you to reprogram controls. Be absolutely sure you're comfortable with the system setup and its use before signing the agreement. Warranties should cover parts and labor for one year and you can opt for a maintenance agreement that covers such extras as emergency service.

After you invest in a security system, check with your homeowner's insurance company. You may be able to get a reduction in your insurance rate.

## GETTING PLUGGED IN

Finally, your security system provider may need a permit and certain components and installation methods may need to comply with local regulations. It's the municipality's call. As the homeowner, you must provide permanent electrical access and a permanent telephone connection.

### WHAT TO CONSIDER WHEN CHOOSING A SECURITY SYSTEM

❖ Do you own or rent?
❖ Is it a house or apartment?
❖ How many entrances and windows?
❖ Are there children or pets in the home?
❖ How often are you around?
❖ Who has access while you're away (housekeeper, etc.)?
❖ Is the neighborhood crowded or isolated?

## SECURITY SYSTEMS

### ADT Security Services Inc.                    3.5    3    4.5    4
47-40 21st Street, Long Island City, NY 11101
(718) 392 - 9335   www.adt.com

*Security systems with central monitoring*

ADT has been helping New Yorkers secure and monitor their homes and businesses for over 125 years.  A well-known national security firm, ADT installs and
maintains systems encompassing burglary, fire, flood and carbon monoxide detection.  Clients describe ADT as "serious security" and praise the efficiency and
quality of the service.  Sources tell us the systems are reasonably priced, but caution that clients shouldn't forget the ongoing monthly fees.

*"If the baby sets off the alarm, there will be two fire trucks at your door, even
if you call ADT!"  "Even though they're a large national company, I still felt like I
got personalized, attentive service."*

### American Security Systems Inc.              3.5    3    4.5    4
18 West 23rd Street, New York, NY 10010
(212) 633 - 8080   www.americansecuritysys.com

*Security systems with central monitoring—video intercoms*

Since 1979, American Security Systems has been protecting homes and businesses in and around the city in a variety of ways.  In addition to its specialty in
alarm systems such as burglary and fire, American also provides video intercoms,
locks, card access systems, telephone entry systems and closed-circuit televi-
sions.  Clients give the firm high marks for the quality systems it installs and
praise American's staff as reliable, skilled with specialty systems and detail oriented.  Numerous clients were impressed that American has its own central
monitoring station for its alarms system, noting that it made a huge difference in
service.  Some clients, however, did note that the technicians can be a bit slow
at times because they are often working on several jobs at once.

*"The manager of my building researched security firms and recommended
American to me as the most responsive.  I've been extremely pleased with the
results—both with the system they installed and the monitoring service."  "They
did an excellent job on a system that had both wire and wireless parts."  "Good,
consistent and reliable."  "They installed a security system with video so I can
watch my kids play while I'm travelling."*

### CJT Inc.                                       3.5    3    4.5    5
35 Tulip Drive, Kings Park, NY 11754
(631) 366 - 4236

*Security systems and telephone systems*

Alarm and telephone systems are CJT's specialties, but this small security firm
also handles computer wiring, heat detectors and other security devices.  Clients
appreciate the creative, intelligent security solutions that CJT offers, as well as its
high-quality systems, reliable, prompt service and trustworthy personnel.  And it
seems there are few surprises when it comes to the bill—actual costs stay close
to projected levels, we're told.

*"Very creative in assessing your security needs."  "Would not change them for
anyone else."  "Prompt and attentive service."*

| | Quality | Cost | Value | Recommend? |
|---|---|---|---|---|
| | ✚ | $ | ◆ | ★ |

## Intelli-Tec Security Services, LLC

| 4.5 | 3 | 5 | 5 |

2000 Shames Drive, Westbury, NY 11590
(516) 876 - 2000   www.intelli-tec.net

*Security and life safety systems, audio/video systems, home automation*

Since 1977, Intelli-Tec has offered a wide variety of security services and products to some of the Northeast's most prestigious residences and businesses throughout New York City and Long Island's East End and North Shore, including some of the area's leading museums and banks. Principal Marty McMillan and his staff of 30 receive high praise for their outstanding work and professional service. Intelli-Tec's work comes recommended by many of New York's high-end contractors as well as security consultants and executive protection firms.

Services offered include security systems, central station monitoring, access control systems, closed-circuit television, engineered fire systems, intercoms, satellite dish and CATV, data cabling, telephone systems, lighting control, sound and A/V systems, home theater and specialized 24-hour protection for high-value paintings and artwork.

*"Comprehensive security services—they've got it all." "Great service! Available 24/7." "Marty's incredible—My walls were open and another company let me down. Marty had workers at my house that same day so my construction could continue." "I have worked with Marty McMillan for more than ten years and find him and his company to be of the highest caliber."*

## L.J. Loeffler Intercom

| 4 | 4 | 4 | 4.5 |

195 10th Avenue, New York, NY 10011
(212) 924 - 7597

*Intercom systems*

In business for 102 years, L.J. Loeffler Intercom receives enthusiastic praise by clients and peers alike. We're told this seven-person firm helps to keep Manhattan buildings safe and looking respectable by providing intercom systems for security (not telephone) purposes. Using a wide variety of intercoms, entrance doors, CCTV systems and roof alarms, L.J. Loeffler makes sure buildings are protected from basement to roof. References highly recommend the company and say its years of experience shine through in its work.

*"I won't use anyone else in the city."*

## Nanny Watch

| 4 | 2.5 | 5 | 5 |

223 Wall Street, Huntington, NY 11743
(631) 423 - 6968   www.nannywatch.com

*Child-care monitoring*

Principal Art DiScala pioneered the use of concealed cameras and recording devices to monitor caretakers and other unsupervised individuals working in someone's home. For parents concerned about keeping an honest eye on their children's care or for protecting family possessions through a procession of new and unfamiliar service professionals and housekeepers, Nanny Watch offers its own state-of-the-art equipment, manufactured by the company since 1994. Its wireless systems, built into such items as a mantel clock that can transmit via the Internet or CCTV, ships out in a day and doesn't need the help of a technician for installation. DiScala's innovations have made their way to homes and businesses as far away as Europe and Australia, and we hear the quality-crafted devices are worth every penny.

*"Professional state-of-the-art equipment at reasonable prices." "You can't put a price on my child's safety." "I sleep better at night knowing I can keep a watchful eye on things."*

| | Quality | Cost | Value | Recommend? |
|---|---|---|---|---|
| | + | $ | ◆ | ★ |

## PD Security Systems

| | 3.5 | 2.5 | 5 | 5 |

1256 71st Street, Brooklyn, NY 11228
(718) 680 - 6216

*Security systems and telephone systems*

Considered an expert home-security-system company since 1986, PD Security can tackle telephone and video installation as well. Clients describe Patrick D'Onofrio and his staff as "wonderful to work with," citing their dependable and responsive service as well as excellent followup practices. We hear this small firm's tidiness in finished spaces and straightforward manner have also contributed to customers recommending PD Security to their friends and family. The company serves clients in New York City and northern New Jersey.

*"They follow up with everything." "Tremendous effort." "Even referred them to my in-laws, who don't like anyone." "Always available and calls back." "They were very patient showing me how to use the system."*

## Scarsdale Security Systems

| | 4.5 | 3.5 | 4.5 | 5 |

132 Montgomery Avenue, Scardale, NY 10583
(914) 722 - 2200   www.scarsdalesecurity.com

*Security systems*

Since 1982, residential, commercial and industrial clients in the regional area have put their trust in Scarsdale Security Systems to keep them safe and secure. From monitored burglar and fire systems to closed-circuit TV and access-control system installations, this firm has proven "exceptional," particularly in high-end residential work. Clients concur that Scarsdale stacks up with some of the best out there, and reserve particular praise for the pleasant and accommodating technicians. Some customers will trust only Scarsdale for their larger projects.

*"They are exceptional and do incredible work. I use them for all my large, high-end jobs." "They go out of their way to do extra things."*

## Scott Security Systems Inc.

| | 3.5 | 4 | 3.5 | 3 |

236 West 30th Street, 10th Floor, New York, NY 10001
(212) 594 - 2121

*Security systems with central monitoring*

For those serious about security, Scott Security offers high-tech solutions, as well as some unique services. The firm specializes in sophisticated alarm systems that include CCTV and access control, which can be integrated into any home system by an on-hand computer specialist. Central monitoring and comprehensive service round out the menu. But what really makes the company unique, according to its clients, are its escorts for the movement of valuables, stable of private investigators and polygraph experts. Started in 1984 and serving New York City, Long Island and New Jersey, this firm deals in commercial and strictly high-end residential security.

| | Quality + | Cost $ | Value ◆ | Recommend? ★ |
|---|---|---|---|---|

## Sonitrol

| | 3 | 2.5 | 4 | 3 |

45 West 34th Street, Suite 900, New York, NY 10001
(212) 967 - 9828   www.sonitrol.com
*Security systems*

Sonitrol, an international company, has been protecting homes since 1977. Although a large outfit with local offices throughout New York State, Sonitrol "comes when you need them," according to clients.  Dealers are responsible for the sales, installation and service of monitored systems to customers.  Sources say that personal attention isn't the firm's forte, but clients will receive home protection at a reasonable cost.

## Speakeasy Intercom & Electric 〰 Service Inc.

| | 2.5 | 2 | 3.5 | 3 |

43-44 162nd Street, Flushing, NY 11358
(718) 939 - 6461   www.speakeasyinter.com
*Intercom systems and security surveys*

This Queens-based firm has been serving residential and commercial clients around New York City for 24 years, focusing on intercom installation and relocation, card access systems and audio/video security systems. Alarm systems are not part of its repertoire, but the company will perform site surveys to assess the security of a client's home and make recommendations for improving it.  Clients are mixed in their reviews about the company—some report concerns about the responsiveness and tidiness of its workers, while others feel that Speakeasy's work is quite good and the service staff knowledgeable.  This firm performs a lot of work for management companies in the city.

*"They seemed competent and completed the job to my satisfaction."  "They were hard to get in touch with, but their work was adequate."*

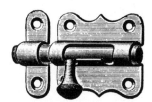

## The SecureCom Group

| | 4 | 2.5 | 5 | 5 |

22-26 College Point Boulevard, College Point, NY 11356
(718) 353 - 3355
*Security systems*

As its name implies, SecureCom is in the business of securing homes and offices against theft, fire and other threats.  This 23-person firm offers wire or wireless security and fire alarm systems, CCTV surveillance systems, card access control and 24-hour service.  We hear that followup training on each system is thorough and clear, provided by the company's helpful and responsive technicians. SecureCom has been in business for five years, serving the regional area.

*"Their central monitoring facility doesn't charge for false alarms, which was certainly a help to my family when we first got the system."  "All of the employees I dealt with were really helpful and pleasant—a plus in my book."*

## U.S. Protective Alarm Services

205 West Houston Street, New York, NY 10014
(212) 645 - 5691
*Security systems*

# Hiring a Telephone Systems Service Provider

It all used to be so simple. One phone. Black. If you weren't around it just rang. If you were on a call, it droned busy. Now, telephone systems appear as high tech as the Space Shuttle program. It's not really rocket science, though, if you know the basics and hire a great service provider.

Local telephone companies now offer a wide array of services: voice mail, call forwarding, three-way calling and caller ID (with or without ID block). The wealth of options combined with the rise of the Internet and the home office has changed the playing field for telephone system service providers. But for systems that integrate multiple phone lines, intercoms and door buzzers to a networked and net-savvy home office, these are still the people to call.

## Plan Ahead and Allow for Expansion

The key to having the perfect phone system for your needs is to think, plan, discuss and think again. Figure out what you want and where. If you're putting in a home office, know how many lines you will need, where the fax and printers are going to be located, which computers will be networked and online and where you're going to sit. If you like to rearrange the furniture from time to time, consider putting phone jacks on both sides of the room. And always run more cable and reserve more lines than you need. Today's bedroom is tomorrow's office. Remember, running that empty conduit gives you enormous flexibility to change with the times down the road. When you run phone, cable and other lines, the wires are usually buried in the walls or hidden behind moldings. This involves messy, disruptive and expensive construction, not to mention the need to redo your decorating touches. Avoid these problems by planning ahead and allowing for expansion. Also, don't overlook unusual spaces in your planning. You can hide that ugly fax machine in a closet, just don't forget to install a phone jack and electrical outlet.

## Check the Brand

Most telephone system service providers have licensing agreements with certain system manufacturers and will only deal with those systems. If you're keen on a particular system, it's a good idea to contact the manufacturer for preferred service providers in your area. On the whole, they all perform the same functions (automated directories, voice mail boxes, multiple lines/extensions, on-hold music, interoffice paging, caller ID) and offer the same accessories (headsets, holsters). It's the brand of the system, sophistication, complexity of integration with other systems and convenience of use that affect the cost. Systems can be purchased outright, leased or financed.

## It's All About Service

What really sets telephone system service providers apart is the quality of their followup service and support. If you're running a business from home, you can't afford to be stranded on the dark side of the moon, cut off from the rest of the planet for days or even hours. If you're just trying to live your life, non-responsive service is still a supreme annoyance. Find service providers with guaranteed response times and emergency service. Know that you'll be able to reach them in a phone-meltdown emergency. A good service provider will suggest and make additions and modifications to your system as times and technologies change. Warranties typically last six months to one year after installation.

## SURF THE INTERNET AT TOP SPEED

Telephone system service providers should also be familiar with what type of Internet connection is best for you. A second line for data is becoming a necessity for anyone who spends time online at home. The speed of this connection is determined by both the type of cable in your home and the type of modem in your computer. Typically, homes are strung in Category 3 (CAT 3) cable. While that is fine for voice, Category 5 (CAT 5) is the way to go for your data lines, and can be had for only a modest increase in price per foot. Modems are a bit more complicated. Plugging a standard telephone or data line into the modem that comes built into your computer gives you about 56K of speed. If you don't have the time or inclination to watch your computer struggle to pull up a web page, you can add modem hardware to increase speed. ISDN provides about double the standard, with 128K. DSL, which is threatening to render ISDN obsolete, starts at 128K and can, if you're willing to pay for it, bring you up to the high-speed commercial level of a T-1 line. A mid-level DSL connection rides in at roughly $50 a month, and can handle streaming audio and video.

### TELEPHONE SYSTEM TIPS

✧ An installer is only as good as his service.
✧ Plan and pre-wire for the future.
✧ Keep in mind a typical phone system lasts five to ten years. Build in excess capacity.
✧ Explore the new variety of telephone ring options—your life may change with a serene, low-key incoming call signal.
✧ Consider sending a request for proposal (RFP) to a number of vendors; having written proposals helps you compare features, service and price.

| | Quality + | Cost $ | Value ◆ | Recommend? ★ |
|---|---|---|---|---|

## Telephone Systems

### Ahl Tone                                    **3.5    2.5    4.5    4**
6749 Fifth Avenue, Brooklyn, NY  11220
(212) 684 - 5959
*Residential phone systems—Panasonic*

Ahl Tone, which operates a retail center in Brooklyn and a sales office in Manhattan, provides end-to-end service of residential phone systems, from sales and installation to maintenance and repairs. We hear the firm is involved in every step of the project, insuring the quality of the end result. Panasonic systems are its focus, and insiders tell us the firm is prepared to take on complex phone systems—like the recent installation of a complete phone system for a four-story Upper East Side brownstone.

Clients applaud the Ahl Tone guarantee of one-day response time on normal service calls, and two-hour response to emergency calls, seven days a week, 24 hours a day. We hear the technicians are helpful, knowledgeable and accessible, and offer polite and friendly service.

*"Good honest guys."*

### AMP Telephone Systems, Inc.              **3      2      4.5    3.5**
57 West 38th Street, Suite 300, New York, NY  10018
(212) 944 - 6720
*Residential and small business phone systems—Telrad*

Insiders say AMP Telephone Systems can wire just about any home for telephone and Internet service with its product of choice—the Telrad system. References tell us that AMP Telephone does excellent work, and we hear that the systems come with warranty and service plans. This firm, which has operated in the area for more than 20 years, frequently does work on brownstone residences in Manhattan.

### Atlantic Office Equipment Inc.           **2      2      4      3**
545 Eighth Avenue, Suite 1502, New York, NY  10018
(212) 643 - 0950   www.atlanticoffice.com
*Residential phone systems—Avaya*

Atlantic Office Equipment relies upon Avaya/Lucent Technologies to meet the communications needs of residential clients. We're told the products offered and serviced by Atlantic include the Partner Advanced Communication System (ACS) as well as other Avaya products like Merlin. Atlantic offers a full range of services for clients, including installation, training and followup technical help. Repairs and maintenance calls are handled on a "next-available" basis, by a group of on-staff technicians.

### Audio by James Inc.
571 Knollwood Road, Ridgewood, NJ  07450
(201) 493 - 7282
*Audio/video installation and service*

See Audio by James Inc.'s full report under the heading Audio/Video Design & Installation

## Automated Answering Systems Inc.   3   3   4   3
875 Avenue of the Americas, New York, NY  10001
(212) 947 - 4155

*Residential phone systems—Avaya*

This Manhattan company has been providing telecommunication services to clients in the city since 1962.  The firm currently sells, installs and services Avaya/Lucent systems, and features the Partner Advanced Communication System (ACS) for residential needs.  Sources say the 20-person staff handles everything from start to finish, and each client is assigned to a technician who programs the system at setup and continues to work with the account on an ongoing basis.  Clients praise the staff's professionalism and efficiency.

## Avaya Technologies Business   3   3.5   3.5   3.5
## Partner-SPS
307 Seventh Avenue, New York, NY  10001
(212) 651 - 9100

*Residential and small business phone systems*

For clients who already know they want an Avaya system (formerly Lucent Technologies), they can now go straight to the source.  Avaya, the equipment arm of AT&T, offers residential systems with digital wireless capabilities (we hear it is the only company to offer this now), including full service and installation.  A 24-hour hotline supplements the service package.

## Birns Telecommunications Inc.   2.5   3   3   3
233 West 17th Street, New York, NY  10011
(212) 633 - 8600   www.birns.net

*Residential and small business phone systems—NEC and Nitsuko*

Since 1973, Birns Telecommunications Inc. (BTI) has been busy answering to clients in the New York metro and northern New Jersey areas.  BTI sells, installs and services only the NEC and Nitsuko systems, which clients say are simple and easy to use.  We're told the company's service is consistent, with certified technicians being routed on a "call-out basis."  References say the technicians are friendly and generally good about cleaning up after themselves.

*"Great spare part availability—called customer service and received a spare part that same day."*

## CBS WhitCom Technologies Corp.   3   3   4   4
2990 Express Drive South, Islandia, NY  11722
(516) 582 - 3200   www.cbswhit.com

*Residential phone systems—Mitel, Nortel, Toshiba*

As an authorized sales agent for Bell Atlantic, this full-service telecom firm, with offices in Manhattan and Long Island, specializes in Mitel, Toshiba and Nortel phone systems.  We hear that in addition to installing and maintaining the phone system, CBS will also work with the local phone company to get the lines activated.  The firm offers repair coverage around the clock, seven days a week, with two-hour response times for emergencies.  While not every account is assigned a specific technician, each client receives an account manager to work with during and after installation.

*"Impressive followup—they consistently check on me to make sure everything is operating to my satisfaction."*

## CJT Inc.
35 Tulip Drive, Kings Park, NY  11754
(631) 366 - 4236

*Security systems and telephone systems*

See CJT Inc.'s full report under the heading Security Systems

| | Quality + | Cost $ | Value ◆ | Recommend? ★ |
|---|---|---|---|---|

## Compushine
30 East 60th Street, Suite 903, New York, NY  10022
(212) 371 - 1525   www.compushine.com
*Computer networking and servicing*

See Compushine's full report under the heading Computer Installation & Maintenance

## Electronic Environments
247 West 37th Street, Suite 704, New York, NY  10018
(212) 997 - 1110
*Audio/video and telephone system installation and service*

See Electronic Environments's full report under the heading Audio/Video Design & Installation

## Fone Booth                    4      3      4.5      5
330 Seventh Avenue, New York, NY  10001
(212) 564 - 0900   www.thefonebooth.com
*Residential phone systems—Panasonic*

In the retail business since 1977, Fone Booth covers all five boroughs, concentrating primarily on the Upper East Side of Manhattan. Panasonic systems are its specialty, and the company offers full installation, training and maintenance services. We are told this four-person firm is responsive and reliable.

*"Very informative, helpful and accommodating—great service." "Installation was done with no disruption to our business."*

## G. Paul Communications Inc.        3      2      4.5      4
143-145 Nassau Boulevard, West Hempstead, NY  11552
(516) 564 - 9600
*Residential phone systems—Avaya, Sprint, Samsung, ITT*

For fifteen years, G. Paul has been busy offering phone systems from Avaya, Sprint, ITT, Samsung, and providing full installation of new systems (including training, followup and service), as well as relocation and upgrades of existing systems. A group of ten certified technicians is assigned to the Manhattan accounts and addresses problems on a "next available" basis. References tell us that the staff at G. Paul Communications offers friendly and helpful service.

*"Courteous people." "Very pleased with service."*

## HED (Home Entertainment Design)
43-22 12th Street, Long Island City, NY  11101
(718) 433 - 4434
*Audio/video and telephone installation and integration*

See HED (Home Entertainment Design)'s full report under the heading Audio/ Video Design & Installation

## Heinz Falkenthal               4      2.5      5      4
P.O. Box 225, New York, NY  10025
(212) 683 - 7040
*Residential phone and intercom systems*

This practitioner of the telecom arts has been praised by clients for his knowledgeable, dedicated service. Heinz works mostly on the Upper East Side of Manhattan, and can work on phone systems, doorbells, intercoms, elevator bells—you name it. We hear he's not really into small talk, but delivers excellent value to his customers.

*"An excellent worker and a master of intercoms!"*

## Intelli-Tec Security Services, LLC

2000 Shames Drive, Westbury, NY 11590
(516) 876 - 2000   www.intelli-tec.net

*Security and life safety systems, audio/video systems, home automation*

See Intelli-Tec Security Services, LLC's full report under the heading Security Systems

## Konanur Inc.

127 West 24th Street, New York, NY 10011
(212) 414 - 0700   www.konanurinc.com

*Computer consulting*

See Konanur Inc.'s full report under the heading Computer Installation & Maintenance

## Lorna/PSI Communications Inc.          3      3.5      3      3

148 West 37th Street, New York, NY 10018
(212) 695 - 6300

*Residential and business phone systems—Nitsuko, Panasonic*

Founded in 1956, Lorna/PSI Communications is a full-service telecommunications company. This 25-person firm relies upon Panasonic, NEC, Samsung and Nitsiko to meet the communication needs of Manhattan clients. The company offers training and followup help with a group of technicians on staff to handle repairs and maintenance calls on a "next available" basis.

## NyCom                                    3      3      4      5

114 East 13th Street, 9th Floor, New York, NY 10003
(212) 477 - 2020

*Residential phone systems*

## PD Security Systems

1256 71st Street, Brooklyn, NY 11228
(718) 680 - 6216

*Security systems and telephone systems*

See PD Security Systems's full report under the heading Security Systems

## Precision Interconnect                   3      3      4      4

161 East 32nd Street, New York, NY 10016
(212) 725 - 9700   www.precisioninter.com

*Home office phone systems*

Since 1972, Precision Interconnect has been offering services in the metro area from its midtown headquarters for phone/voice communications and data network cabling. The company focuses on home offices, providing products and services for Avaya, Nortel and Toshiba. With the prompt dispatch of field technicians and a full cache of warehoused equipment and parts, response time is fairly quick, we're told.

## Reliable Voice & Data Systems            3      3      4      4

366 East Meadow Avenue, East Meadow, NY 11554
(212) 319 - 6109

*Residential phone systems—Avaya, Toshiba*

Featuring Toshiba and carrying Avaya systems, Reliable provides residents and small businesses with end-to-end services. The firm provides sales, installation and maintenance of phone systems, with a group of technicians dedicated to Manhattan clients, though not assigned specifically to accounts. Reliable provides remote maintenance and service 24 hours a day, seven days a week.

*"Prompt response." "They were extremely professional throughout the installation, and have followed up quickly when I've run into problems with my system."*

## S&S Interconnect ◼

| | 4 | 3 | 5 | 5 |
|---|---|---|---|---|

3975 Sedgwick Avenue, Suite 3G, Bronx, NY 10463
(718) 548 - 3333

*Residential phone systems—Panasonic*

Clients, contractors and architects alike say Stu Schulman and his small team of installers do outstanding work with residential and small business phone systems, from the very simple to the complex. They also agree that Schulman is a pleasure to work with, making note of his reliability, honesty and likable character.

*"Stu is very knowledgeable, patient and accommodating." "Really knows his stuff—I wish I could say the same about my contractor." "Stu is a saint! We need to clone him."*

## Tele-Dynamics

| | 3.5 | 3 | 4.5 | 3.5 |
|---|---|---|---|---|

330 Seventh Avenue, 21st Floor, New York, NY 10001
(212) 594 - 7333   www.tele-dynamics.com

*Residential phone systems—Avaya, Toshiba*

Robert Pullman and his team have been helping New Yorkers talk to each other for more than 24 years. As a full-service telecommunications company, Tele-Dynamics installs and maintains Avaya and Toshiba phone systems for residents and small to mid-size businesses in the regional area. Technicians are all union certified and factory trained and we're told the staff is friendly and courteous. Clients report Tele-Dynamics to be a timely service.

*"The technician knew what he was doing, and did his work quickly and efficiently. He was also polite—a bonus in my book."*

## Ultimate Sound & Installation Inc.

36-16 29th Street, Long Island City, NY 11106
(718) 729 - 2111   www.ultimateinstallations.com

*Audio/video, home automation, lighting control and telephone systems*

See Ultimate Sound & Installation Inc.'s full report under the heading Audio/Video Design & Installation.

# HIRING A TILE, MARBLE & STONE SERVICE PROVIDER

Tile, marble and stone can transform a room. Granite kitchen counters make beautiful surfaces on which to work. Marble brings a dramatic flair to the bathroom, and what could be more elegant than a travertine fireplace in the hearth of your home? Colorful, artistic tiles can brightly define the style of a kitchen—Spanish, French, Scandinavian. These materials come in a staggering range of types, qualities, shapes and colors. Tiles, for example, range in size from five-eighths of an inch square to one square-foot and up. Marble can come in tile form or in slabs that can be as small or as large as you need. Slabs—pieces of stone larger than 24 inches square—can be cut in various sizes and shapes to fit the area.

## WHERE DO I START?

The kind of tile that you choose will depend on your specific needs. For example, if you are selecting tiles for a high-traffic area like an entryway or kitchen, you'll want durable tiles that will not show wear and tear. If you are tiling your kitchen, you might consider a durable stone such as granite or a ceramic tile that is easy to clean and maintain. Smaller tiles tend to be used for decorative purposes because they are more laborious to install and harder to clean, while the larger tiles are used for more practical purposes such as covering a floor. Remember, each kind of tile has its advantages and drawbacks. The installer that you choose should be able to help you explore what kind of tile will work best for you.

Tiles, either man-made or natural, can be as plain as classic bathroom-white ceramic or as intricate as hand-painted/embossed pieces from Portugal. Man-made tiles are generally porcelain or ceramic and are durable and resistant to stains. Some manufacturers rate ceramic tile on a scale from 1 to 4+, from least to most durable. Porcelain is considered more durable than ceramic because porcelain is not glazed. Note that porcelain is actually a form of ceramic, but is fired at such high temperatures that it is denser than the material labeled ceramic. Porcelain is vitreous, or glass-like—water cannot penetrate it—and this is one reason why porcelain is stronger than ceramic. Because of the firing process that ceramic tile undergoes, the color as well as the shape of the tile is permanent.

## NATURAL TILE AND STONE

Most natural tiles—such as marble, granite, limestone and slate—will last forever. That doesn't mean it will look like new forever. Marble is one of the most classic, desired and expensive stones, and because it scratches and stains easily it must be sealed after installation. Even after the marble is sealed, it will still be more vulnerable to scratching than other stone, such as granite, so be prepared to care for and maintain a marble installation. There are many types of seals to choose from: a matte seal preserves the stone's natural color or texture, a glossy seal makes the stone appear shiny and smooth and gives it a more formal appearance, and a color enhancement sealer brings out the stone's colors and beauty.

Like marble, granite is a natural stone that comes in both tiles and slabs. Granite is one of the strongest stones, but it also needs to be sealed after professional installation. Granite is more impervious to stains than marble, and also less expensive.

In general, marble and granite slabs are more expensive than tile because the slabs are customized and take more of the installer's time. Slabs are commonly used for areas such as countertops and around fireplaces. Installing slabs requires different skills than installing tile; therefore, you should ask a potential installer if he normally installs tile or slab.

## ON COST

With the exception of hand-painted tiles, tile is generally priced per square foot. This simplifies price comparisons of tiles that differ greatly in size or shape: once you know how many square feet you need for your area, it's easy to calculate the difference in total cost between tile choices. Basic ceramic and porcelain tiles range from $2 to $20 per square foot. Hand-painted tiles can cost anywhere from $8 to $150 each.

On the whole, stone tiles like marble and granite are more expensive than their ceramic counterparts. The price of marble and granite depends on color and type. Natural stone is quarried all over the world, and a particularly desirable origin can make it more expensive. Some stone is easier to find and is not considered as rare as other types of stone. Like ceramic tiles, natural stone tiles are priced per square foot. Marble and granite slab, however, is priced per project because there are so many variables in slab work. The price depends on the edges, customization and amount of work that goes into the actual installation. Slabs also have to be cut to fit the area precisely. The pricing of slab work depends on how difficult the stone was to get and how large the slab is. The larger the slab, the more expensive it is going to be to transport.

Tile and stone installers generally charge per project. The more custom work they have to do, such as edges and corners, the more expensive the project. Also, note that more artistic tile installation, such as creating mosaics, is much more expensive. Hiring a larger company can be cheaper because much work can be done in house, and the company can buy in bulk to save on materials. Also, installers will not have to be subcontracted and the materials will often be in stock. If you order from a smaller company and they do not keep a particular, expensive tile in stock, the price could be higher than from a larger company. With any installer, tile or marble that has to be ordered can significantly delay your project.

## WHO INSTALLS THE TILE, MARBLE AND STONE?

Some of the service providers in this guide use their own installers and some subcontract the work out. If you choose a company that uses installers that are not in house, make sure that the company has used them before and ask for references. Some companies also keep a list of installers that they use on a regular basis.

## QUALIFICATIONS

No professional certification is required to install tile, marble and stone, but there are other ways of screening potential installers. For example, they should have a business license and, ideally, a general contractor's license. An excellent way to evaluate a potential installer is to ask for references, speak to them, and look at photographs of previous installations. Membership in professional organizations may also confer credibility to this service provider. These associations can offer general information as well as answer some of your simple questions about tile and marble installation.

The main professional associations to contact for information are:
The Marble Institute of America (614) 228-6194 www.marble-institute.com
Ceramic Tiles Distributors Association (800) 938-2832 www.ctdahome.org
The Tile Council of America (864) 646-8453 www.tileusa.com
The Ceramic Tile Institute of America (805) 371-TILE www.ctioa.com

Whether you decide to install simple ceramic tile in your shower or rare marble in your living room, the entire process will go more smoothly with a basic understanding of these special materials as provided above.

## Decorative Ideas

❖ For tile in the kitchen or high-traffic areas, consider a darker grout for easier up-keep and a more formal appearance.

❖ Install tile mosaics around kitchen windows and, add a tile inlay to your floors and walls or scatter tiles with a thematic print (herbs for a kitchen or shells for the shower).

❖ Use a stone or tile molding to crown your master bathroom or mix marble countertops with a ceramic tile backsplash.

❖ For the children's bathroom, use hand-painted tiles in favorite colors to make washing more fun or give the playroom some pizzazz with a bright tile chair-rail or "homemade" mosaic.

❖ Too traditional? Exotic stones such as quartzites, slates and alabasters can offer a unique alternative to other natural surfaces and are just as functional!

❖ Don't overlook the nouveau! Some of the latest metallic and glass tiles are made to refract light, giving a glimmer to the dullest spaces.

# TILE, MARBLE & STONE

### A&G Marble
132-19 34th Avenue, Flushing, NY  11354
(718) 353 - 9415

*Marble and granite installation*

| | | | |
| :---: | :---: | :---: | :---: |
| 3 | 3 | 4 | 4 |

### Alcamo Marble Works Inc.
541 West 22nd Street, New York, NY  10011
(212) 255 - 5224

*Slab work and antique marble restoration*

| | | | |
| :---: | :---: | :---: | :---: |
| 4 | 3.5 | 3 | 4 |

Sources reluctantly tell us that Alcamo has been a closely guarded secret of area architects and designers.  This firm specializes in custom slab work for floors, walls, countertops, columns, fireplaces and mantles.  Alcamo will work with marble, granite, onyx, slate and limestone, and occasionally does restoration work on antique pieces.  Sources say these professionals can be pricey.

### Andy's Marble & Granite Shop
55 Craven Point Avenue, Jersey City, NJ  07305
(201) 451 - 9383

*Marble and tile installation*

| | | | |
| :---: | :---: | :---: | :---: |
| 4 | 3.5 | 4 | 4.5 |

The professionals at Andy's Marble receive high praise for their job commitment and reliability.  Sources say that since there is minimal stock in the showroom, the staff will actually escort clients to the stoneyards to purchase project materials. Industry members report that these artisans have a reputation for completing jobs in an impressive time bracket and fix any mistakes until everything is perfect. Andy's generally works through contractors and designers, accepting residential projects on occasion.  Overall, references agree the company produces high quality work, although some say Andy's prices have climbed a bit recently.

*"Truly excellent work."  "I just completed a brownstone with Andy. Of course there were some mistakes, but I tell you, it didn't matter."  "I call his workmen 'magic elves'—they had everything fixed almost overnight!"*

### Ann Sacks Tile & Stone
5 East 16th Street, New York, NY  10003
(212) 463 - 8400  www.annsackstile.com

*Handcrafted tiles and luxury bathroom fixtures*

| | | | |
| :---: | :---: | :---: | :---: |
| 5 | 5 | 4 | 5 |

Clients and industry insiders alike say that Ann Sacks is an industry leader in tile and stone, calling the firm "creative and adventurous." Ann Sacks stores can be found in prime locations across the continental United States, including Manhattan, Chicago, Los Angeles, San Francisco, Denver, Dallas, Portland and Seattle, with plans for further expansion.  Specializing in handcrafted tile, limestone slab, antiquated stone and terra cotta custom mosaics, Ann Sacks has an ever-changing palette of products displayed on the showroom floors.  In fact, we hear that Sacks' unique offering now extends to luxury plumbing products, bathroom fixtures and exclusive tile collections by Barbara Barry and Rebecca Gore. While they do not install, they recommend those who do.

*"Every time I set foot in the showroom I'm like a kid in a candy store because there is just so much to marvel at."*

| | Quality + | Cost $ | Value ◆ | Recommend? ★ |
|---|---|---|---|---|

## Avarino Tile & Marble Inc.

| | 3 | 2 | 4 | 3 |

1023 65th Street, Brooklyn, NY 11219
(718) 680 - 0628

*Imported tiles, granite and marble installation*

Professional customer service and good-quality work has earned this family-run firm a fair rating amongst references. Avarino does all types of installation—residential and commercial—in all five boroughs of New York City. The firm specializes in imported materials—specifically marble, tile and granite.

## Bathrooms Restored

| | 3 | 2 | 4 | 4 |

415 East 9th Street, New York, NY 10009
(212) 533 - 8413

*Tile installation, maintenance, repair and cleaning*

Described by clients as fun, polite and reliable, William Zulkoski has been in the business for 21 years, providing installation, maintenance and repair work. Since he books only one job at a time, clients say Mr. Zulkoski is able to devote his full attention to each project. Client references remark on his positive energy and integrity, granting Zulkoski their full confidence for any job.

Zulkoski works on the Upper East and Upper West Sides of Manhattan, with the majority of his clientele consisting of repeat business or referrals. His work comes with a one-year guarantee, and references stand by the service, confirming that he delivers good value for the money. Bathrooms Restored tends to work most frequently with Bella Tile (American Olean Tile), but is open to other suppliers.

*"The tiling job was beautifully done." "Since he's a one-man show, the job took a while to be completed, but it was worth the extra time."*

## Bollella Tile & Marble

| | 3 | 2 | 4 | 4 |

63 Bleecker Street, New York, NY 10012
(212) 614 - 6628

*Cork flooring, custom coloring, tile sales and installation*

Straightforward and honest, we hear the staff at Bollella Tile and Marble really knows their installation capabilities, and perform accordingly. This firm specializes in cork flooring and custom coloring, and deals with homeowners as well as the trade. Bollella has a showroom, which is open to the public and features among its tile products: glass mosaics, ceramics, porcelain, rubber and vinyl.

Sources say Bollella has a respectable work history including a project at the Guggenheim and the retail store at the Met, not to mention many other high profile projects. Bollella's dedicated, friendly staff, along with good value reports, has some calling this firm a "rock solid" operation.

*"The job was done when it was supposed to be done—no question." "With all these new color trends in the industry, Kenny really comes through with matching the flooring to custom specs."*

## Ceramica Arnon Tile Setting

| | 4 | 3 | 4 | 4 |

134 West 20th Street, New York, NY 10011
(212) 807 - 0876   www.ceramicaarnon.com

*Specialty tiles, custom tile murals, fabrication and installation*

A third-generation artist, Arnon Zodak of Ceramica Arnon, has more than three decades of experience fabricating and installing handcrafted tile murals for residential clients in the metropolitan area. We are told that these specialists have worked with some of the city's more notable designers in addition to homeowners. Ceramica Arnon's showroom features an array of products on display from ceramic and glass tiles to metallic tile mosaics. The company also carries newer lines, including a series of French-Gothic and rustic Moroccan tiles.

| | Quality | Cost | Value | Recommend? |
|---|---|---|---|---|
| | + | $ | ◆ | ★ |

Ceramica's contract division installs not only its own custom creations, but stock products as well, and all installation work is guaranteed for a year. Clients report that their service team is reliable and the pricing is appropriate.

*"I guess you could call Arnon a temperamental artist, but that's overlooked. He is just so focused on perfecting everything!" "Very honest, meticulous craftsmen ..."*

### Certified Marble & Ceramic                3.5    2    4.5    4
24 Demacrest Avenue, West Haverstraw, NY 10993
(212) 967 - 5898

*Tile and marble installation*

The client consensus is that Certified's Joe DelBiondo delivers quality work— no kidding! This one-man operation offers installation, to maintenance and repair services, working with homeowners and the trade. After fifteen years in the business, insiders say DelBiondo is hired most often through referrals, and shies away from advertising. We hear he's "willing to travel anywhere for a job" when given the opportunity and the proper accommodations. References call DelBiondo skilled, trusting him with a range of projects from placing a simple backsplash, to the highly-detailed installation of century-old tile.

*"I always recommend him and I'll continue to do so." "Joe is honest and explains all of my options to me, taking into consideration certain aspects of my lifestyle." "I'm comfortable working with him because he's so down-to-earth."*

### Chess King Marble                4    3    4    3.5
20 Herrick Drive, East Rockaway, NY 11518
(212) 488 - 8930

*Residential and commercial installation and waterproofing*

Chess King Marble specializes in the installation of tile, marble, stone, glass and ceramics. The company also does waterproofing. Insiders say the firm's work is "top quality," and although the duration of some projects may drag, principal and perfectionist Arthur Kormacki is always available to address questions and concerns. We hear the majority of the firm's projects are residential, but Chess King's work can be seen in numerous Manhattan restaurants.

### Country Floors Inc.                4    3    4    5
15 East 16th Street, New York, NY 10003
(212) 627 - 8300   www.countryfloors.com

*Handmade and imported tile sales and installation*

We hear that Country Floors is not only a great source of hard-to-find tiles, but some swear it's "the source for any flooring need." The company carries a wide variety of handmade and imported tiles, from rustic to sleek, including those it manufactures—such as its popular Mediterranean and French floral tiles, both client favorites. References say the showroom staff is reliable and efficient. Overall, we hear that the experience of working with the company is a pleasurable one. Although Country Floors does not do installations, references say that its outsourced installers are dedicated and exacting.

*"Great source for hard-to-find tiles." "The installers were excellent—they were right on the ball with everything from start to finish." "Surprisingly, there were no time issues or delays."*

## D.M.S. Studios

4    3.5    3.5    4

5-50 51st Avenue, Long Island City, NY  11101
(718) 937 - 5648

*Traditional marble and stone fabrication, carving and sculpting*

Known best for its custom fireplaces, D.M.S. has been creating and carving custom stonework for more than 20 years.  Owner Daniel Sinclair has earned a reputation by his clients as the "beautifier of stone."  We are told Sinclair creates unique fireplaces and mantles by combining traditional methods of hand craftsmanship with genuine marble and limestone from its quarries in Europe and America.  We hear that the firm specializes in all areas of stone carving, fabricating and sculpting, and insiders say D.M.S. is taking on more complicated and elaborate jobs such as artistic and architectural detailing.  Because fireplaces and mantles are handmade, it may be longer for a project to be completed, but according to clients, "that's the price for a true work of art."

*"Daniel is an old-world technician—all he uses is a hammer and chisel." "Amazing detail work." "I'd say his only shortcoming is his lack of technology.  Not having the proper machinery can slow him down."*

## David Garbo Tile Works

4    2    4.5    4

5 Tudor City Place, Suite 737, New York, NY  10017
(212) 856 - 9481

*Highly-detailed tile installation, stone and glass mosaics*

Industry insiders say David Garbo's tile work is reminiscent of old European styles, especially of the Portuguese and Italian traditions.  He is known primarily for his work with handmade and stone tiles, but has recently taken to more projects involving glass mosaics.  Garbo learned his craft in San Francisco, and has been practicing for more than 20 years.  Clients refer to him as detail-oriented and confirm that he is trustworthy and personable.  Many consider David Garbo the man to call for extraordinary tile work, some of which has been featured in *Architectural Digest*.

*"Not only does he work well with everyone, but there is a definite exchange of trust between David and and his clients." "I am the pickiest person at my firm and I think David is the best of the best."*

## Dionysus Inc.

3    2.5    3.5    4

1189 Lexington Avenue, New York, NY  10028
(212) 861 - 5616

*Marble and tile sales, installation, maintenance, repair, plumbing and electrical work*

Clients really appreciate the personalized service given to them by the staff at Dionysus Inc.  Mike Giordas and his wife Joanna have been in the business for the past eleven years, and those who have worked with them praise their "infinite patience."  The staff at Dionysus takes care of everything from design to installation of materials such as ceramic, marble, limestone, mosaic, and even does plumbing and electrical work.  Other services include creating cast iron bases for consoles and tables, restoration of marble and ceramic vases, and fabrication of custom fireplaces.  Maintenance and repair work is available to all customers and although the firm's services are limited to the city, Dionysus will sell and ship their materials to any location.

*"Very involved in helping you find what you're looking for." "They give you the attention that larger companies can not offer."*

## Enright Tile & Marble

3    2    4    5

53-55 70th Street, Flushing, NY  11378
(718) 424 - 7900

*Marble and tile installation*

| Quality | Cost | Value | Recommend? |
|---------|------|-------|------------|
| + | $ | ◆ | ★ |

References say the professionals at Enright really deliver on good quality at a reasonable cost. For almost a decade, this company has been installing, repairing and doing maintenance work on tile and marble for both homeowners and the trade. Although there is no formal guarantee, we hear that Enright stands behind its products and services, ensuring that all client needs are met, even years after project completion.

*"A conscientious, respectable business."*

### Fordham Marble
**5  3  5  5**

421 Fairfield Avenue, Stamford, CT  06902
(203) 348 - 5088

*Marble sales and installation, kitchen countertops and flooring*

According to sources, this firm has a reputation for high-quality work and an even higher grade of customer service. Since 1905, Fordham Marble has expanded from its original Bronx-based showroom to a second location in Stamford, Connecticut. Nearly a century later, the team now services Manhattan, Fairfield County and everything in between. We hear the company will outfit clients with the appropriate materials to fit each individual project—offering personalized guidance to architects, designers and homeowners. Even though its workmen don't provide any general maintenance or repairs, the company does offer a one-year guarantee of its services.

*"Basically, there is no one better."*

### Formia Marble
**3  2.5  4  4**

44-36 21st Street, Long Island City, NY  11101
(718) 482 - 0606

*Granite and stone slab work and countertop installation*

In business since 1981, Formia sells and installs a wide range of products including tiles, countertops and customized fittings. Customers consider Formia a good place to get marble and granite, either by the slab or for a particular installation, but forewarn potential customers that the company does not provide repair or maintenance services. Insiders say that stone or marble tile is often manufactured and customized right in Formia's warehouse—where the firm also has a limited supply of ceramics. Formia services both homeowners and the trade, and the company offers a guarantee on all of its installations.

*"They have a great setup and a reliable team of workers at the showroom and the warehouse." "I'm pleased with the work but a little disappointed knowing that they won't repair."*

### Homeworks
**3  2.5  4  3**

132 West 17th Street, New York, NY  10011
(212) 620 - 7070

*Kitchen and bath design, marble, stone and tile installation*

See Homeworks's full report under the heading Kitchen & Bath Design

### Ideal Tile & Stone Gallery

110 West End Avenue, New York, NY  10023
(212) 799 - 3600

*Natural stone and hand-painted tile sales and installation*

We hear that Ideal sells and installs stone and ceramics to homeowners and the trade. All of its products are natural and include terra cotta, mosaic, tumbled and medallion—no synthetic materials are used. In addition to the installation service, they offer patio frost-proofing, stone fabrication and slab work. Custom hand-painted tiles and stone created by Ideal's on-site artist are also available and the staff is said to be informative and pleasant. Ideal serves the New York metro area.

| | Quality  | Cost $ | Value ◆ | Recommend? ★ |
|---|---|---|---|---|

## J&I Marble & Granite Inc.
121 Hausman Street, Brooklyn, NY 11222
(718) 384 - 5106

*Marble, tile and stone installation, fabrication and architectural detailing*

Quality 3 Cost 2 Value 4 Recommend? 4

Insiders say that J&I Marble is on the cutting edge—literally. Using the latest machinery allows these craftsmen to create an impressive selection of edges on marble, onyx and other types of stone and tile. The company factory cuts custom stone slabs to meet client specifications and specializes in the fabrication of kitchen countertops. J&I receives favorable reports for customer service.

## Jimmy Woo
(516) 829 - 0701

*Tile and mosaic floors*

Quality 4.5 Cost 3 Value 4 Recommend? 5

Woo wins rave reviews from references who praise his dedication and skill with tile and mosaic floors. Well known among customers and the trade alike, we hear Woo's work is fabulous and he can be counted on to get the job done right, even redoing the work if necessary. When calling for information, potential clients shouldn't be discouraged by the answering machine—just leave a message and speak slowly—Jimmy will return the call.

We're told that Jimmy Woo doesn't have a public showroom, but sources say his work is coveted by some of the most well respected contractors in the city.

*"Best tile work I have ever seen!"* *"Looked at a design and made it when the product manufacturers were late."* *"A magician with tile."* *"Perfection—made a huge difference in the texture of my apartment."*

## Joseph Corcoran Marble Inc.
50 West Hills Road, Huntington Station, NY 11746
(516) 423 - 8737

*Marble, tile and stone installation*

Quality 4 Cost 2.5 Value 4.5 Recommend? 5

Since 1984, Joseph Corcoran has serviced clients in the New York City area, providing installation from countertops to flooring. Still, the firm does not limit its services—insiders confirm that the company will accept some jobs in Westchester and Fairfield counties. The Huntington Station showroom displays a selection of high quality limestone, slate, granite, marble, travertine and tile. Those who have worked with Joseph Corcoran are quick to report on their high quality work at lower-than-market prices.

*"Beautiful work...and everything fell right within my budget."*

| | Quality | Cost | Value | Recommend? |
|---|---|---|---|---|
| | ➕ | 💲 | ◆ | ★ |

## K&K Marble Importers
17 Seaman Avenue, Bethpage, NY 11714
(516) 932 - 5630

**Quality 4  Cost 2  Value 5  Recommend 5**

*Imported marble sales, fabrication and installation*

We hear this firm will go to great lengths to meets each client's specific and sometimes unusual requirements. With its sister branch in Greece, K & K has been importing fine marble from its Greek quarries for eighteen years. Both residential and commercial clients say that the Long Island showroom is well appointed, with up to 72 colors of marble in stock. A polite and professional staff along with the company's 100 percent guarantee has many insisting that they would "highly recommend" K&K's services.

*"The quality is self-explanatory, just visit the showroom." "They stand behind their product and deal well with clients." "Altered the slabs to fit my color and size specifications."*

## Lodestar Statements In Stone
231 East 58th Street, New York, NY 10022
(212) 755 - 1818

**Quality 5  Cost 4  Value 5  Recommend 5**

*Semi-precious stone and tile mosaics, design and installation*

For those searching for a true master in the art of Byzantine and Florentine mosaic work, references say the search ends with Stewart Ritwo and his select staff of artisans at Lodestar Statements in Stone. What makes this firm unique, according to clients, is the incorporation of semi-precious stones such as onyx, malachite, sodalite and quartzite into their infamous tabletops, decorative floors and murals. In addition to private clients, insiders say Lodestar's commissions can be found in some of the world's most elegant hotels and restaurants, and that a visit to Lodestar's showroom and gallery is worth the trip.

Prices are based on three variables—the stones used, intricacy of the design, and size of the panel. While Lodestar's work is not within everyone's budget, clients who have seen this star have been known to stretch in its direction.

*"Stewart works with the precision of a jeweler."*

## Manhattan Marble Company
276 Elizabeth Street, New York, NY 10012
(212) 226 - 4881

*Decorative mosaics, marble and tile installation*

In addition to installation, Manhattan Marble specializes in decorative mosaic work and stone inlay. This fifteen-year-old firm works with homeowners and with the trade in the New York City area. The company uses stone and marble for the majority of their work, incorporating some tile and slab "specialty work" into its projects. Manhattan Marble does not offer free consultations, but the staff is willing to speak with clients and give price quotes over the phone.

## Marble, Tile & Terrazzo
305 Douglass Street, Brooklyn, NY 11213
(718) 802 - 1512

**Quality 3  Cost 2.5  Value 3.5  Recommend 4**

*Terrazzo flooring, marble and tile installation and maintenance*

This fabricator has a solid reputation among clients who applaud its quality work at a reasonable price. Some typical projects include custom-made marble tables, marble mosaics, countertops, bathrooms, kitchens, building lobbies and terrazzo floors and tables. In addition to fabrication, we hear that the firm's talented craftsmen install, polish, clean and maintain tile and marble surfaces. Consultations are available by appointment only.

*"Carlo and his staff have a great service and they really deliver on quality. I have already recommended them several times."*

| | Quality | Cost | Value | Recommend? |
|---|---|---|---|---|
| | ✚ | $ | ◆ | ★ |

## Michael R. Golden Design Inc.

**Quality** 5 **Cost** 3.5 **Value** 5 **Recommend?** 5

37 West 20th Street, Suite 303, New York, NY 10011
(212) 645 - 3001

*Tile mosaics, hand-carved stone, terrazzo and scagliola treatments*

Michael R. Golden is revered by clients who claim he will fly out to install tile anywhere in the country. Those who have worked with him rave about his superior service and high-quality work, calling both "amazing." Golden's company provides installation of tile and tile mosaics, decorative and hand-carved stone, and even incorporates treatments such as scagliola and terrazzo into his work. Michael's work ranges from bathroom tile-shopping with clients to planning and producing elaborate reproductions. After nine years in the business, we hear that he has paved his way into some impressive residences, working with everyone from well-known professional athletes to top interior designers.

*"Michael has expert knowledge of his field which helped us get through difficult situations with ease." "He has designed quality of life into our home. He has given us art."*

## Quarry Tile, Marble & Granite Inc.

**Quality** 2.5 **Cost** 3 **Value** 3.5 **Recommend?** 3.5

132 Lexington Avenue, New York, NY 10016
(212) 679 - 8889

*Custom-made counter tops*

We hear that Quarry Tile has more than 3,000 samples available in their public showroom located at 128 East 32nd Street between Park and Lexington. This company specializes in custom-made countertops, doing mostly commercial projects and some residences. Working with various architects, builders and decorators in the New York metro area, Westchester County and the Hamptons, this twenty-year industry veteran fabricates counter-tops from tumbled marble, tile, limestone and granite.

## R.G. New York Tile

**Quality** 3 **Cost** 2 **Value** 4 **Recommend?** 4

225 West 29th Street, New York, NY 10001
(212) 629 - 0712

*Tile installation and marble countertop fabrication, kitchen and bath design*

R.G. New York Tile gets glowing reports from clients who praise it for speedy service and a friendly staff. This company installs tile and ceramics, fabricates kitchen countertops and sells tile and marble. All of these products are on display in the company's showroom, and further services include kitchen and bath design and installation. Clients say this high-end work comes at a reasonable price, and the staff is remarkably efficient.

*"Excellent! Fast."*

## Stone Source

**Quality** 4 **Cost** 3.5 **Value** 4 **Recommend?** 4.5

215 Park Avenue South, Suite 700, New York, NY 10003
(212) 979 - 6400  www.stonesource.com

*Natural stone and tile importing, fabrication and installation*

With locations in New York, Massachusetts, Philadelphia and Washington DC, insiders tell us Stone Source is long reputed to be a primary source of natural stone for top designers and architects in the northeast. We hear this firm is the largest importer of limestone in the eastern United States and has its own warehouse and fabrication shop in Brooklyn, where it receives frequent deliveries of granite and marble from Italy. Insiders say the firm carries a large selection of alternative stones and tile materials, including award-winning Veneto Glass Tiles. Stone Source will also do slab work. The firm deals mainly with the trade—much of its work is for architects—but will service some high-end residential clients. References assess the firm's staff as knowledgeable and helpful.

*"Generous with showroom samples." "Very honest in educating about true quality and the best uses for different stones." "The showroom itself is a veritable tool for gathering ideas and researching the options." "Trustworthy—which is more than I can say about most." "My one reservation was not receiving enough followup calls, but then again, it's New York, and everyone's busy."*

## TILES-A Refined Selection Inc.    3    2.5    3.5    3
227 East 59th Street, New York, NY 10022
(212) 813 - 9391   www.tiles-arefined.com
*Tile sales and installation, custom design*

We have received word that Tiles is best described as "a custom house with extensive capabilities." Professional, helpful and attentive, Tiles' showroom staff is said to take the time to work with clients, offering full services with free consultation available.

This company works with well-established clients all over the East Coast from two locations in New York City, one in Boston and the newest in Westport, Connecticut. Tiles will do full kitchens, baths or any other project, and carries a wide selection of materials—from the basics to the latest trends. Many clients assert that the company excels in dealing with private homeowners, although Tiles does work with the trade. However, there are some reports that communication and followup could be better.

*"The showroom was a good resource, but the staff was not as responsive as I would have expected." "Everything arrived as ordered and on price. I was very pleased."*

## Vladimir Obrevko Stoneworks Inc. 🛍    4.5    2    5    5
15 Walworth Street, Brooklyn, NY 11205
(718) 855 - 4602
*Custom stone fabrication and installation, fireplace and sculpture restoration*

Amiable is not a word heard everyday to describe craftsmen, but it is one used time and again by clients in describing Vladimir Obrevko of Stoneworks. For several years before coming to the United States, Obrevko worked restoring cathedrals in Old St. Petersburg, Russia—a trade he learned from his father. Now Obrevko's architectural stonework can be seen in elaborate homes and commercial locations throughout New York City, Long Island and Westchester and Fairfield counties. For example, Obrevko's own onyx wall is prominently displayed at Metrazur, a restaurant in Grand Central Station. Clients laud his pleasant demeanor and dedicated work ethic, calling him personable and true to his craft.

Stoneworks offers fabrication and installation services in marble, granite, limestone and slate. It also does specialty work such as fireplace and sculpture restoration.

*"A very driven artisan." "I always refer him. His work is flawless and his templates are true to size." "Our clients use him all the time." "We wouldn't hire anyone else for our countertops—he does a magnificent job!"*

## Wholesale Marble & Granite    ▱  ▱  ▱  ▱
150 East 58th Street, New York, NY 10155
(212) 223 - 4068   www.wholesalemarbleandgranite.com
*Granite and marble sales and installation*

Don't be fooled by the name. Although Wholesale Marble & Granite deals mostly with the trade, it does offer fabrication and installation services to residential clients all over New York City. In addition to its Manhattan location, Wholesale Marble encourages clients to visit its showroom and gallery at 31 Cobek Court in Brooklyn.

# HIRING AN UPHOLSTERY & WINDOW TREATMENT SERVICE PROVIDER

Do the window treatments in your newly painted or designed living room need a makeover? Did you find a gorgeous set of Federal chairs at the flea market that need reupholstering? Would you like to transform your aging—yet amazingly comfortable—armchair into a spectacular piece that matches your sofa and decor? Or are you ready to buy a complete set of custom-upholstered furniture for your living room? Whether you are thinking about the design and construction of your piece or which fabric to choose, upholstery and window treatment experts are the professionals to call.

Many high-end upholsterers who do specialized work deal exclusively with the trade (decorators and architects). We have clearly noted these professionals in our reviews. These service providers primarily focus on custom work—creating a piece from scratch rather than reupholstering. In the case of window treatments, high-end specialists do custom work rather than installing materials from retail stock.

## WHAT TYPE OF UPHOLSTERY SERVICE DO I NEED?

Your three basic choices are custom upholstery fabrication, reupholstery and custom slipcovers. You may not need a completely new piece of furniture. Depending on the condition of your frame and webbing, you may choose to reupholster or have custom-made slipcovers as a less expensive alternative. A favorite decorator trick is to use a Crate & Barrel frame and upgrade the fillings to create a well-priced custom piece. An upholstery professional will be able to assist you in assessing the structure of your existing piece.

To help narrow down the service you need, determine how the furniture will be used. Is it a seating piece that is frequently used by the family and guests (and pets), or a more stylized piece that is located in a less frequently used space? If it will receive heavy use, you'll choose springs and cushioning that will stand up to this treatment as well as a fabric that is durable and easy to clean.

## KNOW YOUR UPHOLSTERY CONSTRUCTION

FRAMES: The frame is the skeleton of your piece, determining the sturdiness as well as overall appearance of the object. The best frames are made of kiln-dried hardwood. Oak, maple and ash are the hardwoods of choice by professionals. Kiln drying removes moisture and sap from the wood which could cause the frame to warp or bend. When assembling the frame, the ideal method involves using dowels and cornerblocks. This is more costly than using nails and glue but will greatly increase the quality and add years to the life of your piece. Tacks are the preferred method for attaching fabric to the frame, although staple guns are sometimes used. Staple guns should never be used in constructing a quality frame, however.

SPRINGS: The main function of springs is to support the furniture's cushioning. The two basic spring systems for upholstered furniture are round coil springs and flat, s-shaped "no-sag" coils. Most traditional pieces use hand-tied steel spring coils, in which coils are tied by hand in six or eight places around the diameter of the spring. S-shaped or zig-zag coils are sometimes used for contemporary pieces and do not provide the same support as spring coils. S-shaped springs can become lumpy or uneven over time.

Cushions: These come in two types: attached and loose. In an attached construction, fiber-covered foam is placed over the spring system, then is covered with fabric. Loose cushions resemble big pillows that are easily fluffed, moved or turned over to prevent signs of wear. Some pieces may also include semi-attached cushions which look much like removable cushions but are actually part of the piece. Both types of cushions can be filled with a wide variety of filling, from luxurious pure down and down blends to synthetic foam fill.

Down is the ultimate cushion filling and comes at a premium price. The typical down-feather blend consists of 80 percent goose down and 20 percent duck feathers. The ultimate puff-look is 100 percent down, which offers almost no support. The biggest drawback of down or down-blend fill is the frequent need to fluff the cushions to keep the shape and comfort. Because of the high level of maintenance and cost required for down, many consumers prefer to go with a combination of down and foam/feather.

In very high-quality cushion construction, springs are individually wrapped, encased in foam, then covered in a down and feather mixture. This is all then encased in a muslin bag in order to contain the fluff before being covered with fabric. This combination provides firmness and helps to hold its shape.

Fabrics: The possibilities are endless when choosing upholstery fabric. With so many options, you can narrow your search by exploring a few basic issues. Prices vary widely, from $10 to well over $250 per yard. The most important issue is how the piece will be used. Do you need a super durable fabric that can withstand daily use? Or is it a not-to-be-touched showpiece that can be covered in a delicate silk? Some fabrics are simply stronger than others. Ease of cleaning should also be considered. Pieces in the TV room or children's bedroom may attract more dirt. Darker, more durable fabric that withstands frequent cleaning would be appropriate for this furniture. Upholsterers handle the issue of fabric in a variety of ways. Some have catalogs and swatches from which you can choose; others insist that you bring in your own fabric choices. This option is known in the trade as COM—customer's own material. If you do not have the time or inclination to shop for your own fabric, make sure you choose an upholsterer who provides this service. Keep in mind that the ease or difficulty of working with a particular fabric will affect the price of the job. You will need more yardage of patterned fabric so the upholsterer can match the pattern in visible areas.

### What to Look for in Quality Upholstery Work

When viewing the work of an upholstery professional in the showroom or someone's home, keep the following points in mind:

- Fabric patterns should match at all seams and should be centered or balanced on any cushions or surfaces. This can be particularly important with more intricate patterns.
- Check to see if any of the seams pucker, such as those along the arm of a sofa or on the back of a club chair. Seams should be perfectly smooth.
- Are the sofa skirts lined? Is the cushion of the slipper chair invisibly secured with clips, and is the welt or trim tightly stitched?

## ON COST

As with any specialized custom work, upholstery prices vary significantly. The more detailed and specialized, the more labor involved and the higher the price. To choose the appropriate expense level, you should assess the application. A chair in your four-year-old's room will probably not require the same quality of fabric or workmanship as a sofa in your living room where you entertain regularly. Most decorators view the "public" (living room, dining room) vs. "private" (bedrooms, playrooms) with two different price points. All the components discussed in the upholstery construction section above directly contribute to the cost. Knowing a little bit about the basic construction will help you understand the real difference between a $700 and $7,000 sofa and help you determine your specific needs.

## WINDOW TREATMENTS

From a simple minimalist panel to a layer-upon-layer, elaborate design, many elements come together to make a window treatment. Carefully selected shades, sheers, curtains and valances may be held together with various trims, chords, brackets and hardware—and possibly finished off with decorative finials. Some upholstery and window treatment professionals also do hard window treatments, which include all types of shades, laminated shades (roller shades, covered in your choice of fabric) and blinds, custom made in your choice of materials to coordinate with your curtains.

## WHERE DO I START?

To help you decide upon the perfect window treatment for your room, many shops can do miracles with photos and magazine clippings. Once you've settled on a basic design (perhaps with the help of your decorator or examples from your upholsterer), you need to take some measurements. Most service providers will come to your home and measure the window as part of their consultation. Some charge a fee to take measurements, others apply this charge once you place the actual order. Others do not charge at all. Ask the window treatment professional about his policy before setting up the in-home consultation.

It is highly recommended that you do not take the measurements—then you will not be responsible when they are twelve inches too short. Letting a professional do the measuring is preferred because there are many factors involved. Most treatments, for example, take up wall space as well as cover your window, and your window treatment specialist will know what to measure for in the entire room. Will you have finials that take up space on each side of the window? Will your drapes open from the center and be secured on each side with hardware? Be clear with your provider if you prefer just panels. All of these factors will need to be considered when measuring and developing the final plans for your window treatments.

## WINDOW TREATMENT FABRIC AND CONSTRUCTION

As with custom furniture upholstery, fabric choices for window treatments are endless. As with upholsterers, some window treatment shops will provide you with a choice of fabrics and others will require you to provide your own. Ask how the service provider operates and if there will be any additional charges if you choose to provide your own fabric (usually there is not). In addition to selecting a fabric for color, texture and print, consider how easy it will be to clean. Curtains and window sills in the city are vulnerable to dust, dirt, grime and soot, whereas the elements are a bit more forgiving in the suburbs.

Most window treatments require more than one layer of fabric. For the most luxurious look, with excellent volume, curtains are lined and interlined. The interlining is commonly made of flannel, which not only provides heft and a bit of structure, but also a measure of soundproofing. This three-layer construction will provide you with material that will drape very nicely. If you are looking for something a bit more simple, a two-layer construction with a single lining will be sufficient.

## ON COST

Your window treatment cost will be determined by some or all of the following: measurement fee, installation fee (will vary according to the complexity of the job), labor charges, fee for providing your own material or cost of fabric from the shop. Two of the most significant factors in the price will be the fabric, which varies widely in price, and the complexity of the construction of the draperies. A three-layer construction, with lining and interlining, will be significantly more expensive to produce than a single or two-layer construction.

### TIPS ON CARING FOR UPHOLSTERED FURNITURE

#### GENERAL CARE

❖ Ask your upholsterer or fabric supplier exactly how to care for your new fabric.

❖ Vacuum often to get rid of dirt particles that cause abrasion and wear.

❖ Don't allow pets on fine fabrics—their body oils rub off on the fabric and are tough to remove.

❖ Protect fabric-covered pieces from the sun to avoid fading and deterioration, if not in use.

❖ Turn over loose cushions every week for even wear.

❖ Beware of sitting on upholstered furniture while wearing blue jeans or other fabric-dyed clothing—the color may "bleed" onto the fabric.

❖ Do not set newspapers or magazines onto upholstered furniture, as the ink may also bleed onto the fabric.

❖ Regular professional cleaning is ideal.

#### SPILLS

❖ Immediately after the spill, blot (don't rub) the area with a clean cloth. Dried spills are more difficult to remove.

❖ Carefully follow the instructions on the cleaning product (don't wing it).

❖ If you can use water for cleaning, be sure it is distilled.

❖ Choose a hidden area on the fabric to pretest the cleaner for color fastness before applying to the spill.

❖ Avoid making a small spill larger by working lightly, blotting out from the center. To avoid rings, "feather" the edges by dampening the edge of the spill irregularly and blotting quickly.

❖ Using a small fan or blow dryer (on low setting), quickly dry the cleaned area.

## UPHOLSTERY & WINDOW TREATMENTS
## SERVICE PROVIDERS

### A. Schneller Sons Inc.

5    4.5    4.5    5

129 West 29th Street, New York, NY 10001
(212) 695 - 9440

*Trade only—High-end custom upholstery and window treatments*

The provenance of this 120-year-old firm is nearly impressive as the absolute top-of-the line custom built, all hand done, upholstery and draperies it creates. While many New York decorators turn to this prestigious shop, A. Schneller Sons is selective with its workload and careful not to overextend itself. This may be the reason so many commend its responsiveness and incredibly gracious service, which some say is the best there is. Clients say each piece is built by hand with "amazing attention to detail" and to the materials used, adding that even the frames are beautiful. Pieces of A. Schneller's upholstery are named for former clients, such as the "Astor sofa," the "Vanderbilt sofa" and the "Whitney sofa." The firm will work only with the trade.

### ABC Carpet & Home 〰

3    3    3    3

888 Broadway, New York, NY 10003
(212) 473 - 3000   www.abchome.com

*Retail—Reupholstery, window treatments, rug cleaning and installation*

This well-known Manhattan retailer offers a range of home services, including reupholstery, refabrication of window treatments, carpet cleaning and reinstallation of the rugs it sells. ABC works all over the New York metropolitan area. While many New Yorkers like ABC, some told us they were "not as thrilled" at being reduced to customer A, B or C, saying the service and value could improve. They also caution that the "workmen could be more careful, particularly on rug installation."

### Albert Menin Interiors Ltd.

4    3.5    4.5    4

345 East 104th Street, 4th floor, New York, NY 10029
(212) 876 - 3041   www.albertmenin.com

*Trade only—Window treatments and wall upholstery*

Highly recommended by the trade for the trade when courting curtains and wall coverings, we hear this firm posts great ideas and delivers high quality on time and with a friendly Russian smile. Clients tell us the firm always comes through, providing service and product at a price "less expensive" than other respected firms.

*"These two Russians are the most professional that I have ever dealt with. I have recommended them to several people in my building and they are in love with them also." "I give strong marks for quality of his work." "Reliable."*

### Aldo Di Roma

4.5    3    4    4.5

327 East 94th Street, New York, NY 10128
(212) 688 - 3564

*Mostly trade—Custom upholstery*

References note that Aldo Di Roma has an "especially strong gift" at starting from ground zero with a picture or concept of an upholstered piece and getting it just right. Easy to work with and straightforward about money, this firm comes recommended for both upholstery and drapery work, and is noted for its reliability and helpfulness. Clients include many excellent decorators and private customers.

| | Quality | Cost | Value | Recommend? |
|---|---|---|---|---|
| | + | $ | ◆ | ★ |

## Alexander Upholstery

**3.5   3   5   5**

1483 Second Avenue, New York, NY 10021
(212) 472 - 0340

*Retail—Custom upholstery and window treatments*

This retail upholsterer comes highly recommended by customers who were at first hesitant to walk into the relatively small shop, but were later impressed with the service, quality and timing. While Alexander's "does not operate at the very top," some of the most discerning homeowners in New York recommend the firm. We hear that these professionals are particularly responsive under tight deadlines and handle problems with ease. There is a related store down the block called Alexander & Sons that customers also recommend for window treatments and draperies.

*"Impeccable. I was so blown away." "I had an upholstery emergency and they were right there to solve my problem in no time flat with surprisingly good work. I was amazed."*

## Anthony Lawrence - Belfair

**4.5   4.5   4   4.5**

53 West 23rd Street, 5th Floor, New York, NY 10010
(212) 206 - 8820   www.anthonylawrence.com

*Trade only—Very high-end custom window treatments and upholstery*

Anthony Lawrence and Belfair Draperies have recently joined forces to provide both custom upholstery and window treatments from one workroom to decorators only. Some of the greatest brand names in decorating have depended on these two companies for generations, and consider this consolidation a godsend.

Extraordinary work quality and outstanding showroom selection (with over 70 floor models) are the strengths Belfair brings to the table, even though some had found the firm "a bit disorganized," especially to the unfamiliar customer. Anthony Lawrence received outstanding reviews for its high-quality custom furniture, professionalism and reliability. Since the merger, we understand that the company still offers some of the highest quality available.

*"Phenomenal quality at not-completely-insane prices." "There was an obvious defect and I cannot imagine why it was not caught and addressed. In short—not a good job." "Fantastic shop. Does hard goods and soft goods."*

## Baron Upholstery

**5   4   4.5   5**

545 West 45th Street, 3rd Floor, New York, NY 10036
(212) 664 - 0800

*Trade only—Custom upholstery and window treatments*

Baron's trade-only subjects tell us the firm lords over production of a product "which is the Rolls Royce of our industry." Designers enjoy working with Baron Upholstery for their creative selection of fabrics and styles, superior skill and "honest and reliable" manner. This family-owned business offers over 4,000 square feet of showroom samples in their new location. They are reportedly very reliable and meet deadlines strictly. Complicated purchase orders are no problem and are always followed. Decorators say that Baron is considered among the very best workrooms in New York and that your money is well spent for the quality you receive. The friendliness of their service creates long-standing, satisfied clients who say Baron is "a joy to deal with."

*"We have worked with this family owned company for 25 years with great satisfaction." "Way up there in terms of quality, reliability and style." "I love the large offering in their catalog and their flexibility." "I can always count on Baron to be honest and fair, which is the bottom line for me." "Delivers a quality product at good prices." "Their work is perfect." "The two brothers, Steve and Paul, are simply the best! Cannot speak more highly of Baron Upholsterers."*

441

## Beckenstein Fabric & Interiors ∿∿

2.5    1.5    3    3

4 West 20th Street, New York, NY  10011
(212) 366 - 5142

*Custom upholstery*

All agree this firm delivers patient, professional installation and good work-manship, but some say it should stick to less demanding jobs.  They recommend the firm for upholstered headboards, and all items for the maid's room, children's rooms and the kitchen.  While some sources also say that Beckenstein is a good resource for straightforward shades or simple inexpensive drapes, the firm is not considered a master at proportion or installation.  Still, most appreciate that its services are quite inexpensive and rendered in a timely, amiable fashion.

*"Pleasant salesmanship, no bull, helpful suggestions."  "Good followup to minor problems."*

## Berthold's Upholstery

4.5    4    4.5    4.5

119 West 25th Street, 4th Floor, New York, NY  10001
(212) 633 - 0071

*Trade only—High-end custom upholstery*

All projects are hand-hewn at this upstart of a former De Angelis manager.  Trade-only, this shop has wooed its fair share of decorators to it's showroom's shores.  While small, with only 10 to 15 pieces, the boys at Berthold's can create anything of quality if you provide a sketch.

*"Bert is a pro. He knows everything about custom furniture. He takes extraor-dinary pride in his work. I've worked with him for almost twenty years."*

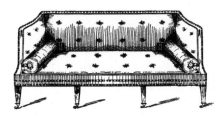

## Billee Dekors International

4    3.5    4    4

93-95  Franklin Street, New York, NY  10013
(212) 274 - 1148

*Trade only—custom upholstery*

We hear that this firm can take a simple picture or sketch and bring it "magi-cally to life."  Billee Dekors is a reliable and frequently used resource for some of the very top decorators and architects, such as Robert Stern.  No detail is too small, as these clients demand the best.  We hear the craftsmen at Billee Dekors are reputed to finish projects swiftly. There's no showroom to speak of, as every-thing is custom.

## Casanova Home Corp.

3.5    2.5    4    4

243 East 78th Street, New York, NY  10021
(212) 639 - 9486

*Retail and trade—Custom window treatments and upholstery*

With just one look clients fall head over heads for Casanova, crooning over the firm's "great taste" and "great service."  The firm has been creating "beautiful" custom window treatments from shades to curtains and doing upholstery work for retail clients in New York and surrounding areas have for sixteen years. A retail showroom offers a wide selection of fabrics at a wide variety of prices and spe-cializing in unique window treatments.  Clients also may bring in their own fabric if they prefer. This firm works in the chosen style of the client or decorator, and we hear that it is typical for each job to begin with a consultation in your home. Clients comment on principal Ana Rosa McGinnis's "calm and pleasant nature."

*"Ana is a dream to work with." "Exquisite workmanship." "Custom finishes on hardware are truly unique and complement the beauty of the overall design."*

## Classic Sofa Ltd.                    2.5    2    3    3
5 West 22nd Street, New York, NY 10011
(212) 620 - 0485  www.classicsofa.com

*Retail and trade—Custom-made, down-filled furniture*

While we hear to expect expedited service and customer-vendor communications, this firm is not a "hand-holder." Classic Sofa offers a wide selection of down-filled furniture and fabrics in its New York City showroom. Clients appreciate the speed with which you can choose a piece from the floor and get it in your home, but they are less impressed with the "uniqueness of the choices." The decision is split as to whether Classic Sofa is open to suggestions for improvement, although the firm is a "quick and reliable" resource when needed, particularly on a basic bedroom. We are told that Classic Sofa produces "decent quality at low prices." The firm sells both to the trade and at retail, with a client list that includes celebrities and top decorators.

*"What you see is what you get, with fast service but limited choices." "Expedient and responsive to quote requests." "Pleasant about changes to the standard fare. Great product."*

## Custom Decorators Service                🗁    🗁    🗁    🗁
415 East Main Street, Denville, NJ 07834
(973) 625 - 0516

*Custom upholstery*

## Custom Design Studio                  3    2    4    4.5
49 Bruckner Boulevard, Bronx, NY 10454
(718) 665 - 0777  www.customdesignny.com

*Retail and trade—Custom upholstery*

This "friendly, helpful and attentive" shop works with several area decorators on a regular basis, as well as directly with clients. The firm specializes in custom upholstery, services that range from custom slipcovers, to antique restoration and furniture restoration and repair. It will do window treatments at client request. Custom Design Studio is has been recommended in recent editions of *New York Magazine* and the *Antiques Newsletter*.

## D&F Workroom Inc.                    3.5    2    4.5    4.5
150 West 25th Street, Suite 2, New York, NY 10001
(212) 352 - 0160

*Trade only—Custom upholstery*

Some of New York's top decorators turn to D&F Workroom for its upholstery work. Most clients also tow the line of this shop, impressed with its professionalism, efficiency and high quality of work. While we hear the firm isn't in the la-la land of decorator schedules, sometimes turning around a piece in a mere two weeks, complaints have been registered to the effect that just getting in contact with the firm to take a new client requires an Olympic effort. Still, one reference felt that small pieces were a "particular area of strength" for D&F and praised its "quick turnaround times" on those items.

*"Excellent quality, reasonable prices." "At the recommendation of an architect, I contacted D&F to redo museum quality contemporary sofas. It took weeks of effort for them to call me back. This company's in the "life's too short" category."*

| | Quality | Cost | Value | Recommend? |
|---|---|---|---|---|
| | + | $ | ◆ | ★ |

## Daleo Upholstery

2.5    2    4    4

2269 First Avenue, New York, NY 10035
(212) 534 - 2700

*Custom upholstery*

Word is this straightforward company provides a mid- to upper-tier performance at a "reasonable price." Clients say Daleo is reliable, easy to work with and delivers a good value.

## Daniel's Custom Upholstery

3    2.5    4    4

422 East 75th Street, New York, NY 10021
(212) 249 - 5015

*Retail and trade—Slipcovers, recaning and antique furniture restoration*

While fundamentally a retail store, Daniel's is also considered a "secret and reliable source" for a number of very high-end decorators who use it primarily for slipcovers and recaning. Clients also seek out Daniel's for antique furniture restoration and fabric wall covering. Patrons may choose from a variety of frames and fabrics (books and samples available in the shop), or may bring their own fabric and ideas.

## David Haag

4.5    4    5    5

114 Horatio Street, Suite 110, New York, NY 10014
(212) 741 - 8557

*Trade only—elegant curtains and slipcovers*

The jury is in and clients declare Haag guilty of consistently pleasing them with the comfortable, casual elegance of his work. With a background in fashion design, David Haag comes highly recommended for his skills in creating window treatments and slipcovers. He is called on regularly by top designers for his "masterful job of executing curtain details." Some add that he is the only one left in New York that knows how to cut fabric the proper way. The beautiful draping of the fabric, pleating,and trimming make it very apparent that he has a background in fashion design.

He only does soft goods—curtains of all styles and levels of detail, slipcovers, tablecloths and decorative bench cushions. It's Haag's vivid appreciation for detail that keep clients wowed. They enjoy working with this reliable and responsible professionals, which may be why one decorator added, "He might be expensive, however, it is well worth it."

*"David's work has a certain style to it. His curtains are not static and contrived looking." "He has always come through for me, fulfilling unrealistic deadlines and installations." "He has great ideas and I know the end result is going to be chic." "David is very reliable and always meets our deadlines."*

## De Angelis Inc.

5    5    3.5    5

312 East 95th Street, New York, NY 10128
(212) 348 - 8225

*Trade only—High-end custom upholstery*

Clients rhapsodize about the fabulous work of De Angelis, while critics are left speechless by the equally fabulous prices. The craftsmen at De Angelis specialize in hand-done work, and clients say their pieces last forever. The service level also receives very high marks, as does the selection of fabrics and trim. Some note that this firm has an impressive showroom with hundreds of pieces to help in your selection, and that it will adjust anything. While several references suggest that comparable quality could be found elsewhere for less, many decorators think De Angelis is in a class by itself adding that it is among the top four in the city.

*"Truly extraordinary furniture at outrageous prices." "Nothing else will do for your top, top-of-the-line client." "If you have the money, do it. The quality of service is amazing." "The place to go for fancy trims and braids."*

| Quality  | Cost $ | Value ◆ | Recommend? ★ |
|---|---|---|---|

### Decorators Workshop
41 West 25th Street, New York, NY 10010
(212) 647 - 0375

*Trade only—Custom window treatments*

### DFB Sales Inc.
21-07 Borden Avenue, Long Island City, NY 11101
(718) 729 - 8310   www.DFBSales.com

*Trade only—Custom upholstery and window shades*

**3   3   4   4**

This large long-established firm manufactures and installs an impressive array of window shading and wall upholstery, predominantly with the trade in the service of notable commercial and high-end residential clients. For over 60 years references have found DFB's window shades to be especially high quality, and a good value for the price. Measurements and installations are performed by the firm's own people, who have been commended for timely service and good project management by its corporate clients. We understand one of DFB's areas of expertise is motorized shades.

### Diamint Upholstery Inc.
324 East 59th Street, New York, NY 10022
(212) 754 - 1155

*Retail and trade—Custom upholstery*

**3.5   3.5   4   4.5**

Located near the D&D building, Diamint is known to work closely in providing custom upholstery to a number of high-end interior designers. We hear that customers have had "excellent results" using the firm for slipcovers and headboards as well. For new custom furniture, Diamint provides a selection of different frames, or the client may bring in a picture of his or her own. Clients are as pleased with the firm's product as its ability to hit schedule.

### Doreen Interiors Ltd.
221 West 17th Street, New York, NY 10011
(212) 255 - 9008

*Trade only—Custom upholstery and window treatments*

**4   4   4   4.5**

Doreen proves a savvy mid-priced alternative for many of the very top decorators in the city. We're told the craftsmen at this firm show diligence and enthusiasm in their customer service and always stand by their products. We've heard that they will even jump on an airplane to the client's residence to resolve a problem or to do repairs on their own work. Some suggest that they are "over-committed and less responsive" to smaller decorators, noting that it is hard to get a call back. Doreen has a few pieces on display, but pictures and sketches are typically used to better define ideas for custom work, which usually takes about twelve weeks.

*"All of my clients enjoy having them to the job site because they exude confidence in their work and people feel comfortable with them." "Minor things are resolved without issue. I have never been disappointed."*

| | Quality | Cost | Value | Recommend? |
|---|---|---|---|---|
| | ✚ | $ | ◆ | ★ |

## E. Polarolo & Sons

| 3 | 3 | 3.5 | 4 |

213 East 120th Street, New York, NY  10035
(212) 255 - 6260

*Retail and trade—Reupholstery work and furniture restoration*

Clients tell us this high-end reupholsterer and furniture restorer is as much of "a gem" as the pieces it restores.  Mr. Polarolo comes highly praised by clients for his "attention to detail and excellent service orientation."  He not only specializes in the restoration and reupholstery of antique pieces, but performs all variants of reupholstery work.  Clients include some of the most notable antique collectors.  Richard Polarolo accommodates both the trade and retail customers, and will try to help anyone out with a quote over the phone.  Pick-up and delivery services are available for those who choose not to brave Polarolo's shop.

*"Mr. Polarolo is a pleasure to deal with. He knows antiques and takes no short cuts—unlike many other upholsterers."*

## Fabric Creations

| 4 | 3.5 | 4 | 4.5 |

45 Old Cedar Drive, Sparta, NJ  07871
(973) 726 - 7866

*Custom wall upholstery*

Fabric Creations specializes in wall upholstery.  Ralph Garcia is described as "so beautifully organized without being persnickety."  Decorators say that he knows how to deal with any fabric, from simple cottons to trickier silks.  Others add that he is the most thorough and neat practitioner they have worked with, describing his work as having perfect depth and lay, just the right amount of padding and with straight seams always turning out perfectly.  One decorator was extremely pleased with Garcia's "can do" attitude, noting a project where he wanted horsehair walls.  Garcia was not sure if he could do it, but the result was fabulous.  This extremely accommodating professional is also said to always be on time.

*"He is the master of this art."*

## Frank Herman Designs

| 4 | 3 | 4.5 | 4 |

150-03 78th Road, Flushing, NY  11367
(718) 591 - 5443

*Retail and trade—Custom upholstery and restoration*

We hear this custom upholstery firm takes pride in its work, down to the very last detail.  Frank Herman Designs does most of its work with the trade, producing top-quality custom furniture and restorations.  The highly skilled craftsmen of this firm take pride in doing all of their work by hand.  Clients seem to "feel the difference," and recommend Frank Herman Design accordingly.

*"Will really try to do whatever the client wants." "I called them to take down window treatments which they had installed five years ago and they did not even charge me."*

## French Needle

| 5 | 5 | 4 | 5 |

152 West 25th Street, 4th Floor, New York, NY  10001
(212) 647 - 0848

*Trade only—Custom curtains and wall upholstery*

With an eye for detail that would make Gustave Eiffil blush, French Needle's custom workroom is used primarily for curtains and wall upholstery by a clan of elite decorators who seek to elevate the quality of their designs to the highest point.  All exclaim the firm is best at working with complicated designs, demonstrated in both elaborate, historic Louis XIV styles and cutting-edge contemporary.

*"Fringe upon fringe, layer upon layer, they really know what they are doing." "Exquisite workmanship."*

| | Quality  | Cost $ | Value ◆ | Recommend? ★ |
|---|---|---|---|---|

### Gracious Home
3.5    3.5    4    5

1217 Third Avenue, New York, NY 10021
(212) 988 - 8990   www.gracioushome.com

*Retail—Reupholstery and window treatments*

This Upper East Side mainstay has minted a Gracious sibling at an Upper West Side Location at 1992 Broadway. While Gracious Home's furniture department does not provide custom furniture or upholstery services, resources report that its reupholstery work is quite good. The store displays a number of fabrics via books, and we are told that you may also provide your own at no additional cost. The design department provides an adequate selection of all hard and soft window treatments—ordered and custom—including laminated roller shades and a variety of curtains. In addition, the ease of one-stop shopping, with an extensive decorative hardware department, lighting, paint, bedding, bath and tabletop departments, and a fabric and window treatment department at each location keep the clients coming back "home."

### Henry B. Urban Inc./Delta Upholstery
4.5    4    4    5

423 West 55th Street, 9th Floor, New York, NY 10019
(212) 265 - 7333

*Trade only—Custom upholstery*

Blue-chip architects and red-hot decorators consider Henry B. Urban Inc./Delta Upholstery one of the best workrooms for curtains in New York. Delta Upholstery was purchased by Henry B. Urban, and now both operate as one company. This shop provides upholstery, drapery and wall-upholstery services. The double-barreled company has pleased customers for years with its incredible attention to detail and reliability.

### Henry Chan
4    3    4.5    4.5

11 East 26th Street, New York, NY 10010
(212) 689 - 1845

*Trade only—Custom upholstery*

Henry Chan's stellar reputation among the city's elite designers is as much a guarded secret the "reasonable price" he charges in comparison to his talented competition. All work is custom and includes furniture upholstery, wall upholstery and window treatments. The showroom includes over 100 pieces for clients to review, and we hear that Chan will create anything the client wants in any size, and does so with an eye to real value. Customers also mention their appreciation of the highly skilled and reliable installers.

*"Unheralded master." "Never anything less than perfect." "Can copy anything."*

### Houston Upholstery Co.
4    3.5    4    4.5

39 West 19th Street, New York, NY 10019
(212) 645 - 4032

*Trade only—Custom upholstered furniture*

Houston never has a problem. This high-end upholstery firm works exclusively with the trade, creating custom pieces for top-lining decorators and architects, many of whom have clients with a real name on the marquee. Houston prefers to do larger jobs with new pieces and steers clear of restoration. In business for 50 years, this family company has the know-how to sew up a full range of upholstery assignments, from traditional to hard-edged contemporary, "with style and grace."

*"The owner makes sure that you always leave happy and completely satisfied."*

447

| | Quality | Cost | Value | Recommend? |
|---|---|---|---|---|
| |  | $ | ◆ | ★ |

## Innovative Touch in Design

3.5   3   4   4

15 Liberty Street, Little Ferry, NJ  07643
(201) 931 - 0500

*Custom upholstery and window treatments*

Be it regarding product or service, this trade-only firm, we're told, is charmed with the right touch.  Innovative Touch provides custom upholstery, window treatments, soft goods and custom furniture to a wide range of top quality decorators. Clients are very pleased with the quality and workmanship put into the projects, and report that the service has direct involvement at all stages.  This firm is distinguished by its ability to offer a wide range of economic flexibility while still ensuring good-to-extraordinary quality with great service.  Though they do not have a showroom, this fifteen-year-old business has a huge workroom.  The staff and installers are reportedly extremely knowledgeable and take pride in their work.

*"Clients are always 100 percent satisfied." "Responsible, creative staff. It is a pleasure working with the people at Innovative Touch in Design." "The attention paid to every detail is incredible! Their workmanship is beautiful!" "We have used their services for years and rely upon them for beautiful window treatments, bed covers, etc., as well and upholstered goods that continually make us look great!"*

## Interiors by Robert

4   4   4   4.5

89-05 130th Street, Richmond Hills, NY  11418
(718) 847 - 2860

*Trade only—Custom upholstery and window treatments*

Clients enthuse this firm offers "extraordinary quality" at reasonable prices. Owner Bob Boccard is known as a "perfectionist," who, we hear, displays a strong commitment to standing behind all work that is done.  Well-respected decorators go to this firm for upholstery work, while its curtains supply some of the finest retail window displays.  The shop doesn't have a showroom, but Boccard and his staff can easily work with sketches or photos.

## Interiors by Royale

3   2.5   3   3

964 Third Avenue, New York, NY  10022
(212) 753 - 4600

*Trade only—Curtains and bedding*

Housed in this firm's shop near the D&D building, clients have discovered a good selection of fabrics and a helpful staff.  The firm does upholstery work at its workshop on Long Island and specializes in window treatments and bedding, all created custom to the client's specification.  Many of the top designers drop by this shop exclusively for draperies.  We hear the product is excellent and the timing is good, with a typical turnaround of six weeks.

## Isak & Andre Upholstery Ltd.

210 East 85th Street, New York, NY  10028
(212) 737 - 1106

*Custom upholstery*

| | Quality | Cost | Value | Recommend? |
|---|---|---|---|---|

## J. Schachter Corp.

**3  2.5  4  4**

5 Cook Street, Brooklyn, NY 11206
(718) 384 - 2732  www.schachtersdowntown.com

*Retail and trade—Custom bedding and bath*

Custom bedding is the name of the game at this firm, which creates custom comforters, pillows, shower curtains and any other items for the bedroom or bath. It also carries an extensive line of imported linens and towels, often at good discounts. The firm works with both retail clients and the trade to deliver what the client has in mind, even monogramming. References say the quality is good and the pricing is reasonable, and note that Schachter's will "happily" pick up and deliver.

## Janovic Plaza Inc.

**3  2  4  4.5**

1150 Third Avenue, New York, NY 10021
(212) 772 - 1400  www.janovic.com

*Paint, wallcoverings and window treatments*

With a multitude of locations throughout New York City, Janovic is outfitted with a kind and accommodating staff and a great selection of all varieties of hard and soft window treatments. Each has a decorator on staff to help customers with their color and window treatment choices. They tell us they were pleased with the quality of Janovic's product, and especially commend the decorator's prompt attention to requests and professional service.

Other locations in Manhattan include: 159 West 72nd Street, 2475 Broadway and 1553 Third Avenue.

*"Very professional and super to deal with." "Will highly recommend."*

## JM Upholstery

**4.5  3  5  5**

10-10 44th Avenue, 5th Floor, Long Island City, NY 11101
(718) 786 - 0104

*Trade only—Custom upholstery*

## Jonas Upholstery

**5  5  4  5**

44 West 18th Street, New York, NY 10011
(212) 691 - 2777

*Trade only—High-end upholstery and curtains*

The city's most discriminating customers can't discuss the highest-quality custom upholstery and drapery without uttering Jonas in the same breath. A substantial percentage of the top decorators agree this high-end practitioner is definitely one of their favorites, noting the personalized service, sophisticated approach, great timing and phenomenal quality. Though prices are excessive, customers know that each piece was made with quality materials and crafted with care. Many decorators enjoy bringing their clients to Jonas' workroom to see how their piece is made. One decorator described it as being like a trip to Santa's workshop—a real treat—adding that everyone is always friendly and informative and even the frames are beautiful. The firm's attention to detail is "superior" and decorators tell us that its professionals are honest and reliable. The firm will only work with the trade.

*"The most comfortable piece of furniture I have ever sat in." "I have been working with Jonas & Sons for eight years. They do 90 percent of my work with skill and quality and design that is unmatched." "They say, 'A good upholsterer makes a good decorator.' I believe that." "Everything is always just as I ordered it." "It's great to work with an upholsterer who can work in different styles to each individual taste of a client." "If one does very high-end design and quality, this is the place to go."*

449

| | Quality + | Cost $ | Value ◆ | Recommend? ★ |
|---|---|---|---|---|

### Jose Quintana
440 Lafayette Street, New York, NY 10003
(212) 358 - 0653

*Custom upholstery*

| | Quality | Cost | Value | Recommend? |
|---|---|---|---|---|
| | 4.5 | 4 | 4 | 4.5 |

### K. Flam Associates Inc.
805 East 134th Street, Bronx, NY 10454
(718) 665 - 3140

*Trade only—Contemporary custom upholstery*

| | Quality | Cost | Value | Recommend? |
|---|---|---|---|---|
| | 4.5 | 4 | 5 | 5 |

A staple (or tack in the case of custom) of New York's most celebrated interior designers with modern inclinations, K. Flam Associates sets the mark for contemporary custom upholstery and window treatments. Clients praise Kenny Flam for the attention he lavishes on clients and the job and mostly for his expertly tailored product. Before starting his own firm he worked exclusively with John Saladino for over 20 years.

*"Delivers the same quality as all of the best upholsterers, but with a modern story." "He is the best in his field." "Incredible workmanship and top-of-the-line service. Would not use anyone else."*

### Kate's Upholstery
325 East 21st Street, New York, NY 10010
(212) 674 - 8813

*Custom upholstery*

(📁 📁 📁 📁)

### La Regence
129 West 29th Street, 12th Floor, New York, NY 10001
(212) 736 - 2548

*Trade only—Curtains*

| | Quality | Cost | Value | Recommend? |
|---|---|---|---|---|
| | 5 | 4.5 | 4 | 5 |

We hear this upholsterer can make even the most simple design perfect—length, proper lining, fullness—and knows the art of draping fabrics like a couture dress. La Regence comes highly recommended by some of the top decorators for curtains and shades. The firm only offers limited upholstery as a courtesy to close-knit clients, most of whom would not consider straying. They exclaim that nothing else compares, saying "you might spend a lot of money but you will never be sorry afterwards."

*"I've used other well-respected firms and La Regence is clearly better. I really love their fabulous curtains." "It is the best investment in town." "Cost is over the top, but worth every penny." "I have never had a dissatisfied client with their curtains." "People deserve the highest quality if they buy the highest quality fabric. La Regence gets it just right."*

### Langsam & Breuer Custom Upholsterers
657 Amsterdam Avenue, New York, NY 10025
(212) 362 - 8600

*Retail—Custom upholstery*

| | Quality | Cost | Value | Recommend? |
|---|---|---|---|---|
| | 4 | 2 | 4.5 | 4.5 |

A primarily retail-based clientele delights in the professionalism exhibited by this firm. They recommend Langsam & Breuer for solid quality, reasonable prices and reliable timing for any reupholstering or custom upholstery. The firm is reputedly organized and reliable. We hear company skipper Leon Breuer provides clients plenty of personal attention and is backed by a good crew—friendly and hard working and apparently loyal. Clients tell us they have seen the same faces working at his shop "all these past years." While the firm does not discount for decorators, its upstanding service keeps this firm's clients coming back.

*"Leon Breuer is charming, honest and flexible. He works with me directly, never through an assistant." "Very pleasant people to deal with—cooperative and*

*dependable on all counts." "I have sent many to friends to Langsam & Breuer and they are just as enthusiastic and pleased as I am." "A pleasure to work with." "The fact that we've gone to him three times attests to our confidence in Leon's work." "Leon Breuer has upholstered or reupholstered my entire brownstone. He has gone out of his way to deliver on time and made necessary alterations."*

## Le Décor Francais      4.5    3    4    4.5
1006 Lexington Avenue, New York, NY 10021
(212) 734 - 0032   www.ledecorfrancais.com
*Retail and trade—Custom upholstery*

The beauty and unusual quality of Jacqueline Coumans, continentally styled work has clients remarking 'ooh-la-la.' This high-end custom upholsterer, with a workroom staff trained in Paris, creates for retail clients and the trade at the same price. She specializes in a wide range of custom projects, including furniture, window treatments, pillows and lampshades. Le Décor Francais also offers its own collection, with a wide selection of uniquely continental fabrics and trimmings. Coumans will give rough estimates over the phone and while she is known to shower clients with attention, turnaround can leave a pressed-for-time project a bit high and dry. Still they tell us her talent is beaucoup worth the wait.

*"Slow but truly beautiful."*

## Lewis Mittman      4    4    4    4
979 Third Avenue, New York, NY 10022
(212) 888 - 5580

*Trade only—Custom upholstery and furniture design*

## Lore Decorators      3.5    2    4    4.5
2201 Third Avenue, New York, NY 10035
(212) 534 - 2170   www.loreupholstery.baweb.com
*Retail and trade—Custom window treatments, upholstery and restoration*

"Competent, highly creative and a joy to work with," clients will recommend Lore to anyone. This family business professes over 40 years of providing custom window treatments, along with reupholstery, custom upholstery and antique furniture restoration services. A great deal of clients mention they were "very satisfied" with Lore's "extremely helpful and time-efficient" service and the "beautiful" finished product. We're told principal Florance Cangelosi will drop by a client's home to discuss fabrics and Lore pick-ups and delivers all pieces in the time frame promised. In addition, clients say "their workers who came to my home were friendly and on time." We hear Cangelosi and crew make a point of following up with clients. Lore does a substantial amount of its work with some of the top interior designers and architects.

*"Lore Decorators provided top-notch service from top to bottom, from the selling process to manufacturing to installation. I would not ordinarily respond to surveys such as this, but I would like anyone else looking for upholstery work or window treatments to have the benefit of my experience with Lore." "They kept to their word." "Lore Decorators is a very professional and dependable company. The quality of work is at a very high standard." "They even came to our apartment to pick up the fabric." "Florence was VERY helpful in helping me choose a fabric for my chairs. We went through many different swatches of colors, textures and prints, and I think I now sit on the best!!!"*

| | Quality + | Cost $ | Value ◆ | Recommend? ★ |
|---|---|---|---|---|

## Luther Quintano Upholstery

| | 4.5 | 4 | 4.5 | 5 |
|---|---|---|---|---|

151 West 26th Street, 4th Floor, New York, NY 10001
(212) 462 - 2033
*Mostly trade—Custom upholstery*

Luther Quintano's performance in the highest-quality custom upholstery rivals the best of the bunch for less maintenance, according to sources. This practitioner, trained at the heralded Jonas Upholstery, comes with excellent recommendations from many of the top decorators, who have noted that Quintano can also do wood carving and is great at creating reproductions to match a client's existing pieces. Located in a spacious industrial loft, Quintano's showroom displays a huge array of choices. Many clients are also quite happy that Quintano has now started to do curtains, too. They commend the firm's professionalism, capacity to "do anything you want" and diligent follow-through. Quintano's incredibly personable nature also wins client comments.

*"Very good job." "His work is definitely worth every penny." "Can make any frame—as good as any one else's."*

## Maglio & Sons

548 West 28th Street, New York, NY 10001
(212) 244 - 4644
*Retail—custom upholstery*

Maglio & Sons is associated with high quality custom upholstery provided with professional service for retail clients at a reportedly reasonable cost. We're told the firm offers a furniture line to choose from.

## Manhattan Glass & Shade Co.

| | 3 | 4 | 3 | 3 |
|---|---|---|---|---|

1297 Third Avenue, New York, NY 10021
(212) 288 - 5616
*Retail and trade—Window treatments*

Trade and retail clients alike are drawn to Manhattan Glass & Shade for window treatments. We hear a wide variety of custom products is available, including hard and soft goods. The quality is agreed to be excellent, but dissenters feel the firm proves less inspired when working with regular clients than decorators. Most however, "think they are great" and were "extremely impressed with the level of service and expertise." The floor staff has received numerous compliments and the installation is regarded as quick, but returning phone calls have left clients hewing "pleas for help."

*"Excellent work, very efficient—if there is a problem they fix it." "My window treatments are outstanding. MS&G's staff was incredible. They made the whole process a pleasant experience." "We had a few out of the ordinary installations which required a little support and advice (but by no means rocket science). After several attempts of calling (with no response to myself or my architect) and dropping by to speak with each of two named proprietors, I vowed to myself to go elsewhere." "It took endless pleading to get them to fix my blinds, which did not work one week after installation." "Easy and knowledgeable."*

## Martin Albert Interiors

| | 2.5 | 2.5 | 3 | 3 |
|---|---|---|---|---|

9 East 19th Street, New York, NY 10003
(212) 673 - 8000
*Custom upholstery and window treatments*

Sources say this firm is best suited for kids' rooms. Middle-of-the-road quality coupled with long lead times and measurement mistakes have dampened designer confidence in larger projects. However, most of the firm's work is still with the trade, doing primarily custom reupholstery and custom-covered furniture. Martin Albert will also do slipcovers and both hard and soft window treatments. Several recent projects have been accomplished at large New York hotels.

*"Very pleasant to work with." "Defensive when work is wrong." "It took them six months to produce a very simple drape and window cushion. Made me look bad."*

| | Quality <br> ✚ | Cost <br> $ | Value <br> ◆ | Recommend? <br> ★ |
|---|---|---|---|---|

## Mary Bright Inc.

4.5    4.5    4    4.5

636 Broadway, New York, NY  10012
(212) 677 - 1970

*Retail and trade—Custom window treatments*

Mary Bright is said to be "the ultimate for exceptional contemporary lines with flair," according to many very high-end architects. Working with both retail clients and the trade, she amazes all with her creativity and innovative utilization of fabrics in the design and fabrication of draperies. We are told she is resolute in her vision of the contemporary genre of her work, and clients say she is always right. Bright's superior service is said to be worth the high costs.

*"Very high-end and equally expensive." "A very creative, interesting person." "Contemporary designs. No swags. No chintz."*

## Master Craftsman

2269 First Avenue, New York, NY  10035
(212) 876 - 6642

*Custom upholstery*

## Miracle Workroom

236 First Street, Yonkers, NY  10704
(914) 423 - 7408

*Custom upholstery*

## New York Drapery (NYD)

4    4    4    4

147 West 25th Street, New York, NY  10001
(212) 229 - 1533

*Trade only—Custom curtains*

Top-of-the-line curtains and intricately detailed handwork have prompted many of the highest-end decorators to sit up and take notice. While NYD is described as "very expensive," the firm gets "tremendous kudos" from clients for its "extraordinary work."

## Peter J. Rizzotto Co. Inc.

4.5    4    4.5    5

30 West 24th Street, 5th Floor, New York, NY  10011
(212) 645 - 1578

*Trade only—High-end custom upholstery and window treatments*

Decorators say that the old-fashioned craftsmanship that comes out of this shop is "hard to find anywhere else." Pete Rizzotto, former lead at "the old De Angelis," is known for his hand-crafted custom-upholstered furniture and window treatments. Everything is created with incredible care, with no shortcuts taken along the way. The shop invites both designers and architects and their clients to visit each of their showrooms so that they may examine the process for themselves. Rizzotto takes pride in the fact that whether he does one room or an entire residence, furniture and draperies are always completed on time. We hear that though his work is "quite expensive," the quality makes it worth every penny.

## Phoenix Custom Furniture Ltd.

4    3.5    4    4

119 West 25th Street, 8th Floor, New York, NY  10001
(212) 727 - 2273

*Trade only—Custom upholstery*

We understand Phoenix did all of the work for the late Renny Salzman, and many decorators of note value the firm for its reliable service and ability to do work "one-half step down" from the very best at quite reasonable prices. The firm creates custom-upholstered furniture for the trade in a variety of styles, providing samples from its showroom or using concepts from the client. Most find the company very "skillful," "consistent" and "easy to work with." The frames it uses are all kiln-dried maple, doweled and corner-blocked. It offers two lines of products— one regular line and one very high-end that includes horsehair fill and other top features. All custom work takes about 8 to 10 weeks to complete.

### Ray Murray Inc.   4   4   4.5   5
121 East 24th Street, New York, NY  10010
(212) 477 - 2121

*Trade only—Custom upholstery and curtains*

Clients confirm this shop does "fabulous work," with "meticulous attention" given to the creation of its product, including many dressmaker details. Dealing with many top designers, Ray Murray specializes in fine custom draperies, upholstery, wall upholstery, headboards and other window treatments. While some mention prices are "a bit high," they add the quality justifies it. Clients find the firm to be highly service-oriented and extraordinarily dependable. We hear that it is developing a second line at a more reasonable price point.

*"Dependable, excellent quality that will not break the bank."*

### Richard's Interior Design   3   3   3   3.5
1390 Lexington Avenue, New York, NY  10128
(212) 831 - 9000   www.richardsinteriordesign.com

*Retail—Custom upholstery and window treatments*

Richard's may not be the ultimate in quality, but New Yorkers who have been using it for upholstery and window treatments for over 20 years recommend it highly for its "wonderful service." The firm has a staff of decorators available for consultations and home visits. Richard's has a good sample of fabrics and upholstery frames on-site. Many of the fabrics the firm carries are produced just for Richard's in the same mills as the big-ticket D&D showrooms, but at much lower prices. (Note, however, that Richard's charges a premium if you bring your own fabrics for curtains or upholstery.) Some mention that this firm is very accommodating in its ability to change the frames to suit the interests of its clients, who include Donna Karan, Stone Phillips, Bette Midler and Bill Murray. Many references praise the firm's "very good solid work," and it's knowledgeable owner, who "takes great pride in the work of the company." Occasional snafus relating to measurement occur, seam and delivery issues are swiftly ironed out.

*"Reliable, dependable service in a pleasant, easy manner." "They offer many valuable suggestions but do not seek to impose their taste on the project. They have been most satisfactory to work with. Any minor problems have been resolved without difficulty." "Well trained and very professional staff." "I could probably find cheaper but they are cooperative and local."*

### Robert Cappa   3   2   5   5
87-15 115th Street, Richmond Hill, NY   11418
(718) 847 - 6030

*Mostly retail—Custom upholstery and curtains*

All one needs is a simple sketch or drawing and this third-generation uphol-sterer can bring that idea to life. We hear he will make house calls, to measure, and brings his pleasing demeanor with him. Most of the work he does is retail—evenly distributed between custom upholstery and window treatments. In the process of computerization, and boasting its own building and trucks, clients tell us, Cappa's operation is as professional as they come. Cappa's prices are known to be quite good.

*"Friendly, listens well." "What a helpful, organized and friendly company."*

### Sandringham Ltd.                    4       3       4       5
224 West 29th Street, 8th Floor, New York, NY 10001
(212) 594 - 9210

*Trade only—Custom upholstery and window treatments*

We hear principal Eric Dahl's agreeable and professional manner complements his firm's flexibility, followup and exceptional skill. Sandringham is a popular choice with many high-end designers for custom upholstery and window treatments. Due to their wonderful quality, they can be quite busy juggling many different projects. Nevertheless, clients report that this firm is very conscientious and reliable with deadlines. One decorator adds that Sandringham always comes through for his office, often on short notice, and the quality of the work is never sacrificed.

*"Especially ready and willing to make last-minute changes that clients inevitably request." "Eric, just a dear. Nice ideas." "Very personable, helpful and easy to work with." "Pleasure to do business with." "Very competitive with excellent capacity to produce anything I sketch."*

### Simon's Upholstery                 3.5     3.5     4       4
601 West 26th Street, 16th Floor, New York, NY 10001
(212) 727 - 7106

*Retail and trade—Custom upholstery and curtains*

We hear this shop does it all, working with both retail and trade customers on custom upholstery and curtains. Its large showroom has over 100 pieces and pro-vides a display of its furniture and window treatments. Decorators and retail clients alike describe Simon's as "upper quality with decent pricing."

*"People who work for him are really sweet. Like a family."*

### Soft Touch Interiors               4       2       5       5
115 Labau Avenue, Staten Island, NY 10301
(718) 448 - 1028

*Retail and trade—Slipcovers, window treatments and bedding*

After 30 years, Harry Berkowitz still has the exuberance and patience to deal with his varied clientele. Specializing in slipcovers, he arrives in your home, fab-ric in hand, knees padded, pins on magnet and very large scissors in his back pocket, ready to work his magic. (He will cover just about anything.) We hear that ideas and concepts are thoroughly discussed and approved before a stitch is sewn. Harvey's wife, Maureen, oversees her husband's endeavors as well as designing draperies, bedspreads and other soft treatments such as lampshades. A recent project, where she draped an outdoor gazebo, appeared on HGTV.

Decorators look to Soft Touch mainly for reupholstery and slipcovers, and describe this team as "efficient, brilliant and a joy to work with," noting that they found the quality and workmanship to be excellent. We hear the staff provides the perfect compliment to Berkowitz's fabulous design concepts and eye for color. KB 2000.

### Sterling Upholstery, Inc.          ▱       ▱       ▱       ▱
135 West 27th Street, 3rd Floor, New York, NY 10001
(212) 8243 - 1878

*Custom upholstery and window treatments*

| | Quality | Cost | Value | Recommend? |
|---|---|---|---|---|
| | + | $ | ◆ | ★ |

## Thomas Pizzillo & Son      5    4.5    5    5
225 East 24th Street, 3rd Floor, New York, NY 10010
(212) 889 - 7070

*Trade only—High-end custom upholstery*

This family-run business has been wowing New York clients for three generations with its top-of-the-line upholstery work, characterized by hand stitching, hand-tied springs and hair construction. Frequently partnered with the absolute best decorators in town, Pizzillo also impresses customers with its "singular focus on customer satisfaction" and the outstanding quality of the custom pieces it creates. Many sources mention their amazement at the speed at which this firm will come to your house and immediately resolve any outstanding issues. Though most of its work is done with the trade, Pizzillo will take on larger retail projects.

"Used by the highest-quality decorators." "They are wonderful, absolute TOP-quality work." "Of unequalled quallity."

## Trade France      4    4    4.5    4.5
127 Madison Avenue, New York, NY 10016
(212) 758 - 8330   www.tradefranceusa.com

*Retail and trade—Custom upholstery*

This firm earns compliments for its ability to stitch and summon exactly what a client envisions, at a level some top-end decorators say almost rivals the best quality in the city. They turn to Trade France for curtains, upholstery and reupholstery. Clients describe this firm as creative with a French flair, noting that it provides "unique and interesting frames" and a wide range of fabric choices. With all work done on site in midtown, Trade France has also been commended for its promptness in delivery, excellent followup and highly skilled workroom, which we hear has incredibly knowledgeable personnel and is able to provide fabulous quality. Most sources also add that working with Trade France could not have been easier, describing the firm's practice of home consultations and willingness to fax sketches back and forth with the client until it turns out "just right."

"The highest quality and creativity makes for a perfect product." "Costly but not insane." "Developed relationship with workman. When I was desperate they came through for me." "Ultimate pleasure at all times." "Very efficient people. Very helpful, creative, competent."

## TriBeCa Upholstery      ▱  ▱  ▱  ▱
103 Reade Street, New York, NY 10013
(212) 349 - 3010

*Trade only—Reupholstery and window treatments*

## Upholstery Unlimited      4.5    4    4    5
138 West 25th Street, New York, NY 10001
(212) 924 - 1230

*Retail and trade—Custom upholstery and curtains*

This shop's "very kind and nice" approach to its clients and superb product has garnered Upholstery Unlimited compliments. A circle of the most discriminating decorators and showrooms in New York, including Brunschwig & Fils rate the firm among the trade's best. Its large workroom provides an opportunity for clients to acquire a sense of the workmanship and style on which Upholstery Unlimited has built its reputation. Clients say that the work is quite expensive, but well worth it.

"Not the cheapest, but the best."

## Versailles Drapery & Upholstery      4.5    4    4    4.5
37 East 18th Street, New York, NY 10003
(212) 533 - 2059

*Trade only—Custom curtains and upholstery*

Versailles' all hand-stitched work keeps it a major destination for many decorators, who praise this custom workroom for its "absolutely remarkable quality" in creating custom draperies and upholstery. Clients also remark upon the shop's experienced and attentive service.

### Werner Ritter, Inc.    4    4    4    5
147 West 35th Street, 11th Floor, New York, NY 10001
(212) 967 - 8717

*Mostly trade-Custom upholstery and curtains*

Clients mention that Werner Ritter's experience "truly shines through" in the finished product. While his firm is most often recruited by the top of the trade, it will work with high-end retail clients who have a specific concept in mind. Customers tell us they are extremely pleased with Ritter's thoughtful and attentive consultation visits. They especially admire his ability to fashion a great product from a simple sketch. While most admire the installation quality, some feel that the firm's timeliness would be better if it had a stronger back office. Not thought to be the cheapest contender, Ritter's work is clearly well worth it.

*"I wouldn't dream of going anywhere else." "Always busy, but manages to fit it all in." "Very reasonable timing and extremely reliable installers for window work."*

### White Workroom    4.5    4    4    5
62 White Street, Suite 5, New York, NY 10013
(212) 941 - 5910

*Trade only—Custom window treatments*

Top-flight designers say it "doesn't get any better than this" when it comes to curtains, White Workroom's specialty. The firm understands fabric in this context, we hear, and offers the ultimate in service for retail and custom work.

*"They are extraordinary when it comes to curtains."*

### Windows Walls & More    3.5    3.5    4    4.5
1595 Second Avenue, New York, NY 10028
(212) 472 - 4800

*Wall upholstery, window treatments, furniture reupholstery*

Described as "solid, helpful, reasonable and reacheable," designers come to this small shop for upholstered walls, window seats, custom window treatments and its reupholstery service. Windows Walls & More provides an abundant selection of fabrics, from basic to Ralph Lauren and some other "top" lines. While the quality is deemed "middle-of-the-road," the staff is as "sweet and friendly" as they come.

### Zelaya Interiors    3.5    3    4    4.5
7321 Broadway, North Bergen, NJ 07047
(201) 868 - 3818

*Retail—Custom upholstery and window treatments*

Trade and retail clients say Zelaya Interiors delivers just the quality one expects of a high-end service professional. The firm specializes in custom upholstery and a full range of window treatments, including some custom work in a private line of shades. Sources say Zelaya, always quite busy, is "great if you are not in a rush." However, we hear that a real effort is made to come through for long-standing customers. Zelaya is known to return extra fabric to the client, and to produce a tasteful end result for a palatable price.

*"Overall a very good experience." "Great upholstery. Great find for the price." "Sent me oodles of my fabric back!" "My designer wanted to charge me $7,000 more for the same job that Zelaya charged me." "Above average work. Great upholstery. Not cheap, not expensive."*

## Hiring a Window Washer

Everyone just adores a magnificent view, and keeping the sites crystal clear in the beautiful edifices in and around sooty New York requires upkeep from professional window cleaners. Window washing may seem like a straightforward project, but because city buildings come in a variety of shapes, sizes and conditions, there are many variables for your service provider to deal with. You'll want to review your situation with the cleaning service before it shows up to do the actual cleaning.

### Do Your Homework

Before contacting any window washers, you should note some facts about your windows. How many do you have? Are they storm windows, French windows or just regular ones? Do they have window guards? How many have grates? Are there panes? How many? Do the windows open in, slide up and down, tip out? Are they old or new? Are they dirty enough that they'll need to be power-washed or scraped? Does your building have hooks outside the window to which the washer can connect himself and his equipment? If so, are they all intact? Taking these factors into consideration, the service provider should give you a rough "guesstimate" over the phone. If you omit any information, the work may end up costing more than the original quote once they come for the formal estimate.

It's customary for window washers to provide a free estimate, but you may want to confirm this on the phone with the service provider, too. Once they inspect the job to be done, they should be able to provide you with a written estimate. Getting the estimate in writing will help prevent unexpected charges later. For example, the service provider could claim that the job was more involved than expected, and try to charge a higher fee after the work is done.

### What Should I Expect?

You'll also want to ask the service provider a few questions before signing any contracts. Inquire about the length of time they have been in business (the longer, the better), where most of their customers are located and whether they can provide references. The references will help you get an idea of how reliable they are: how long it takes to schedule an appointment, whether they get the work done on time and thoroughly, whether they clean up after themselves. We discovered that the window washers we listed didn't vary enormously—you might have to wait longer for an appointment with one company than another, but they all received good reviews from customers.

Be sure that your service provider is fully insured and can show proof of worker's compensation and liability insurance. If they do not have this coverage, you may be responsible for any accidents that happen on your property. There is no specific license or certification for window cleaning companies other than filing to operate as a business with the Department of Labor.

### On Cost

There are three general methods of pricing: per window, per job or per hour with an estimate of the time necessary to complete the job. In addition, some companies have minimums and/or charge for estimates. The most common method of pricing is a basic rate per window that is usually based on window size. It is a good idea to inquire about a discount if you have a larger job (20 or more windows), as many vendors will negotiate a better price if there is a substantial amount of work to be done. For a basic 6-over-6 window (a window that has two frames that slide up or down, each with six separate panes) with no window guards, paint or unusual amounts of dirt, you can expect a price range from $4 to $15 per window, with the majority of vendors charging $8 to $10. However, factors like location (Are you in the city or borough?), type of window (Do you have thermal panes, storm windows, French, etc.?), type of building (Do you live in a high-rise or a low-rise building?), accessibility (Are the windows hard to reach? Do you have hooks or crevices for the window washer to attach himself to?) and amount of dirt should be considered and discussed as these might affect the final estimate.

## Preparing for Window-Washing Day

Once you have set up an appointment, clear a path to the windows to prevent mishaps. Move that antique table with the priceless lamp. Clear objects that may obstruct access from sills and benches. Draw back your curtains and window treatments. Most service providers will show the utmost respect for your home and will protect your carpets and walls from drips and spills. If it makes you more comfortable, schedule free time for yourself on window-washing day so you can keep an eye on the process.

## Cleaning Calendar

A professional window cleaning twice a year is usually sufficient, but if your residence is particularly exposed to the elements of city life you may need cleaning more often. Spring and fall are generally the busiest times of the year for this industry: An early spring cleaning will remove any dirt and grime left by winter rains, snow and frost, and a scrub in the fall will wash away spring and summer's pollen, bugs and dirt. Be sure to call well in advance if you want your windows cleaned at peak times.

## Something Extra

Window cleaners often offer a variety of other services, from cleaning screens and blinds to waxing and sanding floors. They might pressure-wash canopies, awnings, sidewalks, garages and greenhouses; do heavy-duty cleaning of gutters, carpets, upholstery and appliances; some do basic handyman services, house painting and clean-up after renovations. If you are pleased with the company, you may have another project for them to do. Now that you can see through your windows again, you might notice all kinds of things.

### Tips for Washing Windows
### Between Professional Service Calls

- ✧ Never wash windows in the bright sunlight. They'll dry too fast and carry a streaky residue.
- ✧ Use a squeegee instead of paper towels.
- ✧ For best results, skip the store-bought spray cleaner and use a mixture of one cup white vinegar diluted in a gallon of warm water.
- ✧ Sponge the cleaning solution onto the window then drag the squeegee across the glass. Wipe the squeegee blade with a damp cloth after each swipe.
- ✧ For extra shine, rub window glass with a clean blackboard eraser after cleaning.
- ✧ If you absolutely *don't* do windows, share these tips with your housekeeper.

## Window Washers

| | Quality | Cost | Value | Recommend? |

### AAA Window Cleaning                    3    2.5    4.5    4
223 East 85th Street, New York, NY  10028
(212) 249 - 7186
*Residential window cleaning*

Talk about standing the test of time.  This family business has been brightening New Yorkers' windows since its founding in 1930.  AAA serves mainly residential clients and only works in Manhattan (below 111th Street on the East Side and 110th street on the West Side).  Pricing is per window, with factors such as size and location considered in the final estimate.

Known as pleasant and professional, this firm has served clients all over Manhattan for 71 years.  Customers say they are extremely satisfied with AAA's work and continue to use the company year after year.

*"Personable, nice and courteous."  "Extremely professional people."*

### American Cleaning Service               3    2.5    4    4
200 West 24th Street, New York, NY  10011
(212) 242 - 8484
*Residential and commercial window cleaning*

American Cleaning Service was established in 1952 and serves mostly commercial clients with an occasional residential account.  With fifteen full-time employees, the firm works in Manhattan and the surrounding boroughs and provides additional services such as blind and curtain cleaning, janitorial services for offices and general cleaning services for households.  The staff will even clean floors and carpets.  The company is fully insured and gives free estimates.

### Apple Window Cleaning                   2.5    2.5    3.5    3
305 West 18th Street, Suite 3, New York, NY  10011
(212) 620 - 0708
*Commercial and residential window cleaning, general cleaning services*

Apple Window Cleaning has been brightening views in the Big Apple since its establishment in 1992.  The firm serves commercial, residential, industrial and maintenance-contract clients throughout Manhattan.  In addition to window cleaning, which is priced per window, this company also offers floor waxing, carpet care, upholstery, blind and curtain cleaning as well as post-renovation cleanup.  Apple Window also pressure-washes canopies and awnings.  References praise the company's professional demeanor and efficient service.  They are also one of the few firms in the city that provides 24-hour service to its customers.

*"Responsive.  Professional and neat."*

### Belnord Window Cleaning Co.             3    2.5    4.5    5
322 Eighth Avenue, New York, NY  10001
(212) 787 - 4969
*Commercial and residential window cleaning*

Solid and reliable are some of the adjectives used to describe this company.  Belnord has a loyal following of both residential and commercial clients in the

Manhattan area, where the company conducts most of its business. Aside from its high-end residential patrons, Belnord includes Harry Winston among its faithful commercial clientele and has been cleaning the store's windows for the past ten years. Sources appreciate the firm's moderate prices and the efficient service that goes with it. Pricing is per window.

*"Sense of humor, yet professional." "Helpful and pleasant."*

### Blue Chip Building Maintenance Inc.          4.5     3     5     4.5
1133 Broadway, New York, NY  10010
(212) 741 - 0008

*Commercial and residential window cleaning*

With a ten-year history of brightening Manhattan's windows, it's no wonder that Blue Chip is a favorite among its satisfied clients. Though mainly a commercial cleaning company, it also serves some residential clients. Aside from window cleaning, the company also does commercial cleaning and building maintenance. They work throughout Manhattan, particularly the Upper East and Upper West Sides for residential projects.

### Careful Cleaning Contractors          3     2.5     4     3
153 Lincoln Avenue, Bronx, NY  10454
(718) 665 - 8314

*Commercial and residential window cleaning*

Since opening its doors in the 1930s, Careful Cleaning Contractors has been satisfying its residential and commercial clients throughout Manhattan. Unlike other window washing companies where prices for windows vary according to size, location or type, this firm charges one flat rate per window of any type or size.

Clients appreciate this company's thorough work and professional attitude. Indeed, this firm has established itself as a dependable window washing service that also offers extermination services.

*"Polite and thorough." "Did a good job."*

### Clear View Window Cleaning Co.          4     2     5     4
450 East 81st Street, New York, NY  10028
(212) 737 - 2913

*Residential window cleaning*

True to its name, Clear View has been giving Manhattanites a better and cleaner view since opening its doors (and windows) in 1929. Mainly serving commercial and residential clients in the Yorkville area, the workmen will also accommodate customers in other areas of the city. The company, along with its sister company, Frank's Window Cleaning also provides additional services that include floor waxing, rug cleaning and general cleaning services.

Insiders tell us they love this firm's reasonable and flat-rate pricing (one rate for any size or type of window) as well as their thorough work. Customers also appreciate the company's diligent followups and organized routine during projects.

*"Quiet. Low key. They do their work and leave." "Very professional. Someone always answers the phones." "Neat and punctual. They get the job done."*

### Crystal Globe Windows Inc.          3     2     4     4
233 East 60th Street, New York, NY  10022
(212) 533 - 6712

*Commercial and residential window cleaning*

Crystal Globe has been providing clients crysal clear windows since its founding in 1993. Owner Igor Tshem exclusively serves Manhattan residential and commercial clients, including high-rise buildings. Aside from window washing, Crystal Globe also cleans screens, blinds, awnings and restores glass. Most of the company's work is on the Upper East Side and Crystal Globe is licensed, bonded and insured. Pricing is per window and there is a moderate minimum amount required. Clients say they appreciate the firm's reasonable prices and efficient and prompt service.

## Dezel Building Services                    4      2.5      4      4
767 Lexington Avenue, New York, NY  10021
(212) 751 - 3005
*General cleaning and flooring services*

We're told Dezel is pleasant to work with, dependable and responsive. Since its founding in 1951, Dezel has been serving both residential and commercial Manhattan clients, including some in upscale buildings on Central Park West and Fifth Avenue. The company also serves areas in Queens, Brooklyn, the Bronx and the Hamptons. The firm has since expanded, creating a sister company, Dezel Floors which is a full-service flooring store. In addition to window washing, the company offers a variety of other services, such as carpet cleaning, general housekeeping, pre- or postmove cleaning and postconstruction cleanup. Satisfied clients have been working with this firm for years and delight in its efficient service and moderate prices that go along with it.

*"Very happy with them." "Have been using them for years and will continue to do so."*

## Frank's Window Cleaning                    3.5     2.5      4      4
450 East 81st Street, New York, NY  10028
(212) 288 - 4631
*Residential window cleaning*

Described as relaxed, but professional and knowledgeable, this family-owned firm has been winning over fans in Manhattan since its establishment in 1929. Now second generation Richard Frank owns and manages Frank's Window Cleaning, concentrating on residential customers (over 90 percent of its business). While the firm mainly serves the Upper East Side, its servicemen will work in other areas of the city as well. The firm also provides additional services such as floor waxing, rug shampooing, wall washing and general cleaning. Clients say they love the quality of Frank's work and consider his prices fair.

*"Quick, helpful, and very reasonable." "Once you hook up with these guys, you will never think again about using someone else." "Neat. Punctual."*

| | Quality | Cost | Value | Recommend? |
|---|---|---|---|---|

## Franklin Madison Building Maintenance Co. Inc.

**3.5    2    4.5    5**

50 East 66th Street, Suite A, New York, NY 10021
(212) 517 - 9797

*Commercial and residential cleaning services*

One of New York's oldest window washing companies, Franklin Madison Maintenance Systems continues to satisfy Manhattanites since its establishment in 1923 by John Stadnyk. Now owned and managed by his grandson and namesake, John, this company also provides services like general office and household cleaning, rug shampooing, floor waxing and facade, sidewalk and canopy power washing. Clients say they appreciate the company's prompt and efficient service at a moderate price.

*"Very satisfied." "As of now, I would not use anyone else."*

## Johnny's Window Cleaning Inc.

**3.5    3    4    4.5**

4459 Broadway, New York, NY 10040
(212) 942 - 0464

*Residential window cleaning*

With more than fifteen years of service to customers in Manhattan, this firm is known for its high-quality work. Although Johnny's serves mostly high-end residential clients, the company also has a number of commercial accounts, which keep this company under contract for months. Much of Johnny's work is on the Upper East Side—however, the firm does serve clients in other neighborhoods throughout the city as well. One measure of the firm's reputation is that a large number of prestigious buildings along Fifth Avenue have relied on Johnny's work for more than ten years.

## Kirk Window Cleaning Co.

**3.5    3    4    3**

123-25 82nd Avenue, Kew Gardens, NY 11415
(212) 353 - 7780

*Commercial and residential window cleaning, flooring services*

Clients have been turning to Stanley Kirk and his team for a better view since 1970. Sources say although the firm does not provide pricing over the phone, the workmen are willing to stop by to give an estimate. Kirk Window also gives discounts on projects that involve cleaning a sizable number of windows. In addition to windows, this company also offers an array of flooring services such as sanding, cleaning and waxing. We hear that this firm is reputable and dependable, serving both commercial and residential customers mainly—but not exclusively—on the Upper East Side.

## Metropolitan Cleaning

**2    2    4    4**

200 West 24th Street, New York, NY 10011
(212) 741 - 0541

*Window and carpet cleaning*

A veteran of the window washing industry, Metropolitan has been serving Manhattan for twelve years. Though mainly a commercial company serving building management firms, this company also has a strong residential following. Clients appreciate this firm's good quality of service and the reasonable prices that accompany it.

### New York Apartment Cleaning

3     1.5     5     3

325 East 88th Street, New York, NY 10128
(212) 534 - 5557

*Residential cleaning*

One of the oldest window cleaning companies in the city, New York Apartment Cleaning was established in 1968 and continues to satisfy residential and commercial clients in Manhattan. We hear that the company will clean anything in your apartment, and sources report that its prices are extremely reasonable—the firm charges by the hour rather than per window. Satisfied customers appreciate the firm's efficient and prompt service, reliability and pleasant demeanor.

*"Very organized." "Good work ethic."*

### Prestige Window Cleaning Co.

3.5     2.5     4     5

408 Woolley Avenue, Staten Island, NY 10314
(212) 517 - 0873

*Residential window cleaning*

Known as polite and easy to work with, Tom Lorenzo can boast of 38 years of experience prior to creating his own company in 1987. Lorenzo works mostly in Manhattan, particularly on the Upper East Side. He works mainly with residential clients and also does residential high rises. Pricing is per window and there is a minimum fee for every project.

Since Lorenzo does most of the work himself, this firm scores high points among his clients who appreciate the personalized service and attention he provides. Sources also describe him as polite, responsive and prompt.

*"Fantastic—tidy and quick." "A real people person." "Special. Cool." "Easy to work with." "Very fair and reasonable. Returned my call within hours."*

### Red Ball Window Cleaning 〰

2     2     3     3

221 East 85th Street, New York, NY 10028
(212) 861 - 7686

*Residential window cleaning*

This family-run business has been a Manhattan fixture for 62 years. Red Ball, along with its sister company AAA Window Cleaning, serves mostly residential clients throughout Manhattan and some parts of the Bronx, Brooklyn and Queens.

While some report delays, spotty service and lack of responsiveness, others compliment the firm's work and reliability and confirm this with repeat business.

*"Excellent service." "Prompt, neat and responsive." "I waited several weeks for someone to show up." "They left halfway through the job with issues over window guards."*

### Shields Window Cleaning 〰

2.5     3     3     3.5

31 Bedford Street, New York, NY 10014
(212) 929 - 5396

*Residential window cleaning*

Shields Window shields Manhattanites' windows from dirt, dust and other elements that block a beautiful view. In business for fourteen years, this company serves mainly residential clients in Manhattan as well as some outer boroughs in New York. Generally known as reliable, prompt and through, the company has built a strong following of loyal clients. Recently, some references have noticed a change in the firm's efficiency and easygoing demeanor, others report that they are very pleased with Shields' work and recommend it without reservation.

*"High quality of work. I recommend them highly." "Efficient. Worked out issues well." "Used to be easy going and pleasant."*

| | Quality + | Cost $ | Value ◆ | Recommend? ★ |
|---|---|---|---|---|

## Skylight Window Cleaning

| | 3 | 2.5 | 4 | 3 |

3 West 46th Street, Suite 311, New York, NY  10036
(212) 721 - 7889

*Residential and commercial window cleaning*

Skylight has been brightening Manhattan's windows since its establishment thirteen years ago. This small firm serves mostly residential clients and a few commercial customers and residential high rises. Pricing is per window and the final estimate would depend on factors like size, condition and location. True to its name, the firm also cleans skylights and greenhouses.

Most references tell us they have come to expect professional and prompt service from this company. We also hear that the company is cooperative and organized.

*"Neat. Clean. Punctual." "Used them several times."*

## Steven Windows Co.

| | 4.5 | 2.5 | 5 | 5 |

342 West 71st Street, New York, NY  10023
(212) 595 - 6620

*Commercial and residential window cleaning*

This window-cleaning company has accumulated some very devoted celebrity clients, including one who flies the principal out to Beverly Hills periodically to take care of his West Coast panes. We hear Steven Windows will cheerfully clean windows for all clients near and far, from Manhattan to Queens to New Jersey to the West Coast. Available for service seven days a week, insiders advise potential clients to call Steven Windows about two weeks in advance to set a date. The firm is owned and run by Steven Trobish who has nine years of experience behind him. Installing and removing air conditioners, repairing glassworks, and doing general housecleaning are some of the additional services that this company provides.

*"Dependable, trustworthy and hardworking." "Simply charming." "Very professional." "Good people." "Used him for several years. Would not consider using anyone else."*

## Window Cleaning Services

| | 5 | 2 | 5 | 5 |

3224 Grand Concourse, Suite F22, Bronx, NY  10458
(917) 701 - 0306

*Residential and commercial window cleaning*

Customers repeatedly heap praise upon Window Cleaning Services and its owner, Thom Castro and recommend him highly. Castro has been servicing residential and commercial clients with what references say is a "wonderful smile and pleasant demeanor" for eighteen years. The firm works mostly in Manhattan, but also in some areas of the Bronx, Brooklyn and will even travel to the Hamptons. Clients across the board agree that Castro is not only extremely professional, thorough and efficient, they say he is also polite, courteous and pleasant. He is said to always arrive on time and work quickly with the greatest respect for the client's interior. Sources say clients with larger projects will find Window Cleaning Services a great value as the company tends to provide a substantial discount for volume.

*"The most reliable window cleaning service I have ever used. Clean, efficient and most agreeable." "A real find!" "Thom's a professional—an excellent window cleaner and such a nice person!" "Flexible in adjusting to my schedule." "Very good at what he does." "He is so trustworthy, you can leave your keys with Thom and forget about it."*

| | Quality | Cost | Value | Recommend? |
|---|---------|------|-------|------------|
| | ➕ | $ | ◆ | ★ |

## WK Window Cleaning Company
163 East 87th Street, New York, NY 10128
(212) 860 - 3454

*Residential and commercial window cleaning*

**3    2    4.5    4.5**

In business for fifteen years, this company has been serving many high-end residential and commercial clients around Manhattan. Sources say this firm has built a solid reputation on careful and thorough work. References tell us they have been very pleased with the firm's excellent service—many satisfied clients have used the company for ten years or longer. We're told that WK Window Cleaning is willing to negotiate rates for clients with large numbers of windows.

*"Nice guys." "Very helpful. They want to do a good job." "Excellent service."*

## Yorkville Window Cleaning
163 East 89th Street, New York, NY 10128
(212) 534 - 3551

*Commercial and residential window cleaning*

**4    2    5    5**

Small, medium, large, French, regular or storm, Yorkville cleans all types of windows. Described as friendly, helpful and attentive, sources say this firm has brightened windows in Manhattan since its establishment in 1975 by Mel Landsman. Now managed by his son, Darren, Yorkville specializes in store fronts (The Gap, Banana Republic, Nine West, Van Cleef and Arpel, Warner Brothers, and Swatch) and works with some residential customers as well. We hear that many of New York's finest buildings have established ongoing maintenance contracts with Yorkville for its services. Aside from window washing, this company also provides janitorial services, power washing, awning cleaning, painting, sign cleaning and metal cleaning as additional services to its clients.

*"Great work ethic. Timely." "Personable. Reliable." "I wouldn't trust our windows to anyone else."*

# HIRING A WINDOW & DOOR
## SERVICE PROVIDER

Are you beginning to resent your windows and doors for not protecting you better against nature's elements? Do you crave a quiet room in your home where you can close the door and leave the world behind? Or are you just plain uninspired by the windows you look through and the doors you walk through? Whether you're looking for better insulation, soundproofing or a new style for your windows and doors, there are some things you'll need to know before you cross the threshold into the realm of home improvements.

Before you take any action, find out what restrictions or regulations your building management has for new and/or improved windows and doors. Then, take some time to figure out exactly what you're looking for. If you're simply discontented with the style of your windows or doors, you'll most likely want new ones. If that's the case, you should sit down with some home magazines to select styles that appeal to you. Next, you'll need to learn about various manufacturers and whether or not you're looking for a custom design or a standard manufactured model.

## A Matter of Form and Function

Believe it or not, purchasing windows and doors can be similar to purchasing a car. Once you've selected a style, the next step is to decide what amenities to include in the package. If you've dreamt of ways to prevent your child's piano practice from permeating the whole house or if you're ready to hurl your shoes out your window at the blaring horns on the street, you're most likely looking for special doors or windows equipped with soundproofing. There are numerous grades of soundproofing, and the cost depends upon the extent of silence you'd like and the type of window or door you're looking for, as well as the complexity of the installation. Keep in mind that as with cars, the more amenities and specifications, the higher the cost. Most vendors will charge a fixed fee for the window or door, with the greatest cost variable being the installation and amenities.

## Is Money Flying Out Your Windows?

Windows and doors, on average, are responsible for approximately 40 percent of your heating bill. If you'd like to make sure that you get the most for your money, it would be wise to consider insulating the new addition to your home, particularly if your curtains have been fluttering in a breeze that mysteriously penetrates your closed windows or door. If you're one of these unlucky people, your home's heating bill is most likely inflated by poor insulation.

Insulating an outside entrance door is relatively simple. Before holding your current door responsible for the unwanted breeze, make sure that the problem is not concentrated in the weatherstripping, doorframe or threshold. Nature's elements may be sneaking in around the door, not through it. If everything is secure, you may want to purchase a heavy mass door or a door that has insulation built into its core.

When looking for a quality door, keep in mind that there is no significant difference between a seven-ply and a five-ply door. There are either two or three layers of ply on each side of a door, with the outermost ply being the veneer and the innermost ply being the core. When all is said and done, the total thickness of ply is the same for seven- or five-ply doors. The most important distinguishing factors in a door are the quality of ply used and the framing and joining.

If you're looking for internal doors to connect one room to another, your major concerns will be style and soundproofing. Depending on your needs and preferences, there are many interior doors to choose from—pocket doors, louver doors, French doors, etc. The complexity of the installation and whether you choose a custom-designed door or a manufactured door will determine the price.

## WINDOW INSULATION BASICS

If you're interested in insulating your windows, you have numerous options. One simple way is to replace single-pane windows with double-pane windows. The dead-air space between the panes provides additional insulation. To maximize the use of dead-air space, you can choose to inject it with either argon or krypton—both are gases that are denser than air, with krypton being denser and more expensive. Argon is the more economical and popular choice for this type of insulation.

You may also choose to use low emittance (Low-E) glass, a virtually clear coating that prevents much of your furnace- or boiler-generated heat from escaping through the glass, while allowing solar heat to enter. Low-E glass works year round, reflecting sunlight in the summer and absorbing it in the winter. Another common term in the window insulation world is U/R Value. This number indicates the quality of insulation. The lower the U value, the better insulated the window or door.

## REPAIRING AND REPLACING

If your antique door looks like your dog tried to dig an escape route through it or your landmark windows have seen better years and need to be replaced, you'll need a specialized repair or reproduction job. Don't worry—the right professional is just a few pages away.

Before calling a professional, however, you should know what type of window or door you're working with. Do you have operable or non-operable windows? Are they single hung (upper portion is fixed) or double hung (both portions open and close)? Is it a steel casement window (unit is hinged at the side, opening vertically) or a landmark building window with its own special configuration?

All of these factors will affect the cost, so be sure to get an estimate for the cost of the window or door, as well as for the installation and labor.

Once you've updated, renovated, or added the ultimate window and door treatments for your home, you'll enjoy rooms that are cozier in the winter and brighter in the summer. Windows are your portals to the sights and sounds of New York, and the professionals in this guide are ready and able to keep the sights in view while keeping the weather and sounds at bay.

### NOISY NEIGHBORHOOD? CONSIDER THESE WINDOW AND DOOR SOUNDPROOFING METHODS

- ❖ **Interior Windows**—made to fit inside the frames of your existing windows, inside the living area, these create a large airspace between the two windows and dramatically reduce noise from the outside.
- ❖ **Window Plugs**—removable sections of matting material or matting-over-board that can be placed snugly over a window to cut noise and light—put them up at night and take them down in the morning. For large windows, plugs can be custom made with handles for easy insert and removal.
- ❖ **Acoustical Curtains**—usually made of polyester with a heavy plastic lining, these curtains are installed on two sets of rods to create a dead airspace between the first set of curtains and the second, which blocks sound. Weighing in at about 18 pounds a panel, these heavy curtains require sturdy rods and expert installation.
- ❖ **Acoustical Doors**—To lessen the noise inside your home, consider replacing ordinary, hollow doors with acoustical doors that reduce escaping noise by about 50 percent. These doors are made of soundproofing layers and special sealing components.

# WINDOWS & DOORS

### Adorn Glass & Venetian Blind Co.    3    3    4    4
408 Greenwich Street, New York, NY 10013
(212) 675 - 2341

*Glass, mirror, window repair—landmark restoration*

Adorn has been providing its clients with window repair and restoration services for 35 years. Qualified to do landmark repairs, Adorn is equally able with glass and mirror restoration. We're told Adorn has done soundproofing for major music studios, and also offers custom shades and blinds. Fees are determined according to the duration and type of project.

### Apple Architectural Windows    📁    📁    📁    📁
231 West 29th Street, New York, NY 10001
(212) 643 - 0080

*Landmark and contemporary window repair*

### Benra Associates Inc.    📁    📁    📁    📁
180 East 94th Street, New York, NY 10128
(212) 427 - 1600

*Repair of landmark aluminum windows and doors*

### Bright Window Specialists    3.5    3    4.5    4
131 Varick Street, New York, NY 10013
(212) 807 - 1968

*Window installation*

Bright Window Specialists has earned a solid reputation in its nine years of business. Sources praise the accommodating and reliable customer service that Bright offers. The firm is also known for its work on landmark buildings.

### CitiQuiet    4    3    4.5    5
32-26 Greenpoint Avenue, Long Island City, NY 11101
(212) 874 - 5362   www.citiquiet.com

*Custom interior noise reduction windows*

CitiQuiet indeed. Specializing in custom interior windows, CitiQuiet offers 100 percent noise elimination—satisfaction guaranteed. The firm's custom-manufactured and installed windows fit inside original windows to be fully operable with no permits required. Besides noise reduction, insiders report that CitiQuiet windows eliminate 99 percent of draft and dirt. Customers can barely contain their enthusiasm for CitiQuiet—one Upper West Side resident compared his now-silent apartment to a tomb. Sources describe the installation process as efficient and praise the full customer service.

*"Out of this world. Absolutely amazing." "I don't hear a thing." "Not cheap, but absolutely worth it." "I totally and utterly would recommend. It was done beautifully. They came with the highest recommendations. No one else came close."*

## Cityproof Corp.   4.5   3   5   5
10-11 43rd Avenue, Long Island City, NY  11101
(718) 786 - 1600   www.cityproof.com

*Custom interior window units for soundproofing, draft and dirt elimination and thermal control*

We hear bountiful praise for Cityproof's custom interior window systems, which provide soundproofing, energy conservation, protection against drafts and dust, as well as thermal insulation.  Cityproof has been operating for 40 years, and we hear of clients who have enjoyed Cityproof windows for 20 years without a single problem.  Sources explain that rather than replacing or modifying existing windows, Cityproof customizes interior windows to fit inside the original exterior window, preserving the appearance, and minimizing complications with landmark regulations.  We are told that the firm's technicians are extremely professional, neat and polite.  Apartment managers praise the way the window installation took place in no time and with no abuse to the building or tenant complaints.  Cityproof has been featured in *New York Magazine* and *The New York Times*, and is used by the Peninsula and Regency Hotels, as well as various hospitals.

*"The workmen were very polite, they were very good.  And they were always on time."  "What sets them apart is their overall quality and professionalism.  There was no abuse to the building, and no complaints from the tenants.  I would absolutely recommend them."*

## Ekcer Window & Home Improvement   3   3.5   3.5   4
305 Madison Avenue, 11th Floor, New York, NY  10165
(212) 472 - 4666

*Window sales and installation*

Ekcer has been selling and installing windows for New Yorkers for 43 years.  This family business offers windows in all price ranges and styles, including double-hung and soundproofed windows.  In addition to its residential work on the Upper East and Upper West Side of Manhattan, we hear Ekcer is qualified for Landmark work.

## Englander Millwork   4   3   4.5   4.5
2369 Lorrilard Place, Bronx, NY  10458
(718) 364 - 4240

*Windows and doors, millwork, historic replication*

Principal Jay Winston runs Englander, which his grandfather started in the 1920s.  Specializing in custom doors, windows and moldings, we hear Englander also excels in replication and installation.  Offering mortise and tenon construction, soundproofing, glass and paneled wood doors, solid oak, and the restoration of antique doors and old glass, Englander has a reputation for effectively executing curvework and other tricky millwork.

Winston typically works for contractors as well as on commercial and institutional jobs, such as Columbia University, but we hear of private clients who have cited him as the only man who could capably do their work. References describe Englander's staff of six as a team of reliable craftsman, but say the organization lacks on matters such as scheduling and billing.

*"Easier to work with than most, and good at returning phone calls." "No one else would even come out here and look, but Englander could do the kind of replication work I needed."*

## Enjo Architectural Millwork    3.5    3    4.5    4.5
16 Park Avenue, Staten Island, NY 10302
(718) 447 - 5220  www.enjo.com

*Architectural millwork—restoration of windows and doors to landmark standards*

Founded in 1962, this third-generation family company specializes in custom door manufacturing for landmark buildings. Enjo also manufactures wood and glass partitions, wainscoting, wood storefronts, trimmed openings and moldings for commercial and residential properties. We hear principals Joseph and John Autovino and their team of twenty qualified professionals carry out their founder's attention to detail with state-of-the-art facilities and reliable service.

## Millwork Specialties    📁    📁    📁    📁
189 Prospect Avenue, Brooklyn, NY 11215
(718) 768 - 7112

*Historic window and door replication*

For the past 34 years, principal Cosmo Cotroneo has been replicating 18th, 19th and early 20th-century windows, doors and moldings. Although Millwork Specialties does not do general repairs, the firm often provides replacement parts for landmark pieces.

## Mr. Shower Door    3.5    3.5    4    3
651 Connecticut Avenue, Norwalk, CT 06854
(800) 633 - 3667

*Shower door manufacturing and installation*

Supplying clients with custom shower doors and installation, Mr. Shower Door is known to deliver a quality product. However, service is not the firm's forte, especially with follow-through repairs. With eighteen years experience in the industry, Mr. Shower Door has a reputation for a high quality product that can probably withstand a few service complaints.

*"When my shower started leaking, Mr. Shower Door offered to send me some tubing, but did not offer to come out and fix it." "I love my new shower door."*

## New York Window Film    4    2    5    5
131 Florida Street, Farmingdale , NY 11735
(631) 420 - 4101  www.nywindowfilm.com

*Glass coating and tinting*

Established in 1990, New York Window Film offers the technology of Vista, Llumar or Magnum brand window coatings to protect homes against ultraviolet rays. Clients say these window treatments protect against furniture fading while conserving energy, reducing glare and increasing privacy. We hear New York Window Film provides attentive service throughout the process. Clients praise the top-quality products and peace-of-mind of one of the largest liability insurances policies in the business. New York Window Film boasts a long list of high-profile clients and jobs, including NBC Studio's "Today" show site, the Theodore Roosevelt National Historic Site, and Walt Whitman's Birthplace.

*"Fabulous service. Very professional."*

## NEWYORKre:views
486 Angel Street, Cliffwood, NJ 07721
(800) 425 - 7181

*Aluminum window replacement and repair*

| 3.5 | 3 | 4.5 | 4.5 |

This husband-and-wife team has been refurbishing and repairing windows, both antique and contemporary, for the past eight years. We hear NEW YORKre:views works on existing windows, to make them fully operable or soundproofed, but does not manufacture new pieces. Glass replacement, screen installation and child protection are also part of the firm's services. Clients call the team a pleasure to work with and say the personalized service is worth the high-end fees. We hear that this firm is preferred by some of the top apartment buildings on the Upper East Side.

*"Very reliable, helpful and nice."*

## Panorama Windows
767 East 132nd Street, Bronx, NY 10454
(718) 292 - 9882

| 5 | 4 | 5 | 5 |

*Installation and repair of steel, wooden, and aluminum windows—landmark work*

President Peter Folsom entered the business as a dissatisfied customer during his own home renovation, determined to bring high quality and service to the market. Indeed, Panorama is known for its customer service and sells, installs and repairs aluminum, wood and steel windows, as well as restores many of Manhattan's landmark buildings. Folsom's personally-developed fiberglass case windows allow for replacing historic steel casements to improve insulation and provide weatherproofing without compromising landmark standards.

Clients compliment Panorama's crew for being neat, tidy and efficient. Folsom and his partner Doug Simpson reportedly return calls promptly and work only in Manhattan so they can assure quality installation and followup services to all clients. The top quality of Panorama's work is undisputed among architects, decorators, elite residential superintendents and homeowners.

*"One of the most pleasant experiences in New York. Doug is a perfect gentleman and a nice and smart guy." "Doug Simpson is the best in the business. So neat you don't even know that they were there, except that you have a new window—like Santas' elves." "Peter was amazingly nice and generous with his time and knowledge."*

## Philippe Besnard Inc.
171 Lincoln Avenue, Bronx, NY 10454
(718) 401 - 0137

*Window and door millwork*

## Seekircher Steel Window Corp.
2 Weaver Street, Scarsdale, NY 10583
(914) 725 - 1904 www.traditional-building.com/brochure/seekir.htm

| 4 | 4 | 4 | 5 |

*Leaded glass restoration and repair*

John Seekircher is relied upon in fourteen states for restoring historic windows. Specializing in English Tudor, leaded windows and steel casements, Seekircher uses his stock of vintage window, door and hardware materials to replace period pieces. He has been known to clean rust, install new steel casements and restore brass hardware to operable condition, all while maintaining the building's historic integrity. Since opening shop in 1977, Seekircher's work has graced some of New York's most prestigious residences and historic buildings, as well as landmarks across the country, most famously, Frank Lloyd Wright's Falling Water. Clients call Seekircher personable and reliable, saying his crew is amenable and timely.

The firm's work has been reviewed in numerous national trade publications, as well as *The New York Times*.

*"The greatest recommendation is that we hired him back." "John was very east to get in touch with, very responsive, conversant, friendly, easy-to-work with, and an-all around nice guy." "He is very reliable, always finishes early, charges reasonably and the crew works long hours to get the job done in a timely fashion."*

## Skyline Windows                                    4.5    4    4.5    4.5
625 West 130th Street, New York, NY 10027
(212) 491 - 3000   www.skylinewindows.com
*Custom manufacture, installation of windows*

Skyline Windows has been manufacturing, installing and repairing high-end custom windows for nearly 80 years. A third-generation family business, Skyline is qualified to work on landmark buildings and luxury high-rises. Additionally, Skyline has its product tested annually by an independent firm. Comparison shoppers report that Skyline stands out for doing the most research on building codes and architectural requirements.

Many clients say Skyline is committed to customer service, which has earned them a high-profile clientele. However, we did hear of instances of sloppy installations. Overall, though, customers speak of an improved quality of life due to their Skyline windows, which they say offer security, soundproofing, and thermal insulation, all while being fully operable and attractive, and matching landmark specifications.

*"They're the best company I've ever used." "I cannot tell you how heartily I recommend Skyline Windows for the security, insulation, look and sound. I plan to use them again." "Window installation in my high-rise was a big job, but Skyline was willing to go through with it 100 percent."*

## Zeluck Windows & Doors                             4.5    4    4.5    4.5
5300 Kings Highway, Brooklyn, NY 11234
(718) 251 - 8060
*Architectural custom window and door manufacturer*

Zeluck is a national company distinguished by its extremely conscientious customer service and high quality product. Zeluck offers an array of exclusive patented technology, but sources divulge that the most popular treatments in Manhattan are Zeluck's sound-resistant and burglar-resistant glazings. With over 100 employees, we hear Zeluck runs a tier-stepped operation with in-house draftsmen and engineers, all apprenticed to be facile with computer-aided design. With such ample facilities, sources say no job is too big for Zeluck, though some may be too small.

Zeluck is a third-generation family business and thought to be the oldest window company in New York City. Zeluck offers repair for products under warranty and insiders tell us they do both commercial and residential projects, with a very exclusive client list. Zeluck doesn't specialize in a particular style, but works with the client, architect and designer on anything from exacting historical criteria to ultra-modern designs. Those in the know report that Zeluck was the first company approved by New York City Landmark Organization.

Zeluck can boast such high profile New York assignments as the Museum of National History, Helmsley Palace, Baruch College and the Mercantile Exchange. Nationwide, the list includes the Smithsonian Castle in Washington, DC. The company's work is featured monthly in *Architectural Design*, *Architectural Record*, and other prestigious publications.

*"At Zeluck quality really means something." "I love my Zeluck windows and the difference they've made in noise-reduction."*

# THE FRANKLIN REPORT™
## The Insider's Guide to Home Services

## FILL-IN REFERENCE REPORT FORM

Client Name:

Client E-mail:       Client Phone:

Service Provider Company Name:

Company Contact:       Company Phone:

Service (i.e. plumbing):

Company Address:

### PLEASE RATE THE PROVIDER ON EACH OF THE FOLLOWING:

QUALITY OF WORK: ❑ Highest Imaginable ❑ Outstanding ❑ High End
❑ Good ❑ Adequate ❑ Poor

COST: ❑ Over the Top ❑ Very Expensive ❑ Upper End ❑ Moderate
❑ Inexpensive ❑ Bargain

VALUE: ❑ Worth Every Penny ❑ Good Value ❑ Fair Deal ❑ Not Great
❑ Poor ❑ Unconscionable

RECOMMENDATION: ❑ My First and Only Choice ❑ On My Short List, Would
Recommend to a Friend ❑ Very Satisfied, Might Hire Again ❑ Have Reservations
❑ Not Pleased, Would Not Hire Again ❑ Will Never Talk to Again

COMMENTS:

# THE FRANKLIN REPORT™
## The Insider's Guide to Home Services

## FILL-IN REFERENCE REPORT FORM

Client Name:

Client E-mail:          Client Phone:

Service Provider Company Name:

Company Contact:          Company Phone:

Service (i.e. plumbing):

Company Address:

## PLEASE RATE THE PROVIDER ON EACH OF THE FOLLOWING:

QUALITY OF WORK: ❑ Highest Imaginable  ❑ Outstanding  ❑ High End
❑ Good  ❑ Adequate  ❑ Poor

COST: ❑ Over the Top  ❑ Very Expensive  ❑ Upper End  ❑ Moderate
❑ Inexpensive  ❑ Bargain

VALUE: ❑ Worth Every Penny  ❑ Good Value  ❑ Fair Deal  ❑ Not Great
❑ Poor  ❑ Unconscionable

RECOMMENDATION: ❑ My First and Only Choice  ❑ On My Short List, Would Recommend to a Friend  ❑ Very Satisfied, Might Hire Again  ❑ Have Reservations
❑ Not Pleased, Would Not Hire Again  ❑ Will Never Talk to Again

COMMENTS: